THE NARRATIVE UNITY OF LUKE-ACTS

THE NARRATIVE UNITY OF LUKE-ACTS

A Literary Interpretation

Volume 2: The Acts of the Apostles

by

ROBERT C. TANNEHILL

Fortress Press
Minneapolis

THE NARRATIVE UNITY OF LUKE-ACTS
A Literary Interpretation
Volume 2: The Acts of the Apostles

Biblical quotations are the author's own translation.

Cover and internal design: Polebridge Press, Sonoma, California.

Library of Congress Cataloging-in-Publication Data

Tannehill, Robert C.
    The narrative unity of Luke-Acts.

    Place of publication for v. 2: Minneapolis.
    Includes bibliographies and indexes.
    Contents: v. 1. The Gospel according to Luke —
v. 2. The Acts of the Apostles.
        1. Bible. N.T. Luke—Criticism, interpretation, etc.
    2. Bible. N.T. Acts—Criticism, interpretation, etc.
    I. Title.
BS2589.T35   1986   226.4'066   86-45224
ISBN 0-8006-2112-3 (v. 1)

ISBN 0-8006-2414-9 (v. 2)

Manufactured in the U.S.A.   AF 1–2414
94   93   92   91   90   1   2   3   4   5   6   7   8   9   10

Dedicated to the modern apostles and martyrs

Contents

BAGD   Bauer, Walter. *A Greek-English Lexicon of the New Testament and Other Early Christian Literature.* 2d ed. Translated, revised, and augmented by William F. Arndt, F. Wilbur Gingrich, and Frederick W. Danker. Chicago: University of Chicago Press, 1979.

BDF   Blass, F., and Debrunner, A. *A Greek Grammar of the New Testament and Other Early Christian Literature.* Translated and revised by Robert W. Funk. Chicago: University of Chicago Press, 1961.

dif.   differs from; i.e., the named Gospel(s) contain(s) a passage which is generally parallel, but the Lukan version differs from the other version(s) in the feature being discussed.

diss.   dissertation

ET   English translation

LXX   Septuagint

NT   New Testament

RSV   Revised Standard Version

sect.   section

s.v.   *sub verbo;* under the word in a dictionary

TDNT   *Theological Dictionary of the New Testament,* edited by Gerhard Kittel and Gerhard Friedrich. Translated by Geoffrey W. Bromiley. 9 vols. Grand Rapids: Wm. B. Eerdmans, 1964–1974.

Books and articles are cited in footnotes by author, short title, and page only. Full information on these works may be found in the Bibliography.

The Acts of the Apostles is full of dramatic events, yet it has failed to capture the interest of many modern readers. There are both confessing Christians and uncommitted students of Christian origins who regard Acts as a backwater, taking them out of the main currents swirling around Jesus and the historical Paul. Indeed, some people who are very attracted to the portrait of Jesus in Luke find Acts to be strange territory. Of course, there are important religious movements to which these remarks do not apply. Protestant evangelicals find in Acts a powerful affirmation of what the church can be if it truly accepts its mission to evangelize the world. Pentecostals find in Acts an affirmation of their own experience of the Spirit. Evangelicals and Pentecostals are not wrong in pointing out the importance of evangelism and experiences of the Spirit in Acts, but Acts could be of considerable interest to people who identify with neither of these religious movements. Explaining this point requires some further comment on Acts and the modern church before we begin the hard work of detailed interpretation.

Acts should be personally interesting to members of groups united by a mission. If some in the modern church find Acts strange and irrelevant, this reaction may in part reflect the church's loss of a clear and compelling mission. In this situation Acts may serve to glorify past heroes, but it does little more. However, groups fired by a mission—such as those Latin American Christians who feel called to liberate the poor—will find much that reflects and clarifies their experience. Experiences of surprising power, radical new understandings of the religious heritage, conflict with established authorities, and martyrdom—all of these are foreign to a church that fits comfortably into the status quo but not to a movement with a mission that sets it at odds with its context. These experiences follow from the call to mission. They are central features of the narrative in Acts.

Honesty may require an establishment church to recognize that it cannot directly identify with the central figures of Acts. Indeed, the establishment church may frequently act in opposition to new prophetic movements such as the mission described in Acts. Recognition of the difference between then and now might become a beneficial critique of the present church.

The quality of the vision that a missionary group serves will finally determine whether it is a blessing or a curse in human history. Luke-Acts has a vision of God's work that deserves our admiration for its inclusive scope. Missioners are called to serve God's goal of bringing salvation to all flesh, in light of the promise that "all flesh will see the salvation of God" (Luke 3:6). Jews and Gentiles, alienated by their religious past, must both be included if this promise is to be realized. In our world religion still alienates. Religiously motivated conflict repeatedly forms the core of persistent, nearly insoluble social problems. Recognizing this may help us to appreciate the relevance of the Lukan conviction that God is calling the peoples of the world to share in a community that includes their enemies and reconciles them with those who worship and live in other ways.

Luke-Acts does more than share a grand vision. It tells a story from which we are able to learn. It can help us precisely because the mission it narrates was not as successful as early Christians hoped. The vision of God's purpose, to be realized through the mission, had to encounter hard reality, especially in the form of Jewish resistance to the new movement. Rejection and resistance are major factors in the unfolding story, and rejection by Jews is most keenly felt. Conflict with unbelieving Jews is a prominent part of Acts. Recently scholars, newly sensitive to the danger of prejudicial anti-Judaism in the New Testament, have discussed whether the prominence of conflict with Jews means that Luke-Acts is fundamentally anti-Jewish.[1] To charge Luke-Acts with anti-Jewish prejudice is, I think, a mistake.[2] Nevertheless, one should not ignore the fact that conflict with unbelieving Jews is a major and persistent feature of the Acts narrative. Jewish rejection is emphasized in Paul's final remarks to the Roman Jews, the last major scene in Acts (28:23–28). This and related scenes indicate that the mission to bring salvation to the Jewish people through the message of Jesus Messiah has fallen short of its goal. Furthermore, the Jewish people have maintained their rejection of the Christian message to this day. The grand vision of salvation for Jews and Gentiles through Jesus in Luke 2:30–32 and 3:6 appears to lead to tragic disappointment.

Luke-Acts shows a keen awareness of the problem, without being able to resolve it. Modern Christians have something to learn from struggles

---

[1] An extreme charge of anti-Judaism has been raised by Jack T. Sanders, *Jews in Luke-Acts*. On this subject see also Lloyd Gaston, "Anti-Judaism and the Passion Narrative," 127–53; S. G. Wilson, "The Jews and the Death of Jesus," 155–64; Robert Brawley, *Luke-Acts and the Jews*; and the articles in *Luke-Acts and the Jewish People,* ed. Joseph B. Tyson.

[2] See my article "Israel in Luke-Acts," 69–85.

with this issue in Acts. They can learn patience and faithfulness in mission in the midst of a world they do not control. The strong experience of resistance and rejection in Acts results in a necessary tempering of the mission. Peter and Paul are meant to impress us as powerful persons, but they are not all-powerful. The imprisonment of Paul is a particularly vivid indication of strong social limitations on the mission, and this imprisonment persists to the end of Acts. It does not change Paul's dedication to his task, as the final verses of Acts indicate, but Paul must learn to work within limits. He does so while maintaining trust in the purpose he is serving and in God's power to reach the ultimate goal. Such trust is supported by a perception of God as a God of surprises, indeed, a God who works by irony, who can use even opponents of the mission to move the divine purpose forward. The mission must work within limits, yet God repeatedly breaks out of these limits in ways that surprise both the church and its critics. Faithfully serving in mission while trusting in a God whose exact moves cannot be anticipated is part of the ongoing struggle of faith. The resulting life of service is a lesson in which we are repeatedly taught to push back our limited views of how God may act and whom God may use for the divine purpose. The church must be confident that it has a valid and important mission, as Peter and Paul are in Acts, yet it must recognize that God has other and surprising ways of working. Such a perspective will make it possible for Christianity to be a contributing part of what the earth must become if it is to survive: a tolerant, pluralistic world culture.

I will argue at various points that the narrator of Acts, like the Lukan Paul, is loyal to Israel and believes the scriptural promises to the Jewish people. The persistence of the mission to the Jews, even when it frequently meets rejection, is a sign of this loyalty. Those who are convinced that the messianic salvation promised to Israel is dependent on acceptance of Jesus as Messiah must persist in offering this salvation to Israel. This mission, in a reduced form, is assumed to continue even beyond the end of Acts, according to my interpretation. I must emphasize and argue this point, since it is denied by many scholars. I caution my readers now that this emphasis does not mean that Acts reflects my own opinion about Christian mission toward Jews. It seems to me that the centuries of history since the writing of Acts should teach Christians something, namely, that God's covenant loyalty and promises for the Jewish people cannot be dependent on acceptance of Jesus as Messiah. I would not myself advocate a Christian evangelistic mission to Jews.

The vital issue in the study of Acts is not whether it is historically accurate but whether it promotes values worthy of respect and presents models worthy of imitation. Since Acts is a narrative, these issues cannot be adequately discussed without knowledge of the ways in which narratives promote values and beliefs. That is, we must study Acts in terms of narrative rhetoric. It is appropriate to speak of narrative rhetoric both because the story is constructed to influence its readers or hearers and because there are particular literary techniques used for this purpose. Luke-Acts is a complex system of influence which may be analyzed in literary terms.[3] I make use of narrative criticism in order to understand this narrative's message, a message that cannot be confined to theological statements but encompasses a rich set of attitudes and images that are embedded in the story and offered for our admiration and imitation. How we study Acts is important for what we will discover. Narrative criticism brings a new set of questions that can lead to new insights. In this volume I seek to use narrative criticism to explore how Acts conveys its complex message. We can thereby understand more clearly what that message is and our options of response.

Studying Acts as a system of influence inevitably leads into some issues that have been subjects of theological debate. If the issue is high on the agenda of Acts, I want to make clear how Acts speaks to it. Some readers may be surprised at the importance of theological issues in what promised to be a literary study. However, when we study a narrative as rhetoric and discover that certain values and beliefs are consistently advocated within it, theological questions cannot be ignored.

I do not understand narrative criticism to be an exclusive method, requiring rejection of all other methods. Methodological pluralism is to be encouraged, for each method will have blind spots that can only be overcome through another approach. I readily draw on past exegesis of Acts. Biblical exegesis has a tradition of detailed textual interpretation that should not be lost as we address literary questions. Nevertheless, in this work I discuss details as they are relevant to the case that I am arguing and make no attempt to deal with all issues or comment on all verses.

I do not explore the possible sources of Acts and seldom comment on the historical events that may lie behind the story, for these interests would lead me away from my main concern with the significance of the narrative in its finished form.[4] Past concern with sources and historical events has sometimes led to hypotheses that stretch beyond the available evidence. Nevertheless, an understanding of first century society and of historical events within it may be important for understanding Acts as a narrative. I

---

[3] On narrative rhetoric see further *Narrative Unity* 1:8.

[4] That is, the finished form in the Alexandrian version. The Western text raises issues that I cannot discuss in this volume.

appeal, for instance, to the conquest of Jerusalem and destruction of the temple to explain an important aspect of Luke-Acts. While readers schooled in the historical study of the Bible may be surprised at how little reference I make to information from sources beyond Luke-Acts, readers accustomed to viewing a literary work as a closed system may be surprised that I refer to such information at all. I believe that study of first-century Mediterranean literature and society may illuminate unspoken assumptions behind the narrative and may also suggest specific reasons for emphases in the text. My discussion of such matters is limited and tentative. Others will be able to carry this aspect of the discussion further. I hope that my work will contribute to theirs, since a good understanding of Acts as narrative is necessary in order to employ it as evidence in relation to social and historical questions. False conclusions can easily be drawn if the scholar does not recognize how a particular passage functions within the larger narrative. Thus the methods of scholarship are not hermetically sealed compartments but mutually correct and supplement one another.

Although I wish to keep attention focused on Acts rather than on its interpreters, this work is implicitly (and occasionally explicitly) a dialogue with past scholarship. References to Ernst Haenchen's commentary on Acts are especially frequent, and these are accompanied by some critical debate. Discussion of Haenchen's commentary should be recognized as a sign of my respect for his work, which was my earliest guide to the interpretation of Acts. His commentary has assumed something of a classical status in critical scholarship and can therefore serve as a rough measure of whether my attempt at a new approach to Acts is actually leading to new results.

In the first volume of this work, four of the chapters traced Jesus' developing relationship with significant groups within the story. To do this, it was necessary to move through the story a number of times. In this way Jesus' role in relation to each of these groups was clarified, and each of these relationships stood out as a narrative strand, though intertwined with others in the narrative. This approach differs from the traditional commentary, which simply comments on sections of a text in the order in which they occur. In this volume I have reverted to the traditional approach of following the text in a single movement from beginning to end. I believe that there are literary reasons why this is more advantageous in Acts than in Luke. The bulk of Luke, like the other Synoptic Gospels, is episodic. A causal continuity among successive scenes is the exception rather than the rule. If there are narrative continuities, they inhere more in the characters and the general roles they play than in a causal connection of events. In Acts, however, there are large stretches of narrative that do show causal continuity. For instance, the healing of a lame man at the temple gate in 3:1–10 causes a crowd to gather, which provides the occasion for a speech by Peter, which offends the temple authorities and causes the arrest of Peter and John. This leads to an interrogation and a command to stop preaching. Failure to heed this command contributes to a second arrest, interrogation, and prohibition of preaching. Thus most of Acts 3—5 traces a sequence of events in which one event causes something else to happen, and the later event presupposes the earlier. This is rather different than Luke 5:17–32, where Jesus' healing of a man who could not walk is followed by the call of Levi and the meal in Levi's house. There is a certain degree of thematic connection among these episodes, but there is no indication that Jesus' healing of the paralytic caused the call of Levi. The comparatively tight plot sequences extending over major sections of Acts make it generally advisable for the commentator to treat each scene in the order in which it occurs in Acts. Nevertheless, there are patterns that link scenes with distant material, and it will frequently be useful to compare one part of Luke-Acts with another.

There are other significant literary differences between Luke and Acts. Acts contains a greater number of major dramatic scenes, usually with a speech of some length. It makes more extensive use of echoes or parallels with previous narratives from Scripture or the Jesus tradition. Characters in Acts frequently reflect on Luke through review of the Gospel story, especially the death and resurrection of Jesus, in the mission speeches.[5] Both the subtle echoes and the explicit reviews in speeches help to tie Acts closely to Luke. Since the narrative of Acts does not focus on the same central actor as Luke, and, indeed, does not have a single central character, other devices to unify it with Luke and within itself become important.

The literary differences between Acts and Luke may raise questions about the narrative unity of Luke-Acts. The issue is not whether they were written by the same author but whether they are really one narrative if the mode of narration is significantly different. We should not leap to a negative answer, however. Any major work is likely to encompass not only variety but some tension. Furthermore, parts of Luke show literary characteristics close to those of Acts. Scenes such as Luke 2:22–39 and 24:13–35 resemble the dramatic scenes in Acts, and there are echoes of scriptural narrative in Luke as well as Acts.[6] Luke 24 resembles the

---

[5] Here we have narrative at a second level. The narrator of Acts narrates a character narrating the story of Jesus. On narrative levels, see Gérard Genette, *Narrative Discourse*, 227–34, and Robert Funk, *Poetics of Biblical Narrative*, 30–33.

[6] See *Narrative Unity* 1:15, 18, 87–88.

connected plot sequences in Acts because it has a series of scenes in which characters refer to what happened in a previous scene of the chapter, or even to what happened much earlier in Luke. On the other hand, there are parts of Acts that are just as episodic as the gospel. Thus some of the differences noted between Luke and Acts can also be found within each of these volumes, considered individually.

While it is possible to read Luke apart from Acts—an approach encouraged by the division of these works in the canon—we will read Luke differently if we read it as part of Luke-Acts, and our understanding of it will be enriched. Studying Luke-Acts as a narrative—and as a single narrative—helps us to appreciate some things that we might otherwise miss. Scripture and an inspired prophet have already indicated early in Luke the comprehensive saving purpose of God that stands behind the events of both Luke and Acts (Luke 2:30–32; 3:6). These passages explicitly indicate the purpose that stretches from the beginning of Luke to the end of Acts, holding the narrative together in spite of the departure of major characters. Recall of these passages puts the events of Acts in proper perspective. These events represent either the progressive realization of God's purpose of salvation for both Jews and Gentiles or show human resistance to this purpose. In either case the individual events are meaningful parts of a single story because they relate to this overarching purpose behind the whole.

Furthermore, central plot lines are not resolved at the end of Luke. This is most obvious in the case of the mission announcement in 24:47–49, which anticipates specific developments in Acts. It is, of course, perfectly possible to announce a mission with no intention of reporting it (Matt. 28:19–20 is an example). Such an ending makes the mission seem unproblematic. It is assumed to follow naturally, for there are no narratives of danger or difficulty. Continuation of the story in Acts is important for removing this impression. There is a whole set of problems to be faced. Furthermore, the speeches of Peter in Acts make clear that the ending of Luke left another unresolved issue: the rejection of Jesus by the people of Jerusalem and their leaders. This is not to be dismissed as an unimportant matter that can simply be forgotten. The matter is not resolved until the people repent, which Peter urges them to do.

There are many other ways in which reading Luke-Acts as a continuous story enriches our understanding of both volumes. Promises of Jesus in Luke come to fulfillment in Acts (cf., e.g., Luke 21:15 with Acts 6:10), and our understanding of characters and events is deepened by suggestive comparisons between parts of Luke and Acts. For instance, Peter escapes from danger through denial in Luke but boldly confesses Jesus before the Sanhedrin in Acts, the contrasting behavior indicating the important change that has taken place. The advantages of reading Luke-Acts as a narrative and as a single narrative will emerge as we study each episode in light of the whole.

In spite of the title of my work, it is not a monograph arguing as a single, central thesis that Luke-Acts is a unified narrative. It presents much evidence of unity in Luke-Acts and shows how unity is maintained through narrative developments, but it neither argues that this unity is perfect nor focuses on this issue as its sole concern. This work is not a monograph but a new kind of commentary. Acts is a complex document, and a commentary upon it must try to preserve some of its complexity. A number of thematic concerns will appear in Acts as we study it. We will try to understand how these concerns and interests are processed through the medium of the narrative.

Quotations from Acts in this work are my own translations. These translations usually preserve the structure of the Greek text as much as possible and will, of course, depart in various ways from the English translations with which most readers are familiar. These translations will help me to show some of the verbal themes in the text and to demonstrate how the text relates to the point being discussed.

TRANSITION AND PREPARATION

Acts, like Luke, begins with a prologue in which the author comments on the act of writing from a point of view external to the narrative. The author speaks in the first-person singular and addresses a certain Theophilus, an "overt narratee"[1] who does not appear in the following narrative. Boris Uspensky discusses "the shift from external to internal point of view as a formal device for the designation of the frame of a literary work."[2] The frame serves to mark the limits of a work and also to ease the transition from the everyday world to the special world of the work, whether literary or pictorial. In Luke the transition between the framing prologue (Luke 1:1–4) and the narrative is abrupt. Acts, in contrast, provides a smooth transition from external to internal perspective. The author begins with a first-person reference to authorial activity, continues with a summary of the first book, compressed to a few verses, and then in vv. 4–5 narrows the focus drastically by referring to a specific statement of Jesus, which is presented first in indirect and then in direct quotation. By this time we are no longer attending to an author's comments on writing; we are attending to Jesus, a character internal to the narrative. The transition from the external world to the world of the narrative has taken place without apparent break. Because the division between prologue and narrative has been erased, a common feature of a prologue, the preview of the book that is beginning, appears instead as part of Jesus' speech (cf. 1:4–5, 8).[3]

Jacques Dupont, in discussing the plan of Acts, calls attention to the advice of Lucian to history writers. They should avoid breaks between sections by interweaving the material and overlapping the edges. Dupont

---

[1] An "overt narratee" is a person to whom the narrative is explicitly addressed by the narrator. See Mikeal Parsons, *Departure of Jesus*, 177 and n. 138.

[2] See *Poetics of Composition*, 146. The quotation is capitalized in Uspensky's work as the heading of a section. I previously referred to Uspensky's idea of a frame in discussing the ending of Luke. See *Narrative Unity* 1:300. For application to Acts 1:1–11 see Parsons, *Departure of Jesus*, 173–78.

[3] Alfons Weiser, *Apostelgeschichte* 1:47–48, lists (1) the dedication, (2) a short indication of the previous book's contents, and (3) a short indication of the new book's contents as regular elements of the scheme used by Hellenistic authors to introduce a new book in a multi-volume work. Weiser quotes examples.

notes that this technique is clearest in Luke-Acts where the division is also clearest: at the juncture of books one and two.[4] The narrator begins with an explicit reference to the scope of the first book, fulfilling expectations for a prologue in a continuing work. Furthermore, "the reign of God" is the topic of Jesus' discourses with the apostles during his resurrection appearances (1:3), a topic that links this teaching with Jesus' teaching prior to his death. Jesus' instructions and commission in 1:4–5, 8 are a variant version of his instructions and commission in Luke 24:47–49. In both Luke and Acts these words of Jesus point forward to crucial events still to come. Finally, Acts 1:9–11 is a final departure scene like the departure scene in Luke 24:50–51. Thus we are told twice of Jesus' instructions and departure.

In Acts this material is adapted to its position at the beginning of a long narrative. The statement about the promised Spirit is expanded (1:4–5, 8; cf. Luke 24:49) in preparation for the Pentecost scene. The departure scene loses its function of bringing the narrative to closure.[5] It is accompanied by a message of angels that points toward the future, and it is followed not by a sense of fulfillment, expressed in joy and the praise of God, but by prayer in preparation for new responsibilities.

When reviewing events previously narrated, the narrator prefers to vary details and emphases. This process can sometimes get out of hand, resulting in actual conflicts.[6] The reference to a forty-day period of resurrection appearances may cause such a conflict, for Luke 24 gives the impression that one event follows immediately upon another in a time span of one day and night. To be sure, only the longer reading in Luke 24:51, a reading that remains uncertain,[7] clearly makes the ending of Luke an ascension scene. Nevertheless, Acts 1:2 seems to indicate that the first book did end with Jesus' ascension. It may be best simply to admit that we have incompatible details. We can understand how this might happen. In the first book the narrator recognized the dramatic value of rushing from resurrection appearance to commission to Jesus' departure in the briefest span of time, a day and night of tremendous change. In the second book a competing desire took control: the desire to emphasize the extent of the resurrection appearances and the thoroughness of the risen Jesus' instruction of his apostles. Therefore, these activities now stretch over forty days.

However, there is another option that should be considered, even if

---

[4] See J. Dupont, "Question du plan des Actes," 223–25; Lucian, *How to Write History* sect. 55.

[5] See *Narrative Unity* 1:298–301 on Luke 24:50–53 as a point of closure.

[6] Note, e.g., that Paul's travel companions stand, in one account (9:7), and fall down, in another (26:14), following the encounter with Jesus on the Damascus road.

[7] See *Narrative Unity* 1:298–301, including n. 42.

certainty is not possible. P. A. van Stempvoort has argued that the verb ἀνελήμφθη ("was taken up") in Acts 1:2 can have the meaning "to die, to be taken up in the sense of pass away, removal out of this world."[8] The related noun is used in Luke 9:51 in a context that requires it to refer, at least in part, to Jesus' death. If this is the sense of ἀνελήμφθη in Acts 1:2, the review of the previous story falls into chronological order: Jesus' ministry (1:1), his departure from life (1:2), the resurrection appearances (1:3). The time limit in 1:2 ("until the day") does not indicate, then, the end of Luke but the end of Jesus' ministry, mentioned in 1:1. The reference to Jesus "having commanded the apostles" would relate not to Luke 24:47–49 but probably to the Last Supper discourse in Luke 22:24–38.[9] If Acts 1:2 does not indicate that the Gospel ended with Jesus' ascension and if we follow the shorter reading in Luke 24:51, there is no necessary conflict between the end of Luke and the beginning of Acts. As I indicated in volume 1,[10] there are literary reasons for the sense of closure in Luke 24:50–53. It is important that the readers sense that this is an appropriate ending to Luke. Literary closure does not necessarily mean that the scene describes the final encounter between Jesus and his followers, and in Acts 1:3 we discover that the appearances continued for forty days.[11]

Both the end of Luke and the beginning of Acts contain important statements in which Jesus commissions his representatives for their new task. These statements are closely related, having the following elements in common: a command to stay in Jerusalem (Luke 24:49; Acts 1:4); references to the coming of the Spirit, described as "the promise of the Father" and as "power" (Luke 24:49; Acts 1:4, 8); the role of Jesus' "witnesses" (Luke 24:48; Acts 1:8); the universal scope of the mission, which begins in the Jewish homeland and reaches out to the entire world (Luke 24:47; Acts 1:8). Thus the new stage in the narrative is introduced by new commission statements that indicate what must now be done if God's purpose is to be realized. Here, as at the beginning of Jesus' ministry, the commission of chief characters is highlighted as their mission

---

[8] See "Interpretation of the Ascension," 32–33, where supporting references are found.

[9] See Mikeal Parsons, "Text of Acts 1:2," 69. Parsons, building on van Stempvoort's observation, presents an interpretation similar in part to the one I am now offering.

[10] See *Narrative Unity* 1:299.

[11] The view just presented may seem to be seriously weakened by the use of ἀναλαμβάνω in 1:11, with clear reference to the ascension. It should be noted, however, that in this instance the speakers make clear what is meant by additional specifications ("from you into heaven"). The Greek verb is not a technical term with a single application. Indeed, it is applied in Acts 7:43; 10:16; 20:13, 14; 23:31 to other actions than a person ascending to heaven. It might also be significant to note that the narrator apparently assumes that Jesus went immediately to paradise at his death (Luke 23:43). This might help to explain why not only the final departure but also the death could be appropriately described as Jesus being "taken up."

begins, enabling readers to understand what is central in the following narrative and rooting these events in the purpose of God and the command of Jesus.

In Acts 1:4–5 Jesus reminds his hearers of several promises of the Spirit made on high authority. The Spirit is first of all "the promise of the Father." But it is also Jesus' promise, for Jesus reminds his followers that they heard this promise from him. Jesus was preceded by John the Baptist in announcing this promise. The structure of the sentence in 1:4–5 permits the view that 1:5 gives the content of what Jesus' followers heard from him. However, this verse paraphrases not what Jesus said but what John said in Luke 3:16. Therefore, it is best to understand Jesus to be referring to a divine promise transmitted by two prophetic spokesmen, himself and John. What "you heard from me" refers, then, to another occasion than Luke 3:16.[12]

God's promises are expressed in Scripture, and Acts 2:17–18 will highlight a specific Scripture in which God promises the Spirit. This text is one expression of the "promise of the Father." But 1:4 speaks of the promise of the Father heard from Jesus. If Acts 1:4–5 and Luke 24:49 are not variant accounts of the same event, the reference could be to the latter verse. However, there is a better possibility. In Luke 11:13 Jesus told the disciples, "Then if you, being evil, know how to give good gifts to your children, how much more will the Father from heaven give Holy Spirit to those asking him." This promise follows (1) the prayer in which the disciples are taught to address God as Father and (2) a parabolic saying about a father's gifts to his son. The importance of Luke 11:13 for the Lukan image of the Spirit is indicated by calling the Spirit the promise of the *Father* in Luke 24:49 and Acts 1:4 (cf. 2:33), although references to God as Father are concentrated in certain contexts in Luke[13] and are rare in Acts (1:4 and 2:33 are two of only three references).[14] The importance of Luke 11:13 is also shown by the repeated references in Acts to the Spirit as God's "gift" (2:38; 8:20; 10:45; 11:17; cf. 5:32).[15] Jesus in Luke 11:13 declared the Father's readiness to give the gift of the Holy Spirit to the disciples, and in Acts 1:4–5 Jesus indicates that the coming of this promised gift is imminent.

The events of Pentecost will show the importance of the Spirit as power for mission. The coming of the Spirit immediately results in powerful

---

[12] Thus I agree with Rudolf Pesch, *Apostelgeschichte* 1:67, that Jesus is not citing his own words in Acts 1:5.

[13] See *Narrative Unity* 1:238–39.

[14] The other is 1:7, where "the Father" may show the influence of Mark 13:32.

[15] "Gift" translates δωρεά in Acts. Δόμα in Luke 11:13 probably reflects the pre-Lukan tradition that Luke shares with Matt. 7:11 (which lacks, however, any reference to Holy Spirit).

preaching and the conversion of large numbers. The Spirit, however, is more than the necessary means to fulfill a task. The connection of the Spirit and the experience of God as Father suggests that the presence of the Spirit is part of a close family relationship with God. The emphasis on the Spirit as gift indicates that the Spirit's presence is a powerful experience of God's grace. Thus the Spirit is not merely a means to an end but part of the blessings of salvation, and it is listed as such in 2:38–40.

While Jesus in 1:4–5 highlights the importance of the event of Pentecost by calling attention to it in advance, the promise of baptism in Holy Spirit, first mentioned by John in Luke 3:16 and recalled by Jesus in Acts 1:5, will continue to be important beyond Pentecost. Peter will recall this promise following the descent of the Spirit on Cornelius' household (11:16), and the distinction in 1:5 between John's baptism and baptism in Spirit provides the background for an incident in Ephesus in 19:1–7. The repeated references to baptism in Holy Spirit in Acts indicate that it does not refer solely to Pentecost but relates to a process in which the Spirit progressively passes to new groups.

The forty-day period of resurrection appearances is a time of intense instruction in "the things concerning the reign of God" (1:3). Since this phrase is not explained in 1:3, we are left to interpret it in light of two sorts of clues: (1) what we are told of the risen Jesus' instruction of his followers in Luke 24 and Acts 1, and (2) what Jesus' witnesses understand and proclaim in the Acts speeches that they did not understand prior to their encounter with the risen Jesus. In Luke 24 Jesus showed his followers that it was "necessary that the Messiah suffer these things and enter into his glory" (24:26)[16] and that these events fulfilled God's plan revealed in Scripture (24:27, 44–46). "The things concerning the reign of God" of which Jesus speaks in Acts 1:3 include this revelation about his own role as the rejected and exalted Messiah, the king through whom God reigns. It is only in this brief phrase that the important instruction concerning Jesus' way to messianic glory and rule is carried over from Luke 24 to Acts 1. Furthermore, the Pentecost speech makes clear what Peter and the other apostles have learned from the risen Jesus. Having been instructed in "the things concerning the reign of God," Peter proclaims Jesus as the Messiah seated on David's throne and the Lord seated at God's right hand in fulfillment of Scripture (Acts 2:30–36). The Davidic Messianism of the Lukan birth story, which carries with it the imagery of Jesus as King and Lord (Luke 1:32–33; 2:11), reappears in the Pentecost speech. Thus the "reign of God" includes the reign of Jesus as Messiah in Acts.

---

[16] On this verse see *Narrative Unity* 1:284–89.

The importance of Jesus' own reign in the narrator's understanding of the reign of God explains the brief summaries of the missionary message that combine the reign of God and Jesus ("preaching good news concerning the reign of God and the name of Jesus Messiah," Acts 8:12; cf. 28:23, 31). These are not two separate topics, for God's reign is established in the world through the rule of Jesus Messiah. Thus the missionary message may also be summarized simply as "the reign of God" (19:8; 20:25). In such cases the christological aspect is not absent; it is included in the Lukan understanding of God's reign.

The major events of the story, understood as the fulfillment of God's purpose, are included in "the things concerning the reign of God." The use of this phrase reminds us that these events are to be viewed as manifestations of God's sovereignty and steps toward God's ultimate purpose. Of course, this phrase also emphasizes the continuity between the instruction of the risen Messiah, leading to the preaching of his witnesses, and the message of Jesus previously presented in Luke. The teaching of Jesus concerning God's reign in Luke is broad in scope, but Acts is a more tightly organized narrative focusing on a narrower set of concerns. As a result, the application of Jesus' teaching to the life of the church is suggested in rather limited ways in Acts. Nevertheless, the resurrection and exaltation of Jesus make the importance of his teaching all the clearer, and the continuing references to the reign of God in Acts may remind us that Jesus' message, including his call to radical obedience, is not obsolete.

Questions of the future completion of God's purpose through Jesus naturally arise as Jesus discusses the reign of God. The question to Jesus in 1:6 concerning the restoration of the reign to Israel is probably to be understood as an attempt to clarify an important point in Jesus' previous teaching about God's reign. The question may also be caused by the announcement of the Spirit's imminent coming in 1:4–5, if the gift of the Spirit is associated with the last days, as 2:17 suggests. Jesus' followers hope that the time has come when all of God's promises, including the promises of a messianic reign for Israel, will be fulfilled.

Jesus immediately rebukes the interest in times and seasons implied in the question and instead directs the questioners' attention to their responsibility for the mission that will soon begin. The rejection of Jesus by many Jews, which will become increasingly apparent in the narrative, will demonstrate that Israel is not yet ready to share in the reign of its Messiah. Thus the question arises from premature hopes and a failure to anticipate the persistent rejection that Jesus and his witnesses will encounter. Premature hopes appeared among Jesus' followers in Luke, and Jesus had to correct the false view that God's reign would appear immediately upon Jesus' arrival in Jerusalem (Luke 19:11).[17] These premature hopes have been revived by Jesus' resurrection, his discussion of the reign of God, and his announcement of the coming Spirit.

The importance of the issue raised in Acts 1:6 becomes clear when we recall the connections of this verse with other parts of the story. Acts 1:6 is not the first indication of concern with God's promises to Israel in the narrative of Jesus' resurrection appearances. In Luke 24:21 the disciples on the road to Emmaus said, "We were hoping that he was the one who was going to redeem Israel." They referred sadly to the same hope that was proclaimed with joy in the birth narratives. The infinitive "to redeem ($\lambda\upsilon\tau\rho o\hat{\upsilon}\sigma\theta\alpha\iota$)" in 24:21 reverts to a word root that has not appeared since Zechariah's Benedictus and Anna's words in the temple. In both cases the redemption in question was explicitly for Israel or Jerusalem (Luke 1:68; 2:38), just as in the statement by the disappointed disciples. Recognition that Jesus is alive removes the disciples' disappointment but does not automatically solve their problem, as Acts 1:6 shows. The resurrection revives the hope for the redemption of Israel but does not fulfill it. The question in 1:6, then, is a further expression of a hope that has already been expressed in important scenes in Luke. Indeed, the hope for a restored reign for Israel is simply another expression of the hope that Gabriel, a messenger with divine authority, aroused in Luke 1:32–33. The narrative does not allow us to forget about this hope now that its fulfillment is becoming problematic through the rejection of Jesus. The expressions of disappointed and revived hope in Luke 24:21 and Acts 1:6 serve to remind us of the importance of this hope for Israel.

Jesus' answer to the question about restoring the reign to Israel denies that Jesus' followers can know the time and probably corrects their supposition that the restoration may come immediately, but it does not deny the legitimacy of their concern with the restoration of the national life of the Jewish people. In Acts 3:20–21 Peter, who is now a reliable spokesman for the implied author, having been instructed by Jesus and inspired by the Spirit, speaks to the people of Jerusalem of the "times of restoration of all that God spoke" through the prophets and links this to a future sending of Messiah Jesus to these people. There is a close connection between the hope expressed in 1:6 and the conditional promise of Peter in 3:19–21, indicated not only by the unusual words "restore" and "restoration ($\dot{\alpha}\pi o\kappa\alpha\theta\iota\sigma\tau\dot{\alpha}\nu\omega$, $\dot{\alpha}\pi o\kappa\alpha\tau\dot{\alpha}\sigma\tau\alpha\sigma\iota\varsigma$)"[18] but also by the references to "times ($\chi\rho\acute{o}\nu o\iota$)" and "seasons ($\kappa\alpha\iota\rho o\acute{\iota}$)" in both contexts. The "times of restoration of all that God spoke" through the prophets include

---

[17] See *Narrative Unity* 1:257–61.

[18] The verb occurs only twice in Luke-Acts; the noun occurs only once in the NT.

the restoration of the reign to Israel through its messianic king.[19] This conclusion is supported not only by the link between these two passages but also by the understanding of God's promises in the Lukan birth narrative, particularly in Luke 1:32–33 and 1:69–71. In the latter passage we find a long and clumsy clause referring to God's promises through the prophets, a clause almost identical to Peter's words (see Luke 1:70 with Acts 3:21), and this clause refers to the promised Davidic Messiah who will bring political salvation to Israel.[20]

Peter's sermon shows that the hope of the Messiah's reign for Israel is not dead. Acts 3:19–21, however, makes fulfillment dependent on repentance. After the mission's initial success in Jerusalem, the emphasis in Acts will fall on Jewish resistance and rejection. Even this does not mean that the hope for Israel is dead. After all, the messianic reign for Israel was promised by God through the prophets. This fact is highlighted in Luke-Acts, and it is unlikely that its author could ever admit that this important aspect of God's purpose has been finally frustrated. But the story in Acts, so far as the author takes us, is not the story of the fulfillment of this hope for Israel as a people but the story of a tragic turn away from fulfillment when it was readily available. The repeated references to Israel's messianic hope during the transition from Luke to Acts remind us that this hope is not yet fulfilled and prepare for future developments.[21]

Other interpreters have understood Acts 1:6–8 to express Jesus' correction of a narrow, nationalistic hope for Israel, replacing it with a universal mission.[22] But persons who are presented favorably in the narrative and who, therefore, appear to be reliable spokespersons for the implied author[23] affirm that the redemption of Israel from its enemies through a royal Messiah is part of God's purpose (see Luke 1:32–33, 68–75; Acts

---

[19] Franz Mussner recognizes that Peter's words in 3:20–21 are evidence against the supposition that Jesus is rejecting the restoration idea in 1:6. See "Idee der Apokatastasis," 298. John Carroll, *Response to the End*, 146–47, notes that the verb ἀποκαθίστημι "became a technical term in the Old Testament for the political restoration of Israel by God." See LXX Jer. 16:15; 23:8; 24:6; Ezek. 16:55; 17:23; Hos. 11:11.

[20] On Luke 1:69–71 in the context of Luke-Acts, see further *Narrative Unity* 1:34–37. David Moessner views the birth narrative differently than I do. He attempts to distinguish between the limited knowledge of Mary and Zechariah and the authority with which Simeon and Anna speak. See "Ironic Fulfillment," 40–41. Zechariah, he says, is discredited by being struck dumb. However, Zechariah's dumbness affects him until he obediently fulfills Gabriel's directions. Then he speaks "filled with Holy Spirit" (Luke 1:67).

[21] See Robert Tannehill, "Israel in Luke-Acts," 69–85.

[22] See, e.g., I. Howard Marshall, *Acts*, 60, who says that the disciples' question "may reflect the Jewish hope that God would establish his rule in such a way that the people of Israel would be freed from their enemies. . . . If so, the disciples would appear here as representatives of those of Luke's readers who had not yet realized that Jesus had transformed the Jewish hope of the kingdom of God by purging it of its nationalistic political elements."

[23] On the function of reliable characters as spokespersons for the implied author, see Wayne Booth, *Rhetoric of Fiction*, 18.

3:20–21). Although Jesus' witnesses must witness "to the end of the earth" and Gentiles will share in the benefits of his messianic rule of peace, the messianic reign for Israel has not lost its significance in Luke-Acts. The central importance of the Messiah promised to Israel in Peter's Pentecost speech (2:25–36) and Paul's synagogue speech (13:22–23, 32–37) will provide further testimony for this view.

Jesus' final words in 1:8 are his commission to those who will carry on his work. The Spirit is again mentioned. Here it is described as a source of power for their work as Jesus' witnesses. Jesus' statement ends with an indication of the scope of the witness to which his hearers are called. Although the final words are often viewed as an outline of Acts,[24] this is true only in a limited way. It is more accurate to say that Jesus outlines the mission, and Acts ends with that mission still incomplete. Although Jesus' references to Jerusalem, Judea, and Samaria correspond roughly to developments in Acts 2—9, important steps in the progress of the mission beyond that point are ignored. There is no reference to the spread of the gospel to Antioch, Asia Minor, or Greece, although each of these steps is significant in Acts. Nor is there any reference to Rome, for there is no firm basis for identifying "the end of the earth" with Rome. The exact phrase "to the end of the earth ($\xi\omega\varsigma$ $\dot{\epsilon}\sigma\chi\acute{\alpha}\tau\sigma\upsilon$ $\tau\hat{\eta}\varsigma$ $\gamma\hat{\eta}\varsigma$)" is rare in ancient Greek, occurring five times in the Septuagint (Isa. 8:9; 48:20; 49:6; 62:11; Pss. Sol. 1:4), twice in the New Testament (Acts 1:8; 13:47), in other Christian writings showing knowledge of Isaiah and/or Acts, but nowhere else in the immense range of ancient Greek literature compiled for computer search in the Thesaurus Linguae Graecae.[25] Isaiah is the source of the phrase in Acts, as is clear from the fact that the second reference there is a direct quotation of Isa. 49:6. This quotation also shows that, for the narrator of Acts, "to the end of the earth" is a key expression from Isaiah's testimony that God intends salvation for all peoples. The use of the same phrase in Acts 1:8 should also be understood in light of Isa. 49:6. The point of the phrase is to eliminate any stopping point (whether Rome or elsewhere) before the whole of the inhabited world has been covered.[26]

---

[24] See, e.g., Hans Conzelmann, *Acts*, 7: "Verse 8b indicates the plan of the book."

[25] The search was conducted on Thesaurus Linguae Graecae Pilot CD Rom C.

[26] As W. C. van Unnik has convincingly argued, the Greek phrase refers "very definitely to the end, the extreme limit, of the world. . . . For ancient people these limits lay at the Atlantic, by the Germans, Scythians, Indians, and Ethiopians." Pss. Sol. 8:15 is sometimes cited in support of a connection with Rome, but van Unnik indicates that this reference to one who came "from the end of the earth" probably means that Pompey came not from Rome but from Spain, where he fought for many years before going to the east. See "Ausdruck $^{\cdot}E\Omega\Sigma$ $^{\prime}E\Sigma XATOY$ $TH\Sigma$ $\Gamma H\Sigma$," 399–400. See also T. C. G. Thornton, "To the End of the Earth," 374–75. Robert Brawley, *Luke-Acts and the Jews*, 32–33, argues that "to the end of the earth" is an ethnic rather than a geographical phrase on the basis of the references to Gentiles that precede and follow 13:47.

Thus Acts 1:8 does not outline the actual course of Acts beyond Samaria, and it envisions a goal that reaches beyond the end of Acts. It is an outline of the mission, but only in part an outline of Acts.

Jesus is detailed in speaking of those areas where his present hearers will have important roles in the mission: Jerusalem, Judea, and Samaria. The rest of the mission is encompassed in a single, sweeping phrase. Jesus is speaking to Galileans (see 1:11) in the context of the Jewish homeland, and his language reflects the difference between what such people know from experience and the large, vaguely known world beyond. These Galileans will not fulfill the mission to the end of the earth by themselves. In spite of the commission now being given them, they will not even be in the forefront of some of the new developments in the mission in its early stages. Others will begin the work in Samaria and Antioch (see 8:5; 11:20). Even Gentiles in or near the Jewish homeland are not evangelized or accepted without additional prodding from God and argument in the church (see 10:1—11:18). Nevertheless, these Galileans will fulfill their commission within certain limits, and others will step in to help. The mission does not develop according to a clear plan worked out by the apostles. There are unexpected twists and turns, and the necessary work will be done by unexpected agents. When Paul and Barnabas announce their mission "to the end of the earth" in 13:47, they are claiming the mission originally given to the Galileans in 1:8. There is no hint of Paul's role in 1:8, but the fact that Paul later makes a major contribution to fulfilling the mission authorized by Jesus is one of many indications of the importance of his work in God's plan.[27]

The departure scene at the end of Luke brings the narrative to temporary closure. The departure scene in Acts has a different function due to its different position in the narrative.[28] It is dominated by Jesus' parting statement and the statement of two angels. Both of these statements (1:8, 11) point forward to future events and are intended to move the Galileans to action. The angels give the Galileans a gentle prod with a rebuking question, "Why do you stand gazing into the sky?" The Galileans must immediately begin to prepare for the responsibility that has been given them.

---

[27] R. Brawley argues that "Luke employs prophetic prediction as a literary device to sanction its fulfillment." That is, those who work to fulfill the prediction are legitimated by this fact. In this sense 1:8 serves to legitimate Paul's ministry. See *Luke-Acts and the Jews*, 49–50.

[28] See M. Parsons, *Departure of Jesus*, 194: "The ascension story in Luke functions in its narrative context as an ending which brings closure to the Gospel, while the ascension account in Acts serves in its context as a narrative beginning. The differences in detail between these accounts may be accounted for largely by the role of each in its respective narrative context."

The relation of the statement about the Parousia in 1:11b to the preceding rebuke is not immediately clear. The rebuke has been interpreted by influential scholars[29] as a warning against the expectation of Jesus' immediate return. Although Jesus' return will not be immediate, it is doubtful that this is the point of 1:11. The angels refer to Jesus' Parousia but say nothing about its timing. The reference to the Parousia fits the context best if it reinforces the angels' preceding rebuke. It does so if we think of the meaning of the Parousia for the disciples according to the servant parables in Luke (see 12:35–48; 19:12–27). These parables portray the disciples as servants who must one day give an account to their returning master. Viewed in this light, the angels' speech no longer falls apart in two fragments. The rebuke is a call to action, and it is supported by a reminder of the responsibility placed upon Jesus' witnesses by the master who will one day call them to account. This view also fits the following narrative. The Galileans return to Jerusalem, the place where they must begin their mission, and prepare themselves through prayer and through filling the vacant office of apostle. As with Jesus' prayers in Luke, the prayer of the community in Acts 1:14 is preparation for an important new development.[30] Thus a message of angels is added to the commission of Jesus to move the Galileans to their first steps in their new mission. This message is the first of many indications in Acts that the church's mission is repeatedly dependent on divine direction and prodding.

The reference to the Parousia in 1:11 may also be a response to the disciples' concern in 1:6 (note the connection between the sending of the Messiah from heaven and the "times of restoration" in 3:20–21)[31] and a basis for Peter's proclamation of Jesus as the future "judge of the living and the dead" in 10:42. The angels are promising that Jesus' exaltation to heavenly rule will be completed by his return as judge. Their words also remind us that the Jesus story has a future dimension that stretches beyond the end of Acts.

The encounter of the Galileans with the angels following Jesus' ascension closely parallels the encounter of the women with the angels at the empty tomb in Luke 24:4–7. The angels are introduced in the same way in both scenes: "Behold, two men . . . (ἰδοὺ ἄνδρες δύο)." Both scenes refer to their special clothing, and the angels begin their message in both by correcting what the humans are doing, asking why (τί) they are doing it. A statement about the absent Jesus follows, accompanied in Luke 24:6–7 by

---

[29] See Ernst Haenchen, *Acts*, 150, and H. Conzelmann, *Acts*, 7.
[30] See *Narrative Unity* 1:205–6.
[31] See Arthur Wainwright, "Luke and the Restoration," 76.

a review of what Jesus had said, while Acts 1:11 provides a preview of
Jesus' return.[32] Thus the "vision of angels" (Luke 24:23) by the women is
repeated for the "men of Galilee" in a later setting, providing a further
link between Luke 24 and Acts 1.

In 1:15 Peter takes the initiative in seeking a replacement for the
betrayer Judas. His words and the believers' subsequent actions show that
a major change has taken place in Jesus' followers. Peter is now an
interpreter of Scripture and of God's purpose for the church. His insight
into Scripture and God's purpose will also be demonstrated in his missionary speeches, but even before the mission begins he is presented as one
who knows what "was necessary" to fulfill Scripture (1:16) and what
Scripture indicates to be "necessary" now (1:20–22). Peter is taking over a
major function of the departed Jesus. It might seem that there has been no
preparation for this sudden shift in role, but that is not true. The language
with which Peter begins his speech in 1:16 echoes the language that Jesus
used when he was last presented as Scripture interpreter: "It was neces-
sary that the Scripture be fulfilled ($\check{\epsilon}\delta\epsilon\iota$ $\pi\lambda\eta\rho\omega\theta\hat{\eta}\nu\alpha\iota$ $\tau\grave{\eta}\nu$ $\gamma\rho\alpha\phi\acute{\eta}\nu$)"; cf.
Luke 24:44, "It is necessary that all that is written be fulfilled ($\delta\epsilon\hat{\iota}$
$\pi\lambda\eta\rho\omega\theta\hat{\eta}\nu\alpha\iota$ $\pi\acute{\alpha}\nu\tau\alpha$ $\tau\grave{\alpha}$ $\gamma\epsilon\gamma\rho\alpha\mu\mu\acute{\epsilon}\nu\alpha$)." At that time Jesus "opened the
mind" of his followers "to understand the Scriptures." The ability demon-
strated by Peter in his first speech in Acts is the result of this opening of
the disciples' minds through the risen Messiah. The disciples could not
understand the scriptural necessity of Jesus' suffering prior to the revelation of the risen Messiah (see Luke 18:31–34). Now they can, and this
permits them to understand many things, including the defection of Judas,
as part of God's way of working in a resistant world. In Luke 24:44–46
Jesus spoke of "all that is written . . . concerning me," including his
suffering. This could include the role of the betrayer, especially when the
first of Peter's quotations in Acts 1:20 comes from Psalm 69, a psalm from
which a number of references to Jesus' passion in the New Testament are
drawn.[33] Thus we are probably to infer that Peter is either reminding his
audience of what Jesus had directly taught them from the Psalms (which
are explicitly mentioned in Luke 24:44) or is following Jesus' lead in
finding references to the events of the passion there.

Faced with Satan's onslaught on the disciples during his arrest and
death, Jesus asked Peter to "strengthen your brothers" following Peter's
own recovery (Luke 22:32).[34] Peter becomes the leader of the early

---

[32] For further discussion of these parallel scenes see Gerhard Lohfink, *Himmelfahrt Jesu*, 195–98.

[33] See John 2:17 = Ps. 69:9 [68:10 LXX], Rom. 15:3 = Ps. 69:9, and the reference to the drink of vinegar in all four passion stories, including Luke 23:36 = Ps. 69:21 [68:22 LXX].

[34] See Gerhard Schneider, *Lukas, Theologe*, 146–52.

church. In this position he may have strengthened it in many ways. But notice that 1:15–22 is the only place in the first four chapters of Acts where Peter is singled out in a scene that concerns the internal affairs of the church. Furthermore, this scene is introduced by a double reference to the church as "brothers," the first applications of this term to the community of disciples since Luke 22:32.[35] What Peter does through his speech in Acts 1:16–22 may seem a rather small thing compared to the momentous events reported before and after. Nevertheless, it can be understood as an important step in strengthening the community in the faith that was shaken by Jesus' arrest and death. Reconstituting the twelve is an important step in preparation for witness to Israel. Choosing a twelfth member of this core group of witnesses implies acceptance of Jesus' commission to be his witnesses in the new situation following his death and resurrection. This is an act of faith in Jesus and a first step in obedience to his new call. The community responds by doing as Peter recommends. Peter's faith inspires the faith of the others.

Since Jesus chose the original twelve, as we were reminded in 1:2, we might expect Jesus to replace Judas during the forty days before his departure. Instead, this business is left to the early church. Even if the decision to follow the latter narrative option was influenced by tradition available to the narrator, its effect is to highlight Peter's responsiveness to Jesus' commission and ability to guide the church in its new task. The story of the replacement of Judas also indicates the church's willingness to support the mission in response to Peter's leadership. In both cases these are the first clear indications of how Peter and his companions will respond to the formidable task given them by Jesus.

The narrator, somewhat awkwardly, has Peter tell the story of Judas' end. In doing so, Peter says in 1:17, "He received the lot ($\kappa\lambda\tilde{\eta}\rho o\nu$) of this ministry ($\delta\iota\alpha\kappa o\nu\iota\alpha\varsigma$)." Later we hear of the one who is to "receive the place[36] of this ministry," and this person is chosen by lot (1:25–26). The unusual way of describing Judas' apostleship emphasizes the similarity between his position and that of the new apostle, Matthias. Perhaps the simple fact that one is replacing the other might lead to this parallel description. When Judas is described as one who was "numbered among us" and received "the lot of this ministry" like the other apostles, however, his betrayal and evil fate can easily become a warning to the others who hold similar positions of leadership in the church. His cautionary story precedes the solemn choice of his replacement.

---

[35] The Lord's appearance to Simon, reported in Luke 24:34, may have strengthened the brothers, but remarkably little attention is given to this event in Luke 24.

[36] Variant reading: "lot."

Judas receives money for his betrayal (Luke 22:5) and uses the money to buy a field (Acts 1:18), which becomes a field of blood. Thus the corrupting appeal of money and property plays a certain role in the story. Later Paul will warn church leaders about desire for possessions by presenting himself as a contrary example (20:33–35).

The description of apostleship as διακονία ("ministry" or "service") is also noteworthy. The closest preceding occurrence of this noun or its related verb is in the Last Supper scene, as Jesus corrects the apostles' rivalry over rank and instructs them in the special quality of their future leadership. The leader, Jesus says in Luke 22:26, must become "like one who serves (ὁ διακονῶν)." Jesus is speaking of the servant who waits on the table, in contrast to the honored participants in a banquet. In Luke διακονία ("service") and διακονέω ("serve") always refer to the work of preparing and serving food, work normally performed by those regarded as social inferiors, such as women and servants (see Luke 4:39; 8:3; 10:40; 12:37; 17:8; 22:26–27). Yet at the Last Supper Jesus not only describes his own role in these terms but also makes such service a norm for the apostles. The repeated description of apostleship as "service" in Acts 1:17, 25 can remind us of this fact and may imply that the early church now recognizes that its leadership must conform to Jesus' way of service.

There must be twelve apostles, not eleven, and the twelve apostles in some way correspond to the twelve tribes of Israel.[37] Do the twelve apostles represent the early church's claim to *be* the new Israel, in place of those falsely so called, or do they represent Jesus' claim, through his apostles, on the whole of the Jewish people? The latter fits the perspective of Luke-Acts best. Israel remains a designation for the Jewish people in Luke-Acts, and this people is characterized by its twelve tribes (Acts 26:7). The twelve tribes suggest Israel in its fullness, not a remnant. As soon as the twelve apostles are restored to their full number, Acts presents a scene in which Peter, "with the eleven" (2:14), addresses a crowd composed of "Jews . . . from every nation under heaven" (2:5), climaxing his speech with an appeal to "the whole house of Israel" (2:36; cf. 4:10). Thus the next scene of Acts presents the twelve apostles performing their role of witnesses to Israel, to *all* Israel. The completeness of the apostolic circle, restored in 1:15–26, corresponds to the completeness of the audience addressed in the Pentecost scene. The Messiah, through the twelve apostles, lays claim to the whole house of Israel. Awareness of this claim will help us to understand why Jewish rejection is such a problem in Acts.

According to 1:21–22 the one chosen as apostle will become a special witness of Jesus' resurrection, but this person must be drawn from those

---

[37] See Jesus' words to the apostles in Luke 22:30.

who accompanied Jesus during his whole ministry. This requirement reflects the fact that the apostles are not simply witnesses to the resurrection but also to the entire ministry of Jesus as recorded in Luke. This double function is confirmed by 10:39–41, where reference to witnesses to the resurrection is preceded by the statement that "we are witnesses of all that he did both in the land of the Jews and Jerusalem." Although the ministry of Jesus is sometimes omitted from the Acts mission speeches, the requirement in 1:21–22 that the chosen witness must have participated in Jesus' whole itinerant ministry shows the continuing importance of this ministry in the witness to Jesus. What "Jesus began to do and teach" (1:1) remains relevant. It has not become obsolete following his death and resurrection. The first leaders of the church must be qualified to bear witness to it, just as the narrator has borne witness to it by writing Luke. Indeed, the witness of the apostles to Jesus' ministry is understood in light of the gospel story as presented in Luke, for the statement in 10:39 that "we are witnesses of all that he did" is preceded by a summary of Jesus' ministry from a uniquely Lukan perspective.[38]

In 1:21 Peter speaks not of being with Jesus but of *going* with him on his journeys. Elsewhere also Luke-Acts gives special importance to Jesus' traveling companions, particularly on the journey from Galilee to Jerusalem. The narrator notes that certain women accompanied Jesus from Galilee (Luke 23:49, 55). The angels at the ascension address Jesus' followers as "Galileans" (Acts 1:11), and according to 13:31 Jesus appeared "to those who came up with him from Galilee to Jerusalem, who are now his witnesses to the people." The special emphasis on the journey from Galilee to Jerusalem corresponds to the great expansion of this travel narrative in Luke, where it stretches from 9:51 to 19:44. This journey was a period of intense instruction of the disciples on subjects important for their future mission.[39] This emphasis on journeying with Jesus, particularly on his final journey to the cross, suggests that the apostolic witnesses are qualified not simply because they happened to be present when something happened and so could report it, like witnesses to an accident. Rather they have been taught and trained by Jesus for their work. They shared Jesus' life and work during his mission. In the process they were tested and discovered their own defects.[40] That discovery may also be part of their preparation. The witness of the Galileans does not arise from casual observation. They speak out of a life and mission shared with Jesus, after being taught and tested. From this group the replacement for Judas is chosen.

---

[38] See below, 140–41.
[39] See *Narrative Unity* 1:232–53.
[40] See *Narrative Unity* 1:253–89.

The narrative will later suggest that being Jesus' witness will mean sharing anew in Jesus' journey to the cross.[41]

Stephen and Paul do not have the qualifications listed in 1:21–22, yet they, too, are called Jesus' witnesses (22:15, 20; 26:16). Paul is not merely a deputy of the apostles, handing on their witness. He is a witness of what he himself has seen and heard (22:15; 26:16). Paul's witness and the witness of the twelve are complementary, each dependent on the other for completion. Paul cannot be a witness to Jesus' ministry like the apostles, but he is the one who does the most to fulfill Jesus' command to be his witness to the end of the earth. The apostles and Paul share the task of witness, but each makes a unique contribution.[42]

Jesus, the central character of the story, departs at the ascension and from that point will appear only briefly in visions. Although one might argue that he is still, in a sense, the central character, because he is constantly mentioned and is the center of conflict,[43] the fact that he is now beyond the range of sight and sound causes major changes in the narrative. The role of the apostles adjusts accordingly. A major transformation takes place in them so that they may continue Jesus' work. Roughly, we may speak of this transformation taking place through (1) remarkable new fulfillments of promises and commands from Jesus or Scripture, (2) overcoming past failures by the disciples, failures highlighted in Luke, and (3) new power to carry on the mission of Jesus, resulting in echoes of the work and suffering of Jesus in the work and suffering of the apostles (and later Paul). In each of these cases careful attention to Luke is necessary to appreciate the new situation in Acts.

Already in Acts 1 we can note some of these developments. The promise of the Spirit is not fulfilled until Acts 2, but its coming is strongly anticipated in Acts 1. Jesus' announcement of a mission to be his witnesses first in Jerusalem and later to the end of the earth does not itself fulfill the promises of salvation for all, Jew and Gentile, in Luke 2:30–32 and 3:6, but it points to a way of fulfilling them. We can already see some remarkable changes at points where the disciples were deficient. To be sure, premature expectation of messianic salvation[44] appears once more in 1:6, but it will now disappear. There is some evidence that Jesus' rebuke

---

[41] For echoes of Jesus' journey to the cross, trials, and death in the experience of his witnesses, see below, 68–72, 99–100, 239–40, 259, 264–66, 274, 281–82, 345–46.

[42] See below, 280–81.

[43] M. Parsons, applying to Acts an idea of Martin Kreiswirth, speaks of the narrative strategy of the "empty center." Here the plot "employs a character who is 'absent but curiously present . . . around which both the major action and the various characters' thoughts revolve.'" See *Departure of Jesus*, 160–61.

[44] See *Narrative Unity* 1:257–61.

of the apostles' rivalry over rank[45] at the Last Supper has taken effect, for the church now thinks in terms of service (1:17, 25), as Jesus recommended, and the narrator is beginning to show its unity and devotion to mutual welfare (1:14; 2:44–46). Furthermore, the failure of Jesus' followers to understand his death as part of God's way of working in the world, revealed by Scripture,[46] has been overcome. Peter's application of Scripture to one aspect of the passion story, Judas' betrayal, is a preliminary indication of this. His Pentecost speech will indicate this clearly (see 2:23). New power to do what Jesus did appears in Peter's ability to interpret events as the fulfillment of Scripture, the witness to God's plan (see 1:16 with Luke 24:44). This power will be more apparent as Peter begins the mission with an inaugural sermon and emerges as a powerful prophetic preacher of repentance and salvation. He will heal as Jesus did and face the Sanhedrin courageously as Jesus did, in sharp contrast to his previous fear and denial. His courage under threat will show that the apostles' unwillingness to face death[47] has been overcome.

---

[45] See *Narrative Unity* 1:254–57.
[46] See *Narrative Unity* 1:277–89.
[47] See *Narrative Unity* 1:262–74.

THE SPIRIT INSPIRES
A CALL TO REPENTANCE

The Pentecost scene begins abruptly with dramatic events for which there is no discernible cause. "Suddenly" there is a mysterious "sound" like "a strong wind," accompanied by "tongues as of fire." Briefly readers may share the puzzlement later expressed by the Jews dwelling in Jerusalem, for we are told first of the mysterious sounds and sights[1] and only in v. 4 are these connected with the Holy Spirit. Here John the Baptist's words about baptism "in Holy Spirit and fire" in Luke 3:16, of which Jesus reminded his hearers in Acts 1:5, are fulfilled.

Thus the promised Spirit initiates the action of the plot by initiating the mission that continues through the rest of Acts. The Spirit's arrival results in an outburst of speech that communicates to Jews "from every nation under heaven" in their own native languages. A particular speech by Peter follows. Peter's speech refers to what has just happened and to the earlier events surrounding Jesus, interpreting these events in a way that shows their significance for his audience. The speech not only interprets what has happened; it causes something to happen. The audience makes a shattering discovery and is moved to repentance in large numbers. Through Peter's speech the mission of Jesus and his witnesses moves to a new level.

The Pentecost scene is introduced with an unusual phrase: "When the day of Pentecost was being fulfilled (ἐν τῷ συμπληροῦσθαι τὴν ἡμέραν τῆς πεντηκοστῆς)." This phrase closely resembles Luke 9:51, the solemn beginning of Jesus' journey to Jerusalem in fulfillment of his passion prophecies. In both cases the fulfillment of a time is emphasized because the days in question bring the fulfillment of prophecy. Just as the announcement of coming fulfillment in Luke 9:51 was preceded by prophecies in 9:22, 31, 44 requiring this fulfillment, so the fulfillment of the day in Acts 2:1 was preceded by repeated prophecies of the coming of

---

[1] Robert Funk, *Poetics of Biblical Narrative*, 110–11, discusses Acts 2:2–4 as an example of the use of "unusual visual or aural signals" as "perception precipitators," resulting in an arrival and perception in v. 6. This is one way in which the introduction to a narrative unit may bring a scene into focus.

the Spirit (Luke 24:49; Acts 1:4–5, 8). The prophecies have prepared us to appreciate the importance of this day.

Jews "from every nation under heaven" are amazed when they hear the "mighty acts of God" being spoken in their own languages by Galileans. The long list of peoples and lands underlines the diversity of this audience. The list is not meant to be exhaustive, for we are told that these Jews come from *every* nation under heaven. The diverse audience serves to verify the language miracle, but both language miracle and audience are indications of an effort to emphasize the intended scope of the mission. When this point has been made, the Diaspora Jews disappear from the narrative.

We should keep in mind, however, that these people are all devout Jews (2:5), and Peter's response to them is clearly designed as a speech to Jews about their promised Messiah. We need not reject the idea that these Jews function as representatives of their homelands, including the Gentile inhabitants, thus providing a hint of the mission's power to cross ethnic and religious lines. The following speech may provide some support for this view through its assurance in 2:39 that the promise is also for "all those far off," but this is a minor note in a speech that is mainly concerned to address all Israel. As the climactic announcement in 2:36 shows, Peter's speech reveals something of crucial importance to "the whole house of Israel ($\pi\hat{a}s$ $o\hat{l}\kappa os$ $'I\sigma\rho\alpha\acute{\eta}\lambda$)." This climax to the speech indicates the significance of the audience of Jews "from every nation under heaven." It represents Israel in its wholeness, including the Diaspora. The connection between 2:14 and 2:36, the opening and closing of the formal speech (although the dialogue in 2:37–40 is an integral part of the message), provides further support for this view. The address in 2:14 includes "all those dwelling in ($\kappa\alpha\tau o\iota\kappa o\hat{v}\nu\tau\epsilon s$) Jerusalem," to whom Peter says, "Let this be known to you." These are the Jews "from every nation under heaven" first introduced in 2:5 as "dwelling ($\kappa\alpha\tau o\iota\kappa o\hat{v}\nu\tau\epsilon s$) in Jerusalem." In his conclusion in 2:36 Peter rephrases what he said in 2:14: "Let the whole house of Israel know assuredly." He is addressing the same groups mentioned in 2:14 and 2:5, the local Jews together with the residents of Jerusalem who have come from every foreign land.

Although every Jew could not be present for Peter's speech, the narrator does not hesitate to depict representatives of the Jews of every land as Peter's listeners. This feature shows a concern not just with Gentiles but with a gospel for all Jews, which can bring the restoration of Israel as a united people under its Messiah.

These residents of Jerusalem from foreign lands have a special status. They represent the Jews scattered throughout the world, but they have been in Jerusalem long enough to know about and share in the events of the preceding Passover, when Jesus was crucified. They are included in

Peter's accusation as participants in Jesus' death (2:23, 36). This accusation results from their presence in Jerusalem during the crucial Passover, not from the simple fact that they are Jews. When Paul later speaks to Diaspora Jews, he does not accuse them of responsibility for Jesus' death but attributes this to "those dwelling in Jerusalem and their rulers" (13:27-28).[2]

The potential scope of the mission, reaching out beyond its small base in the church to all Jews and the gentile world, seems particularly to cause anticipatory elements in the narrative that strain against the limited historical contexts in which they are found. At the very beginning of his ministry Jesus spoke to the people of Nazareth about prophetic mission among Gentiles (Luke 4:25-27),[3] and the story of the great catch of fish in Luke 5:1-11 is a symbolic narrative about the future mission.[4] The presence of Jews from every nation under heaven at Pentecost introduces a similar symbolic dimension into that narrative, suggesting first that it is the goal of the gospel to address all Israel, scattered throughout the world, and second that it must also address the gentile inhabitants of the lands from which these Jews come.

Susan Sniader Lanser points out that "the authority that the text gives to a particular point of view" depends in part on "the degree to which a given stance is reinforced," and reinforcement takes place when the stance is expressed by multiple voices in the narrative.[5] There is an interesting interplay between the narrator's voice and characters' voices in the Pentecost scene, demonstrating such reinforcement. The narrator's introduction in 2:1 hints at the fulfillment of God's purpose and Scripture. Peter will reinforce this perspective in 2:16-21. In 2:4 the narrator interprets the sounds and sights described in 2:2-3 as manifestations of the Holy Spirit. Peter does the same in 2:16-18, 33, using the prophet Joel as an additional reinforcing voice. The narrator's description of the language miracle is reinforced by the crowd of Jews from every nation. First the narrator says that "they were hearing, each one, in their own language ($\tau\hat{\eta}$ $i\delta\acute{\iota}\alpha$ $\delta\iota\alpha\lambda\acute{\epsilon}\kappa\tau\omega$)" (2:6); then the crowd says, "How is it that we hear, each of us, in our own language ($\tau\hat{\eta}$ $i\delta\acute{\iota}\alpha$ $\delta\iota\alpha\lambda\acute{\epsilon}\kappa\tau\omega$)" (2:8). The narrator's statement of their amazement is also reinforced by the questions from the crowd in 2:7-8. In 2:6-13 the narrator permits the crowd to become a focalizing character. That is, we are experiencing the event through the

---

[2] Jack Sanders, *Jews in Luke-Acts,* 233-35, notes that Peter is addressing representatives of all Jews but fails to note the distinction concerning responsibility for Jesus' death in 13:27-28.

[3] See *Narrative Unity* 1:70-71.

[4] See *Narrative Unity* 1:203-4.

[5] See *Narrative Act,* 220.

perceptions, thoughts, and feelings of the crowd.[6] This approach encourages us to share in the crowd's amazement.

The puzzlement and misunderstanding expressed in 2:12–13 create a narrative need for the following speech. Peter must explain what is happening. He comments in inverse order on the subjects that concern him and his audience. First, he responds to the mockery (2:15), then interprets the manifestations of the Spirit (2:16–21), then the recent events of the death and resurrection of Jesus (2:22–36). When we compare Peter's speech and the surrounding events with the beginning of Jesus' mission in Luke, a cluster of similarities emerges. In both cases endowment with the Spirit in response to prayer (Luke 3:21–22; Acts 1:14; 2:2–4) leads to an inaugural speech containing a Scripture quotation of some length, which, among other things, refers to the preceding endowment with the Spirit (Luke 4:18; Acts 2:17–18). In both cases the Scripture quotation provides important clues concerning the mission that is beginning, and the subsequent narrative provides reminders that the mission is fulfilling the prophecies of this Scripture.[7] According to both speeches the mission offers "release" ($\check{\alpha}\phi\epsilon\sigma\iota\varsigma$, Luke 4:18) or "release of sins" ($\check{\alpha}\phi\epsilon\sigma\iota\varsigma\ \tau\hat{\omega}\nu\ \dot{\alpha}\mu\alpha\rho\tau\iota\hat{\omega}\nu$, Acts 2:38). Jesus' sermon in Nazareth is immediately followed by his rejection. This aspect of the pattern develops more slowly in Acts, but Acts 4—5 shows the apostles in sharp conflict with the Sanhedrin, and in Acts 7 the first Christian martyr dies, followed by a great persecution. The cluster of similarities is even more extensive, as later discussion of the healing of the lame man (Acts 3:1–10) will indicate.[8] These parallels are not drawn in a rigid and wooden way, which would impair the verisimilitude and freshness of the Acts narrative. However, the appearance of a whole cluster of similar themes, which, in each case, are emphasized and developed, suggests a significant pattern. As a result of this pattern the story of Jesus as told in Luke becomes a paradigm for the mission of Jesus' witnesses.[9]

The importance of the quotation from Isaiah in Luke 4:18–19 suggests that we should look closely at the quotation from Joel in Acts 2:17–21 to see whether it has similar importance. We can best detect the "active" parts of the quotation, that is, the parts that have special significance for the narrative, by noting which parts relate to events and statements in the story. In doing so, it becomes apparent that the Joel quotation does not refer exclusively to the coming of the Spirit at Pentecost but is understood

---

[6] On a character as focalizer, see S. Lanser, *Narrative Act,* 141–42.

[7] On Luke 4:18–19 see *Narrative Unity* 1:60–68, 103–9.

[8] See below, 49–52.

[9] On parallels between Luke 3—5 and Acts 1—5, see Charles Talbert, *Literary Patterns,* 15–19. On the use of such patterns in Luke-Acts and other ancient Mediterranean literature, see C. Talbert, *Literary Patterns,* and G. W. Trompf, *Idea of Historical Recurrence.*

as a divine promise that is realized progressively, but only partially, in Acts as a whole.

The quotation interprets the speaking "in other tongues" and Peter's speech at Pentecost as prophetic speech, inspired by the outpouring of God's Spirit.[10] The statement at the end of 2:18, "And they will prophesy," is not found in Joel and may indicate repetitive emphasis on this point (already made in 2:17) by the narrator of Acts. The reference to women in 1:14 prepares for Joel's statements of gender inclusiveness in 2:17–18 ("your sons and your daughters"; "my menservants and my maidservants"), indicating that this point is also important to the implied author. However, Pentecost is only a partial realization of Joel's words, for the divine promise says, "I will pour out from my Spirit on all flesh." This promise is a variation on the promises of worldwide salvation in Luke 2:30–32 and 3:6 ("All flesh will see the salvation of God"). Much more is meant than the coming of the Spirit to a relatively small group at Pentecost. The subsequent narrative shows an interest in the full realization of this promise, for the response of new groups to the word of God brings similar outpourings of the Spirit in progressive movement toward realization of the promise for all.

We should note the following steps in the movement beyond the initial gift of the Spirit to the Galileans. Each of these passages is linked to the larger movement through one or more key themes associated in Luke-Acts with the Spirit: (1) The Spirit received by the Galileans at Pentecost is promised to the listening crowd if they repent and are baptized (2:38). It is described as a "gift," in accord with Luke 11:13. In Acts 2:39 Peter speaks of the "promise," which must include the "promise of the Father" (= the Spirit) of which Jesus spoke (Luke 24:49; Acts 1:4) as well as Joel's promise of the Spirit quoted in 2:17–18. This promise is "for you and your children and for all those far off," a statement that develops Joel's statement about the Spirit being poured out "on all flesh."[11] (2) When the mission moves beyond Jerusalem and a new group, the Samaritans, receives the word of God, special attention is given to the passing of the Holy Spirit to them (8:15–17). In the context (8:20) the Spirit is described as "the gift of God." (3) The coming of the Spirit to Gentiles is a crucial aspect of the Cornelius episode, where the parallel with the Pentecost event is explicit and emphatic (see the comparisons to Pentecost in 10:47; 11:15, 17). The Spirit is again described as God's "gift" (10:45; 11:17), and the Gentiles who received the Spirit were "speaking in tongues and

---

[10] Peter's speech is closely linked to the Spirit-inspired speaking in 2:4 by the repeated use of the verb ἀποφθέγγομαι ("declare," 2:4, 14). The content of the speaking in other tongues ("the mighty acts of God," 2:11) is also closely related to the content of Peter's speech.

[11] The reference in 2:39 to the Lord calling may be dependent on a part of Joel 3:5 LXX (= 2:32 ET) omitted from Acts 2:21.

magnifying (μεγαλυνόντων) God" (10:46), a combination that recalls
2:11 (note μεγαλεῖα, the "mighty" or "magnificent acts" of God). In 11:16
Peter recalls the Lord's promise of baptism in Holy Spirit (1:5), which
was fulfilled at Pentecost and now among the Gentiles. (4) In 19:1–7 the
contrast between the baptism of John and baptism in Holy Spirit, found
in 1:5 and 11:16, reappears. This scene is a reminder that baptism in Holy
Spirit is continuing to spread to new groups and places, now through the
mission of Paul. Paul does what Peter and John did in Samaria, convey
the Spirit by the laying on of hands. As a result people in Ephesus "were
speaking in tongues and prophesying" (19:6), a description that recalls
Pentecost, where speaking in tongues is interpreted as prophetic speech.
Thus the spread of the Spirit to new groups through the mission is given
thematic importance in Acts by these interrelated scenes.[12] The narrative
encourages belief that God's promise to pour out the Spirit "on all flesh" is
meaningful and relevant even though it exceeds present experience, for it
can be linked to a series of new breakthroughs that move toward the final
goal.[13]

The importance of the final sentence of the Joel quotation (Acts 2:21) is
also clear, for Acts 2—5 provides an exposition, in narrative and characters' commentary, of the promise that "everyone who calls on the name
of the Lord will be saved." In these chapters we find repeated reference
both to the name of Jesus and to salvation through him. These themes
occur already in 2:38, 40, and continue to appear in 3:6, 16; 4:7–12, 17–
18, 30; 5:28, 31, 40–41. The development of these themes in the narrative
will be given further attention below.[14] It is noteworthy that references to
the "name" of Jesus are less frequent after Acts 5 and that words of the
cluster "save, salvation, savior" do not appear after Acts 5 until 11:14,
except in one reference to Moses (7:25). The passages cited in Acts 2—5
are part of an interconnected narrative sequence that is shaped with the
prophecy of 2:21 in mind. The divine promise through the prophet passes
into narrative, which displays its fulfillment.

The significance of the words from Joel in Acts 2:19–20 is less clear, for
Joel seems to be referring to disruptions in nature that are signs of the
coming eschatological day of the Lord. Such signs are mentioned in Luke
21:25–27 but not in Acts, apart from the passage in question. It should be
noted, however, that the reference to "signs" is not found in the Septuagint
of Joel, which is followed rather closely in the Acts quotation. This
insertion creates the word pair "wonders (τέρατα)" and "signs (σημεῖα)."
In the first verse after the quotation this word pair recurs as part of a

---

[12] See Richard Zehnle, *Peter's Pentecost Discourse*, 126–28, for a similar view. A continuing
communal experience of the Spirit is indicated in Acts 4:31, 9:31, and 13:52.

[13] See the comments on Luke 3:6, a similar sweeping promise, in *Narrative Unity* 1:40–41.

[14] See 49, 53–54, 60–61.

description of Jesus' wondrous works during his ministry. First the "mighty acts" of Jesus are mentioned, repeating a term used in Luke, then the phrase "wonders and signs" is added. This phrase represents a significant transition in terminology, as there is no reference to "wonders" in Luke. It occurs immediately after the Joel quotation in which "wonders" and "signs" are mentioned and will reappear frequently after 2:22 (2:43; 4:30; 5:12; 6:8; 7:36; 14:3; 15:12),[15] always with reference to the wonders worked by Jesus and his followers (or, in 7:36, by Moses). The first reference to the miracles of the apostles in Acts also describes them as "wonders and signs" (2:43). Thus following the Joel quotation the phrase "wonders and signs" twice appears, once in reference to Jesus and once to the apostles. This is a new formulation not found in Luke-Acts prior to the Joel quotation, and in 2:22, 43 the two nouns occur in the same order as in the quotation. This is evidence that the phrase is meant to indicate fulfillment of the quotation.[16]

The application is, to be sure, strange as wonders, according to Joel, will occur in heaven; explicit reference to the sun and the moon follows. The narrator, however, may understand Joel's poetic parallelism to mean that wonders and signs will occur both in heaven and on earth. The narrator then goes on to indicate that the wonders and signs on earth are already occurring through Jesus and his apostles, even if the heavenly wonders and signs are still future. This earthly application would be encouraged by the conviction that Jesus is the "prophet like Moses" (3:22; 7:37), who also performed signs and wonders (Exod. 7:3; Deut. 34:11; Ps. 105:27 [104:27 LXX]).

Thus major portions of the Joel quotation are "active" in the surrounding text of Acts, which narrates the progressive fulfillment of the divine promises in Joel. The Joel quotation, like the Isaiah quotation in Luke 4:18–19, provides important clues to the purpose that gives events in the story their meaning, thereby providing a guide to understanding the narrative.

The description of both Jesus and his followers as workers of signs and wonders points to a significant similarity between them. This is part of a larger cluster of similarities that has led Luke Timothy Johnson to say that "all the main characters of Acts are described according to a particular model" and can be designated "Men of the Spirit" or prophets.[17]

---

[15] The order of the two nouns varies.

[16] See Richard Dillon, "Prophecy of Christ and His Witnesses," 553, n. 12, for a similar view. See also Leo O'Reilly, *Word and Sign*, 163–66. Both Dillon and O'Reilly note that "signs and wonders" is the normal order in the LXX, which makes the connection of Acts 2:22, 43 with the Joel quotation all the clearer, as they follow the same unusual order.

[17] See *Literary Function of Possessions*, 38, 40.

Johnson concludes, "We found . . . that all the figures in this category shared a certain stereotyped description, which included being filled with the Holy Spirit, speaking God's Word, performing signs and wonders, and stimulating a response of acceptance/rejection." Not only the apostles and Paul but also Moses and Jesus are described in these terms.[18] The rejection of the prophet has an important place in this model. We have already heard of rejected prophets in Luke 6:22-23, 11:47-51, and this theme was applied to Jesus in Luke 4:24, 13:31-35, 24:19-20. It will reappear in Acts 7:35-41, 51-53 in connection with the death of Stephen, who, along with Peter, the other apostles, and Paul, will encounter rejection and suffer the consequences. Johnson's model should be kept in mind, for in the characterization of the main figures of Acts the narrator seems less concerned with individuality than with a recurrent pattern that places these figures in a revelatory tradition.

When Peter begins to recall the story of Jesus in 2:22, he moves into themes that will be repeated, with variation, in a series of speeches (3:13-26; 4:10-12; 5:30-32; 10:36-43; 13:23-41). The repetition is not wooden, for the themes appear in different sequence, with different emphasis, and with variety of expression. One aspect will be treated lightly (or even omitted) in a particular sermon but will receive expanded treatment in another. Acts 2—5 presents two longer speeches to the people by Peter and two shorter speeches to the Sanhedrin. The two short speeches develop different aspects of the Pentecost speech, 4:8-12 referring to salvation through Jesus' name (see 2:21) and 5:29-32 referring to Jesus' exaltation at God's right hand and the gift of the Holy Spirit (see 2:17-18, 33, 38).[19] Thus these sermons are, in part, complementary, and the fullest understanding of their message results from considering them as a group. This approach has been followed in previous scholarship.[20] But narrative criticism of Acts must ask how these speeches function in the narrative. They are a major part of the interaction among characters and contribute to the developing plot. We must note carefully the audience addressed, the relation of this audience to the developing mission at a particular stage of the narrative, signs of adaptation of the message to the audience, and the effects of the speech.

The speeches in Acts 2—5 (and also Stephen's speech in Acts 7) are part of a developing crisis and conflict in Jerusalem, which the speeches interpret and provoke. They are intended to be appropriate to the audi-

---

[18] See *Literary Function of Possessions,* 77.

[19] On the relation of 3:12-26 to the Pentecost speech, see below, 58.

[20] See Martin Dibelius, *Studies in the Acts,* 165-67; Eduard Schweizer, "Concerning the Speeches," 208-16; and especially Ulrich Wilckens, *Missionsreden.*

ence addressed and to focus on the primary issue emerging at this stage in
the story. I mean, of course, appropriate in the eyes of the narrator, which
does not guarantee historical accuracy in the presentation of the early
Jerusalem church. Although the speeches doubtless have some relevance
for later times, it is dangerous to assume that Peter, for all practical
purposes, steps outside his narrative context and preaches the gospel
directly to the narrator's situation.[21] When Peter accuses his audience of
denying and killing Jesus (2:23, 36; 3:13–15), he is not using a preaching
theme that can be applied to any audience whatever, as the restriction of
the accusation to Jerusalem in 13:27–28 indicates. Through the narrative
listeners of later times are overhearing Peter speak to the Jerusalem Jews.
Questions of relevance must take that setting into account.[22]

The plot of a work can often be illuminated by considering the major
conflict or conflicts within it.[23] Although Jesus' witnesses face other
conflicts, the central conflict of the plot, repeatedly emphasized and still
present in the last major scene of Acts, is a conflict within Judaism
provoked by Jewish Christian preachers (including Paul). Acts 2:1—8:3
traces the development of this conflict in Jerusalem.

The speeches in this section of Acts reflect on this matter and provoke
reactions that move the crisis to a new stage. They are strongly retrospective, interpreting events that have already happened in the story.
These events concern Jesus, but they also involve the audience addressed.
Peter speaks not only of what God did through Jesus but also of what
"you" did, namely, reject and kill God's Messiah. Before Peter begins to
speak, the plot is already in crisis, a crisis that carries over from the
passion story. The resurrection does not resolve the problem but only
uncovers the critical situation of Peter's audience. Because this crisis
already exists and an escape is needed, Peter speaks as he does to the
Jerusalem Jews.

The interpretation of the death and resurrection of Jesus primarily in
terms of human rejection and divine vindication in Acts 2—5 fits with the
developing crisis that is central to the plot. Peter's sermons in Jerusalem

---

[21] According to M. Dibelius, Acts is presenting a type of Christian sermon customary in the
author's day, with the implication, "This is how the gospel is preached and ought to be
preached!" See Studies in the Acts, 165.

[22] Two speeches outside Jerusalem, Peter's speech in 10:34–43 and Paul's in 13:16–41, repeat
themes from the Jerusalem speeches. However, there are also significant differences. In
10:39 the crucifixion is reduced to a single clause, and the speech ends not with an appeal to
repentance but to faith. Also in 13:38–41 the concluding appeal is not motivated by the need
to repent from a previous rejection of Jesus.

[23] See the analysis of conflicts in the plot of Mark by David Rhoads and Donald Michie,
Mark as Story, 73–100. See also Laurence Perrine, Story and Structure, 50: "The analysis of
a story through its central conflict is likely to be especially fruitful, for it rapidly takes us to
what is truly at issue in the story."

constantly emphasize the sharp contrast between the hearer's role in denying and killing Jesus and God's vindicating act of resurrection (2:23–24, 36; 3:13–15; 4:10–11; 5:30), using successive clauses with "you" and "God" as subjects (e.g., 2:23–24: "This Jesus . . . you did away with, whom God raised up"). Peter in his speeches concentrates on what the death and resurrection of Jesus mean for those who rejected him in Jerusalem (although 10:39–40 and 13:27–30 show that Jerusalem's blind rejection is not forgotten as the crisis enters a new phase).[24] The contrasting pattern of speech used by Peter is designed to awaken his audience to their critical situation, for it emphasizes the conflict between the actions of the audience and God.

Indeed, we can say that the function of the Pentecost speech is to disclose to the Jerusalem Jews that they have blindly rejected their own Messiah and must repent. The beginning and ending of the main body of the speech emphasize the function of disclosure. Peter begins, "Let this be known to you," and concludes, "Therefore, let the whole house of Israel know assuredly . . . ," forming an inclusion (2:14, 36). In the context this is a new disclosure, for it is the first public proclamation of Jesus' resurrection and its significance. Acts 2:22–36 is a compact, carefully constructed argument leading to the conclusion in v. 36: "God made him both Lord and Christ, this Jesus whom you[25] crucified." Peter not only proclaims Jesus' authority but also reveals the intolerable situation of the audience, who share responsibility for Jesus' crucifixion. The Pentecost speech is part of a recognition scene, where, in the manner of tragedy, persons who have acted blindly against their own best interests suddenly recognize their error. For the speech is precisely designed to produce the effect described following the disclosure in 2:36, "Hearing, they were cut to the heart" (2:37), an indication that the hearers have, in fact, recognized their error and are ready for the call to repentance that follows. The effect of the speech is dependent on the preceding plot and the role of a specific group in that plot. The Jerusalem Jews are led by the speech to recognize their error committed in "ignorance" (3:17) and the critical, perhaps tragic, situation in which they are involved. The well-known dramatic device of the recognition scene has been used to present this vividly.[26]

---

[24] While the motif of atoning death is absent from these mission speeches, we should, perhaps, be cautious about concluding that the narrator did not know this motif or found it unacceptable. It may be replaced by the alternate motif of rejection and vindication through death and resurrection because the latter highlights the crisis in the plot. However, an atoning death is not essential to the preaching; the mission preachers in Acts proclaim forgiveness of sins in Jesus' name without it.

[25] This "you" is emphatic in the Greek.

[26] Modern discussion of the recognition scene is dependent on Aristotle, who describes "recognitions" or "discoveries (ἀναγνωρίσεις)" as one of the two most important elements in tragic plot (*Poetics* 1450a). Aristotle also notes the role of "ignorance (ἄγνοια)" in the tragic

We can also say that the Pentecost speech is designed to move the Jerusalem Jews to repentance. The discovery does not lead to an immediate, tragic denouement, with the plot at a dead end. An avenue of escape is still open, as Peter indicates with his call to repentance and offer of release of sins (2:38). A call to repentance and an offer of release of sins are integral parts of the speeches in Acts 3 and 5 (see 3:19, 26; 5:31). The separation of these elements from the rest of the Pentecost speech is caused by the emphasis on audience reaction in 2:37, which in turn highlights Peter's call to repentance in the following verse. The pressure built up by the conflict between the treatment of Jesus in the passion story and Jesus as now vindicated by God must be released in action. Peter's call to repentance and baptism points to the necessary action. It is supported in 2:39 by the statement "To you is the promise" (with the pronoun in the emphatic first position in the sentence). This pronoun balances the emphatic pronoun in the accusation of 2:36 ("whom *you* crucified"). Both accusation and promise are emphatically applied to the specific audience in order to move it to repentance. These emphatic pronouns will reappear in later statements to Jews.[27] When the promise is rejected, this emphasis will produce pathos, for the promise that belongs especially to Israel, the people of the promise, is being lost to them. However, the Pentecost speech is powerfully effective. Many respond to Peter's call and are baptized (2:41).

The disclosure is also a disclosure about God. God is declared to be the hidden actor behind each stage of Jesus' story: his mighty acts (2:22), his death (2:23), his resurrection (2:24, 32), his exaltation and pouring out of the Spirit (2:33–34), his appointment as Lord and Messiah (2:36). God's action nullifies and reverses the rejection of Jesus expressed in the passion story. Although the residents of Jerusalem "denied" Jesus (3:13, 14) and their rulers "despised" him (4:11), God "exalted" (2:33–35; 5:31) and "glorified" (3:13) him. This reversal is also implied in the repeated statements that "you" killed him but God raised him up.

Human actors are held responsible for Jesus' death, as Peter's accusations and call to repentance make clear. Yet Jesus' death took place "by the fixed purpose and foreknowledge of God" (2:23) and in fulfillment of what God "foretold through the mouth of all the prophets" (3:18; cf. 13:27). These are strong statements of divine sovereignty in events that

---

plot (*Poetics* 1453b–54a). According to Acts 3:17 and 13:27 the Jerusalem Jews acted in ignorance. The discovery of what they have done constitutes a recognition scene. See R. Tannehill, "Israel in Luke-Acts," 79.

[27] First- or second-person pronouns referring to the audience are placed first in their clauses, and thereby emphasized, in 3:25, 26; 13:26, 46. See R. Tannehill, "Israel in Luke-Acts," 77–78.

have the contrary appearance. The two themes of human responsibility and divine sovereignty may seem to conflict, but both are necessary to produce the ironic view of Jesus' death that is typical of Luke-Acts.[28] The residents of Jerusalem and their rulers, blind to God's purpose, act to rid themselves of Jesus and are responsible for their actions, but this very act contributes to God's purpose of enthroning Jesus as Messiah. There may be a connection, for the narrator and others, between a sense of irony and a sense of divine transcendence. God's transcendence is displayed in the world when a surprising grace or a surprising justice appears that transcends, and may contradict, human intentions and powers. The Pentecost speech is primarily the disclosure to its audience of God's surprising reversal of their intentions, for their rejection has ironically resulted in Jesus' exaltation as Messiah, Spirit-giver, and source of repentance and forgiveness.

A reminder of the previous discussion of Luke 24:26 ("Was it not necessary for the Messiah to suffer these things?") may suggest why it would seem natural to include Jesus' death in God's "fixed purpose and foreknowledge." His death was no surprise to God, nor should it be to those who meditate on the pattern of prophetic destiny that the narrator finds in Scripture and recent history. The destiny of God's prophets includes suffering and rejection, for they must speak God's word to a blind and resistant world and must bear the brunt of this resistance. Their suffering is part of God's "fixed purpose and foreknowledge," that is, it fits God's established way of working in a resistant world. God's way of working through suffering prophets applies especially to Jesus as Messiah and prophet like Moses.[29]

Peter's interpretation of the story of Jesus in the Pentecost speech places primary emphasis on Jesus' resurrection and exaltation, the events in the story that are new to his audience. Peter refers first to the resurrection (2:24–32) and then to Jesus' exaltation to the right hand of God (2:33–35). A Scripture citation is attached to each, and each is associated with a title ("Messiah," 2:31; "Lord," 2:34). The conclusion in 2:36 combines these titles, emphasizing what the resurrection, ascension, and coming of the Spirit, taken together and seen as fulfillment of Scripture, disclose about Jesus.

Acts 2:36 is clearly the conclusion and climax of the preceding argument[30] and must be interpreted in light of it. This concluding verse forms

---

[28] On God as a God of irony in Luke-Acts, see *Narrative Unity* 1:283–84.

[29] For further explanation see *Narrative Unity* 1:284–89.

[30] On the structure of the argument and the argumentative use of Scripture, see William Kurz, "Hellenistic Rhetoric in the Christological Proof," 182–84; Barnabas Lindars, *New Testament Apologetic*, 36–59; Jacques Dupont, *Salvation of the Gentiles*, 106–15, 124–26, 147–50; Donald Juel, *Messianic Exegesis*, 139–40, 146–49.

an inclusion with the beginning of the speech (2:14) and recalls 2:23 as well as the statements about the "resurrection of the Messiah" (2:31) and Jesus' exaltation as "Lord" (2:33–34). The concluding affirmation of Jesus as Lord is crucial to the argument and to the mission in the following chapters, for it implies that Jesus is the Lord mentioned by Joel (see Acts 2:21), the Lord whose name brings salvation.[31] Thus the christological argument in 2:22–36 is still related to the Joel quotation.

The connections indicated show that Acts 2:36 should not be separated from the rest of the speech as a fragment of an early adoptionist Christology that conflicts with the narrator's views. The "therefore" in this verse indicates that it is drawing a conclusion about Jesus based on the preceding statements about the Messiah and Lord. These statements refer to resurrection and exaltation. Thus the context strongly suggests that "God made him both Lord and Messiah" is a christological conclusion drawn from the preceding statements that "God raised" him and said, "Sit at my right hand." The centrality of the resurrection for the affirmation in 2:36 is also indicated by comparing it with 2:23–24 and related statements. These passages present the same contrast between what God did and what "you" did. The act of God in 2:24 that corresponds to God making Jesus Lord and Messiah is the resurrection. Parallel passages in 13:33 and 5:31 must also be considered. In the former, Jesus is declared to be God's Son through resurrection;[32] in the latter, Jesus exercises the functions of "leader and savior" as a result of his exaltation to God's right hand.[33] Finally, the idea that Jesus is given a new status and power through his resurrection and exaltation does not appear suddenly in Acts. In Luke 19:12 Jesus tells of a man who goes "to a distant country to receive royal rule," a clear anticipation of his own departure. The Scripture quotations in Luke 20:17, 42–43 anticipate Jesus' exaltation to a new status following his death, and Jesus speaks of himself in similar terms in 22:69. Acts 2:36 is the announcement that these anticipations have been fulfilled.

Specifically, 2:36 refers to God's enthronement of Jesus as messianic king through resurrection and exaltation. The theme of enthronement is important in the preceding speech. The "resurrection of the Messiah" is necessary to fulfill God's "oath" to David to "seat" a descendant of David

---

[31] See D. Juel, *Messianic Exegesis,* 147.

[32] On 13:33 see further 170.

[33] This parallel is emphasized by Emmeram Kränkl, *Jesus, der Knecht Gottes,* 161–62. He also refers to Acts 4:11, 13:33, and Luke 19:12 to support the view that Jesus' kingship is associated with his exaltation and that this is Luke's own view, not a remnant of early church tradition.

"on his throne" (2:30–31). This oath is fulfilled when God says, "Sit at my right hand" (2:34). This enthronement theme may help to explain why the narrator can permit the proclamation of Jesus as Savior, Messiah, and Lord at his birth (Luke 2:11) and yet can have Peter say that God exalted Jesus as Savior at God's right hand (Acts 5:31) and made him Lord and Messiah through resurrection and exaltation. Just as there are several important stages in the life of a king, from birth as heir to the throne, to anointing (which is separated from enthronement by some time in both the story of David and in the Lukan story of Jesus),[34] to actual assumption of the throne, so in the life of Jesus according to Luke-Acts. Although Jesus was called Lord and Messiah previously, the full authority of these titles is granted only through death, resurrection, and exaltation. Peter's concluding statement in 2:36 makes clear that something new and important has happened through these events. Jesus has been enthroned as Lord and Messiah for Israel, to fulfill all the promises made to it. This newly enthroned ruler will also offer salvation to the world, having been granted universal power to rule and judge.

The ruling power of Jesus is saving power. Through the enthroned Messiah benefits are "poured out" or "given" to the Messiah's people. The presentation of this in the Acts speeches suggests continuity with the saving work of Jesus during his previous ministry, for the beneficial power that Jesus then showed to the limited number of people who encountered him will now be offered to all. Thus the Spirit, which rested on Jesus but not on his followers during his preresurrection ministry, has been poured out on others by the exalted Jesus (2:33), and this benefit will be extended to new groups as the mission expands.[35] Repentance and release of sins are associated with Jesus' exaltation in a similar way, for "God exalted" Jesus "at his right hand to give repentance to Israel and release of sins" (5:31). These gifts will be offered universally. When the Gentiles later receive the Spirit, the Jewish Christians acknowledge that "to the Gentiles also God has given repentance unto life" (11:18). This is an extension of Jesus' work during his earthly ministry, in which release of sins had a central place.[36] Hence we find repeated references in Acts to some benefit associated with Jesus being "poured out" or "given" following Jesus' exaltation.

The saving "name" of Jesus is viewed in a similar way in 4:12. It is the "name . . . given . . . by which we must be saved." This is another reference

---

[34] See 1 Sam. 16:1–13; Luke 3:21–22; 4:18; Acts 10:38, and William Kurz, "Acts 3:19–26 as a Test," 316 and n. 32.

[35] See above, 30–31.

[36] See *Narrative Unity* 1:103–9.

to the benefits of the enthroned Messiah.[37] His name is a source of salvation, in fulfillment of Joel's prophecy that "everyone who calls on the name of the Lord will be saved" (2:21). The "name" of Jesus represents his royal power and authority, which is invoked by his subjects, and, as Hans Conzelmann points out, "The acts performed by virtue of the name are in conformity with what is recorded of the ministry of the historical Jesus, for it was this that set the pattern for the future."[38] Through baptism in the name people receive the Spirit (2:38), the apostles speak and teach in the name (4:17–18), wonders take place through the name (3:6, 16; 4:7, 10, 30), and release of sins is received through the name (10:43; cf. Luke 24:47). In all of these ways the benefits that Jesus promised or granted during his earthly ministry are now given by the enthroned Messiah. These benefits not only continue but are greatly extended, for they are now part of a universal mission to Israel and the world.

As we have seen, the benefits of the Spirit, repentance, release of sins, and probably also salvation through the name are viewed as consequences of Jesus' exaltation and enthronement. As the one exalted to God's right hand, Jesus is able to extend the benefits of his ministry to all Israel and the world. Thus we may say that God saves by establishing through Jesus the messianic reign, which is the time of salvation promised Israel in Scripture, a time of salvation that the Gentiles may share. Jesus is Savior as the ruling Messiah,[39] who, in fulfillment of the promise to David, mediates the benefits of God's rule. The Spirit, repentance and release of sins, and salvation through Jesus' name are all part of these benefits. Peter at Pentecost announces the opportunity to share in these benefits (2:21, 38–40).[40]

It is possible that the Pentecost scene is meant not only to fulfill John the Baptist's words about baptism in Holy Spirit (Luke 3:16; cf. Acts 1:5) but also to suggest that Peter is a successor of John in preaching a message of repentance.[41] John proclaimed a "baptism of repentance for release of sins" (Luke 3:3). Peter proclaims, "Repent and be baptized . . . for release of your sins" (Acts 2:38). John's preaching evokes the question, "What should we do? (Τί ποιήσωμεν)" (Luke 3:10, 12, 14), and so does Peter's preaching (Acts 2:37). John's message of repentance is associated with a

---

[37] Note the reference to Jesus' exaltation in 4:11.

[38] See *Theology of St. Luke,* 178.

[39] In both Luke 2:11 and Acts 13:23 the title σωτήρ ("Savior") is used in contexts that clearly refer to the Davidic Messiah.

[40] This manner of thinking probably reflects the ancient social system of benefaction and patronage. See Frederick Danker, *Luke,* 28–46. For an introduction to patronage, see John Elliott, "Patronage and Clientism," 39–48.

[41] On the continuation of John's work through Jesus' disciples in Luke, see *Narrative Unity* 1:229–30, 233–35.

quotation from Isaiah that refers to straightening what is "crooked (τὰ σκολιά)" (Luke 3:5). The only other use of this word in Luke-Acts is in Peter's call, "Be saved from this crooked generation" (Acts 2:40).[42] Perhaps the description of the church as having all things in common (Acts 2:44) shows the fulfillment of John's demand that his hearers demonstrate their repentance by sharing possessions (Luke 3:11). Whether these subtle connections are caught by readers or not, Peter in this and subsequent scenes functions as a preacher of repentance. Filled with the Spirit, he presents a prophetic challenge to a crooked generation. In doing this, he assumes the role of his predecessors, John the Baptist and Jesus.

The Pentecost speech is one of the most carefully constructed speeches in Acts. It is carefully shaped as a persuasive appeal to the kind of audience pictured in the narrative.[43] One sign of rhetorical art is the repeated use of accusatives referring to Jesus in emphatic position at the beginning of a clause (in the Greek text): "Jesus . . ." (2:22), "this one . . ." (2:23), "this Jesus . . ." (2:32), "him both Lord and Messiah . . . , this Jesus . . ." (2:36). Jesus is both the focus of attention and the object of statements concerning God's and the audience's actions upon him. This technique of emphasis helps to make Jesus vividly present to the audience as a special kind of person.[44] In his argument Peter appeals to his hearers' own experience, to what they themselves know, see, and hear (2:22, 29, 33), which can be an especially convincing basis for an argument. Peter also appeals to Scripture. This mutually recognized authority provides an important basis of argument with the Jewish audience, but the appeal to Scripture also reinforces communion between speaker and audience through reference to their shared tradition.[45] Because Peter's accusation of his audience threatens this communion, communion needs to be reinforced. The accusation is balanced by emphasis in 2:39 on the promise "for you and your children" (with emphasis on "you" through its position

---

[42] The phrase "crooked generation" occurs in Deut. 32:5 and Ps. 77:8 LXX, and Acts 2:40 may reflect these passages. See G. Schneider, *Apostelgeschichte*, 1:278, n. 144. The choice of this phrase still creates an additional link between Peter's preaching and the ministry of John as described in Luke 3.

[43] The diverse audience "from every nation" must now be addressed as a single group, which involves considerable simplification. It is assumed that the Septuagint is authoritative, as arguments are based on this version of Scripture, but the audience is also acquainted with events in the Jewish homeland, such as Jesus' wonders and signs (2:22).

[44] See Ch. Perelman and L. Olbrechts-Tyteca, *New Rhetoric*, 117: "It is not enough indeed that a thing should exist for a person to feel its presence. . . . Accordingly one of the preoccupations of a speaker is to make present . . . what is actually absent but what he considers important to his argument."

[45] See Ch. Perelman and L. Olbrechts-Tyteca, *New Rhetoric*, 14, 177: "For argumentation to exist, an effective community of minds must be realized at a given moment." "Often . . . communion [with the audience] is achieved through references to a common culture, tradition or past."

in the sentence) and by modes of address that stress the shared heritage and common bond uniting speaker and audience. While Peter begins with the comparatively cold address "Jews [or "Judeans"] and all dwelling in Jerusalem," he later calls his audience "Israelites" (2:22) and "house of Israel" (2:36), recalling the biblical heritage, and also "brothers (ἄνδρες ἀδελφοί)" (2:29; cf. 2:37). Since Christian leaders address the church as brothers (1:16; 6:3; 15:7, 13), this term affirms a significant bond.

Educated authors would want to compose speeches for their narratives that, in their opinion, were appropriate to the speaker and audience, for appropriateness was an important criterion of a good speech in Greco-Roman rhetoric.[46] Furthermore, in Greco-Roman education students were trained in *prosopopoeia*, "the art of suiting speeches to a historical, fictional or stereotypical figure." They were taught to "consider what kind of character the speaker is, his age, the occasion, etc.," and to compose a suitable speech.[47] Our narrator strives to provide an appropriate speech and may well have received preparatory training for this task.

---

[46] See Cicero, *Orator* 21.71: "The universal rule, in oratory as in life, is to consider propriety. This depends on the subject under discussion, and on the character of both the speaker and the audience." See also Donald Clark, *Rhetoric in Greco-Roman Education,* 100: "Language should be appropriate to the speaker, to the audience, and to the subject."

[47] See W. Kurz, "Hellenistic Rhetoric in the Christological Proof," 186, who refers to Theon.

THE COMMUNAL LIFE
OF THE JERUSALEM BELIEVERS

The narrative now shifts from description of particular events on a particular day to general description of the life of the early Jerusalem church. This shift is brief, for in 3:1 the narrator will return to narration of a particular event. Here the narrative illustrates the alternation between "scene" and "summary" that is common also in novels.[1] A "scene" describes a particular occasion in some detail, usually with dialogue between characters, and the amount of time taken in narration equals by convention the amount of time occupied by the narrated event. The "summary" combines events so that the time of narration is less, often much less, than the time of the events.[2] However, the summary in Acts 2:42–47 is more than just a bridge between the main events because it introduces new material of some importance for the Jerusalem section of Acts.

We may speak of major and minor themes in Acts 2:1—8:3. The major story line is carried by a series of connected dramatic scenes (2:1–41; 3:1—4:31; 5:17–41; 6:11—8:1a). This material depicts the mission and its impact. It will increasingly emphasize the opposition to the mission by the Sanhedrin. It is united thematically, and the connections are especially close in 3:1—4:31, 5:17–41, for these sections present a continuous narrative with causal connections among events and retrospective references by characters to previous events. Primary attention is directed by the narrator to the events in this major story line. There is other material in Acts 2—6, however. This material, although sometimes presented in summary form, is more than filler and bridge between scenes. Especially the two summaries in 2:42–47 and 4:32–35 introduce a distinctive emphasis on unity and sharing in the community. This is a significant minor theme in the Jerusalem section of Acts, for it is emphasized by repetition in these summaries and spawns related scenic material in 5:1–11 and 6:1–6.

---

[1] See Gérard Genette, *Narrative Discourse,* 109–10: "The real rhythm of the novelistic canon . . . is thus the alternation of nondramatic summaries, functioning as waiting room and liaison, with dramatic scenes whose role in the action is decisive."

[2] See G. Genette, *Narrative Discourse,* 94, and see 86–112 for a broader discussion of "duration," i.e., the pace of narration compared to the time span of the story.

Because the confrontation with Ananias and Sapphira and the dispute between the Hebrews and Hellenists represent threats to unity, all of this material (and the brief report about Barnabas in 4:36-37) concerns unity and sharing of possessions. Evidently the church's unity and the community of goods that expressed that unity most tellingly were of special interest to the narrator, who emphasizes them in the first two summaries and introduces related scenes.

Benjamin Hrushovski notes how Tolstoy shifts from one segment of narration to another, "without seeming to be systematic." Shifts of theme, "little threads of plot," and "semantic chains running discontinuously through parts of the text" are "major forms of dynamization" of the text, producing "the impression of a fluid, irregular and natural situation."[3] In a simpler way the narrator of Acts has broken the threads of plot and semantic chains, inserting the minor theme into the major theme at 2:42–47, returning to it in 4:32—5:11, and again in 6:1-6. This procedure introduces pauses into the main thread of plot but does not destroy its continuity.

Acts 2:42-47 describes the community life of those who responded to Peter's offer of release of sins and the gift of the Spirit at Pentecost. As the second summary of community life follows a renewed outpouring of the Spirit, there may be a suggestion that the Spirit not only inspires bold preaching and wonders (4:29-31) but also devotion to others and their needs (4:32). Acts 2:42-47 presents in brief compass a number of characteristic activities that reappear elsewhere in Acts 1—7. Besides the themes of unity and sharing possessions, to be discussed below, we hear of the "teaching of the apostles"[4] (2:42; 4:2, 18; 5:21, 25, 28, 42), the "prayers" (1:14, 24; 2:42; 4:24-30; 6:4, 6), gathering in the temple, which evidently serves as a place of prayer and teaching (2:46; 3:1, 11; 5:12, 20-21, 25, 42; cf. Luke 24:53),[5] "fear" (2:43; 5:5, 11), "wonders" and "signs" (2:19, 22, 43; 4:16, 22, 30; 5:12; 6:8; 7:36), and the favor of the people (2:47; 4:21; 5:13, 26). In light of these repetitions it is somewhat surprising that the breaking of bread is not mentioned between 2:42, 46 and 20:7, 11. The final sentence in 2:47 also makes clear that the community continues to

---

[3] See *Segmentation and Motivation*, 32.

[4] Peter's speeches in Acts 2—5 provide examples of this teaching, which is directed to outsiders as well as the community. See 4:2; 5:28.

[5] These verses and Acts 21:26 show that Jesus' followers are not opposed to the temple, despite the opposition from the temple authorities that will soon develop. On the case of Stephen, see below, 92–95. This observation fits into a larger picture of respect for the patterns of Jewish life. J. Bradley Chance contrasts the Lukan view of the temple with the "dominant pattern" in early Christianity of reserving no place for a literal temple or temple city because these have been replaced by the Christian community or by Jesus. See *Jerusalem, the Temple, and the New Age*, 33, 45.

grow through conversions—another repeated theme (2:41, 47; 4:4; 5:14; 6:1, 7)—and that people are receiving the salvation promised in 2:21, 40 (see also 4:9, 12). All of these aspects of the summary in 2:42-47 are emphasized through repetition elsewhere.

The narrator places special emphasis on the church as a sharing community in the summaries in 2:42-47 and 4:32-35. "They were continually devoted . . . to the communal life ($\mathring{\eta}\sigma\alpha\nu$ δὲ προσκαρτεροῦντες . . . τῇ κοινωνίᾳ)" (2:42), and their "heart and soul" were "one" (4:32). This communal life appears in the early church's assemblies, for the believers spent a great deal of time together in prayer, hearing the apostles' teaching, and at meals (2:42, 44, 46; cf. 1:14; 2:1; 4:24). However, the most impressive sign of the believers' devotion to each other is the fact that they had "all things in common," a sign of unity that receives special attention in 2:44-45 and is the central concern of 4:32-37. The ways in which the community of goods are described suggest that the narrator saw in this both the realization of Greek ideals and the fulfillment of the scriptural promise of God's blessing on an obedient people. It is probably not an accident that the phrases "all things in common" and "one soul" (2:44; 4:32) recall sayings listed by Aristotle as "proverbs" concerning true friendship.[6] David Mealand points out that "nothing one's own" and "all things in common" appear in Plato's discussion of the ideal state, and the theme continues in later writers.[7] Not only Greek ideas of friendship and the ideal state but the promises of Jewish Scripture influence the description of the early church in Acts. The statement that "there was not any needy person among them" (4:34) recalls Deut. 15:4, where this happy situation is promised as God's blessing if the people are obedient and do not harden their hearts against the needy.

Community of goods in the early church also represents wholehearted obedience to Jesus' teachings about possessions in Luke. Thus community of goods is not a mere curiosity, interesting in itself but unconnected with the central concerns of Luke-Acts. It relates directly to a major topic of Jesus' teaching in Luke. Jesus told the rich ruler, "Sell (πώλησον) all that you have and distribute (διάδος) to the poor" (18:22). Jesus also told the disciples, "Sell (πωλήσατε) your possessions and give (δότε) alms" (12:33). In the early Jerusalem church those with lands and houses were following Jesus' commands, and two key verbs from the command to the rich ruler reappear in Acts 4:34-35: "Selling (πωλοῦντες) . . . it was being

---

[6] *Nicomachean Ethics* IX.8.2 (1168b). The proverbs cited by Aristotle include μία ψυχή ("one soul") and κοινὰ τὰ φίλων ("The property of friends is held in common"). See further J. Dupont, *Salvation of the Gentiles,* 87-91, 95-99, and G. Schneider, *Apostelgeschichte* 1:290, n. 1; 365, nn. 15-16.

[7] See "Community of Goods," 96-99.

distributed (διεδίδετο)."[8] The same process is described in 2:45, using different but synonymous verbs. Selling pieces of property and distributing the proceeds are the characteristic features of all four of these passages. Later Acts will show that this practice of the Jerusalem church is not the only way of sharing in the church, but it is the most direct application of Jesus' commands to those with possessions. The emphasis placed on this method of providing for the needy in the two summaries in 2:42–47 and 4:32–37 shows that the strong concern in Luke for the poor and challenge to the rich do not abruptly disappear in Acts. Acts gives remarkably little attention to the internal life of the church. The principal exception in Acts 2—7 is the emphasis on believers selling their property in order to care for the needy.

Perhaps Jesus' commands are fulfilled not only by the selling of possessions but also by the caring unity of which this is a sign. In Luke the disciples were quarrelsome, disputing among themselves who was the greatest, and Jesus corrected them (9:46–48; 22:24–27). In Acts, however, the apostles act as a unified group (cf. 2:14; 5:29; 6:2–4), and there is distinct emphasis on the heartfelt unity of the whole community, demonstrated in acts of sharing. In place of fractiousness there is "one heart and soul."

The community of goods is mentioned only in connection with the early Jerusalem church. It is part of the narrator's picture of the ideal church at the beginning. Already at the time of writing there was probably a clear difference between this ideal picture and the actual practice of Christians. Nevertheless, this ideal is emphasized. We need not suppose that the narrator expected later churches to be transformed into the ideal community described. Such an expectation is not required for the ideal to be relevant. The ideal can function as critique of a complacent church with narrow vision, content with its own obedience, and this constructive criticism may find a response among individuals, if not in a church as a whole. If Jesus' call and this ideal picture of the church lead some Christians with assets to recognize that they can and should give those assets to the poor, something important has happened.[9] Such responses by individuals may not in themselves produce the ideal community of the narrator's vision, but they do recognize the needs of the poor as a moral claim, as did the early church, according to Acts.[10]

---

[8] The verb διαδίδωμι is found only four times in the NT, with three of these occurrences in Luke-Acts. The connection between Luke 18:22 and Acts 4:34–35 is noted by Schuyler Brown, *Apostasy and Perseverance*, 101–2.

[9] Didache 4:8 and Barnabas 19:8 use language similar to Acts in exhortation. The ideal pictured in the Acts narrative becomes a moral imperative addressed to individual Christians. These texts are quoted by J. Dupont, *Salvation of the Gentiles*, 99.

[10] On the social context of the Lukan concern with rich and poor, see Philip Esler, *Community and Gospel*, 164–200.

Even in the Jerusalem church wholehearted concern for others and unity are threatened by Ananias and Sapphira (5:1–11) and the dispute between Hebrews and Hellenists (6:1–6). However, the apostles act with dispatch to deal with these threats, and the integrity of the church is restored.

Later the narrator will call attention to other ways of sharing material goods, ways that, although less radical, are probably regarded as worthy of emulation. Tabitha, a woman "full of good works and charities," is honored for making clothing for the needy (9:36, 39). The church of Antioch sends famine relief to the Christians of Judea (11:27–30). In his farewell address to the Ephesian elders, Paul comments on his attitude toward money and possessions during his ministry (20:33–35). Paul did not covet the money and clothing of others but worked to support himself, his co-workers, and those in need. Paul's practice of working and earning may seem a long way from the community of goods in Jerusalem, but it represents a new application of Jesus' teaching to the situation of church leaders who might claim community support. It is motivated by the same wholehearted devotion to the welfare of others that characterized the Jerusalem church.[11]

The portrait of the church and its situation in 2:42–47 is very positive. It not only describes high enthusiasm among the believers but also indicates that "all the people" viewed them with "favor" (2:47). There is no indication of tension here, either within the church or in relation to its social context. In following chapters this favorable situation will change as first the temple authorities, then Diaspora Jews in Jerusalem (6:9–14) emerge as opponents of the new movement, finally arousing the people (6:12) and instigating a "great persecution" (8:1). The story will move from harmony between believers and Jewish society through developing conflict to a major crisis. This development dominates the narrative from 3:1 to 8:3. We must note the factors that contribute to it, according to the narrator.

---

[11] See below, 260–61.

PETER HEALS A LAME MAN
AND CONTINUES HIS CALL
TO REPENTANCE

The summary in 2:42–47 prepares for the scene that follows. According to 2:46 the believers were "daily . . . in the temple," and 3:1–10 begins by reporting that Peter and John were going to the temple. In 2:43 we were told of "many wonders and signs" taking place through the apostles, and 3:1–10 tells of a specific wonder. Peter's declaration in 3:6 that he has no silver or gold presupposes a renunciation of possessions similar to that described in 2:44–45, although Peter and John left their possessions long before (cf. Luke 5:11).[1] Finally, Acts 4:4 declares that "many . . . believed" as a result of Peter's preaching, continuing a theme from 2:41, 47.

The healing of the lame man at the temple gate initiates a connected sequence of events involving the apostles, the people, and the Sanhedrin in 3:11—5:42.[2] The healing causes "all the people" to gather (3:11), which becomes the occasion for Peter's speech in 3:12–26. This speech in turn provokes the temple authorities to arrest Peter and John (4:1–3). The whole sequence of events in 3:1—4:22 takes place on an afternoon and the next day and is directly caused by the healing of the lame man and by Peter's speech to the crowd attracted by this event. There are repeated references to the healing of the lame man in this section as Peter and John explain its significance and the Sanhedrin struggles to respond to what has happened (3:12, 16; 4:7–12, 14, 16). The section ends as it began with a reference to the healing of the lame man and its effect on the people (4:21–22). Thus the sequence of events in 3:1—4:22 is unified causally, one event provoking the next. It is unified temporally by the short span of time. It is also unified by the persistent presence of the healed man with Peter and John. Remarkably, the lame man is physically present even at the hearing before the Sanhedrin after the apostles' arrest (4:14). He is a persistent reminder of the power of Jesus' name.

---

[1] The role of the apostles as custodians of community funds for the needy is introduced later (4:35, 37). This role is not presupposed in Acts 2—3.

[2] On coherence and segmentation in Acts 3:1—4:31, see R. Funk, *Poetics of Biblical Narrative,* 75–97. Some parts of the following discussion of Acts 3 were originally published in the *Society of Biblical Literature 1984 Seminar Papers,* ed. Kent Harold Richards (Chico: Scholars Press, 1984), copyright 1984 by the Society of Biblical Literature. See Robert Tannehill, "The Composition of Acts 3—5," 218–22, 229–31. Used by permission.

The causal chain does not end at 4:22. The hearing of Peter and John before the Sanhedrin concludes with the threats of the Sanhedrin, who are trying to force the apostles to stop speaking in Jesus' name. The prayer of the church that follows in 4:23–31 is a response to this threat, and following a second arrest and hearing, the Sanhedrin complains that the apostles have disobeyed the command not to teach in Jesus' name (5:28). They attempt again to enforce their order, but their efforts are ineffective. Acts 5:17–42 is tied to 4:5–31 because it is the continuation of the story of the Sanhedrin's threats to the mission. The one section also reduplicates the other, each moving from arrest to hearing to release, thereby emphasizing the courage of the apostles and the inability of the Sanhedrin to respond effectively.

Acts 2—5 is also united by frequent references to the "name" of the Lord or of Jesus Messiah, references that are especially characteristic of this section of Acts. The references begin with the Joel quotation in 2:21 ("Everyone who calls on the name of the Lord will be saved"). Peter also speaks of being baptized "in the name of Jesus Messiah" in 2:38. Then the name of Jesus Messiah is presented as the effective power behind the healing of the lame man (3:6, 16; 4:7, 10, 12), and there are repeated references to Jesus' name as the apostles encounter the rulers' threats (4:17, 18, 30; 5:28, 40, 41). In following chapters the "name" of Jesus is also important. Christians are described as those who "call upon the name" (9:14, 21; 22:16), a reminder of the quotation in 2:21 with which the theme is introduced. Following Acts 2—5 references to the name of Jesus are first associated with the mission of Philip in Samaria (8:12, 16) and then with Paul's call and early preaching (9:14, 15, 16, 21, 27, 28 [29 RSV]), perhaps to emphasize the continuity of the preaching of Philip and Paul with the preaching of the apostles. After Acts 9 references to Jesus' name become less frequent and more scattered, occurring at 10:43, 48; 15:26; 16:18; 19:5, 13, 17; 21:13; 22:16; 26:9. The comparative infrequency of references to Jesus' name in Acts 10—28 supports the view that the frequent references in Acts 2—5 and 8—9 are not merely the result of habits of expression but show deliberate emphasis in a section of Acts where this theme contributes to narrative continuity. The lame man becomes a paradigm of salvation through the name of the Lord (cf. 4:9–12), in fulfillment of the scriptural promise quoted in 2:21, and the promised salvation then passes to others through the missions of the apostles, Philip, and Paul.

Our experience of the story is greatly enriched when we note that Acts 2—5 (and other parts of Acts) can produce a complex echo effect. Characters and events in Acts echo characters and events already presented in the Gospel, and remembrance of these earlier characters and events suggests a complex set of similarities, differences, and fulfillments that deepens our experience of the story. In this way the narrative takes on resonance. The previous story resonates with the new events, so that significance is both amplified and enriched. We can also say that the previous story provides commentary on the current story. At some points this commentary seems clear and specific, so that the echo effect serves to control interpretation. The echo adds emphasis, helping to specify central meanings and ensure their communication. But the echoes multiply, producing tantalizing hints of meaning that are difficult to control. Echo added to echo produces a resonance that surrounds the central meanings with overtones that the author cannot fully control and readers or listeners cannot easily exhaust.

We are discussing what is often called "parallels" between Luke and Acts (and also within Acts).[3] In discussing such parallels, we should remember that they serve to enrich narrative lines that keep moving into the future. Absolute sameness would bring movement to a halt. The parallels always suggest *similarity* in events that are not the *same*, each event retaining the uniqueness appropriate to its special time and place. Furthermore, the discovery of similarity may also accent important differences, and exploring these differences may also contribute to the significance of the story. We become aware of similarities and differences together as comparisons come to mind. Significant comparisons may multiply. The discovery of similarities between two events does not preclude connections with other events as well. Nor do the related events all occur between the birth of Jesus and Paul's preaching in Rome. The story also awakens echoes of Old Testament figures.

A first set of similarities appears when we compare the beginning of the apostles' mission with the beginning of Jesus' mission.[4] In each case we must consider not single scenes but a development through several chapters, encompassing a group of scenes that have thematic connections. Both the mission of Jesus and the mission of the apostles begin with prayer and the coming of the Spirit, followed by an inaugural speech that relates the coming of the Spirit to the new mission through a Scripture quotation. The inaugural speech also proclaims "release ($\check{\alpha}\phi\epsilon\sigma\iota\varsigma$)."[5] Soon afterwards we are told of the healing of a paralytic or lame man, which becomes the occasion for a fundamental disclosure concerning Jesus' saving significance. The disclosure also involves the interpretation of

---

[3] For recent discussion of such parallels, see C. Talbert, *Literary Patterns*, and G. Trompf, *Idea of Historical Recurrence.* Both argue that patterns of balance or recurrence are widespread in Hebraic and Greco-Roman writings of the ancient world.

[4] See C. Talbert, *Literary Patterns,* 16.

[5] For more detail see above, 29.

something from the Scripture quotation in the inaugural sermon. This same healing is the occasion for the first expression of opposition to the new mission from religious leaders.

The first opposition from Pharisees and teachers of the law appears when Jesus offers release of sins to a paralytic (Luke 5:17–26), an important fulfillment of Jesus' commission to proclaim release (cf. 4:18 in Jesus' inaugural speech). The healing of the paralytic is both the beginning of a continuing conflict with the scribes and Pharisees and a proclamation of Jesus' authority to release sins (5:24), an authority basic to his ongoing ministry, as indicated by the narrator's tendency to link later scenes with Luke 5:17–32.[6] The narrative in Acts 3—4 is linked to Peter's inaugural sermon by references to the saving power of Jesus' name (2:21; 3:6, 16; 4:7–12). This theme is developed through the healing of a lame man. Although there are some similarities of expression between the two healing stories, these similarities might simply reflect the fact that both stories report the healing of a man who could not walk.[7] The connection between the two stories becomes striking, however, when we consider the function of the stories in the larger narrative. Both stories, placed early in the respective missions, contain or lead to a basic proclamation of Jesus' saving significance, a proclamation important for the continuing mission, and both provoke opposition from religious leaders, which will continue into the following chapters. The healing of the lame man in Jesus' name leads up to the general proclamation of salvation in Jesus' name in 4:7–12, thereby explaining the offer of salvation to those who call upon the name of the Lord in 2:21. The healing of the paralytic in Luke 5:17–26 is also linked to the preceding inaugural sermon (through the theme of "release") and develops the significance of Jesus' work announced there by proclaiming Jesus' authority on earth to release sins (5:24). This general claim is made in the face of opposition already expressed by Jewish leaders, just as Peter speaks to the temple authorities about Jesus after he and John have already been arrested. In both cases the opposition from Jewish leaders has just appeared but will continue in scenes that follow closely.

Thus the similarity between Jesus' healing of the paralytic and Peter's healing of the lame man lies less in the healing itself than in the function of these scenes in the larger narrative. In both cases the healing becomes the occasion for a fundamental claim about Jesus' saving power, emphasizing its importance and general scope ("on earth," Luke 5:24; "under heaven," Acts 4:12). In both cases the healing leads to proclamation of a

---

[6] See *Narrative Unity* 1:103–9.

[7] The similarities in wording are clearer between Acts 3:1–10 and 14:8–11 (Paul's healing of a lame man) than between Acts 3:1–10 and Luke 5:17–26.

saving power that goes beyond physical healing. In both cases the claim is made in the face of new opposition and is directly related to the mission announced in the Scripture quotation in the inaugural speech.

Conviction that these similarities are not accidental increases when we note a third similar sequence at the beginning of the section of Acts devoted to Paul (13:1ff.).[8] The sequence includes a healing of a lame man (14:8–10) that is described in language similar to Peter's healing at the temple gate, although the function of the healing in the narrative is not fully comparable.[9]

The narrator emphasizes the lame man's "leaping" immediately following Peter's healing, using the rare word ἅλλομαι and its compound form ἐξάλλομαι together in 3:8.[10] This leaping not only demonstrates the healing vividly but, for those as familiar with the prophecies of Isaiah as our narrator is, recalls Isaiah 35:6, part of a passage that probably influenced the summary description of Jesus' mighty acts in Luke 7:22. In the context of Acts 3, this allusion to Isaiah would support Peter's claim that "all the prophets . . . proclaimed these days" (3:24).

The events of Acts 3 are set in the temple or at its entrance, and this setting is significant. It helps the plot move without interruption from a healing at the temple gate, to a speech in the temple, to the immediate reaction of the temple authorities. The appearance of the apostles in the temple shows their attachment to this symbolic center of Jewish religion. It is the appropriate place for prayer and teaching by followers of the one destined to fulfill the promises to Israel. However, this positive attachment will also lead to conflict. The apostles do not hesitate to teach publicly in the temple, and what they say does not please the authorities (cf. 4:2, 17; 5:28). The result is a conflict of authority, for the temple rulers question the apostles about their authority (4:7), and the apostles refuse to recognize the authority of the temple rulers when they attempt to block the mission (4:19–20; 5:29). The unifying center of Jewish religion, properly a place of prayer and instruction (cf. Luke 19:46–47), is on its way to becoming again a place of strife and danger, as it was for Jesus (Luke 19:45—21:38).[11]

In his second speech Peter responds to the amazed crowd that gathers after the healing of the lame man. Peter begins by correcting a possible false impression, that the apostles had "made him walk by our own power

---

[8] See C. Talbert, *Literary Patterns,* 23.

[9] See below, 177–78.

[10] ἐξάλλομαι occurs only here in the NT. ἅλλομαι is used in Acts 14:10 in Paul's healing of a lame man. Elsewhere in the NT it is found only at John 4:14.

[11] The temple has both positive and negative associations in Luke-Acts. These are discussed by Joseph Tyson, *Death of Jesus,* 84–113. See also P. Esler, *Community and Gospel,* 131–63. Concerning Stephen's comment on the temple, see below, 92–95.

or piety" (3:12). In Acts, Peter and Paul do mighty works similar in kind to those performed by Jesus in the Gospel. Therefore, it is important to make clear that these mighty works do not stem from the disciples' own power but show the power of Jesus' name, as Peter will explain in 3:16. The same sort of correction is made more dramatically when Paul heals a lame man, for Paul and Barnabas must stop the people of Lystra from sacrificing to them as gods (14:14–15). Peter, too, must correct a Gentile who treats him as more than human (10:25–26). The care with which Peter and Paul distinguish between themselves and the power at work through them contrasts with the claims of religious charlatans like Theudas and Simon Magus, who claim that they themselves are "somebody" or "somebody great" (5:36; 8:9). The sensitivity Peter and Paul show on this issue is also an indication of the change that has taken place in Jesus' followers through the appearance of the risen Christ and the gift of the Spirit. Whereas in Luke the disciples engaged in disputes over who was the greatest, even at the Last Supper (Luke 22:24; cf. 9:46), Jesus' warning that "everyone who exalts himself will be humbled, and the one who humbles himself will be exalted" (Luke 14:11; 18:14; cf. 9:48; 22:26) has now taken effect in the lives of Jesus' witnesses.

After correcting false impressions, Peter explains the true cause of the healing: God "glorified his servant Jesus" through this sign (3:13).[12] Having announced this, Peter recalls the death and resurrection of Jesus. He then attributes the healing to faith in Jesus' name (3:16). This verse may seem to be awkwardly inserted into the speech, having little to do with the preceding train of thought. It refers, however, to a representative sign of the power of Jesus' name now that he has been installed at God's right hand as Lord and Messiah. Thus the speech moves in order from Jesus' death to his resurrection, then to the present result of his new status, demonstrated in a specific case. Acts 3:16 is an overloaded and awkward sentence, but close inspection suggests reasons for its awkwardness. It places great emphasis on faith and on Jesus' name as the keys to the healing of the lame man. First a prepositional phrase linking the two key concepts is placed at the beginning of the sentence as a heading: "on the basis of faith in his name." This is followed by two linked sentences with "his name" and "faith" as subjects, arranged in chiastic form so that these two key terms are brought together: τοῦτον . . . τὸ ὄνομα αὐτοῦ, καὶ ἡ πίστις ἡ δι' αὐτοῦ . . . ("this one . . . his name, and the faith that is

---

[12] It is also possible to understand God's glorification of Jesus as taking place in his resurrection and exaltation. The two interpretations may not be exclusive. Just as the pouring out of the Spirit is a public sign of Jesus' exalted position at the right hand of God (2:33), so is the healing of the lame man. The Messiah entered "his glory" (Luke 24:26) through resurrection and exaltation, but that glory is publicly manifested through the gift of the Spirit and the continuation of Jesus' healing work in spite of his apparent absence.

through him . . .")`. The result is emphasis on "faith" and "his name," and
on their close connection with each other, through repetition, through
making them active causes of the healing, and through word order.[13] The
emphasis on faith is a belated addition to the healing story, as it is not
obvious that the lame man is an example of faith, but this addition is
important if the healing of the lame man is to be understood as a paradigm
of salvation through Jesus.

We should note that the so-called connection to the situation,[14] the
direct reference to the narrative setting, sometimes regarded as secondary
and artificial, occupies the first eight verses of the Pentecost speech,
reappears in 2:33, and is also found in the middle of Peter's temple speech
in 3:16, as well as in 3:12–13. These are indications of the importance that
this feature has in these speeches. Peter is not only explaining the death
and resurrection of Jesus but is also interpreting specific manifestations of
his power, described in the preceding narrative. Apart from some signs of
Jesus' power, the offer of salvation in Jesus' name would seem vague and
remote.

The speech is also connected to its situation because it calls a specific
group of people, Jews dwelling in Jerusalem, to repentance. Even more
clearly than the Pentecost speech, the speech in Solomon's portico calls the
audience to repentance because of a specific crime. The speech stresses the
special involvement of Jerusalem Jews in what has happened and is
happening. They are involved in two ways, the first negative, the second
positive: (1) They "delivered up and denied" Jesus, asked for a murderer
in his stead, and "killed" him (3:13–15). The accusation is made vivid by
the repeated verbs and by descriptive details from Luke's passion story
(Pilate's decision to "release [ἀπολύειν]" Jesus, cf. Luke 23:16; the crowd
asking for Barabbas, the "murderer," cf. Luke 23:18–19). The audience's
responsibility receives further stress through the double use of the emphatic nominative pronoun "you (ὑμεῖς)." (2) Emphatic second-person
plural pronouns return at the end of the speech, now emphasizing the
audience's share in the promised blessing (3:25, emphatic nominative
pronoun; 3:26, dative pronoun in emphatic position at the beginning of
the sentence). This emphasis may suggest that the rather frequent use of
the second-person plural pronoun throughout 3:19–26 is also significant.[15] The reference in 3:20 to Jesus as "the Messiah chosen for you" is

---

[13] On 3:16 see G. Schneider, *Apostelgeschichte* 1:320–21.

[14] See U. Wilckens, *Missionsreden,* 37.

[15] The three occurrences in the following sentence are especially striking: "The Lord *your* God
will raise up a prophet for *you* from *your* brothers, a prophet like me" (3:22; my emphasis).
The first "your" is textually uncertain. The LXX of Deut. 18:15 has singular rather than
plural pronouns in all three cases. Jacques Schlosser recognizes the importance of the
second-person pronouns in 3:22, 25–26. See "Moïse, serviteur du kérygme," 19.

also a significant indication of a desire to make clear the audience's stake in what is happening.

In this manner, the application of the message to this audience is emphasized, especially near the beginning and end of the speech. The audience is involved negatively, for it bears responsibility for rejecting and killing Jesus. Nevertheless, the final result can be positive, for God is now working through Jesus and his witnesses to fulfill the covenant promise to these people. To be sure, there is a hint at the end of the speech that the promised blessing is not for them alone, but it is for them *first*. They have a preeminent place in God's plan to bless "all the families of the earth," for they are "the sons of the prophets and of the covenant" (3:25–26). The promised blessing rightly belongs to them. It is still available to them, if they repent.

The stress on the audience's involvement, negatively and positively, in God's work through Jesus heightens both danger and opportunity. It discloses a situation of high tension, a tension that can be released only through turning away from past rejection and accepting the promised blessing through Jesus. The speech is shaped to fit its narrative setting and to move its narrative audience to respond. It is meant to call the people of Jerusalem to repentance.

Peter still hopes, and encourages the people of Jerusalem to hope, that they will share in the "times of restoration of all that God spoke" through the prophets. This will include a further sending of their Messiah to them, provided they repent (3:19–21). Peter's hope includes the hope expressed by Jesus' followers in 1:6, as the shared wording indicates. That is, it includes the restoration of Israel's national life through the reigning Messiah.[16] The prophetic words of Zechariah in Luke 1:69–75 have not been forgotten.[17]

The anticipated sending of the Messiah is not a coming in judgment but part of the restoration for Israel. The images are hopeful ones: "seasons of refreshment," "restoration of all things that God spoke" through the prophets. The "seasons of refreshment" and even the "times of restoration" need not relate exclusively to the final coming of the Messiah.[18]

---

[16] See above, 14–17.

[17] John Carroll, *Response to the End*, 140, notes that there are a series of verbal contacts between Luke 1:70–75 and Acts 3:19–26 and concludes that the latter recalls the former "by design." However, he denies that "the parousia is contingent upon the repentance of Israel" in 3:19–21 (p. 144). This allows Carroll to loosen 3:19–21 from a concern with Israel's restoration (cf. 147). I would emphasize that the subjunctive verb ἀποστείλη ("send") is part of the purpose clause in v. 20. The people of Jerusalem are urged to repent *in order that* God may send the Messiah to complete the restoration of Israel as a nation.

[18] Dennis Hamm argues that the healing of the lame man is a symbolic narrative, representing the restoration of Israel, which is already under way. He bases his view, in part, on the

They can refer to the Messiah's benefits already available in the gift of the Spirit and release of sins. However, 3:21 indicates that the restoration of *all* things coincides with the final coming of the Messiah. Until then "heaven must receive" Jesus.

Both 3:19-21 and 3:25-26 express the speaker's appeal to the audience, an appeal to repent accompanied by an offer of great benefits. The former passage indicates that the realization of Israel's hopes is still possible. Even those judged to be directly responsible for Jesus' death may share in the promises, if they repent. The latter passage goes further. The thought shifts from a possible future sending (3:20) to a realized one: "God, having raised up[19] his servant, sent him to you first" (3:26). Saying "to you first" implies a progressive mission, the mission traced in the rest of Acts.[20] God has sent the risen Jesus on this mission. Jesus is actively present in it, a thought that not only concludes and climaxes Peter's temple speech but also Paul's speech before King Agrippa (26:23). In this mission Jesus, God's servant, is actively blessing the people in fulfillment of the covenant promise made to Abraham. This blessing will come to "all the families of the earth," but it rightly comes first of all to those who are "sons of the prophets and the covenant." Addressing the audience in these terms highlights the fact that the promised blessing is rooted in their own history. It would be strange and tragic if this people who received the covenant promise from their ancestors and have long cherished it should miss the promised blessing when it is given. As part of this blessing Jesus is creating repentance among the people, "turning each" of them from their former wickedness. Thus repentance is not only a requirement, as in 3:19, but is the intended result of the active intervention of God and God's servant through the mission. God does not simply wait for repentance but seeks to create it.[21]

The positive appeal is accompanied by a negative threat in 3:23. This threat develops from a reference in 3:22 to the prophet like Moses, whom Israel must hear, as Moses insisted. Whoever "does not hear that prophet

---

connection of the healing with Isa. 35:6 and the fact that one possible meaning of "restoration" is healing. See "Peter's Speech and the Healing," 199–217.

[19] This is a reference to Jesus' resurrection. See Robert O'Toole, "Some Observations on Anistēmi," 85–92.

[20] Both the word order and 13:46 speak against taking "first" with "his servant," as R. O'Toole proposes. See "Some Observations on Anistēmi," 90–91.

[21] The phrase ἐν τῷ ἀποστρέφειν ἕκαστον in 3:26 is ambiguous because the verb can be either transitive ("in turning each") or intransitive ("when each turns"). The latter could imply a condition that must be fulfilled to receive the blessing. The transitive sense fits both the sentence, in which the focus is on God's action through Jesus, and other Lukan passages, for God through Jesus not only demands repentance but "gives" it (5:31), and John the Baptist was sent to actively "turn many . . . to the Lord" (Luke 1:16). We have noted signs that John's work continues in the mission of the apostles. See above, 40–41.

will be destroyed from the people."[22] This statement makes acceptance of Jesus, the prophet like Moses, decisive for the people of Jerusalem. We are not told, however, when this threat will take effect for those who refuse to repent or accept God's servant. As long as God continues to send the servant to bless the people through the mission, there is hope that the refusal will change to obedient hearing. Jesus' witness will still be struggling to make a deaf people hear at the end of Acts.[23]

Whether the immediate decision is final or not, the harsh warning in 3:23 may anticipate the imminent turn for the worse in the relation between the apostles and the temple authorities. Directly following Peter's speech, the temple authorities will demonstrate their refusal to hear the prophet like Moses and Peter, his witness (4:1–3). Such anticipation of rejection in a speech prior to its actual appearance occurs elsewhere in Luke-Acts (see Luke 4:23–30; Acts 13:40–47).

The statement with which Peter closes, "To you first . . . God sent his servant," indicates that the offer of salvation to the Jerusalem Jews is only the first stage of a longer process. This should be no threat to Peter's audience. They are included in the promised blessing,[24] and those who know the prophecies of Isaiah should also know that God intends to bring salvation to Gentiles as well as Jews. In any case, inclusion of Gentiles is a cause of conflict only after the gentile mission actually begins.

In 3:17 Peter says, "Brothers, I know that you acted in ignorance, just as your rulers did."[25] This failure to recognize and accept God's servant requires repentance, as Peter goes on to say, but it is something that can be forgiven. The new possibility is dramatized by the story of Jesus' followers in Luke, for until they encountered the risen Christ, the disciples shared the ignorance of the people of Jerusalem. They were ignorant of ($\dot{\eta}\gamma\nu\dot{o}o\upsilon\nu$) Jesus' meaning when he spoke of his coming rejection and death (Luke 9:45; cf. 18:34). The ignorance of both the disciples and the people of Jerusalem included a failure to understand what was written by the prophets (Luke 18:31; 24:25–27, 32, 44–46; Acts 13:27; cf. 3:17–18). Thus Peter, in speaking to the people of Jerusalem, is trying to convey the new and revolutionary understanding that removed his own blind ignorance when he was instructed by the risen Christ. Furthermore, Peter accuses the Jerusalem Jews of having "denied" Jesus

---

[22] The language appears to reflect Lev. 23:29, although the reason for the threat in Leviticus is quite different.

[23] On 28:17–31 see below, 344–57.

[24] Use of πᾶσαι αἱ πατριαί ("all the families") in 3:25, rather than πάντα τὰ ἔθνη ("all the nations" or "Gentiles") as in Gen. 18:18; 22:18; 26:4 LXX, avoids the misunderstanding that the promised blessing does not apply to Israel. See Nils Dahl, "Story of Abraham," 149.

[25] On "ignorance" and recognition scenes in a tragic plot, see above, 35–36.

(3:13–14) yet "is himself a reformed denier"[26] (cf. Luke 22:34, 54–62). Peter's record suggests that he knows something of the need and possibility of repentance and can speak to his audience from this experience. Similarly, Paul's mission will be associated with bringing light and opening eyes (13:47; 26:18, 23), but first he himself must be stopped in his tracks by a blinding light and receive new sight.

Although both the Pentecost speech and the temple speech call to repentance, review the story of Jesus, and cite Scripture, they are complementary rather than simply repetitive. Different aspects are emphasized and new perspectives are introduced, broadening the picture of Jesus' significance for the people of Jerusalem. We must view the two speeches together in order to understand Peter's message in its full scope. The Pentecost speech emphasizes Jesus' resurrection and exaltation, but the temple speech recalls details of Jesus' trial. The Pentecost speech briefly refers to Jesus' earthly ministry, but the temple speech anticipates the Parousia. The Pentecost speech emphasizes God's oath to David; the temple speech recalls God's promise to Abraham and refers to the Mosaic prophet. The Pentecost speech focuses on the titles "Messiah" and "Lord"; the temple speech introduces other titles—"servant ($\pi a\hat{\imath}s$)," "holy and just one," "leader of life." The Pentecost speech cites a prophetic book and the Psalms, but the temple speech cites the Pentateuch.[27] The Pentecost speech sees God's "fixed purpose and foreknowledge" behind Jesus' death; the temple speech expresses a similar thought in a different way, referring to "what God announced beforehand through the mouth of all the prophets." The Pentecost speech offers salvation through the name of the Lord and the gift of the Spirit; the temple speech refers to "seasons of refreshment," "times of restoration," and the promised blessing. Both speeches emphasize repentance and release of sins, but the wording is mostly different. Both speeches refer to the future participation of others in the salvation (2:39; 3:26); again the wording is different. Thus the two speeches are complementary, probably deliberately so, even though they address the same type of audience about the same situation. A much broader and richer understanding of Christian preaching to Jews emerges from hearing two speeches rather than one.

---

[26] See D. Hamm, "Peter's Speech and the Healing," 207.

[27] Some scholars regard "glorified his servant" in 3:13 as an allusion to Isa. 52:13. It is not, however, a citation.

CONFLICT WITH
THE TEMPLE AUTHORITIES

The temple authorities are the first opponents of the new mission. An indication of their reasons appears in 4:2. They were disturbed because the apostles "were teaching the people and proclaiming in Jesus the resurrection of the dead." Probably the offense is a double one. The apostles were usurping authority to teach in the temple, and the content of their teaching conflicted with denial of the resurrection by the Sadducees, an important group in the temple leadership. The apostles' authority to teach will be a continuing subject of discussion in Acts 4—5. The question of the resurrection will reemerge when *Paul* appears before the Sanhedrin (cf. 23:6–10) and will be an important subject in Paul's defense speeches.[1] Later we will learn that the high priest and his party are "filled with jealousy" at the influence of the apostles on the people (5:17), and the high priest will make further accusations. The apostles have refused to obey a specific prohibition and try to convict the temple leaders of wrongly killing Jesus (5:28), something that the temple leaders refuse to admit. Thus the battle is joined.

The attitude of the people is quite different. The narrator continues to note the powerful effect on the people of the apostles' preaching and wonders (4:4; 5:12–16), resulting in multitudes of new believers. The "people," indeed, "all the people," saw the healed man and heard Peter's speech, a point made clear through the term λαός ("people"),[2] used no less than five times just before and just after the temple speech.[3] This term is especially frequent in Acts 2:47—6:12 and plays a role in a significant development. In 2:47 we are told that the Jerusalem Christians were viewed favorably by "all the people." This favor continues. When the temple authorities begin to oppose the apostles, they are unable to act

---

[1] On the theme of hope and resurrection in Paul's defense speeches, see below, 286–91, 299–301, 316–20.

[2] On this term as a way of referring to the Jewish people in its distinctiveness, see *Narrative Unity* 1:143–44.

[3] Much of the following discussion of Acts 4—5 was originally published in the *Society of Biblical Literature 1984 Seminar Papers*, ed. Kent Harold Richards (Chico: Scholars Press, 1984), copyright 1984 by the Society of Biblical Literature. See Robert Tannehill, "The Composition of Acts 3—5," 222–29, 232–40. Used by permission.

effectively because the apostles enjoy the people's support (4:21; 5:13, 26). The situation mirrors the passion story, where the people support Jesus as he teaches in the temple and prevent the authorities from taking action against him (Luke 19:47–48; 20:19, 26; 21:38; 22:2). In Acts the people are a fertile field for the Christian mission, yet, just as in the passion story, they are fickle and easily swayed by false charges. A first indication of change is found in the Stephen story. Opponents are finally able to arouse the people by false charges against Stephen (6:11–14). In Jesus' trial before Pilate the people, despite their previous support, suddenly shift their attitude and join in calling for Jesus' death (Luke 23:13–25).[4] We will be reminded of this aspect of Jesus' trial in Acts 4:25–28. The role of the people in Stephen's death is not as clear as in the passion story, but following this event, the Jewish people of Jerusalem will appear as opponents, which represents a significant shift from the way in which they are presented in Acts 2—5. In 12:3–4, 11 "the people of the Jews" is a threatening group, from which Peter must be rescued. In this passage Herod and the Jewish people stand together as persecutors, just as another Herod and the people of Israel joined together against Jesus, according to Acts 4:25–28. When Paul is arrested in Jerusalem, references to the "people (λαός)" reappear with sudden frequency (21:28, 30, 36, 39, 40), and the people cry for Paul's death (21:36; 22:22). The charge that the Christian mission is an anti-Jewish movement (21:28) is false, as Paul will reiterate as late as 28:17. Nevertheless, the "people" of Jerusalem who have not become disciples, although they favor the Christian mission in Acts 2—5, will act primarily as opponents following the death of Stephen. This shift indicates a major change in the mission's environment.

The arrest and release of Peter and John in Acts 4 is the first of a series of arrests and releases of Jesus' witnesses in Acts. The later narrative suggests that there is good hope of rescue from imprisonment, either through human action (5:33–40) or some greater cause (5:17–21; 12:6–11; 16:25–26), but the narrator also knows that the missionary does not always escape. Acts ends with Paul still a prisoner. The basic belief is in the power of God's purpose to reach its goal in spite of, or even by means of, the suffering caused by human opposition. Imprisonment provides a graphic image for human efforts to confine the word, preventing its spread, but in one way or another these efforts fail.

It is only as the apostles stand before the Sanhedrin, facing the first powerful opposition, that the full significance of the promise in 2:21 and the healing of the lame man is made clear. The promise from Scripture

---

[4] On the role of the people in Luke's passion story, see David Tiede, *Prophecy and History*, 103–18.

quoted in 2:21, "Everyone who calls on the name of the Lord will be saved," is reflected in the exhortation of Peter to "be saved" in 2:40 and in the reference to "those being saved" in 2:47. These general references, however, are not enough. In Acts 3—4 the healed lame man, who in his leaping demonstrates the fulfillment of the prophecies (cf. Isa. 35:6), becomes a paradigm of salvation through Jesus' name. The healed man takes on this significance through the speeches following the healing. Peter's statement in 3:12 that he and John had not healed the man "by our own power" raises the question of whose power is behind this wonder. A first answer is given in 3:13, 16, but the question appears again in the interrogation of Peter and John. They are asked in 4:7, "By what power or by what name did you do this?" This reference to "power" and "name" picks up language previously used by Peter in connection with the healing (cf. 3:6, 12, 16), thereby connecting this scene to the preceding narrative and providing a perfect setup for Peter's disclosure of the healing's full meaning.[5] Answering the question by whom this man "has been saved ($\sigma\acute{\epsilon}\sigma\omega\tau\alpha\iota$)," Peter proclaims that it was "by the name of Jesus Messiah." The verb just translated "saved" can, of course, refer to healing (RSV: "has been healed"), but 4:9 prepares for use of the same word in 4:12 in a broader sense. Peter's climactic statement in 4:12 interprets the healing as a symbol of a multidimensional salvation that includes all the benefits previously promised to those who repent and call on Jesus' name (cf. 2:21, 38–40). The name of Jesus, according to Peter, is the means "by which we must be saved ($\delta\epsilon\hat{\iota}\ \sigma\omega\theta\hat{\eta}\nu\alpha\iota\ \acute{\eta}\mu\hat{\alpha}\varsigma$)." Not only lame people but all can find salvation through it, for the salvation that the lame man received repre-sents a greater salvation offered to "everyone who calls on the name of the Lord." Indeed, Jesus' name is the inescapable decision point concerning salvation for Peter's hearers, because "there is no other name under heaven" given to people for salvation.[6] For Peter's audience this salvation does not mean healing of lameness but the gifts of repentance and release of sins, and the blessings of messianic rule. The healed lame man is the continuing symbol of the salvation for all offered in Jesus' name.

According to 4:13, Peter's words in 4:8–12 are a demonstration of $\pi\alpha\rho\rho\eta\sigma\acute{\iota}\alpha$ ("boldness," especially boldness of speech in circumstances that

---

[5] Admittedly, this is a bit too neat for modern ideas of verisimilitude in narrative.

[6] The $\delta\epsilon\hat{\iota}$ ("must," "it is necessary") in 4:12 probably refers, as elsewhere, to a necessity that derives from God's purpose, which ultimately aims at salvation for "all flesh" in accordance with the promise of Isa. 40:5 (cf. Luke 3:6). The frequent instances of Jewish refusal in the subsequent narrative and the church's experience through the centuries should cause us to ask whether Peter's enthusiastic statement about salvation through Jesus alone may have unfortunate consequences. Does it not place inadmissible limits on God's possibilities and block the very goal that the narrator wishes to affirm, the inclusive salvation for all peoples prophesied by Isaiah?

might inhibit frank speech). Peter demonstrates boldness both in his proclamation of the name of Jesus and in his blunt accusation of the rulers for their rejection of Jesus. The short speeches in 4:8–12 and 5:29–32 are important because the former develops the theme of salvation in Jesus' name and the latter reminds us of other themes from the Pentecost speech, thus rounding off the series of speeches by the apostles in Jerusalem. These short speeches are also important because they dramatically demonstrate *persistent* speaking in the face of opposition. It is dramatically important that the apostles repeat what they have said in spite of threats from the powerful. The importance of boldness in the face of opposition is made clear by the church's prayer for such παρρησία and by the answer to that prayer (4:29, 31), as well as by the bold declarations of allegiance to God's command, rather than the Sanhedrin's, in 4:19–20 and 5:29.

The authorities marvel at the boldness of Peter and John, who are unskilled laymen, trained neither in Scripture interpretation nor rhetoric (4:13). The apostles' speech, inspired by the Holy Spirit (4:8), is beyond their own human capacity. Embarrassed by the healed lame man, the public sign of Jesus' saving power, the authorities try to control the damage being done. They command the apostles to stop teaching in the name of Jesus and back this command with threats (4:17–18). This move heightens tension and provides a further test of Peter and John, a test they immediately pass, defiantly announcing that they cannot stop preaching, for they must listen to God rather than the Sanhedrin (4:19–20). Their defiant words are a reaffirmation of the commission to be Jesus' witnesses, received from the risen Messiah (Luke 24:48; Acts 1:8). The statements in 4:19–20 epitomize the apostles' stance in a dramatic situation, which helps to give the declaration impact. This declaration will be repeated in 5:29, again drawing the contrast between God and human authorities, and even Gamaliel will warn the Sanhedrin that it must respect the difference between what is "from God" and what is "from humans" (5:38–39). The repetition of this contrast between divine and human authority in several dramatic scenes and from the mouths of both the apostles and Gamaliel indicates emphasis, suggesting that we are encountering narrative rhetoric that is meant to convey a message not only between characters in the story but also from the implied author to the implied reader. This message indicates approval of those who, in proclaiming the name of Jesus, obey God rather than humans and suggests their boldness as a model for others. It is also a message about how the story is to be interpreted. This is a story about what happens when a purpose which is "from God" is recognized by persons willing to obey God in spite of human hostility.

The defiance of Peter and John in 4:19–20 reveals the impotence of the Sanhedrin, for it can only make additional threats and release the apostles. Nevertheless, the narrative leaves open the question of what the Sanhedrin will do if the apostles not only state their defiance but also disobey the Sanhedrin's command to stop preaching. This uncertainty enables the conflict to develop, moving to a new stage in 5:17–42.

The prayer scene in 4:23–31, in which the church prays for boldness to speak God's word in the face of threats, shows the source of the boldness already demonstrated by Peter and John. This scene also places the developing conflict in the context of sacred paradigms provided by Scripture and the passion story of Jesus.[7] The church appeals to God both for the power to speak the word boldly and for the continuation of the signs and wonders through Jesus' name (4:29–30). The importance attributed to the healed lame man as a sign of Jesus' saving power, a sign recognizable even by outsiders and opponents, suggests why signs and wonders have an important role in strengthening a mission under pressure, in the narrator's view. Both aspects of the church's appeal are answered. Bold and powerful speaking is recorded in 4:31, 33. "Many signs and wonders" are reported in 5:12–16, along with the addition of new believers to the church. Individual healings are not reported, but details emphasize the eagerness of the multitude, who come even from surrounding cities, bringing their sick, all of whom were being healed. This summary leads into the next stage of the conflict with the Sanhedrin. Just as the healing of the lame man and Peter's preaching to the crowd led to the first arrest, so now the continued preaching and healing, attracting multitudes, lead to a second arrest and the attempt of the high priest's party to enforce the previous prohibition of preaching in Jesus' name.

The importance of the conflict with the temple authorities is made clear by the space devoted to it in Acts 4—7. The conflict develops in three stages (the third focusing on Stephen), and each stage is dramatized through a face-to-face confrontation between the temple authorities and Jesus' witnesses, with speeches in direct discourse. The narrative makes the similarity between the confrontations in Acts 4 and 5 especially clear. Similar wording is used in 4:1–3 and 5:17–18 to introduce the two episodes. A similar sequence of events follows these introductions: the arrest of the apostles, their appearance before the Sanhedrin (including short speeches that both reaffirm the apostles' message about Jesus [4:10–12; 5:30–32] and declare that the apostles will obey God rather than the Sanhedrin [4:19–20; 5:29]), deliberation by the Sanhedrin without the

---

[7] See below, 71–72.

apostles present (4:15–17; 5:34–39), and the release of the apostles with a prohibition of speaking in Jesus' name. Although the sequence of events is so similar, it is clear that the second arrest and hearing builds upon the first, for the second interrogation by the Sanhedrin begins with the accusation that the apostles have disobeyed the rulers' command in the first hearing (5:28), and the second response of the apostles to the Sanhedrin puts them in danger of death (5:33).

Charles Talbert believes that the pattern of correspondences is more extensive. He compares 1:12—4:23 with 4:24—5:42.[8] It does seem significant that in both of these sections of Acts we hear of the church gathered at prayer (1:14; 4:24–30), then filled with the Holy Spirit and speaking by the Spirit's power (2:4; 4:31). The two descriptions of communal life that follow the outpourings of the Spirit are also closely related (2:42–47; 4:32–35), and the signs and wonders of the apostles are noted before each of the arrests (2:43; 3:1–10; 5:12–16). This pattern of reduplication contributes to the story of the developing conflict between the church and the Sanhedrin. It helps to build suspense as the resolve of both parties to the conflict is tested under increasing pressure. It shows the apostles and the church holding firm under this pressure. That the apostles repeat what they have already said makes the point of their firmness in the face of the threats. The tension also increases, however. The rulers, frustrated in their attempts to silence the apostles, must either give up their authority or take more drastic action. That the narrative is building to a climax through these patterns of reduplication becomes clear when we have a third sequence of arrest and trial before the Sanhedrin (6:8—7:60), this time resulting in the death of Jesus' witness and the scattering of the church (8:1).

Thus the narrator makes use of similar sequences to present an evolving conflict that moves toward a crisis. The repetitive sequences contribute to the development, for the situation in Acts 5 is not exactly the same as in Acts 4. Both parties must deal with the fact that the apostles have defied the command not to teach in Jesus' name (cf. 5:28). The stakes have increased since the first encounter. Certain differences in detail between Acts 4 and 5 show this increase in tension. In Acts 5 the apostles in general, not just Peter and John, are arrested. There is imminent danger of death (5:33), and the apostles do not escape without physical suffering through flogging (5:40). Furthermore, the high priest and his party are reacting not only to the apostles' refusal to keep silent but also to the accusation that the Sanhedrin is responsible for Jesus' death (5:28). The teaching they are trying to suppress is not only a word about Jesus

---

[8] See *Literary Patterns*, 35–39.

but also a stinging word about themselves. The apostles repeat their charge and their offer of repentance and forgiveness (5:30–31), bringing the narrative to the brink of crisis, for the hearers are infuriated and want to do away with them (5:33). Then the tension relaxes as Gamaliel intervenes.

This, however, is not the end of the conflict. After a brief narrative that introduces Stephen, we find a third scene in which a witness of Jesus[9] is brought before the Sanhedrin (6:11—8:1). To be sure, a new protagonist is introduced, the accusations against him are new, and Stephen's speech develops the accusation against his hearers at great length. Nevertheless, this is a new phase of the same conflict, with the Sanhedrin still trying to suppress the witness to Jesus. This time the conflict comes to the brink of crisis and spills over. The action contemplated in 5:33 is carried out against this new witness: Stephen is killed. The continuity is made clear by the use of the same verb of strong emotion in 5:33 and 7:54, the verb διεπρίοντο (literally, "they were being sawn through" = RSV "they were enraged").[10] In the one case this leads to the desire to "do away with" the apostles (5:33). In the other case it leads to the actual "doing away with" Stephen (8:1). Thus in Acts 4—7 we have a continuous narrative that depicts a series of similar confrontations, each representing a surge toward the crisis marked by Stephen's death and the great persecution that follows.

Acts 5 adds to the sequence of events in Acts 4 a rescue from prison by an angel. This, however, is narrated briefly and without dramatic emphasis. As much attention is given to the angel's command to continue speaking in the temple as to the opening of the prison. The command to speak in the temple makes no sense if the main purpose is escape, for the apostles are still in danger there and will still be brought before the Sanhedrin. This command shows a reluctance to concede the temple to the mission's opponents.

The release from prison sets up the following scene (5:21b–26), which is developed with direct discourse and dramatic detail despite the fact that the apostles are not present. This scene is an ironic description of the embarrassment and confusion of the high priest and his party when they discover that the imprisoned apostles have vanished.[11] The scene is introduced with a solemn formality that contributes to its burlesque quality ("the Sanhedrin and all the senate of the sons of Israel," 5:21). It focuses on the reports of messengers who tell the Sanhedrin what readers already know, provoking smiles at their surprise and confusion. In 5:23, part of

---

[9] Stephen, like the apostles and Paul, is called Jesus' "witness." Cf. 22:20.

[10] These are the only uses of this verb in the NT.

[11] Luke Johnson notes the irony. See *Literary Function of Possessions,* 196–97.

the first messenger's report, we find some of the descriptive detail that we might have expected in the earlier narrative of rescue from prison. The messenger indicates that the expected security measures were carried out, yet the apostles are gone. The narrator's focus on the report to the Sanhedrin, rather than on the rescue itself, shows that the primary interest here is not in miraculous rescues as such but in the impotence of human authorities to control the course of events. Although the apostles end up just where they would have been apart from the prison release— standing before the Sanhedrin accused of disobedience—the threat from the Sanhedrin has been undermined by irony and burlesque. The point made later by Gamaliel ("If it is from God, you will not be able to destroy them," 5:39) has already been made by the narrator through the rescue from prison and the ensuing scene of discovery. Here we have an instance of reinforcement through reiteration. A message is first suggested by an event and then clearly stated in the interpretive commentary of a story character.[12]

Again the bold persistence of the apostles is expressed in a brief speech that repeats the proclamation concerning Jesus (5:30–32). This speech briefly summarizes themes from previous speeches, including some that have not been mentioned since Pentecost ("God exalted him at his right hand," cf. 2:33; "the Holy Spirit which God gave," cf. 2:33, 38). The authorities are again accused of killing Jesus, but this accusation is followed by the proclamation of repentance and release of sins, a gift of God through the exalted Messiah that is still valid for Israel.[13] The sermons with their persistent themes demonstrate the persistence of the apostles, who neither crumble before powerful opponents nor despair of the possibility of repentance.

The release of the apostles in 5:40 shows that in Acts 5 there are two rescues: one by an angel and the other by a human being, Gamaliel. Gamaliel, a person of insight and reason, intervenes as the plot moves toward crisis and corrects those carried away by their murderous passions (5:33). The speech of Gamaliel shows that there are still cool heads within the Sanhedrin. Not only is Gamaliel properly cautious; he is able to persuade the Sanhedrin that the apostles should not be put to death.

---

[12] Susan Rubin Suleiman presents an elaborate classification of types of narrative "redundancy" in "Redundancy and the 'Readable' Text," 119–42. In one of her types "an event is redundant with the interpretive commentary made by a C [character] . . . concerning it" (128). Gamaliel may not be interpreting the prison rescue directly, but it is at least an illustration of his point.

[13] L. Johnson believes that the offer of repentance and release of sins no longer applies to the leaders, who have already rejected Jesus a second time. See *Literary Function of Possessions,* 69. However, no distinction is made between the leaders and the rest of Israel in 5:30–32. The apostles speak to the leaders as if there were still hope of repentance.

There are several indications that Gamaliel, although he does not speak as a Christian, serves as spokesman for the implied author. As I have indicated, the point made by Gamaliel in 5:39a has already been supported by the narrator, who chose to highlight the impotence of the temple authorities in 5:21–26. Furthermore, in speaking of the two possibilities of "this purpose or this work" being "from humans" or "from God," Gamaliel shifts from the conditional sentence with ἐάν and subjunctive to εἰ and indicative. The latter construction often, as here, comes close to the causal meaning "since."[14] The shift in construction suggests that "this purpose" really is from God, showing that the implied author's view is being placed in the mouth of Gamaliel.[15] Also, the contrast between what is "from humans" and what is "from God" in 5:38–39 continues a theme in the responses of the apostles, who have demonstrated which side they stand on by declaring, "It is necessary to obey God rather than humans" (5:29; cf. 4:19). Gamaliel also seems to recognize that Jesus' followers are different than Theudas' and Judas the Galilean's supporters, who disappeared with the death of their leaders. Gamaliel's whole speech is a warning against rash action in light of the serious possibility that the Sanhedrin may prove to be foolish "fighters against God" (5:39). His argument is persuasive on this occasion, but the danger of which he warns will reappear in the trial of Stephen.

Gamaliel is introduced as a Pharisee in 5:34. In Acts Pharisees are consistently presented as either open in attitude toward Christians or as having actually accepted the Christian message (cf. 15:5; 23:6–9; 26:5). This is a different picture than that presented in Luke. Although Pharisees had no part in the temple conflicts[16] or death of Jesus, they were frequent opponents of Jesus previously. Jesus' resurrection may make the difference in the portrait of the Pharisees. Paul will appeal to Jews on the basis of "hope and resurrection," and Pharisees will defend him (23:6–9).[17] The difference noted in the presentation of the Pharisees may suggest that this group, so strongly opposed to Jesus' teaching, may nevertheless be open to faith in Jesus after, and as a result of, his resurrection.

To this point I have emphasized narrative development in Acts 4—5, seeking to show the narrator's methods of building toward a crisis. This approach can contribute much to explaining why the story is told as it is. Our appreciation of the narrative will be greatly increased, however, if we

---

[14] See BDF, no. 372, 1. R. Brawley, *Luke-Acts and the Jews*, 89, notes that 5:38b-39a refers to conflicting claims. If the second conditional clause merely expressed the claim of the apostles, the first should use the same construction to express the claim of the opponents.

[15] This is the opinion of H. Conzelmann, *Acts*, 43, and E. Haenchen, *Acts*, 253.

[16] Note the difference between Mark 12:13 and Luke 20:20.

[17] Later scenes develop Paul's appeal to the "hope of Israel" into a major theme. See below, 286–87, 299–301, 316–20.

note the subtle echo effect that accompanies the narrative development. While focusing our attention on a particular development that is partly unique, the narrator has also laced the narrative with reminders of earlier narrative segments. Listening carefully for these echoes of the past can help guide and deepen our response to the narrative in Acts 4—5.

We have already noted similarities between Acts 1—4 and a series of important events near the beginning of Jesus' ministry in Luke.[18] There are also a number of similarities between the Jerusalem section of Acts and the Jerusalem section of Luke, a second set of echoes of the Jesus story. Reading Acts 1—7 against the background of both the beginning and ending of Jesus' ministry in Luke adds greatly to the resonance of the Acts account.

Four speeches of Peter in Acts 2—5 explicitly recall the rejection and death of Jesus, and we have especially noted the detailed reference to the trial scene before Pilate in Acts 3:13-15.[19] Furthermore, there is continuity of characters between the passion story in Luke and the Jerusalem section of Acts. The high priest and the Jerusalem Sanhedrin are available to play the same role in both the confrontation with Jesus and with the apostles. This continuity makes it easy to suggest that similar situations are recurring, and the narrator takes advantage of this opportunity. After Peter recalls the circumstances of Jesus' death in his first two speeches, a sequence of events takes place that partially reduplicates the passion story. Like Jesus, Jesus' witnesses are arrested and called to account before the Sanhedrin. The third sequence of arrest and trial in Acts will lead to a death. The report of Stephen's death both recalls and parallels the narrative of Jesus' death in Luke. Stephen's speech ends by recalling Jesus' death (7:52). Stephen's next words recall Jesus' words to his accusers about the exalted Son of Man (Luke 22:69; Acts 7:56). His final words parallel Jesus' words from the cross (Luke 23:34,[20] 46; Acts 7:59-60). Thus the sequence of arrests, trials, and death in Acts 4—7 reaches its climax in a scene in which the connections with Luke's passion story are quite clear.

Details of description in Acts 4 also suggest connections with the passion story. Note the following similarities between the description of the arrest and examination of the apostles in Acts 4 and the arrest and examination of Jesus in Luke: Acts 4:1 refers to "the captain ($\sigma\tau\rho\alpha\tau\eta\gamma\acute{o}s$) of the temple"; Luke 22:52 also refers to "captains of the temple" (dif.[21]

---

[18] See above, 29, 49–52.
[19] See above, 54.
[20] On the textual problem in this verse, see *Narrative Unity* 1:272.
[21] This abbreviation indicates that Luke *differs from* Matthew and/or Mark in the feature discussed, although Luke has a passage that is generally parallel.

Matthew, Mark). The temple officials "laid hands on (ἐπέβαλον τὰς χεῖρας)" the apostles (Acts 4:3; 5:18); the same phrase is used in reporting the frustrated attempt of scribes and high priests to arrest Jesus in Luke 20:19 (dif. Matthew, Mark). Acts 4:5 places the examination on the morning after the arrest, as with Jesus (Luke 22:66, dif. Matthew, Mark), and Acts 4:5–6 agrees further with Luke 22:66 in referring to the component groups of the Sanhedrin being "gathered together" (aorist passive of συνάγω). The reference to "rulers (ἄρχοντας)" in Acts 4:5 corresponds to Luke 23:13, 35; 24:20.[22]

Most of Jesus' speaking in Jerusalem is done prior to his arrest, and the primary location of his teaching is the temple. The narrative in Acts recalls some of this material in shaping the dialogues between the rulers and the apostles, who also teach in the temple. In Luke 20:2 Jesus was asked, "By what authority are you doing these things?"; in Acts 4:7 Peter and John are asked, "By what power or what name did you do this?" The same group poses the question in the two instances. Peter, in responding to the question, refers to the stone scorned by the builders that has become head of the corner (Acts 4:11), repeating (with some variation in wording) a Scripture quotation used by Jesus in Luke 20:17. This quotation follows Jesus' accusation of the rulers for wishing to kill God's greatest messenger, an accusation expressed in the indirect form of a parable. This accusation is directly made in the Acts speeches. So the Scripture reference to the stone in Acts 4:11 recalls the rejection and vindication of Jesus in imagery already used by Jesus. In both Luke and Acts the "people (λαός)" support Jesus or the apostles, preventing the rulers from taking action against them (Luke 19:47–48; 20:19; 22:2; Acts 4:21; 5:26). This will delay, but not prevent, the death toward which the narrative is moving.

The similarities between Acts 4—5 and the Jerusalem narrative in Luke help to make clear that the conflict in Jerusalem over Jerusalem's Messiah has not been resolved. It simply enters a new phase, with the apostles as Jesus' witnesses. The apostles now assume the risky role of proclaiming Jesus and calling the people of Jerusalem and their rulers to repent of their blind error. Their new role shows that the apostles have changed in important ways. Given a second chance, this time they show their faithfulness. The similarity of the situation (arrest and trial) and the continuity of the opposition (the high priests and others associated with the temple or Sanhedrin) highlight the difference in the behavior of the apostles before and after the resurrection and sending of the Spirit. Luke alone reports Peter's declaration that he was ready both to die and to go "to prison" with Jesus (Luke 22:33). He failed to keep this promise when

---

[22] Neither Matthew nor Mark applies this term to the Jewish authorities in Jerusalem.

he denied Jesus. In Acts Peter no longer denies Jesus, although threatened by powerful authorities, and he does go to prison. His boldness before the rulers is the opposite of his previous denial. The boldness of the apostles helps the rulers to recognize that Peter and John "were with Jesus" (Acts 4:13). This is what Peter denied, according to Luke 22:56–60.

Having been transformed by the risen Jesus and the Spirit, the apostles are now able to follow the instructions about facing opposition given by Jesus during the journey to Jerusalem. In following his instructions, they also experience the fulfillment of his promises. Several descriptive details in the narrative of the apostles' arrests recall Jesus' teaching about persecution in Luke 12:11–12 and 21:12–15. Jesus prophesied in Luke 21:12 that "they will lay their hands on you" (see Acts 4:3; 5:18), "handing you over . . . to prisons . . . because of my name" (see the emphasis on Jesus' name in Acts 3—5). Jesus promised, "It will lead to witnessing" (Luke 21:13; see Peter's witness before the rulers in Acts 4:8–12 and 5:29–32). The promise that the opponents will not be able to "contradict (ἀντειπεῖν)" them (Luke 21:15) is fulfilled in Acts 4:14, and the related promise that they will be taught by the Holy Spirit what they should say (Luke 12:12) is fulfilled in Acts 4:8.[23] The inability of the opponents to reply to or contradict the apostles also fits an emphasis within stories of Jesus, for Jesus had silenced his opponents both during his temple teaching (Luke 20:26, 40) and earlier (Luke 13:17; 14:6). The points noted show that the similarities between the situation of Jesus in the passion story and the situation of the apostles in Acts 4—5 serve in part to highlight the transformation of the apostles, who were unable to face danger courageously but now are able. This, in turn, makes possible the fulfillment of specific promises of Jesus to his witnesses.

The theme of persecution because of Jesus' "name," developed as a prophetic preview in Luke 21:12–19, reappears in Acts 5:40–41, and there may be additional points of contact between this conclusion to the apostles' arrest and Jesus' teaching about persecution in Luke. The apostles leave "rejoicing (χαίροντες) . . . because they were counted worthy to be dishonored on behalf of the name" (Acts 5:41). In Luke 6:22–23 Jesus instructed his disciples to "rejoice (χάρητε)" at persecution, a strikingly odd response shared by these two passages in Luke-Acts. The verb "dishonor (ἀτιμάζω)" is found not only in Acts 5:41 but also in the parable of the wicked vineyard tenants (Luke 20:11). Because it is a rare word in Luke-Acts, occurring only twice and on both occasions associated with

---

[23] Does the rulers' judgment that the apostles are uneducated and untrained (Acts 4:13) in part reflect the fact that they did not plan a polished oration in advance, in accordance with Jesus' instructions in Luke 12:11, 21:14?

beatings, this link suggests that Jesus' parable of the wicked tenants may still be working in the imagination of the author,[24] who sees the beaten and dishonored servants of the vineyard owner as an apt image for the apostles. These points of contact reveal particular aspects of the story of Jesus that had sufficient appeal to the author's imagination to shape the vision of the early church in Acts.

Connections between Acts 4—5 and the passion story become explicit when the church responds to its first crisis by turning to God in prayer (4:23–31). The church prefaces its petition with a reference to the passion story, interpreted as fulfillment of Scripture. This preface is relevant because Jesus' situation, threatened by rulers and peoples, is viewed as essentially the same as the church's situation, faced with the threats of the Sanhedrin. The prayer moves directly from a reference to "Herod and Pontius Pilate with the Gentiles and peoples of Israel," those who gathered against Jesus the Messiah, to a petition concerning "their threats," meaning the threats of the Sanhedrin just encountered by the apostles. Ernst Haenchen speaks of a "rift between verses 27 and 29" because "their threats" do not refer to threats by Herod and Pilate, as verses 27–28 would seem to suggest.[25] However, the train of thought in the prayer depends on the elimination of the distinction important to Haenchen. The opponents of Jesus and the opponents of the church are viewed as one continuous group, a simplification facilitated by the Sanhedrin's leading role in both situations.[26] Although the connection drawn in 4:27–29 may seem strange to some modern interpreters, these verses disclose a basic mode of thought presupposed throughout Acts 3—7, as shown by the numerous echoes of the passion story in this section of Acts.

The prayer of the church contains a citation of Ps. 2:1–2. This prayer (and the Stephen scene in Acts 7) reveals that there is actually another level of echoes. In listening to the story of the apostles, we can hear echoes of the passion story, but in both we are meant to hear echoes of Scripture.

The explicit parallel in the prayer between Jesus' passion and the church's situation provides important evidence that the similarities with the passion story already noted are not accidental. This parallel should also encourage us to ask whether the church's prayer has a more specific connection with material in the passion story. In Luke 22:39–46, just before Jesus' arrest and just after Peter's assertion of readiness to suffer, Jesus urged the disciples to pray in order that they might not enter into

---

[24] We have already noted reminiscences of Luke 20:17, 19, parts of the conclusion to this scene.
[25] See *Acts*, 228.
[26] Rather than Herod representing the "kings" and Pilate the "rulers" of 4:26 (so E. Haenchen, *Acts*, 227), there is some evidence that the "kings" are political authorities and the "rulers" religious authorities, i.e., the Sanhedrin, which is otherwise not mentioned in 4:26–27. Compare 4:26 with 4:5. Both verses use the aorist passive of συνάγω.

temptation. Instead, the disciples fell asleep and were unprepared for the following crisis. In Acts 4:23–31 Jesus' followers are again confronted with the dangerous opposition of the Sanhedrin. Now they pray as they had previously been told to do. As a result they receive power from God to continue the mission despite the opposition. We have already noted that Peter's boldness before the Sanhedrin in Acts contrasts with his denial of Jesus in Luke. The church in Acts, finding power for witness in prayer, also contrasts with the disciples who slept instead of praying in Luke. These contrasts contribute to the narrator's picture of a dramatic transformation in Jesus' followers.

The Acts speeches repeatedly affirm God's active presence in the story of Jesus. God continues to be active in the life of the church, and the narrative has various ways of signaling this active presence of God: angels, visions, messages from the Spirit, and so forth. One further way of bringing God into the narrative is to report a prayer and its answer. This is an opportunity to show how God responds to the characters and events of the narrative.

Prayer is also an opportunity to characterize God more fully, so that we have a clearer impression of the God who is acting through the human events of the story. The church's petition in 4:29–30 is preceded by a five-verse preface that is basically characterization of God. God is creator of all things and therefore sovereign ($\delta\epsilon\sigma\pi\acute{o}\tau\eta\varsigma$) over all. This sovereignty is revealed as God announces in Scripture a preordained purpose and brings it to fulfillment. God's sovereignty is even more clearly revealed when opponents of God's purpose become instruments of its realization. The chief instance of this is celebrated in 4:25–28: Jew and Gentile—gathered in opposition to God and God's Messiah—ironically fulfilled God's purpose.[27] Here the narrator's theological vision of a God who works by irony again surfaces. Reality conflicts with appearance. Blind human actors commit themselves to a course of action, only to discover that its meaning and result are quite different than anticipated. The narrator traces the work of God in a series of such ironies. The irony of God's purpose realized through Jesus' rejection provides the interpretive key. The church at prayer recalls this event, which enables it to trust in the sovereign God in its time of danger. It prays for the power to continue the mission in the face of the Sanhedrin's threats, and its prayer is answered. Remaining faithful to its mission, it will again discover that the sovereign God can twist the opponents' plans, yielding the opposite, as the "great persecution" in Jerusalem (8:1) leads to the spread of the word to new

---

[27] Note that 4:28 repeats and reemphasizes the assertion in 2:23 that God's preordained purpose was realized in the death of Jesus.

areas and the most devoted persecutor of the church, Saul, becomes a witness of Jesus to all people.

The effort to control history by armies and nuclear weapons appears foolish if we believe in such a God, but it never seems foolish to fearful people. In a time of threat, prayer can be a rediscovery of the sovereign God who wins by letting our opponents win and then transforming the expected result. This rediscovery can keep God's witnesses faithful in spite of threats.

The first opposition to the church's mission comes from the Jewish rulers in Jerusalem. However, the Psalm quotation in 4:25–26 refers also to Gentiles, and Gentiles are included in the application to Jesus' death in 4:27. The church has not yet experienced opposition from Gentiles, but it will. Paul's arrest and imprisonment in Philippi (16:16–24) and the riot in Ephesus (19:23–40) are dramatic accounts of such opposition. I am suggesting that the church's prayer in 4:23–31 relates not only to the specific situation of the apostles' arrest by the Sanhedrin and the previous situation of Jesus' rejection and death. It also anticipates the recurrent opposition from Jews and Gentiles encountered by the mission from this point on. Furthermore, the church's prayer for power to speak the word with "boldness ($\pi\alpha\rho\rho\eta\sigma\iota\alpha$)" and for signs and wonders is not answered solely by the outpouring of the Spirit in 4:31. These character traits of bold and powerful speech, accompanied by wondrous works, are passed on from the apostles to Stephen (6:8–10), Philip (8:4–7), and Paul (9:27–29; 14:3) as the narrative progresses. Indeed, Acts ends with the imprisoned Paul faithfully preaching "with all boldness" (28:31). The powerful and hardy witness the Spirit inspired in response to the church's prayer persists to the very end of Acts and appears in the narrator's last statement. The prayer scene in Acts 4 prepares for this by attributing to the Spirit not only the beginning of the mission (cf. 2:1–21) but also the bold speaking that maintains the witness despite all opposition and danger.

In discussing echoes of Luke in Acts, we should also note the similarities between Luke 6:17–19 and Acts 5:12–16, passages that include summary descriptions of multitudes coming and of works of healing and exorcism, even through touching the healer or lying in his shadow. There is similar material in the story of Paul, but it is divided between 14:3 (which also recalls Acts 4:29–30) and 19:11–12.

Having previously considered echoes of the beginning of Jesus' ministry in the early chapters of Acts,[28] we have been discussing echoes of Jesus' temple teaching and passion in Acts 4—5. Themes associated with

---

[28] See above, 29, 49–52.

the beginning of Jesus' and the apostles' mission also appear in the story of Paul's mission,[29] and Paul's final journey to Jerusalem, arrest, and trials will echo Jesus' journey to Jerusalem and final days there.[30] These two sets of repetitive patterns are overlaid with a third within Acts 4—5 itself: the pattern of arrest, witness before the Sanhedrin, deliberation, and release in 4:1-22 and 5:17-42.[31]

Various types of repetition in narrative have been discussed by some recent theorists under the heading of "redundancy." Redundancy, far from being strange and unusual, is a necessary aspect of effective communication. In narrative it may take many forms. Susan Rubin Suleiman has proposed an elaborate classification of the possible types of redundancy in realistic narrative.[32] Many of her types of redundancy occur in Luke-Acts. In our discussion we have noted (1) the repetition of the same type of event or sequence of events happening to different characters (Jesus, Peter, and Paul begin their missions empowered by the Spirit and comment on their missions by quoting Scripture), (2) similar events or sequences of events happening to the same characters (apostles are twice arrested and appear before the Sanhedrin), and (3) similarity in the interpretation of events by the narrator and by a character. Examples of the last type of redundancy are the narrator's interpretation of the noise and tongues of fire as the coming of the Holy Spirit in 2:4, an interpretation repeated in Peter's speech (2:15-17) despite brief reference to an alternative view (2:13, 15), and the ironic portrayal of the Sanhedrin's impotence in 5:17-26, followed by Gamaliel's statement, "If it is from God, you will not be able to destroy them" (5:39).

What is the function of the rather elaborate patterns of repetition or "redundancy" we have noted? Why would one compose a narrative in this way? The answer must be complex, embracing at least the following points:

(1) Information theorists note that every channel of communication is subject to "noise," that is, "disturbances . . . which interfere with the faithful transmission of signals," and "a certain degree of redundancy is essential . . . in any communication system in order to counteract the disturbing effects of noise."[33] In Luke-Acts one major source of "noise" is the length of the narrative, offering a large opportunity to forget what has already happened. Redundancy combats the tendency to forget.

---

[29] See below, 161–62.
[30] See below, 239–40, 259, 264–66, 274, 281–82, 345–46.
[31] See above, 63–64.
[32] See "Redundancy and the 'Readable Text'," 126–32.
[33] See John Lyons, *Semantics* 1:44. Quoted by Fred Burnett, "Prolegomenon to Reading Matthew's Eschatological Discourse," 93–94 and n. 4.

(2) Repetition is a means of emphasis. Selective emphasis enables narrators to convey the views they regard as most important for correct interpretation of the narrated events. Thus emphasis serves the "education of the reader"[34] in what is central to understanding the story. Because a particular interpretation is being promoted, other options are being ignored or rejected, reducing the amount of indeterminacy in the text. However, the closing of options may guide the reader to an interpretation the author regards as particularly rich, with its own broad field of meanings, a field not likely to be explored if the reader is not guided to it. Because repetition conveys interpretation through emphasis, it is important for us to take careful note of *what* is repeated. Interpretation takes place through *selective* repetition.

(3) Repetition has a persuasive effect. The events, characters, or assertions seem "right" because they fit what is already known. As Susan Wittig says, "The creation . . . of a multi-level set of expectancies not only allows the audience to predict the occurrence of successive items, but also provides for that audience's *assent* to the sequence, for if the listener can predict the next item (perhaps he may even repeat it silently before it occurs) he will be more likely to accept it and agree to it."[35]

(4) Characters in Acts who show qualities and patterns of behavior similar to Jesus and to scriptural models take on some of the authority of these authoritative figures. This is true of Peter, Stephen, and Paul, whose missions and sufferings resemble those of Jesus, and Jesus' mission and rejection reflect the experience of Moses with the rebellious Israelites (see Acts 3:22; 7:22–39).[36]

(5) Reading is a constant process of forming and revising expectations, both "focal expectations" in the immediate context and "global expectations," stretching over large sections of the work.[37] The continual need to revise expectations involves the reader actively in the work and can be a major means of holding the reader's interest. To be most effective, the reader must have some basis for anticipating events, perhaps through suggestive patterns of repetition, but must lack certainty. The lack of certainty pertains not only to what will happen but also to how, when, and why it will happen. Furthermore, the process of building and revising expectations in reading can be used effectively to guide readers toward a

---

[34] The subtitle of Fred Burnett's essay (see the preceding note) is "Redundancy and the Education of the Reader."

[35] See "Formulaic Style and the Problem of Redundancy," 131. Quoted by Janice Capel Anderson, "Double and Triple Stories," 84. Emphasis by Wittig.

[36] Charles Talbert understands the parallels between Jesus and his witnesses in Luke-Acts as a way of indicating who are the authentic successors of Jesus. See *Literary Patterns,* 125–36.

[37] These terms are used by J. Anderson, "Double and Triple Stories," 83.

climax in the narrative. Confirmation of expectations through a growing repetitive pattern allows the reader to anticipate a climactic instance of the pattern, fulfilling expectations in the highest degree, as in the triple pattern of arrests and confrontations with the Sanhedrin that lead up to Stephen's death.[38]

(6) The same or related characters may be presented in similar situations in order to highlight an important change. The similarities make the differences stand out sharply, suggesting an important development in the narrative. In Acts 4—5 Peter and the other apostles face situations similar to Jesus' arrest and trial in Jerusalem, a time when the apostles failed Jesus. The contrast in their behavior highlights the apostles' transformation. Now Peter responds to the Sanhedrin's threat by boldly confessing Jesus, while this threat causes the church to turn in prayer to God, the source of power to withstand opposition.

(7) Repetitive patterns preserve narrative unity in spite of significant developments. Very important changes take place as the mission moves from Nazareth to Jerusalem to the gentile world, but the narrator succeeds in presenting all this as the manifestation of a single purpose of God, in part through the recurrence of unifying patterns distributed through the sections of the narrative. The narrator is careful not to allow innovations to disrupt the continuity of the narrative.

(8) Repetitive patterns in narrative encourage interaction among characters and events in the reader's experience. The character or event is experienced not in isolation but against a background that gives it "resonance." That is, we are able to detect overtones and echoes of other characters and events that add suggestive richness to the narrative episode now being read. Such resonance is not entirely controllable by an author. Once some parallels have been suggested in the narrative, other related ones may occur to the reader, whether intended by the author or not. This is especially true when possible interconnections multiply, with several systems of echoes working at once, as in Acts 1—7. Thick layers of background produce resonance through activating the reader's imagination. The reader is sent actively exploring the rich associations of similarity and contrast that may exist among characters and events. Resonance is a cumulative experience in reading. Connections among narrative materials build up, so that more and more are available as background for exploring those nodal points of narrative where many connecting lines cross.

When a narrator emphasizes certain images and patterns through

---

[38] See the discussion of "building" (along with emphasizing, echoing, and complicating) in chapter 2 of Bruce F. Kawin, *Telling It Again and Again*.

repeated use, much will depend on the capacity of the selected material to grow in significance as the narrative progresses. Repetition without growth soon becomes monotonous. However, a narrator may convince us of the value of central images and patterns if we discover that they expand in meaning. This may happen as we find that they encompass more and more of human experience, including, perhaps, our experience. It may also happen as we are led to a deeper grasp of their implications. The discovery of an expanding symbol is a powerful enticement to explore a new perspective on life. Repetition may lead us to deepening discovery of such symbols, as familiar material returns in new contexts with new significance. Having experienced the power of the symbol to expand in the story, we are more likely to believe that it hides treasures that will reward further exploration.[39]

In Acts 4—5 the repetitive patterns emphasize and enrich a vision of God as one who works by irony, subverting and overruling the human powers who appear to be in control. Because of this God, there can be a mission in which courageous people speak boldly of realities denied and rejected by these human powers.

As previously noted,[40] the narrative shifts between major and minor themes. At 4:32 the narrator turns to the minor theme of unity expressed through community of goods, emphasizing an aspect of the church's life previously presented in 2:44–45.[41] According to 4:35 the apostles have a direct role in administering the distribution of goods. Proceeds from the sale of property are placed "at the feet of the apostles" and then are distributed, presumably by the apostles. The apostles oversee relief for the whole community only temporarily. In 6:1–3 we learn that part of the community is being neglected, and the apostles themselves recognize that a new arrangement, sharing responsibility with seven others, is necessary. Thus there is no attempt to suggest that only the twelve could administer the community's resources. On the contrary, the task proves too large for them. As others are introduced into the narrative, they will share this role. It is probably significant that the apostles, Stephen, Philip, Barnabas, and Paul, although primarily preachers of the word in Acts, are all briefly given a direct role in the distribution of material goods within the

---

[39] The remarks concerning the expanding symbol were suggested by E. K. Brown, *Rhythm in the Novel*, 33–59. According to Brown, "the expanding symbol is repetition balanced by variation, and that variation is in progressively deepening disclosure" (57). "By the use of an expanding symbol, the novelist persuades and impels his readers towards two beliefs. First, that beyond the verge of what he can express, there is an area which can be glimpsed, never surveyed. Second, that this area has an order of its own which we should greatly care to know" (59).

[40] See above, 43–44.

[41] See the discussion above, 45–47.

community (cf. 4:35–37; 6:3–5; 11:27–30; 12:25). These brief references indicate that the leading preachers gave active support to this important feature of the church's life.

The Spirit-inspired speaking in 4:31 continues in the apostles' powerful testimony to Jesus' resurrection (4:33). The special emphasis on Jesus' resurrection in their preaching fits the preceding narrative, including the Pentecost speech, the reference to Jesus as the "originator (ἀρχηγόν) of life, whom God raised from the dead" in the temple speech (3:15; cf. 3:26), and the note in 4:2 that the temple authorities and Sadducees were provoked especially by proclamation of the resurrection. In spite of the authorities' threat, the apostles continue with renewed power the proclamation that provoked their opponents.

In 4:36–37 a certain Joseph Barnabas is introduced as a concrete illustration of those who sold property and brought the money to the apostles for distribution. The two verses give no indication that Barnabas will later play an important role in the story. Barnabas is a first example in Acts of the tendency to introduce an important new character first as a minor character, one who appears and quickly disappears. Philip (6:5) and Saul (7:58; 8:1, 3) are similarly introduced before they assume important roles in the narrative. This procedure ties the narrative together, and in each case the introductory scene contributes something significant to the portrait of the person.

By giving him the name Barnabas, the apostles recognized Joseph as a "son of encouragement (υἱὸς παρακλήσεως)." This honorary name, together with the indications that he has roots both in Judaism (he is a Levite) and in the Diaspora, foreshadows his future role as mediator between Jewish and gentile Christians and encourager of the gentile mission. In 11:23 and 14:22 we find Barnabas "encouraging" (both passages use παρακαλέω) communities that include Gentiles. He is trusted by the Jerusalem church but is more than its errand boy. He exercises independent judgment in supporting the recently converted Saul against initial suspicion (9:26–27), and in Antioch he is the one who must decide whether "the grace of God" is at work in a new kind of community (11:22–23). Through his support of these new developments and service with Paul, Barnabas proves to be a "son of encouragement" in ways that extend beyond the apostles' original meaning in giving this name to a dedicated disciple.

Barnabas' positive example of dedication to the community's welfare is followed by the negative case of Ananias and Sapphira (5:1–11). The contrast introduces a cautionary note, suggesting that even a Spirit-filled community so united in heart and soul that people would sell their property to support needy members may be corrupted by counterfeits.

Although the outward act may appear to represent a heart and soul united with others in mutual care, hidden motives may be at work. Such is the case with Ananias and Sapphira.

Repetition of key phrases encourages us to read 5:1–11 in contrast to the preceding description of community life. Immediately after we are told that Barnabas sold property and placed the proceeds at the feet of the apostles, we learn of a married couple who did the same (5:1–2),[42] but Ananias falsely retained part of the sale price, with his wife's knowledge. This was a calculated deception, and Peter calls it lying to the Holy Spirit (5:3). The later dialogue with Sapphira (5:8–9) confirms that the couple was trying to represent the partial offering as the full price of sale. Thus the outward act appears to be the same as with Barnabas, but the orientation of the heart is quite different. Treating all things as common property is meant to express oneness of heart (4:32), in which the hearts of all are directed to the welfare of others. The term "heart ($\kappa\alpha\rho\delta\iota\alpha$)" reappears in 5:3–4 but in a negative setting. Satan has filled Ananias' heart, producing a counterfeit of the heart united in mutual care.

In Luke Jesus was portrayed as a prophet who revealed the hidden thoughts of hearts.[43] Now Peter is the prophet who exposes and rebukes the deceptive heart. In this case the rebuke is followed by immediate death. This is a much more drastic result than the temporary blinding of Elymas (13:9–11) or the beating of the sons of Sceva by the possessed man (19:16). Although the exact relation between Peter's rebukes and the following deaths is unclear, this scene shows no compassion toward Christians who lack complete commitment. The double death clearly emphasizes the seriousness of the threat to the church represented by Ananias and Sapphira. It is a threat of a particular kind, one that arises from inside, is deceptive, and attacks a central aspect of the church's life, as presented by the narrator: the heartfelt devotion to others demonstrated in the community of goods.

Thus the early church not only faced an external threat from the temple authorities but also an internal threat. An internal problem will also appear in the dispute between Hebrews and Hellenists in 6:1–6. These internal problems occupy much less of the narrative than the external conflict, for they are quickly and decisively resolved in single scenes. However, it is significant that there *are* problems in the internal life of even the earliest church. The portrait is not so idealized as to deny the necessity of clearly facing problems in order to preserve and restore the life to which the church has been called.

---

[42] R. Pesch carefully notes the similar words and phrases in 4:32, 34–35, 37 and in 5:1–4. See *Apostelgeschichte* 1:196.

[43] See *Narrative Unity* 1:43–44.

CLIMAX OF THE CONFLICT
IN JERUSALEM

This section continues the story of the conflict between the mission and the temple authorities, a conflict that first appeared in 4:1–3. It brings that story to a climax with Stephen's lengthy speech before the Sanhedrin and his death, accompanied by a persecution that scatters the Jerusalem church. The section begins, however, with an incident in the internal affairs of the church. In this scene new characters are introduced, and two of them, Stephen and Philip, will have continuing roles in the narrative. Thus one function of 6:1–6 is to introduce Stephen and Philip, thereby preparing for Stephen's speech and martyrdom in Acts 7 and for Philip's mission in Acts 8.

The seven are appointed to solve a specific problem in the Jerusalem church. The values emphasized in previous descriptions of the Jerusalem church show that it is an important problem. In 4:32, 34 we were told that the church's "heart and soul were one," and "there was no needy person among them" because property owners were willing to sell their goods and share. Now we hear of a "complaint" or "grumbling" (6:1) that disturbs the church's unity. The threat to unity appears precisely in the area of the church's life where unity had been most clearly demonstrated: the sharing of wealth with the needy. This is the second threat to the caring unity the Jerusalem church demonstrated through sharing possessions, for Ananias and Sapphira had previously injected deceit into the process of sharing (5:1–11). In both cases there is a decisive response to the threat. In the case of the Hellenists' widows, the twelve act with dispatch to solve the problem and restore unity. In doing so, they show a willingness to share community leadership with others (according to 4:35 the twelve have been in charge of community funds for the needy) and sensitivity to the feelings of all parties, arriving at a solution satisfactory to all (6:5).[1]

This will not be the last internal church problem noted by the narrator. Threats from internal corruption, suspicion, and conflict continue to

---

[1] Joseph Tyson discerns a literary pattern of peace / threat / resolution / restoration in Acts 4:32—5:11 and 6:1–7, as well as other passages. See "Problem of Food in Acts," 69–76.

appear (cf. 8:18–24; 9:26–28; 11:1–18; 15:1–35; 21:20–26). These problems do not dominate the narrative, however, for in each case (except, perhaps, the last) the problem is addressed and a solution is found. The early church had problems but, according to Acts, it also had leaders who moved swiftly to ward off corruption and find solutions to internal conflicts, supported by people who listened to each other with open minds and responded with good will. When we recognize that Acts is not primarily concerned with the internal life of the church in the first place, we will also recognize that its idealizing tendency appears less in avoiding internal church problems than in exaggerating the ease with which they were solved.[2]

The conflict within the church between "Hellenists" and "Hebrews" grows out of a difference in language and culture, even if both are Jews. Problems and suspicions caused by differences in cultural background reappear later when Gentiles enter the church. These problems are handled with considerable care in 10:1—11:18 and 15:1–35, where specific proposals for resolution of problems are advocated. In 6:1–6 we find an advance indication of the narrator's concern to show the church overcoming cultural divisions through communal consideration of fair proposals leading to solutions supported by all.

The resolution of the conflict is framed by references to the continuing growth of the church (6:1, 7). In 6:7 the narrator places special emphasis on this growth by noting that "the number of the disciples in Jerusalem was being multiplied greatly," and even "a large crowd of the priests were obedient to the faith." These statements fit the picture of the powerful appeal of the word of God and the rapid growth of the church in Jerusalem presented since the Pentecost speech. Peter's two public speeches are followed by mass conversions (2:41; 4:4), and the church's growth is supplemented by daily additions of new converts (2:47; cf. 5:14). The strong statement in 6:7 shows that the Sanhedrin's opposition has not stopped the mission's remarkable progress. Although there may be a change in atmosphere, even the great persecution following Stephen's death does not stem the church's growth. According to 9:31 "the church throughout all Judea and Galilee and Samaria" was still "being multiplied by the encouragement of the Holy Spirit," and later James will refer to "myriads" of Jewish believers (21:20). Whatever the situation at the time of its composition, Acts does not picture the church as a gentile body

---

[2] Although the specific causes of conflict in 11:1–18; 15:1–33; and 21:20–26 differ, it is possible to understand these passages as manifestations of a single conflict over the meaning of the mission for Jews and Gentiles, a conflict that persisted and was not easily solved. The emphasis in 11:1–18 and 15:1–33, however, seems to be on harmonious resolution.

with a withering Jewish arm, for the mission in the Jewish homeland is very successful, and the church there is vigorous.[3]

In 6:7 the narrator speaks not only of the multiplication of the disciples but also of the growth of the word of God. These are two ways of speaking of the same development, but the narrator directs attention first of all not to the church but to the creative force behind its growth, the word of God. In Exod. 1:7 both the verb "grow ($a\dot{v}\xi\acute{a}v\omega$)" and the verb "multiply ($\pi\lambda\eta\theta\acute{v}v\omega$)" are used to describe the rapid growth of the people of Israel as the time of exodus approached. The reference to Exod. 1:7–8 in Acts 7:17–18 is further evidence of its influence in Acts. Application of these verbs to the growth of the word and the church in 6:7 may suggest a parallel between the church's situation and the situation of Israel as the promised time approached.[4] This connection makes it all the more striking, however, that the word, not just the people, grows. This metaphor (which reappears in 12:24; 19:20) shows the continuing influence in Acts of Jesus' parable in Luke 8:4–15, where a sower's growing seed represents the word of God.[5] This metaphor becomes a vehicle for understanding the word of God as an active force in the world, full of its own vitality. It is not just a human report of God's activities but the way in which God continues to act in fulfilling the divine purpose.

This reference to the word's growth without reference to a human speaker separates the appointment of Stephen to care for the widows from the report of his mission, involving wonders and powerful speech. At this point there is a shift in Stephen's role for which we were not prepared by 6:1–6. The twelve draw a clear distinction between two types of service, serving tables ($\delta\iota\alpha\kappa\sigma\nu\epsilon\hat{\iota}v$ $\tau\rho\alpha\pi\acute{e}\zeta\alpha\iota\varsigma$, 6:2) and the service of the word ($\delta\iota\alpha\kappa\sigma\nu\acute{\iota}\alpha$ $\tau\sigma\hat{v}$ $\lambda\acute{o}\gamma\sigma v$, 6:4). Because they believe that the former is now interfering with the latter, the twelve propose a division of labor. They will now concentrate on prayer and the word and let others distribute food, a reasonable plan that is accepted by the whole community. However, the growing word has its own ways. Stephen, chosen because he was "full of Spirit and wisdom" (6:3), uses that Spirit and wisdom not just to organize charity but in speaking (6:10), and he performs wonders and signs as the apostles have been doing (2:43; 5:12; 6:8). The division of labor breaks down in the face of Stephen's demonstrated power in a mission to Hellenistic Jews. So much for human plans as to how the

---

[3] See Jacob Jervell, *Luke and the People of God*, 44.

[4] The word $\sigma\phi\acute{o}\delta\rho\alpha$ ("greatly") in Acts 6:7, a word found only one other time in Luke-Acts (Luke 18:23), occurs repeatedly in Exod. 1:7, 12, 20. On the connection of Acts 6:7 with Exodus and the promise to Abraham, see Paul Zingg, *Wachsen der Kirche*, 25, 174.

[5] Only Mark's version of the parable contains the verb $a\dot{v}\xi\acute{a}v\omega$ (Mark 4:8), which is found, however, in the Lukan version of the mustard seed (Luke 13:19). The influence of the parable of the sower is noted by Jerome Kodell, "Word of God Grew," 517.

mission should proceed! Philip's ministry will show the same surprising shift. Appointed to serve in the distribution of charity, he becomes a missionary who takes a bold new step in fulfilling part of the apostles' commission before they are ready to do so.[6]

The qualifications of Stephen and his companions are indicated by four similar phrases consisting of paired nouns that are (in three of the four cases) dependent on πλήρης ("full") (6:3, 5, 8, 10). The greatest emphasis is placed on the endowment with "Spirit" and "wisdom," because both of these nouns are repeated. Because Stephen and Philip are new characters in the story, it is important to establish their credentials for the roles they are about to play. The stress on "wisdom" is the most striking, as σοφία is found only four times in Acts, with all these occurrences in chapters 6 and 7 (6:3, 10; 7:10, 22). In 6:10 Stephen's wisdom is manifest in his speech, suggesting that the stress on wisdom is meant to guide the reader's reaction to the speech presented at 7:2–53. It is a speech by one full of Spirit and wisdom. In particular, it demonstrates Stephen's wisdom as an interpreter of the biblical story.[7] Moreover, Stephen's wisdom links him to Joseph and Moses, scriptural figures who also share with Stephen the qualities of "grace" and "power" (6:8; 7:10, 22).[8] We should also compare the references to Jesus' endowment with "wisdom" and "grace" or "favor" in Luke 2:40, 52. Stephen, although his role is comparatively brief, shares the qualifications of leading figures of Scripture and of leading figures in Luke-Acts, suggesting that his words and actions have great importance for the story. Furthermore, Stephen, like Jesus, the apostles, and Moses (7:36), does wonders and signs (6:8). His face was like the face of an angel as he spoke before the Sanhedrin—probably a parallel to Moses' shining face.[9] Jesus' promise is fulfilled for Stephen, as it was with the apostles. His opponents are unable to "withstand the wisdom and Spirit by which he was speaking" (6:10), fulfilling Jesus' words in Luke 21:15.[10] There is no sign that the power of the witness weakens as others begin to share what has been the work of the apostles, for Stephen shares qualities with God's most important messengers.

The appointment of the seven in 6:1–6 resembles a group of Septuagint stories about appointing to authority a person or persons who have wis-

---

[6] See below, 102–4, 107–11.

[7] See Earl Richard, *Author's Method*, 350–51.

[8] E. Richard concludes that "the important relationships established between Stephen and various personalities of Jewish history are clearly intentional." See *Author's Method*, 238.

[9] See François Bovon, "La figure de Moïse," 82.

[10] Cf. Acts 4:14 for the apostles. Acts 6:10 is linked to Luke 21:15 both by σοφία and ἀντιστῆναι. The latter word occurs only one further time in Luke-Acts (Acts 13:8). Luke 12:11–12, which is almost a doublet of 21:12–15, relates fearless witness to the Spirit instead of to wisdom. Acts 6:10 combines wisdom and Spirit and is thereby linked to both passages.

dom and Spirit, another use of scriptural precedent to support Stephen's authority. Joseph and Moses play the chief roles in these stories, for they concern Pharaoh's appointment of Joseph as governor of Egypt and Moses' appointment of tribal leaders and of Joshua as his successor.[11] The echoes of these scriptural stories strengthen the similarities between Stephen, on the one hand, and Joseph and Moses (or Joshua, Moses' successor), on the other. Joseph and Moses, of course, are important figures in Stephen's speech. The echoes of these scriptural stories also strengthen the sense of authorized continuity in the early church, not only between the twelve and the seven but also between the church and the Israel of Scripture, thus undermining in advance the credibility of the charge that Stephen is one who speaks "blasphemous words against Moses and God" (6:11).

The plot will follow the same basic course as in Acts 4 and 5: after performing wonders and signs, Jesus' witness will be arrested and interrogated before the Sanhedrin. There are also important differences, however, not only in the outcome but also in the material that leads up to Stephen's speech. First, a new group of opponents is introduced, Diaspora Jews who dispute with Stephen and then take action against him. Thus the new protagonist is paired with new opponents, who probably share his background. These opponents are the instigators of action against Stephen, but they succeed in doing away with Stephen only because of the Sanhedrin's emotional and violent reaction to Stephen's speech. The Diaspora Jews begin by spreading accusations against Stephen and arousing "the people and the elders and the scribes." Then they seize Stephen and bring him to the Sanhedrin (6:11-12). Those aroused do not include the high priests, perhaps because their opposition to the Christian mission has already been made clear. The reference to arousing the people ($\lambda a \acute{o} s$) is probably significant. In 4:21 and 5:26, the people favored the apostles, providing a counterforce that prevented the high priestly party from taking decisive action against them. Stephen will not have the same protection. Stephen's opponents are able to poison the minds of sufficient numbers that the people's sympathy begins to shift. This development parallels the shift in the attitude of the people in the passion story, for after supporting Jesus and preventing his enemies from acting, they join in shouting for Jesus' death before Pilate (cf. Luke 23:13-25).[12]

A second important difference from the previous arrest accounts concerns the charges made against Stephen. The accusation in 6:11 of speaking "blasphemous words against Moses and God" becomes more

---

[11] See Gen. 41:33, 37-38; Num. 27:16, 18-19, 22-23; Deut. 1:10, 13-15; 34:9. These passages are noted by G. Schneider, *Apostelgeschichte* 1:422, and E. Richard, *Author's Method,* 349.

[12] See *Narrative Unity* 1:164-65.

precise in 6:13–14: Stephen speaks against the temple and the law, claiming that Jesus "will destroy this place and change the customs that Moses delivered to us." Stephen is accused of attacking the foundations of Jewish life: temple and Torah, God and Moses.

The high priest asks Stephen to respond to these charges, and the speech follows. The speech is clearly not intended to soothe its audience and thereby escape punishment. It also has a line of thought that is not determined by the specific charges. Nevertheless, the charges are not ignored. The opponents claim blasphemy against Moses, and Stephen speaks at length about Moses, emphasizing his importance in God's purpose and revealing the real nature of the opposition he faced. Although there is no detailed discussion of the law, it is recognized as "living oracles" of divine origin (7:38). Thus Stephen acknowledges the law as well as Moses, although he turns both into bases for accusations of disobedience (cf. 7:39). The guilty history of disobedience to the law is reemphasized in the speech's final verse (7:53). Finally, the temple is a topic of considerable importance in Stephen's speech. Early in the speech Stephen acknowledges God's promise that Abraham's offspring would "worship me in this place" (7:7), and he returns to the topic of Israel's sanctuaries, including the temple, near the end of the speech (7:44–50). Discussion of these passages must wait until later.[13] At this point we can say that Stephen does give some response to the accusations, for the law, Moses, and the temple, especially the latter two, are significant topics in his speech. However, his speech is not calculated to secure acquittal on the charges; instead, he turns the charges into an indictment of his audience.

The issues of the temple and the law do not disappear with Stephen's death. Charges similar to those against Stephen are shouted against Paul when he is apprehended in Jerusalem (21:28). They include the accusation that Paul teaches "against this place" (the temple). Furthermore, conflicts over the Jewish law or "customs," both with non-Christian Jews and within the church, keep appearing in the story. These sensitive and persistent issues first appear in Acts in the Stephen episode.

Stephen's speech may seem remarkably different from the other Acts speeches. Stephen refers directly to Jesus only in 7:52 (cf. also 7:37), there is no call to repentance and forgiveness, and the bulk of the speech consists of the retelling of the scriptural story of Israel from Abraham to Solomon. Stephen is not merely citing Old Testament prophecies of Jesus; he is retelling Israel's story, step by step. Closer consideration, however, reveals important similarities to other speeches. There are connections between the speeches in Acts 3 and 7 because a Moses-Jesus parallel is important

---

[13] See below, 88–95.

in both.[14] Furthermore, there is a connection between Stephen's speech and the previous accusations by Peter against those who rejected and killed Jesus. Stephen repeats the accusation of killing Jesus (7:52) but precedes this with a long review of Israel's rejection of God's messengers, including Moses and the prophets. Previous accusations are strengthened and broadened through being placed in this historical context. We must also take account of 7:55–60. Important elements of the Pentecost speech occur after the speech is interrupted by dialogue (cf. 2:37–40). Similarly, elements that are important in previous speeches occur after the audience reaction to Stephen's speech in 7:54. Reference to Jesus' death is balanced by testimony to his exaltation in 7:55–56, completing the basic elements of christological witness. The call to repentance and forgiveness that follows the accusations in the speeches of Acts 2 and 3 is not found in Stephen's speech. The audience's angry reaction in 7:54 to the accusation does not permit Stephen to continue. The prayer in 7:60 serves as a substitute for the missing offer of forgiveness. Stephen cannot speak of forgiveness to an audience that has stopped its ears (7:57), but as his last act he prays for their forgiveness, thus expressing his desire for their good and testifying to God's saving possibility.

The emphasis in Stephen's speech on past and present rejection of God's messengers fits the speech's setting. Opposition to Jesus' witnesses and to the message of repentance and forgiveness in his name is about to become deadly. Stephen's death will be accompanied by a great persecution that will scatter the Jerusalem church. These events represent a significant hardening of the opposition. Stephen's speech interprets this hardening opposition while it is still taking shape. As Luke Johnson indicates, "The speech functions as a prophecy for the narrative"[15] because the following events dramatically manifest the attitude being condemned. Stephen is addressing the high priest, the assembled Sanhedrin, and the witnesses against him, not the people in general.[16] However, these are powerful leaders, and Stephen aligns their attitude with widespread rejection of Moses in the past, at least raising the possibility that the leaders will infect the people with their virus. Insofar as Jewish rejection is emphasized in the following narrative, we may say that Stephen's words also interpret in advance this broader rejection.

Stephen's speech builds toward the final words of accusation in 7:51–53, where the application is made through the principle "as your fathers did, so do you." These verses also contain the harshest words of the speech. Even here, however, Stephen remains within the scope of the appeals and

---

[14] See Richard Zehnle, *Peter's Pentecost Discourse*, 76–78.
[15] See *Literary Function of Possessions*, 76.
[16] Correctly noted by L. Johnson, *Literary Function of Possessions*, 51.

denunciations addressed to Israel within its own Scripture and tradition. Stephen speaks in the mode of Pentateuch and prophets as he denounces Israel's unfaithfulness.[17] Furthermore, the reference to the persecution of the prophets in 7:52 reflects a theme that Odil Hannes Steck has identified as an element of the Deuteronomic view of history, rooted in Hebrew Scripture but traceable also in later Jewish and Christian literature. Steck describes this Deuteronomic view of history as follows: the repeatedly disobedient people is admonished by the prophets, whose words are rejected, bringing God's judgment. To this pattern, found in 2 Kings 17:7–20, a reference is added in Neh. 9:26 to the prophets being killed, and 2 Chron. 36:14–16 indicates that they were scoffed at.[18] The theme of repeated resistance to the Spirit who speaks through the prophets, culminating in the rejection of the "righteous one," is not only the climax of the speech but also its main idea, for the story of Moses, the most detailed section of Stephen's speech, is shaped to make the same point. Steck's work indicates that this theme, too, is based on Jewish Scripture and tradition.[19]

The negative note, emphasizing the failure of the people to understand and obey, begins to be obvious only at 7:25.[20] It appears that Stephen comes to his point only here, whereas 7:2–22 seems a leisurely summary of the story of Israel, material with which Stephen's audience would be well acquainted and quite irrelevant to the issues of the moment.[21] It is

---

[17] "Stiff-necked"—Exod. 33:3, 5; "uncircumcised heart"—Lev. 26:41, cf. Jer. 9:25 (ET 9:26); "uncircumcised ears"—Jer. 6:10; "resist (ἀντιπίπτω)"—Num. 27:14 LXX. The charge of being stiff-necked first occurs right after the incident of the golden calf, suggesting that there is continuity between Acts 7:40–41 and 51. Noted by M.-E. Boismard, "Le martyre d'Étienne," 186.

[18] See Israel und das gewaltsame Geschick, 66–68, 74–77. Compare the references to the persecution of the prophets in Luke 6:22–23; 11:47–51; 13:33–34, and see Narrative Unity 1:97–99. Ulrich Wilckens, Missionsreden, 208–24, discusses the significance of Steck's work for the interpretation of Stephen's speech, and Steck (265–69) had already discussed Acts 7:52 as an example of the traditional theme.

[19] However, the statement that they "always" resist the Spirit and the implication that all the prophets were persecuted (7:51–52) is exaggeration that may not be helpful even in prophetic rhetoric.

[20] Earl Richard, "The Polemical Character of the Joseph Episode," 255–67, has argued that 7:9–16 has a polemical intent, like the bulk of the speech. It is true that 7:9 presents Joseph's brothers, the "patriarchs," in a negative light, and the jealousy they show may be intended to mirror the jealousy the high priestly party and other Jewish opponents show in relation to the Christian mission (see 5:17; 13:45; 17:5). However, this negative view is not maintained. If, as Richard asserts, their "tribulation" in 7:11 is a sign of God's disfavor, their rescue from the famine through Joseph shows God's continuing care. Furthermore, it is not clear to me that the reference to "Shechem" in 7:16 is polemical, as Richard asserts (259–60).

[21] See Martin Dibelius, Studies in the Acts, 167: "The irrelevance of most of this speech has for long been the real problem of exegesis. It is, indeed, impossible to find a connection between the account of the history of Israel to the time of Moses (7:2–19) and the accusation against Stephen: nor is any accusation against the Jews, which would furnish the historical foundation for the attack at the end of the speech, found at all in this section."

possible to account for the present speech by the hypothesis that the author
has added material with a negative tendency to a prior "neutral"
account.[22] However, describing much of the material as a neutral account
of Israel's history is equivalent to saying that it has no function in its
present context. It would be strange for a skilled writer (even if working
from a source) to retain so much irrelevant material at such a moment of
high drama. Perhaps we need to broaden our understanding of Stephen's
approach to his subject. The speech gains its full power only because
Stephen can use a shared history and a shared set of values to call the
audience to account, and this shared perspective enables Stephen to contrast the great promise of Israel's beginnings with its failure at the time of
fulfillment, conveying a sense of tragic error and loss. The so-called
neutral account of Israel's history in 7:2-22 (actually it is largely *positive*
in tone, not neutral) contributes to the power of the speech in these ways,
as I will attempt to explain.

Chaim Perelman and L. Olbrechts-Tyteca remind us that, "for argumentation to exist, an effective community of minds must be realized at a
given moment." There must be an "intellectual community,"[23] a shared
set of perceptions and values that can be the subject of discussion.
Highlighting these shared perceptions and values can be an important
step in rhetorical argument. In Stephen's speech the commonly acknowledged history of Israel, which defines its existence and purpose, provides
the basis for the concluding prophetic indictment. We can be more
specific: Stephen presents Israel's history as a story of promise and
(flawed) fulfillment by highlighting God's promise to Abraham in 7:5-7.
This promise has a key function in the speech,[24] for the speech concerns
the fulfillment of this promise and Israel's failure to respond properly.
The promise contains three elements: (1) the land as Israel's possession
(7:5), (2) rescue from slavery (7:6-7), (3) subsequent worship "in this
place" (7:7). All of these are basic elements in Jewish self-understanding,
which is precisely why they are important to all parties in the argumentative situation.

A community's past may, of course, be understood as an affirmation of
its present, as a way of supporting a people and its leaders and displaying
their greatness.[25] At the beginning Stephen's retelling of Israel's story can

---

[22] See E. Haenchen, *Acts*, 288–89.

[23] See *New Rhetoric*, 14.

[24] The key function of 7:6-7 was noted by Nils Dahl, "Story of Abraham," 143–47. See also
Jacques Dupont, "Structure oratoire du discours d'Étienne," 163–66, who indicates that v. 6
anticipates vv. 9–22, the first part of v. 7 anticipates vv. 23–43, and the end of v. 7
anticipates vv. 44–50.

[25] This would be a case of what James A. Sanders calls "constitutive" hermeneutics, in contrast
to the hermeneutics of prophetic critique (here practiced by Stephen). See "Hermeneutics,"
405.

be understood in this way, but when he begins to talk about Moses' mission, he makes clear that there is a negative side to Israel's history, which is well supported by biblical incidents such as the making of the golden calf (and by the recurrent biblical pattern of events that we discussed as the Deuteronomic view of history). Starting with the shared story, its meaning shifts as it is retold. When Stephen finally speaks of recent events (7:52) and interprets them in light of this negative side of Israel's history, neither this history nor the institutions to which it gave rise can be used to support the authority of Stephen's audience.

We might compare the strategy of Stephen's speech to that of a political speech that begins by recalling the history of the American people, together with some of the purposes and promises expressed in its foundation documents and pledges. Recalling the promise of "liberty and justice for all," the speaker might retell the story of America as the story of this promise—and the story of its perversion because, at decisive points, Americans have turned away from the promise and have rejected the leaders who called them to live by this promise. This is how Stephen speaks to his audience.

I referred above to a sense of tragic error and loss. The emphasis on God's great promise to Israel in the first part of the speech contributes to a sense of tragic loss when the fulfillment encounters rejection. Vivid awareness of Israel's great expectations and anticipation of fulfillment as it draws near contribute to a sense of tragedy if the expected fulfillment is rejected. The greater the expectations, the sharper the sense of tragic loss in such a situation. I have argued elsewhere that the implied author has a tragic vision of Israel's history.[26] In such a perspective both the positive emphasis on the great promise and the negative emphasis on rejection have important functions within the speech, which can now be understood as a skillfully crafted unity rather than the wanderings of one who somehow can't get to the point.

This interpretation of the speech is supported by the close connection between the first (7:2–8) and last (7:39–50) sections of Stephen's account of Israel's history. What is promised in the former is lost or perverted in the latter, emphasizing the tragic reversal of Israel's situation. In 7:5–7 Stephen refers to God's promise to Abraham that his seed will possess the land, be rescued from the enslaving oppressor, and "worship[27] me in this place." In 7:39–43 the people's rejection of God's redemption through Moses causes something to go wrong with each of these promises. Although they had come out of the land of slavery, "they turned in their

---

[26] See "Israel in Luke-Acts," 69–85.
[27] The Greek word λατρεύσουσιν refers to cultic service of God, as in the temple worship.

hearts to Egypt" and made the golden calf (7:39–41). In response "God turned and delivered them up to worship the host of heaven" (7:42), a perversion of the promised worship. Finally, God declares, "I will deport you beyond Babylon" (7:43), evidently as a result of their idolatrous worship. The promises of freedom, possession of the land, and true worship of God in it are all affected. They are replaced by an inner return to the life of Egypt, idolatrous worship, and exile.

Stephen does recognize a continuing history of the worship of God by Israel, leading up to the building of the temple (7:44–47). Even here there is a problem, however, which surfaces in 7:48–50. This passage, too, suggests tragic loss when read, as I think it should be, against the background of the destruction of the temple by the Romans.[28]

Tragic reversal[29] is expressed through repeated use of key terms first in a positive and then in a negative sense. According to 7:4 God "resettled (μετῴκισεν)" Abraham "to this land." The only other use of this verb in the New Testament is in 7:43, which declares that God "will resettle" or "deport" the people because of their idolatry, this time *away* from the promised land.[30] In 7:7 God promises Abraham that his descendants "will worship (λατρεύσουσιν) me in this place." In 7:42 God delivers up the people "to worship (λατρεύειν) the host of heaven."[31] True worship of God turns into idolatry, and the use of the same word highlights this shift. The reference to the "covenant of circumcision" in 7:8 prepares for a similar reversal, for at the end of the speech Stephen declares that his audience is "uncircumcised in hearts and ears" (7:51). Circumcision, too, has gone bad. Thus three key words or word roots associated with God's saving work and promise in the Abraham section of the speech recur toward the end of the speech with a negative meaning.[32] This literary device leads us to compare the great promise of Israel's beginnings with the failure of its later history, thereby highlighting the tragic disparity. The tragedy is increased by knowledge the author and readers share but that Stephen and his audience do not, the knowledge that Israel's attempt to throw off a foreign oppressor has failed and the central place of worship ("this place" promised in 7:7)[33] has been destroyed. The tragic force of

---

[28] See below, 93–95.

[29] Reversal in the plot is a central device of tragedy. See R. Tannehill, "Israel in Luke-Acts," 78–81, with reference to Luke-Acts and Aristotle.

[30] The verb is found in the LXX of Amos 5:27, which is being quoted. Stephen's speech prepares for this quotation by use of the same word in 7:4. E. Richard notes the connection between 7:4 and 43 and also notes that this brings the Israelites back to where Abraham began. See "Creative Use of Amos," 42. The reference to Babylon in 7:43 is not found in the quoted section of Amos.

[31] These are the only uses of λατρεύω in Acts until 24:14; 26:7; 27:23.

[32] See E. Richard, *Author's Method*, 205.

[33] On the meaning of this phrase, see below, 92–93.

this event is also underscored by the divine promise in 7:7, where God promises the place of worship that no longer exists.

The Abraham and Moses stories are not unrelated incidents but are connected as promise and fulfillment. God spoke to Abraham of enslavement and exodus (7:6–7). The section on Moses is introduced by a clear statement that the time of the fulfillment of this promise was drawing near (7:17). Fulfillment of prophesied events is indicated by carrying over the verb κακόω ("mistreat") from 7:6 to 7:19. Later God is identified at the burning bush as the "God of Abraham" (7:32) and speaks of the "mistreatment (κάκωσιν) of my people" (7:34), who are about to be rescued through Moses. The story builds to a high point of expectancy in 7:34 as Moses is sent to redeem the people and fulfill the promises. However, it does not continue as expected by reporting the exodus. Instead, Stephen contrasts the divine commission Moses received with the people's rejection of him and God (7:35–41). Just as the promises are coming to fulfillment, the people reject the chosen redeemer and turn away from God. The story turns on a fateful decision in a moment of great opportunity. The great opportunity and the negative response combine to create dramatic and fateful events.

The story of Moses is the most fully developed section of Stephen's speech. It comes to a high point in 7:35–38, where strong rhetorical emphasis appears in setting "this one," referring to Moses (οὗτος in accusative or nominative), at the beginning of each sentence. This emphasis supports a contrast between Moses' role in God's plan and the rejection of him by the people, for v. 35 begins and v. 38 is completed (in v. 39) with references to such rejection.

Although Stephen's story of Moses contains no direct mention of Jesus, comparing the description of Moses here and descriptions of Jesus in other Acts speeches reveals a remarkable series of similarities. The story of Moses is being used to interpret the story of Jesus and vice versa. Moses was sent by God as "ruler and redeemer (ἄρχοντα καὶ λυτρωτήν)," and through his hand God was giving "salvation" (RSV: "deliverance") to the people (7:25, 35). Similarly, God exalted Jesus as "leader and savior (ἀρχηγὸν καὶ σωτῆρα)" (5:31). However, the people did not understand the divine commission of these two redeemers (3:17; 7:25). They "denied" Moses as they did Jesus (3:13, 14; 7:35, using ἀρνέομαι in all three cases). The strong contrast between divine affirmation and human denial in Peter's speeches is also strong in Stephen's retelling of Moses' story. Both Jesus and Moses are rejected in spite of the fact that they do wonders and signs for the people (2:22; 7:36). And in case any should miss the connections between Moses and Jesus, Stephen cites the Scripture about the coming prophet like Moses (7:37), which has already been applied to

Jesus in 3:22. The similarities between Moses and Jesus are only part of a larger similarity. Both Stephen's interpretation of Israel's history and the Lukan story of Jesus and his witnesses proclaim salvation for Israel and then report the tragic rejection of this salvation just as it is coming to fulfillment. In both cases a long-awaited promise is being realized, but this realization is seriously damaged by blind refusal from its intended beneficiaries. Thus it is not only the figures of Moses and Jesus that are similar but also the trajectories in which they have key roles. The whole movement from great hopes to great loss in Stephen's description of Israel's history prefigures the story of Israel and Jesus in Luke-Acts, which begins by proclaiming the fulfillment of Israel's hopes in Luke 1—2 and ends with bitter words about a people that cannot hear or see (Acts 28:26–27).[34] In both cases we have a story of tragic reversal of fortune.[35]

As the story of Israel's blindness and rebellion develops in Stephen's speech, certain individuals stand out in contrast. Each is introduced as one especially favored by God. In the case of Joseph we are told that "God was with him" (7:9). Moses at birth was "pleasing ($\dot{\alpha}\sigma\tau\epsilon\hat{\iota}os$) to God" (7:20). David "found favor before God" (7:46). These individuals are the instruments of God's saving purpose for the people, but Joseph, at first, and Moses, more fundamentally, are rejected by them. These outstanding Israelites contrast with the rebellious people and resemble Jesus and Stephen.[36]

Stephen was accused of speaking "against this holy place" (6:13), and he responds by commenting on Israel's sanctuaries, especially the temple (7:44–50). There is a further indication of the importance of this issue: the promise to Abraham, which, as we noted,[37] has a key function in the speech, ends with the statement that "they will worship me in this place." Israel's worship and its "place" are here viewed as the goal of God's saving purpose. This statement is derived from Exod. 3:12, which, however, speaks of worshiping God on "this mountain." The substitution of "place" is significant. "This place" is related to "this land" (7:4) to which Abraham came and could refer to the land in general. However, $\tau\acute{o}\pi os$ ("place") is used in a special sense in the larger context. Stephen's accusers used the same phrase "this place" to refer to the temple (6:13, 14). The

---

[34] On the function of Luke 1—2 within the plot of Luke-Acts, especially in connection with salvation for Israel, see *Narrative Unity* 1:20–44. The words of Zechariah in Luke 1:73-75 are closely related to Stephen's speech, for they interpret the promise to Abraham in terms of political freedom resulting in unhindered worship (using $\lambda\alpha\tau\rho\epsilon\acute{v}\epsilon\iota\nu$). Cf. Acts 7:6-7.

[35] Compare Meir Sternberg's discussion of foreshadowing in Hebrew narrative through "analogical organization," which "directs the reader to apply the lessons of the past" to a new situation. See *Poetics of Biblical Narrative,* 268–70.

[36] See above, 83–84.

[37] See above, 88.

same phrase with the same reference recurs in the accusation against Paul in 21:28. It appears to be well known to the narrator as a way of speaking of the temple.[38] This phrase is deliberately used in 7:7. The continuity with the accusation should be recognized. The promise in 7:7 anticipates a specific place of worship within the land, and that place will be the temple.

This observation implies that Stephen's statement in 7:47–50 is neither a rejection of the temple nor a criticism of Solomon for building it. The "place" of worship is an important part of the promise to Abraham. The fulfillment of this promise through building the temple was appropriate. Nevertheless, there is a distinct note of warning in 7:48–50. The setting of the speech implies that this warning is relevant to Stephen's audience, a group headed by the high priest (7:1) that is willing to take legal action against anyone speaking "against this holy place" (6:13) or prophesying its destruction (6:14).

Stephen warns against any implied restriction of God to the temple. With the assistance of Isa. 66:1–2, he proclaims the transcendence of God.[39] God is not dependent on works of human hands, nor do temples of human construction define God's location or "place of rest." God is the maker of all things; humans do not make things for God, as if God were in need of anything. This view will later be argued before a pagan audience by a reliable spokesman for the implied author, suggesting that it is a fundamental theological axiom (17:24–25). This declaration of God's independence of the Jerusalem temple is also a declaration of God's availability to all with or without the temple. The temple was a special provision for the Jewish people in fulfillment of God's promise, but it is not needed in order to worship God, for God's presence spans heaven and earth, and all creation bears God's fingerprints. This was a point of acute relevance in the author's historical setting, in which memory of the temple's destruction was still painful for any who honored Israel's tradition and respected the devout men and women who worshiped in its temple.[40]

The repeated references to the conquest of Jerusalem and destruction of the temple in Luke (cf. 13:32–35; 19:41–44; 21:5–6, 20–24; 23:27–31)[41]

---

[38] On the temple as the holy "place" in Hebrew Scripture, LXX, and NT, see Helmut Koester, "τόπος," 196–99, 204–5.

[39] Dennis Sylva provides supporting arguments for the view that the point of 7:46–50 is not the rejection of the temple but God's transcendence of the temple. See "Meaning and Function of Acts 7:46–50," 261–75.

[40] A positive picture of temple worshipers emerges both from Luke 1—2 and from the close association of the early church with the temple in Acts 2—5.

[41] On these passages see David Tiede, *Prophecy and History*, 70–96, 105; R. Tannehill, "Israel in Luke-Acts," 75.

indicate that this is part of the information shared by author and reader as background for Stephen's speech. In part the speech explains why the temple is dispensable. This is not apparent from 7:48–50 alone, for a prophet might proclaim God's independence of the temple even if the temple continued to exist. However, the context of the speech does contain a reference to the destruction of the temple. Stephen said, according to his accusers, that Jesus "will destroy this place" (6:14). It is often noted that the narrator has transferred an accusation against Jesus from the passion story, where it is found in Matthew and Mark, to the Stephen episode. If the motive were embarrassment at the charge, it could have been eliminated altogether. Our narrator is keenly concerned with the temple's fate. Therefore, the charge is not eliminated but is transferred to a context that provides more freedom for theological comment than the passion story, namely, the Stephen episode with its extensive speech. I am suggesting that 6:14 is an important indication of the agenda being considered as Stephen speaks of the temple.[42] The continuity between the accusation in 6:14 and the comments on the temple in 7:48–50 may be indicated by the description of temples as "things made with (human) hands" (using $\chi\epsilon\iota\rho\sigma\pi\sigma\acute{\iota}\eta\tau\sigma\varsigma$) in 7:48, for this word is used of the temple in the Markan version (Mark 14:58) of the accusation quoted in Acts 6:14.[43]

This reference to the temple's destruction contains both truth and falsehood (the speakers are "false witnesses," according to 6:13). There are no indications in Luke-Acts from authoritative characters that Jesus will destroy the temple. However, he did state that there would not be a stone of the temple "which will not be thrown down" or "destroyed" (Luke 21:6, using $\kappa\alpha\tau\alpha\lambda\acute{\upsilon}\omega$ as in the charge in Acts 6:14). Furthermore, Jerusalem's destruction is linked with its failure to recognize "the time of visitation" at Jesus' arrival (Luke 19:44). Although Jesus does not destroy the temple, the temple is destroyed because of the blindness of those who reject Jesus and his witnesses. An ironic situation results: people who are zealous for the temple manifest the blindness that brings its destruction.

Earlier I related Acts 7 to Odil Hannes Steck's discussion of the Deuteronomic view of history and the persecution of the prophets.[44] One element of the Deuteronomic view of history, the judgment through catastrophe (such as the Assyrian and Babylonian conquests), is missing in Stephen's speech. Stephen ends with strong accusations, but there is no reference to an impending judgment. Nevertheless, those conditioned by

---

[42] See John Kilgallen, *Stephen Speech,* 32, 39.

[43] Noted by D. Sylva, who argues that "Acts 7:46–50 is an answer to the temple accusation found in Mark 14:58 and partially referred to in Acts 6:14." See "Meaning and Function of Acts 7:46–50," 270.

[44] See above, 87.

the Deuteronomic pattern would expect rebellion against God to lead to catastrophe, indeed, just such a catastrophe as the fall of Jerusalem. At this point the readers' knowledge of Jerusalem's recent conquest and the temple's destruction would come into play.[45] Steck, in discussing the further development of the Deuteronomic view of history, notes that the element of judgment once associated with the capture of Jerusalem by the Babylonians is later associated with Jerusalem's capture by the Romans,[46] and C. H. Dodd and David Tiede discuss how Scriptures that referred to the first destruction of Jerusalem were reapplied to the second.[47] Thus there is evidence that Scripture operated as pattern in the way just suggested.

It is quite likely that the speech, considered in the context of Luke-Acts, presupposes the destruction of the temple. It is also likely that this event is viewed in light of the Deuteronomic pattern as God's punishment on a disobedient people who have rejected the prophets and the Messiah (cf. Luke 19:44, which attributes the destruction of Jerusalem to the city's failure to accept Jesus). This punishment, severe as it is, does not mean that unbelieving Jews have been eliminated from God's people once and for all. Those who continue to reject the prophet like Moses will indeed be rejected, according to Acts 3:23, but the conquest of Jerusalem is not the end of the Jewish people. Their history continues beyond this catastrophe, which permits some hope of a change of heart. The implied author's hope does not die easily, even in the face of contrary evidence, for it rests on divine promises in Scripture of salvation for the Jewish people.[48]

Stephen's accusation is directed at his audience, the high priest, Sanhedrin, and the opponents who have brought charges against him. Yet he has been discussing the history of the people ("our fathers" [7:38–39], which becomes "your fathers" as Stephen makes the application to his audience [7:51–52]), emphasizing its rebellion against Moses and God. Widespread rejection has not yet appeared in Acts, but scriptural precedent plays a powerful role in the implied author's perspective. We may guess that Stephen's speech interprets in advance a story of spreading

---

[45] Some of my readers may be disturbed by my appeal here to knowledge of an extratextual event. However, all communication, including narrative communication, rests on a bed of presupposed knowledge that is not explicitly cited. One possible subtlety of narrative is suggesting a connection with known extratextual events without disrupting the characters' world through intrusive statements, a possibility I see realized here. Moreover, the knowledge in question is extratextual only in the sense that an event clearly anticipated in Luke has actually happened.

[46] See *Israel und das gewaltsame Geschick*, 104.

[47] See C. H. Dodd, "Fall of Jerusalem," 69–83; D. Tiede, *Prophecy and History*, 4–7, 65–70.

[48] Simeon's vision, based on Isaiah, of salvation, light, and glory for both Israel and the Gentiles (Luke 2:30–32) expresses an understanding of God's purpose that remains central to Paul's preaching as late as Acts 26:23. On continuing hope for Jewish conversions at the end of Acts, see below, 350–53.

resistance. The development will take place step by step. The immediate effect of Stephen's death is simply the movement of the mission beyond Jerusalem. It will spread to the Samaritans but will also continue among Jews. Each Jewish community must make its decision about the word of God.

Rejection by the Jerusalem authorities will become part of a pattern of rejection that appears when we note connections between the Stephen episode and the series of scenes in which Paul, in the face of Jewish rejection, turns to the Gentiles (cf. 13:44–48; 18:5–6; 28:23–28). Stephen's speech is linked to the first of these scenes (and thereby to the series as a whole) when Paul repeats words used by Stephen to describe the wilderness rebellion and its consequences. Stephen described how the Israelites "pushed" Moses "aside" (7:27, 39; using ἀπωθέομαι). This word is used only one other time in Luke-Acts, in Paul's description of how the Jews of Antioch treated the word of God (13:46). In both passages it is associated with the idea of turning (expressed by στρέφω). The Israelites pushed Moses aside and "turned in their hearts to Egypt," making gods for themselves. As a result "God turned and gave them up to worship the host of heaven" (7:39–42). When the Antioch Jews "push aside" the word of God, Paul and Barnabas also "turn," now in a positive direction. In light of their mission mandate, they "turn to the Gentiles" (13:46).[49] Thus pushing aside God's message or messenger results in a fateful turning, in which the people turn away from God's purpose while God's purpose turns in a new direction. This pattern, applied by Stephen to the people in the wilderness and the Jewish leaders of Jerusalem, is applied by Paul to Diaspora Jews. Thus this important aspect of Stephen's speech prepares for later developments in the narrative.

In 7:51–53 Stephen summarizes and applies his account of Israel's history to the present. In doing so, he quickly extends the history of Israel's rebellion to include the persecution of the prophets, the murder of the "righteous one," and failure to keep the law. Borrowing the fierce invective of Scripture,[50] he directly accuses his audience, which provokes a violent reaction. The effect of Stephen's speech on his hearers is described in vivid language: "They were sawn through in their hearts and were gnashing their teeth" (7:54). Thus the scene comes to the same pitch of tension as in 5:33, where the same rare word διεπρίοντο ("they were sawn through") was used. In 5:33 anger leads to a desire to kill but not to the actual deed. In Stephen's case the emotion will become violent deed. We are reaching the climax of the story of the confrontation between the

---

[49] The verb στρέφω is used only in these three verses in Acts, and in both 7:39 and 13:46 it is associated with ἀπωθέομαι.

[50] See above, 86–87.

Sanhedrin and the Christian mission in Jerusalem. Violent reaction to Stephen's accusations was not the only possibility, as the previous narrative showed. In 2:36–37 Peter accused the people of Jerusalem of having crucified Jesus. They were "cut to the heart" and were ready to repent. The speeches to the people of Jerusalem and their leaders produce emotional responses, either of repentance or of passionate opposition. Although the narrator has shown the positive possibility of repentance, we have also been carefully prepared for the negative response of violent rejection. There has been repeated conflict with the high priest and his associates, and Stephen in his speech called attention to the long history of rejection of God's messengers. The "great persecution" of which Stephen's death is a part continues the rebellious behavior of those who "persecuted" the prophets in the past (cf. 7:52; 8:1).[51]

The narrator imposes story on story on story, building up mutually interpretive layers of similar events. The rejection of Moses resembles the rejection of Jesus, which resembles the rejection of Stephen. On the positive side, Stephen resembles Jesus and the apostles as he speaks courageously before the Sanhedrin, which has been the consistent opponent of Jesus and his witnesses. Stephen is "full of Holy Spirit" (7:55) as he faces his opponents, as was Peter (4:8) and as Jesus promised his followers they would be (Luke 12:11–12).

Stephen not only interprets rejection of Jesus and his witnesses in light of Israel's past but also bears direct witness to Jesus as the exalted Lord. The angry reaction to his accusations is separated from the violent action against him by one further event: Stephen sees Jesus standing at the right hand of God and announces this to his hearers (7:55–56). The violent action that follows is not only an angry response to Stephen's accusations but also a rejection of this announcement. Stephen's announcement corresponds to Peter's witness to the exalted Lord at God's right hand (cf. 2:33–35; 5:31). Stephen does not appeal to apostolic tradition or Scripture to make his point but bears direct witness on the basis of his own vision. As a recipient of divine visions he resembles Abraham and Moses. An "angel" appeared to Moses, and he heard the "voice of the Lord" (7:30–31). "The God of glory" appeared to Abraham (7:2); Stephen sees the "glory of God" (7:55).[52] Because of his vision Stephen, like Peter, can bear witness to Jesus as the one exalted at God's right hand as leader and savior (5:31–32; cf. 2:32–36). Visions of the exalted Jesus are a continuing possibility after the ascension of Jesus, and these visions have an important function in qualifying Stephen and Paul as witnesses. This is clearly stated in the case

---

[51] E. Richard, *Author's Method,* 327, notes the connection in wording.
[52] See E. Richard, *Author's Method,* 230.

of Paul, whose role as witness is more extensively discussed than
Stephen's. Paul, who sees the righteous one and hears his voice on the way
to Damascus, is called to be "a witness . . . of what you have seen and
heard" (22:14–15; cf. 26:16). Although only Jesus' companions during his
ministry are qualified to bear witness to his words and deeds prior to
Easter and the apostles' witness to the resurrection remains important, the
Lord's appearance enables Paul to be a witness to the exalted Lord.
Stephen, who is also called a "witness" (22:20), has the same qualification.
In 7:56 Stephen proclaims Jesus' exalted place in heaven and his
centrality in God's purpose. It is this proclamation that leads to the final
action of Stephen's hearers. It receives special emphasis through
placement at this climactic moment.

Stephen, in announcing his vision, confirms what Jesus asserted at his
own trial before the Sanhedrin: "From now on the Son of the Human One
(ὁ υἱὸς τοῦ ἀνθρώπου) will be sitting at the right hand of the power of
God" (Luke 22:69). Stephen's confirmation of Jesus' claim is part of an
ongoing struggle that continues to the end of Acts and comes to dramatic
expression in trial scenes. It is a struggle between the claims of the one
who has been exalted to God's right hand and those who refuse to acknowledge these claims. The frequent and lengthy trials of the apostles,
Stephen, and Paul are not concerned only with the fate of these persons;
they are concerned with the claims of the exalted one and with the
acceptance or rejection of those claims in the world.[53] In these trials two
visions of reality clash. Stephen appears weak before the threatening
authorities, yet he acts as if he were in the position of strength. He
proclaims what his audience does not see, the Son of the Human One at
the right hand of God's power. He thereby reveals the true balance of
power. The rulers do not see what Stephen sees, and they refuse to hear
his witness. "They stopped their ears," the narrator says (7:57). This is a
dramatization of the refusal to see and hear that Paul laments in the
words of Isaiah at the end of Acts (28:26–27).

It is very unusual to have the title "Son of the Human One" (RSV: "Son
of man") applied to Jesus outside the Gospels.[54] The close connection of
Acts 7:56 with Jesus' statement before the Sanhedrin in Luke 22:69
provides one explanation of the use of this title. There may also be a
connection with the saying in Luke 12:8–9, where this title is also
important. In teaching his disciples about coming persecutions, Jesus
promised that the Son of the Human One would confess before God those
who confessed Jesus before humans. Stephen is making this dangerous

---

[53] Jerome Neyrey refers to "Jesus' trials in Acts" because the trials there continue the trial of
Jesus with new witnesses appearing in Jesus' behalf. See *Passion According to Luke,* 89.
[54] Only here is it clearly used as a title. Cf. Heb. 2:6; Rev. 1:13; 14:14.

confession. His vision of Jesus as Son of the Human One standing before God perhaps serves, in part, as assurance of Jesus' supportive witness in the heavenly court.[55]

At the crucial moment of Stephen's stoning, the narrator momentarily directs our attention away from Stephen to a young man named Saul (7:58b). The appearance of Barnabas in 4:36–37 has already provided an example of the narrator's tendency to introduce an important new character first as a minor character, a literary method that helps to unify the narrative.[56] However, attention to Saul at this climactic moment shows a special concern to associate Saul with Stephen's death. This is one detail in the portrait of Saul as persecutor. Later we will see, however, that there is also a positive resemblance between Stephen and Saul,[57] as there is between Stephen and Jesus. Because of these resemblances, it is interesting that here (and here alone) Jesus, Stephen, and Saul—three suffering prophets important to God's ongoing purpose—appear together in one scene.

Stephen follows the pattern of Jesus in facing death. All three of the last words of the martyr recall statements by Jesus in Luke's passion story. We have already noted the connection between Acts 7:56 and the words of Jesus before the Sanhedrin in Luke 22:69. Stephen's prayers in Acts 7:59 and 60 correspond to prayers of Jesus on the cross, one immediately after crucifixion, the other at the moment of death. Jesus prayed that his crucifiers might be forgiven (Luke 23:34),[58] and Stephen prays for the forgiveness of those stoning him (Acts 7:60). The dying Jesus commended his spirit to God's care (Luke 23:46); Stephen dies with a similar expression of trust in a care extending beyond death (Acts 7:59).[59] In both of his prayers Jesus addresses God as "Father," and Stephen addresses the "Lord Jesus," the one who has just appeared to him in his heavenly vision. Both Jesus and Stephen shout their final prayer "in a great voice ($\phi\omega\nu\hat{\eta}$ $\mu\epsilon\gamma\acute{\alpha}\lambda\eta$)" (Luke 23:46; Acts 7:60). These similar responses in a similar situation show that Stephen is a true follower of Jesus. They also emphasize important points in the implied author's understanding of martyrdom. The martyr bears witness to the exalted Lord, ruling with heavenly

---

[55] This may explain the enigmatic "standing" in Acts 7:56, which differs from the "sitting" of Luke 22:69. The standing position may indicate that Jesus is giving or about to give his testimony before the heavenly court. See G. Schneider, *Apostelgeschichte*, 1:475.

[56] See above, 78.

[57] See below, 100, 273.

[58] On the textual problem in this verse see *Narrative Unity* 1:272.

[59] In 7:59 Stephen is "calling upon" or "appealing to ($\dot{\epsilon}\pi\iota\kappa\alpha\lambda o\acute{\upsilon}\mu\epsilon\nu o\nu$)" the Lord Jesus. We have already seen that the scriptural promise cited in 2:21 ("Whoever calls upon the name of the Lord will be saved") continues to influence the narrative that follows it. The narrator's phrasing in 7:59 suggests that this promise holds good for Stephen and extends beyond death.

power, whom the opponents cannot see. The martyr trusts in a divine care reaching beyond death and shows no animosity toward the killers, instead interceding for them. In these ways the martyr follows the example of the Lord Jesus. An impressive picture of a faithful follower of Jesus results, a picture that probably had considerable appeal in the early Christian era.[60]

The gap left by Stephen's death is quickly filled by other witnesses. Stephen's preaching will be carried on and extended by Philip, and his role of suffering witness will be taken over by the young man Saul, introduced at the moment of Stephen's death. The experience and work of Stephen and Saul will be similar, and both of these figures resemble their Lord. Saul, like Stephen, encounters the Lord Jesus in a vision. We are told that Saul "must suffer ($\delta\epsilon\hat{\iota}$ . . . $\pi\alpha\theta\epsilon\hat{\iota}\nu$)" (9:16) in language previously used by Jesus to announce his own suffering (Luke 9:22; 17:25; 24:26). The description of Saul debating with Hellenists in Jerusalem, people who try to kill him (9:29), recalls the description of Stephen and his opponents in 6:9–12. Saul is, in fact, taking up the work of Stephen. Paul's final journey to Jerusalem contains anticipations of his coming suffering and reminiscences of Jesus' final journey and death (20:22–23; 21:10–14).[61] At the instigation of Diaspora Jews Paul is seized in the temple, and his opponents shout charges against him similar to the charges against Stephen (6:13–14; 21:28). Paul responds with a speech that begins like Stephen's speech (7:2; 22:1) and mentions Stephen's death (22:20). Paul's speech, like Stephen's, would have been followed by his death, had not the Romans been present (22:22–24).[62] A series of trials follows, resembling the series of trials in Luke 22—23 and Acts 4—7. So the reference to Saul at Stephen's death not only ties Saul to Stephen's killers but also prepares for these positive connections between Stephen and Saul. The continuity between Stephen and Saul could encourage the conviction that the Lord will continue to have powerful witnesses despite human opposition, which cannot halt the divine purpose.

Stephen's death does not affect him alone. It is the beginning of a "great persecution" that falls on the Jerusalem church, so that "all were scattered" to the countryside of Judea and Samaria, except for the apostles (8:1). This is the low point of the entire narrative of Acts. The early church is in danger and disarray. There are only a few signs of hope, but they are important. We are told that "devout men buried Stephen," with "great lamentation" (8:2). These devout men are evidently non-Christian

---

[60] Charles Talbert refers to Greco-Roman, Jewish, and early Christian views of martyrdom that suggest that the death of martyrs like Stephen would have persuasive power, legitimating Jesus and the Christian cause and supporting evangelistic outreach. See "Martyrdom in Luke-Acts," 103–6.

[61] See below, 259, 264–66.

[62] See E. Richard, *Author's Method*, 258–59. On 21:27—22:29 see below, 271–84.

Jews because the Christians, except for the apostles, have left Jerusalem. The opponents of Stephen do not represent all the Jews of Jerusalem. Some openness and sympathy toward the gospel and its witnesses remain.[63] Furthermore, Stephen's prayer for forgiveness opens a possibility even for his persecutors. Even those who have rejected Jesus a second time, with violence against Jesus' witness, need not be excluded from God's salvation for Israel, for Stephen prays that "this sin" not be held against them. That repentance and forgiveness are still possible, even for those who have rejected the risen Lord and have persecuted his witnesses, is made clear by the case of Saul, who is associated with Stephen's killers, vigorously persecutes the church as the agent of the high priest (8:3; 9:1–2), and yet is accepted as the Lord's witness. Stephen's prayer points to an open possibility, and that possibility is effectively realized in the case of Saul. God's possibilities are not exhausted when humans reject the offered salvation with violence.

The other sign of hope appears as the plot moves on. The scattering of the Jerusalem church results not in the disruption and weakening of the mission but in the spread of the word of God to new areas. The narrator links the scattering of the persecuted church to the spread of the mission by repeating the key word "scattered" in connection with new movements of the mission (cf. 8:1, 4–5; 11:19–20).[64] Here again there is an ironic turn. The efforts of the Sanhedrin to halt the preaching of the word, carried to an extreme in the stoning of Stephen, result in the spread of the word in Judea, Samaria, and Antioch.

---

[63] Mishnah Sanh. 6,6 forbids public lamentation for one who has been executed (noted by G. Schneider, *Apostelgeschichte* 1:479). If we can assume that this rule was recognized at the time of Acts and would apply to Stephen's death, the burial may represent not only sympathy for Stephen but public protest against the Sanhedrin's action.

[64] "Scatter (διασπείρω)" is found only in these three places in the NT.

SAMARIA
AND THE END
OF THE EARTH

The death of Stephen affects the church as a whole, for a "great persecution" breaks out and "all" are "scattered" (8:1). The apostles are the sole exception. Note that the effect of the persecution is not limited to the Hellenists, according to Acts. All except the apostles leave Jerusalem. Historically, this is strange, for we would expect persecution to fall most swiftly on the leadership. However, this description of the apostles fits with the emphasis on their perseverance in the face of threats in Acts 4—5. It also suggests the special attachment of the apostles to Jerusalem, an attachment that will persist throughout the narrative.[1] Although Peter and John appear in Samaria and Peter appears in the coastal plain, these are temporary visits from which they return to Jerusalem (8:25; 11:2). As a result of this persistent attachment to Jerusalem, the apostles lose their role as initiators of the mission in new areas.

This is an unexpected development. In 1:8 Jesus told the apostles (perhaps in the presence of other "men of Galilee," 1:11) that they were to be his witnesses "in Jerusalem, and in all Judea and Samaria, and to the end of the earth." The mission does unfold in these geographical stages, but the apostles do not initiate the mission to Samaria and the end of the earth. Philip does. From this point on the apostles must repeatedly catch up with a mission that is sparked by other persons and other forces. This shift does not make the apostles unimportant. They become the stabilizing, verifying, and unifying element in a mission that moves to new areas and groups without their planning or control. As the mission begins to move beyond Jerusalem and Judea, it is useful to distinguish two roles within it: the role of the *initiator* and the role of the *verifier*. The apostles shift at this point from the former to the latter role. That is, their function is reduced to recognizing and confirming the work of the evangelists who bring the gospel to new areas and groups, or to working as evangelists in areas already opened for mission (cf. 8:25; 9:32–42).[2]

---

[1] This point is noted by Jacques Dupont, *Nouvelles études,* 151.

[2] The episode of Peter and Cornelius (Acts 10) is a partial exception. (Partial because of Philip and the Ethiopian; see below, 107–11.) Here one apostle does play an important role

The narrative in Acts 8—11 contains a series of twists in the plot and surprises for any who expected the mission of Jesus' witnesses to follow a smooth course. The effect is irony. Humans belatedly discover what they did not expect, for developments do not follow their plans. This effect is emphasized, on the one hand, by repeated references to divine initiatives, and, on the other, to human resistance to these initiatives. Resistance to familiar relations with Gentiles in the Cornelius scene and resistance to acceptance of Saul as believer and preacher are examples. In other cases we are simply told of major new developments by freelance evangelists (as in Samaria and Antioch). The fact that these took place without authorization or supervision by the apostles appears from the fact that they must send representatives to check on these developments after the event. The apostles are reacting to developments that take place without their planning or control. The real initiative is not in earthly hands. This is true of Philip's mission also, even though there are no references to divine directions until the scene with the Ethiopian.

The irony deepens when we note that the breakthrough in Samaria (and later in Antioch) is the result of the persecution in Jerusalem, which scattered the disciples. Not the church's planning but adverse circumstances lead to important new fields of mission.

The twelve intended to perform the "ministry of the word" themselves while the seven cared for the daily ministry of serving tables (6:2–4), but now those scattered, including Philip, appear as preachers of "the word" (8:4), with no indication that the twelve have authorized this.[3] The contrast between the apostles' expectations and Philip's actual role is more sharply drawn than with Stephen. Stephen performs wonders and signs and then is drawn into disputes with Hellenistic Jews (6:8–10), leading to his major speech before the Sanhedrin. Philip is not responding to critics. As soon as the narrative begins to focus on him, he is presented as an evangelist, and the words used to describe his activity were previously used of the missions of Jesus and the apostles. Philip, and others who were scattered, "preach good news" (using the verb εὐαγγελίζομαι; Acts 8:4, 12; cf. Luke 4:18, 43; 9:6; Acts 5:42 of Jesus and the apostles). The object of this preaching is the "word" (λόγος; Acts 8:4, 14; cf. Luke 5:1; 8:11, 21; Acts 4:29, 31; 6:2, 4). Philip "proclaims" (κηρύσσω; Acts 8:5; cf. Luke 4:18, 19, 44; 8:1; 9:2). Philip preaches concerning "the reign

---

in a mission initiative, which must then be verified by others in Jerusalem (11:1–18). However, there is striking stress on Peter's reluctance to play this role. The new step is clearly not the result of Peter's or the other apostles' plan.

[3] Michel Gourgues recognizes the importance of this shift. See "Esprit des commencements," 378.

of God" (ἡ βασιλεία τοῦ θεοῦ; Acts 8:12; cf. Luke 4:43; 8:1; 9:2) and the "name" of Jesus (ὄνομα; Acts 8:12; cf. Acts 4:17, 18; 5:28, 40). Thus the narrative emphasizes that Philip is performing the same kind of preaching mission as Jesus and the apostles. The mission begun by Jesus is continuing through a new instrument of God.

Furthermore, Philip's preaching is accompanied by signs, as was the preaching of Jesus and the apostles, and these signs are described in terms that recall the early ministry of Jesus and the ministry of the apostles. Philip exorcises "unclean spirits crying out with a loud voice" (Acts 8:7; cf. Luke 4:33; Acts 5:16) and heals the "paralyzed" (cf. Luke 5:18; Acts 9:33) and "lame" (cf. Luke 7:22; Acts 3:2). Lest Philip's healings be underrated in comparison with others, there is repeated emphasis in 8:7–8 on the "many" who were healed and the "much" joy that resulted (πολλοί . . . πολλοί . . . πολλή). The summary of Philip's healings in 8:13 describes them as "signs (σημεῖα)," a term applied to the apostles' works from Acts 2:43 on, and "acts of power (δυνάμεις)," a word applied to Jesus' works in Luke 10:13; 19:37; Acts 2:22. Philip's mission of preaching and healing is described in ways that suggest its similarity to and continuity with the mission of Jesus and the apostles. What they did he is now doing, but he does it in a new area and with a new ethnic group. The fulfillment of Jesus' commission in 1:8 does not wait until the apostles are ready to include Samaria. While they are trying to maintain Jesus' claim on Jerusalem, the mission moves forward through Philip.

When the apostles in Jerusalem hear about Philip's successful mission, they send Peter and John (8:14). The following narrative concerning the coming of the Spirit to the Samaritans through the laying on of the apostles' hands can be profitably considered from two perspectives: what it means for Philip's mission and what it means for Peter and John.

First, Philip's mission: Faith and baptism are incomplete without the gift of the Spirit, which means that Philip's mission is incomplete until the coming of Peter and John. Although Philip initiated the mission on his own, the apostles have an important role to play in completing Philip's work. The point is not that the Spirit can be received only when apostles lay on their hands, for in later scenes it comes in other ways (cf. 10:44) or through other persons (cf. 19:6). Rather, through the arrival of Peter and John, and through their important action in behalf of the Samaritans, the mission becomes a cooperative undertaking. Philip is the initiator, but Peter and John also make an important contribution. Philip's mission does not become an independent operation, for the apostles quickly establish contact and help the Samaritans to share in the Holy Spirit. The result is a cooperative mission in which an established church affirms and contributes to the establishment of new churches.

Second, the effect of the visit on Peter and John: In 10:44–48 the coming of the Holy Spirit is a visible sign that God wants to include the Gentiles in the salvation that Jesus brings (cf. 11:15–18). Those who have clearly received the Spirit cannot be rejected even if they belong to alienated groups. The coming of the Spirit to the Samaritans is a similar sign that God has already begun to include the Samaritans in salvation through Jesus. The apostles come to Samaria in order to verify Philip's mission.[4] This does not mean that they are being portrayed as strongly skeptical. They prove to be open to signs of God's working among these people. Through their own actions they receive such a sign, and the Samaritan mission is confirmed. The resulting change in the apostles is indicated in 8:25, for Peter and John now join in Philip's mission and preach to many villages of the Samaritans.

The narrator deliberately depicts the new mission in Antioch as a parallel case (11:19–26). Again the new initiative is the work of those scattered following Stephen's death. Again the church in Jerusalem sends an emissary, this time Barnabas, when it hears of this development. Barnabas is qualified to be a verifier not only because he is sent by the Jerusalem church but also because "he was a good man and full of Holy Spirit and faith" (11:24). Such a man is capable of "seeing the grace of God" and affirming it when it appears among new groups and in new areas, and so Barnabas does. The situation in Samaria is similar except that a special sign is given to confirm the presence of God's grace among the Samaritans: the initial coming of the Holy Spirit in recognizable form. This sign is all the more convincing in that Peter and John are not only present when it happens but actively participate in this event. Both factors help to confirm the reality of the Spirit's arrival. The apostles' willingness to lay their hands on the Samaritans shows that they, like Barnabas, are open to the possibility that God is already at work among a new group through a mission that the apostles did not create.

Both Philip (8:9–13) and the apostles (8:18–24) encounter a certain Simon, who is described as "practicing magic" (8:9; cf. 8:11). Simon has several functions in the narrative. On the one hand, the narrator emphasizes the greatness of Philip's signs by contrasting them with Simon's magic. After we are told that Simon was "astounding ($\dot{\epsilon}\xi\iota\sigma\tau\dot{\alpha}\nu\omega\nu$)" the Samaritans by his magic and was even called "the power ($\delta\dot{\nu}\nu\alpha\mu\iota\varsigma$) of God that is called great ($\mu\epsilon\gamma\dot{\alpha}\lambda\eta$)" (8:9–10), Simon himself "was astounded ($\dot{\epsilon}\xi\dot{\iota}\sigma\tau\alpha\tauο$), seeing signs and great acts of power ($\delta\upsilon\nu\dot{\alpha}\mu\epsilon\iota\varsigma$ $\mu\epsilon\gamma\dot{\alpha}\lambda\alpha\varsigma$) happening" through Philip (8:13).

On the other hand, Simon represents serious dangers that the mission

---

[4] See M. Gourgues, "Esprit des commencements," 379.

must avoid. His magic is not described, but the narrator gives him two negative characteristics: he claims that "he himself is someone great" (8:9) and he thinks that he can obtain by money the power to control the Holy Spirit (8:18–19). His proposal to pay evokes a strong rebuke from Peter, making clear that this is a serious error. His claim to be someone great aligns him with Theudas, one of those who temporarily seems great but does not represent the purpose of God (5:36–39),[5] and contrasts with the attitude of the apostles and Paul, who carefully distinguish between the power of Jesus' name and their own power or greatness (3:12; 10:26; 14:14–15). A concern over corrupt religion appears in these comments about Simon. They suggest that religion becomes corrupt whenever humans attempt to use God's power to make themselves powerful or great in human eyes. Because this is a continual temptation, the leaders of the mission must make clear, whenever the crowd gets false ideas, that they themselves are neither divine nor great. Simon took the opposite attitude.

Money—a form of human power—is another factor in the human corruption of religion, one that receives special attention in Luke-Acts.[6] Simon thinks that money can give him the power to confer the Holy Spirit on whomever he chooses. He views the Spirit as a commodity in human commerce that humans may trade for their own advantage. Peter replies that Simon and his money can go to hell ($\epsilon\ddot{\iota}\eta$ $\epsilon\dot{\iota}s$ $\dot{\alpha}\pi\dot{\omega}\lambda\epsilon\iota\alpha\nu$). The Spirit is "the gift of God." It is not subject to human buying and selling. Peter rejects Simon abruptly when he discovers that Simon thinks he can control the Spirit by money. Nevertheless, forgiveness may be possible—if Simon repents.

It is often important to recognize whether an expression represents the point of view of the narrator or the point of view of a character. Expressions of a character's point of view are not limited to that person's direct discourse. There are also cases of free indirect discourse in which the narrator freely summarizes the perceptions of a character. We find an example in 8:18—"Simon, seeing that the Spirit is being given through the laying on of the apostles' hands. . . ." The narrator is telling us how Simon interpreted what he had seen, and this is not to be taken as simple truth. Indeed, Peter corrects this interpretation when he calls the Spirit "the gift of God" (8:20, emphasized through first position in the Greek clause). Simon supposes that the Spirit is given through the laying on of

---

[5] In the Greek, the claim of Theudas in 5:36 closely resembles the claim of Simon in 8:9.

[6] Recall Judas (1:18), Ananias and Sapphira (5:1–11), the owners of the soothsaying girl (16:16–19), and Demetrius the silver worker (19:24–27). Money is a factor in the evil acts attributed to each of these persons.

human hands and does not recognize the deeper truth that it is the gift of God.[7]

Simon evidently had a significant amount of money in order to make this offer. He is not asking for the Spirit for himself but for the power to confer it on others through his hands. This would both make him the equal of the apostles and would be valuable magic that others would pay for. In offering money, Simon is still thinking like a magician, for magicians would charge a fee for the use of their powers.[8] Because Simon could make money with such power, he was willing to invest money to obtain it.

This passage (along with 13:6–12 and 19:18–20) makes clear that the narrator wishes to distinguish the mission sharply from the magic practiced in the Greco-Roman world, but the point is potentially broader. Whenever religion is used to make its leaders seem great and powerful, and whenever religion becomes a commodity by serving the interests of those who have or want money, it has become corrupt. Because Simon has been baptized when he makes his offer, the possibility of such corruption within the church is clearly recognized. Although miracles are ascribed to Peter and Paul in Acts that seem close to magic, the line between their mission and tendencies toward self-promotion and the use of religion for financial benefit, typical of magicians and other corrupt dealers in the supernatural, is clearly drawn through Peter's confrontation with Simon.

The story of the Ethiopian eunuch in 8:26–40 is linked to preceding events because Philip remains a central character. However, in terms of the progress of the mission, it does not represent the next logical step, a "stepping-stone" between the conversion of the Samaritans and the Gentiles,[9] but a leap to the extreme. Ethiopia was on the edge of the known world. This scene anticipates the power of the gospel to reach "the end of the earth" (1:8). Although it may seem out of order if we anticipated a step-by-step progression of the mission from Jerusalem, the sequence of Samaria and the end of the earth fits Jesus' instructions in 1:8. This view of the scene is defended below.

Philip's encounter with the Ethiopian is not a causal factor in a sequence of events that moves toward the end of the earth. Indeed, this scene has no consequences in the narrative. The Ethiopian is not mentioned

---

[7] K. Haacker recognizes 8:18 as a case of "erlebte Rede," in which the narrator is not expressing the situation objectively but as a participant experiences it. See "Einige Fälle von 'erlebter Rede'," 70–77. On complexities arising from combinations of authorial speech and the speech of characters, see Boris Uspensky, *Poetics of Composition*, 32–50. On free indirect discourse in Hebrew Scripture, see Meir Sternberg, *Poetics of Biblical Narrative*, 52–53.
[8] For supporting quotes from ancient literature, see C. K. Barrett, "Simon Magus," 287–88.
[9] See E. Haenchen, *Acts*, 314.

again, and there is no indication that the Jerusalem church learns of his conversion. There is no discussion in Jerusalem of the propriety of baptizing an Ethiopian eunuch as there is after the baptism of Cornelius. Philip's encounter with the Ethiopian takes place on a "desert" or "deserted" road (8:26), and it remains a private event within the narrative. The scene is important for what it anticipates and symbolizes rather than for its consequences. It is prophetic of the gospel's reach.

In this scene Philip is richly endowed with characteristics of prophet and preacher of the word previously attributed to the apostles. He receives instructions from an angel and the Spirit (8:26, 29), and when his task is complete, he is snatched away by the Spirit like the prophets Elijah and Ezekiel (cf. 1 Kgs. 18:12; 2 Kgs. 2:16; Ezek. 11:24).[10] Philip can disclose the hidden references to Jesus the Messiah in Scripture (8:32–35), just as Peter does in his preaching after his mind was opened by the risen Lord (Luke 24:45). As one who is divinely directed, Philip acts with authority. Although there might be hindrances to baptism of this eunuch in the eyes of many, Philip responds to his request by baptizing him without consulting the apostles. To be sure, the narrator does not present these events as the result of human plans, Philip's or the apostles'. Philip is following divine instructions, and events unfold by divine providence (note the suitability of the text the eunuch is reading and the presence of water at the right time for baptism). Furthermore, the eunuch is eager. His invitation, questions, and request lead Philip on to the baptism (8:31, 34, 36).[11] Nevertheless, Philip is the human instrument by which the mission spreads to a very different kind of person. He is the initiator of the mission not only in Samaria but to the end of the earth.

An Ethiopian eunuch is a very strong representative of foreignness within a Jewish context. He comes from the edge of the known world, of the black race, is a castrated male, and probably a Gentile. Each of these characteristics requires some discussion.

It is important to note, first, that the sequence in 1:8 (Jerusalem, Judea, Samaria, the end of the earth) is geographical. To be sure, the locations imply at least three different religious groups (Jews, Samaritans, and Gentiles) who would predominate in the different locations, but these groups are represented by places that they inhabit. The Ethiopian is introduced by his geographical origin, and it is one that fittingly represents the end of the earth. As W. C. van Unnik has convincingly argued, the Greek phrase "to the end of the earth (ἕως ἐσχάτου τῆς γῆς)" refers "very definitely to the end, the extreme limit, of the world. . . . For ancient

---

[10] In Acts 8:39 it is πνεῦμα κυρίου that snatches Philip up, as with Elijah in 1 Kgs. 18:12 and 2 Kgs. 2:16. For further points of similarity with 2 Kgs. 2, see E. Haenchen, *Acts*, 313.

[11] See B. Gaventa, *From Darkness to Light*, 105.

people these limits lay at the Atlantic, by the Germans, Scythians, Indians, and Ethiopians."[12] The conviction that the Ethiopians lived at the ends of the earth is well documented in ancient literature.[13] The view that "the end of the earth" in 1:8 refers to Rome, because that is where Acts ends, is without real support.[14] Although Acts follows a number of geographical advances in the spread of the mission, it is not able to report that preachers of the word have reached the end of the earth. Because this goal remains important, an anticipatory scene is substituted. Philip baptizes an Ethiopian who is passing through Judea. Philip initiates the mission not only to Samaria but also to the end of the earth, for the Ethiopian represents those who are at the end of the earth, whether he is a Gentile or not.

When told that a man was Ethiopian, people of the ancient Mediterranean world would assume that he was black, for this is the way that Ethiopians are described by Herodotus and others.[15]

The man was a eunuch.[16] This reinforces his position as an outsider, for in Deut. 23:2 (ET, 23:1) castrated persons are forbidden entrance into the assembly (ἐκκλησία) of the Lord. In spite of this, eunuchs are promised a place in God's house in Isa. 56:5, overcoming previous exclusion. This passage may well stand in the background of our scene, for Isa. 56:3–8 is concerned with two excluded classes: the eunuch and the foreigner. The Ethiopian eunuch is both. The narrator's acquaintance with this passage is suggested by the fact that it comes from the section of Scripture most heavily used in Luke-Acts (Isaiah 40—66), and this acquaintance is confirmed by the reference to Isa. 56:7 in Luke 19:46.

From the fact that he is an Ethiopian eunuch, we are probably meant to conclude that he is a Gentile. His origin in one of the remotest regions of the known world would suggest this, and the prohibition against admitting eunuchs to the assembly of Israel in Deut. 23:2 (ET, 23:1) makes it unlikely that he had become a proselyte.[17] To be sure, he has come in order to worship in Jerusalem, and he is reading the prophet Isaiah. Cornelius also is presented as a devout worshiper of the God of Israel

---

[12] "Ausdruck 'ΕΩΣ 'ΕΣΧΑΤΟΥ ΤΗΣ ΓΗΣ," 400.

[13] See Homer, *Odyssey* 1.23; Herodotus III.25, III.114; Strabo, *Geography* I.1.6, I.2.24; cited by T. C. G. Thornton, "To the End of the Earth," 375.

[14] See above, 17, n. 26.

[15] See Herodotus II.22, III.101; Philostratus, *Life of Apollonius* VI.1. See also E. Dinkler, "Philippus und der ANHP ΑΙΘΙΟΨ," 90–91.

[16] Although E. Haenchen notes that "eunuch" can denote high political and military officers, not necessarily implying castration (see *Acts*, 310), H. Conzelmann rightly notes that the man's official status is described by what follows, suggesting that "eunuch" indicates castration. See *Acts*, 68.

[17] J. Schneider concludes that the Ethiopian was not a proselyte but one of those whom Luke calls God-fearers. See "εὐνοῦχος," *TDNT* 2:768.

(10:2), yet he is clearly a Gentile. The narrator shows special interest in such God-fearers.[18]

The main reason that many scholars hesitate to recognize the Ethiopian eunuch as a Gentile is the disturbance this would cause to a prior conclusion: that the narrator intends to present Peter as the initiator of the Gentile mission in the story of Cornelius' conversion. Thus E. Haenchen says, "Luke cannot and did not say that the eunuch was a Gentile; otherwise Philip would have forestalled Peter, the legitimate founder of the Gentile mission!"[19] But this assumption about Peter must be questioned. The conversion of Cornelius remains important. It is the story of how Peter and the Jerusalem church came to accept Gentiles for baptism.[20] The baptism of the eunuch has no effect upon them because it remains a private event. Through the conversion of Cornelius, Peter learns something that has permanent value for the church and affects the future course of the mission. In this sense the story of Cornelius and Peter initiates something new, and the importance of this event is reflected in the extent of the Cornelius episode. Its importance does not derive from the fact that Cornelius is the first Gentile converted. Rather, the two scenes of the Ethiopian eunuch and Cornelius are related to each other according to a pattern established in the Samaritan mission and later repeated in Antioch (cf. 11:19-24): the new step is taken by someone other than the apostles, and the apostles must then catch up with events that are happening independently of them. In the process the rightness of the new move is verified. Philip initiates the Samaritan mission, while Peter and John verify what has happened. Philip also initiates the Gentile mission. Peter and the Jerusalem church do not investigate the conversion of the eunuch, but they are later brought to recognize that Gentiles can now be accepted through the conversion of Cornelius. Thus the new step is verified for the leaders in Jerusalem.

There are significant similarities between the stories of Philip and the eunuch, on the one hand, and Peter and Cornelius, on the other. Similarities, once noted, encourage comparison for further similarities and contrasts. If the narrator wished to avoid the implication that what Peter did Philip had already done—convert a Gentile[21] —it would be important to

---

[18] Philip Esler discusses God-fearers who worshiped in Jerusalem and emphasizes that they were marginalized by the prohibition of passing beyond the outer court. See *Community and Gospel,* 154-57.

[19] *Acts,* 314.

[20] In 15:14 James refers to the Cornelius episode as God's "first" act in taking Gentiles as God's people. This reflects the viewpoint of James and the apostles. For them it was a "first."

[21] See E. Haenchen, *Acts,* 315, who says, "The story of the eunuch is the Hellenistic parallel to Luke's account of the first Gentile-conversion by Peter: its parallel—and rival. As such, of course, Luke could not accept it, in view of the importance of the twelve Apostles in his eyes."

discourage comparison by minimizing similarities. The narrator chooses the opposite course, presenting two similar scenes in which the missionary, receiving strong divine guidance,[22] makes contact with a foreigner, which leads to preaching and the foreigner's baptism. Details support the general similarity of the story line. In both cases an angel initiates events (8:26; 10:3). Later the Spirit gives specific instructions to make contact with the foreigner (8:29; 10:19–20). In response to an invitation, Philip and Peter preach the gospel, and their sermons are introduced in the same way: "And Philip [Peter], opening the mouth . . . (ἀνοίξας δὲ ὁ Φίλιππος [Πέτρος] τὸ στόμα)" (8:35; 10:34). Then in 8:36 and 10:47 the baptism of the foreigner is introduced by a question, asking whether anything prevents baptism (using the verb κωλύω). The emphasis on baptism, and the similar way in which the issue of obstacles to baptism is raised, is especially striking. When Peter baptizes Cornelius, readers may well remember that Philip was earlier led to baptize a foreigner.

The interpretation of Scripture plays an important role in the eunuch's conversion, and an extensive quotation is included in the narrative (8:32–33). However, the quotation is not interpreted. We are only told that Philip used it as a basis for preaching about Jesus. The story provides the narrator with the opportunity to include one more of the passages that Jesus presumably would have had in mind when he referred to "all the things written concerning me in the law of Moses and the prophets and psalms" (Luke 24:44). The best guide to the intended interpretation is previous interpretation of Jesus' rejection and exaltation in the light of Scripture in the Acts speeches. The one who opens not his mouth is Jesus as he accepts the necessity of his death according to "the fixed plan and foreknowledge of God" (Acts 2:23). His life taken up from the earth would refer to Jesus' resurrection and exaltation to God's right hand. The preceding question ("Who will describe his family?") probably indicates wonder at the vast progeny of believers that will result from Jesus' exaltation as Messiah. In the first line of v. 33, ἡ κρίσις αὐτοῦ ἤρθη may mean either "His condemnation was taken away" (a reference to God's vindication of the rejected Jesus) or "His justice was taken away" (a reference to the unjust treatment of the innocent Jesus, as in 3:13–15). In spite of some uncertainty in details,[23] the quotation seems to fit the interpretation of Jesus' death and exaltation according to Scripture in

---

[22] E. Haenchen comments on the story of the eunuch, "Acts contains but one other story distinguished . . . by this same feature of divine direction determining the course of events at every turn: the story of Cornelius." See *Acts*, 315.

[23] On 8:32–33 see further P. B. Decock, "Understanding of Isaiah," 111–33. Decock examines the text in light of the Jewish tradition of the vindication of the suffering just person.

preceding speeches in Acts, broadening the base of Scripture quotations that support this interpretation. Within its present context the quotation may also suggest a contrast between Jesus' past role as silent sufferer ("He opens not his mouth," 8:32) and Philip's present role as proclaimer of Jesus ("Philip, opening his mouth . . . ," 8:35).

In 8:39–40 the Philip section of the narrative is rounded off by repeating themes from its beginning. As there was "much joy in that city" in 8:8, so the eunuch "went his way rejoicing" in 8:39. As those scattered "passed through preaching good news (διῆλθον εὐαγγελιζόμενοι)" in 8:4, so Philip, "passing through, was preaching good news (διερχόμενος εὐηγγελίζετο)" in 8:40. This final verse also resembles the closing summary of Peter and John's preaching mission on their return to Jerusalem (8:25). The narrator leaves Philip in Caesarea, where Paul will find him in 21:8.

SAUL THE PERSECUTOR
BECOMES A PROCLAIMER
OF JESUS

Acts 9—11 continue to trace new stages of the mission. After Philip carries the word to Samaria and makes the first contact with a representative of peoples at "the end of the earth" (Acts 8), the narrative focuses on a key character in the spread of the mission (Saul) and on key events in the development of a sustained mission to the Gentiles. Saul's role in relation to Gentiles is indicated in the story of his transformation (9:15). The narrative will continue with the story of Peter's conversion of the Gentile Cornelius. Temporal relations between the Cornelius episode and the preceding stories of Philip and Saul are very vague, and no causal sequence is indicated, for Peter does not react to Cornelius in light of what has already happened to Philip and Saul. It would have been quite possible for the narrator to place the material in 8:26—9:30 after the Cornelius episode. This reversal would be preferable if the narrator wished to make the point that the gentile mission is initiated through Peter. Instead we hear of divine initiatives in the lives of Philip and Saul, pointing toward the gentile mission, before we hear of Peter's encounter with Cornelius. Preparatory steps toward the mission to the Gentiles and the end of the earth are taken before Acts 10, and these initiatives do not take place through Peter. We will also note that Saul begins his preaching mission in Damascus without the prior approval of the apostles, just as Philip launches a mission in Samaria of which the apostles hear only later (8:14). The Jerusalem leaders have a role in verifying these missions. They are not their initiators or directors.

Although Acts 8—10 focuses in turn on three different leading characters—Philip, Saul, and Peter—there is some similarity in the events presented. The narrator is depicting a period of important new developments in the mission and does so by presenting three different scenes in which a believer is sent to an unexpected person, resulting in a conversion.[1] In each case there is strong emphasis on divine direction through an angel, the Spirit, or the Lord. As a result the church is led to include

---

[1] See Beverly Roberts Gaventa, "Overthrown Enemy," 443.

two foreigners (the Ethiopian and the Roman centurion) and its bitter enemy Saul.

In 9:1 the narrator picks up the thread of the narrative about Saul, who was introduced in 7:58 and last mentioned in 8:3. In 8:3 Saul began to take a major role in the persecution of the church. In 9:1–2 we are told that Saul is "still" a fearsome threat. He wants to extend the persecution beyond Jerusalem to Damascus. However, while carrying out this project, he is confronted by the exalted and persecuted Lord.

Descriptions of the roles of Saul link him with the Stephen scene and, to a lesser extent, with Philip. Saul is introduced in connection with Stephen's death (7:58; 8:1), and this link is later recalled in 22:20. Those who kill Stephen demonstrate that they belong to the "stiff-necked" people who "persecuted" the prophets and are "murderers" of the righteous one (7:51–52). Saul is first associated with Stephen's killers and then becomes the major representative of the attitude condemned by Stephen in 7:51–52. In 9:1–5 Saul is described in language that recalls 7:51–52:[2] he is "breathing threat and murder" ($\phi\acute{o}\nu o\nu$ 9:1; cf. $\phi o\nu\epsilon\hat{\iota}s$ 7:52); he is a persecutor ($\delta\iota\acute{\omega}\kappa\epsilon\iota s$ 9:4, 5; cf. $\dot{\epsilon}\delta\acute{\iota}\omega\xi\alpha\nu$ 7:52) not only of Jesus' followers but of Jesus himself. The Lord's striking reproach in 9:4–5, accusing Saul of persecuting *him* (not just his followers) may be due less to an assumed identity between the risen Lord and the church as his earthly body, or between the Lord and his messengers (cf. Luke 10:16), than to a desire to identify Saul with those previously accused of Jesus' rejection and death in the speeches of Peter and Stephen.

When he is transformed, the characterization of Saul shifts from aligning him with the killers of Jesus and Stephen to aligning him with Jesus and Stephen as suffering proclaimers of the word. The Lord's statement to Ananias about what Saul "must suffer for my name ($\delta\epsilon\hat{\iota}$ . . . $\pi\alpha\theta\epsilon\hat{\iota}\nu$" (9:16) uses language characteristic of Jesus' passion predictions in Luke (cf. 9:22; 17:25; 24:26).[3] Stephen, too, shares Jesus' fate, for the story of Stephen's death echoes the passion of Jesus.[4] We have already noted that Saul, when he returns to Jerusalem, assumes the role of the fallen Stephen, debating with Hellenistic Jews, who plot to kill him (9:29; cf. 6:9–11). Later Paul will face accusations similar to the accusations against Stephen (21:28; cf. 6:13).[5] When Stephen is killed, the important role of leading advocate of Jesus among Hellenistic Jews in Jerusalem

---

[2] See B. R. Gaventa, *From Darkness to Light*, 55.

[3] On further echoes of Jesus' way of suffering in descriptions of Paul, see below, 239–40, 259, 264–66, 274, 281–82, 345–46.

[4] See above, 99–100. David Moessner emphasizes that not only Jesus but also Stephen and Paul fit the pattern of the rejected prophet like Moses in Acts. See "Paul and the Pattern of the Prophet like Moses," 203–12, and "Christ Must Suffer," 220–56.

[5] For more detail on the similarities between Stephen and Paul, see above, 100.

falls vacant. This role carries with it the threat of death. When Saul is in Jerusalem, he takes up this role.

The similarities between Saul and Philip are less distinctive, for they relate to their general roles as evangelists. Nevertheless, it may be worth noting that the first statement of their preaching missions is similar: in Samaria Philip "was proclaiming (ἐκήρυσσεν) to them the Messiah" (8:5); in Damascus Saul "was proclaiming (ἐκήρυσσεν) Jesus, that he is the Son of God" (9:20). In light of the fact that references to the "name" of Jesus tend to cluster in Acts 2—5 and 8—9, rather than being evenly distributed throughout the work,[6] it is significant that both Philip's and Paul's preaching are associated with Jesus' name (8:12; 9:15,[7] 27-29). This feature suggests the continuity of their work with the apostles' speaking and teaching in Jesus' name in Jerusalem (4:17-18; 5:28, 40). In addition, Saul will suffer for Jesus' name (9:16) as the apostles did (5:41). Furthermore, in Acts only the preaching of Philip and Paul is said to be about "the reign of God" (8:12; 19:8; 20:25; 28:23, 31), and the relation of 8:12 to 28:23, 31 is especially close. In brief summaries these verses relate the message of Philip and Paul both to Jesus and to the reign of God. The references to the reign of God emphasize the continuity of the message with the message of Jesus as it is carried forward by messengers who had no contact with the preaching of the earthly Jesus. Finally, Philip's conversion of the Ethiopian anticipates the mission that Paul will accept (as announced in 13:47): to bring salvation "to the end of the earth."

Shifts in the central character of the narrative (from Peter to Stephen to Philip to Saul) could fragment the narrative, but the narrator stresses the similarity of the mission that central characters share, calling this similarity to our attention through similar descriptive phrases. This procedure unifies the narrative and gives this mission central thematic significance.

The episode of Saul's conversion in 9:1-19a differs from the two later accounts of the same events in Acts 22 and 26 in that it is told directly by the narrator, not by a character within the story. Furthermore, in Acts 9 the Lord appears not only to Saul but also to Ananias, and the narrative recounts a longer dialogue with Ananias than with Saul. Ananias is an important figure in Acts 9. He is more than a messenger. His reaction to events is important. The narrator takes time to present this reaction and the Lord's corrective response. Therefore, this episode is more than the story of Saul; it is the story of Saul and Ananias, a story of how the Lord encountered both and brought them together. This required changes in

---

[6] See above, 49.
[7] On this verse see below, 117-19.

both. Not only must Saul's aggression toward the disciples be curbed but Ananias' fear of the persecutor must be overcome.

The reconciliation of enemies takes place through the literary device of the "double vision."[8] The appearance of the Lord to Saul directs him into Damascus, where an important task will be revealed to him (9:6). Apart from this further communication to be brought by a human messenger, Saul is left in limbo. His helplessness is strongly expressed through his blindness. He must be led by the hand even to enter the city. In v. 12 there is reference to a supplementary vision by Paul. While praying he sees the man who will come and enable him to begin his new life.

Similarly, Ananias' vision directs him toward Saul. The Lord has a task for Ananias to perform, and it specifically concerns Saul. However, the Lord's command elicits Ananias' protest, for Ananias knows Saul's reputation and purpose in coming to Damascus. This protest must be overcome by the Lord's repeated command and announcement of the quite different future that the Lord has in store for Saul. Each of the three versions of Saul's conversion in Acts highlights the Lord's commission that will direct Saul's life from that point on, but these commission statements are presented within different dialogue segments of the narrative. The Lord is speaking to Ananias in 9:15–16, Ananias is speaking to Saul in 22:14–15, and the Lord is speaking to Saul in 26:16–18. Yet these are closely related previews of Saul's future role. The direct transmission of the commission from the Lord to Saul in Acts 26 speaks against the view that the narrator wishes to subordinate Saul to the apostles and the Jewish church before him, through which Paul's commission must be mediated.[9] Instead, the placement of Paul's commission in the dialogue between the Lord and Ananias in 9:15–16 should be explained from the narrator's interest in the reaction of Ananias to the Lord's command. Ananias must be persuaded to do his job. The disclosure of Saul's future role serves this purpose in 9:15–16. The use of this material for this purpose indicates the narrator's interest in Ananias' resistance to approaching Saul and in the overcoming of this resistance.

Resistance to receiving Saul reappears when he goes to Jerusalem (9:26). The Jerusalem church is afraid of him because they do not believe that he is a disciple. The repetition of this motif is a further sign of its importance. Human disbelief highlights the amazing transformation of Saul worked by the Lord, as E. Haenchen recognizes. Then he continues,

---

[8] On the double vision see Gerhard Lohfink, *Conversion of St. Paul,* 73–77. The term refers to something more specific than the occurrence of two visions in a narrative. As Lohfink explains, "what is essential to the motif is that both of the visions or dreams *correspond with each other, refer to each other or, again, work together toward a single purpose or goal*" (75, emphasis by Lohfink).

[9] See Günter Klein, *Zwölf Apostel,* 145–51.

however, "Luke has no thought of portraying the devout Jewish Christian Ananias as refractory to God's command!"[10] Here Haenchen trivializes the issue with which the narrative is dealing. The disciples are not prepared to obey the Lord because they are afraid of their persecutor. This shows a misdirected fear of the persecutor rather than God (cf. Luke 12:4–5). It also shows the problem that humans have in keeping up with the Lord's work. The Lord's work is revealed through events that overthrow human expectations. Humans calculate the future on the basis of their normal experience. These calculations leave them unprepared for the appearance of the Overruler, who negates human plans and works the unexpected. This is a problem not only for the rejecters of Jesus but also for the church, which, as our narrative indicates, is led by the Lord into situations beyond its fathoming. The narrator's sharp sense of God (and the exalted Messiah) as one who surprises appears again in this episode, and the reaction of Ananias (and in 9:26 the Jerusalem disciples) shows that the church, too, has difficulty keeping up with such a God.

The narrative seeks to heighten the sense of surprise by rhetorical reversal in the dialogue between Ananias and the Lord. Ananias protests that Saul has come to inflict suffering on "those calling upon your name," but the Lord replies that Saul is a chosen instrument "to bear my name" and he himself "must suffer for my name" (9:14–16).[11] The persecutor is about to become not only a Christian but also an outstanding example of one who endures persecution in order to fulfill his mission, much to Ananias' surprise.

Previously it has been helpful to note carefully the commission statements that disclose and govern the missions of leading characters in Luke-Acts.[12] These preview the course of the narrative, emphasize central features of it, and, if the commission comes from an ultimate source, contain norms for judging whether the character is fulfilling the Lord's will. The Lord's words in 9:15–16 provide a first statement of Saul's commission.

To be sure, Gerhard Lohfink has argued that 9:15–16 does not describe Saul's preaching mission but refers only to confessing Jesus' name in situations of persecution and public accusation.[13] Suffering is clearly indicated in v. 16, and the use of the conjunction $\gamma \acute{\alpha} \rho$ ("for") to connect this verse with the preceding one associates the bearing of Jesus' name with this suffering. Noting this implication has a further advantage. We may

---

[10] See E. Haenchen, *Acts*, 324.

[11] See E. Haenchen, *Acts*, 324–25.

[12] On the importance of commission statements for recognizing major themes that unify the narrative, see *Narrative Unity* 1:21–22, 61, 295–98.

[13] See "Meinen Namen zu tragen," 108–15.

find here, in the first statement about Saul's Christian career, a preview of the extensive series of defense and trial scenes in Acts 22—26. This connection is supported by the somewhat surprising reference to "kings" in 9:15, for in Acts 26 Paul appears before a king. If these defense scenes and Paul's lengthy imprisonment are already in mind in 9:15–16, their importance in the Lukan portrait of Paul is clear.[14]

However, it is a mistake to divorce this preview of suffering from a call to mission. The suffering that Saul must face will come as a result of his preaching. The immediately succeeding scenes make this clear. The narrator knows that the encounter with the Lord on the Damascus road creates not just another Christian but an outstanding missionary. Saul immediately engages in preaching (9:20), and that leads to threats to his life (9:23–25, 29–30). The same pattern will recur in the later narrative.

The later reviews of Saul's conversion in his speeches clearly refer to a call to be Jesus' witness, either delivered to Saul by Ananias or given directly by the Lord (22:14–15; 26:16–18). Although there may be a progressive heightening and clarification of Paul's call to mission in these later scenes, as Lohfink argues,[15] Paul, as a reliable character, provides an interpretation of the Damascus road encounter that should not be ignored. We should assume that Paul's call to be a witness in 22:15 and 26:16–18 is at least implicit in the words about Saul's future in 9:15–16.

Several details of phrasing in 9:15 support this contention. The Lord speaks of Saul as a "chosen instrument" (literally, "instrument of election [σκεῦος ἐκλογῆς]"). Although ἐκλογή occurs only here in Luke-Acts, Lukan usage of the related words ἐκλέγομαι and ἐκλεκτός is informative. Apart from Luke 18:7 and, perhaps, Acts 13:17, these words do not refer to God's choice of a people for covenant or for salvation. When applied to the choice of persons, these words much more frequently refer to choice for a special role or mission that not all disciples share. Thus ἐκλέγομαι is used of the choice of the twelve (Luke 6:13; Acts 1:2, 24), the seven (Acts 6:5), Peter as God's instrument in converting Cornelius (Acts 15:7), and the representatives of the Jerusalem church who will go to Antioch (Acts 15:22, 25). These observations already imply that Saul is called the Lord's "chosen instrument" for a special reason, not just because he will be converted and numbered among the disciples.[16]

This conclusion is confirmed by the reference to "Gentiles and kings and sons of Israel" before whom Saul will "bear my name." These words do not refer to the life of an ordinary Christian who may happen to be

---

[14] As Volker Stolle says, "An arc stretches from the encounter with Christ before Damascus to the judicial conflict in Jerusalem and Caesarea." See *Zeuge als Angeklagter*, 164.

[15] See "Meinen Namen zu tragen," 114.

[16] See B. R. Gaventa, *From Darkness to Light*, 62.

accused because of his or her faith. Saul's future role will have unusual scope. It will comprehend Gentiles as well as Jews, and officials of the highest rank. Although Paul will be accused and attacked by both Jews and Gentiles, the reference to Jews and Gentiles corresponds first of all to descriptions of Paul's mission. In the narrative of Paul's mission beginning with Acts 13, he commonly preaches first to Jews and then to Gentiles.[17] According to 22:15 Paul will be a witness "to all persons" and in 26:17 he is sent by the Lord to both the (Jewish) "people" and to the "Gentiles."[18] If Paul must confess Christ before Jewish and gentile accusers, that is because his mission is directed to both of these groups. The reference to "Gentiles" and "sons of Israel" in 9:15 is a first indication of the comprehensive scope of Paul's mission. The inclusion of both is a major theme in the Lukan description of Paul's mission and is characteristically Lukan, for the historical Paul described his mission as a mission to Gentiles (Gal. 2:7–9).

Thus when we interpret 9:15 in the context of the larger document in which the narrator has placed it, both Paul's mission and its resulting dangers appear to be implied. Paul is a "chosen instrument," that is, chosen for a special task, and that task will concern both Jews and Gentiles, the groups to whom Paul is sent in later descriptions of his mission.

In order to gain clarity on the Lukan conception of Paul's role, it is helpful to compare the various summary statements of Paul's mission in Acts. We find in these statements a series of paraphrases of recognizably similar themes, just as the mission speeches to Jews paraphrase the same themes. This observation enables us to clarify phrases by comparing them with similar phrases in other summaries of Paul's mission. In the following table of repeated themes, I am not only drawing upon the commission statements in the three accounts of Paul's conversion but also on Paul's statement about his mission in 13:46–47 and his retrospective summary of his mission in the farewell address to the Ephesian elders (20:18–35).

1. Paul was chosen by the Lord
   9:15   "a chosen instrument of mine"
   13:47   "I have appointed you"
   20:24   "the ministry that I received from the Lord Jesus"
   22:14   "the God of our fathers chose you"
   26:16   "for this I appeared to you, to choose you"

---

[17] The order in 9:15 is the reverse of this. Putting Gentiles first probably emphasizes this word. This is appropriate because it indicates a new development at this point in the narrative.

[18] The εἰς οὕς in 26:17 refers to both the people and the Gentiles, as 26:19–20 (a statement of the fulfillment of this commission) shows.

2. Paul is sent as witness to both Jews and Gentiles
   - 9:15   "to bear my name before Gentiles and kings and sons of Israel"
   - 13:46–47 "to you [Jews] it was necessary that the word of God be spoken first. . . .
     I have appointed you for a light of Gentiles"
   - 20:21   "bearing witness to both Jews and Greeks"
   - 22:15   "you will be a witness for him to all persons"
   - 22:18–21 "they [the people of Jerusalem] will not receive your witness. . . . I will
     send you far away to the Gentiles"
   - 26:16–17 "I appeared to you to choose you . . . as a witness . . . the people and the
     Gentiles, to whom I send you"
3. Paul's mission will encounter rejection and require suffering
   - 9:16   "how many things he must suffer for my name"
   - 13:46   "since you reject it [the word of God]"
   - 20:19   "testings that happened to me by the plots of the Jews"
   - 20:23   "bonds and tribulations await me"
   - 22:18   "they will not receive your witness"
   - 26:17   "rescuing you from the people and the Gentiles"
4. Paul will bring light
   - 13:47   "I have appointed you for a light"
   - 26:17–18 "to whom I send you to open their eyes, so that they may turn from
     darkness to light"
   - 26:23   Paul testifies on the basis of Scripture that the Messiah "is going to
     proclaim light both to the people and to the Gentiles"
5. Paul will preach repentance
   - 20:21   "bearing witness . . . of repentance to God"
   - 26:18   "to open their eyes, so that they may turn from darkness to light"
   - 26:20   "I was proclaiming to repent and turn to God"
6. Paul's witness to Jesus will be based on what he has seen and heard
   - 22:14–15 God "chose you . . . to see the just one and to hear a voice from his mouth,
     for you will be witness for him . . . of what you have seen and heard."
   - 26:16   "I appeared to you to choose you . . . as witness to what you have seen and
     to what I will appear to you"

Notice that Paul's mission is repeatedly presented as a comprehensive mission, including both Jews and Gentiles. In this mission Paul acts as Jesus' witness, just as the apostles do, a subject that will require later discussion.[19] Paul will bear witness to what he has seen and heard, that is, to his encounters with the exalted Messiah. This task presupposes that Paul saw the Messiah, not just the light. The impact of rejection and suffering on Paul's mission will be highlighted in passages beyond those listed here.[20] We will also see more clearly that Paul's message continues the message of repentance and release of sins committed first to the apostles in Luke 24:47. Indeed, Paul's preaching of repentance will continue the work of John the Baptist.[21]

---

[19] See below, 280–81.
[20] See below, 239–40, 264–66, 274, 281–82, 345–46.
[21] See below, 324–25.

The association of Paul with the theme of light requires some further discussion. The brilliant light is emphasized in all three versions of the Damascus road story, and in the first two Paul is blinded and then has his sight renewed. This feature of the story might be only a dramatic way of depicting the Lord's heavenly glory, but other passages indicate that light has symbolic significance for the narrator. In 13:47 one of the "light of the Gentiles" passages from Isaiah is applied by Paul and Barnabas to their mission. In this quotation of Isa. 49:6 "light" is parallel with, or results in, "salvation." Acts 13:47 ties the mission of Paul both to the commission of Jesus in 1:8 ("to the end of the earth") and to Simeon's proclamation of salvation and light in Luke 2:30-32 (which is also based in part on Isa. 49:6 and the related statement in Isa. 42:6).[22] The comprehensive hope of salvation for both Israel and the Gentiles prophesied in Isaiah is celebrated by Simeon as it approaches fulfillment. However, fulfillment of this hope requires a messenger who will be "light of the Gentiles." Therefore, references to this scriptural hope recede until Paul and Barnabas begin their mission to Jews and Gentiles in Acts 13. The reference to this hope early in the narrative and its reappearance at an appropriate but much later place show how important it is to the narrator.

The reference to the light on the Damascus road could still be only a traditional device with dramatic value. However, the final version of this story (26:12-18) suggests that the brilliant light is part of the scriptural symbolism that links light with salvation available to all peoples, for here the Lord encountered in brilliant light speaks immediately of a mission that brings light: "I send you to open their eyes, so that they may turn from darkness to light" (26:17-18). This is a mission directed both to the "people" and the Gentiles. This symbolism is reemphasized at the close of the speech, where Paul states that he bears witness to the Messiah who "is going to proclaim light both to the people and to the Gentiles" (26:23). The sequence of thought in this speech suggests that the light in which the Messiah appears is symbolic of the light that he proclaims and that he sends his messenger to proclaim. The mission also involves opening eyes (another theme from Isaiah),[23] which is easily linked with the restoration of Paul's sight in Damascus (reported in the first two versions of the story). Thus the one who is called to be a light of the nations and to open the eyes of Jews and Gentiles has encountered the Messiah in light and is himself a healed blind man, forced by the Messiah's light to recognize his own blindness and to receive his sight through him.[24] The story of Paul is

---

[22] See also the light and darkness imagery in Luke 1:78-79.

[23] The reference to "light of the Gentiles" in Isa. 42:6 is followed by "to open eyes of the blind." See further *Narrative Unity* 1:66-67.

[24] This conclusion does not imply that the narrator did not understand the story of Paul's

necessary to complete the story begun in Luke 1—2, for it is with Paul that the crucial prophecy of light for the Gentiles, as well as for Israel, begins to be fulfilled as the gospel moves through the Mediterranean world. The narrator will later link the light on the Damascus road with this saving light, as we have noted.

The episode is not over with Saul's healing and baptism. Saul stays in Damascus, "and immediately in the synagogues he was proclaiming Jesus, that he is the Son of God." Saul has become not only a Christian but also a missionary through the preceding events, and the narrator emphasizes that he begins this new role "immediately." This emphasis excludes the assumption that he must first receive extensive instruction in the church's tradition before he can be a missionary. Just as with Philip, the work of this new missionary begins without the appointment or approval of the apostles. When Saul goes to Jerusalem, he is a preacher with a record in Damascus to which Barnabas can point (9:27). E. Haenchen distorts the picture when he speaks of Luke's "conviction that Paul must have lost no time in seeking out the Twelve, the fount of all legitimacy."[25] Saul does not hurry from Damascus to seek out the twelve. He engages in a mission of some length, leaving Damascus only when he is in danger.

Saul will preach in Jerusalem as well as Damascus, and events will follow the same pattern in the two places. In each case Saul's preaching leads to a plot to kill him, but this plot becomes known, and Christians arrange Saul's escape (9:20–25, 28–30). The similarity in this sequence of events is underscored by the wording in vv. 28–29. After Barnabas relates how Saul "spoke boldly ($\epsilon\pi\alpha\rho\rho\eta\sigma\iota\acute{\alpha}\sigma\alpha\tau o$) in the name of Jesus in Damascus" (v. 27), the narrator uses the same language to describe Saul in Jerusalem: "speaking boldly ($\pi\alpha\rho\rho\eta\sigma\iota\alpha\zeta\acute{o}\mu\epsilon\nu o\varsigma$) in the name of the Lord." Furthermore, the plot "to do away with ($\dot{\alpha}\nu\epsilon\lambda\epsilon\hat{\iota}\nu$)" Saul in Damascus is echoed through repetition of the same word in Jerusalem (9:23, 29).

The brief narratives of Saul's work in Damascus and Jerusalem show the Lord's words about Saul being quickly fulfilled. In his preaching and in the resulting plots on his life, we see Saul bearing Jesus' name and suffering for his name (9:15–16). The references to Saul speaking boldly in Jesus' "name" in 9:27–29 particularly recall the references to bearing "my name" and suffering for it in 9:15–16. When the narrative returns to

---

conversion literally. The narrative of Acts encourages us to read the story on two levels at the same time. On vision as metaphor in the Gospel of Luke, see Dennis Hamm, "Sight to the Blind," 457–77. B. R. Gaventa notes that "imagery about blindness and the giving of sight appears frequently in Luke-Acts," citing Luke 2:30; 4:18; 24:16, 31; Acts 9:8, 18, 40; 13:11; 28:27. See *From Darkness to Light*, 85.

[25] See *Acts*, 336.

Paul's mission in Acts 13 and later chapters, the sequence of preaching, danger, and escape will recur. The "plot (ἐπιβουλή)" of the Jews in Damascus is the first of a series. Toward the end of his free ministry, Paul will reflect on the past, emphasizing the trials that came upon him "in the plots (ἐπιβουλαῖς) of the Jews" (20:19). Although this refers first of all to his Asian ministry, the Asian ministry is not unique in this respect.

Other characteristic features of Paul's ministry are suggested in the narrator's description of Paul's first preaching. Paul's bold speaking (cf. 9:27–29) is reemphasized in Antioch of Pisidia (13:46) and again at the very end of Acts (28:31; see also 14:3; 19:8; 26:26). Paul's bold speech matches that of the apostles, who had to show the same courage in face of the threats of the Sanhedrin (4:13, 29, 31). The references to plots "to do away with" Paul also link him to his predecessors, for the same verb is used in Acts of the death of Jesus (2:23; 10:39; 13:28), threats against the apostles (5:33), and the death of Stephen (22:20; cf. 8:1). Saul quickly joins this illustrious company.

We noted previously that the fear of Saul shown by the Jerusalem disciples (9:26) is a repetition of the fear shown by Ananias.[26] The Jerusalem church, too, cannot immediately adjust to the Lord's latest surprise. Barnabas functions as intermediary. He was previously introduced as a "son of encouragement" (4:36) and later will be praised as "a good man and full of Holy Spirit and faith." He will demonstrate these qualities by recognizing "the grace of God" at work in new ways among the Gentiles in Antioch and encouraging these new Christians (11:23–24). He shows the same openness to new developments in the mission when he brings Saul to the apostles. Saul needs someone to testify in his behalf (note the reference to "attested" or "approved" men in 6:3; 10:22; 16:2; 22:12); Barnabas is willing to do this. He does so by telling Saul's story to the Jerusalem apostles, as Peter will later report what happened to himself and Cornelius to the Jerusalem church (11:1–18). In both cases hearing the story changes attitudes. The summary of Barnabas' account emphasizes two things: the encounter on the road, which included seeing the Lord and being addressed by him, and Saul's bold preaching in Damascus. The change in Saul is traced back to the Lord, a Lord whose surprising power is already known to the apostles, and the authenticity of the encounter is supported by Saul's subsequent behavior. Thus Barnabas helps the leaders of the church to recognize the unexpected work of the Lord and accept Saul, not only as a Christian but also as a partner in mission, who accompanies the apostles and begins to preach in Jerusalem

---

[26] See above, 116–17.

as he had in Damascus. Through Barnabas the Jerusalem church is able
to recognize the grace of God working in surprising ways.

Note that Barnabas says that Saul "saw the Lord" (9:27). This clarifies
a point in the previous narrative. In 9:3-6 it is not clear whether Saul saw
Jesus or only the brilliant light. Barnabas' statement agrees with the later
accounts of Paul's call, which emphasize that Paul was chosen "to see the
just one" (22:14), to be "a witness . . . of what you have seen" (22:15; cf.
26:16). That Paul has seen the Lord will enable him to be a witness of
Jesus Messiah, as the apostles have been.

Saul is sent off to Tarsus (9:30). When he next appears in the narrative,
Barnabas will find him there (11:25). This illustrates a narrative technique that is used more than once. Geographical locations are used to
create links in narrative lines that will be broken by other material. One
section of the story of Saul ends by placing him in the location where the
next section of his story will find him. Philip was handled in the same
way. Acts 8 ends by placing Philip in Caesarea, which prepares for a later
scene in which Philip is briefly mentioned. It takes place when Saul comes
to Caesarea and Philip is his host (21:8-9). Similarly, 9:43 places Peter in
Joppa, where Cornelius' messengers will find him in the next scene. This
technique may be especially useful in Acts 8—12, where the narrator is
switching among a number of leading characters.[27]

In 9:31 the section closes with a summary statement reviewing the
situation of the church in light of preceding events. The summary calls
attention to the expansion of the church into Judea, Galilee, and Samaria,
marking a significant step beyond the previous summary of growth (6:7),
which focused on the church in Jerusalem. The peace of the church and
the church's continued growth are emphasized in 9:31. The peace results
from the end of the persecution that began with Stephen's death and
continued through the efforts of Saul. The growth results from the surprising power of the word to find new opportunities in spite of resistance.
This power has been demonstrated in the case of Philip, who began a new
Samaritan mission when the Jerusalem church was scattered. It has also
been demonstrated in the case of Saul, who has been transformed from
persecutor to preacher of Jesus in preparation for his important later role.
The reference to the church being multiplied also prepares for the scenes
that immediately follow, which report several miracles of Peter that have
an evangelistic effect in towns of the coastal plain.

---

[27] Possible exceptions to the narrator's general care in placing characters in locations
appropriate to the next step in the narrative are 12:25, a confusing statement that Barnabas
and Saul returned to Jerusalem (if that is the correct text), and the sudden reference to Silas
in Antioch in 15:40, after he had returned to Jerusalem in 15:33.

PETER CONTINUES
THE PROPHETIC MINISTRY
OF HEALING

The narrator's attention now shifts to Peter. Before the major scene of Peter's encounter with Cornelius, we are told of two occasions on which Peter was able to help when faced with paralysis and death. The two persons helped were probably Christians. Tabitha is described as a "disciple" (9:36), and Peter found Aeneas when he came "to the saints living in Lydda" (9:32-33). Presumably Aeneas was one of those saints. If so, special attention is given in this section to the value for the church itself of the healing power given to its leaders. Nevertheless, both scenes end by emphasizing the evangelistic effect of the mighty act performed by Peter.

Peter's visit to Lydda is part of a tour of all the new Christian communities (9:32). Even though there is no indication that Peter founded the churches in Lydda and Joppa (8:40 suggests that this area was first evangelized by Philip), he evidently feels a sense of responsibility for these groups. This is demonstrated in the narrative not through presenting Peter as an administrator with power to make decisions but through presenting him as one who can offer help in the face of physical need.

These scenes reemphasize the signs and wonders first performed by the apostles in Jerusalem (2:43), most vividly represented by Peter's healing of the lame man at the gate of the temple (3:1-10). These wonders respond to specific needs of individuals and communities, and these needs are presented in the stories. Aeneas had been lying on a mat for eight years because of his paralysis (9:33). The widows were weeping because of the loss of Tabitha (9:39). Here we again find the tendency toward pathos that we noted in the healing stories in Luke.[1] Although most recipients of healing in New Testament healing stories are nameless, Aeneas and Tabitha are named, which helps them to stand out as persons who deserve attention as individuals. Tabitha is more fully characterized than Aeneas, for her life of charity is noted (9:36) and then reemphasized through the garments (9:39), which are the lasting emblems of her charitable life. Because Tabitha is characterized in an attractive way, the sense of loss increases and with it the pathos of the scene.

---

[1] See *Narrative Unity* 1:90, 92.

The tendency to present women and men in pairs, which we noted in Luke,[2] reappears in these paired scenes. We should also note Peter's healing word in 9:34—"Aeneas, Jesus Messiah heals you." This statement recalls Peter's previous strong emphasis that the healing power is due to the name of Jesus Messiah and not to Peter's own power or piety (3:6, 12, 16). In the case of Tabitha, the narrator may make a similar point in a different way. Peter prays before raising the woman (9:40). Prayer is an appeal to a higher power.

Luke-Acts has previously reported Jesus' resurrection of a widow's son and of Jairus' daughter (Luke 7:11–17; 8:41–42, 49–56), and these stories show resemblances in detail to the story of Elijah raising the widow's son (1 Kgs. 17:8–24).[3] In Acts 9 the narrator not only presents the same general kind of event happening through Peter but also tells the story of Tabitha with details that parallel one or more of the previous stories. The narrator is not copying any one of these stories, but various features of the set of stories may have influenced the narration, consciously or unconsciously. The result is meaningful in the context of the narrative; it indicates that the prophetic power demonstrated by Elijah, Elisha, and Jesus continues in the life of the early church.

Note the following similarities between the stories of raising dead people by Elijah (1 Kgs. 17:17–24 = 3 Kgdms. 17:17–24 LXX), Elisha (2 Kgs. 4:18–37 = 4 Kgdms. 4:18–37 LXX), and Jesus (Luke 7:11–17; 8:41–42, 49–56),[4] on the one hand, and Peter's raising of Tabitha, on the other: The dead person's body is placed in an "upper room (ὑπερῷον)" (3 Kgdms. 17:19; Acts 9:37). The healer is absent and must be summoned (4 Kgdms. 4:22–25; Luke 8:41–42; Acts 9:38). The healer encounters people weeping (using the verb κλαίω) (Luke 7:13; 8:52; Acts 9:39). The healer excludes the public (4 Kgdms. 4:33; Mark 5:40;[5] Luke 8:51; Acts 9:40) and prays in private (3 Kgdms. 17:21; 4 Kgdms. 4:33; Acts 9:40). There is a command to rise (Luke 7:14; 8:54; Acts 9:40).[6] After this command or a healing action, the dead person's eyes open (4 Kgdms. 4:35; Acts 9:40). The dead person sits up (ἀνεκάθισεν in both Luke 7:15 and Acts 9:40). The healer either grasps the hand of the dead person or, after revival, gives her a hand (Luke 8:54; Acts 9:41). The healer calls relatives or friends of the dead person to show the person alive (4 Kgdms. 4:36; Acts

---

[2] See *Narrative Unity* 1:132–35.
[3] See *Narrative Unity* 1:88, n. 25.
[4] See also Mark's parallel to the last story, Mark 5:22–24, 35–43.
[5] Furthermore, Mark 5:40 and Acts 9:40 use the same words: "putting them all out (ἐκβαλὼν πάντας)."
[6] Furthermore, commentators frequently note that the command in Acts 9:40, if translated into Aramaic, differs in only one letter from the Aramaic command in Mark 5:41. See, e.g., E. Haenchen, *Acts*, 339.

9:41). The report of the resurrection went out in a "whole (ὅλος)" area (Luke 7:17; Acts 9:42). The stories being compared are similar because they report a resurrection by a religious healer. This general similarity is bolstered by a series of shared details. Thus Peter's resurrection of Tabitha echoes a number of stories of the miracle-working prophets of Scripture and stories of Jesus. Peter, like Elisha and Jesus, is a prophet "powerful in work and word" (Luke 24:19). The ongoing mission has not lost this prophetic power.

According to Mark 5:37 and Luke 8:51, Peter was one of three disciples permitted to see Jesus heal Jairus' daughter. The narrator may have assumed that this would prepare Peter to repeat Jesus' miracle. Acts 9:36–42 shares a number of details with Elisha's raising of the Shunammite woman's son in 4 Kgdms. 4:18–37. However, the method of resurrection is by command, not bodily contact. At this point Acts 9:36–42 follows the synoptic resurrection stories. However, when Paul raises Eutychus, there is no command to the dead person, and there is bodily contact (20:10). These stories of Peter and Paul are both related to the story of Elisha's raising of the Shunammite woman's son. However, the Paul story imitates an aspect of the Elisha story that the Peter story ignores.

The stress on Tabitha's works of charity, especially to widows, adds a unique dimension to this resurrection story. Although details of the internal life of the church are scanty, the narrator emphasized the sharing of wealth with the needy in the early Jerusalem church (2:44–45; 4:32–37). This included a daily provision for widows (6:1). As the mission moves into new areas, the narrator finds opportunities to hold up further models of active concern for the needy. We hear of Tabitha's work for the widows in Joppa, the offering of the Antioch church for their fellow Christians in Judea (11:27–30), and of Paul in Asia working with his hands not only to support himself but to share with others (20:34–35). As the gospel spreads, people like Tabitha appear in these new areas, showing the power of the gospel through lives "full of good works and charities" (9:36). This remark about Tabitha also provides a bridge to the story of Cornelius, who practices charity, although he is not yet a Christian (10:2).

The narrator integrates the healing of Aeneas and the resurrection of Tabitha into the larger story of the spread of the mission in "Judea and Galilee and Samaria" (9:31) by noting the evangelistic effect of these wonders. In the conclusions to the two scenes the inhabitants of the area learn what has happened and are impressed. The people of Lydda and Sharon "turned to the Lord." In Joppa "many believed in the Lord." These are parallel statements of new conversions as a result of the signs and wonders given by God to Jesus' witnesses.

JEWISH CHRISTIANS DISCOVER
THAT GOD HAS DECLARED
THE GENTILES CLEAN

Divine messages and actions play an important role in the lengthy episode in 10:1—11:18, and because of this E. Haenchen levels a pointed criticism of Acts:[1]

> Here stands revealed a peculiarity of Lucan theology which can scarcely be claimed as a point in its favour: in endeavouring to make the hand of God visible in the history of the Church, Luke virtually excludes all human decision. Instead of the realization of the divine will *in* human decisions, *through* human decisions, he shows us a series of supernatural interventions in the dealings of men: the appearance of the angel, the vision of the animals, the prompting of the Spirit, the pouring out of the ecstatic πνεῦμα. As Luke presents them, these divine incursions have such compelling force that all doubt in the face of them *must* be stilled. They compellingly prove that God, not man, is at work. The presence of God may be directly ascertained. But here faith loses its true character of decision, and the obedience from faith which Luke would have liked to portray turns into something utterly different: very nearly the twitching of human puppets.

Even though the story of Peter and Cornelius has characteristics that may impress modern people as naive, we will see that it is considerably more subtle in tracing the process of discerning the divine will than Haenchen recognizes.[2]

The episode begins with scenes that focus in turn on two characters who are separated by some distance: first Cornelius, then Peter. Each has a vision and receives a divine message. These are best called divine promptings because they are incomplete in themselves. They require human action or reflection. The message to Cornelius is that he must send for a certain Simon Peter. Only sufficient information to locate Peter is given, and apart from human response to this prompting nothing would

---

[1] See *Acts*, 362. Richard Pervo makes a similar criticism. According to Pervo, "The verifiability of God's 'providence' is constitutive for the theology of Luke." This is an "unreflective" and "popular" theology that shares the naive view of sentimental fiction that God will cause virtue to triumph. See *Profit with Delight*, 74.

[2] I have been helped to see this by the sensitive discussion of this matter by Luke T. Johnson in *Decision Making in the Church*. Johnson brings a fresh perspective to the question of divine guidance and human decision in his interpretation of Acts.

be accomplished. Peter's vision concerns clean and unclean animals, with a command to kill and eat. At the end of it, Peter is "at a loss" concerning its meaning (10:17). Unless Peter discovers something more, it will have no effect.

Peter does discover something more because Cornelius obeys the divine prompting and sends messengers. At this point in the narrative the conjunction of events appears to play a role in divine guidance. When the messengers call out at the gate, Peter is pondering the meaning of his vision. Then he hears the Spirit direct him toward these men. The conjunction of two remarkable events, the vision and the appearance of Cornelius' messengers, is understood as revelatory[3] and becomes the occasion for further divine prompting toward discovery of the vision's meaning. Now Peter, in turn, must obey. Only then will either Cornelius or Peter discover the purpose of their visions.

Interestingly, there is some reflection on human factors in the receipt of divine messages. Cornelius' vision occurs while he is at prayer (10:30), that is, while his mind is directed toward God. More strikingly, a vision in which Peter is commanded to eat comes to him when he is hungry (10:10). Peter is also praying (10:9). Later he hears the Spirit speaking to him while he is pondering his vision, that is, actively seeking its meaning (10:19). However, the connection between the vision and the messengers to whom Peter is directed is still unclear at this point. Peter will discover the meaning of his vision only if he follows the Spirit's prompting.

The sudden appearance of the Spirit in demonstrative form (tongues speaking) in 10:44–46 may seem to be the clearest justification for Haenchen's complaint, for it is viewed as a decisive indication of God's will, which humans would be foolish to oppose (10:47; 11:17). Even so, the Spirit, although surprising to the Jewish Christians,[4] appears in a humanly appropriate setting: a setting of eager expectation of a divine message to which Peter responds by preaching the good news of the Messiah whom God anointed "with Holy Spirit and power" (10:38). Furthermore, the Jewish Christians recognize the Spirit in these events not because they are forced to do so by God but because this manifestation of the Spirit fits their own experience. They recognize that the Gentiles have "received the Holy Spirit just as we did" (10:47). The Jewish Christians are led to draw a surprising new conclusion not because they

---

[3] Note Peter's emphasis on the temporal conjunction of the two events in 11:11: "And behold, immediately three men. . . ."

[4] "Even on the Gentiles" in 10:45 is free indirect discourse, indicating the surprise of Peter's companions. It is not labeled as this group's thought or speech, yet it represents their viewpoint, not the narrator's. On free indirect discourse see above, 106–7.

are being treated like puppets but because they discover Gentiles who share their own experience of God.

Study of the composition of the narrative also reveals another important factor in discernment of the will of God: the sharing of divine promptings with other persons. Through this process the divine message is clarified and completed. Roland Barthes offers a structural analysis of Acts 10:1— 11:18, being interested not in theological issues but in the major linguistic "codes" used in the narrative. He notes the large number of résumés in this narrative,[5] for characters are repeatedly telling other characters what the narrator has already told the reader. This characteristic contributes to the unusual length of this section of Acts. It is not enough for the reader to be told, or for the reader to be told that a character was told (through a summary statement to that effect). The sharing of what has happened with additional persons is sufficiently important that it is highlighted with repeated direct discourse. After we are told of Cornelius' vision, this event is retold three more times, by the messengers to Peter (10:22), by Cornelius to Peter (10:30–32), and by Peter to the Jerusalem church (11:13– 14). After we are told of Peter's vision, Peter refers to it again in 10:28 and repeats the story in detail in 11:5–10. Later we will discover that Peter again summarizes and interprets the whole of Acts 10 for the Jerusalem church (15:7–9). The text is concerned not just with what happened but with the transmission of what happened, as Barthes notes.[6]

It is through this process that the recipients of the initial visions discover the purpose of their visions. As previously indicated, the visions are incomplete in themselves. Peter does not know what to make of his vision. He receives a first clue when the messengers appear at the gate and the Spirit nudges Peter to make a connection between the vision and the request of these messengers. Their request is supported by the first repetition of the story of Cornelius' vision (10:22). Peter does not commit himself to an interpretation of his vision at that point. He waits until the situation is clear, having met Cornelius and the "many" in his house. However, it is on the basis of the previous series of events, including the report about Cornelius' vision, that Peter draws a conclusion about the meaning of his own vision in 10:28: God has shown him that he must not "call any person common or unclean." Cornelius then repeats his vision in greater detail and expresses his eagerness to hear Peter's message. This

---

[5] See "L'analyse structurale du récit," 33–34.

[6] See "L'analyse structurale du récit," 35–36. R. Funk analyzes the narrative levels in 10:1— 11:18 (e.g., the narrator of Acts narrating Cornelius' vision; Cornelius narrating Cornelius' vision; Peter narrating Cornelius' report of Cornelius' vision). See *Poetics of Biblical Narrative*, 150–56. Funk notes that the narrative retains a mimetic quality through these shifts of level.

prompts Peter to draw a further conclusion about his vision. It not only reveals how he must act toward Gentiles but also reveals *God's* acceptance of Gentiles (10:34–35), which Peter is now willing to recognize.

Karl Löning believes that the Lukan redaction has spoiled the recognition scene in 10:27–36 by letting Peter learn of Cornelius' vision earlier from the messengers (10:22).[7] It is true that the motivation of Peter's question in 10:29 is weak because he has already been informed by the messengers. Nevertheless, the summaries of Cornelius' vision in vv. 22 and 30–32 have a function in both locations, in the one case to explain why the messengers have come, in the other case to prepare for Peter's speech, which is to be understood as the fulfillment of what Cornelius has been led by God to seek. The drama of the scene in Cornelius' house is also heightened by having Cornelius himself testify of his vision, and he does so in greater detail than his messengers. I do not agree with Löning's statement that Peter's reaction in v. 34 is "unmotivated, because it was possible already previously." Peter's reaction is motivated not simply by the report of Cornelius' vision but by the whole series of events since 10:9. This includes the discovery of a whole group of Gentiles prepared by God to receive his message (emphasized in v. 33).

There are several more stages in Peter's transformation: The gift of the Spirit to the Gentiles persuades Peter that they must be baptized (10:44–47). Then Peter becomes the advocate of the Gentiles in 11:5–17 and, in a more theological way, in 15:7–11.

In the course of these events Cornelius is also discovering the purpose of his vision. In 10:5 he is simply told to send for Simon Peter. However, later statements are more explicit: Cornelius is to hear a message through Peter (10:22), things "commanded by the Lord" (10:33). The nature of the message is not clear until Peter speaks in 10:34–43. When he does so, his first statement is about the Gentiles and is based on his own vision and the events that have helped him to understand it. This statement is an important new insight for Peter. It is also crucial for Cornelius and his group, for it opens the door for them.

The narrative presents a more sophisticated and complex account of humans discerning the will of God than Haenchen thought. This account includes the following elements: divine promptings of persons in a state of receptivity, obedient responses by those persons even though they do not fully understand, and openness to other persons, with mutual sharing of visions. Indeed, the visions in question here have the specific purpose of opening a relationship between persons of different cultures. Each is a vision that leads its recipient to be open to a stranger's experience of God.

---

[7] See "Korneliustradition," 14.

God works from two sides at the same time to achieve this goal. Peter discovers the purpose of his vision through meeting Cornelius and hearing his story. Its purpose is the kind of relationship that he has with Cornelius when he recognizes that Cornelius is not unclean. Cornelius discovers the purpose of his vision when he meets Peter and hears the story Peter can tell, both about his vision and about Jesus (10:36–43). Its purpose is a full relationship with God, as well as with Peter and his company.

There are further stages to this process of discerning God's will: the new insight and relationship must be justified publicly before the church (11:1–18), and its implications must be worked out in public debate with contrary understandings of God's will (15:1–29).[8]

The narrator's original account of the visions is not treated as a sacred text that must be exactly repeated by the characters. Indeed, paraphrase is preferred in repetition. For instance, the angel's statement about Cornelius' prayers and alms is differently worded in Cornelius' report (10:31) than in 10:4. Cornelius also adds the detail about the angel's shining clothing (10:30). Furthermore, the messengers know that the purpose of Peter's coming is so that Cornelius may "hear words from" him (10:22). Cornelius makes a similar point in 10:33, but the original account of the vision does not indicate this. Peter's report in Jerusalem is even more explicit. According to Peter, the angel told Cornelius to send for Peter, "who will speak words to you by which you and all your house will be saved" (11:14). In light of events Peter is confident that this was the purpose of the sending. He does not hesitate to report the angel's words in a way that makes this clear. Subsequent events are taken to be a valid basis for interpreting the angel's message. Note also that the three types of creatures in the great sheet, according to 10:12, become four types in Peter's report in 11:6.

Although the divine command in 10:15 is paraphrased in 10:28, it is repeated exactly in 11:9. The rhetorical form of the command in 10:15 encourages repetition, for the command is concise, forceful, and memorable. The words "What God cleansed do not you defile (ἃ ὁ θεὸς ἐκαθάρισεν σὺ μὴ κοίνου)" contain a concise and pointed antithesis that helps make these words challenging. Additional words would make the contrast between the two subjects ("God" and "you") and the two antithetical verbs ("cleansed" and "defile") less prominent. The command gains its force by presenting a sharp warning of the potential conflict between divine and human action. The form of the words mirrors this conflict, attaching contrary actions to God and the person addressed and allowing the contrast to stand out in full relief through omission of all

---

[8] See below, 183–93.

distractions.[9] The rhetorical force of these words is appropriate to their function as climax of Peter's vision, and the antithesis between God and Peter prepares for Peter's later statement that he could not withstand God (11:17).

The emphasis on Cornelius' piety is a noteworthy feature of the narrative rhetoric of this episode. Cornelius is clearly an uncircumcised Gentile (cf. 11:3), yet his piety parallels that of a devout Jew. He is "devout and fearing God with all his house, performing many charities for the people and praying to God constantly" (10:2). The Jewishness of this non-Jew does not stop there. He is favored with a vision of an angel of God, and the narrator presents the encounter in a form common in the Old Testament and previously used in Luke-Acts to describe divine messages to faithful Jews like Mary (Luke 1:26–38) and Ananias (Acts 9:10–17).[10] Furthermore, the angel speaks of Cornelius' piety in language appropriate to a devout Jew: "Your prayers and your charities have ascended for remembrance before God" (10:4).[11] Thus Cornelius is addressed like a Jew by the angel and portrayed like a Jew by the narrator. The narrator is not presenting a character as distant as possible from the Jews in order to display the potential of the gospel to reach all. Rather the narrative uses a persuasive rhetoric that would be appropriate for Jewish Christians like Peter and those with him. They meet a character who has the central qualities that they recognize as true piety. When Peter notes in 10:47 that Cornelius and his company "have received the Holy Spirit just as we have," this is the capstone of a series of similarities between Cornelius and devout Jewish Christians. It is more difficult for Jewish Christians to reject the divine promptings by declaring Cornelius unclean and unacceptable to God when they recognize so much of what they honor and emphasize in this man. Everything in the narrative conspires against maintaining the barrier between Jews and this Gentile.

When the narrator calls Cornelius "devout" (10:2), we have direct characterization by epithet, which is also common in Hebrew Scripture.[12]

---

[9] See my discussion of antithetical aphorisms in *Sword of His Mouth*, 88–101. Acts 10:15 closely resembles Mark 10:9 (see *Sword of His Mouth*, 95–98), for both prohibit human action that would conflict with God's action, referring to the latter in a relative clause and the former in the main clause.

[10] See Benjamin Hubbard, "Commissioning Stories in Luke-Acts." Hubbard cites parallels in the Old Testament and other ancient Near Eastern literature. The following elements in Acts 10 are characteristic of the form: the introduction (vv. 1–2), the confrontation (v. 3), the reaction (v. 4a), the reassurance (v. 4b), the commission (vv. 5–6), and the conclusion (vv. 7–8).

[11] On the Old Testament–Jewish background of the references to prayers ascending and God's remembrance, see W. C. van Unnik, "Background and Significance." Van Unnik concludes, "That which Cornelius has done as a heathen, is treated as if he had been an Israelite" (253).

[12] See M. Sternberg, *Poetics of Biblical Narrative*, 328–41.

Such an epithet is not meant to be subtle, but it does not exclude later subtleties in characters and complexities in the situations they face. The epithet can serve to "nail down" a characteristic that will contribute to a later development. In this case the clear statement that Cornelius is devout contributes to the central problem for Jews like Peter: how do we respond to a Gentile who (to our surprise) is a devout worshiper of God and the recipient of an angelic message?

Peter at first resists the command in his vision (10:14) and later indicates that he would not normally associate with Gentiles (10:28). It is only because of convincing signs of God's will that he baptizes Gentiles (10:47; 11:17). It is important to be clear about the issue highlighted in the narrative by these indications of resistance, for there is a possibility of confusion. If Peter is being portrayed as opposed to the whole idea of Gentiles sharing in salvation through Jesus, the narrator has either forgotten something important, breaking the narrative's coherence, or the narrator is portraying Peter as imperceptive and forgetful. The apostles were clearly told by Jesus that the mission must include "all the nations" and be carried "to the end of the earth" (Luke 24:47; Acts 1:8). It is unlikely that Peter is being portrayed as forgetful of this key aspect of the Lord's commission. Peter's early preaching in Jerusalem contained indications that he was aware that the promise fulfilled in Jesus is also relevant to the Gentiles. In 2:39 he declared that the promise is not only for the Jews being addressed but "for all those far away,"[13] and in 3:25-26 he recalled the promise that "all the families of the earth will be blessed" and indicated that God's servant had been sent to the people of Jerusalem "first," hinting at a later sending to others. Paul will use similar language when he turns from Jews to Gentiles in his preaching (13:46). So Peter did not forget the comprehensive dimensions of God's purpose in Jesus. Yet he is portrayed in Acts 10 as learning something new (10:34-35) after some resistance. The general idea of salvation for Gentiles and a gentile mission would not be something new. The actual issue in the narrative must be more specific.[14]

Furthermore, we have seen that the episode of the Ethiopian eunuch undermines the view that the narrator wishes to make Peter responsible for the first gentile convert.[15] The Ethiopian eunuch is a better representative of the gospel's reach "to the end of the earth" than Cornelius is. Yet

---

[13] See the reference to Gentiles "far away (μακράν)" in 22:21.

[14] J. Jervell recognizes this and also notes the passages just mentioned from Peter's speeches in Acts 2 and 3. See *Luke and the People of God*, 57–58, 65.

[15] See above, 108–11. The references to the eunuch worshiping in Jerusalem and reading Scripture do not make him a Jew. The Gentile Cornelius is also a worshiper of the God of Israel.

the Cornelius episode is broadly developed and must be dealing with an important issue. That issue is not whether there should be a Gentile mission—the Lord commanded his witnesses to preach to all the nations —but how that mission can be conducted in the face of a serious obstacle.

Philip has converted an Ethiopian and Saul has been chosen for a mission that will include Gentiles (9:15), but the apostles, the initiators of the mission in its first phase, have made no move to fulfill the Lord's command to preach to Gentiles. This may not appear remarkable. Acts follows a mission that moves step by step into new areas. So far the church has been established only in Judea, Galilee, and Samaria (9:31). The need to strengthen and extend the work with Jews may indicate that it is simply not time yet for a gentile mission. However, the appearance of Cornelius reminds us that there were Gentiles within these areas, yet no attempt has been made to include them. The Cornelius episode indicates that this omission is not merely the result of the apostles' desire to work in an orderly fashion but results from an obstacle that makes Peter and others reluctant to begin. In the Cornelius episode we are told how that obstacle was removed.

The obstacle is gentile uncleanness, which prevents Jews from associating freely with Gentiles. The central importance of this issue is clear if we consider the general structure of the episode. Cornelius has been instructed by the angel to send for Peter. The divine purpose can only be fulfilled if Peter comes, but when the scene shifts to Peter, the issue of uncleanness appears.[16] In his vision Peter is instructed to eat indiscriminately from unclean and clean animals, but he refuses (10:11-14). The heavenly voice commands that he not defile what God has cleansed (10:15). The point of this command must be understood in light of the following narrative, which directs attention not so much to the problem of unclean foods as to the problem of association with the Gentiles, who are unclean people. Peter states the problem clearly in 10:28 and then announces what he has learned through the vision. Although it is unlawful for a Jew to associate with non-Jews because of their uncleanness, God has removed this obstacle. God has shown Peter that Gentiles can no longer be regarded as unclean, which frees Peter to come to Cornelius' house (10:29). In his later interpretation of the Cornelius episode, Peter again will emphasize that God has "cleansed" the Gentiles (15:9). Because the extreme opposite of the unclean is the holy, the descent of the Holy Spirit on the Gentiles in 10:44-47 may complete their change

---

[16] Whether or not it is correct to designate 10:9-29a as a "sub-plot," Mark Plunkett rightly sees that Peter's resistance to social contact with Gentiles, gradually overcome in this section, functions as an obstacle to the fulfillment of the agenda established by Cornelius' vision. See "Ethnocentricity and Salvation History," 470-71.

of status. Those previously regarded as unclean have been granted a share in the holy.[17]

Although Peter's vision is applied to unclean people rather than unclean foods, the question of hospitality and shared meals plays a role in the text.[18] Both the Gentiles' entry into the house where Peter is staying and Peter's entry into Cornelius' house are noted (10:23, 27). If we recall the previous story about a gentile centurion who said, "I am not worthy that you enter under my roof" (Luke 7:6), these acts of entry appear to be significant. They are accompanied by acts of reciprocal hospitality. First Peter received the gentile messengers as guests overnight (10:23). Later he is invited to stay some days with Cornelius (10:48). It is assumed that this would include not only lodging but also shared meals, a point highlighted in the accusation in 11:3: "You entered to uncircumcised men and ate with them." Because God has declared that no person can any longer be called unclean, Jewish Christians can freely associate with them, which includes reciprocal hospitality. This relates not only to fellowship among Jewish and gentile Christians in the church. It applies also to Gentiles who have not yet received the gospel. It opens the possibility of Jewish Christians conducting a mission among Gentiles. If Jewish Christians must guard against unlawful association with Gentiles, as Peter stated in 10:28, such a mission would be difficult or impossible. Now this obstacle to the gentile mission has been removed.

It may seem that the objection in 11:3 is not dealt with in Peter's following discourse. Peter by narrative enables his critics in Jerusalem to experience what he experienced, leading to the conclusion "Then to the Gentiles also God has granted repentance unto life" (11:18), but this says nothing directly about eating with Gentiles. However, at the conclusion of the Cornelius episode, 11:18 means more than a general recognition that God, sometime and somehow, will enable Gentiles to find salvation. It means that a mission by Jews to Gentiles can begin because, as Peter has seen, God has removed the social barrier between Jews and Gentiles. Peter's narrative summary does speak to the question of whether Jewish Christians may enter gentile houses and eat with them because it allows the Jerusalem church to understand how he came to the conclusion in 10:28–29 that he may now freely associate with Gentiles. He carefully repeats his vision and the subsequent prompting of the Spirit that led him

---

[17] While Peter in 15:9 says that God "cleansed" the Gentiles' hearts "by faith," in 26:18 Paul speaks of those "sanctified by faith (ἡγιασμένοις πίστει)," which includes them among the holy.

[18] This is noted by B. R. Gaventa, who adds, "By means of the issue of *hospitality*, Luke demonstrates that the conversion of the first Gentile required the conversion of the church as well." See *From Darkness to Light*, 109. Emphasis by Gaventa.

to go with the messengers and enter Cornelius' house (11:5–12). The coming of the Holy Spirit on the Gentiles is a further ratification of his decision. When we recognize that the main issue is the social barrier to mission among Gentiles, the objection in 11:3 fits into the larger picture, and it receives an appropriate answer.

It is possible to hear a subtle echo of Jesus' critics in 11:3. Jesus was also accused of eating with or lodging with the wrong kind of people. Repetition of this story element resulted in a characteristic "type-scene" in Luke.[19] Now Peter must face the kind of criticism that Jesus faced, arising this time from the circle of Jesus' disciples.

Even though Peter does not convert the first Gentile, the Cornelius episode is a breakthrough for the Gentile mission. The conversion of the Ethiopian was a private and isolated event that had no effect. The conversion of Cornelius has consequences in the following narrative, as the reference back to it in Acts 15 makes clear. It is a breakthrough not simply because Peter and the Jerusalem church now accept Gentiles for baptism but also because they recognize the right of Jewish Christians to freely associate with Gentiles in the course of their mission. The story focuses on the attitudes of Peter and the Jerusalem church toward mission among Gentiles, although Peter and the apostles will not take the leading role in this mission. Others, especially Paul, will take over this task. It is still important that Peter and the Jerusalem church approve of this mission. The narrative of how they came to do so allows the narrator to inject interesting reflections on the transformation of a church that has a universal mission but is caught in ethnocentric isolation, and on the inter-action of divine promptings and human reactions in that transformation.

Peter's speech in Cornelius' house (10:34–43) shares some themes with Peter's previous speeches but also differs from them in significant ways. The opening statement in vv. 34–35 is clearly related to the context, but the reason why Peter speaks to Gentiles as he does in vv. 36–43 is less clear. In vv. 34–35 Peter publicly announces the conclusion to which he has been led by preceding events. This conclusion is closely related to Peter's previous statement that he has been shown that he must not call anyone unclean (10:28), but it goes beyond it. Although v. 28 speaks of attitudes and behavior toward other persons, vv. 34–35 speak of God. The God who commanded Peter to call no one unclean cannot be one who discriminates among nations, choosing one as a favorite and excluding the others. Therefore, the door is open to anyone who fears God and works righteousness, as Cornelius does (cf. 10:22). Such a person is "acceptable"

---

[19] See Luke 5:30, 15:2, 19:7 and *Narrative Unity* 1:170–71. Both eating and entry into the house are causes of objection in Acts 11:3. The former is mentioned in Luke 5:30 and 15:2; the latter in Luke 19:7.

to God. The effect of this declaration is to include Cornelius and all those
like him among those who may share in the fulfillment of God's promises
through Jesus Messiah. Those acceptable to God may share in God's
gifts, the gift of "repentance unto life" (11:18), "release of sins" (10:43),
and even the gift of the Holy Spirit (11:17).

Peter begins his speech by saying, "In truth I perceive that God is not
one who plays favorites." That God is impartial was not a new assertion
in the ancient world.[20] However, when Peter says that he now sees God's
impartiality "in truth," he means that this accepted view of God has taken
on new meaning. He now sees God's impartiality more sharply and
clearly, for it is being demonstrated in a new way. Peter is beginning to
understand how God is going to implement God's impartial goodness as
salvation for Gentiles as well as Jews. Peter's statement in vv. 34–35 is
important for Cornelius, but it is also important for Peter and his church.
Peter's new clarity enables him to affirm a universal mission conducted
freely, without social barriers.

After this affirmation we would expect Peter to begin this mission by
presenting the gospel to Cornelius in a way that reflects its significance for
Gentiles. The rest of the speech may not fit our expectations. In v. 36
Peter refers to the word sent "to the sons of Israel," not to the Gentiles.
Furthermore, the connection of this verse with what precedes and follows
is obscured by grammatical difficulties.[21] Whatever the solution to these
difficulties,[22] the statement "he is Lord of all" indicates that there is a
connection in thought between vv. 34–35 and v. 36. In v. 36 the speech
does not turn abruptly to another topic, unless we assume that Peter is
portrayed as suddenly remembering another way of affirming God's openness to Gentiles and belatedly inserts it in an inappropriate place. Why does
v. 36 begin, however, by referring to the word sent to the sons of Israel?

It is important to recognize that v. 36 is a summary of the angel's
announcement of Jesus' birth to the shepherds in Luke 2.[23] Note the
following similarities in wording: The angel says, "I preach good news
($\epsilon\dot{v}\alpha\gamma\gamma\epsilon\lambda\acute{\iota}\zeta o\mu\alpha\iota$)" concerning the birth of "Messiah Lord ($X\rho\iota\sigma\tau\grave{o}s$

---

[20] See Jouette Bassler, "Luke and Paul on Impartiality," 546–52. According to Bassler, Paul's
statement of divine impartiality in Rom. 2:11 is based on the Jewish axiom of God as
impartial judge. In contrast, she understands the statement in Acts 10:34 to be influenced by
Greco-Roman ideas of universalism.

[21] Clarification for those who are not following the Greek text: The "you know" that the RSV
places at the beginning of v. 36 is actually found at the beginning of v. 37. The translators
have understood "the word" at the beginning of v. 36 as an object of "you know" in v. 37.
This is possible but not certain. Furthermore, the parentheses around "he is Lord of all" in
v. 36 have been added by the translators because these words seem to interrupt the train of
thought.

[22] For further comment see below, 139–40.

[23] See Christoph Burchard, "Note on 'PHMA," 290–94. See also G. Schneider, *Apostelgeschichte* 2:75, n. 149.

κύριος)." Then the angel chorus proclaims "on earth peace" (Luke 2:10–14). According to Acts 10:36 God, in sending a message to the sons of Israel, was "preaching good news of peace[24] through Jesus Messiah," who is also "Lord." This is a good summary of the message to the shepherds. However, Peter says that Jesus Messiah is "Lord of all." This goes beyond the shepherds' scene and reflects Peter's new insight at this point in the narrative. The one who is Lord as Davidic Messiah, who will bring joy to "all the people" (Luke 2:10), is Lord not just of the Jewish people but of all. Peter's recent experience leads him to a theological insight in vv. 34–35 and to a christological insight in v. 36. Both concern the universal scope of God's purpose in Jesus.[25]

This connection with the birth narrative explains several peculiarities of Acts 10:36: It refers to the word sent "to the sons of Israel" because it is referring to the message to the shepherds in Luke 2. It refers to God's word, not Jesus' word, because it has in mind not Jesus' preaching but messages received before Jesus was active.[26] Moreover, it refers to preaching good news of peace, not preaching good news to the poor, even though 10:38 clearly has Isa. 61:1 in mind, where the latter phrase is used.

"He is Lord of all" expresses Peter's new insight in v. 36. It is probably also the main statement in the verse, not a parenthetical remark. Although there are several possible solutions to the grammatical difficulties in the first part of Peter's speech,[27] I am inclined to follow the suggestion of C. Burchard that τὸν λόγον should be understood as an accusative of respect.[28] The verse is then a separate sentence and can be translated as follows: "With respect to the word which he sent to the sons of Israel, preaching good news of peace through Jesus Messiah, he (Jesus Messiah) is Lord of all." This places the emphasis where it belongs, on the assertion that Jesus is Lord of all, which is the main clause of the sentence. This is

---

[24] This phrase may echo Isa. 52:7. Its connection with the annunciation to the shepherds does not exclude this possibility. The language of Second Isaiah has permeated the narrator's own thinking and vocabulary and is freely used in key passages of Luke-Acts.

[25] Although this universal dimension goes beyond the shepherd's scene in Luke 2, it is present in Simeon's oracle in 2:29–32. Furthermore, there are thematic connections between these two parts of the birth narrative (see *Narrative Unity* 1:42–43). Peter's insight will not be a surprise to readers who remember the Simeon scene. However, Simeon's oracle is spoken privately before Jesus' parents. Peter is speaking of a word sent to the sons of Israel, i.e., a public announcement like the announcement to the shepherds.

[26] "Through Jesus Christ" modifies "peace." It does not designate the preacher.

[27] The solution of Harald Riesenfeld, "Text of Acts X. 36," 191–94, deserves attention. He understands τὸν λόγον ὃν κτλ. in apposition to the ὅτι clause in vv. 34–35 and as the object of καταλαμβάνομαι. Then vv. 34–36 are a single sentence. This reading would imply that the word previously sent to Israel was not only good news of peace but also indicated God's impartial openness.

[28] See "Note on ʿPHMA," 293. On the accusative of respect see BDF, no. 160. We find a similar sentence in Rom. 8:3: an accusative of respect extended into a fairly lengthy phrase, followed by the main clause of the sentence.

not a parenthetical remark. Thus the continuity of thought with vv. 34–35 is clear, and v. 36 can be seen as a key disclosure of the theological perspective that dominates Luke-Acts as a whole: the messianic Lordship of Jesus, which brings peace to the Jewish people in fulfillment of scriptural promises, applies to all peoples, for they are invited to share with Israel in this messianic peace.

There is a further interesting consequence of this understanding of v. 36. If v. 36 refers to Luke's birth narrative, the whole of vv. 36–43 presents a summary of Luke's Gospel in chronological order, from the birth of Jesus to the commission to the apostles at the end of Luke 24. In v. 37 Peter reminds Cornelius and his company of what happened "throughout the whole Jewish land." This was a public event of major importance, and Peter assumes that even gentile residents of the area have heard about it ("you know"). It began with "the baptism that John proclaimed" (cf. Luke 3:3) and Jesus' ministry in Galilee. Jesus' ministry is described in words that recall his announcement of his commission in the Nazareth synagogue: Jesus, a man from Nazareth, was anointed by God with Holy Spirit and power (Acts 10:38; cf. Luke 4:18, "Spirit of the Lord is upon me because he anointed me").[29] Jesus' healing ministry is summarized, and the reference to help for those oppressed by the devil may indicate one way in which Jesus brought "release for the captives" (Luke 4:18). Peter and others are chosen witnesses of Jesus' ministry and of the resurrection that followed his crucifixion. In vv. 39–41 the story of Jesus continues, and there is special concern with the witnesses to these events, represented by Peter. The twofold object of this witness—ministry of Jesus and resurrection—corresponds to the qualifications for an apostolic witness specified in Acts 1:21–22. The meal with the risen Christ is recalled in v. 41 (cf. Luke 24:43;[30] Acts 1:4). Finally, Peter refers to the Lord's command to proclaim and bear witness. He is speaking of the Lord's commission to his witnesses in Luke 24:46–48, for he refers to a command "to proclaim" (see Luke 24:47: "that repentance be proclaimed") and "bear witness" (see Luke 24:48: "you are witnesses"). In Acts 10:43 (which continues to describe what the apostles were commanded to proclaim) the reference to the witness of all the prophets corresponds to the reference to Scripture in Luke 24:46.[31] In both Acts 10:43 and Luke 24:47 we find reference to the release of sins and the name of Jesus. The command to proclaim repentance for release of sins "to all the nations" in Luke 24:47 becomes an offer of release of sins to "everyone who believes"

---

[29] See also the reference to "the power of the Spirit" in Luke 4:14.

[30] On this verse see *Narrative Unity* 1:290–92.

[31] The proclamation of the release of sins to all nations is to be understood as part of what is written. See *Narrative Unity* 1:294.

in Acts 10:43. Peter's narrative of Jesus stretches from the birth narrative to the penultimate scene of Luke's Gospel and especially recalls three specific scenes: the angel's announcement to the shepherds, Jesus' announcement in the Nazareth synagogue, and the risen Jesus' commission to his witnesses.

Even though it is a separate sentence, v. 43 continues the thought of v. 42, explaining further what Peter and the other apostles were commanded to proclaim. This is shown by the fact that v. 43 matches the command received in Luke 24:47. The final phrase (in the Greek = "everyone who believes in him"), in its position of emphasis, indicates that the offer of release of sins in Jesus' name applies also to Cornelius and his company. Thus the end of the speech returns to the thought of the beginning (an *inclusio* or envelope structure) with its emphasis on God's acceptance of Gentiles and Jesus as Lord of all. The frame formed by this beginning and end indicates that the story of Jesus, as summarized by Peter, is significant also for Gentiles.

The reference in v. 42 to Jesus as the one "appointed by God as judge of the living and the dead" probably supports this new application of the Jesus story. Jesus as judge of the living and the dead is universal judge, judge of all people whatever their status. This universal scope is clear in the closest parallel in Acts to this statement. At the close of his speech in Athens Paul refers to the day on which God "is going to judge the world ($\tau\grave{\eta}\nu$ οἰκουμένην) in righteousness by a man whom he appointed" (17:31). Thus the reference to Jesus as "judge of the living and the dead" balances the reference to him as "Lord of all" in v. 36 and is part of the envelope structure.[32] Furthermore, this interpretation suggests that Peter ends his speech by noting a twofold responsibility given by Jesus to his witnesses: They must preach to the Jewish people and they must bear witness that Jesus has been appointed as universal judge, who already exercises his authority by offering to release the sins of everyone, Jew or Gentile, who believes in him. This pairing of a witness to the people with a witness of universal scope probably corresponds to the descriptions of Paul's commission, for Paul must testify to both Jews and Gentiles (cf. 9:15; 26:17). However, 10:42–43 does not clearly claim a mission to the Gentiles for the apostles. They are to proclaim to the people, and they are to bear witness that Jesus' authority applies to all and his benefits are open to all (as Peter does in defending gentile Christians in 15:7–11). This does not necessarily imply that they will conduct the gentile mission themselves. The ending of Peter's speech may represent a modification of Luke 24:47–48 in light of

---

[32] See Polycarp 2.1, where Jesus is called κριτὴς ζώντων καὶ νεκρῶν in a context that emphasizes his universal lordship.

the fact that the apostles will largely play the role of verifiers, not initiators, in the gentile mission.

If we recall that this is Peter's last mission speech in Acts, the emphasis placed on the apostolic witnesses, those who could testify to Jesus' ministry as well as his resurrection, may not be surprising. Anticipating a transition, the narrator emphasizes the permanent value of this witness. The last mission speech of Peter is also an appropriate place for a comprehensive review of the Jesus story, from birth to the commission of the risen Lord, a feature of this speech that distinguishes it from previous ones. However, something new and important is being said through this review. By telling this story to Cornelius and his company, and by placing it in a frame that affirms Jesus' universal significance, Peter is affirming that the story of the Jewish Messiah also has relevance for Gentiles. What the speech as a whole affirms is succinctly stated in v. 36: that God sent good news to the people of Israel about the peace now available through their Messiah, and this Messiah is Lord of all, offering peace to all. Peter reviews the Jesus story as told in Luke in order to say to Cornelius that this story is a word of salvation for him also.

In telling the story, Peter retains its Jewish setting. Note the frequent geographical references: the whole Jewish land (καθ' ὅλης τῆς Ἰουδαίας), Galilee, Nazareth, the land of the Jews and Jerusalem. Peter does not transform Jesus into a Gentile, living in a Gentile environment, in order to speak to Cornelius. It is Jesus the Jew through whom God is working for all, and the witness of his first followers who accompanied him "in the land of the Jews and Jerusalem" has permanent value. In telling the story, Peter also retains its full scope. Peter presents only a sketch of what we can read in much greater detail in Luke's Gospel, but it is a sufficient sketch. Its comprehensive parameters (from birth to the risen Lord's commission) indicate that the whole story is important. Certain events may disclose Jesus' significance with special clarity, but the story is not reduced to a single event. Nor is the story replaced by a series of christological propositions. The story is full of interpretation and will give rise to much further interpretation, but it retains its integrity as a story, capable of inspiring different and complex human responses. Peter offers this story to Cornelius. In doing so, "the word" first sent "to the sons of Israel" (v. 36) becomes "the word" for Gentiles also (v. 44).

The descent of the Holy Spirit on the Gentiles is depicted as a repetition of Pentecost. When Peter refers to the Gentiles as receiving the Spirit "as we also" did (10:47), he is clearly referring to Pentecost, as connections in wording indicate. The Jewish Christians refer to the "gift" of the Holy Spirit (10:45), as in 2:38. This gift has been "poured out" (see 2:17), causing the Gentiles to speak in tongues and magnify God (see 2:4, 11).

The narrator clearly wants us to recall the Pentecost scene and acknowledge that Gentiles have been chosen by God to receive the same gift
and the same power as Jesus' first followers received at the beginning of
their mission. Peter's statement in 2:38 suggests that in the mission the gift
of the Spirit normally accompanies or follows baptism. In the Cornelius
episode the order is reversed so that the appearance of the Spirit becomes a
divine sign that guides the church to the acceptance of Gentiles.

After Stephen and Philip enter the narrative, the apostles are seldom
presented as initiators of new stages of the mission. Rather the apostles
and the Jerusalem church respond to what others are doing and affirm it.
This is the case with the mission in Samaria in Acts 8, and it will be the
case with the new developments in Antioch (11:19–26). The role of
verifying and affirming new developments is an important one, for the
new developments must be able to convince the larger church, judging on
the basis of its past experience, that they represent extensions of God's
purpose. However, the initiative in extending the mission to new areas or
groups generally does not come from the apostles.

The Cornelius episode is the major exception to this division of responsibility. Even here, to be sure, Peter's initiative was preceded by Philip's
conversion of the gentile eunuch.[33] However, this was a private event that
had no effect on the Jerusalem church. Peter must start over again,
becoming a second human initiator of Gentile mission. He then must
convince the apostles and brothers in Jerusalem, who act as verifiers.
Peter is a reluctant initiator, for he begins with the presuppositions of the
objectors in 11:3. Nevertheless, he is the one who takes the new step that
requires the Jerusalem church to reexamine its relation to Gentiles.

It is not enough that Peter takes the new step. The Jerusalem church
must be convinced of its rightness. The importance of this process is
indicated by the fact that the narrator devotes a scene to it which largely
consists of retelling the events of chapter 10.[34] The events are familiar, but
they are now being told to a new group. There are also some interesting
differences in the way they are told. Peter is the speaker, and the narrator
recognizes that this makes a difference in how the story should be told.
The narrative is now presented from Peter's point of view. He is the
focalizing character.[35]

In response to the objection in 11:3, Peter does not begin by arguing
through logical inference but retells the narrative of his own experience. It

---

[33] See above, 108–11.

[34] This is comparable to the enactment-report sequence that M. Sternberg notes in the
Hebrew Bible. See *Poetics of Biblical Narrative*, 376–78, 380–82.

[35] On "focalization," a term that she prefers to "point of view," see Shlomith Rimmon-Kenan,
Narrative Fiction, 71–85.

is this narrative that will prove convincing, for on the basis of its past experience the Jerusalem church will be able to recognize divine guidance and faithful human response in these events. The narrator indicates that Peter presents the narrative "in order" (11:4). The order is a narrative order, but it is not the same as the order of events in chapter 10. Peter begins not with Cornelius' vision but with his own vision. He is presenting events in the order in which he experienced them, so Cornelius' vision will appear later, at the time when Cornelius told Peter about it (11:13-14). The Jerusalem audience is like Peter, beginning with Peter's previous assumptions about the way a Jew should behave. A sequence of events led Peter to change his mind. Now his audience is being led through the same sequence of events so that they can appreciate and share Peter's new insight.

As Peter retells the story, he also interprets it in light of his previous experience. The indication in 11:14 that Peter will speak to Cornelius "words by which you will be saved" goes beyond previous indications of the purpose of sending for Peter. It is not an obvious formulation of the purpose of Peter's speech in Cornelius' house, which is less clearly formulated as a direct appeal to the audience than the speeches in Acts 2 and 3, ending as it does with a general reference to "everyone who believes" rather than an appeal to "you." However, the reference to being saved recalls Peter's preaching at Pentecost, when the offer of salvation in the name of the Lord was a major theme (2:21, 40, 47).[36] Peter saw the Gentiles receive the Spirit "just as we did" at Pentecost (10:47). Now he also interprets the purpose of his preaching in light of his Pentecost preaching. This may represent a gradual sharpening of Peter's perception of his own role in recent events.

Peter also interprets events by recalling a word of the Lord in 11:16. Although most of Peter's report repeats what we already knew, 11:16 introduces a new point. Peter now indicates that the sudden appearance of the Spirit reminded him of one further element of his past experience: Jesus' promise of baptism in Holy Spirit. This promise was first spoken by John the Baptist in Luke 3:16. Jesus made it his own promise in Acts 1:5, in preparation for Pentecost. By recalling this promise now, Peter interprets the new experience of the Spirit by the Gentiles as another stage in the history of this promise, integrating the new experience into the larger story and also broadening the promise's meaning. For "you will be baptized with Holy Spirit" now means Gentiles, too. This new understanding of Jesus' promise fits the scriptural promise quoted in 2:17 ("I

---

[36] Between Acts 2 and 11 the terms "save," "salvation," and "savior" appear only in 4:9, 12; 5:31 (and 7:25, which refers to salvation through Moses).

will pour out from my Spirit on all flesh"), even though Peter does not recall this in Acts 11. Memory and recent events interact, producing new understanding. Recent events are understood on the basis of their correspondence to past experiences and promises, and the promise is newly understood on the basis of recent events. A growing understanding of the breadth of God's purpose and the depth of God's power is the result.

Not only the order of the narrative but also the references to Pentecost (11:15), Jesus' promise of the Spirit (11:16), and Peter's Pentecost preaching (11:14) show Peter interpreting his experience as a unified story with a divine purpose. He is speaking to people who share key aspects of his experience. His interpretation is effective for them. They, too, are able to see recent events as a fulfillment of the saving purpose of God (11:18).[37]

---

[37] Compare 11:18 with 5:31, a similar statement about the gift of repentance to Israel.

Acts 11:19-30

THE NEW MISSION BASE
AT ANTIOCH

The summary of the establishment of the church in Antioch presents an important new development, both geographically and ethnically. The gospel reaches a major city of the empire and finds a ready response from people of Greek culture, including Gentiles.[1] The narrator pulls together threads from the preceding narrative, especially chapters 2 and 8, and weaves them into a tapestry to describe the new phase of the mission.

The new development is, first of all, presented as the continuation of the gospel's spread resulting from the scattering of believers by the persecution at the death of Stephen. Key words in 8:4 are repeated in 11:19 to indicate this. The mission of Philip in Samaria was the first result of this scattering noted by the narrator. The work of Philip, one of those appointed to serve the Hellenistic Jewish Christians of Jerusalem (6:1-6), is continued in new areas by other Hellenistic Jewish Christians, the men of Cyprus and Cyrene who came to Antioch. It is important to note that the arrival of the gospel in Antioch is the result of the scattering of Christians following Stephen's death, not the result of a mission organized by the Jerusalem church. Nor is it caused by the conversion of Cornelius. The Cornelius episode justifies a gentile mission for those who have problems with gentile uncleanness, but the narrator reaches back behind it when indicating the human factor that brought the gospel to Antioch. Neither the plan nor the permission of the Jerusalem church plays a role.

---

[1] The manuscripts are divided on whether to read "Greeks" or "Hellenists" in 11:20. The contrast with "Jews" in 11:19 has persuaded some leading interpreters to choose the reading "Greeks," even though the other reading appears to have stronger manuscript support. See E. Haenchen, *Acts*, 365, n. 5; H. Conzelmann, *Acts*, 87; G. Schneider, *Apostelgeschichte* 2:86. On the other hand, Bruce Metzger argues for "Hellenists" (see *Textual Commentary*, 386-89), interpreting this to refer to "the mixed population of Antioch in contrast to the Ἰουδαῖοι of ver. 19" (389). However, this makes a poor contrast if "Jews" are included in this mixed population. The choice of the rare word Ἑλληνιστής, applied to Hellenistic Jews in 6:1, may be the result of a desire to be inclusive, but those included would not be "Jews" but proselytes (note the addition of "proselytes" to "Jews" in 2:10-11; 13:43), Gentiles attracted to the synagogue, and any other Gentiles. Not only the contrast with Jews but also the demand for circumcision of Antioch disciples in 15:1 supports the inclusion of Gentiles. Nowhere prior to 15:1 has the narrator noted the presence of Gentiles in the Antioch church, unless it is in 11:20.

146

The time relation between the events in 10:1—11:18 and 11:19-21 remains unclear. Because the latter is caused by the scattering, an event placed some time before Peter's visit with Cornelius, it is possible to assume that the conversion of Cornelius and the spread of the gospel to Antioch were taking place in the same time period. In any case, the one did not cause the other.

The Jerusalem church does have a role after the initial work is done. Not only the scattering as cause of the mission's spread but also subsequent events in Acts 8 provide a pattern for events in Antioch, as 11:22 shows. In both cases we find a secondary establishment of a relation with Jerusalem through the sending of an emissary. The language is similar: when those in Jerusalem "heard" what had happened, they "sent" a representative (8:14; 11:22).[2] The emissary (Barnabas, in this case) demonstrates Jerusalem's interest in the new Christian community, establishes a relation between it and the Jerusalem church, and also confirms the fact that God is actively present in this new work. In Samaria this confirmation took place through the appearance of the Spirit. In Antioch it happens when a disciple qualified to judge these matters (Barnabas is "good" and "full of Holy Spirit and faith")[3] recognizes "the grace of God" in the new community. Barnabas (and those who sent him) have experienced the grace of God. It is assumed that they are competent to recognize its presence. This gives Barnabas a certain authority. However, confirmation of the presence of God's grace also involves a commitment by Barnabas and Jerusalem. Barnabas sets to work to support this community, and through him the Jerusalem church is being led into the gentile mission, not because it planned this course of action but because it recognizes that what it values most highly is present also in the lives of others.

Barnabas rejoices at what has already happened and shows his care for the future of these new Christians by urging them to "stick with ($\pi\rho\sigma\mu\acute{e}\nu\epsilon\iota\nu$) the Lord" (11:23). This is one of a number of statements that indicate the missionaries' concern to support new converts and young churches after the initial conversions (cf. 13:43; 14:22; 15:32, 41; 16:5; 20:1-2). The narrator also notes that many more "were added to the Lord" (11:24). The Antioch church is going through a period of rapid growth similar to the initial growth of the Jerusalem church. The same language is used to describe it, for references to people being added, or to the Lord adding people to the church (using $\pi\rho\sigma\tau\acute{\iota}\theta\eta\mu\iota$), form a repeated

---

[2] With 8:14 see also 11:1. There is no sending in 11:1 because Peter is going to return to Jerusalem.

[3] This is a clear case of the narrator's evaluation in direct commentary.

theme in the narrative of the early Jerusalem church (cf. 2:41, 47; 5:14).[4]
There may also be a connection between the dedication of the Jerusalem
disciples "to the teaching of the apostles and the fellowship" in 2:42 and
the dedication of Barnabas and Saul according to 11:26. This dedication is
emphasized by the amount of time that they gave to the task. They met in
the assembly "even for a whole year" and taught a good-sized crowd. The
reference to teaching and the communal setting of their work (they "came
together in the assembly" for a whole year) suggest that this verse and 2:42
at least reveal a common set of concerns.

There is another possible similarity between the new church in Antioch
and the first church in Jerusalem. The narrator portrayed the early
Jerusalem Christians as fully devoted to each other, to the point that those
with property were willing to share their wealth whenever others were in
need.[5] The Christians of Antioch demonstrate the same concern and carry
it one step further: they share with another community. Those who have
more than enough to cover immediate needs ($\epsilon\dot{v}\pi o\rho\epsilon\hat{\iota}\tau\acute{o}$ $\tau\iota\varsigma$ = when
"anyone was having plenty") share with those in special need (11:29). The
recipients are regarded as "brothers," a somewhat weaker form of the
unity of heart and soul demonstrated by the sharing of goods in the
Jerusalem church (4:32), and there is emphasis on the free decision of
individual disciples ("each of them determined") to share in this way with
their fellow disciples in Judea. They decide to send something to Jeru-
salem for "service" or "aid ($\delta\iota\alpha\kappa o\nu\acute{\iota}\alpha\nu$)," thereby showing the same gen-
erous concern as in the daily "service" or "aid" in the Jerusalem church
(6:1).

Barnabas was the only individual used as a model of the Jerusalem
church's sharing (4:36–37), and he now plays a role in Antioch's sharing
with Jerusalem (11:30). He forms a personal link between the demon-
strations of selfless generosity in these two churches. Not only Barnabas
but also other preachers and leaders in the early church play an active part
in the church's efforts to help the poor. The apostles (4:35, 37), Stephen
and Philip (6:1–6), and now also Saul (11:30) have leading roles in the
various efforts of the church to help those in need.[6]

In 11:25–26 the story line of Saul is picked up where it was dropped in
9:30. Saul is in Tarsus, and Barnabas fetches him from there. For a
second time Barnabas is instrumental in introducing Saul to a place of

---

[4] In the first eleven chapters of Acts, this verb occurs only in these passages and 11:24. All
four of these passages describe the growth of the respective churches.

[5] See above, 45–46, 77–78.

[6] John Koenig makes the related point that "the historical Jesus/risen Christ . . . , the
Jerusalem apostles . . . , and Paul . . . are all shown to be simultaneously preachers and
teachers on the one hand and stewards of material goods . . . on the other." See *New
Testament Hospitality*, 110.

mission (cf. 9:26–29). Acts 11 ends by highlighting Barnabas and Saul as a team, serving as representatives of the Antioch church. Their work together in Antioch prepares for their shared mission from Antioch that begins in chapter 13.[7]

In the preceding discussion we have noted that the description of the founding of the Antioch church is modeled on preceding descriptions of Jerusalem and Samaria. The way that the gospel spread in Samaria and its effect in the lives of the new church in Jerusalem are repeated as the mission moves to this major city of the empire. The concern for the needy shown by the Jerusalem disciples (2:44–45; 4:32–37) is shared by the Antioch Christians, and there seems to be a similar emphasis on devotion to teaching in the fellowship (2:42; 11:26). The mission in Antioch was the result of the persecution after the death of Stephen, as was the mission in Samaria in Acts 8, and both Philip and the unnamed disciples in 11:20 dared to take the gospel to new ethnic groups. In both cases the validity of the new development is confirmed later by representatives of the Jerusalem church. These repetitions (with variations) suggest patterns of how the mission develops in new areas. We have also noted the repetition of the helpful role of Barnabas in introducing Saul to a place of mission and the first indications of their role together. Material from the preceding narrative is being reprocessed in preparation for the mission that will begin from Antioch in Acts 13.

The mission of the apostles is based in Jerusalem. That base never changes. Peter and John visit Samaria but return to Jerusalem (8:25). Peter visits towns of the coastal plain, including Caesarea, but he returns to Jerusalem and reports what has happened to people there (11:2–18). The remaining appearances of Peter and the apostles will be in Jerusalem. Antioch, however, will become a new mission base for Paul and Barnabas. In 13:1–3 they are commissioned for their missionary journey in Antioch, and they return to Antioch and report when it is over (14:26–27). The trip to Jerusalem that follows is not required by this mission. It has a new and special cause: the demands of some disciples from Judea that Gentile Christians be circumcised (15:1). Furthermore, Paul and Barnabas are sent to Jerusalem as emissaries of the Antioch church (15:2–3).[8] After the meeting they return to Antioch and spend some time there (15:35). It is from Antioch that Paul's new missionary journey begins (15:36, 40). In 18:22–23 the narrator indicates Paul's return to Antioch, even though there are no events in Antioch to report. Although the

---

[7] Agabus (11:28) returns in 21:10–11. However, he is introduced afresh ("a prophet by the name of Agabus") on this second appearance. In both cases Agabus is the source of a specific prophecy.

[8] Home base for a character is where that character returns naturally, without a special cause.

reference to "going up and greeting the church" may indicate a visit to Jerusalem, this visit is subordinated in two participles, while the main verb reports the return to Antioch. Paul also spends some time in Antioch, but "greeting the church" suggests a brief stay in Jerusalem. Good relations with Jerusalem are important, but Antioch is Paul's home base. Paul makes major decisions about his mission without consulting Jerusalem. He works with Barnabas and Silas, both of whom came from Jerusalem, but Paul emerges as the leading figure. Thus two mission bases appear in the narrative, Jerusalem and Antioch, and these are the centers of two missions, those of the apostles and of Paul.[9] It is important that Jerusalem and Antioch not come into conflict. Acts 15 deals with this possibility and how it was avoided.

---

[9] As B. N. Kaye notes, "The focus of the story shifts in Acts xi 19 ff. from Jerusalem (with excursions out from there) to Antioch (with excursions from there)." See "Acts' Portrait of Silas," 16. The first excursion from Antioch is back to Jerusalem to bring the collection of the Antioch church. This event shows the concern of Antioch for the "brothers in Judea" and indicates harmony between the two churches. The narrator, as if accompanying Barnabas and Saul, uses the shift in location as an opportunity for one further story concerning Peter in Jerusalem.

PETER IS RESCUED
FROM PRISON

Peter's rescue from prison is an unusually vivid episode in Acts even when simply taken as a story about Peter. Because it is not connected with events in the chapters immediately before and after it, however, it may seem rather isolated and unimportant for Acts as a whole. Yet it becomes more than a vivid account of an isolated miracle when we probe below the surface, for this story is an echo of other stories in Luke-Acts and in Jewish Scripture. An event that is unique, and vividly presented as such, takes on the importance of the typical when it reminds us of other similar events. It recalls the power of God to rescue those chosen for God's mission, a power repeatedly demonstrated in the past.

Acts 12 presents the second of three rescues from prison in Acts (cf. 5:18-20; 16:23-29). These three scenes, plus the sea rescue in Acts 27, show the narrator's interest in stories of divine rescue.[1] The references to divine rescue and help in Paul's review of his ministry before King Agrippa confirm this interest (cf. 26:17, 22). To be sure, only in Acts 12 is the prison rescue the central event of the narrative episode. In Acts 5 the apostles are briefly released but are brought again before the Sanhedrin. In Acts 16 Paul and Silas do not even leave the open prison until the jailer brings them out; the primary effect of the opening of the prison is the jailer's conversion. In Acts 12, however, Peter is saved from almost certain death by an angel's intervention.

Not only Jewish religious leaders but also political rulers appear in the narrative as potential threats to the mission. Jesus warned that his followers would be led away to kings and governors (Luke 21:12). The Jerusalem church, when the apostles were threatened, recalled the role of Herod and Pilate in Jesus' death (Acts 4:25-29). Paul is commissioned to bear Jesus' name before kings (9:15) and eventually appears before governors and kings on trial for his life (Acts 23:33—26:32; cf. 27:24). Jesus and Paul appear as prisoners both before the Sanhedrin and before political rulers. In Acts 4—5 Peter was imprisoned and appeared before

---

[1] On the generic aspects of these four scenes, studied against the background of other ancient literature, see Reinhard Kratz, *Rettungswunder*.

the Sanhedrin. Now he is also imprisoned by a political ruler. Both the
religious rulers and the political rulers can be dangerous, and sometimes
these threatening forces work together.

Herod the king is the chief threat to Peter. He has killed James the
brother of John, and Peter, in prison, faces a similar fate. Readers of
Luke-Acts, in the first century as well as the twentieth, should be
pardoned if they think that this is the same Herod who killed John the
Baptist and was ominously interested in Jesus.[2] The two rulers are
associated by the common name and act in a similar way: they endanger
God's messengers.[3] The opposition of one Herod to the Lord's Messiah
was recalled in Acts 4:27. Now another Herod threatens the life of the
leading apostle. The narrator will demonstrate the final impotence of this
seemingly powerful ruler.

The description of the threatening situation in 12:1–4 already contains
a number of suggestions that this is a familiar situation. Together they
serve as reminders of some previous occasions of God's rescue from evil
rulers, helping the skilled imagination to construct the layers of background that give this episode its deeper meaning. The echoes of other
times and places suggested by this narrative add to its resonance. It gains
in power and richness as it reechoes earlier, paradigmatic stories of divine
rescue from threatening rulers. The vivid specificity of many concrete
occasions persists in this process alongside a sense of harmonious pattern
that reaches beyond any past occasion and offers hope for the future. The
occasions remain specific, yet they become suggestive of the typical.

We have already discussed several passages in Acts in which the narrative situation was understood against the background both of Scripture
and the story of Jesus. This was quite clear in the church's prayer in 4:25–
30 and in Stephen's speech and death scene (Acts 7).[4] Acts 12 is similar.

Other sections of Acts demonstrate the narrator's interest in echoes of
Jesus' arrest and trials in the experiences of his witnesses.[5] The same interest appears in Acts 12. Peter has been arrested and faces almost certain
death. His situation is the same as that of Jesus after Jesus' arrest in Luke
22:47–54. The Greek word for "arrest" in Acts 12:3 ($\sigma\upsilon\lambda\lambda\alpha\mu\beta\acute{\alpha}\nu\omega$) is
also used of the arrest of Jesus in Luke 22:54 and Acts 1:16. We are more

---

[2] The narrator does distinguish them to this extent: the latter Herod is a tetrarch (Luke 3:1,
19; 9:7; Acts 13:1), while the Herod of Acts 12:1 is a king. On Herod in Luke see *Narrative
Unity* 1:53, 196–97. Recall that only Luke's passion story contains a scene in which Jesus is
examined by Herod (Luke 23:6–12).

[3] The association is probably intentional. According to H. Conzelmann, *Acts,* 93, Agrippa I is
called Herod only by Luke. On the other hand, Agrippa II, who is presented more
favorably, is called Agrippa (25:13).

[4] On these passages see above, 71–72, 91–92, 97–100.

[5] On the arrests of the apostles in Acts 4—5 see 68–72. On the arrest and defense scenes of
Paul see 264–66, 274, 281–82.

likely to note the connection because the narrator interrupts the sentence[6] to indicate that the arrest took place during "the days of unleavened bread" and then refers to the Passover in the following verse. The interruption of the sentence indicates the importance of this date. One of its functions is to signal the connection between Peter's arrest and Jesus' arrest at the feast of unleavened bread (Luke 22:1, 7). After the Passover Herod intends to "bring him [Peter] forward to the people." As E. Haenchen notes, "The people had no voice in any regular legal process. In this detail the description probably follows the model of the Passion story."[7] In other words, it is because Pilate presented Jesus to the people according to the passion story that this detail appears in the Peter story.

Further details support a connection both with the passion story and with other arrests of Jesus' followers predicted by Jesus: The scene begins by saying that Herod "laid hands on ($\epsilon\pi\epsilon\beta\alpha\lambda\epsilon\nu$ . . . $\tau\grave{\alpha}\varsigma\ \chi\epsilon\hat{\imath}\rho\alpha\varsigma$)" some Christians with evil intent. The same phrase is used of an attempt against Jesus in Luke 20:19, in a prophecy about Jesus' disciples in Luke 21:12, in descriptions of the high priest's arrest of the apostles in Acts 4:3; 5:18 and of the attack of the crowd on Paul in Acts 21:27. The verb $\dot{\alpha}\nu\alpha\iota\rho\epsilon\omega$ ("do away with") is used to describe the killing of James in Acts 12:2. It is used of Jesus in Luke 22:2; 23:32; Acts 2:23; 10:39; 13:28 and of threats against the apostles and Paul in Acts 5:33; 9:23, 24, 29. In Acts 12:4 Herod "delivers" Peter to the soldiers (using the verb $\pi\alpha\rho\alpha\delta\dot{\imath}\delta\omega\mu\iota$). This verb is frequently used in the gospels in connection with Jesus' betrayal and death. The closest parallels to Acts 12:4 in the rest of Luke-Acts are the references to Jesus being delivered to those who will kill him (Luke 9:44; 18:32; 24:7), to Pilate and the Jewish rulers delivering Jesus to his death (Luke 23:25; 24:20), and to followers of Jesus being delivered to prisons (Luke 21:12; Acts 8:3; 22:4). The narrator tends to use a fixed vocabulary in describing the arrests and threats of death that Jesus and his followers encounter. In Acts 12 this vocabulary supports a more striking connection between Peter's and Jesus' arrests: the dating of both at Passover.

The reference to the days of unleavened bread and the Passover suggests another event—the exodus from Egypt—which enriches the significance of Peter's rescue. This connection does not compete with the connection to Jesus' death. Indeed, Luke 9:31 previously suggested a relation between the exodus, on the one hand, and Jesus' death and resurrection, on the other, by its reference to Jesus' "exodus ($\xi\xi o\delta o\nu$)" in Jerusalem. The establishment of the Passover is embedded in the exodus narrative

---

[6] In the Greek v. 4 is not an independent sentence but begins with a relative pronoun referring to Peter.

[7] See *Acts*, 382.

and commemorates this saving event. In addition to the date, the first verse of the scene and Peter's two summaries of what the Lord has done for him (12:11, 17) contain phrases that recall the Septuagint account of the exodus. Because the words in question are common in the Septuagint, it is important that they are not common in the New Testament, yet are used again in Acts with explicit reference to the exodus from Egypt. Thus Acts itself indicates that its narrator associates these words with the exodus.

When Peter realizes what has happened, he exclaims that the Lord "rescued me from the hand (ἐξείλατό με ἐκ χειρός) of Herod" and the people. Later he tells the Christians in Mary's house "how the Lord brought him out of (αὐτὸν ἐξήγαγεν ἐκ) the prison." When God appeared to Moses in the burning bush, God said (according to the Septuagint), "I have come down to rescue them from the hand (ἐξελέσθαι αὐτοὺς ἐκ χειρός) of the Egyptians and bring them out (ἐξαγαγεῖν αὐτοὺς ἐκ) of that land" (Exod. 3:8). In the previous verse God said, "I have seen the mistreatment (κάκωσιν) of my people," a statement that is quoted in Acts 7:34. This noun or the related verb κακόω is also used of the oppression of the Egyptians in Gen. 15:13; Exod. 1:11; 5:23 and in Acts with the same application in 7:6, 19, 34. When the narrator begins the episode by stating that Herod began "to mistreat (κακῶσαι) some of the church" and then refers to the days of unleavened bread, a significant hint has already been given that the exodus rescue may be repeated.

That God "rescued" the people "from the hand (ἐξείλατο ἐκ χειρός)" of their oppressor is also a repeated statement within Exodus. It occurs four times in the scene in which Jethro, Moses' father-in-law, rejoins him (Exod. 18:4, 8–10).[8] The introduction to this same scene repeats the statement that "the Lord brought out (ἐξήγαγεν) Israel from Egypt" (Exod. 18:1). Acts 13:17 also states that God "brought out" Israel from Egypt,[9] and Acts 7:36, 40 indicates that Moses "brought out" the people (as in Exod. 32:1, 23). Acts also repeats the statement that God came down "to rescue" Israel from Egypt (Acts 7:34 = Exod. 3:8). Thus the three phrases in question, concerning mistreatment, God's rescue, and God bringing out the people, are used repeatedly in the Septuagint in connection with the exodus. The narrator of Acts also applies these phrases to the exodus. Then they reappear in the story of Peter's rescue from prison. The God who "brought out" Israel "from the house of

---

[8] Exodus 18:8 states that the Lord rescued Israel "from the hand of Pharaoh and from the hand of the Egyptians." Acts 12:11 also states that Peter was rescued from both ruler and people. Furthermore, Exod. 18:8–9 states that Moses "narrated (διηγήσατο)" to Jethro what the Lord had done, and Jethro "was amazed (ἐξέστη)." The same verbs are used in Acts 12:16–17 (but in reverse order).

[9] The reference here to God's "uplifted arm" suggests a connection with the statements concerning the exodus in Exod. 6:6–7 and Deut. 26:8, which also use ἐξάγω.

bondage (ἐξ οἴκου δουλείας)" (Exod. 13:3, 14; 20:2) and Peter from
Herod's prison is still the God of rescue and exodus for oppressed people
who bear faithful witness to Jesus.[10]

In light of the evidence above, it is possible that August Strobel is
correct when he relates Acts 12:7–8 to the Passover account in Exodus
12.[11] The angel's commands to Peter to rise quickly, gird himself, and put
on his sandals make good sense apart from any symbolic background.
Although not strictly necessary to the narrative, they make the moment
vivid and help the audience to picture a befuddled Peter struggling to put
himself together without waking the sleeping guards. However, it happens that the commands also correspond to the regulations for Passover.
The Israelites who are about to be rescued must be ready for the journey
that will follow. They must eat the Passover with their loins girded and
sandals on their feet. And they must eat in haste (Exod. 12:11).[12]

In discussing the prison rescue in Acts 5:17–26, we noted that the
narrator emphasized the irony of the situation. The rescue itself was
reduced to the minimum and had no lasting effect on the course of events,
but the confusion of the officials who could not find the imprisoned
apostles was broadly depicted.[13] There is an ironic tendency to prison
rescue stories as such. Opponents take strong, even elaborate measures to
prevent any escape, yet all of this merely proves the futility of human
effort in the face of divine power.[14] Although this irony may have become
conventional, the narrator elaborates on it in 5:21–26.

The irony in 5:21–26 is at the expense of the apostles' opponents; their
confusion at the disappearance of the apostles is strongly depicted. A
somewhat comparable scene is found in 12:18–19, but the main focus of
irony shifts elsewhere. In Acts 12 it is primarily Peter and the church who
fail to understand and are taken by surprise. The surprising twist in the
course of events is unexpected and initially unbelievable for insiders as
well as outsiders. Hindsight may detect holy precedents for the wonder,

---

[10] I was stimulated to explore echoes of the exodus in Acts 12:1–17 by the following articles:
Walter Radl, "Befreiung aus dem Gefängnis," 81–96; Jacques Dupont, "Pierre délivré de
prison," *Nouvelles études*, 329–42. Dupont (338–39) cites a Jewish midrash (Ex. R. 12, 42)
that dates a series of famous rescues on Passover night. This night, Dupont concludes, is
"the privileged moment of interventions of God" for the persecuted.

[11] See "Passa-Symbolik," 212–13.

[12] It is quite possible that Peter's rescue from prison also awakened echoes for the narrator
from familiar passages in Second Isaiah. Following a reference to the servant as "light of the
nations" (see Luke 2:32; Acts 13:47), we read: "to bring out (ἐξαγαγεῖν) from bonds those
bound and from a house of prison those sitting in darkness" (Isa. 42:7). Recall the reference
in Acts 12:7 to the light that shown in Peter's prison. See further Isa. 49:9; 52:2; 61:1
(quoted Luke 4:18).

[13] See above, 65–66.

[14] See R. Kratz, *Rettungswunder*, 441, 444–45, on elements of the prison rescue miracle in
ancient literature. These include describing the measures taken to ensure secure custody.

but in the midst of the event normal human expectations control perception. The narrative makes the incongruity between human expectations and divine action stand out sharply through its portrait of Peter and the Christians gathered in Mary's house. They are like the disciples on the Emmaus road, blind to what has happened even though the evidence of God's power stands before them.[15] This ironic perspective on central characters is a way of celebrating God's power. It also serves to remind humans, including the insiders favored by the narrator, of the continuing gap between human understanding and the wonder of God's ways. The church, too, experiences God ironically. New discoveries of the wonder of God are also discoveries of its own myopia.

The narrative reinforces the effect by doubling it. First Peter does not believe that he is really being released. Then the Christians in Mary's house refuse to believe that Peter has been released. Peter, left knocking at the door, gets a second taste of his own skepticism in the reaction of his friends inside. Twice the narrative leads up to a moment of recognition. Peter in the prison blindly follows the crisp instructions of the angel, thinking it is only a vision (v. 9). We are told each stage of the procedure: Peter dressing, passing the first guards, the second guards, through the iron gate, to the first cross street, all the while Peter not recognizing that this is really happening. Then the angel disappears but Peter's freedom does not. Finally, Peter is convinced and makes his statement of recognition: "Now I know truly that the Lord sent out his angel and rescued me from the hand of Herod and from all the expectation of the people of the Jews." The beginning corresponds to the narrator's statement in v. 9: "He did not know that what was happening through the angel was true."

Peter's slowness to recognize the Lord's work reappears in the behavior of the Christians in Mary's house. Several details underscore the new irony. The iron gate of the prison swung open for Peter with no effort on his part, but now he cannot get past the gate of his friends because they will not recognize his presence.[16] The church has been praying fervently for Peter (v. 5), and as Peter approaches the disciples are still praying (v. 12). When the maid announces the fulfillment of their prayer, they say she is crazy. Finally the gate is opened, and the disciples are astonished to find Peter there. Peter can then make his second confession of the Lord's saving work (v. 17; cf. v. 11) as he relates his story to his friends. The importance for the community of this new story of God's saving work is

---

[15] On irony in the Emmaus narrative see *Narrative Unity* 1:282–84, 288–89.

[16] See R. Kratz, *Rettungswunder*, 470, who notes that v. 14 ("she did not open the gate") contrasts with v. 10 (the gate "opened by itself").

indicated by Peter's instructions to pass it on to "James[17] and the brothers."

Herod is presented as an evil ruler who not only persecutes the church but also is willing to accept divine honors and is punished for his hubris (12:22–23).[18] In his persecution he has the support of Judean Jews. Here the portrait of the Jewish people of Judea takes a negative turn. Prior to the appearance of Stephen, the "people (λαός)" of Jerusalem are portrayed as sympathetic and interested in the apostles' message (2:47; 4:21; 5:13, 26), even though it required them to repent for their share in Jesus' death. However, Stephen's enemies were able to arouse the people against him (6:12). Saul also is in danger in Damascus from "the Jews" and in Jerusalem from "the Hellenists" (9:23, 29). Now we are told in 12:3–4 that the killing of James the brother of John was pleasing to "the Jews," so that Herod is encouraged to arrest Peter and bring him before "the people." After his release from prison, Peter indicates that he has been rescued not only from Herod but also from "the expectation of the people of the Jews" (12:11). Not only Stephen and Saul but even Peter are out of favor with the non-Christian Jews of Jerusalem. Attitudes have changed. The early openness to the apostles and their message has ended, and a wall of suspicion separates the disciples from others in Jerusalem, so that "the Jews" can be used to refer to a hostile group. Later "the people" in Jerusalem will show its hostility to Paul as well (21:30, 36). The narrator leaves us to speculate about the causes of this important change.

The story of the conversion and early ministry of Saul the persecutor was rounded off with a summary statement concerning the church, which was being "built up" and "multiplied" (9:31). The story of Herod's persecution ends with a similar statement: "The word of God was growing and being multiplied" (12:24).[19] Through the Lord's remarkable help, the word and the church are able to continue their growth in spite of persecutions. The final verse of the chapter prepares for the next stage of the narrative. The narrator shifts back to Barnabas and Saul, who are now accompanied by John Mark. John Mark's mother was mentioned in

---

[17] Here as elsewhere a significant character is introduced in passing, providing some preparation for the more important role the character will later play. See 15:13–21; 21:18.

[18] According to Mark Strom, Acts 12:20–23 is dependent on Ezekiel 28. See "An Old Testament Background," 289–92. H. Conzelmann, *Acts*, 96, discusses Dio Cassius 62.20.5, where the crowd honors the divine voice of Nero, as a possible parallel to Acts 12:22 but rejects it. Nevertheless, this citation might be relevant to understanding Acts. It might suggest that the report of Herod's death has more than Herod in mind. If it was widely known that Nero encouraged people to treat him as Herod was treated in 12:22, Nero falls under the same judgment, and his flight and suicide could be understood as the fulfillment of that judgment. Nero is the Caesar that Paul must appear before (27:24).

[19] On the word as vital and growing, see above, 82.

12:12. Thus attention has already been drawn to him. These two references in Acts 12 prepare for the brief role that he will play in Paul's mission, as noted in 13:5, 13. John is a Jerusalemite (12:12; 13:13) who at first supports Paul's mission, but Paul finds him to be unreliable (cf. 15:38).

PAUL AND BARNABAS BEGIN
THEIR MISSION JOURNEY

From Acts 13 on, Paul is the central character. The narrator follows Paul's journeys and shows Paul fulfilling his divine commission. The Lord has chosen Paul to play a key role in the fulfillment of a mission that begins with John the Baptist and Jesus and stretches on beyond the apostles and Paul into the future. Paul's place in this mission is defined in scenes that disclose the nature of Paul's commission to figures of the narrative and to us. The statement of the Lord concerning Paul in 9:15–16 was such a disclosure. There we were told that Paul has been chosen "to bear my name before Gentiles and kings and sons of Israel," and he "must suffer for my name." Because the narrator regards the Lord's voice as authoritative, there is little doubt that all of this will come to pass. Suspense remains, however, concerning *how* this will come to pass, especially in light of the remarkable scope of Paul's work, according to these words. Paul's commission is not entirely unique, for he participates in a mission that began before him and will end after him. The nature and conditions of this mission require similar acts and similar experiences by the various people called to share in it. Nevertheless, Paul has a central role at the point where missionaries begin to act intentionally in light of the comprehensive claim and gift of God inherent to the good news they bring. In chapter 13 the narrator shows how an intentional mission to new areas is launched by Paul and Barnabas, reaching out to both Jews and Gentiles.

This mission begins with the choice of the missioners. In 13:1–3 we have a commissioning scene. We already know in a general way that Paul has been chosen as the Lord's special instrument (9:15). Now the Holy Spirit makes known to prophets and teachers in Antioch that Paul and Barnabas have been chosen for a particular "work" (13:2). The nature of this work is clarified by the rest of Acts 13—14, which reports a missionary journey beginning in Antioch and ending with a return to Antioch. The brief summary of the return in 14:26–27 includes a reminder of the commissioning scene in 13:1–3, an indication that "the work" is now fulfilled, and a report to the Antioch church. Thus Acts 13—14 is a major narrative segment with its own introduction and conclusion, the latter rounding off the section by a return to the beginning point and an announcement of the successful completion of the task.

The initiative for this new mission comes not from the apostles but from the Holy Spirit active in the Antioch church. The Spirit indicates through a small circle of prophets and teachers that two of their number should be selected for a particular task. The reference to Paul as a prophet provides background for the next scene, in which Paul speaks as a prophet, filled with Holy Spirit (13:9–11).

Paul has been preaching and teaching for some time and in several places (in Damascus, Jerusalem, and Antioch, at least). Nevertheless, this mission journey from Antioch is highlighted as an important new beginning through echoes of the beginning of Jesus' and the apostles' missions. We have noted that the sequence of events at the beginning of the apostles' mission in Acts 1—4 contains echoes of the similar sequence at the beginning of Jesus' mission in Luke 3—5.[1] The narrator suggests the importance of Paul's missionary journeys by including reminders of these two previous momentous beginnings in the narrative of Paul's first missionary journey.

By itself the commissioning scene in 13:1–3 would probably not remind us of the beginnings of Jesus' and the apostles' missions. However, readers alert to such things may begin to pick up clues when they come to the impressive scene of Paul preaching in the synagogue of Pisidian Antioch (13:14–41). Like Jesus (Luke 4:18–21) and Peter (Acts 2:14–40), Paul makes a major statement near the beginning of his new mission. His speech resembles that of Jesus in setting (a synagogue service with reading of Scripture) and resembles Peter's in points of content.[2] The three speeches either contain or lead to a Scripture quotation that interprets the mission that is beginning (Luke 4:18–19; Acts 2:17–21; 13:47). They lead immediately (Luke 4:24–30) or in due course (Acts 4:1–3;[3] 13:45–52) to an outbreak of opposition. The inclusion of Gentiles in God's salvation is mentioned and may be part of the provocation (Luke 4:25–28; Acts 2:39; 3:25–26; 13:45–48[4]). Furthermore, a scene in which a lame man is healed follows shortly after the scene in which the mission is announced (Luke 5:17–26; Acts 3:1–10; 14:8–10).[5]

---

[1] See above, 29, 49–52. M. Sternberg calls this "analogical organization" and gives examples from the Hebrew Bible. See *Poetics of Biblical Narrative*, 268–70.

[2] See below, 170, 174.

[3] Peter gives two speeches in close order. Together they function as provocation for the high priestly party.

[4] Note the repetition of "to you first" in Acts 3:26 and 13:46.

[5] The first two of these healings have the same function. They raise the general issue of Jesus' saving power. See above, 51–52. On the similarities in wording between Acts 3:1–10 and 14:8–10, see below, 177–78.

The commissioning scene in Acts 13:1-3 is also part of the pattern. The beginnings of the missions of Jesus and the apostles are preceded by references to prayer (Luke 3:21; Acts 1:14), which provides opportunity for action of the Spirit (Luke 3:22; Acts 2:1-4), and the Spirit leads directly to mission (Luke 4:14, 18;[6] Acts 2:5-41). The commissioning scene in Acts 13:1-3 follows a pattern already established when it presents a situation of worship and prayer that leads to the action of the Spirit initiating a mission. The mission journey of Paul and Barnabas, like the missions of Jesus and the apostles, is born out of the searching and alertness of prayer and is empowered by the Spirit.[7]

The narrator briefly reports the preaching of Paul and Barnabas in Jewish synagogues on Cyprus (13:5). Dramatic portrayal of this preaching is reserved for the major scene that follows in 13:14-43. First we are told of the conversion of the Roman proconsul of Cyprus and of Paul's remarkable display of prophetic power when he confronts a false prophet and magician. It is understandable that the narrator would not want to pass over a story of the conversion of a proconsul, the highest official of a Roman province. Much attention is directed, however, to Paul's encounter with Elymas the magician.

The larger narrative suggests that two interests may have led to this focus on Elymas. First, the narrator repeatedly shows concern with corrupt and degenerate religion, whether Jewish, pagan, or Christian. There are several related subthemes: magic, money, and hubris. Religion is corrupted by the desire to make money and to be viewed as someone great. Religion is also corrupted when it degenerates into magic. Elymas is the second magician encountered in Acts, for Simon of Samaria also practiced magic (8:9, 11). Even after baptism Simon had to be sharply rebuked by Peter for his debased thinking about the Spirit (8:18-24). Later Paul's work in Ephesus will result in the burning of many magic books (19:18-19). Elymas is another representative of the false attempt to manipulate nonhuman power through magic, and Paul's scathing words express the implied author's perception of great danger in such practices and strong rejection of them. Evidently magic was a threat of some importance.

Second, if the mission of Paul is to be comparable to the missions of Jesus and Peter, the narrator must not only demonstrate his power as a preacher but also as a worker of signs and wonders. Each of the three

---

[6] Luke 4:18 is an interpretation of 3:22 as an anointing for a particular mission. See *Narrative Unity* 1:57-58.

[7] On the analogical pattern discussed in the last two paragraphs, see C. Talbert, *Literary Patterns*, 16-19, 23-26. W. Radl, *Paulus und Jesus*, 101-2, suggests in addition that there may be a parallel between the temptation scene in Luke 4:1-13 and Acts 13:4-12, which occupy the same position in the pattern. Note that Elymas is called a "son of the devil" (Acts 13:10).

missions begins with a major scene including a summary of the preacher's message, but the beginnings of the missions also present the key characters as workers of signs and wonders. Peter's Pentecost sermon was followed by a reference to the "many wonders and signs" happening through the apostles (2:43), and the account of a specific wonder was placed soon after (3:1–10). Jesus' announcement in Nazareth was followed by his mighty acts in Capernaum. The two settings fit together, presenting complimentary aspects of his mission.[8] The first reported wonder of Jesus in Luke is preceded by the statement that the people of Capernaum "were amazed at his teaching" (Luke 4:32). It is remarkable that the first story of a wonder by Paul ends with the statement that the proconsul was "amazed at the teaching of the Lord" (13:12). In both places a wonder and amazing teaching are associated in an unusual way.[9] In Acts 13 both Paul's preaching and his wonder-working are presented, as at the beginning of the missions of Jesus and the apostles. The major scene of preaching follows rather than precedes the wonder-working, the reverse of Luke 4 and Acts 2. Nevertheless, both are present. Because there were previous references to Paul's preaching but not to his mighty acts, presenting the latter first may have been advantageous.

Elymas is introduced not only as a magician but also as a false prophet (13:6). He is the false counterpart of Barnabas and Paul, who are counted among the prophets in Antioch (13:1).[10] The conflict between Paul and Elymas is similar to the conflicts between prophets with rival messages for king or people in the Old Testament (see Micaiah and the opposing prophets in 1 Kgs. 22; Jeremiah and the opposing prophets in Jeremiah 28—29 [= Jeremiah 35—36 LXX]).[11] Paul's rebuke of Elymas is uttered while "filled with Holy Spirit" and uses the rhetoric of invective. It moves from denunciation to judgment, announcing that Elymas will become blind. It is a word of power, for the announced judgment immediately happens.

Jeremiah also denounced the false prophets and announced a harsher judgment: death.[12] Although Paul's words are harsh, the judgment invoked is comparatively temperate, especially because the blinding is

---

[8] See *Narrative Unity* 1:82–83.

[9] Luke 4:32 and Acts 13:12 are the only places in Luke-Acts where teaching (διδαχή) is a cause of amazement (expressed by ἐκπλήσσω).

[10] Elymas is also named Bar-Jesus, that is, son of Jesus. E. Haenchen, *Acts*, 402, believes this would be an embarrassment and is a clear sign of pre-Lukan tradition. However, the name would be functional in the present narrative if it suggests that Elymas also claims to be a follower of Jesus. See Günter Klein, "Synkretismus," 61–67.

[11] The LXX repeatedly refers to the prophets opposing Jeremiah as "false prophets (ψευδοπροφῆται)." Cf. Jer. 33:7–8, 11, 16; 34:9; 35:1; 36:1, 8.

[12] See Jer. 28:15–17 (= 35:15–17 LXX), 29:21–23 (= 36:21–23 LXX). See also Deut. 18:20: a false prophet shall die.

temporary. It serves as a revelation to the proconsul, and perhaps to Elymas himself, of the blindness of this supposed seer.[13] The nature of the judgment is interesting for another reason. Through Paul the same judgment falls on Elymas as Paul himself received on the Damascus road.[14] Paul and Elymas, two opponents of the mission, are both blinded temporarily. An added detail underlines the helplessness of both: they need others to lead them by the hand (9:8, χειραγωγοῦντες; 13:11, χειραγωγούς). These words are applied only to Paul and Elymas in the New Testament. Thus there is a connection between Elymas and Paul's old self.[15] And the power that Paul encountered on the Damascus road (called in 13:11 the "hand of the Lord") continues to operate through Paul, exposing the blindness of the opposition to the "straight ways of the Lord."

Although references to "straight" and "twisted ways" (using εὐθύς or διαστρέφω) are common in the Septuagint, the accusation that Elymas is "twisting the straight ways of the Lord" has specific points of contact within Luke-Acts. The image of the "way of the Lord" was introduced in connection with John the Baptist, who was its preparer (Luke 1:76; 3:4; cf. 7:27), and in the Isaiah quotation that prefaces John's ministry it is connected with straightening what is crooked (Luke 3:4–5). Later in Acts 13 John's ministry will be explicitly recalled (13:24–25), and at several stages the narrator indicates that the missionaries continue the work of John (the seventy-two, see Luke 7:27; 9:51–52; 10:1; Peter, see Luke 3:3, 5, 10 with Acts 2:37–38, 40; Paul, see Luke 3:3, 8 with Acts 26:20).[16] The "straight ways of the Lord" refer to the renewal movement based on repentance and release of sins begun by John the Baptist and now continuing under the authority of the exalted Messiah. Elymas is trying to twist this movement from its purpose, on this occasion through trying to block its effect at high levels of government.

---

[13] With the reference to darkness in 13:11, compare the parallelism between darkness and the authority of Satan in 26:18, from which the opening of people's eyes will bring release.

[14] Noted by E. Richard, "Old Testament in Acts," 333.

[15] This could be interpreted psychologically, if one were so inclined. Paul in denouncing Elymas is rejecting his own former personality and value structures, which remain threatening potentialities within himself.

[16] See *Narrative Unity* 1:229–30, 233–35.

PAUL'S SYNAGOGUE SPEECH

Although we are frequently told that Paul is speaking, on only three occasions during Paul's ministry as a free man does the narrator devote more than a few verses to reporting his speeches. The three speeches that are more extensively reported differ in their audience and content. In 13:16–41 Paul speaks to Jews and God-fearers in a synagogue, in 17:22–31 he speaks to cultured Gentiles in Athens, and in 20:18–35 he delivers a farewell address to leaders of a Christian community. These three speeches give us an impression of how Paul responded to three major aspects of his mission. They are widely distributed in the narrative of Paul's mission journeys, the first and third occurring near the beginning and end of this section of Acts, and each dominates its context.[1]

In the course of his mission journeys, Paul repeatedly enters synagogues and speaks to Jews. The speech in the synagogue of Pisidian Antioch provides a model of what he said on those many occasions. Most of the summary indications of the content of Paul's later preaching to Jews match aspects of this model speech. Thus the content of the Antioch speech is summarized in 13:43 as "the grace of God," which the responsive Jews now must "stick with." Paul's message is also summarized in terms of God's grace in 14:3; 20:24, 32. Paul argues that the Messiah had to suffer and be raised from the dead (17:3) and that the Messiah is Jesus (17:3; 18:5). Both of these statements fit the Antioch speech. He argues from the Scripture (17:2, 11), as in the Antioch speech, and the emphasis on faith in Jesus in 20:21 echoes 13:39.[2] The speech of Paul in the Antioch synagogue has special importance because here the narrator provides an extended statement of the message that Paul repeatedly preaches to Jews of the Diaspora.

I have already discussed the place of this speech in the similar pattern of events at the beginnings of the missions of Jesus, the apostles, and Paul.[3]

---

[1] See Donald Miesner, "Missionary Journeys Narrative," 212–14.

[2] The references to the reign of God in 19:8 and 20:25 also fit the Antioch speech when it is recognized that the enthronement of Jesus as royal Messiah through resurrection is a major step in the coming of God's reign. See 13–14, 351–52.

[3] See above, 160–62.

In this pattern Paul's speech in the Antioch synagogue (and his announcement about his further mission in 13:46–47) corresponds to Jesus' announcement in the Nazareth synagogue and Peter's Pentecost speech. Just as these speeches have central significance in understanding the missions of Jesus and Peter, so the speech and following events in Antioch have central significance for understanding Paul's work.

The speech and Paul's response to Jewish jealousy a week later must be viewed together. They stand in tension with each other, for, on the one hand, Paul announces that the word of salvation has been sent to his synagogue audience (13:26), and, on the other hand, he announces that he is turning to the Gentiles in the face of Jewish rejection. The speech concerns the fulfillment of God's promise to the Jewish people, bringing them salvation. We must not forget the message of the speech when we hear that Paul is turning to the Gentiles. Both aspects together, when each is given its full weight, express a central problem that pervades the following narrative: God has acted for Israel's salvation, but the effects of that saving work are limited by repeated rejection.

The speech is directed to Israelites and other synagogue worshipers. Paul's approach to his audience in Athens is distinctly different, showing awareness that Gentiles untouched by Judaism require special preparation to appreciate the Christian message. In reading or hearing the Antioch scene, Gentiles would be in the position of outsiders overhearing what Paul is saying to another group. Nevertheless, the scene might be important for them, too, as part of an education in which Gentiles become Godfearers, honoring Scripture and appreciating the importance of God's dialogue with Israel.

The speech is carefully crafted to be persuasive for the audience the narrator envisions. Such crafting is necessary for an effective speech, and the narrator wants to present Paul as an effective preacher before Jews. As C. Perelman and L. Olbrechts-Tyteca assert in their adaptation of traditional rhetoric, "For argumentation to exist, an effective community of minds must be realized at a given moment." This requires adaptation to the audience, for "no orator, not even the religious orator, can afford to neglect this effort of adaptation to his audience." Argument must begin with shared premises, for "the unfolding as well as the starting point of the argumentation presuppose . . . the agreement of the audience."[4] Marcel Dumais, citing Perelman and Olbrechts-Tyteca, studies Paul's synagogue speech in Acts 13:16–41 in light of this requirement for effective rhetorical argument.[5] According to Dumais, the orator does not

---

[4] Quotations from C. Perelman and L. Olbrechts-Tyteca, *New Rhetoric*, 14, 24, 65.
[5] See *Langage de l'évangélisation*, 259–61.

passively accept all of the hearers' presuppositions but is actively selecting those presuppositions that will lead to the desired understanding, while correcting other presuppositions.[6] This selection process will be guided both by the orator's (or narrator's) sense of truth and by the concern to be persuasive in addressing the audience.

Paul's speech begins with a brief summary of the story of Israel from the patriarchs to David (13:17–22). This section is not intended to convey new information to the audience, but neither is it simply a "reference to the depicted situation" (a regular feature of the mission speeches in Acts).[7] It intends to affirm the community relationship that connects speaker and audience (see the reference to "our fathers" in 13:17) and to make present some shared presuppositions that will be important for the following argument.[8] The beginning and end of 13:17–22 highlight two important premises that bind speaker and audience and that will form the foundation of the speaker's argument. They are the election of Israel (God is "the God of this people Israel" and has "chosen our fathers") and the election of David, who is recognized as the king pleasing to God to whom (as v. 23 goes on to say) God made a particular promise, that the Messiah would come from his offspring and sit on his throne (cf. 2:30). Paul makes a transition in v. 23. He expresses a central premise on which agreement is expected—God's promise of the Davidic Messiah—but, as Dumais notes,[9] he also introduces something new and potentially controversial. Paul speaks in the past tense of the Messiah who has already come to Israel and identifies the Messiah with Jesus.

Both setting and content make clear that this is a speech by a Jew to Jews, for it concerns God's promise to the Jewish people.[10] Paul addresses his audience as "Israelites" and "sons of the family of Abraham" (13:16, 26). He also stresses his own position in this family by calling his audience "brothers" (13:26, 38). The speech is addressed to this particular people and those who have chosen to associate with it ("those who fear God," 13:16, 26). Once David is mentioned, the speech focuses on him and his promised heir. The speech is basically the announcement, with support-

---

[6] See *Langage de l'évangélisation*, 279.

[7] See U. Wilckens, *Missionsreden*, 53.

[8] C. Perelman and L. Olbrechts-Tyteca emphasize the importance of "presence, . . . the displaying of certain elements on which the speaker wishes to center attention in order that they may occupy the foreground of the hearer's consciousness. Before even starting to argue from particular premises, it is essential that the content of these premises should stand out against the undifferentiated mass of available elements of agreement." See *New Rhetoric*, 142.

[9] See *Langage de l'évangélisation*, 155.

[10] Parts of the following discussion of Acts 13:16–52 were first prepared for my article "Rejection by Jews and Turning to Gentiles" in *Society of Biblical Literature 1986 Seminar Papers*, edited by Kent Harold Richards (Atlanta: Scholars Press, 1986), 130–41. Used by permission.

ing argument, that the promised heir has come and has been installed as Messiah through resurrection. The coming of the Messiah in fulfillment of God's promise is first announced in v. 23. The word "promise (ἐπαγγελία)" in this verse becomes a theme word when it reappears in vv. 32–33 in a more forceful proclamation of the fulfillment of the promise. The narrative concerning Jesus (vv. 27–31) leads up to this proclamation that the promise has been fulfilled through Jesus' resurrection, and vv. 33b-39 develop the significance of this event through Scripture and an invitation to forgiveness. Thus the fulfillment of the promise to Israel of an heir to David's throne is the leading idea of the speech.[11]

Having committed himself to the surprising proposition in v. 23, Paul must now defend it. However, he retains through most of vv. 24–31 the narrative mode with which he began in v. 17.[12] Now the narrative focuses on Jesus, the fulfiller of the promise to David. This applies also to vv. 24–25, for this brief review of John's message leads up to his announcement of the one coming after him. It is significant that John is included in Paul's narrative. His proclamation "to all the people of Israel" is viewed as valid and important for this audience.

The narrative is interrupted by a renewed, more intense address of the audience in v. 26, emphasizing the significance of what is being said for them: "To us[13] the word of this salvation has been sent out." This renewed address prepares for and highlights the review of the Jesus story that follows, yet there is narrative continuity with vv. 24–25. Without a real break in continuity the speaker seeks to intensify the audience's involvement in his message as he approaches the crucial narration of Jesus' death and resurrection. Application to the audience and appeal for their response is not reserved for the end of the speech but is interspersed with the narration and scriptural argument. It develops from the reference to the savior[14] for Israel in v. 23, to the announcement of the word of salvation for the audience in v. 26, to the proclamation of the fulfillment of the promise in vv. 32–33, ending with the emphasis on the resulting opportunity and danger in vv. 38–41.[15] In the meantime the arguments are de-

---

[11] Verses 23, 32, 33a formulate the *Leitgedanken* of the speech, as indicated by Matthäus Buss, *Missionspredigt*, 29.

[12] I am proposing a somewhat different analysis of the speech into narration, proposition, and proof (recognized parts of a speech in Greco-Roman rhetoric) than that given in the brief rhetorical analysis of Paul's synagogue speech by George Kennedy, *New Testament Interpretation*, 124–25. The mingling of narration and proof in vv. 24–25, 27–31 and the development of the proposition in v. 23 through repeated applications of it to the audience in vv. 26, 32–33a, 38–41 seem important to me for understanding the speech's strategy. See the following discussion.

[13] Alternate reading: "to you." The pronoun is emphasized by being placed first in the clause.

[14] Associating Jesus' role as "savior" with his role as Davidic Messiah is typical of Luke-Acts. Cf. Luke 1:69, 2:11.

[15] Note the references to "you" in vv. 32 and 38.

veloped, first indirectly through narrative (vv. 24–25, 27–31) and then directly through Scripture (vv. 33–37). The narrative contributes to the argument. John's witness in vv. 24–25 is assumed to carry weight. His announcement about the one coming "after me" is connected with Jesus by placing John and Jesus in temporal sequence: John preached "before the face of his [Jesus'] entrance." In vv. 27–29 the condemnation and killing of Jesus is twice related to the fulfillment of Scripture. Furthermore, Jesus' innocence is asserted, and the condemnation of Jesus by the people of Jerusalem and their leaders is viewed as a sign of ignorance. In vv. 30–31 Jesus' resurrection by God is announced, and witnesses of this event are cited. This announcement will become the basis of the proclamation in vv. 32–33a and the argument from Scripture that follows. Thus the narration contributes in a variety of ways to the argument that Jesus is the promised savior from the seed of David.

Not only the promise to David but also the election of Israel remains an important premise of the speech as a whole. Israel's election is not stated in v. 17 only to be forgotten. In the context of the speech God's election of Israel means that God is committed to Israel's salvation. That commitment appears in God's new action. Note the emphasis on the fact that Jesus means salvation for Israel: God "brought a savior, Jesus, to [or "for"] Israel" (v. 23). "To us the word of this salvation has been sent out" (v. 26). The promise to the fathers has been fulfilled for the children of those fathers through Jesus' resurrection (vv. 32–33). Of course, this salvation does not work automatically. Israel's response is needed. But the fact that the Antioch episode will end with Paul's announcement that he is turning to the Gentiles in the face of Jewish rejection does not lessen the importance of God's election of Israel and God's commitment to Israel's salvation, strongly indicated in the speech.

In the discussion of Stephen's speech I argued that the story of Israel is presented as an ascent toward fulfillment of God's promise and a tragic fall at the time of realization. The episode in Pisidian Antioch is similar, but only the final verse of the speech hints at a tragic turn. The story of God and Israel is positively presented in the speech and climaxes in God's fulfillment of the promise. The tragic turn appears a week later when the Jews become jealous as the general population shows interest in Paul's preaching. The connection that I am suggesting is supported by the use of the rare word ἀπωθέω ("push aside") to describe the act of rejection in both Stephen's speech (7:27, 39) and the Antioch episode (13:46). These are the only occurrences of this word in Luke-Acts, and both occurrences are followed by references to a "persecution (διωγμός)" (8:1; 13:50). The development is tragic because these Diaspora Jews are rejecting what belongs to them and means salvation for them. The scene ends with unresolved tension between their rejection of the word of salvation and God's commitment to bring salvation to Israel, as presented in the speech.

In v. 27 the same sense of ironic fulfillment of Scripture and God's plan appears as in 2:23; 3:17–18; and 4:27–28. Acting in ignorance and intending to get rid of Jesus, the people of Jerusalem actually played a destined role contributing to the exaltation of Jesus as Messiah. Acts 13:27 refers only to the inhabitants of Jerusalem and their rulers. Other Jews are not blamed for Jesus' death. However, if the hearer relates v. 27 to vv. 40–41, the former can be understood as an advance warning not to repeat the blind rejection of the Jerusalemites.

Commentators have interpreted vv. 31–32 as evidence that those accompanying Jesus from Galilee have a role as resurrection witnesses that Paul does not share. E. Haenchen comments, "As Luke saw history, only the Twelve, who were with Jesus during his earthly life as well, were fully valid witnesses of his resurrection."[16] The denial of this role to Paul rests on shaky evidence. The emphatic nominative pronoun at the beginning of v. 32 (καὶ ἡμεῖς, "and we") calls attention to the present role of Paul and Barnabas alongside the role of the witnesses from Galilee described in v. 31.[17] Not only are the Galileans witnesses to the risen Jesus but "we" preach good news, and the content of that good news according to 13:32–37 is essentially the same as Peter's message about the risen and exalted Jesus in 2:24–36. It includes Jesus' resurrection (13:33). Although this observation does not completely settle the issue of whether Paul is a "witness" of the risen Jesus, later statements about Paul's encounter with Jesus on the Damascus road indicate that this event qualifies him as a witness of the risen Lord (22:14–15; 26:16). Although Paul does not share the Galileans' witness to the ministry of Jesus, he does share their witness to the risen Lord. This should be taken into account when interpreting 13:31–33. These verses do not intend to contrast Paul with the Galilean witnesses but to make them companions in witness.

There is one significant difference in the witness of Paul and the Galileans. This concerns the scope of the witness. According to v. 31 the Galileans are Jesus' witnesses "to the people." In 10:41–42 Peter also spoke of his role as a chosen witness and his commission to proclaim "to the people." Paul will soon reveal that the Lord has commanded him and Barnabas to be a "light of the Gentiles," bringing "salvation to the end of the earth" (13:47). The apostles were originally designated as witnesses

---

[16] See *Acts*, 411. H. Conzelmann, *Acts*, 105, and G. Schneider, *Apostelgeschichte* 2:137, also distinguish Paul from the Galilean witnesses because Paul is not an eyewitness of the resurrection.

[17] Henry Cadbury presents evidence suggesting that the nominative pronoun here is indeed emphatic. He shows that in Luke the author tends to omit unemphatic personal pronouns found in the synoptic parallels. See *Style and Literary Method*, 191–92.

"to the end of the earth" (1:8).[18] Now we discover a shift in strategy, although the goal remains the same. The apostles focus their witness on the Jewish people. Paul also preaches to Jews, as in the Antioch synagogue, but he becomes the chief instrument by which the gospel reaches out to the Gentiles and the end of the earth. Thus his witness is comprehensive, as the later designation of him as Jesus' "witness to all persons" indicates (22:15). There are surprises on the way to fulfillment of the Lord's commission. Paul and his companions take on a major role while the mission of the apostles becomes limited and specialized.

Paul in 13:32–33 is speaking of the promised king of David's line, as is shown by the further references to David in 13:34, 36, and by the close connection of this section of Paul's sermon to Peter's Pentecost sermon. The reference to Ps. 16:10 (15:10 LXX) in 13:35–37 is a brief reminder of the more extensive quotation and application of this psalm in Acts 2:25–31. There Peter argued that David was not speaking of himself but of his descendant, concerning whom God had sworn an oath to seat him on David's throne (2:30). It is Jesus, risen and seated at God's right hand, who fulfills this promise. The oath of which Peter spoke is equivalent to the promise of which Paul speaks; both refer to the expected Davidic king for Israel. Peter connected the resurrection of Jesus to the oath that God would seat David's descendant on David's throne and proclaimed Jesus, seated at God's right hand, as the promised Lord and Messiah. Similarly, Paul proclaims God's resurrection of Jesus (ἀναστήσας ᾽Ιησοῦν, 13:33) as the fulfillment of the messianic promise. Through resurrection and exaltation[19] Jesus is declared to be God's Son, which is equivalent to the enthronement mentioned in 2:30. The context strongly supports the view that 13:33 refers to Jesus' resurrection as the fulfillment of the messianic promise, for Jesus' resurrection is the subject throughout 13:30–37.[20]

The messianic significance of Jesus' resurrection is developed through the scriptural quotations in 13:34–35.[21] There Paul indicates that the risen one is "no longer going to return to corruption." This places

---

[18] M. Buss, *Missionspredigt,* 137–38, points out that the verb ἐντέλλομαι is used in Acts only at 13:47, referring to Paul and Barnabas' commission, and 1:2, referring to the apostles' commission. The content of the apostles' commission is explained in 1:8.

[19] The narrator distinguishes between the resurrection and exaltation of Jesus in Acts 1 in order to emphasize Jesus' careful instruction of the apostles. However, when Jesus' messianic enthronement is the main concern, this distinction can be ignored.

[20] For further argument supporting the view that 13:33 refers to Jesus' resurrection, see J. Dupont, "Filius meus es tu," 528–35; Evald Lövestam, *Son and Saviour,* 8–10; Emmeram Kränkl, *Jesus der Knecht Gottes,* 137–38; Robert O'Toole, "Christ's Resurrection in Acts 13,13–52," 361–72. On the Messiah being "raised up" in the messianic "promise tradition" of Judaism and early Christianity, see Dennis Duling, "Promises to David," 55–77.

[21] M. Dumais compares the scriptural interpretation in the speech to Jewish midrash, arguing that the methods of interpretation as well as the themes are appropriate to the Jewish synagogue. See *Langage de l'évangélisation.*

emphasis on a continuing freedom from death, an emphasis that is supported by reference to "the holy things of David which are faithful," that is, lasting.[22] The emphasis in 13:34 fits well with the description of the Messiah in the angel's announcement to Mary. Mary's baby will not only be called God's Son and receive "the throne of David his father." He will also "reign over the house of Jacob forever, and of his reign there will be no end" (Luke 1:32–33).[23] Because the Messiah has been enthroned through resurrection, he is no longer threatened by corruption and his reign will have no end.

The significance of this messianic promise for the Jewish people is expressed by the quotation of Isa. 55:3 in Acts 13:34, a quotation that usually receives too little attention. The plural "you ($\dot{v}\mu\hat{\iota}v$)" shows that this promise is not a promise to the Messiah but to the Jewish people (in the context of the speech, to Paul's audience). The application of Paul's message to his audience is strongly stressed through first- or second-person plural pronouns, sometimes in emphatic position, in 13:26, 32, 33, 38. The pronoun in the quotation in 13:34 fits with these other pronouns and refers to the same group. Because the verb in the quotation has been changed from the verb in Isa. 55:3 LXX and the pronoun is the indirect object of that verb, it too could easily have been changed if it did not serve the narrator's purpose. Instead, the pronoun has been allowed to stand. Paul through this quotation affirms the promise of the messianic kingdom for the Jewish people and acknowledges that this promise is firmly rooted in Scripture.

The verb in the Isaiah quotation has been changed so as to match the verb in the Psalm quotation that follows. The words these two quotes have in common, as well as the way they are introduced, indicate that they are to be interpreted together. Indeed, they are understood to be the positive and negative expression of the same basic promise, and the parts correspond: "I will give to you" / "You will not give"; "the holy things of David" / "your holy one"; "which are faithful" / "to see corruption." The connection between the last two phrases, which is not apparent in the wording, is established by the introduction of the Isaiah quotation in 13:34: the messianic kingdom is "faithful" because the risen Messiah is "no longer going to return to corruption" but will rule over an eternal kingdom. The reference to "the holy things of David" helps to make clear that "your holy one" refers to the Davidic Messiah. Although the strange

---

[22] See H. Conzelmann, *Acts*, 105, who interprets τὰ πιστά as "imperishable." E. Lövestam detects a double aspect to the promise in 13:34: "The covenant promise to David had . . . a *firm* and *irrevocable* nature. This promise similarly concerned *permanent* dominion." See *Son and Saviour*, 79. Emphasis by Lövestam.

[23] M. Buss rightly emphasizes the close terminological and thematic connection of the Antioch speech with Luke 1—2. See *Missionspredigt*, 146.

phrase τὰ ὅσια Δαυίδ is open to several interpretations, the reference to something belonging to David in a promise applying to people of Paul's time naturally calls to mind the promised rule of David's heir, especially after 13:22–23, 32–33.[24]

As the speech draws to a close, we find the common offer of release of sins, which in this case is paraphrased in traditional Pauline language (being "justified [δικαιωθῆναι]" = RSV "freed"). Justification is open to "everyone who believes" (13:39). Peter's speech to the Gentiles ended with the same phrase (10:43). In Paul's speech also it probably indicates openness to Gentiles along with Jews. The continuation in 13:44–48 supports this view.

The offer of forgiveness and justification is balanced by a prophetic warning, which ends the speech. Justification is offered to everyone who believes, but in Hab. 1:5 the prophet addressed "scoffers" who "will certainly not believe" God's work if it is disclosed to them (13:41). In the context of the preceding speech this "work" may be understood as the fulfillment of the messianic promise through Jesus' resurrection. In the context of what follows it may be understood as the inclusion of the Gentiles in the eternal life of the messianic reign. Perhaps both of these key developments are included in God's surprising work.[25] However, it is significant that the Jewish audience is portrayed as interested and responsive until the next Sabbath when "nearly the whole city," including the Gentile population, is attracted to Paul's message. The Jews react with jealousy and begin to oppose Paul. Thus the narrative suggests that the discovery of Gentiles as fellow citizens in Jesus' messianic state is the major stumbling block for the Jews of Antioch, turning them into "scoffers" who refuse to believe God's "work." The final words of the speech foreshadow this negative development. In his major synagogue scene Paul anticipates the possibility of rejection, as Jesus did in the Nazareth synagogue (Luke 4:24). In both cases people finally "cast out (ἐξέβαλον)" God's messenger (Luke 4:29; Acts 13:50).[26]

When the Jews oppose them, Paul and Barnabas solemnly declare that they are turning to the Gentiles (13:46). What are the implications of this

---

[24] Walter Bauer interprets τὰ ὅσια as divine decrees, in contrast to human ones. See BAGD, 585. J. Dupont objects to this. He says that use of the phrase to mean religious duties, in contrast to social duties, is well established, but the meaning "divine decrees" is doubtful. See "ΤΑ ῾ΟΣΙΑ ΔΑΥΙΔ ΤΑ ΠΙΣΤΑ," 95. Dupont's criticism leads me to suggest that the narrator may have understood τὰ ὅσια to refer to the religious duties of David as king and therefore to what we would call the "office" of king. This royal office will be established for the Jewish people through the coming of their Messiah, according to 13:34.

[25] Furthermore, God's "work" also becomes the "work" of Paul and Barnabas. M. Buss, *Missionspredigt,* 133, notes that ἔργον is applied to the mission of Paul and Barnabas in 13:2, 14:26.

[26] Noted by Gerhard Krodel, *Acts,* 250.

announcement? Certain interpretations must be eliminated because they do not fit the rest of the narrative. The announcement cannot mean that Paul will never again preach to Jews, for as soon as he reaches the next town, he begins his mission by preaching in the synagogue to Jews (14:1). He preaches to Jews repeatedly in his continuing mission. Paul's announcement also cannot mean that Gentiles are offered the word of God only because of Jewish rejection, as an afterthought or as a second choice. The narrator of Luke-Acts has made clear ever since the birth narrative that the purpose of God that shapes this story intends to work salvation for all peoples. This was announced by an inspired prophet (Luke 2:30–32) and proclaimed as God's purpose in a banner quotation of Scripture (Luke 3:6). Then an inclusive mission of preaching was entrusted by the risen Messiah to his apostles (Luke 24:47; Acts 1:8). Preaching to the Gentiles is part of God's saving purpose announced long ago in Scripture and is a task entrusted by the risen Messiah to his witnesses. It is also part of the commission that Paul received from the risen Lord, governing his ministry (9:15; 22:15; 26:16–18). It is not an afterthought, nor does it need to be justified by Jewish rejection. In the narrator's view, salvation for the Gentiles is firmly rooted in Scripture, the witness to God's ancient purpose, as the Antioch scene also makes clear. In 13:47 Paul and Barnabas quote Isa. 49:6 and describe it as a command of the Lord that governs their ministry, obligating them to bring light to the nations and salvation "to the end of the earth" ($\xi\omega s$ $\dot{\epsilon}\sigma\chi\acute{a}\tau o\upsilon$ $\tau\hat{\eta}s$ $\gamma\hat{\eta}s$ as in the command to the apostles in 1:8).

In order to understand why turning to the Gentiles is nevertheless a special event that deserves a dramatic announcement, we must consider the first part of this announcement: "To you it was necessary that the word of God be spoken first" (13:46). The mission is universal, but it must follow a prescribed order. The Jews must be addressed first. If they reject the gospel, the missionaries are free to begin the second phase of their mission.

Why was it "necessary" that the preachers speak to the Jews "first"? Recall the two premises of Paul's synagogue speech that bind the speaker with his audience: the election of Israel and God's promise of a Messiah for Israel. The seriousness of Paul's (and the narrator's) commitment to these premises is shown by the acceptance of the difficult obligation of preaching to the Jews first. At this point it is important to keep the complete Antioch episode in mind, giving full weight both to the synagogue speech and to the announcement on the following Sabbath, for the poignancy of the announcement depends on the content of the synagogue speech. Interpretation that forgets the speech when discussing the announcement will miss the unresolved tension in the narrator's attitude toward unbelieving Jews, a tension to which the total scene gives powerful expression.

The Antioch scene repeats themes from both of Peter's first two speeches, an example of the common Lukan practice of sounding important themes more than once. The Pentecost speech, as we have seen, helps us to understand Paul's reference to Jesus' resurrection as the fulfillment of God's promise to David. The speech in Solomon's portico helps us to understand the necessity of Paul speaking first to the Jews. Peter, after making clear that God will still send the messianic "times of refreshment" and "restoration" if the people of Jerusalem repent (3:19–21), ends his second speech by saying, "To you first God, having raised up his servant, sent him" (3:26). This is explained by the preceding reference to his hearers as "sons of the prophets and of the covenant which God covenanted with our fathers" (3:25). The covenantal promise is described as a blessing that "all the families of the earth" will share, but it is clear that the Jewish people are meant to share in this blessing as "first" (3:25–26). The way that this priority is highlighted in Acts and its connection with the Jewish people as "sons of the prophets and of the covenant" show that the narrator still understands the scriptural promises quite concretely as promises to the Jewish people, even though Jewish Scripture also promises salvation for all nations. The narrator affirms God's promise to the Jewish people found in Scripture and is therefore willing to have one of his chief characters say that God sent his servant "to you first." This determines the course of the mission. If God sent the risen Messiah and his blessings to the Jews first, in fulfillment of promises to their ancestors, Paul must speak to the Jews first, as he indicates in 13:46.

The risen Messiah's instructions to his apostles also recognize this. The extension of the mission to the Gentiles is clearly stated in the two versions of the commission to the apostles, but both also indicate where the mission must begin: in Jerusalem, the center of Jewish life (Luke 24:47; Acts 1:4, 8).

The preceding discussion should make clear that the narrator of Acts is not merely giving a Jewish coloring to Paul's Antioch speech to make it fit the synagogue setting. Paul's preaching reflects a view that characterizes Luke-Acts from its beginning, the view that Jesus is the Davidic Messiah who fulfills specific promises of God to the Jewish people. These promises are found in Scripture, which the narrator accepts as the revelation of God's saving purpose for Israel and the world. However, what happens if the Jews, or at least most of them, reject the gospel? Here we enter difficult terrain for the implied author, who has no clear and easy answers. If one believes in a powerless God, or one prone to easy changes of heart, one could assume that Jewish rejection is the last word and that

God's saving purpose for them has no effect. God in Luke-Acts, however, relentlessly works for salvation even by means of human rejection, and Jesus' witnesses, including Paul, proclaim God as one who has chosen Israel and keeps promise with this people. We might be content to say that God's defeat with the Jews is not so bad because the Gentile mission will be a great success. Even Jewish rejection is not complete, for Acts affirms the success of the mission among some Jews, especially in Jerusalem. However, Acts does not allow us to ignore Jewish rejection. The Antioch episode ends by highlighting Jewish rejection in a dramatic scene, and this is only the first of a series of similar scenes. Indeed, the last scene in Acts is still preoccupied with this problem. The repeated appearance of this problem, especially in major scenes like those at Antioch of Pisidia and Rome, shows that the implied author is not content with past success among the Jews and is not ready to forget about those who have rejected the gospel. God's power to save and the scriptural promise to Israel are too important in the author's theology. We are left with an unresolved problem. Acts does not mitigate the problem and reduce the tension by weakening the witness to God's saving purpose and scriptural promise to the Jewish people. Apparently, living with the tension is preferable to ignoring either of two fundamental realities: God's promise to Israel, fulfilled in Jesus, and Israel's rejection.

Several aspects of the context need to be noted to help us understand the circumstances behind the announcement of turning to the Gentiles. First, Paul began by speaking in the synagogue to the Jewish assembly. Turning to the Gentiles means the end of such preaching in the Antioch synagogue. Second, the situation changes because Jews "were contradicting the things being said by Paul, reviling them" (or "blaspheming" the Lord Jesus—the object of βλασφημοῦντες is not specified). Resistance is openly expressed and involves personal attacks that would make continued preaching in the synagogue difficult or impossible. Third, when they are thrown out, Paul and Barnabas shake off the dust of their feet and go to another city. In doing this, they are following the instructions Jesus gave to the twelve and the seventy-two (Luke 9:5; 10:11), instructions that apply when a *city* fails to receive the mission. The context in Acts 13:51 is the same, for this gesture is used as the missionaries leave one city and go to another, where the mission to the Jews will begin again. So the announcement of turning to the Gentiles applies first of all to the city of Antioch. Of course, we must also note that the narrator has given a great deal of space to what happened at Antioch, suggesting that it has special importance for understanding Paul's larger mission. Its importance is underscored by the similar pattern of events found in later scenes (cf. 18:5–7; 19:8–9; 22:17–21; 28:23–28).

ENCOUNTERS
WITH PERSECUTION
AND IDOLATRY

The extensive treatment of Paul's ministry in Pisidian Antioch is followed by a summary account of his ministry in Iconium. There are similarities between the two accounts. Both begin with preaching in the synagogue and end with a crisis that forces Paul and Barnabas to leave the city. Nevertheless, Acts 14:1–6 does not simply report rejection by Jews and success with Gentiles, as Paul's announcement in 13:46–47 might lead us to expect. Details of the narrative prevent us from reducing Paul's ministry to this simple formula.

Note first that the preaching in the Iconium synagogue was a great success. "A great multitude of both Jews and Greeks believed" (14:1). The "Greeks" here are evidently Gentiles previously attracted to the synagogue. There is also resistance, however, from some Jews, who are able to gain support from Gentiles (14:2). Paul and Barnabas continue their preaching in the face of this resistance, with the result that "the multitude of the city was split" between support for "the Jews"[1] and the missionaries. Gentiles as well as Jews oppose Paul and Barnabas, for 14:5 reports an effort "of both Gentiles and Jews, with their rulers," to stone the missionaries. In this case the Gentiles are mentioned first. So Iconium is a divided city, but not on an ethnic basis. There are Jews and Gentiles on both sides of the division, and there are Gentiles among the active persecutors. Paul's statement in 13:46–47 is not meant to establish a rigid pattern of Jewish rejection and Gentile acceptance. Even in 13:50 the Jewish opponents are able to drive out Paul and Barnabas only because they gain the support of leading Gentiles in the city. The following description of the Iconium mission suggests that there is some variety in the responses encountered in various locations.

The schematic description of the mission in Iconium follows the pattern of the mission in Jerusalem more closely than the pattern of the mission in Antioch of Pisidia. To be sure, it adds an important role for Gentiles. As in 14:1–2 the Jerusalem mission was a great success (2:41; 4:4; 5:14) but

---

[1] In vv. 1–2 the narrative distinguishes between believing and unbelieving Jews. "The Jews" in v. 4 refers to the latter.

also aroused opposition (beginning in 4:1–3). The description of Paul and Barnabas' response echoes events in Jerusalem. The reference to bold speaking supported by the witness of signs and wonders can be understood as indication that the Lord continues to act as previously when the Jerusalem church prayed in response to the first opposition. They prayed that the Lord might "give to your servants to speak your word with all boldness, while you stretch out your hand for healing and signs and wonders to continue happening" (4:29–30). References to the Lord giving, to speaking with boldness (μετὰ παρρησίας πάσης λαλεῖν, παρρησιαζόμενοι), and to signs and wonders happening (σημεῖα καὶ τέρατα γίνεσθαι) are found in both 4:29–30 and 14:3.[2] The best parallel to opposition from "both Gentiles and Jews, with their rulers" (14:5), is found as part of this same prayer of the Jerusalem church, which includes "the rulers (οἱ ἄρχοντες)" along with Gentiles and "peoples of Israel" in the opposition to Jesus, which is now reawakening (4:25–27). The reference to stoning (planned in 14:5, performed in 14:19) also recalls the stoning of Stephen.[3] Thus the apostles and Stephen's bold witness and the accompanying power of the Lord reappear in the mission of Paul and Barnabas as they encounter opposition.

The echoes of the Jerusalem mission continue into the following account of Paul healing a lame man. The narrative is briefly told, and the narrator focuses primary attention on the crowd's reaction to it. However, both the manner of the telling and its relation to its setting echo the healing of the lame man at the temple gate in 3:1–10. Although any two stories of healings of lame men may have elements in common because of the subject matter, some phrases in these two scenes are strikingly similar. In 14:8 "a certain man . . . lame from the womb of his mother" exactly repeats the introduction of the lame man in 3:2. The responsive gaze of the healer is mentioned (ἀτενίσας in both 14:9 and 3:4). The reference to Paul seeing the man's faith is more like Luke 5:20 (Jesus' healing of the paralytic) than anything in 3:1–10, but in 3:16 Peter does relate the healing to faith. The commands to rise or walk and the report that the lame man did walk are expected elements, but the shared references to leaping (3:8; 14:10) are not. These are the only references to a lame or

---

[2] The reference to signs and wonders in 14:3 also resembles 5:12, a verse that indicates the answer to the prayer in 4:30.

[3] The rare noun ὁρμή (only here in Luke-Acts, once more in NT) matches the verb in the description of Stephen's stoning (7:57). Stephen's hearers "rushed" together, cast him out of the city, and stoned him. I would suggest that ὁρμή in 14:5 refers to the "onrush" of a mob and συνιδόντες in 14:6 means not that Paul and Barnabas heard of this indirectly but that the mob actually came within range of their vision. See H. Liddell, R. Scott, H. Jones, *Greek-English Lexicon*, on these two words. If so, this is a much more dramatic escape than the pale translation in RSV indicates.

paralyzed man "leaping" (using ἄλλομαι or ἐξάλλομαι) in the New Testament. They are followed in both cases by indications that the people or the crowds saw and responded, leading to the next stage of the narrative.[4]

Some further observations show that we are not merely dealing with common elements of healing stories: (1) Consider the location of the stories. In both cases they are the first specific act of healing by the apostles, on the one hand, and by Paul, on the other. We have already seen that Paul's healing is preceded by material recalling the Jerusalem mission of the apostles and Stephen, and the speeches of Peter in Acts 2 and of Paul in Acts 13, both highlighted at the beginning of new missions, are similar in content and have similar positions before the healing.[5] (2) Both healing stories are in contexts of gathering opposition (4:1–3; 14:5–6, 19–20). (3) Both lead to an encounter with the crowd in which the missionary must begin with a rebuke, "Men [of Israel], why . . . ("Ανδρες ['Ισραηλῖται], τί)" (3:12; 14:15). (4) The healing results in a similar problem, although expressed in a Jewish setting in the one case and a pagan setting in the other. There is a tendency to confuse the power that heals with the healer himself, and the healer acts immediately to set the record straight.[6] In 14:15 the necessary rebuke leads into Paul's main message, for he goes on to proclaim a God who is neither like human beings nor like the "vain things" that humans create. It may seem that Paul is reacting to gross superstition, but 3:12 suggests that even people who abhor idolatry may sometimes dangerously confuse saving power with its human medium.

The crowd's mistaken identification of Barnabas and Paul with Zeus and Hermes and the plan of the priest of Zeus to offer sacrifice provide a dramatic setting for Paul's short speech to Gentiles untouched by the Jewish synagogue. These people are not like Cornelius, "devout and fearing God" (10:2), that is, the one God of the Bible, nor like the God-fearers who come to the synagogues. Here the mission takes a new step, and Paul faces a new challenge. In this scene the problem of mission among such people appears in sharp focus.[7] Far from suggesting that the further the mission moves from Judaism the more receptive people will

---

[4] G. Schneider, *Apostelgeschichte* 1:307–8, provides a chart comparing Luke 5:17–26; Acts 3:1–10; and 14:8–11.

[5] See above, 160–62, where other points of similarity between the beginning of the mission of the apostles and the beginning of Paul's mission in Acts 13—14 are noted.

[6] The sensitivity of Peter on this issue also appears in the Cornelius story, where Peter corrects Cornelius for treating him as more than a man (10:25–26).

[7] G. Krodel, *Acts*, 257, comments, "If the faith of the lame man illustrates the promise of the Gentile mission, then the reaction of the crowd points out the problem of pagan superstition which the mission encounters."

be, the narrator sees a special obstacle where people do not believe in the one God who has created all. The mission must begin with a call to "turn to a living God" (14:15) from idols. This is a call to repentance from past ignorance of God (see 17:30). Although the reason for repentance is quite different than in Peter's sermons to the people of Jerusalem, repentance is necessary in both cases. The crowd's ignorance of God is dramatically demonstrated in the scene as they confuse Barnabas and Paul with divine beings and prepare a very inappropriate sacrifice.

Both this brief speech and the longer speech in Athens (17:22–31) show careful reflection on the problem of approaching Gentiles who do not share the biblical story nor Judaism's belief in one God, major premises for other speeches in Acts. Paul in Lystra recognizes that various peoples have had various religions and does not harshly condemn their religious histories. He says, "In past generations [God] permitted all the nations to go in their ways" (14:16), but Paul assumes that he stands at a turning point in world religion. The time of ethnic permissiveness in religion, a time of ignorance and trust in "vain things," is drawing to a close. As Paul will say in Athens, now God "commands people that all everywhere repent" of their idolatry (17:30). Idolatry diminishes the divine to human size (as in the mistaken identification of Barnabas and Paul with divinities) and makes God dependent on human actions and subject to human control. Concerns over these issues will be clearer in the Athens speech, where not only the making of images is rejected but also the location of God in temples and the supplying of divine needs through sacrifices. When Gentiles do repent of their idolatry, they will find the God who always has been the basis of their life and the source of the good gifts that they constantly receive. God is their creator also, and the gifts of nature have always been a witness to God's goodness. Although they have not been part of Israel's history, the sustaining fruitfulness of nature can be understood by all as witness to the goodness of the universal creator whom Paul preaches. This affirmation of nature as witness to the goodness of the transcendent God is rare in the New Testament. However, it recalls Old Testament themes.[8] It also provides a point of contact between the biblical tradition and other traditions, enabling Jesus' witnesses to speak to Gentiles untouched by the Bible. Although their varying histories tend to divide peoples, the sustaining goodness of nature is a shared experience of many peoples, testifying to God's goodness across ethnic lines.[9] In speaking to these Gentiles, Paul affirms Jewish monotheism but makes

---

[8] See Ps. 145:15–16 (144:15–16 LXX); 147:8–9 (146:8–9 LXX); Jer. 5:24. The description of God as creator in Acts 14:15 repeats Exod. 20:11; Ps. 146:6 (145:6 LXX).

[9] Partly for this reason, nature may have an importance in interreligious dialogue that it has, in large part, been denied in traditional Christian theology.

clear that the Jewish God is no tribal divinity with parochial concerns. Gentiles, too, are the beneficiaries of the sustaining goodness of the universal creator.

The narrative quickly shifts to the appearance of Jews from Antioch and Iconium, who are able to gain local support and stone Paul, leaving him for dead (14:19). Attributing this act to Jews from Antioch and Iconium connects the references to opposition in the previous two cities to this event in Lystra, making it the climax of a narrative sequence. The opposition builds from Antioch, where Paul and Barnabas are cast out, to Iconium, where there is an attempt to stone them, to Lystra, where Paul is actually stoned. Some of the same opponents are behind these actions. They persist in their opposition until they think they have succeeded in ridding the area of Paul. The interest shown in the persecution of Paul and Barnabas in the sequence of three cities, coming to a climax in an actual stoning, indicates the importance of this theme for the narrator.[10] Paul's first mission journey, like his ministry in Damascus and Jerusalem, shows the fulfillment of the Lord's prophecy of how much Paul "must suffer for my name" (9:16). Paul and Barnabas conduct a successful mission, but persistent opponents are able to mobilize dangerous opposition and reach out beyond their own cities to attack Paul.

As soon as Paul revives, he returns to the city. Then, after work in Derbe, Paul and Barnabas return to Lystra, Iconium, and Antioch. This return shows courage and commitment to their calling because these places have proved to be dangerous.[11]

Paul and Barnabas return to the new churches in order to strengthen the disciples there. The missionaries do not abandon the churches but continue to show pastoral care. Paul's role as pastor to Christians is most fully presented in his farewell speech to the Ephesian elders (20:18–35), but its importance is also indicated by repeated brief references to care for established churches by Paul, Barnabas, and others. This care is called "strengthening" the disciples (using ἐπιστηρίζω 14:22; 15:32 [by Judas and Silas], 41; 18:23; cf. 16:5). It involves urging disciples to "persevere in" or "stick with" the faith (ἐμμένω 14:22; προσμένω 11:23 [by Barnabas]; 13:43). There are also repeated references to leaders exhorting or encouraging the churches (using παρακαλέω 11:23 [by Barnabas]; 14:22;

---

[10] This observation counts against E. Haenchen's contention that Luke intends to play down Paul's sufferings. See *Acts*, 434. R. Pervo satirizes this scene, calling Paul "the typical superhero, able to shrug off a beating that would have killed any ordinary man, then return without hesitation or delay to his appointed task." See *Profit with Delight*, 26. However, the abbreviated report of Paul's recovery in v. 20 allows us to picture the scene as we will, with either a vigorous Paul marching back to town or a battered one limping between supporting colleagues.

[11] See J. Dupont, *Nouvelles études*, 350.

15:32 [by Judas and Silas]; 16:40; 20:1, 2). In interpreting the parable of the sower, Jesus contrasted those without root who would believe only for a time with those who will hold fast the word and bear fruit with endurance (Luke 8:13, 15). Paul and Barnabas are working to build churches full of the latter kind of Christian.[12]

Paul and Barnabas also tell the disciples, "Through many oppressions we must (δεῖ) enter into the reign of God" (14:22). Why is this particular warning placed at this point in the narrative? It is no doubt intended to prepare the disciples to face oppression that may come in the future, but it also relates to the oppression that Paul and Barnabas (especially Paul) have already experienced. The preceding narrative has not emphasized the suffering of local Christians but the persecution that Paul and Barnabas have experienced in three different cities. Thus their warning about the necessity of facing oppression is a warning based on their own experience. It epitomizes the narrative sequence of persistent persecution in 13:50—14:20. It does so in a way that not only recalls the Lord's prophecy about Paul's suffering but also recalls what Jesus said about the necessity of his own suffering. In both kinds of statements δεῖ ("must") was an important word (Luke 9:22; 17:25; 24:7; Acts 9:16). Because the oppressions are the required way to "enter into" the reign of God, the formulation is especially close to Luke 24:26, where the Messiah's suffering is the required way for him to "enter into his glory" (expressed with the past tense of δεῖ). Jesus suffered in accordance with a pattern of prophetic destiny that applied not only to him but to other prophets before him.[13] The same destiny of suffering applies to Paul and Barnabas, and in 14:22 they warn that it will apply to other Christians, too.

The care of Paul and Barnabas for the churches also leads to the choice of elders as local leaders. Paul's dedicated care for a church will be more fully presented in his speech to the Ephesian elders, which also develops the theme of suffering (14:22; 20:22-24) and repeats the act of entrusting the church or its leaders to God or the Lord Jesus as Paul departs (14:23; 20:32). The brief reference to Paul strengthening the churches at the end of the first missionary journey becomes a scene with a major speech at the end of the last missionary journey. There we will hear more about Paul's commitment to the churches and his exhortation to persevere in the faith.

The return to home base brings the missionary journey to an end. Antioch is described as the place where they "had been delivered to the grace of God for the work that they fulfilled" (14:26), a reminder of 13:1-3. This description calls attention to the *inclusio* or envelope pattern that

---

[12] See J. Dupont, *Nouvelles études,* 351.

[13] On Luke 24:26 and the prophetic destiny of suffering, see *Narrative Unity* 1:284-89.

characterizes the missionaries' movement. They "had been delivered to the grace of God," and their report of "how many things God had done with them" showed that the grace of God was effective in their work. The successful mission of Paul and Barnabas is viewed as a significant sign of the power and purpose of God behind the mission that they conducted. The importance of the completed mission as testimony to God's purpose appears from the repetition in Jerusalem of this report about "how many things God had done with them" (15:4; cf. 15:12).

Paul and Barnabas especially conclude that God has "opened for the Gentiles a door of faith." This is not the only important thing that happened on the journey. The emphasis placed on Paul's synagogue speech and on the missionaries' suffering should not be forgotten. This epitomizing statement is highlighted at the end of the journey because it leads to the next development, the conflict in Acts 15 over the status of Gentiles in the church. The reference to a "door of faith" prepares for the emphasis that Peter will place on faith as the means of cleansing for Gentiles and the way of salvation for both Jews and Gentiles (15:9, 11).

Acts 13—14 presents a representative picture of Paul's mission and includes many themes that we will encounter again.[14] He preaches first in the Jewish synagogue but turns to the Gentiles when synagogue preaching is no longer possible. He announces the one God to Gentiles who have had no contact with Jewish monotheism. He repeatedly encounters persecution and moves on when necessary, but he does not abandon his mission. He works signs and wonders. He strengthens the new churches. In this mission Paul is fulfilling the Lord's prophecy that he would "bear my name before Gentiles and kings[15] and sons of Israel" and "must suffer for my name" (9:15–16).

---

[14] Edwin Nelson writes of the anticipatory nature of the first missionary journey and sees it as typifying what Paul will face throughout his ministry. See *Paul's First Missionary Journey as Paradigm*, 70–71, 101–2.

[15] Recall Sergius Paulus in 13:6–12. Paul has not yet appeared before a king, but he has converted a high Roman official.

A DISPUTE RESOLVED
IN JERUSALEM

A crisis between the Antioch church and the church of the Jewish homeland arises when some come from Judea and claim that gentile Christians
must be circumcised in order to be saved (15:1). This demand produces
"no little dispute" (the narrator's way of saying a *big* dispute), and the
Antioch church takes action, sending Paul, Barnabas, and some others to
Jerusalem. Paul and Barnabas are official representatives of the Antioch
church in this matter (cf. 15:2). If the Jerusalem church supports the
demand for circumcision and if no resolution of the dispute can be found,
then the relation of friendly support between the churches in Antioch and
Jerusalem will be gravely threatened.

On their journey Paul and Barnabas report the conversion of the
Gentiles through their mission; disciples in Phoenicia and Samaria
respond with joy. The gentile mission of Paul and Barnabas has widespread support outside Judea, but the support of the Jerusalem church is
now in question. Upon arrival in Jerusalem the delegates from Antioch
are received, but some believers from the Pharisees immediately repeat
the demand of circumcision made in Antioch, adding that Gentiles must
keep the law of Moses (15:5). The result again is "much dispute" (15:7).
The crucial significance of the following statements by Peter and James
becomes fully apparent when we realize that they are responding to a
dispute that has been carried on with considerable vehemence, threatening the unity between the Judean church and the new mission areas.
The mission faces a major crisis.

Paul and Barnabas are received not only by "the apostles and elders"
but also by "the assembly" (ἐκκλησία = "church" in RSV), according to
15:4. Only the apostles and elders are mentioned in v. 6, but the meeting is
evidently open to all disciples, for v. 12 refers to "all the multitude"[1] and
"the whole assembly" participates in the decision in v. 22.[2] Peter and
James play important roles in the decision, but the scene gives the impres-

---

[1] In 15:30 the Christian assembly is also called τὸ πλῆθος ("the multitude").
[2] The participation of the whole community is emphasized by A. Weiser, "'Apostelkonzil,'"
163–64.

sion that their authority is informal—resting on the respect they have gained and lasting as long as they can persuade their fellow apostles and elders, and the assembly as a whole, to follow. The speeches in 15:7–21 are the necessary means of persuasion. It is also important that the decision in Jerusalem is accepted by the church in Antioch (15:31).

The dispute is resolved through three speeches that together present a single persuasive interpretation of God's purpose. The problem is resolved by reviewing the indications of God's purpose in the past. First, Peter reviews what he learned through the Cornelius episode (10:1— 11:18). Then Barnabas and Paul review their recent mission (13:1— 14:28). This review is confined to a single verse because these events have recently been narrated. Furthermore, Barnabas and Paul do not need to make a theological case, for Peter and James will do that for them. Nevertheless, specific signs of God's work among the Gentiles in an effective mission constitute part of the evidence on which a decision must be based, and v. 12 reminds us of the importance of this evidence. Finally, James shows that Scripture agrees with the experience of the church in its mission. Adequate clarity comes when the experience of those active in the mission correlates with those aspects of the biblical tradition that present the saving purpose of God in its widest dimensions. The speeches mesh into a coherent understanding of the purpose of God with respect to the Gentiles, providing the basis for the church's decision.

Peter reminds the assembly of things well known, although some are failing to apply this knowledge to the present issue. He begins, "Brothers, you know . . . ," and reviews what he learned through his encounter with Cornelius. In a sense he regards the issue as having been decided long ago, but to demonstrate this, Peter must carry his own thinking about the past further than he has before. In 11:5–17 Peter recounted the story of Cornelius and himself in some detail in responding to criticism of his association with Gentiles. In 15:7–11 Peter approaches the same events from a different perspective. Acts 11:5–16 is personal narrative, recounting events as Peter experienced them, with a brief theological conclusion in v. 17. Acts 15:7–11 is a distinctly theological statement. In vv. 7–9 Peter indicates what God was doing in these events. He says that God chose, God testified, God did not discriminate, correlating each of these actions of God with a part of the Cornelius episode. God's act of choosing resulted in Peter's preaching and the Gentiles' faith (cf. 10:34–43). God's testimony appeared in the unexpected gift of the Spirit to these Gentiles (cf. 10:44– 47). God's refusal to discriminate against Gentiles (see the related statement about God in 10:34) is revealed in the removal of the Gentiles' uncleanness. God's cleansing of the Gentiles (15:9) recalls the heavenly voice in Peter's vision (cf. 10:15). Peter is drawing emphatic theological conclusions from specific aspects of his past experience. He applies them to the present issue in 15:10–11, asserting that the demand for Gentiles to be circumcised and obey the Mosaic law puts God to the test, provokes God, when God has made clear that Gentiles have already been accepted on a different basis. These concluding verses speak directly to the claims that caused the dispute, for v. 10 refers to the demand in v. 5 that Gentiles keep the law and v. 11 refers to what is required in order to be saved (cf. v. 1).[3]

Putting God to the test by demanding that Gentiles obey the law is roughly equivalent to trying to "hinder" God's clear purpose, something that Peter recognized he could not do (11:17). In both 10:1—11:18 and 15:7–11 the fact that God treated the Gentiles the same as the Jews, giving both the Holy Spirit, plays an important role in convincing Peter and his fellow Jews (10:47; 11:15–17; 15:8–9). Peter will finally conclude that Jews and Gentiles are saved on the same basis and that obedience to the law is not a factor in either case (15:10–11).

Thus the issue at hand leads Peter to draw a far-reaching conclusion about the basis of salvation. This conclusion applies to Jews as well as Gentiles. God has taught Peter through his experience with Cornelius that both Jews and Gentiles are saved by grace received in faith: "But through the grace of the Lord Jesus we have faith so as to be saved,[4] just as they do" (15:11). Salvation is here linked not only to grace but also to faith.[5] It is a mistake to understand πιστεύομεν ("we believe, have faith") in the weakened sense of "we think, are convinced," for Peter has already emphasized faith in the preceding speech. His conclusion in v. 11 must be understood in light of this emphasis. In v. 7 Peter spoke of God's choice that through Peter the Gentiles should "hear the word of the gospel and believe (πιστεῦσαι)." In v. 9 he developed this, saying that God had "cleansed their hearts by faith (τῇ πίστει)." In v. 11 he concludes that all are saved by faith through grace. Both the emphasis on the similarity of Jews and Gentiles and the reference to believing in this concluding statement develop themes from vv. 8–9.

Peter's interpretation of the Cornelius episode in 15:7–11 considerably strengthens the emphasis on faith. Peter did end his sermon before Cornelius by stating that "everyone who believes in" Jesus receives release of sins (10:43), and in 11:17 receiving the Spirit is related to believing. However, the statement that the cleansing of the Gentiles takes place

---

[3] See E. Richard, "Divine Purpose," 191; J. Dupont, "Un peuple d'entre les nations," 331, n. 17.

[4] Infinitive of result. Cf. BDF, no. 391,4.

[5] See J. Nolland, "A Fresh Look at Acts 15.10," 112–13. Nolland notes that believing and being saved are linked in Luke 8:12 and Acts 16:31, as well as in the healing stories in Luke 8:50; 17:19; Acts 14:9.

through faith is new, and the statement that salvation for both Jew and Gentile comes through grace and faith, not through the law, expresses the matter with new sharpness.

The closest previous parallel is the end of Paul's synagogue speech, where Paul speaks of the inadequacy of the law and says that in Jesus "everyone who believes is justified" (13:38–39).[6] The thinking of the historical Paul about the law survives only in a much weakened form in Acts, but I have no doubt that the narrator intends to preserve Paul's message of justification by grace through faith in these two passages. It is not a minor point, for 15:11 is the epitome of what Peter has been taught by God through his experience with Cornelius. It is also the central insight that should guide the Jerusalem church in its decision.

Peter's speech produces a change in the audience. Previously there was "much dispute" (15:7), but the multitude is now silent (v. 12) and willing to listen further to Barnabas and Paul's account of God's activity in their mission among Gentiles. Then James speaks. James is not introduced to the reader either in 15:13 or previously in 12:17. Evidently the narrator assumes that he is a well-known figure. James refers to Peter by the Semitic name Symeon, which indirectly shows that James is a representative of the Aramaic-speaking church. At this point the narrator is using the rhetorical art of "impersonation ($\pi\rho o\sigma\omega\pi o\pi o\iota\acute{a}$)," composing a speech appropriate to the narrative character and the setting.[7]

James begins by referring to Peter's speech, which he supports by citing Scripture. His summary of Peter's speech throws new light on the Cornelius episode. In v. 7 Peter said that "God chose ($\grave{\epsilon}\xi\epsilon\lambda\acute{\epsilon}\xi\alpha\tau o$)," but it was not entirely clear whether this was a choice of Peter for a special role, a choice that the Gentiles should receive the gospel, or both. Now James describes the event as God's choice of a people, using language reminiscent of God's choice of Israel according to Scripture: "God visited to take from the nations [or "Gentiles"] a people for his name." God's choice pertains not only to Peter but to a people. The events directing Peter and Cornelius to each other and the subsequent coming of the Spirit have the same meaning for Gentiles as the election of Israel has for the Jewish people. The God who chose Israel continues to act in the same way, calling a people as a special possession, now from non-Israelites also. This

---

[6] This connection is noted by K. Löning, "Paulinismus in der Apostelgeschichte," 226, in discussing 15:11. However, he ignores $\pi\iota\sigma\tau\epsilon\acute{u}o\mu\epsilon\nu$ in this verse.

[7] Training in "impersonation" was one of the prescribed "elementary exercises" in Greco-Roman education. D. Clark, *Rhetoric in Greco-Roman Education,* 199, explains: Students were asked to "compose an imaginary monolog which might appropriately be spoken or written by a historical, legendary, or fictitious person under given circumstances." See also W. Kurz, "Hellenistic Rhetoric," 186.

expansion of the people of God began when Peter and Cornelius were guided to their encounter.

Note the weighty language used in 15:14 and in a related passage in 18:10. Contrary to the narrator's normal pattern of reserving the term λαός ("people") for Jews,[8] these two passages apply the term to Gentiles. As J. Dupont has argued, these two applications of λαός to Gentiles do not weaken the sense of the word but use it with its full theological force.[9] The speakers are making the important affirmation that Gentiles can be God's λαός in the full sense that Israel is. In 18:10 the Lord says, "There is a large people for me (λαός ἐστί μοι πολύς) in this city." Similar formulations with the verb εἰμί and a dative complement are found in Pentateuchal passages that affirm Israel's place as the chosen people. In Exod. 19:5 we read, "You shall be for me a special people from all the nations[10] (ἔσεσθέ μοι λαὸς περιούσιος ἀπὸ πάντων τῶν ἐθνῶν)" (cf. Exod. 23:22 LXX; Deut. 7:6; 14:2). This statement resembles Acts 18:10, but it also resembles Acts 15:14 in its reference to the "nations." However, in 15:14 "from the nations (ἐξ ἐθνῶν)" indicates the origin and nature of those being chosen. They are Gentiles, not Jews, yet they are now God's people. Other phrases used in the Septuagint to describe God's choice of Israel at the exodus resemble Acts 15:14. According to James, Peter related how God "visited (ἐπεσκέψατο)," a word previously used in Luke-Acts of God's concerned approach to save Israel through sending Jesus Messiah (Luke 1:68, 78; 7:16; cf. 19:44). The Septuagint also speaks of God's visitation of Israel at the time of the exodus (Exod. 3:16; 4:31).[11] James says that God "visited to take a people for his name." This resembles God's instructions to Moses, who is to say in God's name, "I will take you for myself as a people for me (λήμψομαι ἐμαυτῷ ὑμᾶς λαὸν ἐμοί)" (Exod. 6:7 LXX; cf. Deut. 4:20, 34).[12]

Thus a series of election texts in the Septuagint provides patterns for the formulations in Acts 15:14 and 18:10. The resulting biblical style is important to the message. The Gentiles now turning to God are God's people in the full sense that Israel is, for the God who long ago chose a people for communion and mission is doing the same now among the other peoples of the world.[13]

What God is doing among the Gentiles fits God's ancient purpose announced in Scripture, according to James. He quotes Amos 9:11–12,

---

[8] On the use of this term in Luke-Acts, see *Narrative Unity* 1:143–44.

[9] See "Un peuple d'entre les nations," 326–29.

[10] This probably means special in comparison with all the other nations.

[11] See L. T. Johnson, *Decision Making in the Church,* 84.

[12] See N. A. Dahl, "A People for His Name," 323.

[13] Zechariah 2:15 LXX (2:11 ET) proclaims that many Gentiles will become God's people, anticipating the statement of Acts 15:14.

which indicates that God will rebuild the hut of David in order that the Gentiles might seek the Lord. How the rebuilding of David's hut serves the cause of the Gentiles is not made clear in this quotation. In fact, this strange sequence of events is the result of a mistranslation in the Septuagint, for the Hebrew text does not refer to "the rest of humans" seeking the Lord.[14] Nevertheless, it is especially this strange sequence of events that James (and the narrator) finds revelatory for interpreting Jesus and the mission of his witnesses. We have noted on a number of occasions the importance of Scripture quotations (especially longer quotations highlighted in a speech) for understanding how the narrative is fulfilling the divine purpose. The present quotation belongs with others that provide important clues to the meaning of the narrative from God's perspective.

Although Acts 15:17 follows the Septuagint of Amos 9:12 fairly closely, the preceding verse retains the basic sense of the Septuagint but differs significantly in wording. Acts 15:16 forms a neat chiasm built around four first-person singular future verbs beginning with the prefix $\dot{\alpha}\nu$-.

> After these things *I will return*
>   And *I will rebuild* the hut of David that has fallen
>   And its demolished ruins *I will rebuild*
> And *I will restore* it.

Not only do the longer interior and shorter exterior lines balance, but also the verbs are placed in balancing positions within those lines.[15] Although the Septuagint twice uses the verb $\dot{\alpha}\nu\alpha\sigma\tau\dot{\eta}\sigma\omega$ ("I will raise up"), this verb does not appear in the version of Amos 9:11 in Acts. It is a verb used repeatedly in Acts of God's resurrection of Jesus (Acts 2:24, 32; 3:26; 13:33, 34; 17:31). The absence of this verb weakens the case of those who interpret the rebuilding of the hut of David as primarily a reference to Jesus' resurrection.[16] There may indeed be a connection with Jesus' resurrection, but that is not the primary point of emphasis in this quotation. The primary point is also obscured when v. 16 is understood to refer to the restoration or gathering of Israel.[17] Here there is too little attention to the rebuilding of the hut of *David* in this verse. In major scenes in Luke-Acts Jesus is proclaimed as the fulfillment of the promise of a restored Davidic kingdom. This central theme cannot be ignored when James

---

[14] The fact that the application to the issue depends on the LXX is a fault in the narrator's attempt at "impersonation" (a fault of which the narrator and most readers were probably unaware). See above, 186.

[15] See J. Dupont, "Je rebâtirai la cabane de David," 24–25.

[16] G. Schneider, *Apostelgeschichte* 2:182–83, understands v. 16 to refer not to the Davidic kingdom or to the true Israel but (quoting Haenchen) to the story of Jesus culminating in the resurrection. E. Richard, "Creative Use of Amos," 44–52, and J. Dupont, "Je rebâtirai la cabane de David," 22–27, explain v. 16 as deliberate Lukan redaction of the LXX. They believe that Luke wanted to avoid using $\dot{\alpha}\nu\alpha\sigma\tau\dot{\eta}\sigma\omega$ with the hut of David as object.

[17] See J. Jervell, *Luke and the People of God*, 51–53; G. Lohfink, *Sammlung Israels*, 59.

speaks of the rebuilding of the hut of David.[18] This theme is repeated in the birth narrative (Luke 1:32–33, 69; 2:10–11) and is highlighted by Peter (Acts 2:30–36) and Paul (13:22–23, 32–34) in their sermons to Jews. The seating of Jesus on David's throne and installation as royal Son of God have already taken place through Jesus' resurrection and exaltation to the right hand of God. Of course, this should also mean the restoration of Israel, for, as Zechariah indicated in Luke 1:68–69, the coming of the Messiah means "redemption for his people" and God's raising of "a horn of salvation for us." However, the question of whether Israel has already been sufficiently incorporated into the Messiah's kingdom is not being discussed by James. The Scripture has been fulfilled because the Davidic heir has been installed as reigning Lord at God's right hand. That is the primary point of Acts 15:16.[19]

Stephen, in relating Israel's history, said that Israel rejected Moses and "turned in their hearts to Egypt." Then God "turned (ἔστρεψεν)" from them (7:39, 42). James carries Israel's story further by citing God's promise that "I will return (ἀναστρέψω)" (15:16; not in Amos 9:11 LXX).[20] This is a new stage of Israel's history in which the separation between the people and its God is overcome. The sign of this is the establishment of the messianic kingdom for Israel. This will also be a new stage of Israel's relation to the Gentiles, who will seek out Israel's Lord. James is proclaiming the Messiah previously announced in Luke's birth narrative, the one who would "reign over the house of Jacob" on "the throne of David his father" (Luke 1:32–33) and bring salvation to Israel (1:69–71) but who was also called a "light for revelation of the Gentiles," bringing salvation to all flesh (2:30–32; 3:6). James recalls the prophecy concerning this Messiah who would be savior of both Israel and the Gentiles, reminding us of opening themes in the Lukan narrative, because the participation of the Gentiles is now in progress and the church must affirm this development.

Next James draws a conclusion from the agreement that he has noted between Peter's interpretation of mission experience and the witness of

---

[18] The reference to a "hut" or "tent" of David is part of the rebuilding metaphor in this verse. J. Dupont understands it as a reference to the "house," that is, family, of David in its diminished state since the end of the monarchy. See "Je rebâtirai la cabane de David," 31. It could also refer to the rule of the Davidic king, represented by the place from which he rules.

[19] J. Dupont, whose interpretation I am adopting, adds other important evidence, including the repeated use of ἀνορθόω ("restore"), which occurs in Acts 15:16 but not in Amos 9:11 LXX, in Nathan's oracle to David (see the LXX of 2 Sam. 7:13, 16; I Chron. 17:12, 14, 24; 22:10) and the association of the Nathan oracle with Amos 9:11 in 4QFlor. See "Je rebâtirai la cabane de David," 27, 29.

[20] E. Richard notes this connection between the version of Amos 9:11 in Acts 15:16 and the setting for the previous Amos quotation in Acts 7:42–43. See "Divine Purpose," 195; "Creative Use of Amos," 49–50.

Scripture. In v. 19 James turns to the issue at hand and concludes that it would be wrong to "trouble" the gentile converts. He seems to agree with Peter's rejection of the demand that Gentiles submit to the "yoke" of the law (v. 10). Nevertheless, there are certain things from which Gentiles should abstain, and these are listed in v. 20. Both the relation of these rules to the Jewish law and the motive for their inclusion in Acts are unclear. They are commonly understood to be a summary of the regulations for Gentiles living in Israel in Lev. 17:8—18:18.[21] This connection is not certain.[22] James does not explain the reason for these rules, except, perhaps, in v. 21. This verse might be understood as support for v. 19, arguing that it is not necessary for Gentiles to follow the law, for Moses still has plenty of supporters and there is no danger that the Mosaic way of life will disappear. However, v. 21 probably supports v. 20. Calling attention to the long-standing and widespread enculturation in Mosaic law through the synagogues, it points to the need for the regulations in v. 20. The underlying point would be that gentile Christians need to find ways of living with people deeply committed to Mosaic law. Jewish Christians may be the primary concern, but v. 21 does not refer only to them. The concern to correct the view that the Christian mission is an attack on Judaism and its way of life, apparent in Paul's defense scenes (cf., e.g., 21:20-28; 22:3; 28:17, 19), may also be a factor here.

There are some further indications that concern for the effect of a gentile church on practicing Jews stands behind the regulations that James is proposing. In 16:1-3 we may have a parallel case. Timothy, whose mother was Jewish but his father Greek, was uncircumcised. Paul "circumcised him because of the Jews who were in those places." An uncircumcised man from a Jewish mother would be an offense to Jews, so Paul is willing to circumcise Timothy. In this case circumcision is not viewed as an improper imposition of Jewish regulations on a Gentile. Rather, Paul, and evidently the narrator, assumes that it is right to take Jewish feelings into account. The story continues in the next verse (16:4) by reporting that Paul and his companions delivered to churches the regulations for Gentiles proposed by James and accepted in Jerusalem. This activity probably arises from the same concern not to offend Jews.[23]

The regulations for Gentiles are recalled a final time in 21:25. The

---

[21] See, e.g., H. Conzelmann, *Acts*, 118-19; G. Schneider, *Apostelgeschichte* 2:187.

[22] See the problems raised by S. G. Wilson, *Luke and the Law*, 84-94.

[23] K. Löning notes that 16:3-4 helps us to understand the purpose of the regulations for the Gentiles proposed by James. See "Paulinismus in der Apostelgeschichte," 228. R. Brawley, *Luke-Acts and the Jews*, 151-52, views the decision of the Jerusalem council and the circumcision of Timothy as instances of a "pattern of conciliatory action . . . for the sake of unity with Jewish Christians." He cites Paul's participation in temple ritual (21:23-26) as a third instance.

setting seems strange at first, but it may actually illuminate the purpose of these regulations. Paul has just arrived in Jerusalem. He learns that Jewish Christians have been told that he "teaches all the Jews living among the Gentiles apostasy from Moses, saying that they should not circumcise their children nor walk by the customs" (21:21). His informants then propose that Paul demonstrate his own fidelity to the cultic law and add that they have already written gentile believers to avoid certain things (repeating the prescriptions of the letter in 15:29). This addition makes sense in context only if these regulations for Gentiles are a relevant response to the accusation in 21:21. The Jerusalem Christians are pointing to two things that can correct this mistaken accusation: Paul's demonstration of his fidelity to the law and the fact that the church has already taken measures to avoid putting pressure on Jews to give up life according to Mosaic law. Acts 21:21 shows that the problem is no longer the demands being made on Gentiles to become Jews but the pressure being felt by Jews to conform to a Gentile way of life. This pressure would strengthen as Gentiles become the majority within the church. Jewish Christians might then have to choose withdrawal into isolation or "apostasy from Moses." The Jerusalem meeting that guarantees the Gentiles' freedom from the law also anticipates the problem that will arise as the gentile portion of the church grows, for James is proposing that Gentiles be asked to abstain from certain things especially offensive to a Jewish sense of cultic purity so that Jewish Christians may remain in the fellowship of the church without being forced to give up their way of life.

The assembly as a whole will accept this proposal and make it part of their letter. Then it will be joyfully accepted in Antioch (15:31) and actively promoted by Paul. Although the letter is addressed only to gentile Christians in Antioch, Syria, and Cilicia (15:23), Paul delivers the regulations for observance by believers in the churches founded on his first missionary journey (15:36; 16:1–4). James' proposal is not accepted reluctantly but is embraced as a solution to an important problem. The Jerusalem council not only recognizes the freedom of Gentiles from the law but also acts to protect the religious culture of Jews.

The narrator demonstrates an active interest in the so-called apostolic decree by the attention it receives in the narrative and the indications of positive response by the Antioch church and Paul. It is fully cited three times in the narrative (15:20, 29; 21:25), the kind of treatment generally reserved for very important material like Paul's call and Cornelius' conversion. After James proposes the regulations, the narrator extends the scene by a full quotation of a formal letter in which these regulations have final position. This evidence that the narrator is not simply recording but actively promoting these regulations also indicates sensitivity to the dan-

ger openly expressed in 21:21, the danger that Jews who have or may
enter the Christian community will be pressured into abandoning their
religious culture. Because Gentiles, as Peter proclaimed, are saved
through grace and faith (15:11), they are not only free from the law but
also free to protect the rights of a minority that honors God by its religious
traditions.

The decision is indicated in 15:22, which begins, "Then the apostles
and the elders, with the whole assembly, resolved."[24] This refers to an
official decision, taken collegially.[25] The resolution transmitted by letter
contains the regulations for the Gentiles proposed by James, but also
more. It begins by rejecting the position of those who came to Antioch and
demanded that the Gentiles be circumcised. Then it indicates the measures that Jerusalem has adopted to solve the problem disturbing the
relationship between the Jerusalem and Antioch churches. These measures include the sending of Judas and Silas as authorized representatives
to communicate directly with the Antioch church, explaining the Jerusalem church's thinking and healing any wounds. They also include the
assurance that no greater burden would be put on the Gentiles than
abstinence from a few things especially offensive to Jews. If the Gentiles
abstain from these things, "you will do well" (v. 29). F. W. Danker notes
the use of similar phrases in the official letters that he has studied and
emphasizes the underlying assumption of reciprocity; that is, acting as
requested will earn the good will of the requesters, to be demonstrated in
future relations.[26]

The letter includes a commendation of Barnabas and Paul (vv. 25–26),
and it conveys Jerusalem's decision to support their mission. There is
special reference to the way that they have risked their lives for the name
of the Lord, a reminder both of the prophecy of Paul's sufferings (9:16)
and of the emphasis on danger and suffering in the mission of Acts
13—14.[27]

Acts 15:30–33 indicates that a harmonious and supportive relation
between the churches has been restored by the decision in Jerusalem. The
Antioch church accepts the rules of abstinence gladly. Judas and Silas do
all that they can to strengthen the Antioch church. They are not just
errand boys; they are prophets who, like Barnabas when he first came

---

[24] On use of the Greek style of decrees and resolutions in 15:22, 24, 25, 28, see F. Danker,
"Reciprocity," 50–52.

[25] Note that both the apostles and elders, on the one hand, and the assembly, on the other,
have a role. F. Danker compares their functions to those of the council and the popular
assembly in provincial cities of the Roman Empire. The council, he explains, made proposals but the assembly voted on them and made amendments. See "Reciprocity," 54.

[26] See F. Danker, "Reciprocity," 52–54.

[27] See above, 180–81. The suffering or risk is "for the name" of Jesus in both 9:16 and 15:26.

from Jerusalem to Antioch (11:22–24), encourage and exhort the believers (παρακαλέω in both 11:23 and 15:32). When they leave, they are
sent off "with peace," an indication that any bad feeling between the
churches has been overcome. Thus a major crisis in the new community of
Jews and Gentiles has been resolved.

PAUL BEGINS
A NEW MISSION
IN MACEDONIA

In 15:36 Paul proposes to Barnabas that they return to the churches previously founded, visiting and strengthening them as they had in 14:21–22. However, developments do not follow Paul's plan. First, there is a dispute between Barnabas and Paul over John Mark, causing a split in the old mission team. The new journey will differ from the previous visitation of churches because Silas will replace Barnabas as Paul's partner. Second, Paul's attempts to expand his previous mission into neighboring areas are frustrated, hindered "by the Holy Spirit" according to 16:6. Paul's plan and God's plan do not coincide at this point. Paul must endure frustrating experiences until the moment of discovery of the new opportunity for mission. This discovery expands Paul's horizons beyond his original plans.

The narrative in 15:36–41 repeatedly recalls the previous journey of Paul and Barnabas. Paul proposes to return with his old partner to every city where they previously preached and established churches (15:36). However, an unresolved problem from the past makes the repetition of the past impossible. Paul's initial proposal founders on conflicting attitudes toward John Mark, who had withdrawn from the mission early in the first missionary journey (13:13). Paul adjusts to this, finds a new partner, and continues with his basic plan to strengthen established churches, as he and Barnabas had done in 14:21–22. The new journey resembles the previous one. It begins from Antioch with the support of the Antioch church. There Paul is "delivered to the grace of the Lord by the brothers" (15:40), a statement that recalls 14:26 (see also the blessing in 13:3). The journey focuses on old areas and is blessed by the Antioch church in the same way. We do not, however, find any directive from the Holy Spirit (comparable to 13:2) inaugurating this work.

Paul's work is successful within the limited scope of his plan. The churches are indeed strengthened and continue to grow (16:5). However, when Paul attempts the next logical step, the expansion of the mission into neighboring areas, he runs into difficulty. Paul and his co-workers "passed through" Phrygia and Galatia, according to 16:6. Because 18:23 refers to disciples in these regions, they must have engaged in a mission that was partially successful, yet the narrator gives no indication of this in 16:6. Instead we are told of the mission's failures. We also find references to the intervention of the Spirit, missing at the beginning of this journey from Antioch, but, remarkably, the Spirit acts as a frustrating force. Both vv. 6 and 7 report journeys, but both indicate that the Spirit blocked some aspect of Paul's plan. Thus blindly, by trial and error, they finally reach Troas, a good shipping point for Macedonia. The obstacles to work in Asia and Bithynia have been guiding them in this direction. There Paul receives a night vision of a Macedonian appealing for them to come, clarifying the next stage of his mission. Finally Paul's troubled journey has clear direction and hope. Once again the narrator shows keen interest in the dialogue between human purpose and divine purpose, indicating that Jesus' witnesses, too, must patiently endure the frustration of their own plans in order to discover the opportunity that God holds open. This opportunity may not be the next logical step by human calculation.

The references to the Spirit and a vision recall the guidance received by Peter in the Cornelius scene (10:10–20) and the initiating role of the Spirit at the beginning of Paul's first mission (13:2). In the second mission journey, signs of divine authorization and guidance do not initiate events but are reserved until the narrator recounts something of the frustrating experience of a mission that has not found its way, thereby indicating that even this frustration may be divine guidance leading to later illumination.[1] For both Peter and Paul, factors of their human situation contribute to the illumination. The Spirit speaks to Peter as the messengers from Cornelius call out; only the messengers' arrival makes the Spirit's guidance meaningful (10:17–20). Similarly, Paul's vision occurs after attempts to turn aside from the course toward Macedonia have been frustrated. Illumination comes at the proper moment, which is defined by the course of human events.

As his new co-workers Paul chooses Silas, a "leading" man of the Jerusalem church (15:22), and Timothy, a son of a Jewish mother and a Greek father from the churches founded on the first missionary journey. The former represents support for Paul's mission from Jerusalem, the latter support from the churches previously founded by Paul and Barnabas, with their mixed Jewish and Gentile membership.[2] Silas not only comes from Jerusalem but is one of the emissaries of the Jerusalem church who brought that church's letter to Antioch.[3] While in Antioch,

---

[1] As G. Krodel, *Acts,* 302, points out, the parallel to the divine commissioning in 13:2–4 is not found until 16:9–10.
[2] This is specifically noted for Iconium in 14:1.
[3] In contrast to the narrator's usual practice (cf. above, 124), neither Silas nor John Mark was left in the proper location for his next appearance in the narrative. In 15:33 Silas

Silas strengthened the believers there (15:32). Thus he showed himself to be an active supporter of the Antioch church, which includes Gentiles.

I would suggest that the partnership of Paul and Silas represents the unity of purpose between Jerusalem and the mission launched from Antioch, a unity achieved through the Jerusalem agreement. The continuing importance of the Jerusalem agreement for Paul's mission is indicated by the fact that Paul promotes observance of the regulations for Gentiles even beyond the specified area of "Antioch and Syria and Cilicia" (cf. 15:23; 16:4). Silas represents the Jerusalem side of this agreement and demonstrates Jerusalem's commitment to support the Jewish-gentile mission led by Paul. Delivering the regulations to the churches (16:4) is part of the process of strengthening them (16:5), for it enables Jews and Gentiles to live together in harmony, with mutual support. Paul, who represented the Gentiles at the Jerusalem meeting, and Silas, a delegate of the Jerusalem church in executing the agreement, work together to make the agreement effective and achieve this harmony.

Silas as well as Paul is seized, beaten, and imprisoned in Philippi (16:19–24). Silas shows that some Jerusalem believers are willing to pay the price of active commitment to the world mission.[4]

The Philippi narrative in 16:11–40 is an integrated episode in which the interaction of characters produces a sequential chain of events. Only the references to Lydia stand somewhat apart. The references to Lydia and her household form a frame around the rest of the episode (cf. 16:14–15, 40) and show an interest in the key role of a patroness of the community and hostess for the missionaries in the founding of a church. Although there have been previous references to local hosts and hostesses in connection with the work of Peter (cf. Simon the tanner in 9:43; Cornelius in 10:48; Mary, John Mark's mother, in 12:12), this is the first such reference since the narration of Paul's mission began in Acts 13. From this point on the narrator mentions other local sponsors of Paul's mission—

returned to Jerusalem, yet he is available in Antioch in 15:40. (The insertion of v. 34 in some manuscripts is a later attempt to account for Silas' presence in Antioch in v. 40.) Similarly, John Mark returned to Jerusalem in 13:13, yet accompanies Barnabas from Antioch in 15:39.

[4] According to B. N. Kaye, "Acts' Portrait of Silas," 26, "Silas denotes the Jewish character, first of the visit to Syria and Cilicia, and then of the extension of this to a journey through Macedonia." This is imprecise and confusing, particularly when Jews have a marginal role in Philippi (Paul and Silas must seek a place of prayer outside the city and find only women there), and the encounter with Roman society is emphasized in the Philippi scene. The presence of Silas does not indicate that Paul's mission has a particularly Jewish focus at that point. Rather, Silas is important because this representative of the Jerusalem church takes the Jerusalem agreement to mean not passive acceptance of Gentiles but active commitment to an inclusive mission, which is the way the narrator would like it to be read. Thus the partnership of Paul and Silas expresses the full meaning of the Jerusalem agreement by showing the unified mission that it makes possible.

Jason in Thessalonica (17:5–9), Aquila and Priscilla and then Titius Justus in Corinth (18:2–3, 7)—as well as hosts on Paul's journeys (21:8, 16). In this way the narrator acknowledges the important role that local sponsors played in the establishment of the church and demonstrates the necessary partnership between traveling missionaries and local supporters.[5]

The main action begins when Paul encounters the slave girl with the "python" (divinatory spirit). From this point events unfold in a single sequence, moving to arrest and then release. Although there is no causal connection with the conversion of Lydia, v. 16a forms a bridge to the preceding scene by placing the encounter with the slave girl on the way to the "place of prayer" where Paul found Lydia.

Paul is an exorcist like Jesus who acts in the name of Jesus, according to 16:16–18. The motif of the possessed person's recognition of God's representatives (16:17) recalls scenes of exorcism in Luke (cf. 4:34; 8:28). The reference to Paul and his companions as "servants of God most high" especially recalls the possessed man's address of Jesus as "Son of God most high" in Luke 8:28.[6] The report of Paul's ministry in Ephesus—the last major scene of work while Paul is a free man—will also refer to Paul's exorcisms and note that Paul was recognized by a spirit (Acts 19:12, 15). Thus the narrative of Paul's mission between the meeting in Jerusalem and arrest in Jerusalem shows some interest in this aspect of his work.

Nevertheless, the exorcism in 16:16–18 is not the main focus of attention. Like the healing of the lame man by Peter and John in 3:1–10 and the healing of the lame man by Paul in 14:8–9, the intervention by God's servants causes a public reaction with consequences for the mission. Thereby issues are raised that transcend the healing, and these issues become the center of attention in the narrative. To be sure, the exorcism of the slave girl does have some special features that contribute to the following narrative. The prophetic spirit within her causes her to repeatedly cry that these servants of God "proclaim to you a way of salvation." This cry can serve as both review and preview: review of a major theme in the narrative—the revelation of God's salvation to all flesh, for which God's servants must prepare the way (Luke 3:4–6)—and preview of following events, in which both the slave girl and the jailer find salvation (Acts 16:30–31).[7]

---

[5] On this partnership in Acts, see J. Koenig, *New Testament Hospitality*, chap. 4.

[6] There are further verbal connections between Luke 8:27–29 and Acts 16:16–18 in describing the encounter, the crying out, and the exorcist's command.

[7] The slave girl's share in salvation is not directly stated, but the exorcism story in Luke 8, which is partially parallel, notes in summary "how the man possessed by demons was saved"

Although the slave girl's witness prepares for the following acts of salvation and places them within the context of God's saving purpose, the exorcism has negative consequences for Paul and Silas. Their situation worsens rapidly through vv. 19–24, for they are seized, accused before the city magistrates (στρατηγοί), beaten, and placed in prison under tight security. The cause is the slave girl's owners, who gain the support of the city magistrates and crowd. There is an interesting interplay between the private and public motive of the owners. When the spirit "went out" of the slave girl, the owners' hope of profit also "went out" (v. 19); this is the real reason for their attack on Paul and Silas, according to the narrator. Before the city officials they state their case differently: Paul and Silas are undermining proper Roman mores by trying to introduce Jewish customs. The accusation is an example of what Meir Sternberg calls "inset rhetoric" (characters trying to influence other characters) in distinction from "framing rhetoric" (the narrator's persuasive shaping of the experience of the readers). As Sternberg has observed in the Hebrew Bible, the narrator often shows characters maneuvering without scruple for their own advantage, the discrepancy between characters' statements and the narrator's statements being a strong way of showing this.[8] Opposition from similar motives will arise in Ephesus, where Demetrius, a leader of the silver workers, will speak frankly to his colleagues about Paul as an economic threat (19:25–26). In both cases economic motives behind present religious practices appear as major sources of resistance to the mission.[9] The accusers' rhetoric also includes labeling to heighten social boundaries: they are Jews, we are Romans (a contrast heightened by the parallel phrases at the end of vv. 20 and 21 in the Greek text).[10] This thrust meets a later parry in v. 37, where Paul announces that he and Silas are Romans and demands to be treated as such.

As in two previous scenes in Acts (5:19–21; 12:6–11) prison doors are opened and prisoners' bonds released without human action, this time through an earthquake. Surprisingly, the open prison doors do not lead to freedom in this case. The earthquake becomes a subordinate part of the story of the jailer. It leads to the jailer's conversion, when Paul intervenes to save his life. It is striking that in Philippi Paul is twice presented with opportunities for freedom (vv. 26, 35–36) and twice refuses them. These

---

(Luke 8:36). Release from demons is one aspect of the salvation that Jesus and his witnesses bring.

[8] See M. Sternberg, *Poetics of Biblical Narrative*, 422–23.

[9] For further examples of the corrupting influence of attachment to possessions, see 106.

[10] Daniel Schwartz understands Ἰουδαῖοι ὑπάρχοντες as concessive ("although they are Jews") and suggests that the accusers are themselves Jews. See "Accusation and the Accusers at Philippi," 357–63. This view ignores the contrast implied by the participial phrases in parallel position at the ends of vv. 20 and 21.

developments focus attention not on the fact of miraculous release but on Paul's reasons for rejecting these opportunities, which involve his relation to the jailer, on the one hand, and to the city officials, on the other.

The city officials, as well as the jailer, are important. The episode does not come to a quick end when the officials send the message to have Paul and Silas released. Instead, there is further negotiation between Paul and the officials, for the conditions of release are important to Paul. This material contributes to reflection on Paul's relation to Roman society, an important concern that I will discuss below.

The command to release the prisoners in v. 35 may seem rather abrupt. No reason is given for this seeming about-face on the part of the city officials. Any narrative, to be sure, is going to contain gaps of information, some of which are temporary (the narrator is withholding information until a time that suits the narrative strategy), some of which are permanent. In discussing this, M. Sternberg distinguishes between "gaps" and "blanks." The former refers to omissions of relevant material, the latter to omissions of material judged by the narrator to be unimportant.[11] It is possible, of course, to supply reasons for the officials' actions. Two possibilities come to mind: (1) They made no connection between the earthquake and the prisoners, thought that a beating and a night in prison were sufficient punishment for a minor offense, and so ordered the release.[12] (2) They did make a connection between the earthquake and the prisoners and decided that the imprisonment was an invitation to divine judgment; the safest thing was to get them out of town as quickly as possible (cf. v. 39).[13] Although attributing one or the other of these motives to the officials would make some difference in our understanding of them (they are ignorant and arrogant in the one case, cowed in the other), the narrator's omission is probably closer to a blank than a gap. Paul's behavior in response to the Roman authorities is a matter of major interest in the story; the character and motives of these officials is a matter of slight interest. Such blanks are not surprising. They should be taken as guides to what does and does not interest the narrator. They are not a major disturbance to the integrity of the narrative.[14]

---

[11] Sternberg writes of "what was omitted for the sake of interest and what was omitted for lack of interest." See *Poetics of Biblical Narrative*, 236.

[12] This is the explanation of K. Lake and H. Cadbury, *Beginnings of Christianity* 4:200.

[13] This is the implication of the Western text, which indicates that the magistrates remembered the earthquake, were afraid, and sent to have Paul and Silas released. See M.-É. Boismard and A. Lamouille, *Texte occidental des Actes* 1:183.

[14] It is hazardous to draw conclusions about sources from such a blank. The lack of reference in v. 35 to the preceding miracle leads H. Conzelmann to conclude that the miracle was not an original part of the narrative. See *Acts*, 133. The following observation by Sternberg suggests that such conclusions are hasty: "The world, every piece of it inexhaustible, will not lend itself to coverage by discourse. Nor would discourse cover it, even if it could, because

There are interesting similarities and differences between this episode and the narrative of the apostles' mission in Jerusalem in Acts 2—5. As in 16:16–40, we have in Acts 3—5 a sequence of healing or exorcism, imprisonment, and divine action that enables release.[15] Additional minor points of connection are praying in the situation of persecution (4:23-31; 16:25) and a healing command "in the name of Jesus Messiah" (3:6; 16:18).[16] The similarities are not limited to healings, imprisonments, and releases. The description of the jailer's conversion echoes elements of the first conversions in Jerusalem. The jailer asks, "What must I do to be saved?" (16:30), a question that combines the question following the Pentecost sermon (2:37: "What should we do, brothers?") with Peter's reply (2:40: "Be saved from this crooked generation"). The word, baptism, and faith are mentioned in both places (2:41, 44; 16:31-34). Less expected, and therefore more suggestive of a special connection between these scenes, is the reference in 16:34 to the jailer preparing a meal and exulting (ἠγαλλιάσατο). The description of the jailer's joy with this unusual and strong verb (it and the related noun occur in Acts only in 2:46; 16:34; and in a Scripture quotation in 2:26) links the jailer with the early converts in Jerusalem (and with the realization of hope announced in the Lukan birth narrative—see Luke 1:14, 44, 47). In both the early Jerusalem church and in the jailer's house this exultation accompanies a meal that is evidently a celebration of salvation. This is especially striking in Acts 16:34, for the jailer serves a meal at a strange time—the middle of the night.

The joyful experience of God's saving work that marked the earliest church appears now in a Roman environment. There is a significant shift in cultural context between Acts 2—5 and the Philippi episode. The account of the mission in Jerusalem was strongly marked by its Jewish setting. The setting of the Philippi narrative is equally important but significantly different. It is not just Gentile but specifically Roman.[17] Philippi is introduced as a κολωνία ("colony"), a Latin loan word (16:12). Roman colonies were originally settlements of Roman citizens, such as veteran soldiers, and by law the colonists had the same legal rights as their fellow citizens in Italy. The colony had a Roman form of local adminis-

---

meaning and value depend on selection. . . . For the message to signify, there must be omissions, absolute and relative" (*Poetics of Biblical Narrative*, 236).

[15] The last is reserved for the second of two imprisonments in Acts 3—5. On the repetitive pattern of imprisonments, hearings, and releases in Acts 3—5, see above, 63–66.

[16] The "name" of Jesus is a major theme in Acts 3—5. See above, 49, 52–54. The name of Jesus also has a special role in exorcism, which may account for the reference in 16:18. See Luke 9:49; Acts 19:13.

[17] Similarly, Paul's healing of the lame man in 14:8–10 echoes the healing of the lame man at the temple gate (see above, 177-78) with a significant shift of cultural context from Judaism to gentile polytheism.

tration and used Roman law in local as well as external matters.[18] This situation is reflected in the Philippi narrative, not just to add local color but because the narrative is centrally concerned with the mission's encounter with the Roman world. The chief officials in Philippi are called στρατηγοί (16:20), a Greek term for the Roman praetors.[19] Later we hear of the ῥαβδοῦχοι (16:35, 38; RSV: "police"), the Roman lictors who attended the highest Roman officials and symbolized their authority by carrying the fasces.[20] The accusation against Paul and Silas is designed to appeal to people who are conscious of their Roman heritage and its privileges (16:20–21). The accusers speak of themselves and their audience as Romans, not Philippians or Macedonians, and contrast Jewish "customs" with Roman customs, a source of Roman solidarity and pride.[21] The narrator reserves the disclosure of Paul's (and Silas') Roman citizenship for this setting (16:37–38). It serves not as protection (the beating from which it should have spared them has already occurred) but as a basis for accusing the magistrates and as proof that Paul and Silas belong to Roman society in spite of the fact that their accusers dismissed them as Jews (16:20–21).

In Philippi Paul and Silas follow the rule of preaching to Jews first, but there is no indication of Jewish opposition. The role of stirring up opposition, attributed to Jews in 13:50 and 14:2, 19, is taken by the Gentile owners of the slave girl, who speak as Romans opposed to subversive Jewish preachers. Here and in the story of the Ephesian riot (19:23–40) we have major dramatic scenes that highlight gentile opposition to the gospel. It is important to keep these scenes in mind lest we attribute to the narrator a one-sided obsession with Jewish resistance. The encounter of the gospel with gentile religion, culture, and government is a repeated concern in Acts 16—19. The concern in the Philippi episode is specifically with the fate of the mission before Roman magistrates, reacting to their proud and suspicious citizens.

The accusation against Paul and Silas in 16:20–21 is one of a series. In Acts 16—19 we find four scenes that feature accusations against Christians, and these accusations are parts of similar sequences of events.[22] The

---

[18] See K. Lake and H. Cadbury, *Beginnings of Christianity* 4:190.

[19] See K. Lake and H. Cadbury, *Beginnings of Christianity* 4:194. BAGD, s.v., adds, "This title was not quite officially correct, since these men were properly termed 'duoviri', but it occurs several times in inscr[iptions] as a popular designation for them."

[20] See K. Lake and H. Cadbury, *Beginnings of Christianity* 4:200.

[21] On the importance that ancient authors attached to Roman customs or mores as a source of Roman greatness, see W. van Unnik, "Anklage gegen die Apostel," 374–85.

[22] The following discussion of the four scenes was developed for my article "Paul outside the Christian Ghetto: Stories of Intercultural Conflict and Cooperation in Acts," in *Text and Logos: The Humanistic Interpretation of the New Testament: Essays in Honor of Hendrikus Wouterus Boers*, edited by Theodore W. Jennings, Jr. (Atlanta: Scholars Press, forthcoming). Used by permission.

sequence contains three basic elements: (1) Christians are forcefully
brought before officials or a public assembly. (2) They are accused, and
this accusation is highlighted by direct quotation. (3) We are told the
result of this attempt to curb the Christian mission. Thus in Philippi the
owners of the girl with the oracular spirit drag Paul and Silas to the
magistrates (16:19) and state their accusation (16:20-21). As a result,
Paul and Silas are beaten and imprisoned (16:22-24). In Thessalonica
Jews raise a mob and come looking for Paul and Silas (17:5). Not finding
them, they drag "Jason and some brothers" to the magistrates (17:6) and
make their accusation (17:6-7). The officials are disturbed and require
Jason and the others to post a bond (17:8-9). In Corinth the Jews bring
Paul before the tribunal of Gallio, the proconsul (18:12), and accuse Paul
(18:13), but Gallio refuses to accept the case (18:14-16). The scene in
Ephesus is the most independent in construction. Here the narrator
presents a longer and more dramatic scene, and the accusation is stated
first, in a speech by Demetrius to other members of his trade (19:25-27).
In this case the accusation motivates action against Christians, which
follows. People rush together into the theater, seizing two of Paul's companions along the way (19:29) and forming an impromptu public assembly. After much confusion and uproar, the assembly is dissolved.

The similarities among these scenes justify speaking of a public accusation type-scene. We may speak of a type-scene when a basic situation,
with similar characters and plot elements, recurs several times in a given
literature.[23] Type-scenes can become an important literary technique in a
narrative. The recurrent pattern suggests similarity, and the variations
prevent monotony. Discovering the pattern repeatedly, we come to view
the situation as common or characteristic and look for it in various guises.
The public accusation type-scene, with its four examples in four consecu-
tive chapters, shows the narrator's strong concern with the way that the
outside world perceives the Christian mission and the effect those perceptions may have on Christians.[24]

Although Paul has frequent disputes in synagogues, in the four cases
we are examining the dispute either does not begin or does not remain in
the synagogue community. It spills over into the public sphere and is
brought to city officials, the provincial governor, or the public assembly.
Jews may or may not be involved as accusers. Of the four scenes under
consideration, Jews are accusers in the second and third (Thessalonica

---

[23] On type-scenes in the Hebrew Bible, see R. Alter, *Art of Biblical Narrative*, 47-62. On
type-scenes in Luke, see *Narrative Unity* 1:18, 105, 170-71.

[24] In her dissertation Marie-Eloise Rosenblatt discusses the "public confrontation type-scene"
in Acts. Her category overlaps mine, although it is defined somewhat differently and
includes a somewhat different list of passages. See *Under Interrogation*, 193-205.

and Corinth), and Gentiles are accusers in the first and fourth (Philippi and Ephesus). This provides a neat balance that may be deliberate. Jews are not the sole source of trouble for Paul's mission. Gentiles also feel threatened and take action against him. Whereas Paul is attacked by Jews for disloyalty to Jewish customs (18:13;[25] cf. 21:20–21, 28), he is attacked in Philippi for preaching Jewish customs in a Roman colony. Caught between two suspicious communities, Paul is a troublesome outsider to both, for he advocates teachings and behavior that threaten their ways of life.

These scenes contribute something new and important to the narrative of Paul's mission. Although Paul faced plenty of opposition in Acts 13— 14, the narrator did not highlight specific accusations by quoting them in scenes before magistrates or a public forum. In Acts 16—19 this is done repeatedly, and the accusations, taken together, provide a brief survey of the problems that the mission creates for its environment. In 16:20–21 Romans accuse the mission of importing Jewish customs that undermine the customs that made Rome great. In 17:5–7 Jews secure public support and accuse Christians before the magistrates of upsetting society and political subversion, as Christians claim that there is another king than Caesar. In 18:12–13 Jews accuse Paul before the proconsul of inciting people to worship God contrary to the law. In 19:25–27 Demetrius the silversmith persuades his companions to oppose Paul on the basis of economic self-interest but also because of a threat to Artemis herself and to Ephesus' position as cult center. The latter argument fires the passions of the δῆμος ("public assembly," although in this case not an authorized one; cf. 19:30, 33, 39–40). Both Jews and Gentiles view the mission as a threat to the customs that provide social cohesion, to the religious basis of their cultures, and to political stability through Caesar's rule. It is somewhat remarkable that these repeated public accusations do not lead to defense speeches. The narrator provides no opportunity for Paul to speak in reply. In 17:6–9 and 19:23–40 Paul is not even present to speak to the issue, and in 18:14 he is cut off by the proconsul just as he is about to make his defense. Defense speeches are reserved for the climactic conflict portrayed in 21:27—26:32 (which begins with a seizure and accusation similar to the scenes just discussed).

Thus the narrative shows awareness of the culture-shaking power of the mission[26] but does not directly address the resulting issues. To be sure,

---

[25] On this verse see below, 226–27.

[26] Other aspects of our narrator's cultural awareness are discussed by K. Löning, "Evangelium und die Kulturen," 2604–46. According to Löning, Luke regards the Jewish law as a cultural phenomenon of the Jewish people and does not deny its legitimacy for them. This position allows cultural diversity within the church. The gospel is neither the enemy of cultures nor the prophet of a particular culture (2627).

the narrative may suggest that the accusation in 16:20–21 is partially due to ignorance. Contrary to the accusers' assumptions, Paul and Silas are not only Jews but Romans (v. 37). We have also been shown that gentile Christians need not adopt the Jewish "customs" in order to share in God's salvation; hence they need not reject all of their old customs. Religion and society were too intermixed in the ancient world for this to be a complete answer, and following scenes show that the narrator is sensitive to areas of continuing conflict between the cultures of the Roman world and the Christian movement.

The narrative of Paul's imprisonment at Philippi suggests a resilient optimism in spite of opposition from society. It holds out the hope that the forces of opposition are open either to conversion (as with the jailer) or correction (as with the magistrates). Paul's response to the jailer and the magistrates requires further discussion.

The conversion of the jailer is not just one more of the many conversions in Acts but the conversion of a member of the oppressive system that is punishing Paul and Silas. The earthquake gives Paul the opportunity to show this jailer the love of enemies that Jesus taught (Luke 6:27). Instead of escaping from prison, as Peter did in Acts 12, Paul remains, which enables him to save the jailer's life. In 16:27 attention shifts to the jailer. The story moves quickly to a dramatic crisis, for the jailer is about to kill himself. Paul intervenes with a shout, and vv. 29–30 portray the strong emotional effect on the jailer of Paul and Silas' refusal to escape. Paul's attention to the welfare of another in the midst of his own suffering—somewhat like Jesus' concern for the criminal crucified beside him—brings to the jailer a share in the salvation that God offers through Jesus. Paul and the narrator do not despair that God will open hearts to their message even among persecutors.

However, the narrative is not just concerned with immediate conversions, as the concluding dialogue with the magistrates (through their messengers) indicates. The command of the magistrates to release Paul and Silas (v. 35) seems to bring the episode to a happy conclusion. The jailer not only informs Paul and Silas of the order but urges them to go in peace (v. 36). His words, containing little new information for the reader, are included in order to add a further voice, this time from a supporter of Paul, to the chorus of those urging Paul to go. However, Paul refuses. He does not agree that all problems have now been solved. He does not immediately grab the offered freedom. Bold and confident, he vigorously protests the previous treatment and demands that the magistrates publicly acknowledge the miscarriage of justice by coming personally to the jail to release the prisoners. He protests the unjust beating, without a proper trial, of Roman citizens (who are protected by law from such treatment).

This was done publicly, and it cannot be undone secretly. The refusal to settle without a public act of vindication shows a concern with the public standing of the mission. Acts of ignorance and injustice must not be allowed to masquerade as truth and justice in the public eye. The portrait of Roman officials is clearly negative in this scene. Paul is not passive in the situation, content to disappear from public view when the opportunity arises, but vigorously demands the rights that Romans claim to respect. Even when the magistrates submit to his humiliating demand, Paul demonstrates his independence. Having been asked to "go away (ἀπελθεῖν) from the city," Paul and Silas instead "went in (εἰσῆλθον)" to the house of Lydia. Only after encouraging the disciples, they "went out (ἐξῆλθαν)" (vv. 39–40).

Paul and Silas, whose fortunes take a sudden turn for the worse when they are seized, accused, beaten, and imprisoned, prove to be anything but helpless victims. They pray and sing hymns to God in prison, and when the sudden possibility of freedom arises, they freely set it aside for the sake of another person, thereby advancing the gospel. They also defend the mission in the public sphere, gaining a public acknowledgment of wrongful treatment from Roman officials.

CONTRASTING RESPONSES
IN THESSALONICA AND BEROEA

After the relatively lengthy episode that concentrates on Paul's encounter with Roman officials at Philippi, the narrator returns to an emphasis on Paul's synagogue preaching and its results. The longer episodes in Acts 16—19 concern the impact of the mission on gentile society (see 16:16-40; 17:16-34; 19:23-40). However, the narrator does not allow us to forget that Paul is committed to the Jewish mission and regularly begins with preaching in the synagogue. In 17:2 we are reminded that it was the "custom" of Paul, arriving in a new place, to go to the synagogue and present the word on the basis of the Scriptures. This impression is reinforced in 17:10b, where arrival in Beroea and going to the synagogue are compressed into a brief statement, as if nothing happened between these two events. Interpretation of the Scriptures plays a key role in Paul's message (17:2, 11). This emphasis, together with the summary reference to the suffering and resurrection of the Messiah in 17:3, recalls the preaching of Paul in the synagogue of Pisidian Antioch (13:16-41) and the sermons of Peter. We can fill in the rest of Paul's message from these previous sermons. The same message of the fulfillment of the messianic promise for the Jewish people remains the focus of Paul's synagogue preaching.

There is also an interesting connection between the summary of Paul's synagogue preaching in Thessalonica and the message of the risen Lord in Luke 24. Paul, basing his discussion on the Scriptures, was "opening (διανοίγων) [the Scriptures] and demonstrating that it was necessary for the Messiah to suffer and arise from the dead" (Acts 17:3). The risen Lord first opened the Scriptures for his disciples, as they confessed in Luke 24:32 ("as he was opening [διήνοιγεν] to us the Scriptures"). The central theme of this revelation was the necessity of the Messiah's suffering and resurrection, expressed in language that returns in the summary of Paul's preaching in Thessalonica. The risen Lord said, "Was it not necessary for the Messiah to suffer these things? (οὐχὶ ταῦτα ἔδει παθεῖν τὸν Χριστόν;)" (Luke 24:26). In Thessalonica Paul demonstrates that "it was necessary for the Messiah to suffer (τὸν Χριστὸν ἔδει παθεῖν)" (Acts 17:3). In Luke 24 the risen Lord later "opened (διήνοιξεν) the mind" of his followers in Jerusalem to understand the Scriptures and repeated his revelation: "Thus it is written that the Messiah suffer and arise from the dead (καὶ ἀναστῆναι ἐκ νεκρῶν)" (24:46). The summary of Paul's message in Thessalonica continues: "And arise from the dead (καὶ ἀναστῆναι ἐκ νεκρῶν)" (Acts 17:3). In opening the Scriptures to the Jews of Thessalonica, Paul is playing the same revelatory role as the risen Lord played on Easter, and the core of his message is the same. Nevertheless, the narrator is aware that Paul is dependent on God or the Lord to "open" hearts or doors for the mission (see 14:27; 16:14).[1]

The scenes at Thessalonica and Beroea should be considered together. They begin in the same way, deliberately present contrasting responses, and are linked by the appearance of Thessalonian Jews in Beroea to continue their opposition to Paul. The two scenes report the results of the preaching in similar sentences (17:4, 12). Even in Thessalonica the work is not in vain, for "some" of the Jews and a "great multitude of the devout Greeks and not a few of the foremost women" were persuaded. The same groups are listed in 17:12, and the result among the Beroean Jews is clearly better: "Many of them believed." This is preceded by a comparative statement. The Jews of Beroea were "nobler" than the Jews of Thessalonica, as demonstrated by their willingness to hear and their serious study of the Scripture in light of Paul's message. The description of the Beroean Jews shows that the narrator has not completely stereotyped Diaspora Jews. Despite repeated emphasis on Jewish opposition, the narrator here inserts a contrasting picture, preserving a sense of local variety of response.

However, the local communities are not isolated. Paul's work in Beroea attracts the attention of Thessalonian Jews, who carry their opposition to Beroea, stirring up the crowds. As a result, Paul must quickly leave Beroea, as he had Thessalonica. This pattern of persistent opposition that reaches beyond the local scene, following Paul on his mission, previously appeared in 14:19, where Jews from Antioch and Iconium attacked Paul in Lystra. Furthermore, the opposition of the Jews from both Antioch and Thessalonica is attributed first of all to their jealousy of the way that Paul is attracting Gentiles (13:45; 17:5). Indeed, 17:1–5 parallels the main steps of the larger narrative of Paul's work in Antioch (13:14–52). Entering the synagogue, Paul preaches from Scripture on the Messiah's death and resurrection. This makes an impact, but Paul's success also

---

[1] The remark about the Lord opening Lydia's heart in 16:14 shows that the Lord continues to do what he did for the first followers in Luke 24:31, 45 (there of the opening of eyes and mind). It is interesting that both Lydia and the Emmaus travelers are said to have "prevailed upon" their guest to stay with them. Luke 24:29 and Acts 16:15 are the only uses of παραβιάζομαι in the NT.

causes jealousy among Jews, who incite others against Paul and force him to leave. In Thessalonica, however, there is no announcement by Paul that he is turning to the Gentiles. Instead, he is abruptly forced to turn to another town. The "brothers" send him away because of the danger, and the mission continues elsewhere among Jews. The narrator uses patterns but varies them, giving some sense of the varied results to which Paul's mission could lead.

The synagogue mission of Paul and Silas finds faith not only among Jews but also among "devout Greeks" and "foremost women" (17:4; see the reference to "prominent Greek women and men" in 17:12). These groups are evidently associated somehow with the synagogue, as are the Greeks mentioned in 14:1. The attention given to women among the converts is noteworthy. There was some notice of the presence of women in earlier stages of the mission, in the earliest community (1:14) and among the converts in Jerusalem (5:14) and Samaria (8:12). Women as well as men suffered from Saul's persecution (8:3; 9:2). There is greater attention to women in Acts 16—18. In 17:4, 12 the narrator speaks specifically of women of high social position, the "foremost" or "prominent" women. "Devout prominent women" were previously mentioned in 13:50, but not as Christians. The references in 17:4, 12 seem to acknowledge that women of economic means and social influence played an important role in the growth of the church in certain localities. Lydia the dealer in purple goods, introduced in the preceding episode as patroness of the mission in Philippi, may be an example of such a prominent woman because she is able to provide hospitality for the missionaries (16:15) and a meeting place for the church (16:40).[2] A woman is named among Paul's converts in Athens (17:34), and Priscilla is repeatedly mentioned in 18:2, 18, 26 as an important supporter of Paul, along with her husband, and as a teacher of Apollos. These are only brief glimpses of the roles of women in the early church,[3] but Acts in this section restricts itself to brief glimpses of everyone except Paul.

After the reference to the jealousy of Jewish opponents in 17:5, the parallels that we have noted with Luke 24, Acts 13, and other material give way to a second version of the public accusation type-scene that appeared in 16:19–24.[4] This time Paul and Silas escape because they are absent at the right time. Instead, "Jason and some brothers" are dragged to the officials. The dangers of the mission extend to local supporters, par-

---

[2] E. Haenchen comments, "Purple materials were a markedly luxury item for rich people; Lydia will have been wealthy herself." See *Acts,* 494.

[3] According to Elisabeth Schüssler Fiorenza, the scarcity of information about women in the NT does not reflect their historical role but is the result of "androcentric selection of historical traditions." See *In Memory of Her,* 48–53.

[4] See above, 201–3.

ticularly those who open their homes to the mission. Jason and the others are not imprisoned but must post a bond. As in Philippi there is a contrast between the private motive of the opponents (jealousy according to 17:5) and their public accusation, which is designed to gain support for their position from those loyal to Rome. The narrator further undermines their claim that Paul and Silas are "disrupting" society (17:6) by indicating that the opponents had deliberately fomented a disturbance (17:5; see also 17:13). The accusation extends and sharpens the accusation in 16:20–21. Although Paul and Silas are accused of disturbing "our city" in 16:20, they are accused in 17:6 of disrupting "the world ($\tau\grave{\eta}\nu$ $o\grave{\iota}\kappa o\nu\mu\acute{\epsilon}\nu\eta\nu$)," which probably means the Roman Empire.[5] The accusers are aware of the work of Paul and Silas elsewhere, such as Philippi (they speak of them being "here also"), and present them as a general threat to Roman society. Furthermore, the accusers sharpen the accusation in 16:20–21 that the mission is a threat to the customs on which Roman society is based. They charge Paul and Silas with sedition, for these troublemakers reject Caesar's rule and support another king.[6]

The instigators of this action are Thessalonian Jews. As noted previously, Paul is twice accused by Jews (17:5–7; 18:12–13) and twice by Gentiles (16:19–21; 19:24–27) in the four scenes of public accusation in Acts 16—19. Paul and Silas are sent to both Jews and Gentiles, and they are perceived as threats by both. Twice the charge is given some credence by public officials (16:22–24; 17:8–9), and twice it is dismissed (18:14–17; 19:35–40). Thus the narrator gives a varied picture of the opponents and of the officials who administer Roman society.

---

[5] So BAGD, s.v., 2.
[6] Cf. Luke 23:2, where Jesus was accused of claiming to be a king and of opposing Caesar's taxes.

ATHENS:
THE UNIVERSAL SCOPE
OF PAUL'S MISSION

In the Athens scene we find the second of three major speeches attributed to Paul during his missionary career as a free man. Careful planning is indicated by the fact that we have three different types of speeches addressed to three different audiences: a mission speech to Jews (13:16–41), a mission speech to Gentiles (17:22–31), and a farewell speech to the elders of the Ephesian church (20:18–35). Like the other two speeches, the significance of the Athens speech reaches beyond the scene in which it is set.

Paul's speech in Athens is strikingly different than the mission speeches to Jews in Acts 2—13. Indeed, at first glance it seems to be related only to Paul's brief speech at Lystra (14:15–17). One might be inclined to regard it as a foreign body or as a temporary experiment with no lasting importance for either Paul or the narrator. This would be a mistake. The speech is important not only as further indication of interest in the mission's encounter with Greco-Roman culture but also as an attempt to deal with issues that emerge from core values affirmed in the narrative as a whole. There is an internal as well as an external impulse toward the viewpoint expressed by Paul in Athens.

Reliable indicators of the implied author's values highlight the universal scope of God's saving work. The birth narrative comes to its climax with the words of the inspired prophet who celebrates God's salvation "prepared before the face of all the peoples, a light for revelation of Gentiles and glory of your people Israel" (Luke 2:30–32). This emphasis is reaffirmed by an explicit Scripture quotation in Luke 3:6. The fundamental importance of these statements for the whole of Luke-Acts is indicated by the appearance of related themes toward the end of Acts. Paul, in a retrospective summary of his call and ministry, speaks of being sent to both the Jewish people and the Gentiles to bring them "from darkness to light." He closes this speech by summarizing the Messiah's mission in similar terms: the Messiah's task is "to proclaim light both to the people and to the Gentiles" (Acts 26:17–18, 23).[1] The narrative of

---

[1] Note also the repetition of the phrase τὸ σωτήριον τοῦ θεοῦ from the Isaiah quotation in Luke 3:6 (see also 2:30) in Acts 28:28. Cf. *Narrative Unity* 1:40–42.

Acts shows the purpose of God and the mission of the Messiah, expressed in these passages, becoming effective in the world. Effective mission, however, requires reflection on theological foundations in order to discover a message that can address the whole world. More than instruction in the Jewish gospel is needed. The mission must discover latent resources within the tradition (discovered, perhaps, in conversation with the larger world) in order to preach a universal message. Otherwise the world cannot hear, and the preachers themselves lose sight of the worldwide dimension of the message they proclaim.

The necessary resources are found through reflection on the relation of the Creator to the creation. This is a relation that transcends every ethnic and racial difference. It is a relation rooted in creaturely existence as such, embracing, therefore, Jews and Gentiles equally. Starting from this theological foundation enables Paul to say "all" and "each one," that is, to proclaim a message that excludes no one. This is a basic thrust of the speech. It moves from proclamation of the God "who made the world and all that is in it, . . . giving to all life and breath and all things" to an assertion of the fundamental unity of humanity (God "made from one every nation of humans") and God's availability to every individual (God is "not far from each one of us"), concluding with the call for "all everywhere to repent" in light of God's coming judgment of "the world ($τὴν οἰκουμένην$)." Paul appeals to the relation of Creator and creature, and to God as universal judge, in order to provide a foundation for a gospel that can address the whole of humanity. The internal impulse for this speech (internal to the implied author's perspective) comes from the need to speak of all humanity sharing an essentially similar relation to God as a basis for an inclusive gospel, a gospel commensurate with the inclusive saving purpose of God announced in Luke 2:30–32.

Nevertheless, this is a speech addressed to a specific audience. Paul speaks to cultured Greeks about their situation before God as universal Creator and judge. This aspect of the speech will be discussed further below. It relates to the external impulse for this speech, the challenge of Greek thought that is already using universal categories.

Initial impressions that the Athens speech is a foreign body in Acts or a twig that departs from the main trunk are also corrected when we consider carefully the relation of parts of the speech to other statements in Acts:[2] (1) Verse 24 speaks of God as Creator of the world and sovereign over it. God's role as Creator was emphasized not only in 14:15, part of a short speech to Gentiles, but also in 4:24 (in a Jerusalem setting). God's

---

[2] Paul Schubert compared the Athens speech systematically to the preceding speeches in Acts. See "Areopagus Speech," 253–59. In the rest of this paragraph I am freely summarizing his discussion and making a few additions.

position as Creator is associated with God's present sovereignty in 4:24, 28 as well as in 17:24. (2) Verse 24b insists that God "does not dwell in temples made with hands." Stephen made the same point to Jews in 7:48. Moreover, the rejection of images formed by "human skill and imagination" in 17:29 is also paralleled in Stephen's speech. The Israelites, too, fell into idolatry, rejoicing "in the works of their hands" (7:41; cf. 7:43). (3) According to v. 26, all people were created from one. Luke, in contrast to Matthew, traces Jesus' genealogy back to Adam (Luke 3:38), suggesting that the biblical story of the origin of all from a single father is also behind Acts 17:26. A good parallel to the reference to "seasons" (RSV: "periods") in v. 26 is found in 14:17, which appeals to nature as a witness to God's gracious care. (4) Verse 30 indicates that the audience must now "repent" of its past "ignorance." This is remarkably similar (remarkable in light of the different character of the ignorance) to the treatment of Jerusalem Jews, who are called to repentance because they showed "ignorance" of God's purpose in Jesus (3:17–19; 13:27). The call to repentance is, of course, a frequent theme in the Acts mission speeches, which carry out Jesus' command that "repentance for release of sins be proclaimed to all the nations" (Luke 24:47). (5) Verse 31 refers to Jesus (although not by name) as the one appointed by God to judge the world. Peter said the same thing in 10:42,[3] adding that this judge has been authorized to proclaim amnesty (10:43). The characteristically Lukan word ὁρίζω[4] appears in both 10:42 and 17:31 to express God's role as the one who has "appointed" or "determined" Jesus to be judge. God is almost always the determiner to which this word refers (so in Luke 22:22; Acts 2:23; 10:42; 17:26, 31). It has an important role in the Lukan presentation of God as the sovereign shaper of destiny according to God's own plan (cf. especially 2:23). Thus a good share of the Athens speech repeats themes already presented in Luke-Acts.

Nevertheless, the speech as a whole contributes something new and important to the narrative. It provides a carefully stated theological perspective not only for Paul's work in Athens but also for his more extensive work in Corinth and Ephesus that follows. Paul and Barnabas were, of course, working among Gentiles on the first missionary journey, and the success of this work was emphasized in 14:27. However, the new mission that began with the vision in 16:9–10 has been based primarily in Jewish settings, even if gentile God-worshipers are involved. This is true of

---

[3] There may be a hint of the role of Jesus as judge in the quotation in 2:20–21. The name of the Lord that saves in 2:21 is understood to be the name of Jesus in the following narrative (see above, 31, 49, 60–61), which suggests that the "day of the Lord" in 2:20 may refer to the day of Jesus' judgment.

[4] Used six times in Luke-Acts, twice in the rest of the NT.

Philippi (the conversion of the jailer is due to exceptional circumstances, not a plan of mission) and also of Thessalonica and Beroea, where Paul's mission was cut short while its synagogue phase was still in progress. In Athens the situation begins to change. Even there Paul speaks in the synagogue with the Jews and their Gentile associates, but at the same time he is speaking in the marketplace with any who happen by (17:17). The rest of the scene, including the mission speech, highlights his encounter with Gentiles who have no relation to the synagogue.

Paul's work in Corinth and Ephesus begins in the synagogue, but the emphasis on extensive mission work beyond the synagogue in these locations is unusual. The extended mission in Corinth is understood as a partial fulfillment of God's plan to take "a people ($\lambda a \acute{o} \nu$) from the Gentiles," recognized by James in Jerusalem (see 15:14 with 18:10). The extended mission in Ephesus enables Paul to reach "all those inhabiting Asia . . . , both Jews and Greeks" (19:10). Paul's mission in Ephesus is a universal mission that reaches all.[5] The order of the narrative invites us to understand Paul's work in Corinth and Ephesus in light of the programmatic speech in Athens. This speech is the charter of a mission that can reach all because it no longer depends on the instruction of Gentiles by the synagogue, which has prepared some to accept the God of Israel revealed in Scripture. Paul speaks to Athenians but proclaims the God of all, who is close to every individual, an uneducated Ephesian as well as a sophisticated Athenian, thus providing the foundation for a mission that reaches beyond Athens. As the Athens speech prepares for this phase of Paul's mission, the farewell speech to the Ephesian elders looks back on it. There Paul declares that he did not fail to announce "the whole plan of God ($\pi \hat{a} \sigma a \nu \ \tau \grave{\eta} \nu \ \beta o \upsilon \lambda \grave{\eta} \nu \ \tau o \hat{\upsilon} \ \theta \epsilon o \hat{\upsilon}$)" (20:27). That is why he is "clean from the blood of all" (20:26). Paul uses similar language to speak of his prophetic responsibility to Jews in 18:6, but in 20:26 he is speaking of his responsibility to "all." If Paul had failed to announce the whole plan of God, God's plan in its universal scope, thereby implying that some group is excluded from God's saving purpose, he would bear guilty responsibility for the blood (i.e., the death) of those persons. The narrator of Acts has been presenting the plan of God through the whole series of speeches to Acts 17. Because, as Paul Schubert said, "the Areopagus speech is not only a hellenized but also a universalized version of Luke's $\beta o \upsilon \lambda \acute{\eta}$-theology," it is probable "that Luke regarded the Areopagus speech as the final climactic part of his exposition of the whole plan of God."[6] This speech presents the relation of God to humanity as a whole and founds God's call

---

[5] On the Ephesian mission, see further 235–36.
[6] P. Schubert, "Areopagus Speech," 260–61.

not on the history of a special group but on the creaturely humanness that is shared by all.

Nevertheless, Paul and the narrator are not renouncing their belief in God's promise to Israel, for this theme will return in the final cycle of speeches after Paul's arrest.[7] The tension between the Athens speech and Paul's statements about God's promise to Israel cannot be easily resolved, for one begins from what all share as God's creatures and the other from God's special history with a chosen people. Both perspectives are important in Acts.

In setting the scene, the narrator is able, in a few bold strokes, to characterize the life of Athens and recall what is typically Athenian. Philosophers are present, including representatives of two of the major schools. The Areopagus is mentioned. The curiosity of the Athenians and their desire for knowledge are noted (17:19–21). There are even hints that Paul is a new Socrates in the description of him as a "proclaimer of foreign divinities" (reminiscent of the charge that Athenians brought against Socrates)[8] and perhaps also in the references to Paul's discussions in the marketplace.[9]

Although the narrator, along with most people of the Greco-Roman world, may honor Socrates, the picture of Athens is not favorable. We are told immediately that Paul was angered when he observed that the city was "full of idols" (17:16). Here we are given advance indication of an important issue that will be addressed in Paul's speech. In 17:18 two reactions of the philosophers to Paul are quoted. One expresses contempt (he is a $\sigma\pi\epsilon\rho\mu o\lambda\acute{o}\gamma os$, a superficial collector of gossip and other people's ideas), the other a gross misunderstanding of Paul's message (Jesus and the resurrection are two deities). Verse 21, an aside to the reader,[10] offers an evaluative generalization to the effect that all Athenians are prone to fads. They are overly fascinated with the latest thing. Their interest in Paul's new teaching is merely a further sign of this weakness. Thus Paul, in responding to the philosophers' request for more instruction, is speaking to a difficult audience. He has already been preaching "Jesus and the resurrection" with no success. In hope of doing better, he must now attempt to present his message in a way that critically engages the cultural world that he has entered.

Within this cultural world knowledge has high value. This appears in the philosophers' requests of Paul: "Can we know?" (v. 19); "We wish to know" (v. 20). Paul responds to these requests by referring to the altar to

---

[7] See below, 286–87, 318–22.
[8] See E. Haenchen, *Acts,* 518.
[9] See E. Haenchen, *Acts,* 517.
[10] On asides to the reader see David Rhoads and Donald Michie, *Mark as Story,* 38–39.

an "unknown God" in Athens, taking this as a sign of Athenian ignorance ("What then without knowing [ἀγνοοῦντες] you worship . . . ," v. 23). He then proceeds to make this God known as the creator of all, who is independent of human creations. At the end of the speech Paul returns to the theme of knowledge and ignorance, describing the past as "the times of ignorance" from which people must now repent if they are to acknowledge the true God (v. 30).[11] Starting from a cultural value acknowledged by the audience enables Paul to engage them in the discourse. Denying that this value has been realized within the present culture and calling for repentance turn this into a critical engagement.

The Areopagus speech may provide a helpful model of the delicate task of speaking outside the religious community through critical engagement with the larger world. A mission that does not engage the presuppositions and dominant concerns of those being approached leaves these presuppositions and concerns untouched, with the result that the message, even if accepted, does not transform its hearers. The fundamental structures of the old life remain standing, and the gospel loses its culture-transforming power. Dialogue with outsiders may be risky, but the refusal of dialogue on cultural concerns results either in the isolation of the religious community or the compartmentalization of religion so that it does not affect society at large.

The critical aspect of the speech seems strong when we notice that it contains three prominent negative statements that expose misunderstandings of God.[12] Paul insists that God "does not dwell in temples made with hands," is not "served by human hands" (through the offerings of the temples), and cannot be represented by images of human creation (17:24–25, 29). In all three cases there is confusion between God and a location or an image that humans create, or with the mutual meeting of needs that characterizes human life. The speech upholds God's transcendence not by implying God's distance from humans (cf. vv. 27–28) but by understanding God's role in creating and giving as irreversible. God gives and creates for humanity; humanity may give and create, but not for God.[13] The rejection of human attempts to represent God by images in v. 29 is

---

[11] On this theme of knowledge and ignorance in the Athens scene, see further J. Dupont, *Nouvelles études*, 411–13. Dupont denies that the speech refers simply to an intellectual ignorance.

[12] The importance of these negative statements is emphasized in J. Dupont, *Nouvelles études*, 392–96, and G. Schneider, *Lukas, Theologe*, 302.

[13] A further detail that seems to support this point: The verb κατοικεῖ (in the phrase "does not dwell," v. 24) becomes thematic when the stem is repeated in v. 26 (κατοικεῖν, κατοικίας). Verse 24 concerns human efforts to provide a dwelling for God, which demonstrates a misunderstanding of God. Verse 26 shows that God instead cares for the human need for a place to dwell. See P. Auffret, "Structure littéraire du discours d'Athènes," 186–87, 192.

Paul's public expression of his displeasure with a city "full of idols," noted at the beginning of the episode (v. 16).

Thus it is clear that Paul is critical of Athenian religion as expressed in temples, cults, and images. It is not so clear that he is critical of the philosophers who have asked for an explanation. Martin Dibelius has shown that much of the speech (until vv. 30–31) parallels what respected thinkers of the Greco-Roman world would affirm. The freedom of God from any need that humans might supply (v. 25) is a frequent theme in Greek philosophy.[14] Furthermore, "the idea that God is related to men has been familiar in philosophy ever since the spread and popularising of the Stoic conception of the wise man."[15] In the speech Paul makes this point by explicitly referring to a line of the poet Aratus written in praise of Zeus (v. 28: "For we are indeed offspring of this one"). Dibelius finds Seneca to be a particularly rich source of parallels. According to Dibelius, "the motifs of Acts 17 constantly recur in Seneca's work: rejection of worship and of every service to the gods, the nearness of God to men, man's relatedness to God."[16] Although the speech is clearly critical of the popular religion of Athens, it seems to go out of its way to find common ground with philosophers and poets.

We might ask, then, whether the narrative properly fits the speech to the depicted audience. Is Paul criticizing his audience for views that they probably would not share? The answer may depend on how we conceive the audience. Paul is responding to the request of some philosophers, who are presumably part of the audience. However, they have "brought him to the Areopagus" (v. 19), and Paul speaks "standing in the midst of the Areopagus" (v. 22). There has been extensive discussion of whether the Areopagus refers to the Hill of Ares, a place (the original meaning of the term), or to the administrative body that took its name from this place.[17] Dibelius, arguing that "the decision must be reached neither by topographical nor by historical, but by literary considerations," decides that the place is meant.[18] However, literary considerations (namely, the assumption that here as elsewhere the narrator intends the speech to fit the audience) incline me to the opposite choice. The speech fits better if Paul is addressing not only the philosophers but also an official body that has responsibility for the city, including its religious facilities and rites.[19]

---

[14] See M. Dibelius, *Studies in the Acts*, 42–43.

[15] See M. Dibelius, *Studies in the Acts*, 47.

[16] See M. Dibelius, *Studies in the Acts*, 53–54.

[17] See K. Lake and H. Cadbury, *Beginnings of Christianity* 4:212–13; E. Haenchen, *Acts*, 518–19.

[18] See *Studies in the Acts*, 67–69, 80–81. The quotation is from 69.

[19] Commenting on the Areopagus as a governing body, K. Lake and H. Cadbury say, "The

Then Paul's comments on the popular religion of Athens are not wide of the mark, for he is addressing a group that bears responsibility for such matters. Paul is telling them that religion in Athens does not live up to the insights of the philosophers and poets. The address of the speech, which is general ("men of Athens," not "philosophers of Athens"), the reference to the sanctuaries that provoked Paul as "your sanctuaries" (v. 23), and the concluding reference to the conversion of an Areopagite (a member of the Areopagus council) provide further support for this view.

The preceding observations help us understand the strategy of the speech in its context. We have already noted that Paul is speaking to a difficult audience, for the philosophers who ask him to explain his teaching have expressed contempt for him or gross misunderstanding of his teaching (17:18) and are motivated by fickle curiosity (17:21). George Kennedy's emphasis on the key significance of the "rhetorical problem" can help us to understand Paul's response to this situation.[20]

In many rhetorical situations the speaker will be found to face one overriding *rhetorical problem*. His audience is perhaps already prejudiced against him and not disposed to listen to anything he may say. . . . The problem may color the treatment throughout the speech, and sometimes a speaker is best advised to lay a foundation for understanding on the part of the audience before bringing up the central problem.

such is the strategy of the Areopagus speech. Paul's problem relates especially to his strange teaching about Jesus and the resurrection. Reference to these problematic subjects is postponed to the very end of the speech, while in the bulk of the speech Paul seeks to "lay a foundation for understanding on the part of the audience." He does so by first advancing views that would not appear ridiculous in the eyes of respected Greco-Roman thinkers.

The desire to emphasize common ground appears not only in the parallels to the speech cited by Dibelius and in the explicit quotation of a Greek poet but also in other features. Paul begins by recalling his tour of Athenian sanctuaries, mentioned by the narrator in v. 16. In that verse we were told that Paul was provoked and irritated ($\pi\alpha\rho\omega\xi\acute{v}\nu\epsilon\tauo$) by what he saw. He does not express that feeling in vv. 22–23. Passing over the many sanctuaries, he focuses on one that provides a point of contact with his audience: an altar to an unknown God. This altar both testifies to the Athenians' rudimentary awareness of the God proclaimed by Paul (who is, then, not a "foreign" divinity) and confesses that this God is unknown

---

control of religious matters was doubtless the one thing it had always retained during the period of its least influence." See *Beginnings of Christianity* 4:213.

[20] See *New Testament Interpretation,* 36. Emphasis by Kennedy.

in Athens. Then Paul proclaims this God in terms that maintain biblical
monotheism but could also gain the respect of many cultured Greeks. The
negative statement about images in v. 29 brings Paul to his concern about
a city "full of idols" (v. 16). Although his criticism is clear, he softens his
statement by saying "we ought not" rather than "you ought not" fashion
idols. This is an effort to avoid the confrontation that results from an "I"
accusing a "you."[21] Yet the connection of v. 29 with v. 16 indicates that
Athenian idolatry is a serious problem for the narrator, and Paul's next
sentence is a call to repentance (v. 30). The Athenians are still ignorant of
God, but the "times of ignorance" should be past because of the new
opportunity and necessity of repentance.

The call to repentance is not pointed specifically at Paul's audience. It
is a call to "all everywhere." Yet Paul's audience must also be included.
Although the speech suggests possible areas of agreement between Paul
and cultured Greeks, these do not excuse the latter from repentance.
Perhaps not only the Areopagus but also the philosophers are held
responsible for the fact that Athens is a "city full of idols" that continues
the confusion between God and human works noted in the negative
statements of vv. 24–25, 29. The philosophers' teaching has not solved the
problem of religions that restrict God to human space and shape, and
some of the wise, perhaps, are not even concerned to reform religious
practices that treat God in this way. Paul, viewing the present in light of a
new action of God, is not willing to accept the past "times of ignorance"
passively. He sees the need and opportunity for a radical transformation
of the religious culture of the Greco-Roman world, for the present is a
new time that requires all to repent. This is necessary preparation for the
coming world judgment.

Although Paul seeks areas of common understanding with his audience, the speech is basically a call to repentance, a call for the Greco-
Roman world to break decisively with its religious past in response to the
one God who now invites all to be part of the renewed world. The culture
that Athens represents is called to repent because it makes God dependent
on human temples, rites, and images (vv. 24–25, 29), but it is also called to
repent because it rightly belongs to God's family. It is important to note
that there is a positive as well as a negative motivation for the call to
repentance in the speech. The positive motivation appears most clearly in
vv. 27–28. According to vv. 26–27, humans were created to seek for God.
In spite of the difficulty of this search for blind humans, who must "feel
after" God, it is not impossible, for God is "not far from each one of us" (v.
27). This statement is supported by v. 28. God is not far, for human life

---

[21] A point noted by Jean Calloud, "Paul devant l'Aréopage," 227.

itself is rooted in God, and (as the poet said) we are God's "offspring" or "family (γένος)." Paul's statements in vv. 27b-28 have an important function in the speech. They recognize and encourage the search for God in the Greco-Roman world, grounding its possibility in human existence as such and in the universally shared relation of Creator and creature.[22]

The description of all humans as members of God's "family" is particularly striking. The term γένος is never used in Luke-Acts to mean simply a "kind" or "species" but always refers to a human group with a common origin and social life. It is sometimes used in introducing new characters when the narrator indicates the "nation" or "people" from which they come (Acts 4:36; 18:2, 24). It is also used of the "highpriestly family" (4:6) and the "family of Joseph," that is, his brothers (7:13). Jews as a whole are a "family" or "people" united by origin. Using γένος, a Jew can speak to fellow Jews about "our family" (7:19) or address them as "sons of the family of Abraham" (13:26). This same family is God's "people (λαός)" (Luke 1:68, 77; 2:32; Acts 7:34; 13:17). In Athens, however, Paul asserts (helped by a pagan poet) that all humans are God's "family." All are embraced by God as God's people and children. The place of Israel as God's people remains important, but it cannot be understood as an exclusive claim, for it is placed within a larger relationship of humanity and God that encompasses all. Being God's family implies that God is "not far," that is, available and responsive to those who seek. As God's relation to Israel carries with it a promise, so all humanity as God's family is promised that God is available to those who seek.[23] Human ignorance of God has hampered this search, but now God is available in a new way, and those who respond with repentance will be able to find their Creator.

The speech constructs a series of delicate balances. The chiasm in vv. 24–25 balances initial and final clauses presenting God as Creator with two internal statements presenting the failure of human religion to properly acknowledge this God.[24] The purpose of such a construction is not to emphasize one part or another but to balance the parts, emphasizing the tension between the frame and the framed. Less clear but still significant is the frame formed by the negative statements about religion in vv. 24–25 and 29. These indications of human ignorance of God frame the encour-

---

[22] J. Dupont stresses the "nuance of skepticism" in the reference to seeking God in v. 27. See *Nouvelles études*, 420. Although this may be found in the reference to people "feeling after" God (expressed in the optative in Greek), it is immediately balanced by what follows. The real possibility that every person may seek and find God is being affirmed.

[23] K. Löning comments that in the Areopagus speech seeking for God corresponds, on a lower level, to Israel's hope. See "Evangelium und die Kulturen," 2635.

[24] I am simplifying the construction somewhat. It begins with two participial clauses, followed by two main clauses, followed again by two participial clauses. See J. Dupont, *Nouvelles études*, 393, and P. Auffret, "Structure littéraire du discours d'Athènes," 187–89.

aging words about being God's "family," from whom God is "not far."
The resulting structure emphasizes the tension between the potentiality
and the reality of religion. These balanced statements then lead to the call
to repentance in v. 30, which returns to a theme of the beginning
(ignorance, v. 23), forming an inclusion.[25]

The speech does not end the mocking of some (v. 32; cf. v. 18). However, others express a willingness to hear Paul further on these matters, so
the speech is not without positive impact,[26] and a few conversions are
recorded. Because the mocking is prompted by the reference to resurrection, it is clear that this remains a point of difficulty. The expressed
desire to hear again "concerning this" (i.e., this man?) may reflect the fact
that the role of Jesus is presented only in a brief and cryptic way in this
speech.

---

[25] As noted by J. Dupont, *Nouvelles études*, 392.

[26] As C. K. Barrett points out, the μέν . . . δέ construction indicates a contrast between the two
reactions. See "Paul's Speech on the Areopagus," 71.

CORINTH:
A LENGTHY MISSION
DESPITE OPPOSITION

Gerhard Krodel contrasts the account of Paul's work in Athens with his mission in Corinth. Although the Athens account is "a carefully structured single scene," in the Corinth report "Luke merely connected four pieces of information" (vv. 1–4, 5–8, 9–11, 12–17).[1] It is true that the Corinth episode is constructed out of a series of short scenes. Even here, however, there are suggestions of narrative links among the scenes, resulting in a sketch of a significant development in Paul's ministry in Corinth. Furthermore, after the introductory verses (vv. 1–4), the materials are shaped into three varieties of type-scenes highlighting three important pronouncements (by Paul, v. 6; by the Lord, vv. 9–10; and by Gallio, vv. 14–15). These scenes are good examples of the narrator's tendency to portray events in typical patterns. The scenes combine to show Paul having a long and fruitful ministry in Corinth in spite of strong Jewish opposition.

Aquila and Priscilla are introduced in 18:2. They are important, first of all, because they enable Paul to work at his trade. Later they will travel with Paul from Corinth to Ephesus (18:18) and will play a role in the mission as teachers during Paul's absence from Ephesus (18:26). Thus they are more than employers. The reference to Paul working with them at a trade in 18:3 prepares for Paul's statement in his farewell speech that he supported himself and others with his own hands (20:33–35). His statement there indicates that he did hand labor not only in Corinth but also later in Ephesus.

Priscilla and Aquila are examples of Christians who not only support a local community but also travel and link communities. Aquila is a native of Pontus who, with Priscilla, came from Italy, works in Corinth, and then will travel with Paul to Ephesus. There they will come in contact with Apollos, an Alexandrian who comes to Ephesus and then goes to Corinth (18:24—19:1). There is a suggestion here of the benefit to the

---

[1] See *Acts*, 341.

mission from folk who are able to travel and who use that opportunity for the mission and the new communities.[2]

The first of the type-scenes that make up the Corinthian sequence is found in 18:5–7. It is widely recognized that this scene follows the pattern of events in Pisidian Antioch, where Paul and Barnabas announced that they were turning to the Gentiles in the face of Jewish rejection (13:44–47). Corinth is the setting of the second such scene, and the final major scene of the work, Paul's preaching and parting words to the Jews of Rome, is a third.[3] In Corinth Paul has been "testifying to the Jews that the Messiah is Jesus." This summary recalls an important aspect of Paul's message in the Antioch synagogue. Then Paul announces, "From now on I will go to the Gentiles." The cause of the announcement closely parallels the situation in Antioch. It is made when the Jews were "resisting and reviling" (or "blaspheming"). Paul shakes out his garments as he makes his announcement, a gesture that parallels the shaking off of dust from the feet in 13:51. Nevertheless, there is a significant difference at this point. Paul does not do this as he leaves the city, as both 13:51 and Jesus' instructions in Luke 9:5 (cf. 10:10–11) would lead us to expect. The following verses will place major emphasis on the fact that Paul is not driven from Corinth by the Jews, as has happened in other places. Still, the announcement and gesture are accompanied by a change of location. Paul has been preaching in the synagogue. When he begins to encounter strong public resistance, he transfers to the house of Titius Justus. Paul's announcement that he is going to the Gentiles indicates a shift from a synagogue-based mission, addressed to Jews and to those Gentiles attracted to Judaism, to a mission in the city at large, where the population is predominantly Gentile. The narrator makes clear that Paul's mission to Jews and gentile God-worshipers had some success, mentioning Titius Justus (who presumably has become a believer because he offers his house for Paul's use) and Crispus, a synagogue ruler, who "believed the Lord with all his house." Indeed, the description of Paul's new base may indicate that Paul yielded as little ground as possible. He is based in the home of a Gentile, but Titius Justus is one of the God-worshipers who participated in the synagogue, and his house "borders on the synagogue" (18:7).

---

[2] F. Beydon notes the interest of Acts in the mobility of some people within the Roman Empire, which is useful to the mission. See "Luc et 'ces dames de la haute société," 338–39.

[3] Although E. Haenchen, *Acts,* 729, speaks of three such scenes and finds their geographical distribution to be significant, a partially similar pattern is also found in 19:8–9 and 22:17–21. On these five passages see my essay "Rejection by Jews and Turning to Gentiles." The next two paragraphs are a modified version of part of this essay, originally published in *Society of Biblical Literature 1986 Seminar Papers,* edited by Kent Harold Richards (Atlanta: Scholars Press, 1986), 130–41.

In 18:6 Paul says, "Your blood is [or "will be"] on your head; I am clean." These words are to be understood in light of the necessity laid on Paul to speak the word of God first to the Jews, as stated in 13:46. References to bloodguilt as responsibility for someone else's death, as in Matt. 23:35; 27:25; Acts 5:28, are not close parallels, for here the Corinthian Jews are responsible for their own blood. *They* are responsible, not Paul, as he emphasizes with the statement, "I am clean." The situation is like that of the prophetic "watchman" described in Ezek. 33:1–9, and Paul borrows the language of Ezek. 33:4 (τὸ αἷμα αὐτοῦ ἐπὶ τῆς κεφαλῆς αὐτοῦ ἔσται = "His blood will be on his head"). The watchman is one who hears a word from God and is obligated to speak it to the people. If he does not, the blood of those who perish will be demanded from the hand of the watchman; if he does, the blood of those who perish will be on their own heads. Paul is clean because he has fulfilled his obligation to speak God's word to God's people.[4] They are now responsible for their own fate. The pattern of speaking first to Jews and only later turning to the Gentiles testifies to Paul's sense of prophetic obligation to his own people. He is released from this obligation only when he meets strong public resistance within the Jewish community. Then he can begin the second phase of his mission within a city, a phase in which the conversion of individual Jews is still possible, although Paul is no longer preaching in the synagogue nor addressing Jews as a community.[5]

With little introduction a report of a night vision and message from the Lord is inserted into the narrative (18:9–10). The narrative moves forward by presenting a second variety of type-scene, an epiphanic commissioning story. Benjamin Hubbard has analyzed these stories, showing that they are common both in Hebrew Scripture and in Luke-Acts.[6] These scenes, in which God or God's representative (usually an angel or the risen Lord Jesus) commissions someone for a task, have typical elements. These include the following elements of 18:9–11: the confrontation (i.e., the appearance of the divine commissioner), the commission to undertake a task, reassurance, and the conclusion (usually, as in v. 11, a statement that the one commissioned carries out the task). The element of reassurance because of the difficulty of the task is especially prominent in 18:9–10: "Do not fear but continue speaking . . . , for I am with you, and no one will attack you to harm you." Previous epiphanic commissionings

---

[4] In 20:26–27 the motif is reused with reference to Paul's inclusive mission, which entails responsibility for both Jews and Gentiles.

[5] This two-phase pattern was not followed in Athens, where Paul apparently conducted simultaneous missions in the synagogue to Jews and in the marketplace to Gentiles. See 17:17.

[6] See "Commissioning Stories in Luke-Acts," 103–26, and "Role of Commissioning Accounts in Acts," 187–98.

in Acts set in situations of danger or difficulty are closely related to 18:9–
11. Note 5:17–21 (the appearance of the angel to the imprisoned apostles,
with the command to "go and . . . continue speaking" in spite of the arrest),
9:10–18 (the appearance of the Lord to Ananias, with the sense of danger
accented by Ananias' protest and description of Saul), and 16:6–10 (the
vision of the Macedonian, who provides divine direction in a difficult
situation after a series of frustrating failures). The element of reassurance
in 18:9–10 will also be strong in later epiphanic scenes when Paul the
prisoner faces threats to his life from human enemies and the sea (23:11;
27:23–24).

The Lord's reassurance is important because the context emphasizes
strong Jewish opposition to Paul's work and because the Lord's command
will eliminate the easy ways out: stopping his preaching or (as Paul has
repeatedly done previously) leaving for another city. Paul must not become silent; he must continue his mission in Corinth, for the Lord has "a
large people in this city." The narrator places this command after the
strong Jewish resistance that Paul encountered in the synagogue, causing
his departure (18:6), and just before the report of a concerted effort by
Jews to eliminate Paul by judicial action. Previous episodes have repeatedly shown how necessary it was for Paul to leave when the situation
became impossible. The Antioch episode, with which the Corinth episode
is linked by the type-scene of turning to Gentiles in the face of Jewish
opposition, ends with Paul and Barnabas being put out of the region
because of Jewish agitation (13:50–51). Philippi and Thessalonica are
linked to the Corinth episode by the public accusation type-scene.[7] In the
former case Paul is released but must leave the city, and in the latter he is
sent away by night for safety (17:10). Neither in 17:10 nor elsewhere
(14:6; 17:14) is there any sense of shame at a quick escape. It is the
obvious requirement in the situation. However, Paul's exit from Corinth
is blocked because the Lord is concerned about the "large people for me in
this city." Paul's stay of a year and six months in Corinth (18:11), an
unusually long time, is a direct response to the Lord's instructions. The
large people requires an extended period of "teaching the word of God."
In the vision scene the Lord intervenes both to require and (through divine
protection) allow a change in the pattern of events that has been common
to this point in Paul's mission. There is to be no quick mission and rapid
escape.

The description of Corinthians, most of them Gentile, as the Lord's
"people (λαός)" applies the statement of James in 15:14 to the present
situation. James, using scriptural language, spoke of how God first began

---

[7] See above, 201–3, 208–9.

"to take from the Gentiles a people for his name."[8] What God began earlier through Peter's conversion of Cornelius is continuing through Paul's work in Corinth; the Lord's people is being gathered in a Gentile city. Again this is expressed in scriptural language, indeed, language specifically reminiscent of the covenant relation between God and the people of Israel. The phrase λαός ἐστί μοι ("there is a people for me") in 18:10 closely resembles the common covenant formula in Jeremiah and Ezekiel: ἔσονταί (or ἔσεσθέ) μοι εἰς λαόν ("They [or "you"] shall be for me as a people," i.e., "shall become my people"), preceded or followed by the statement that "I will be for them [or "you"] as God."[9] The scriptural style conveys meaning: the Lord's "large people" in Corinth is now part of the one covenant people that began with Israel, not by accepting Israel's circumcision but through being cleansed by faith (15:9).

Jacques Dupont, while emphasizing that λαός has its full theological force when applied to Gentiles in Acts, also warns against the notion that there can be two peoples of God.[10] Nevertheless, two historic peoples of God, Judaism and Christianity, will be the result of the development that Acts is tracing. The narrator's discomfort with this development shows in the persistence of appeals to Jews. Some interpreters would see the threat of exclusion from God's people in 3:23 as an effort to solve this problem by eliminating unbelieving Jews once and for all. However, we are not told when that threat will take effect. We remain within the parameters of Lukan thought if we say that it applies whenever the rejection of God's prophetic messenger becomes definitive and irreversible, a possibility that must be continually tested by calls to repentance.

Scriptural language is not confined to the reference to the Lord's people. The Lord speaks to Paul in the way that God spoke to Jeremiah when calling him as a prophet. Jeremiah was called to be a "prophet to the nations (ἔθνη)." When he protested that he did not know how to speak, the Lord responded, "Whatever I command you, you shall speak (λαλήσεις)." This was followed by assurance of the Lord's protection: "Do not fear . . . , for I am with you to rescue you (τοῦ ἐξαιρεῖσθαί σε)" (Jer. 1:5–8; cf. 1:19). The reference to rescue is replaced with the statement that "no one will attack you to harm you" in Acts 18:9–10, but the whole of the Lord's statement (up to the reference to "a large people") can be understood as a paraphrase of Jeremiah's call to be a prophet to the nations (one who will suffer at the hands of his own people). It is true that similar words of divine assurance occur in other passages (Gen. 26:24; Isa.

---

[8] See above, 186–87.

[9] See LXX Jer. 7:23; 11:4; 24:7; 38:1, 33; 39:38; Baruch 2:35; Ezek. 11:20; 14:11; 36:28; 37:23.

[10] See "Un peuple d'entre les nations," 329.

41:10 [addressed to God's servant]; 43:5), but the influence of Jeremiah's call on the narrator's portrayal of Paul appears again in the account of Paul's call in Acts 26:16–17, with the key word "rescue": "I appeared to you to choose you . . . , rescuing you (ἐξαιρούμενός σε) from the people and from the Gentiles, to whom I send you."[11] The Lord's promise of rescue plays a significant role in the narrator's presentation of Paul.

The placement of the night vision is significant, for it is related both to what precedes and what follows. The promise that "no one will attack you to harm you" is fulfilled when Paul escapes from a critical situation in vv. 12–17 and is able to continue his work in Corinth (v. 18). The statement concerning the Lord's large people in Corinth is related to v. 8, where we are told that "many of the Corinthians . . . were believing and being baptized." This statement of success comes before the vision. Thus the reference to a large people is not a prediction of something new but an interpretation of what is already underway. Paul's daytime experience (success in mission) and nighttime experience (the vision) confirm each other in this case. The vision interprets both the mission's success and the escape from danger as manifestations of the Lord's purpose and power. The statement "I am with you" highlights the hidden actor in the narrative.

The narrative continues with a third type-scene, a scene of public accusation before an official, similar to 16:19–24 and 17:5–9. The situation is similar, but the outcome is different. Rather than being beaten and put in prison (as in Philippi) or having to put up a bond (as with Jason in Thessalonica), Paul is released when the accusation is rejected out of hand, a turn of human events that appears as the Lord's providential care in light of 18:10.

There are several difficulties in understanding the Gallio scene. One concerns the accusation brought by the Jews in v. 13: "This fellow incites people to worship God contrary to the law." Are the accusers referring to Roman or Jewish law? According to Hans Conzelmann, Luke pictures the Jews as deliberately ambiguous in an attempt to deceive Gallio.[12] This view strains credulity, however. The Jews speak of worshiping God (using the singular). It is unlikely that any official would forget that Jews have their own way of worship according to their own law. It seems, then, that the Jews are straightforwardly appealing to Gallio for protection of their religious community against a disturbing intruder. Paul's relation to the Jewish law will become an important concern when he arrives in Jerusalem for the last time. There he must respond to accusations that he

---

[11] Perhaps Joseph provides another model of God's protection. See Acts 7:9–10: "God was with him and rescued him."

[12] See *Acts*, 153.

teaches against the law (21:21, 24, 28; cf. 22:3; 24:14; 25:8; 28:17). The accusation in 18:13 can be understood as a forerunner of this later theme. In Ephesus there will be a complaint about Paul's harmful effect on Ephesian religion (19:25–27). In Corinth the Jews complain about his harmful effect on their religion, hoping for some protection from the Roman proconsul. The reference to inciting people "to worship God (σέβεσθαι τὸν θεόν) contrary to the law" may also fit the context if it arises especially from Paul's effect on people like Titius Justus, a "God-worshiper" (σεβομένου τὸν θεόν; 18:7) who might have accepted the law under the influence of Corinthian Jews but who would not do so as a Christian.

The reference to Paul's vow in 18:18 may also indicate a concern with Paul's attitude toward the Jewish manner of life, regulated by the law. The reference is very brief, and the purpose of Paul cutting his hair and making a vow is obscure. The vow may relate to the Lord's rescue of Paul from danger in Corinth or anticipate danger on the trip that Paul is beginning.[13] However that may be, the narrator regards a vow concluded by the cutting of the hair as a practice of pious Jews who live according to the law. This is clear in the second reference to such a vow in Acts, when Paul is urged to participate in the completion of the Nazirite vow of four men. Paul's participation will demonstrate in the face of contrary accusations that he is a good Jew who lives according to the law (21:23–26). Readers somewhat familiar with Jewish practices would get the same impression from 18:18. Indeed, in one respect the point is made more clearly in 18:18; here Paul has acted without outside pressure. Even if Paul does not believe that gentile God-worshipers must live according to the law (see the accusation in 18:13), his position does not arise from contempt for Jews and their way of life.

A second set of problems concerns the attitude of Gallio toward the Jews and the attitude of the narrator toward Gallio. Many would share the view of Ernst Haenchen that "Luke makes Gallio occupy that standpoint which he himself considers as the correct one and which he passionately desires that Rome herself should take as her own: that Christianity is an inner-Jewish affair in which Rome does not meddle."[14] There is no doubt that the narrator is glad to have Paul escape further trouble. That the narrator hoped to persuade Romans to view Chris-

---

[13] See I. H. Marshall, *Acts,* 300: "Jews made vows to God either in thankfulness for past blessings (such as Paul's safekeeping in Corinth) or as part of a petition for future blessings (such as safekeeping on Paul's impending journey); the present context inclines towards the former interpretation."

[14] See *Acts,* 541.

tianity as "an inner-Jewish affair" is doubtful, however, as is Haenchen's tendency to make Gallio an inner-textual representative of the narrator.

At the end of the scene "all" seize Sosthenes, the synagogue ruler, and beat him "in front of the tribunal." Gallio shows no concern at this. The fact that the beating took place "in front of the tribunal" and the final statement about Gallio's unconcern make clear that Gallio saw and could have stopped the beating. So the final verse is an important indication of Gallio's attitude. The statement that "all" seized Sosthenes and beat him leaves a gap in the text that must be filled by the reader. The problem was experienced by manuscript copyists, for there are a number of manuscripts that read "all the Greeks" and a few that read "all the Jews." Both of these are secondary attempts to eliminate an ambiguity. Although the short reading "all" is probably original, it is still possible to interpret the assailants as either Jews or Gentiles. In either case we must read between the lines, supplying something that is not explicit (a common necessity in reading). In the one case we must guess at a motive for Jews suddenly turning on their own leader. In the other case we must identify a new group, a group of Gentiles not previously introduced in the narrative. Because the setting of the scene is a public area, the presence of such a group is not surprising, even if reference to it is sudden. Furthermore, the spatial configuration in vv. 16–17 seems to support the view that the assailants of Sosthenes are Gentiles. According to v. 16, Gallio "drove away" the Jews "from the tribunal." However, the beating takes place "in front of the tribunal." If one Jew, Sosthenes, is still in front of the tribunal, it is because he has been seized by the gentile crowd. If all the Jews are still there, a conflict appears with the forceful removal indicated in v. 16.

Gallio's rejection of the Jews' accusation might simply be the result of good political and legal judgment. The beating at the end, however, suggests that a less noble motive is involved. By refusing to intervene, Gallio gives implicit approval to gentile hostility toward Jews. In that case, his negative attitude toward Jews may also have been a factor in his legal decision.[15]

The narrator shows an interest in the beating of Sosthenes, adding it even though it has no effect on the outcome of the scene for Paul. Implied evaluation of this incident is more difficult to detect, perhaps, but the final sentence of the scene does not present Gallio as a clearheaded administrator, guided by a strong tradition of Roman justice, but only as a Roman official who is indifferent to the suffering of a troublesome Jew. We

---

[15] Thus there seems to be justification for E. Haenchen's description of Gallio as anti-Semitic. He also notes that Gallio's brother Seneca was anti-Semitic. See *Acts,* 536, 541.

should be careful not to assume that a minor character who happens to favor Paul is therefore approved by the narrator in other respects. The city official at Ephesus who ends the Ephesian riot is a similar case. Although the narrator and other Christians would no doubt thank this official for cooling pagan tempers, he does not speak from a Christian perspective. Indeed, he argues that the Christian challenge is inconsequential (19:35–36), hardly the narrator's view. The official is either speaking from ignorance or hiding what he knows in order to quell the riot.[16] Christians sometimes benefit, but it is not because the officials are wise, speak honestly, and consistently uphold justice. In both Corinth and Ephesus the narrative provides a glimpse of the complexity of human events, in which good results and flawed motives mix.

In describing the Ephesian riot, the narrator notes the hostility of pagans to Jews as well as Christians (19:33–34). Another instance of hostility to Jews by the dominant culture appears at the beginning of the Corinthian episode: Aquila and Priscilla come to Corinth because Claudius has expelled the Jews from Rome (18:2). Of these three cases of gentile hostility to Jews, the Gallio incident might be interpreted as satisfying to the narrator (a case of a Jewish opponent getting what he deserved). However, the other two cases decrease this possibility, for they show Jews and Christians facing the same hostility from pagans, or Jewish Christians oppressed by the Romans along with other Jews. Hostility to Jews within the Roman Empire is a reality recognized in the narrative and a significant factor in the Gallio scene. Indications of other types of bias will appear in the descriptions of the Roman governors who will later hold Paul prisoner.[17] Paul is released by Gallio, and this is the result of the Lord's promised protection. Nevertheless, the human instrument of this protection is no model of just and enlightened policy.

---

[16] See further below, 243–44.
[17] See below, 301–4, 306–14.

EPHESUS:
CLIMAX OF PAUL'S MISSION
AS A FREE MAN

Paul's trip from Corinth takes him first to Ephesus, where the narrator notes an initial contact with the local Jews. Instead of continuing this work, Paul refuses the Jews' invitation to stay longer and leaves Ephesus, promising to return, "God willing." Then 18:21–23 reports a major journey, although it occupies only two and a half verses. Why record such a journey when 18:24 will again direct our attention to Ephesus, about which the narrator has much to say? Paul's return trip to Jerusalem[1] and Antioch must have some importance. It need not indicate a subordination of Paul to the apostles (as if Paul had to report to his superiors),[2] but it probably does indicate a concern to maintain contact with the church's old centers. Paul is not a loner, founding a separate, Pauline church, but a major figure in the one mission that began in Jerusalem and was effectively continued from Antioch. Antioch actually receives the greater emphasis in the description of the journey. When Paul leaves Corinth, his goal is Syria (18:18). In Jerusalem he simply greets the church, but in Antioch he spends some time (18:22–23). The stay in Antioch appropriately rounds off a missionary journey that began there (15:35–41). Thus there is some basis for speaking of Paul's three missionary journeys, with a division at this point.

There is a further indication that 15:36—18:22 is to be understood as a major missionary journey like the journey in Acts 13—14. Paul's work includes both the conversion of new disciples and the later strengthening of these disciples. Once churches have been established in an area, Paul will visit them again in order to strengthen them. Only then is Paul's work in an area relatively complete. The motif of strengthening the churches is used at the end and beginning of the missionary journeys, thus serving as a mark of division. At the end of the first missionary journey, Paul and Barnabas return to the cities of southern Asia Minor where they have

---

[1] "The church" in 18:22 must refer to the Jerusalem church because Paul goes up from Caesarea and then goes down to Antioch. See the use of ἀναβαίνω and καταβαίνω of travel to and from Jerusalem in Luke 2:42, 51.

[2] See G. Klein, *Zwölf Apostel*, 175. Klein argues extensively that Luke subordinates Paul to the twelve.

worked, "strengthening the souls of the disciples" (14:21-22). The beginning of the second journey again emphasizes Paul's concern to visit and strengthen established churches (15:36, 41; 16:5). When Paul leaves Antioch for the third time in 18:23, he again is "strengthening all the disciples." This refers, however, to Galatia and Phrygia, not to the churches of Macedonia and Greece established on the second journey. There is an unfinished task in these areas that Paul will complete when he ends his work in Ephesus and leaves for Jerusalem, for he will not go directly but by way of Macedonia and Greece (19:21; 20:1-3). Thus the reference to leaving Antioch and strengthening the disciples in 18:23 suggests another missionary journey. Nevertheless, Paul's work before and after this return to Antioch is more closely connected than his first and second missionary journeys are. Not only does the Jerusalem conference form a more imposing division than the travel summary in 18:18-23 but also Paul's review of the churches in Macedonia and Greece is postponed until after his work in Ephesus. Paul's work in Macedonia, Greece, and Ephesus is completed as part of the final journey to Jerusalem, as Paul visits these churches for the last time or speaks to their leaders (the Ephesian elders, 20:17-38). Thus Paul's work on the second and third journeys is completed through a single sequence of final visitation, which binds these areas of work closely together. Although the second and third journeys are distinct, the narrative also encourages us to consider Paul's work in the Aegean region as a whole.

The third journey is a journey of new mission only in a limited sense. In the first two journeys the emphasis was on the founding of new churches. In 18:23 Paul begins a journey to strengthen established churches. We hear of missionary preaching only in Ephesus, and even there some previous work had been done. We really have a settled mission in Ephesus incorporated into a journey of church visitation. This observation should alert us to one of the main effects of the division imposed by Paul's return to Antioch in 18:18-23: it sets off Paul's Ephesian ministry. Ephesus is not just another stop in a series. It is Paul's last major place of new mission work; indeed, it is the sole center of mission noted in the last stage of Paul's work as a free man. The special importance of Ephesus appears already in 18:19-21, where Paul's brief visit to the Ephesian synagogue is indicated even though there is little to report except an initial responsiveness and Paul's promise to return. The fact that Paul's farewell speech will be addressed to the Ephesian elders is further indication of the special importance of Ephesus.

Before the narrator returns to Paul's synagogue preaching in Ephesus, we are told about Apollos and about some anonymous "disciples" who had not received the Spirit. The two sections are linked by the indications that

Apollos and the "disciples" had received only "the baptism of John" (18:25; 19:3). We must attempt to understand what these sections contribute to the narrative.

Michael Wolter has recently argued that Acts here reflects the Corinthian controversy discussed by Paul in 1 Corinthians 1—4, a controversy caused by followers of Apollos who claimed to be pneumatics. Luke constructs Paul's trip from Ephesus to Antioch and back in order to deny any contact between Paul and Apollos, making clear that Paul did not transmit the Spirit to him.[3] That Apollos knew "only the baptism of John" (18:25) indicates a deficiency, to be sure, one that includes incomplete understanding of God's way in Jesus (later rectified by Priscilla and Aquila). But Wolter's explanation founders on the fact that everything else in the episode is highly favorable toward Apollos, especially when he reaches Corinth (the site of the controversy). Apollos is not being set down as a troublemaker in the church for whom Paul must have no responsibility. Knowing only the baptism of John is a deficiency in a man who otherwise has great gifts for the mission and is already putting them to use. Apollos is an ἀνὴρ λόγιος (a "learned" or, more likely, "eloquent man"), "powerful in the Scriptures," acquainted with "the way of the Lord," able to teach "accurately the things about Jesus." He speaks out boldly in the synagogue. All this is true although he knows only the baptism of John. Before he goes to Corinth he has the further benefit of Priscilla and Aquila's instruction. "The brothers" in Ephesus support Apollos' plan to work in Achaia, writing and asking believers there to welcome him. Arriving in Corinth (see 19:1), he helps the believers there "much," for with the new insights gained from Priscilla and Aquila he can use his power of Scripture interpretation to great effect. "Vigorously" he is able to refute the Jews and show through the Scriptures that the Messiah is Jesus. The Christian community in Ephesus supported him, and the Corinthian community benefited from him. Apollos is not a problem but an asset.

In v. 25 the narrator refers to "the spirit" in connection with Apollos' speech. There is debate whether this refers to his personal temperament (his spirit was "boiling" = fervent, and this was demonstrated in his speech) or to the effect of the Holy Spirit on his speech.[4] In either case the remark underscores Apollos' power as a speaker, but this is especially true if, as I think likely, the Holy Spirit is meant. Two reasons support this view: First, this would explain a significant difference between Apollos and the "disciples" of 19:1-7. Although both know only the baptism of

---

[3] See "Apollos und die ephesinischen Johannesjünger," 49–73.
[4] See E. Haenchen, Acts, 550, who refers to representatives of the two opinions.

John, the latter alone are baptized and receive the Spirit. If it is obvious that Apollos already has the Spirit apart from Christian baptism,[5] his situation is quite different than that of the disciples who are ignorant of the Spirit (19:2). Second, 18:25 is describing Apollos' speech, and there is a good deal of attention to manifestations of the Holy Spirit through speech in Acts.[6] As parallels to 18:25 we should consider not just Rom. 12:11 but also references to speaking "in" or "by the Spirit," such as 1 Cor. 14:2 and especially Acts 6:10. There Stephen is speaking by the Spirit (τῷ πνεύματι ᾧ ἐλάλει; a construction similar to 18:25).[7] The powerful Apollos, refuting the Jews through Scripture, resembles Stephen, whose opponents could not withstand "the wisdom and the Spirit by which he was speaking" (6:10) and who interpreted Scripture to the Sanhedrin. Thus there is significant evidence, both from Acts 18:24—19:7 (which is concerned with those who lack the Spirit but does not raise this issue for Apollos) and from related references to speaking by the Spirit that Apollos' gifts include a strong manifestation of the Spirit in his speech.

However, the conjunction of two passages referring to people who know only the baptism of John suggests that the issue is not just Apollos but also John the Baptist and his heritage. The narrative shows the continuing effect of John's work, while presenting two different pictures of the result. Apollos is presented much more favorably than the "disciples" encountered by Paul in 19:1. Both know only the baptism of John, but they differ at two significant points: (1) The effect of the Spirit is manifest in Apollos' speech, but the disciples in Ephesus have not even heard that there is a Holy Spirit (19:2).[8] (2) Apollos, "knowing only the baptism of John," is nevertheless able to teach "accurately the things concerning Jesus." In contrast, Paul must instruct the other group that John's baptism of repentance was meant to prepare the people for faith in Jesus, the one coming after John (19:4). In the case of Apollos, John's baptism led him to teach about Jesus because he accepted John's testimony about the coming one and recognized Jesus as its fulfillment. However, the response by the so-called disciples to Paul's first question in 19:2 seems to lead him to doubt whether they even know about Jesus and the need for faith in him (19:4). John's "baptism of repentance for the people"

---

[5] The narrator is aware of such people. John the Baptist is among them (Luke 1:15), as well as Elizabeth (1:41), Zechariah (1:67), and Simeon (2:25–27).

[6] See 1:16; 2:4, 17–18; 4:8, 25, 31; 6:10; 10:44–46; 13:9–10; 19:6; 21:4, 11.

[7] In light of 1 Cor. 14:2 and Acts 6:10, it is quite possible that τῷ πνεύματι in 18:25 goes with ἐλάλει rather than ζέων. Even if it is the complement of ζέων, the participial phrase still modifies ἐλάλει, suggesting that this sentence is merely an emphatic variant of the references to speaking by the Spirit that we have noted.

[8] Perhaps this means that they have not heard that there is a new outpouring of the Spirit through Jesus, making the Spirit available to all. Then again, a statement of gross ignorance may be intended: they have never heard of the Holy Spirit at all.

has an important role in preparing the people for the coming of their Messiah, and John's mission is both recalled and continued in the preaching of Peter and Paul.[9] For a Jew to be baptized into John's baptism is in itself a very positive thing, but much depends on whether this leads one on to anticipate and accept the coming Messiah who will baptize with Holy Spirit, of whom John spoke (Luke 3:15-16). Apollos had accepted John's witness to the coming Messiah and Jesus as its fulfillment, even though he had not received Christian baptism.[10] However, Paul shows serious doubt about the group that he discovers at Ephesus. The problem is solved by clarifying the relation of John's work to Jesus. Hearing about faith in Jesus, the "disciples" are baptized into his name and receive the Holy Spirit. John's heritage is still influential, and it still has great value, provided it is properly understood. Apollos understood before he came to Ephesus. He only needed some further instruction from Priscilla and Aquila to be a very powerful spokesman for Jesus.[11] The group Paul met had received John's baptism but did not understand the purpose of John's mission. They represent a degenerate form of John's heritage, from the viewpoint of Paul and the narrator. Even so, John's heritage helped lead them to recognize what they had missed.

In Antioch of Pisidia and Corinth, Paul announced that he was turning to the Gentiles after meeting resistance in the synagogue (see 13:45-47; 18:4-7). Although there is no such announcement in 19:8-9, Paul left the Ephesian synagogue for the school of Tyrannus after encountering similar resistance. The change took place when "some were becoming hardened and disobedient, speaking evil of the way before the multitude." Even though the opposition came from only "some" of the Jews, it was vocal and public, perhaps including heckling and disruption of the assembly. Under these circumstances Paul moved his mission to another setting and also "separated the disciples." The last statement suggests the fateful consequences of the required shift of mission locations: Christian disciples began to form a separate religious community. The repeated references to resistance in the synagogue, followed by a shift to another location, suggest that the narrator is adjusting to a hard fact. The Christian message belongs in the synagogue, because it is first of all a message to Jews about their Messiah, but, under the circumstances, the synagogue cannot be a place of Christian preaching.

The most persistent element in the similar scenes in 13:45-47; 18:4-7;

---

[9] See *Narrative Unity* 1:48-50.

[10] Apollos knew "the way of the Lord," according to 18:25. This theme was first introduced in connection with John the Baptist (see Luke 1:76; 3:4; 7:27) and seems to function here as a summary of John's heritage understood as preparation for Jesus.

[11] Francis Pereira draws a parallel between Apollos and John the Baptist when he comments that Apollos prepared the Ephesian Jews to hear Paul's message as John had prepared for Jesus. See *Ephesus: Climax of Universalism,* 60-61.

and 19:8–9 is the shift from the synagogue as a place of preaching because of "reviling" or "evil-speaking" by Jews. In the first two instances the shift is accompanied by Paul's announcement that he is turning to the Gentiles. In Ephesus such an announcement is missing, for a good reason. What follows is not an exclusively Gentile mission. Jews cannot be addressed as an assembly, but they can still be addressed as part of the public that Paul encounters in his work. The narrator emphasizes that Paul's mission in Ephesus was comprehensive and inclusive, for "all the inhabitants of Asia heard the word of the Lord, both Jews and Greeks" (19:10). This statement does not mean that Paul preached to all the Jews before leaving the Ephesian synagogue, then preached to all the Gentiles. It is placed after Paul's withdrawal from the synagogue and in context indicates the result (see ὥστε) of two years of preaching based in the school of Tyrannus. Acts 19:10 makes no distinction in time or place between Jews and Greeks as recipients of the word. It is speaking of the spreading effect of Paul's continuing contact with both groups (perhaps including secondary contacts through converts) until the whole province is covered. Any attempt to limit preaching to Jews to Paul's three months in the synagogue also introduces an unnecessary difficulty. The narrator may exaggerate, but there is no need to increase the exaggeration by imagining that all the Jews of Asia could be reached through three month's work in one synagogue. A broader and longer mission is envisioned.

The strong statement about the scope of Paul's mission in 19:10 is supported in 19:26, where Paul's enemy Demetrius testifies to his influence in "nearly all of Asia." Moreover, the phrase "Jews and Greeks (᾽Ιουδαίους τε καὶ ῞Ελληνας)" is a formula used repeatedly in connection with the mission in Ephesus and used only there of preaching outside the synagogue. It also occurs in 14:1 and 18:4, but both passages refer to preaching in the synagogue, indicating that the "Greeks" are Gentiles who have already been attracted to Judaism. Thus the mission is not yet a general one. In the Ephesian mission, however, the formula applies to *all the inhabitants* of Asia (19:10) or Ephesus (19:17). It will recur in 20:21 as part of Paul's summary of his Ephesian ministry in his farewell speech. That Paul's mission outside the synagogue reaches out to all, both Jews and Greeks, is a point of special emphasis in the narrative of Paul's work in Ephesus.[12]

In Ephesus Paul had a lengthy ministry (longer, even, than in Corinth)

---

[12] F. Pereira understands Ephesus to represent a new kind of mission for Paul, a universal mission in which Jews and Gentiles are approached on equal footing outside the synagogue context. See *Ephesus: Climax of Universalism*, 138–76. The vagueness of descriptions of some of Paul's previous work makes it difficult to say whether this mission strategy is completely new. Furthermore, I would disagree with Pereira's hasty conclusion that a universal mission in Ephesus means that special concern with the promises to the Jewish people (a concern represented by preaching "first" to the Jews) has now been set aside.

through which the word of the Lord reached all the inhabitants of the province, both Jews and Greeks. This description is one important indication that the narrator presents Ephesus as the climax of Paul's missionary work, the place where Paul most fully realizes his calling to be Jesus' "witness to all persons" (22:15). Paul's later address to the Ephesian elders (20:18–35) suggests that this description of Paul's work at Ephesus is also meant as a lasting model for the church after Paul's departure.[13] There are other indications that the Ephesian narrative is intended to be a climactic presentation of Paul as a channel of divine power and servant of the Lord's word. These indications will be reviewed below. For the moment I would note that the special importance of the Ephesian mission is supported by references back to Ephesus in the Jerusalem narrative. The fateful event in Jerusalem that leads to Paul's trials is his seizure by the mob in the temple. "Jews from Asia" incite this riot, and they do so partly because they believe Paul has brought "Trophimus the Ephesian" into the temple (21:27–29; cf. 24:19). The narrative suggests that the attack on Paul in Jerusalem is especially the result of his work in Ephesus. Two factors may help to explain this: (1) Ephesus is presented as the climax of Paul's work, the place where he is most effective and the Lord's power is most fully manifest in him. (2) In Ephesus Paul separated Jewish disciples from the synagogue when he left under pressure. This act threatens the Jewish community, who stand to lose not only gentile God-worshipers but also ethnic Jews. This additional comment, not found in the related passages in Pisidian Antioch and Corinth, may help to explain the strong accusations against Paul in Jerusalem, accusations by Asian Jews that he is "against the people" (21:28) and by others that he teaches Diaspora Jews "apostasy from Moses" (21:21). Although Paul does not *teach* apostasy from Moses, Jewish Christians will find it difficult to maintain Jewish identity and the Jewish way of life while mixing with Gentiles and isolated from the synagogue.

Special emphasis on Paul as a channel of divine power, with benefits for the mission, appears in a number of features of the Ephesian narrative. The encounter with "disciples" who have not received the Holy Spirit provides the opportunity to present Paul transmitting the Spirit to them through laying on of hands (19:6). This reminds us less of Pentecost than of the apostles' conferral of the Spirit on the Samaritans through laying on of hands (8:17). The connection with this scene is one of a series of hints that Paul is fully equipped with the remarkable powers that appeared in the missions of Jesus and Peter.

It is noteworthy that Paul's synagogue preaching in Ephesus concerned

---

[13] See below, 254, 256–57.

"the reign of God" (19:8), a reminder of Jesus' own preaching, and that Paul performed remarkable δυνάμεις ("mighty acts," 19:11), a term used of Jesus' healings and exorcisms (Luke 10:13; 19:37; Acts 2:22) that is rarely applied to the marvels performed by a missionary in Acts.[14] Furthermore, 19:11–12 emphasizes that the kind of mighty acts performed "through the hands of Paul" were of an "extraordinary" kind, for diseases and evil spirits departed when handkerchiefs and work aprons were taken from Paul to the sick. Although this may impress us as crude, it is clearly intended as a very strong indication of God's power at work through Paul. It echoes similar statements in summaries of Jesus' and the apostles' healing work. Luke 6:18–19 refers to Jesus' work of healing and then adds, "All the crowd was seeking to touch him, for power was going out from him and healing all." A summary statement of signs and wonders "through the hands of the apostles" adds that the sick were even seeking contact with Peter's shadow (Acts 5:12, 15–16). Healing through touching Jesus is extended to indirect contact with the source of power through Peter's shadow or pieces of cloth taken from Paul to the sick. The power found in Paul at Ephesus is comparable to the power found in Peter at Jerusalem.

The story of the Jewish exorcists who use the name of Jesus further highlights Paul's power by contrast. The Jewish exorcists attempt to do what Paul is doing, with disastrous results. The evil spirit knows the power of Jesus' name but also knows the difference between the true exorcist and the counterfeit. The sons of Sceva attempt the exorcism through "Jesus whom Paul proclaims." Their words indicate their distant, indirect knowledge of Jesus. The evil spirit's reply ("Jesus I recognize and Paul I know, but who are you?") underscores the futility of their attempt while bearing witness to Jesus and also to Paul as Jesus' chosen representative.[15] This scene is somewhat like Paul's encounter with the Jewish false prophet in 13:6–12, for in both cases Paul's power is highlighted in contrast with a false counterpart. In both cases the issue of magic appears in the context (13:6, 8; 19:18–19). This scene also resembles Peter's encounter with Simon Magus in Samaria (8:18–24). Here also the issue of magic appears (8:9, 11), and Simon, like the sons of Sceva, wants to exercise the same power as Jesus' witnesses, falsely believing that it can be manipulated through formulas or money.

The connection noted between the sons of Sceva and the Jewish false

---

[14] The only other use of the plural in Acts (besides 2:22 and 19:11) is to refer to Philip's mighty acts in 8:13.

[15] Here the evil spirit's special powers of recognition (as in Luke 4:34, 41; 8:28; Acts 16:17) result in public testimony.

prophet Elymas should also remind us that 13:6–12 demonstrates Paul's miraculous power at the beginning of his missionary journeys. Furthermore, this power and Paul's mission are connected with the Holy Spirit (13:2, 4, 9; cf. Paul as transmitter of the Spirit in 19:6). Here we seem to have ring or envelope composition, for themes in the last major setting of Paul's mission repeat themes at the beginning of Paul's missionary journeys.

We have already noted the connection of 19:6 with the passing of the Spirit to the Samaritans through Peter and John, the connection of 19:13–16 with the same Samaritan episode, and the connection of the summary of healing in 19:11–12 with 5:12, 15–16. These observations suggest that the last major station of Paul's evangelistic work mirrors to a high degree the work of the apostles, especially Peter, in Acts 2—8. There is further evidence to support this view. The narrator emphasizes the strong impression that the incident with the sons of Sceva made on the whole city, both Jews and Greeks. When they learned of it, "fear fell on them all, and the name of the Lord Jesus was being magnified" (19:17). Many who had already believed were also moved to confession (19:18). It is surprising that this incident should have such a wide effect. It appears that the narrator is repeating a motif used early in Acts, first following Peter's Pentecost sermon ("Fear [φόβος] was coming on every soul," 2:43) and then following the death of Ananias and Sapphira (5:5, 11). In the latter case the "fear" affects "all the church" and also "all those hearing these things." Especially the indication that the fear came upon *all* links these passages with 19:17. The use of the unusual verb "magnify" (μεγαλύνω; RSV: "extol") in 19:17 is another link with the early chapters of Acts, where it is used to describe the reaction of the general populace, greatly impressed by what was happening (5:13). The echoes of the apostles' successful work in Jerusalem and Samaria in the early days of the mission suggest that the word of the Lord is equally powerful in Paul's Ephesian ministry and that the Christian mission can be equally successful in the pluralistic world of Greeks and Diaspora Jews represented by Ephesus.

The response of the Ephesians in 19:17–19 shows the powerful impression that Paul's deeds made on the people of Ephesus. The narrator's glowing picture of Paul's power appears indirectly in the mirrors of the Jewish exorcists' failure and the response of the impressed crowd. Many are moved to repentance, especially repentance from magical practices.

The reference to the word's powerful growth in 19:20 picks up the reference to the word of the Lord in 19:10, thus forming a frame around the intervening material. The narrator is not simply glorifying Paul. It is finally the power of the word of the Lord, or the name of the Lord (19:17), that stands behind these events. A strengthened form of a familiar refrain reappears in v. 20, one that has been used to mark significant steps in the progress of the mission. This refrain appeared in 6:7 as a summary of the mission's progress in Jerusalem and again in 12:24 to summarize developments just before Paul begins his missionary journeys. In 19:20 the refrain highlights the success of Paul's mission to this point, especially in Ephesus, where the power mentioned in 19:20 was prominently displayed through Paul's ministry. The use of the refrain at this point brings a sense of closure that will be reinforced by the travel plans in the next verse, which begins with a statement of fulfillment ("When these things were fulfilled . . . ") similar to 14:26 at the end of the first missionary journey.[16] The ring composition noted above reinforces this sense of closure, as endings are commonly indicated by a return to themes of the beginning. Paul's missionary journeys come to a climax and a point of relative closure through the narrator's description of his powerful ministry in Ephesus.

In v. 21 a preview of the rest of Acts mentions two locations that will be the goals of Paul's remaining travels: Jerusalem and Rome. The decision to go to Jerusalem and then Rome is presented in unusually solemn fashion. Paul's decision to go to both cities corresponds to the divine will. Paul says that he "must (δεῖ) also see Rome," using a word characteristic of God's purpose in Jesus' and the church's experience.[17] To this corresponds the statement that Paul "decided in the Spirit" to go to Jerusalem. Although the phrase ἐν τῷ πνεύματι ("in the spirit") could refer either to the human spirit or the Holy Spirit, there is reason to believe that the latter is at least included. It would be strange to attribute the journey to Jerusalem to a human decision while linking the trip to Rome to divine necessity, especially when Paul says he "must also" see Rome, implying some comparability between the two trips. Furthermore, in 20:22–23 Paul refers to the same decision and speaks of himself going to Jerusalem "bound in the Spirit" and of the Holy Spirit testifying in every city of coming suffering. More than a strong human resolve is indicated.[18] A reference to the Holy Spirit in 19:21 would also attribute this new journey to the same divine initiative as Paul's first journey from Antioch (13:2, 4).

Solemnity and a sense of divine purpose are also added to this preview by its functional similarity to Jesus' passion announcements and the beginning of Jesus' journey to Jerusalem. In spite of Paul's success in Ephesus, we have an indication here that Paul's life is not a simple success

---

[16] The placement of a major scene in Ephesus following these verses requires a special explanation. See below, 241–42.

[17] On this term see especially Charles Cosgrove, "The Divine Δεῖ in Luke-Acts," 168–90.

[18] E. Haenchen agrees, although he does not apply this to 19:21, despite the common reference to going to Jerusalem. See *Acts*, 568, 591. See also F. Pereira, *Ephesus: Climax of Universalism*, 220–21.

story. To be sure, we are not told in 19:21 that Paul's journey will mean suffering. Rather, a mystery surrounds this trip, for its purpose is not explained. Those who catch the echo of Jesus' journey to Jerusalem, guided by divine necessity, might suspect that suffering will follow. For Paul, too, 19:21 may state a partial insight, an awareness of the goal but not yet an awareness of the attendant suffering, which is disclosed to him as he travels, according to 20:22–24. Walter Radl discusses the parallel between Acts 19:21 and Luke 9:51 as part of a series of parallels between Jesus' journey to suffering and death and Paul's journey to suffering.[19] This connection may extend even to the following references to sending representatives ahead to prepare (Luke 9:51–52; Acts 19:22).[20] To be sure, there is also a slight difference in function. Luke 9:51 is the actual beginning of a journey to Jerusalem; Acts 19:21 is not. It is a first indication of the necessity of this journey, corresponding in this respect to Jesus' passion announcement in Luke 9:22 (with which it shares reference to the divine "must [δεῖ]") and to the reference to Jesus' "exodus" that he is going "to fulfill in Jerusalem" that quickly follows (9:31). Thus Acts 19:21 is not exclusively related to Luke 9:51. It is related to the turning point in the gospel narrative that follows Luke 9:18, a section in which Jesus recognizes, announces, and begins to fulfill a divine destiny that will take him to Jerusalem. The sense of divine necessity that surrounded Jesus' final trip to Jerusalem reappears as the narrator anticipates Paul's trip. This necessity was a dark cloud, impenetrable to the disciples, because it led Jesus to suffering and death.[21] Foreshadowings of suffering and danger will soon become strong in the narrative of Acts.

J. Bradley Chance protests against the view that Luke is "portraying Christianity as a religion straining to sever its ties with Jerusalem." Rather, "Luke is continually bringing the church back to Jerusalem."[22] Chance is correct, and Paul's periodic returns cannot be explained simply as required reports to the Jerusalem apostles. The apostles have disappeared before Paul's last journey to Jerusalem, and there will be relatively little attention to the Jerusalem church when Paul arrives. Attention will center on Paul's relation to the Jewish people, their leaders and institutions. Jerusalem functions as the symbolic center of Judaism, to which Paul remains loyal. However, his journey is not a happy trip home. The spiritual home is now a threatening place, a place of conflict, arrest, and possible death, as it was for Jesus and Stephen.

---

[19] See *Paulus und Jesus,* 103–26.
[20] See F. Pereira, *Ephesus: Climax of Universalism,* 67. The "two" sent in 19:22 may correspond to Luke 10:1.
[21] See *Narrative Unity* 1:226–27, 279–89.
[22] See *Jerusalem, the Temple, and the New Age,* 101.

THE WORSHIPERS
OF ARTEMIS PROTEST

In spite of the announcement of Paul's travel plan in 19:21, the narrative does not move immediately to the journey. First an extensive dramatic scene, a good example of what Eckhard Plümacher calls Luke's "style of the dramatic episode,"[1] is inserted. The narrator wants to tell more about Paul's effect on Ephesian society and religion.

Paul is not a major actor in 19:23-40, appearing only in vv. 30-31. However, the whole episode indirectly demonstrates the powerful effect of Paul's work in Asia through the emotional reaction of people who feel threatened by it. The angry protest in Ephesus is the reverse side of the powerful impression Paul has made. In v. 26 Paul is specifically cited as a threat by Demetrius, the instigator of the protest. In this respect the episode supports 19:10-20, the description of the power of the word in Ephesus and Asia through Paul's ministry. It is also connected with earlier scenes in which public accusations were made against Paul and his supporters. The speech of Demetrius in 19:25-27, even though it is not made before city officials, has a role analogous to the accusations made in Philippi (16:20-21), Thessalonica (17:6-7), and Corinth (18:13). These accusations were accompanied by mob action and further stirred the crowds to angry protest against Paul. Angry protest is more vividly portrayed in 19:23-40. In Philippi the accusers protested the mission's effect on Roman customs, and in Thessalonica they claimed a conflict with the decrees of Caesar. In Ephesus the protest has a religious aspect. It concerns Paul's harmful effect on the established religion that helps to give Ephesus its importance and prosperity. The Ephesian riot is further evidence that the mission is perceived as a serious challenge by both Gentiles and Jews. The resulting protests are social realities that Jesus' followers must face. They make the mission dangerous but not impossible, for surrounding society is not viewed as a monolithic front of opposition.

Placed after the reference to Paul's impending journey, the Ephesian riot is set off somewhat from the preceding description of Paul's work in Ephesus. Furthermore, this episode has not only links backward with

---

[1] See *Lukas als hellenistischer Schriftsteller,* 98–100.

previous scenes of accusation and protest, as just noted, but also a significant link forward to events in Jerusalem. The Ephesian riot will be followed by a second riot in the Jerusalem temple, with greater consequences for Paul. Both of these riot scenes begin with claims that Paul is a threat to the religion—especially the temple—of a society, and the development of the riot is described in similar terms. Thus the protest by Jerusalem Jews in 21:27–36, which determines Paul's situation for the rest of Acts (Paul is never released from the resulting arrest), is preceded by a similar protest by Gentiles in Ephesus. The result is not the same, but there is similarity and balance between the scenes of angry protest. Paul must be rescued from both the people and the Gentiles, as the Lord told him (26:17), for his work is perceived as a threat by both groups.

Let us compare the two riot scenes in greater detail. In both cases the riot is instigated by a limited group that moves others to action (Demetrius and his co-workers in Ephesus; the Asian Jews in Jerusalem). Both scenes highlight an accusation and call to action (19:25–27; 21:28) that indicate the motives of the protesting group, and these statements contain some similar elements. They refer to the negative effect of Paul's preaching or teaching, the great extent of its influence (19:26, "nearly all Asia"; 21:28, "all everywhere"), and its harm to the local temple. In the narrator's portrait the particularism of the Ephesians is every bit as clear as with Jews. Artemis is one whom "the world worships," but she is still "Artemis of the Ephesians" (19:27–28), and the honor that Ephesus gains from being her temple keeper is a main concern. The honor of goddess, temple, and city mingle.[2] The accusations and calls to action cause a similar sequence of events in the two scenes. The narrator describes protesters shouting (using κράζω; 19:28, 34; 21:28, 36), the crowd stirred up and tumultuous (using συγχέω; 19:32; 21:27, 31), and twice uses the phrase ἄλλοι . . . ἄλλο τι ἔκραζον (or ἐπεφώνουν; RSV: "Some cried one thing, some another") to describe the confused shouting (19:32; 21:34). The whole city is affected, rushes together, and someone is seized (19:29; 21:30). Thus the description of the developing riot is partially similar, and the reason for the riot is also similar: members of an established religion are protesting the effect that Paul's mission is having on their religion and its temple.

The scenes of protest in the narrative heighten dramatic tension and also highlight issues of conflict between the new way and its environment.

---

[2] G. Schneider notes that the description of Demetrius' audience as "full of anger" in 19:28 parallels the reaction of the people of Nazareth in Luke 4:28. See *Apostelgeschichte* 2:275. We can go further. The people of Nazareth and Ephesus show the same kind of attitude. The people of Nazareth, who want Jesus to use his powers at home (see *Narrative Unity* 1:68–73), show the same narrow self-interest as the Ephesians, who cheer for the cult that brings them fame and profit.

The Jewish protest sets the agenda for much of the narrative in Acts 22—26 and 28. The gentile protest occupies less space but is still important. To be sure, the narrative undermines the validity of the protest from the beginning by having Demetrius reveal his self-interested motives. Demetrius speaks persuasively to the artisans being addressed, appealing to concerns that they are likely to share, but the outside observer sees another instance of the profit motive corrupting religion. Demetrius first appeals to commercial interests and then to the honor of the temple and its Goddess. Later the shouting crowd seems to be moved as much by local pride as by religious piety. Thus commerce, narrow patriotism, and religion mingle, resulting in an unsympathetic portrait of Demetrius and his followers.

Nevertheless, Demetrius should be taken seriously when he presents Paul as a threat. What Demetrius says about Paul is justified by what Paul himself has said in the earlier narrative. We must assume that during the two years at Ephesus Paul shared some of the negative views of popular religion expressed in the Athens speech, for Demetrius knows Paul's claim that gods made with hands are not gods (19:26). Paul stated this in other language in 17:29, and the reference to "hands" recalls a related point: the gulf between God and temples or cult, the work of "human hands" (17:24–25). If we accept the narrator's claim that Paul's teaching has already made considerable headway in the province, Demetrius is right to worry about its effect both on his own trade and on the worship of Artemis.

In passing, the narrative notes that a Jew named Alexander attempts to make a speech before the crowd but is shouted down. Indeed, the appearance of this Jew unifies a crowd that had been confused about its purpose (19:32–34). Gerhard Schneider assumes that Alexander intended to defend Jews by dissociating them from Paul and the Christians.[3] It is equally possible that he intended to give a courageous defense of the Jewish rejection of idols. Even if his intentions are not clear in the narrative, the crowd's reaction is. This Jew provokes the same cheering for Artemis as Demetrius' speech about Paul, for all Jews (not just Paul) reject the worship of idols. In other scenes Jews and Christians are in conflict. Here they stand for the same thing and face the same angry protest from their neighbors.

There are two speeches in the episode, one by Demetrius and the other by the executive secretary ($\gamma\rho\alpha\mu\mu\alpha\tau\epsilon\acute{v}s$; RSV: "town clerk") of Ephesus. The first speech incites the riot; the second ends it. The first says Paul is a danger; the second says that these Christians are no real threat to

---

[3] See *Apostelgeschichte* 2:277.

Ephesus' importance as cult center for Artemis. While the executive secretary is speaking to the crowd, he is indirectly replying to Demetrius, whose speech states the motivation for the protest. Demetrius said that both his business and the worship of Artemis are in danger (κινδυνεύει, 19:27). The secretary reassures the crowd about that danger and insists that the real danger is something else: "We are in danger (κινδυνεύομεν) of being accused of revolt" because of this disorderly assembly (19:40).[4] The secretary's speech is designed to end the protest and succeeds. He first reassures the crowd and then turns the crowd's attention to its own behavior. Because there is no basis for charges of sacrilege or blasphemy against the two Christians Gaius and Aristarchus and because the courts and the lawful assembly are available for settling other disputes, the disorderly assembly has no justification and those participating in it may be open to serious charges. With this subtle threat the protest ends.

There is further subtlety to the two speeches because both agree partly—but only partly—with the narrator's values and beliefs. Demetrius is clearly an opponent of Christianity, yet he takes seriously what Paul says about idol worship. In contrast, if we take the first part of the secretary's speech at face value, he is a naive Ephesian who assumes that the Christian criticism of idol worship has no importance. He clearly adopts the perspective of those acclaiming Artemis. He makes the crowd's shout his own by speaking of the "great Artemis" and uses key words of the city's religious ideology: the city as "temple keeper" and the goddess' image as "fallen from the sky." To be sure, it is possible to interpret these words as strategic flattery rather than naiveté.[5] The following indications of overstatement might support this view: "What person is there who does not know . . . ? These things being irrefutable . . ." These phrases play to the crowd but completely ignore the existence of Christians and Jews, who are the cause of the whole protest. On two other matters the secretary is close to the position of the narrator. He recognizes the innocence of the two Christians seized by the crowd, and he recognizes that the crowd is responsible for an unjustified riot. The latter point fits with the tendency in Acts to make opponents responsible for disturbances, even when they make this charge of Christians (see 17:5-9; 24:5, 12). The recognition of innocence may indicate some knowledge of the "way" and a moderately favorable impression of it. If we are to infer this, the secretary's position is close to that of the Asiarchs who act as Paul's "friends" and seek to protect him (19:31).

---

[4] R. Pesch notes this play on the motif of danger. See *Apostelgeschichte* 2:182-83.

[5] E. Plümacher, *Lukas als hellenistischer Schriftsteller*, 99, speaks of the secretary's "flattery."

THE FAREWELL JOURNEY BEGINS

When Paul decided "in the Spirit" to go to Jerusalem and then to Rome, a prior journey through Macedonia and Achaia was also mentioned (19:21). We have previously noted that Paul not only founds churches on his journeys but also visits them again to strengthen them.[1] Because he has not yet revisited the churches of Macedonia and Achaia, this must be done before leaving for Jerusalem. The journey will continue with visits to Christian communities down the coast on the way to Jerusalem.

This journey of visitation is also a farewell journey. Paul's farewell to the Ephesian elders in 20:17–38 is one of a series of farewell scenes that continue until Paul reaches Jerusalem. As Paul nears Jerusalem, emotional scenes of parting become prominent (20:36–38; 21:5–6, 12–15). The scene with the Ephesian elders stands out from the others only because it contains a farewell speech. The narrator refers to Paul's encouragement and admonition of the communities at various stops on the trip. The farewell speech to the Ephesian elders provides a model that, with proper modification for local circumstances, can be applied to other occasions of admonition and farewell in the places Paul is visiting.

Acts 20:1–12 emphasizes the thoroughness of Paul's efforts in encouraging and admonishing the churches. The beginning of the section twice refers to Paul "encouraging" the churches (using $\pi\alpha\rho\alpha\kappa\alpha\lambda\acute{\epsilon}\omega$; 20:1, 2).[2] The general statement in v. 2 about Paul's activity in Macedonia and Greece stresses that he encouraged the churches extensively (literally, "with much discourse [$\lambda\acute{o}\gamma\omega\ \pi o\lambda\lambda\hat{\omega}$])." This summary is developed in the scene at Troas, which stresses both at the beginning and end the extensiveness of Paul's address, prolonged first to midnight (20:7) and then to dawn (20:11). The scene ends with the statement that the believers "were greatly encouraged" or "comforted ($\pi\alpha\rho\epsilon\kappa\lambda\acute{\eta}\theta\eta\sigma\alpha\nu$)." This refers in part to the effect of finding Eutychus alive, but there is renewed emphasis on Paul's dedicated preaching (along with the breaking of bread) in the

---

[1] See above, 180–81, 194, 230–31.

[2] This verb means to encourage, both in the sense of urge on and in the sense of comfort in the face of difficulty.

preceding verse. Paul's words also encourage the church. Verse 12 reports the success of Paul's work and words of encouragement, rounding off a section that began by emphasizing this activity as characteristic of Paul's journey (vv. 1–2).

The narrator's account, especially at Troas, of Paul encouraging the churches at length before departure, prepares for the speech to the Ephesian elders in 20:17–35. This speech is an example of the departing Paul encouraging the churches, even though it is not labeled as such. It shares themes with 14:22–23 ("elders" are chosen, believers are "commended to the Lord"), where Paul and Barnabas are described as "encouraging (παρακαλοῦντες)" the disciples "to persevere in the faith."[3] Paul is doing the same thing on his farewell journey. The emphasis on Paul's dedicated thoroughness in executing this task (20:2, 7, 11) prepares for the speech to the Ephesian elders. Looking back at his previous work in Ephesus, Paul emphasizes his dedicated thoroughness, which did not allow him to omit anything beneficial and led him to teach both publicly and in homes, both night and day (20:20, 27, 31). Material in 20:1–16 also prepares for the reference in 20:19 to "the plots of the Jews," for 20:3 refers to a specific "plot" of the Jews (ἐπιβουλή is used in both passages).

When Paul begins his journey from Greece to Jerusalem, he is accompanied by seven named companions, whose origins are also noted (20:4). They represent the fruit of Paul's labors in the various areas of his work. They also resemble the companions of Jesus, who journeyed with him to Jerusalem. Trophimus will be cited later as a partial cause of the Jerusalem riot (21:29), which is a protest against Paul's work among Diaspora Jews and Gentiles.

When the actual journey to Jerusalem begins (departing from Greece), the narrator shifts to the "we" style (20:5), which continues until the arrival in Jerusalem (21:18), except for the scene in Miletus, where the focus of attention is solely on the relation between Paul and the Ephesians (20:16–38). By using the first-person plural during the journey to Jerusalem, events are experienced through a focalizing character who accompanies Paul but is distinct both from the seven named companions (note the different locations of "us" and the seven in 20:5) and from Paul himself (see 20:13–14). This focalizing character is both anonymous and plural ("we," not "I"). The anonymity of the group decreases its value as eyewitness guarantor of the report,[4] but an anonymous and plural first-

---

[3] Acts 11:23 also speaks of disciples being encouraged to persevere. The verb παρακαλέω overlaps with "strengthening" in 14:22 and 15:32.

[4] Susan Praeder also sees a "lack of authorial concern for eyewitness support" in the anonymous and "colorless" portrayal of the first-person companions of Paul. See "First Person Narration in Acts," 198.

person narrator is well suited to increase imaginative participation in the narrative by readers or hearers of it. The anonymous "we"—a participant narrator—is a special opportunity for us and others to enter the narrative as participants and to see ourselves as companions of Paul as he prepares the churches for his absence and resolutely approaches the danger in Jerusalem. A first-person narrator is a focalizing channel through whom the story is experienced. Our experience of events is limited to the experience of the first-person narrator, and this common perspective creates a bond of identification. The anonymous "we" is a focalizing channel without clear definition, except as companions of Paul, making it easy for many individuals, and even a community, to identify with the narrator. "We" as fellow travelers both share Paul's experience and receive his legacy as he travels toward his passion.[5] The narrative also heightens our experience of the journey as such, for the "we" narration includes passages that simply present the journey with sufficient detail to make us aware of it as experience of a special type, with its own stages, decisions to be made, and goal (see 20:13–16; 21:1–3).

The journey to Jerusalem is dated in relation to Jewish festivals, "the days of unleavened" bread (20:6) and "the day of Pentecost" (20:16). In 20:16 Paul adds to the spatial goal (Jerusalem) a temporal goal (arrival by Pentecost). The importance of this festival to Paul is an early indication of the stress on Paul as a loyal Jew in the remainder of the narrative.[6]

Paul's farewell at Troas includes the account of Eutychus, the youth who fell from the window and was taken up as dead. There are some general similarities between this account and the story of Peter's raising of Tabitha in 9:36–42. Both are stories of death and life, both concern a Christian disciple who is named, and both refer to an "upper room (ὑπερῷον)." The stories are placed toward the end of the recorded ministry of Peter and the free ministry of Paul. Most details, however, are quite different. Nevertheless, in the light of the tendency to show Paul exercising the full powers demonstrated by the apostles, noted in the discussion of Paul's Ephesian ministry,[7] it may be significant that both Peter and Paul enable the Christian community to discover life in the face of death.

---

[5] S. Praeder, however, says, "There is little in this portrayal of Paul's first person traveling companions to invite readers to involve themselves with them and their travels. Parts in conversations, scenes, and speeches, personal information, reports of inner processes, and other elements of characterization that invite reader involvement are used sparingly or not at all." See "First Person Narration in Acts," 199. In my view the role of first-person narration itself invites identification. This identification is not with the "we" narrator as speaker or actor who has "parts in conversations, scenes, and speeches" but with the narrator as silent observer and listener to Paul, who remains the focus of attention.

[6] See also 18:18 and 226–27.

[7] See above, 236–39.

In discussing the story of Tabitha, I noted a series of similarities between that story and the stories of the raising of dead people by Elijah and
Elisha, on the one hand, and by Jesus, on the other.[8] Peter's raising of
Tabitha shares a number of details with Elisha's raising of the Shunammite woman's son in 4 Kgdms. 4:18–37. The story of Paul and Eutychus
is related to this same story, but to a different aspect of it. Whereas Peter
raises Tabitha by a command, following the pattern of resurrection stories
in Luke, Paul "fell upon (ἐπέπεσεν)" Eutychus and embraced him and
then announced that he was alive (20:10). If there is a healing act here, it
is by bodily contact, not by word, and follows the pattern of the Elisha
story (2 Kings 4:34 = 4 Kgdms. 4:34).[9] Peter and Paul are similar in part
because they fit a common scriptural type. Through both, the prophetic
power of Elijah and Elisha continues to be available to the church.

The scene at Troas is an interesting example of a narrative with
significant gaps of information permitting multiple readings. The gaps
are permanent; they are not eliminated by later disclosures. The result is
tantalizing ambiguity that calls for active imagination from readers.[10]
One gap concerns a significant fact: was Eutychus really dead? The other
concerns the presence of multiple dimensions to the narrative: is there a
second, symbolic meaning?

After falling from the third story, Eutychus was "taken up dead" (20:9).
If this is a statement of the omniscient narrator, there is no ambiguity, for
we are meant to understand that Eutychus was dead.[11] Ambiguity
appears when we recognize the possibility of free indirect discourse in the
Bible. In free indirect discourse the view expressed is not directly attributed to a character yet actually represents the limited perspective of a
character. This limited perspective is embedded in the narrator's discourse.[12] Examples of this can be found in Acts. Philip's encounter with
the Ethiopian eunuch is described by the narrator with these words: "And
behold a man, an Ethiopian . . ." (8:27). "Behold" is an indicator of a
significant discovery and, according to M. Sternberg, a "marker of biblical
free indirect thought."[13] Although these are the narrator's words, Philip's

---

[8] See above, 126–27.

[9] The reference to bodily contact is missing from the LXX account of Elijah's raising of the
widow's son, which indicates instead that Elijah breathed on the boy. See 3 Kgdms. 17:21.

[10] On gaps in narrative that require creative activity by readers, see Wolfgang Iser, *Implied
Reader,* 34, 38, 40, 208, 214, 280. M. Sternberg distinguishes between temporary and
permanent gaps, and between gaps (omissions relevant to interpretation) and blanks
(irrelevant omissions). See *Poetics of Biblical Narrative,* 230–31, 235–37.

[11] The question of historical probability of a resurrection should not be introduced here. I am
not discussing a historical event but the implication of this narrative.

[12] For an example of free indirect discourse in Hebrew Scripture, see M. Sternberg, *Poetics of
Biblical Narrative,* 52–53.

[13] See *Poetics of Biblical Narrative,* 53.

experience is incorporated in them, for it is Philip, not the narrator, who is making the significant discovery. Similarly, 10:45 states that "the believers from the circumcision were amazed . . . that even on the Gentiles the gift of the Holy Spirit had been poured out." "Even on the Gentiles" underscores the surprise of this discovery. It is not the narrator but Peter's Jewish companions who are surprised.[14]

In the Eutychus story, the passive verb "was taken up" implies an actor, a group of Christians who have rushed down to find Eutychus. "He was taken up dead" can easily be understood as their judgment about Eutychus' condition, an example of free indirect discourse rather than a statement of the omniscient narrator. The following statement of Paul, "His life is in him" (rather than "His life has returned to him"; cf. 1 Kings 17:21 = 3 Kgdms. 17:21), also permits this view. The narrator has not taken a clear stand on whether Eutychus was dead. This ambiguity may have value as a reflection of believing experience. Believers may recall experiences of discovering life when only death was apparent, but they seldom really know what happened to cause this change, or how it happened.

Whether Paul has performed a resurrection miracle or not, his role remains important. His prophetic power is still shown by his detection of life where others see only death.

There is a further significant ambiguity: the narrative permits, but does not require, a symbolic reading. Such a reading has been developed by Bernard Trémel,[15] who notes, among other things, the statement about the numerous lamps in 20:8. The sparse narrative style of most biblical narrative does not encourage irrelevant details, yet the significance of the lamps for the action in the scene is not indicated. Trémel proposes a symbolic reading: the place of the word and breaking of bread is a place of abundant light, but when Eutychus falls asleep, he falls into a place of death and darkness. This is not the only way in which the many lamps can be understood.[16] However, Trémel can produce a reading that coheres with the rest of the scene and with Luke-Acts as a whole. The role of Paul, who does not give up when others despair over the one who has fallen but discovers that there is still life in him, may contribute to the picture of Paul as a dedicated pastor and a model for others, as in 20:31. The larger context provides more support for his reading than Trémel indicates. Trémel does note connections between the Troas scene and Paul's later

---

[14] See also 106–7 on 8:18.

[15] See "À propos d'Actes 20,7–12," 359–69.

[16] A more common interpretation is offered by R. Pesch: the many lamps heat the room and foul the air. Therefore, Eutychus went to the window. See *Apostelgeschichte* 2:191. Both Trémel and Pesch are filling a gap in the text by supplying a missing motivation for the reference to many lamps.

speech in Miletus, including the exhortation there to "keep awake (γρηγορεῖτε)" (20:31),[17] but exhortations to wakefulness play a larger role in Luke. This theme is found in a parabolic exhortation in Luke 12:37 (preceded by the command "Let your lamps be burning"; 12:35) and in the eschatological exhortation in Luke 21:36. Also, the disciples' partial or complete failure to respond faithfully and perceptively is indicated by sleep in Luke 9:32 and 22:45–46. The length of Paul's preaching may incline us to sympathize with sleepy Eutychus. The well-developed synoptic theme of wakefulness puts a different perspective on the matter. Falling asleep is a serious failure with potentially grave consequences. Paul's dedicated preaching makes demands on his audience. They must be dedicated listeners who hear the word and "bear fruit with perseverance (ἐν ὑπομονῇ)" (Luke 8:15). Eutychus failed and fell.

Light and darkness also have a symbolic function in Luke-Acts (Luke 1:78–79; 2:32; Acts 13:47). As Paul later explains, he was sent so that people might "turn from darkness to light" (Acts 26:18), and the Messiah, also, has come "to proclaim light" (26:23). Trémel's symbolic interpretation of the well-lighted room where Paul instructs the church is not strange when viewed in this context, but neither is a symbolic interpretation forced on us by a narrative that makes little sense otherwise. It remains an option, perhaps an opportunity, in interpreting a narrative that preserves a tantalizing ambiguity.

The church at Troas was "greatly encouraged" both by Paul's discovery of life where they could see only death and by Paul's persistent and careful instruction. The Troas scene provides a dramatic example of how Paul was able to encourage the churches as he visited them on his farewell journey. Paul's instruction was accompanied by the breaking of bread. This practice has not been mentioned in Acts since the days of the early Jerusalem church (2:42, 46), where it contributed to the picture of a committed group of believers who were "devoted to the teaching of the apostles and the fellowship" (2:42). The believers in Troas show the same devotion and unity in response to Paul. In the description of Paul's Ephesian ministry, there were indications that the early mission of the apostles and its results were being reproduced in a different cultural setting by Paul.[18] The reference to breaking bread in Troas is a further indication of this. It appears a second time in v. 11 immediately before Paul's departure, showing that it has importance in its own right. Breaking bread is not merely the occasion for the Eutychus story, as v. 7 might suggest. Because Paul is departing, the community's breaking of bread

---

[17] See "À propos d'Actes 20,7–12," 364.
[18] See above, 236–39.

becomes a farewell meal, resembling Jesus' farewell meal with his apostles, when he "took bread" and "broke" it (Luke 22:19). The echoes of Jesus' Jerusalem journey and its consequences that begin in Acts 19:21 and continue thereafter[19] may suggest that this resemblance has some importance, even though it is not developed.

---

[19] See 239–40, 259, 264–66, 274, 281–82, 345–46.

PAUL'S LEGACY:
THE FAREWELL ADDRESS
TO THE EPHESIAN ELDERS

Paul's farewell to the Ephesian elders at Miletus is one of a series of scenes of visitation and farewell on Paul's journey to Jerusalem in Acts 20—21. It has special importance, however, because it contains a speech by Paul in which he reviews his past ministry and previews future events.[1] Through this review and preview, Paul's significance for his churches is highlighted, and the narrator provides orientation in the course of the narrative, recalling and clarifying key aspects of Paul's past ministry and alerting us to key developments in the future.

This speech is significantly different than the mission speeches of Peter and Paul. It is the only extensive speech of Paul to Christians that Acts presents. It has elements resembling farewell speeches in the Old Testament and other ancient Jewish literature: the speaker, anticipating his death, calls together a circle of associates, points out the exemplary character of his past life, gives exhortations to those who will be left behind, and prophesies the future.[2] In Luke the Last Supper scene was expanded into a farewell speech by Jesus.[3] The comparable farewell speech of Paul is placed not on the night before his death or at the end of Acts, but at Paul's final parting with the leaders of the church where he last worked extensively, with the greatest success, for the speech concerns Paul's legacy to his churches and the responsibility of those he leaves behind.

Scholars present conflicting proposals for understanding the outline of the speech.[4] In my opinion, confusion can be reduced if we recognize that two principles are operative in the speech at the same time. On the one hand, the speech moves forward from an initial statement about Paul's past ministry (vv. 18–21) to announcements about a new situation that is

---

[1] On the importance of reviews and previews, see *Narrative Unity* 1:21.

[2] See Hans-Joachim Michel, *Abschiedsrede des Paulus*, 48–54, 68–71, for further details.

[3] See *Narrative Unity* 1:263. J. Neyrey discusses the similarities between the two farewell speeches. See *Passion According to Luke*, 43–48. See also G. Krodel, *Acts*, 382.

[4] Four different proposals may be found in the following writings: J. Dupont, *Nouvelles études*, 424–45; Cheryl Exum and Charles Talbert, "Structure of Paul's Speech," 233–36; J. Lambrecht, "Paul's Farewell-Address," 318; Franz Prast, *Presbyter und Evangelium*, 49–50.

about to arise, with warnings and exhortations. Temporal phrases at the beginning of sentences mark the emphasis on the new situation and its requirements ("And now behold," vv. 22, 25; "And now [καὶ τὰ νῦν]," v. 32). References to Paul's past ministry mingle with references to the new situation in vv. 22–35, but these past references support statements and exhortations that bear on the present and future. Verse 25b adds poignancy to the imminent parting, v. 27 justifies an assertion about the present (v. 26), and in vv. 31, 33–35 exhortations to the elders are supported by references to the past.[5] Thus Paul's past ministry is understood as a resource that can help the elders face their future responsibility.

As Paul's past ministry is a resource for the continuing work of the elders, so Paul's initial statement about his ministry in vv. 18–21 is a resource for the rest of the speech, resulting in another pattern that overlays the pattern just discussed. Paul repeatedly draws elements from vv. 18–21 for use in the rest of the speech. Consequently, a number of words and phrases from the first part of the speech reappear in the latter part of the speech. To some extent these repetitions fall into a chiastic pattern, as follows:

> 18–19: "You know . . ., serving the Lord with all humility"
>> 18b–20: "the whole time . . . tears . . . in public and from
>>> house to house"
>>> 20: "I did not shrink from announcing"
>>>> 21: "bearing witness"
>>>> 24: "to bear witness"
>>> 27: "I did not shrink from announcing"
>> 31: "three years night and day . . . with tears"
> 34: "You know that these hands served"

In part the related phrases use the same Greek words, in part synonyms. In the chart above I assume that the reference to Paul serving the Lord with humility in v. 19 is related to his service with his own hands in v. 34 because the willingness to do hand work instead of taking the clothing and money of others is a signal demonstration of humility. The phrase "in public and from house to house" in v. 20 is related to "night and day" in v. 31 because these phrases demonstrate the completeness of Paul's efforts, first on the spatial plane and then on the temporal. There is some flexibility in this chiasm, as the material parallel to v. 31 is spread over vv. 18–20 and mingles with phrases that parallel vv. 27 and 34. Furthermore, this chiasm does not account for all the verbal links within the speech. Paul's reference to his "ministry" or "service (διακονία)" in v. 24 picks up his reference to "serving the Lord" in v. 19. Similarly, "the word of [God's]

---

[5] "I have shown you" in v. 35 indicates that vv. 33–35 function as exhortation to the elders.

grace" in v. 32 recalls the reference to "the gospel of the grace of God" in v. 24, and "to remember" in v. 35 recalls the reference to "remembering" in v. 31.

The bulk of the repeated material is first found in the initial long sentence of the speech (vv. 18-21). Thus this initial sentence about Paul's past ministry serves as a base to which the rest of the speech repeatedly refers, taking elements from it and relating them to the new situation that arises with Paul's departure. In this process deeper significance is found in the initial description of Paul's ministry. What the future demands of both Paul and the elders is interpreted in light of Paul's past record.

In vv. 18-21 very strong emphasis is placed on Paul's total devotion to his task of teaching and bearing witness. Although it would be impossible to detail all of Paul's efforts in short compass, vv. 20-21 suggest the fullness of Paul's efforts through a rhetorical fullness of word pairs: "to announce and to teach"; "publicly and in homes"; "both to Jews and to Greeks"; "repentance and faith." Paul's devotion to his task is an example to the elders. When Paul warns of the coming dangers that they will face, he continues, "Be alert, therefore, remembering" the devoted ministry of Paul (v. 31). They can meet the crisis if they follow Paul's example. The dangers described in vv. 29-30 are not the only ones. The authority granted to the elders carries with it the temptation of misuse for personal gain, especially economic gain. Paul warns against this, again pointing to his own example. "I have shown you," he says, that instead of seeking church support the elders should work to support themselves and to help others financially (v. 35). Paul also speaks of his past and future trials, facing opposition that threatens his freedom and life. The speech does not indicate that Paul's willingness to face these trials is also an example to the elders, but this implication is quite possible.

Through vv. 22-24 we learn something new about what is likely to happen in Jerusalem. We have been told of Paul's decision "in the Spirit" to go to Jerusalem and then to Rome (19:21), but this is the first indication that imprisonment awaits him in Jerusalem. Paul reports to the elders something that the narrator has not previously shared with us: as Paul travels the Holy Spirit is bearing witness to him that imprisonment awaits him (20:23). Subsequently, the narrator will present specific examples of these prophecies (21:4, 10-11). This foreknowledge permits Paul to demonstrate his determination to complete the course that he has begun (20:24).

With a second "and now behold" (v. 25; cf. v. 22) Paul clarifies the significance of what he has just said for the elders: this parting will be the final one. This announcement has consequences both for Paul's ministry and for the ministry of the elders. Paul's ministry in Ephesus is now complete. He considers it in light of this fact and declares that he has fulfilled his responsibility (vv. 26–27). Then he considers the situation of the elders who must take over responsibility for the church and begins to warn and exhort them. He commends them to God and the word of God's grace (v. 32) but, before ending, adds a further exhortation that applies a hitherto neglected aspect of Paul's manner of ministry described in vv. 18–21 to the situation of the elders.[6]

Paul's legacy to the church as presented in the speech is not only the manner of his ministry—his devotion to his calling, his acceptance of suffering, his willingness to work with his hands—but also the gospel that he preached and the vision of God's purpose that it contained. Paul's gospel is described in a number of ways in the course of the speech: He bore witness to "repentance to God and faith in our Lord Jesus" (v. 21). He bore witness to "the gospel of the grace of God" (v. 24) and proclaimed "the reign [of God]" (v. 25). He announced "the whole purpose of God" (v. 27). Finally, Paul refers to "the word of [God's] grace" (v. 32). It is to God and this word of grace that Paul commends the elders in parting, for this word of grace "is able to build up and give the inheritance" to the elders and the church for which they are responsible. The church's security is not the elders as such, although the speech assumes their importance. The elders cannot provide security, for they themselves are threatened. Paul must warn them urgently. He even says, "From you yourselves men will arise speaking twisted things" (v. 30).[7] The elders must be entrusted to a greater power, to God and the word of God's grace. What is meant when Paul's preaching is summarized as "the gospel of the grace of God" and "the word of [God's] grace"? It is important to grasp the dimensions of these phrases in light of the preceding narrative. The varied descriptions of Paul's gospel in the speech contain some reminders that help us to do that.

The "gospel of the grace of God," in spite of its Pauline ring, is not specifically Paul's gospel, according to Luke-Acts. It is a gospel shared with Jesus and Peter, although its full implications have been worked out only through a lengthy story that involved new discoveries. The continuity of Paul's gospel with the preaching of Jesus is suggested in vv. 24–25. The

---

[6] On vv. 33–35 see below, 260–61.

[7] Discussion of the nature of the troubles anticipated in vv. 29–30 should take note of the suggestion of Robert Brawley, *Luke-Acts and the Jews,* 79–83, 157. He views the external opponents as Jews and the internal opponents as Jewish Christians or Gentiles under the influence of Judaism. This view has the advantage of allowing the following narrative (see the charges against Paul in 21:20–21, 28) to interpret Paul's cryptic reference to opponents, rather than speculating about opponents on external grounds. As Brawley notes, 21:27–28 is linked to the warning in 20:29–30 because it expresses the opposition of Jews from *Asia.* The necessity of presenting Paul's defense suggests that the charges against him by Jews are still an important factor in the author's situation.

noun εὐαγγέλιον ("gospel" or "good news") occurs only twice in Luke-Acts, here and in Acts 15:7 as a summary of Peter's preaching to Cornelius (a connection that will be discussed below). However, the verb εὐαγγελίζομαι ("preach good news") is common and appears in key locations, including the quotation from Isaiah 61 that interprets Jesus' ministry in Luke 4:18. Furthermore, the people of Nazareth responded to Jesus' application of Isaiah to himself by speaking of the "words of grace" that they had just heard (Luke 4:22). Jesus' announcement of good news for the poor and the captives is a "gospel of grace" that provides a foundation for Paul's. It is also a gospel of God's reign, for when the terms of Luke 4:18–19 were reused in 4:43–44, Jesus spoke of "preaching good news of God's reign."[8]

However, Jesus' followers had to learn the full implications of this gospel of grace by steps. Only after Jesus' resurrection did they learn that the message must be "proclaimed to all the nations" (Luke 24:47), and Jesus' witnesses did not begin this task immediately. First they had to discover the deeper implications of the gospel of the grace of God. Peter summarized this discovery when he referred to his preaching before Cornelius as "the word of the gospel" (Acts 15:7; the only reference to "gospel" in Luke-Acts besides Acts 20:24) and concluded his speech by saying that "through the grace of the Lord Jesus" Jews "believe in order to be saved," just as Gentiles do (15:11).[9] In 15:7, 11 we find the two key terms in Paul's summary of his preaching as "the gospel of the grace of God" (20:24). The "word of the gospel" that Peter preached was one that placed God's word to Israel and Jesus' announcement in the Nazareth synagogue in the context of the realization that God welcomes Gentiles as well as Jews (10:34–43).[10] The "word of the gospel," then, is a message announcing that "the grace of the Lord Jesus" provides a way for both Jews and Gentiles to share in God's salvation on the same basis. Paul has been faithfully proclaiming this gospel. This is the message called "the gospel of the grace of God" in 20:24.

On the one hand, the speech emphasizes that Paul's message is a gospel of grace. On the other hand, it emphasizes the word's inclusive scope: it is a message for all, whether Jew or Gentile. These two facets of the word are related. Because it is a message of grace, it is open to all equally, as 15:11 indicated. The inclusive scope of Paul's message appears in 20:21, which refers to Paul "bearing witness both to Jews and to Greeks." This is

---

[8] This passage contains the word κηρύσσων ("proclaiming"), which reappears with the reference to God's reign in Acts 20:25. The connection between Acts 20:24–25 and Luke 4:18, 22, 43 was noted by Franz Prast, *Presbyter und Evangelium*, 103, 106, 114, 265.

[9] On this key assertion that salvation is open to all on the basis of grace and faith, see above, 185–86.

[10] See above, 137–42.

a reminder of Paul's Ephesian ministry, which reached "all the inhabitants of Asia . . . , both Jews and Greeks" (19:10). The reference to Jews and Greeks in 20:21 completes a statement that Paul "did not shrink from" his duty of announcing the gospel. The similar statement in 20:27 indicates that Paul "did not shrink from announcing the whole purpose of God (πᾶσαν τὴν βουλὴν τοῦ θεοῦ)." This statement also refers to the inclusive scope of Paul's message. "The whole purpose of God" is an understanding of God's purpose of salvation that recognizes its world-embracing dimensions. God's saving purpose does not stop short with a select group of people but moves into the whole world seeking all. Paul did not shrink from announcing this.

The context substantiates this interpretation of 20:27. Verse 27 supports v. 26. Paul declares that he is "clean from the blood of all, for (γάρ)" he announced "the whole purpose of God." If he had not announced the *whole* purpose of God, he would bear guilty responsibility for the death of some, for he would be presenting a gospel that excluded some. A partial purpose of God would be a purpose that reached so far and no further. Paul, however, proclaimed God's saving purpose without limit. The reference to "the blood of all" distinguishes 20:26 from the similar statement in 18:6, which speaks of "your blood," referring to the Corinthian Jews. In the farewell address Paul is assessing his responsibility in the broadest terms. It is a responsibility to all that arises from a gospel that offers salvation to all.[11] The emphasis on the inclusive scope of the mission also continues into v. 28. "The whole flock" corresponds to "the whole purpose of God." It is the inclusive church of Jews and Gentiles that results from announcing God's saving purpose for all. The elders must care for this inclusive church that results from Paul's work of bearing witness to "the gospel of the grace of God" and announcing "the whole purpose of God."

Paul's legacy to the church, then, is not merely his example as a devoted minister but also the inclusive gospel of grace that he proclaimed. Indeed, Paul receives so much attention in Acts partly because his mission best expresses the inclusive purpose of God at work in the world, a purpose emphasized by the narrator as early as Luke 2:30–32 and 3:6. The narrator has shaped this farewell scene so that Paul will be remembered in these terms. Paul is clearly being presented as a model for the later church at a number of points in this speech. Surely the narrator also intends the church to share Paul's understanding of the universal scope of God's saving purpose and his sense of responsibility for sharing this with all. This observation speaks against the view, often based on Acts 28:25–

---

[11] Compare the description of Paul's commission in 22:15: "You will be a witness for him to all persons."

28, that the narrator is willing to abandon a mission to part of the world, namely, the Jews.[12]

The speech is addressed to the Ephesian elders. In part it reflects points emphasized in the preceding description of Paul's Ephesian ministry; in part it reflects features of Paul's ministry noted in other locations. The speech shades from a summary of the Ephesian mission into a summary of Paul's mission in general. The following features seem to be reminders of the Ephesian mission in particular: the reference to Asia in 20:18; the reference to "both Jews and Greeks" in 20:21, which is related to the special emphasis on the scope of Paul's mission in 19:10; the reference to "going to Jerusalem, bound in the Spirit," a reminder of 19:21; the reference to proclaiming God's reign in 20:25, a reminder of 19:8, the only previous reference to God's reign as the content of Paul's message; the reference to "three years" in 20:31, a reminder of the unusual length of the Ephesian ministry that approximately fits 19:8, 10, plus a period following 19:21. In contrast, the following features of the speech are most closely related to incidents elsewhere than Ephesus: the reference to "the plots of the Jews" in 20:19, which reminds us of the "plot by the Jews" shortly before in Greece (20:3); the assertion that Paul is "clean from the blood of all" (20:26), which recalls a similar assertion in Corinth (18:6); the reference to admonishing at night as well as during the day (20:31), which is illustrated in the Troas narrative (20:7-12); the reference to supporting himself with his own hands (20:34), which is illustrated by his work with Aquila and Priscilla in Corinth (18:2-3). Perhaps the narrator assumes that these were common features of Paul's mission that occurred in Ephesus also. To some extent it may also be true that the Ephesian elders represent the Pauline churches in general.

The Holy Spirit has appointed the elders as "overseers to shepherd the church of God, which he obtained through the blood of his own" (20:28). There are strong echoes of Septuagint descriptions of Israel and its leaders in this statement. In prophetic passages that refer to the good and evil shepherds of Israel we find repeated reference to the need to "inspect" and thereby care for the people (using the verb ἐπισκέπτομαι; see Jer. 23:2; Ezek. 34:11; Zech. 10:3; 11:16). This is the function of the elders, indicated by their title "inspectors" or "overseers (ἐπισκόπους)." The reference to the "church" or "assembly of God (ἐκκλησίαν τοῦ θεοῦ)" also reflects Septuagint language, where the term "assembly" is frequently used (sometimes with "of God" or "of the Lord" added) in describing Israel (see Deut. 23:2-3; Judg. 20:2; 1 Chron. 28:8; Mic. 2:5). The Ephesian church belongs to God; it is God's possession, which God

---

[12] For further discussion see below, 344–53.

"obtained" or "acquired (περιεποιήσατο)."[13] It is quite clear here that God's relation to the mixed church of Jews and Gentiles is being understood after the pattern of God's relation to Israel in Scripture. In this respect 20:28 develops and emphasizes the implications of 15:14 and 18:10, where Gentiles are called God's "people (λαός)," sharing that designation with the ancient people of God.

We have already noticed that Paul's "gospel of the grace of God" is a continuation in a universal context of the good news that Jesus preached.[14] The portrait of Paul in the farewell speech also suggests that he faithfully follows the example and commands of Jesus in facing suffering, in humble service, and in giving rather than taking material goods. In each case there is continuity between master and disciple but also a new twist, suggesting a creative hermeneutical process of discovering new meanings in new situations.

The testimony of the Spirit about Paul's fate in Jerusalem echoes Jesus' passion announcements about his rejection and death in Jerusalem. This is especially clear in 21:11 (cf. Luke 18:31–32) but applies also to 20:23. The reference to being "bound in the Spirit" (20:22) is a variation on the theme of the divine necessity of the final journey, previously expressed with δεῖ ("it is necessary," "must") in 19:21 and, with reference to Jesus, in Luke 13:33 (see also Luke 9:22; 17:25; 24:7, 26). Luke 13:32 and Acts 20:24 are connected by using τελειόω ("complete," "accomplish") of the divinely determined goal. Paul's statement that he places no value on his ψυχή ("life") in Acts 20:24 may also paraphrase and apply Jesus' call to be willing to lose one's ψυχή in order to save it, first expressed in Luke 9:24, soon after the first passion prediction (see also Luke 14:26; 17:33).[15] Although Paul is answering Jesus' call to surrender his life and thereby reenacting Jesus' journey to suffering and death in Jerusalem, there is also a difference. Paul will not die in Jerusalem. Indeed, he "must" reach Rome (Acts 19:21). His sufferings extend over a long period of imprisonment and stretch from the Jewish to the Gentile capital. Paul follows his master in suffering, but there is a new twist that corresponds to the new dimensions of Paul's universal mission.

Jesus also demonstrated and taught a way of service. At the Last Supper he told the apostles that the leader must become like one who serves and added, "I am in your midst as one who serves (ὁ διακονῶν)" (Luke 22:26–27). Paul's farewell speech stresses his servant role. He has

---

[13] Compare God's statement in Isa. 43:21: λαόν μου ὃν περιεποιησάμην ("my people whom I obtained").

[14] See above, 255–58.

[15] The connection of Acts 20:24 with Luke 13:32 and 9:24 was noted by F. Prast, *Presbyter und Evangelium*, 95.

been "serving the Lord with all humility" (Acts 20:19), his hands "served" not only his own needs but those of others (20:34–35), and he describes his mission as his "service" or "ministry (διακονία)" received from the Lord (20:24). Paul's mission is a particular fulfillment of Jesus' command, in continuity with Jesus' own life and death. Again there is a new twist that indicates a creative application, however. In Luke the verb διακονέω and the noun διακονία are used exclusively with relation to a servant's or woman's role of preparing food and serving at table. This is no longer true in Acts, where positions of leadership in church and mission are called διακονία, as in 20:24. The humble service that Jesus commended by including himself among the waiters and waitresses is now being carried out through Paul's dedicated service to the Lord and others in his mission.[16]

Jesus in Luke speaks repeatedly about the dangers of possessions[17] and commands his disciples to sell their goods and give charity (Luke 12:33). Paul's attitude toward possessions is emphasized at the end of the farewell speech, and his behavior is even presented as an example of how Jesus' statement that "it is more blessed to give than to receive" can be put into practice (20:35).[18] Again there is a twist in the application. Paul does not follow Jesus' teaching by selling his possessions and distributing the proceeds. Instead, he gives by working with his hands. This is a new application of Jesus' teaching to fit the situation of church leaders such as the elders being addressed. Church leaders who do not work to support themselves will have to be supported by the church. Because Paul did not want to take other people's money and clothing (20:33), he worked with his own hands so that he could give rather than receive from others, in accordance with Jesus' teaching. His willingness to do hand work demonstrates his freedom from the desire for riches and his commitment to contribute to others, for (1) it ends the necessity of taking contributions from others and (2) enables Paul to help his co-workers ("those with me," 20:34) and the sick or economically weak (20:35). To apply Jesus' teaching on possessions in this way may seem to some a capitulation to bourgeois society. It suggests, however, that the narrator took Jesus' teaching on possessions seriously enough to want to find realistic applications in the life of the church. In light of the fact that most church leaders today are actually supported by their churches, it may still be radical enough to be disturbing.

---

[16] According to F. Prast, *Presbyter und Evangelium*, 193–94, use of διακονία of official functions in the church expresses a conscious attempt to distance the church from the conception of offices in the profane world.

[17] See *Narrative Unity* 1:127–32, 246–48.

[18] Although this saying of Jesus is not found in the Gospels, the command to give is repeatedly found in Luke. See 6:30, 38; 11:41; 12:33; 18:22.

New application of the teaching of Jesus may also be demonstrated by the warnings to "watch out for yourselves" and "keep alert" in 20:28, 31, for the same words are used in eschatological warnings in Luke 12:37 and 21:34. The possible connection is strengthened by the fact that the eschatological parable of the steward in charge has been applied in Luke 12:41–48 to leaders of the church.[19]

---

[19] Jesus' teaching to the disciples in Luke 12:1–53 emphasizes faithful fulfillment of leadership responsibility, willingness to suffer, and a right attitude toward wealth. These themes are also important parts of Paul's example to the elders, according to Paul's farewell speech. See *Narrative Unity* 1:250–51.

ACCEPTING THE LORD'S WILL
AS IMPRISONMENT APPROACHES

As Paul continues his journey to Jerusalem, the anticipations of an imprisonment that will deprive the church of Paul, which previously surfaced in 20:22–25, come to dominate the narrative. The narrator continues to note stops along the way where Paul meets with disciples. These contacts stretch beyond the areas of Paul's mission. Paul is recognized and welcomed in Tyre and Caesarea as he was at earlier stops on his trip,[1] and the disciples in these places show great concern for Paul's safety. Widespread respect for Paul is also indicated by the attention that he receives from figures associated with the mission in its early days: Philip the evangelist (21:8), Agabus the prophet (21:10; cf. 11:28), and Mnason, an "early disciple" (21:16). Their attention and support balance the ambiguous reception of Paul in Jerusalem, where Paul is welcomed gladly (21:17) but then is informed of widespread suspicion among Jewish Christians (21:20–21). During the journey the reception of Paul is all positive. Nevertheless, a struggle is taking place between Paul and those who love and honor him.

The shared recognition of the danger that Paul faces in Jerusalem produces conflicting perceptions of how Paul should respond. Paul finds himself in conflict with his own friends, who try to dissuade him from completing his trip. Both prophetic messages and human advice play important roles in this conflict, and the narrative reveals some of the difficulties in using either to determine God's will for human life.[2] The conflict is finally settled when Paul states conclusively his resolve to go to Jerusalem and his decision is finally accepted as the Lord's will (21:13–14). Prior to this Paul's resolve is tested, not by Satan, but by his own well-meaning friends.

The Miletus episode ended with an emotional scene of weeping because of Paul's announcement that his friends would not see him again (20:37–38). This weeping demonstrated the great affection that the Ephesian

---

[1] When Paul finally reaches Italy, he will be welcomed by local Christians in a similar way. See 28:14–15.

[2] See François Bovon, "Le Saint-Esprit, l'Église et les relations humaines," 339–58.

elders had for Paul. It was an appropriate and natural human response. However, it can become a form of pressure on Paul that could turn him from his purpose.[3] When we again hear of Paul's friends weeping, they are urging Paul not to go up to Jerusalem. Their weeping is an emotional reinforcement of their appeal, and Paul must reproach them, saying, "What are you doing, weeping and breaking my heart?" (21:12–13). The affection of friends who do not understand his decision greatly increases Paul's difficulty in holding to his purpose, and he seeks to end their appeal with an unequivocal statement of his resolve.

Prophetic revelations also play a role in the conflict. Paul has been receiving these revelations prior to his address in Miletus, for he referred there to the Spirit "bearing witness to me city by city, saying that bonds and tribulations await me" (20:23). This is preceded by the statement that he does not know what will happen to him in Jerusalem. Thus the Spirit's revelation is surrounded by uncertainties. In particular, Paul seems to anticipate the possibility that he will die in Jerusalem, for he affirms his willingness to do so in 21:13. This will not happen. In the narrative the Spirit's witness is understood as opening an area of foreknowledge that remains surrounded by mysteries. During Paul's journey the Spirit's messages continue, delivered by Christian prophets. In Tyre some disciples, speaking "through the Spirit," tell Paul "not to embark for Jerusalem" (21:4). Paul does the opposite, for he persists in believing that it is the Lord's will for him to go to Jerusalem. This is an interesting case of conflict in understanding the Spirit's directions. The conflict can, of course, be reduced to the human level. The more extensive statements of the Spirit's revelations in 20:23 and 21:11 simply indicate what will happen to Paul if he goes to Jerusalem. The message in 21:4 goes further, drawing the conclusion that Paul should not leave for Jerusalem. Perhaps the Spirit's message is consistent, but the prophets in Tyre have mixed their own conclusion with the Spirit's message.[4] The use of indirect discourse in 21:4 removes the message a step from the Spirit's direct expression. Nevertheless, it is interesting that the narrator has allowed to surface at least a superficial contradiction in the divine guidance that Paul is receiving, an indication that it is seldom easy to separate divine revelation from human interpretation. Appeal to divine guidance is not an easy escape from the ambiguities of human life.

When the Spirit's revelations are understood as they are in 21:4, they become further pressure on Paul to abandon his journey. This pressure peaks in the final scene of prophetic revelation before Paul reaches

---

[3] As noted by F. Bovon, "Le Saint-Esprit, l'Église et les relations humaines," 352.
[4] This is apparently the view of H. Conzelmann. See *Acts,* 178.

Jerusalem. The prophetic revelation, the appeal to Paul to abandon his journey, and Paul's response are presented here in their fullest form. In Caesarea the prophet Agabus appears, performs a prophetic sign by binding his own feet and hands with Paul's belt, and interprets this with the Spirit's message that the Jews in Jerusalem will bind Paul and deliver him into the hands of the Gentiles (21:10–11). Both Paul's travel companions (including the "we" narrator) and the local Christians draw an immediate conclusion from this: Paul must not go up to Jerusalem.[5] They appeal to Paul to change his mind, but he rejects their appeal with a final affirmation of his willingness to accept whatever awaits him in Jerusalem. At this point his friends finally accept his decision with the statement, "Let the will of the Lord be done."

Up to this point the narrative has preserved two options for Paul, the one expressed through Paul's original intention to go to Jerusalem, the other expressed through his friends, who attempt to dissuade him. The Spirit's messages do not resolve this conflict; rather they heighten it, as we see from the effect of Agabus' prophecy. The conflict comes to a head at the last recorded stop on the way to Jerusalem, which becomes the scene of a final decision. Paul, aware of the suffering and danger ahead, must make the same decision in Caesarea that Jesus made in the prayer scene before his crucifixion. In the prayer scene Jesus expressed the two options himself in internal debate: "Take this cup from me; nevertheless, let not my will but yours be done" (Luke 22:42). In Paul's case his companions and friends express the option of escape and appeal to Paul to choose it. Paul chooses the other option. The conflict finally ends when Paul's friends recognize that they cannot persuade him and say, "Let the will of the Lord be done" (21:14). These words, which recall Jesus' words just quoted, remind us of the similarity of the situations of Jesus and Paul. As the anticipated suffering nears, there is a final struggle pitting the natural human desire for freedom and life against the conviction that imprisonment and death must be accepted. Paul, like Jesus, commits himself to imprisonment and death, and the passion story moves forward.

Not only the final words of Paul's companions in 21:14 but also Paul's words in 21:13 recall statements in the Lukan passion story. They resemble Peter's pledge, "Lord, I am ready to go with you both to prison and to death" (Luke 22:33).[6] Peter's pledge differs from the parallels in Matt. 26:33, 35; Mark 14:29, 31, and it resembles Paul's words in Acts 21:13 in

---

[5] Note that the "we" narrator is not omniscient but shares the limited insight of Paul's companions.

[6] Walter Radl, in discussing Acts 21:13–14, notes the connection of 21:14 with Luke 22:42 but not the connection of Acts 21:13 with Luke 22:33. Radl wants to link an Acts scene with a single scene in Luke, but the links are actually more complex. See *Paulus und Jesus*, 159–68.

mentioning prison as well as death and in speaking of readiness (ἕτοιμος, Luke 22:33; ἑτοίμως, Acts 21:13). Peter fails to keep his pledge; Paul does not. Although a similar situation has returned and we are reminded of this by the use of similar words, Jesus' followers have moved beyond the faithlessness and blindness of the disciples prior to Jesus' resurrection.[7] What Peter then promised but did not do, Paul now promises and will do. In this way he will also fulfill the destiny of suffering announced by the Lord in the narrative of Paul's conversion (9:16). Even Paul's companions who press him so strongly to abandon his plan finally come to recognize that the coming events in Jerusalem are the Lord's will. The human problem in facing suffering and death has not vanished. Acceptance of such a fate is still a struggle, which well-meaning friends can make even worse. However, there are now persons in the church who can make the decision to accept this fate and live it through to the end.

It is not only the concluding exchange between Paul and his friends (21:13-14) that reminds us of the Lukan passion story. Agabus' prophecy is also formulated in a way that echoes the passion prophecies of Jesus in Luke. Jerusalem will not be the scene of Paul's death but will be the place where Paul begins a long imprisonment. Therefore, both the symbolic action and the accompanying words emphasize the binding of Paul. The rest of Agabus' prophecy shows the influence of Jesus' passion prophecies, even to the extent of weakening the correspondence to the later fulfillment. Paul replies to Agabus' prophecy that "the Jews will bind" him in Jerusalem by saying that he is ready "to be bound." The same form of the same verb (δεθῆναι) is found in the arrest scene in 21:33, but it is not the Jews who bind Paul but the Roman tribune. Likewise, the Jews do not literally "deliver" or "hand over" Paul to the Gentiles, as Agabus states in 21:11. Rather the Romans seize Paul from Jews who are intent on killing him. Two forces are tugging on Agabus' statement: the desire for correspondence with the fulfillment and the desire for correspondence with Jesus' prophecies. The result is a compromise. Agabus' statement that they "will deliver" Paul "into the hands of the Gentiles" mimics Jesus' statements that he "is about to be delivered into the hands of humans" (Luke 9:44) and that "he will be delivered to the Gentiles" (Luke 18:32).[8] A role for both Jews and Gentiles is specified in Acts 21:11, even though these roles do not precisely correspond to subsequent events. That Paul "was delivered into the hands of the Romans" will be repeated in a review statement in 28:17, showing the importance of this

---

[7] On this see *Narrative Unity* 1:226–27, 253–74.

[8] The view of W. Radl differs slightly. He links the reference to the Jews in Acts 21:11 to Luke 9:22, while connecting the last part of Agabus' prophecy to Luke 18:31–33. See *Paulus und Jesus*, 153–54.

phrase for highlighting the correspondence between Jesus' and Paul's fate at Jerusalem.

We have noted a series of indications that prophecy is incomplete (20:22–23), inexact (21:11), and may even lead to false conclusions (21:4). Agabus' prophecy is also viewed as conditional by the story characters: it will come true only if Paul insists on completing his trip in spite of Agabus' warning (cf. 21:12). Paul does insist, which suggests that he has a very powerful reason for going to Jerusalem.

This reason, however, remains obscure. The collection for Jerusalem, so important in Paul's letters, is not mentioned until 24:17, if there. It is not presented as a major factor in Paul's plans. Instead, we find references to what Paul decided in the Spirit (19:21), to the fact that he felt bound in the Spirit (20:22), and to his plan as the will of the Lord (21:14). The lack of an obvious human reason for going to Jerusalem makes the sense of divine purpose all the stronger. Nevertheless, there are a few hints in the narrative of how Paul's final journey to Jerusalem fits with his basic mission. In his farewell speech Paul said that he was willing to risk his life in order to "complete my course and the ministry which I received from the Lord Jesus, to bear witness to the gospel of the grace of God" (20:24). The journey to Jerusalem is necessary to complete the ministry to which he has been called. Because Paul goes to Jerusalem aware of what will befall him there, his arrest and trials are not an unexpected interruption of his plans but a part of what he must face to complete his ministry.

Thus the completion of Paul's ministry apparently requires the extensive defense of his work against religious and political accusations that actually follows in the narrative. Paul is facing the cultural consequences of his previous ministry, which has disturbed religion and society, with their guardians, by introducing a new understanding of God's work as reaching out through Jesus Messiah to both Jew and Gentile, breaking down the barrier between them. The mounting accusations that Paul has "upset the world" (17:6; cf. 16:20–21; 18:13; 19:25–27) now come to a climax. The world discovers that the challenge is really serious when it learns that the ministers of the new gospel are willing to face the consequences of their own disturbing words. This is a crisis that cannot be avoided without damage to the mission. Paul's decision to go to Jerusalem and to Rome is a decision to face this crisis. Jerusalem and Rome are the centers of the two powers that Paul has disturbed and to whom he must give a reckoning. He heads for the centers of power, where he will defend his ministry and carry his witness to the high authorities who embody that power.[9] The narrator avoids suggesting that Paul goes to Jerusalem for

---

[9] Paul's defense is not neatly distributed between Jerusalem and Rome, as we might expect. A

ordinary, human purposes. Paul is controlled by a larger purpose. Whether he is fully conscious of this or not, he goes to do what he will in fact do: defend his ministry before angry Jews and confused Romans and carry his witness to the centers of power. In doing so, Paul is also seeking a way for the gospel to move forward in spite of the opposition it has caused.

---

very important part of it actually takes place in Caesarea. Nevertheless, it is a defense before Jews and Romans, and their capitals of Jerusalem and Rome remain symbolically important in the narrative (cf. 23:11).

PAUL'S ARREST AND
FIRST DEFENSE SPEECH

Initial indications of Paul's reception by the Jerusalem church are quite positive. Paul is received gladly, and leaders of the Jerusalem church respond to Paul's report of his ministry by praising God (21:17, 19–20). In v. 20, however, there is a sharp shift in tone as the Jerusalem church leaders express a problem. It concerns an accusation against Paul circulating among Jewish believers. Paul is accused of teaching Diaspora Jews "apostasy from Moses." Specifically, Paul, according to the charge, advocates that Jews stop circumcising their children and walking "by the customs," that is, the law. Because the Jewish Christians are "all zealots for the law," this charge must be immediately laid to rest. The Jerusalem church leaders propose a way of doing so.

Presentation of this problem develops into a short speech in 21:20–25. The narrative highlights the problem as the most important subject of discussion at the meeting of James, the elders, and Paul, for no other subject is presented in direct discourse. Furthermore, the problem grows in importance through its relationship to important developments in the larger narrative. Looking backward in the narrative, we can see that this scene presents the third in a series of church conflicts that arise from a mission that includes both Jews and Gentiles. The issue of the baptism of Gentiles was settled in 11:1–18. The demand that Gentiles be circumcised and obey the Mosaic law was rejected in 15:1–31. Now the commitment to include both Jews and Gentiles in the mission generates a third problem: overt or covert pressure on Jewish Christians to abandon their Jewish manner of life.[1] There are some similarities between 21:17–25 and the conference in Acts 15. James and the elders are again present. Paul reports on his past mission as he did in 15:4, 12 and there is an explicit reference in 21:25 to the result of the previous conference. This reference recalls a measure already taken to enable Jews and Gentiles to live together in the church and ease the problems of Jews who want to

---

[1] Joseph Tyson perceives a change from the earlier church conflicts. Now the opposition is powerful, and there is no settlement of the dispute, with the result that the picture of the Jerusalem church contrasts sharply with the harmony of believers in the early days. See "Problem of Jewish Rejection," 135–36.

maintain their way of life.[2] Verse 25 may also serve as assurance thther n speaking of keeping the law, the Jerusalem leaders are not reopening the question of the Gentiles. That issue has been settled. The new issue is distinct: is Paul leading Jewish Christians to abandon their Jewish way of life?

This time the issue is sharpened by laying the charge directly at Paul's door. He has been teaching apostasy from Moses, the charge states. The previous narrative has given no indication of Paul doing this. Nevertheless, the way in which this problem is highlighted here, when it could easily have been avoided altogether, suggests that it is more than a mere misunderstanding with no foundation in the church's experience. Although the narrator may wish to absolve Paul of responsibility, one of the effects of the growth of the gentile mission is the inclusion of Jewish Christians in social groups that no longer support their Jewish way of life. In churches that are predominantly gentile, Jewish practices become a mark of foreignness. The desire to identify fully with the group results in subtle pressure to conform to the practices of the majority. When Paul separated the disciples from the Ephesian synagogue in 19:9, he was also separating Jewish Christians from a social world that supported their Jewish manner of life. Even if Paul did not teach these Jewish Christians to abandon circumcision and the Mosaic customs, the new social situation would encourage this development. In response to this problem, James, the elders, and Paul wish to demonstrate that Paul supports the right of Jewish Christians to live as Jews, just as gentile Christians live as Gentiles.

The importance of the charge against Paul is also underlined when we look forward in the narrative. To be sure, the Jerusalem church will drop out of the narrative after this scene, and the charge in 21:21 may seem to disappear with it. In reality, the charge is absorbed into a larger accusation of continuing importance throughout the rest of Acts. This accusation comes from Jews and claims that Paul teaches "against the people and the law and this place [the temple]" (21:28), that is, that Paul and his mission are anti-Jewish. The reference to the temple reflects the temple setting of the scene. The references to the people and the law parallel the charge in 21:21, for circumcision is the distinctive mark of the Jews as God's special people. Abandoning it and the Mosaic customs means the dissolution of the Jews as a separate and unique people. The charge that Paul leads Jewish Christians to abandon their Jewish way of life can disappear because it is one aspect of a larger issue: Paul's attitude toward Judaism in general. This larger issue does not disappear. Again and again

[2] See above, 190–92.

in the following chapters Paul will seek to convince his hearers that he is a
loyal Jew and that his mission is not an anti-Jewish movement. He will
still be arguing his case in 28:17-20, after he arrives in Rome. The
importance of this issue in Acts 21—28 is one major indication of the
importance throughout Luke-Acts of the problem of Judaism, a problem
that becomes acute because of the conflict between the promise of God to
the Jewish people and Jewish rejection of its fulfillment through Jesus.[3]
When Paul reaches Jerusalem, he becomes the lightning rod through
which the pent-up energy surrounding this issue is discharged.[4]

The Jerusalem leaders have a concrete plan for dealing with the
suspicions aroused by the charges against Paul. They urge Paul to pay the
expenses for the sacrifices associated with the Nazirite vows of four men
and to consecrate himself so that he can share in this temple ritual. These
acts will demonstrate that Paul keeps the law, including the ritual provi-
sions. This proposal may seem questionable both from the viewpoint of
Paul's critics and from the viewpoint of Paul, if he were being honest.
How can support of and participation in a temple ritual demonstrate that
Paul keeps the law? Recall that Paul is charged with *teaching* against the
Jewish customs. The question of the moment is less a matter of Paul's
general behavior than what he advocates. Therefore, participation in the
temple ritual can demonstrate that he believes it appropriate for Jews to
participate in the temple and follow the regulations of temple holiness.
Indeed, Paul's agreement to the proposal can be understood as a sign of
his respect for his Jewish heritage and his desire to lay claim to it. Thus
the ritual will be a sort of confessional act, a confession of the validity of
law and temple for the Jewish people.

It is less easy to dismiss Paul's response as a superficial sop to the
complainers when we realize that the proposal involves real risk. Recall
that Paul on the way to Jerusalem was repeatedly told that "bonds and
tribulations await" him (20:23; cf. 21:4, 11). The proposal does not allow
Paul to play it safe in hopes of at least postponing the realization of the
prophecy, for it calls for a public demonstration (cf. v. 24: "And all will
know") in the temple. It involves "announcing" in this public place the
time when his days of sanctification will be completed (v. 26), thus
enabling Paul's enemies to plan action against him with full knowledge of
where Paul will be on a particular day. Paul's action may seem superficial

---

[3] For an overview see R. Tannehill, "Israel in Luke-Acts," 69–85.

[4] It is no accident that the figure of Paul, who presented a radical theological defense of a
worldwide mission, is at the center of this problem, and there is justification for Robert
Brawley's view that a major concern of Acts is to defend Paul. See *Luke-Acts and the Jews,*
51–83. See also John Carroll, "Luke's Apology for Paul," 106–18. In defending Paul, the
narrator of Acts tries to take seriously some of the Jewish charges that arise from the success
of the gentile mission that Paul promoted.

in itself, but in the context Paul is risking his life in order to make clear that he affirms the right of Jewish Christians to live according to the law. As a result Paul is nearly killed in the temple, is seized as a prisoner, and is never again a free man. The perspective of Acts has been called a "theology of glory" because the many imprisonments and dangers encountered in the mission are simply the occasions for the demonstration of extraordinary power and courage, with quick releases from prison, rather than real experiences of weakness and suffering.[5] If previously there was some truth to this charge, there is a significant change with Paul's arrest in Jerusalem. Paul is still a hero, but he is heroic through enduring an imprisonment that goes on and on. There are no more wondrous prison releases, as in 5:17–21; 12:1–17; and 16:25–30. Although Paul is rescued from danger, he remains a prisoner. Paul's references to his bonds (26:29; 28:20) keep this fact before us. Paul enters this bondage because he is willing to put himself at risk in order to support Jewish Christians who treasure their Jewish heritage. Later he will say to Jews, "For the sake of the hope of Israel I wear this chain" (28:20). This enlarges the point: Paul's whole imprisonment is an act of loyalty to Israel.[6] Paul's lengthy imprisonment and the witness that this prisoner bears to Israel's hope are signs of his loyalty to Israel, although he is being attacked as a renegade. Imprisonment is not just an opportunity for an amazing escape.

By human calculations the proposal for Paul to share in the temple ritual was not a good one. Rather than clearing Paul of a charge before Jewish Christians, it leads to a lengthy imprisonment with repeated accusations and trials. There is irony here at the expense of the church. There is also irony in the charge made against Paul in the temple. When he is demonstrating his loyalty to his Jewish heritage and has consecrated himself to participate in the temple worship, he is accused of being a renegade Jew and defiling the temple (21:28) and then is attacked. However, the seemingly disastrous result of the proposal by the leaders of the Jerusalem church will not end Paul's witness. Indeed, it will enable him to bear witness before governors and kings.[7]

The accusation in 21:28 indicates the motive for the attempt on Paul's life. It contains one specific charge—that Paul has defiled the temple by bringing Greeks into it—but this is preceded by a sweeping charge that relates to Paul's whole mission. Paul teaches "all everywhere against the people and the law and this place." According to the accusers, Paul's mission is an anti-Jewish movement, for the special place of the elect

---

[5] See R. Pervo, *Profit with Delight,* 24, 27.

[6] See further below, 344–45.

[7] See Jean Zumstein, "L'apôtre comme martyr," 387, who sees this as another instance of the "theme of the providential defeat (échec)" that actually leads the mission forward.

people, the life of obedience to the Mosaic law, and the temple worship are defining characteristics of Judaism. This sweeping charge is not a superficial error, for the narrative provides some support for it. Both Stephen and Paul have declared that God does not dwell in temples made with hands (7:48–50; 17:24–25), which relativizes the importance of the Jewish temple, and Jesus has been associated with the temple's destruction (Luke 19:41–44; 21:5–6, 20–24; Acts 6:14). With respect to the law, the church includes Gentiles who are permitted to live outside the law (15:1–29), and even Jewish Christians are troubled by the possibility that the Jewish Christians of the Pauline churches are being lured away from the way of Moses (21:20–21). If true, this would also be an attack on "the people," undermining what makes the Jewish people distinctive. Finally, a movement declaring that Gentiles participate in God's salvation in the same way as Jews inevitably reduces the importance of being a Jew. This movement can be seen as an attack on the religious basis of Israel's uniqueness. The cry of the accusers in the temple is the cry of a people trying to maintain itself against a perceived threat to its identity. The fact that Paul in the remaining chapters of Acts repeatedly speaks of his relation to Judaism shows that the narrator has heard this cry and is trying to shape a response. This is especially apparent in the two major speeches in Acts 22—26, placed at the beginning and ending of this series of defense scenes. Both are addressed to Jews—the former to a Jewish mob and the latter to a Jewish king—and give an account of Paul's call and mission in response to Jewish accusations.

The problem is so important and so difficult because the narrator is committed to a vision of God's saving purpose that includes both Jews and Gentiles, as announced in Luke 2:30–32 and 3:6, and recognizes that the scriptural promises of salvation refer first of all to the Jewish people. Instead of being satisfied with the fact that some Jews have accepted Jesus, the narrator concludes the second volume by wrestling with the fact that many Jews have not. The threat perceived by Jews is not easily removed. Paul and the narrator want to be loyal to Israel, but they are committed to an understanding of God's saving purpose that reaches beyond Israel, which necessarily relativizes Israel's place in the scheme of things. They are not willing to allow Jewish rejection to stand in the way of the world mission. In this situation, is there still a way to appeal to Israel? To a large extent Paul's defense speeches are an attempt to find a way. The continuing attacks on Paul underscore the great difficulty of the attempt.

The charge that Paul defiled the temple by bringing Greeks into it does not have the same importance as the sweeping charge that precedes it. It is a mistake made by suspicious people, who "were supposing" that Paul brought Trophimus into the temple simply because they had seen them together in the city (21:29). This error does not exclude the slight possibility that there is a symbolic truth to the charge because Gentiles, "cleansed" and "consecrated" by faith (15:9; 26:18), can now approach the holy God like Jews.[8]

The charges of teaching against the law and the temple parallel the charges against Stephen in 6:13. The charge of teaching against the people can now be added because of the growth of the gentile mission, which threatens the special position of the Jewish people.[9] There are other similarities between the unfolding scene and the Stephen episode. Both Stephen and Paul are seized and then deliver speeches that cause an angry and violent response (7:54–58; 22:22–23). The similarity to Stephen's martyrdom, plus the description of Paul being beaten by the mob (21:30–32), shows how close Paul has come to death.[10] Although the content of the speeches is different, the speeches of Stephen and Paul begin with the same address ("Brothers and fathers, listen"; 7:2; 22:1), and Paul's speech contains an explicit reference to Stephen's death (22:20).[11] Action against both Stephen and Paul is incited by Diaspora Jews (6:9–12; 21:27; cf. 9:29).

The references to the Asian Jews and to Trophimus the Ephesian (21:27–29) help to preserve continuity between events in Jerusalem and Paul's previous ministry. The uproar in Jerusalem is a direct reaction to Paul's previous mission, especially the recent and extensive mission in Ephesus.

The tribune who seizes Paul and puts him in chains has a significant role in Acts 21—23. He is the first of a small group of Roman officials who go through a process of learning about Paul. The development is most fully displayed in his case. He starts from complete ignorance and tries to learn something from the crowd, without success (21:33–34). Then he begins to learn little by little, through trial and error. He guesses that Paul is the Egyptian who recently led a revolt (21:38) and learns that he is instead a Jew from Tarsus. He plans to examine Paul by torture but quickly changes his mind when he learns that Paul is a Roman citizen (22:24–29). He continues his investigation by bringing Paul before the

---

[8] E. Haenchen rejects a similar view of Overbeck because "Luke does not work with such allegories." Cf. *Acts*, 616, n. 4. I think that Luke 5:1–11 is evidence to the contrary. See *Narrative Unity* 1:203–4. However, the indications are not as clear in Acts 21:28–29.

[9] See Volker Stolle, *Zeuge als Angeklagter*, 227.

[10] The intervention of the tribune is one of a series of scenes that portray last-minute rescues. R. Pervo cites these to indicate Luke's interest in "adventure." See *Profit with Delight*, 14–17, 22.

[11] The connections between the two speeches are noted by Benoît Standaert, "L'art de composer," 325.

Sanhedrin (22:30), and from the response to Paul's shout before that body
he learns that the real issues are disputes of the Jewish law (23:28–29).
By the time that the tribune Claudius Lysias sends Paul to Felix the
governor, he is able to form a sound opinion about him that differs greatly
from his initial assumptions (see his letter to Felix in 23:26–30). Thus the
narrator offers a little subplot: the education of a Roman.

When Paul is taken away by the Romans, "the multitude of the people"
follow shouting, "Get rid of him (αἶρε αὐτόν)" (21:36), a cry repeated
after the speech with clear indication that they are calling for his death
(22:22). The same cry appears in the trial of Jesus (Luke 23:18), along
with the cry "Crucify." Reuse of the cry against Jesus seems to be a clear
attempt to parallel the attitude of the people of Jerusalem toward Paul
with their attitude toward Jesus at the time of his death. "Get rid of him"
(applied to Jesus in Luke's passion story but not in Matthew or Mark) is
broad enough to fit the situations in both Luke and Acts, while "Crucify"
would not apply to Paul. Thus there are connections between this scene
and both Jesus' death and Stephen's death. Furthermore, all three of these
events take place in Jerusalem, where the conflict between God's prophets
and God's people comes to a head, as Jesus anticipated in Luke 13:33–34.

Jesus goes to his death without a defense speech. It is not so with Paul.
The issue raised by the opponents' charge in 21:28 requires discussion,
and the narrator immediately arranges an opportunity, even though Paul
has just been beaten by an unruly mob. The speech differs markedly from
Paul's previous mission speeches. It is autobiographical, a review of his
own life. In the farewell speech in 20:18–35, Paul gave an account of his
ministry to church leaders. Now he will give an account of his life to
Jewish opponents. The desire to do this suggests that important issues are
involved and that these issues focus specifically on Paul.

Paul's defense speech to the Jewish crowd begins a lengthy section of
Acts in which Paul is responding to Jewish resistance to his mission. This
difficult problem will be highlighted even in the final scene of Acts (28:23–
28). The fact that the narrator devotes so much of the speech material
from Acts 22—28 to this problem shows its seriousness. If the narrator
were prepared to dismiss the Jews with an indication that they are simply
fulfilling the role foreordained for them in Scripture (cf. 28:26–27), the
matter could be handled much more briefly. The dominance of the last
section of Acts by this intractable problem should make us hesitate to
speak of Lukan "triumphalism," a charge repeated recently by Richard
Pervo.[12] "The verifiability of God's 'providence,'" he claims, "is constitutive for the theology of Luke," resulting in a simplistic "popular"

---

[12] See *Profit with Delight,* 137–38.

theology akin to "sentimental fiction," in which "virtue triumphs over evil because God is on the side of the virtuous."[13] Yet this last section of Acts makes clear that the mission has not triumphed with the Jews, a problem so serious that it cannot be ignored. The narrator wrestles with it at length in the scenes in Acts 22—26 and again in Acts 28. All of this material must be considered in order to understand the narrator's complex response.

An account of Paul's encounter with the Lord on the Damascus road is a prominent part of Paul's autobiographical speech in Acts 22. We were first told of this encounter in 9:1–18, and it will appear a third time in 26:9–18. The triple narration of this event is an indication of its key importance for understanding Paul's mission. The placement of the three accounts supports this observation. The first appears at the beginning of Paul's mission as its foundation, the second and third in the two major defense speeches at the beginning and end of the defense sequence in Acts 22—26, all prominent positions.[14]

The most important differences between the account of Paul's call in 22:4–16 and the account in 9:1–18 are due to two factors: (1) In 22:4–16 the point of view shifts because Paul is narrating his own story. (2) The account in 22:4–16 is part of a defense speech and is meant to refute the charge that Paul is a renegade from Judaism. Both of these points require further explanation.

In 11:5–17 Peter retells a story that has just been told by the narrator of Acts, the events leading to the baptism of Cornelius. Peter tells the story from his own point of view. This is particularly apparent in the different ordering of the events in Acts 10 and 11. Peter tells of events as he learned of them, while the privileged narrator of Acts 10 speaks as though present with both Cornelius and Peter.[15] There is a similar shift in point of view between the accounts of Paul's encounter with the Lord in Acts 9 and 22.[16] In Acts 9 the privileged narrator speaks as though present with Paul and then with Ananias as the Lord addresses each. Paul, however, does not claim the narrator's privilege. He is giving personal testimony and focuses on what he himself experienced. Paul does not tell what the Lord said to Ananias when Paul was not present. Therefore, the narration of

---

[13] See *Profit with Delight*, 74.

[14] M.-E. Rosenblatt speaks of the accounts as three "poles. The first in Acts 9 and the second in Acts 22 circumscribe the period of Paul's active mission and the growth of the Church. The second in 22 and the third in 26 frame Paul's testimony as a prisoner subject to interrogation and trial." See *Under Interrogation*, 116.

[15] See above, 143–45. It is customary to speak of the privileged narrator as "omniscient" and "omnipresent."

[16] Robert Funk discusses the order of events in Paul's report in Acts 22, using G. Genette's categories. See *Poetics of Biblical Narrative*, 204–6.

Paul's commission shifts from a message of the Lord to Ananias to a message of Ananias to Paul, and the Lord's appearance to Ananias drops out of the narrative. We learn of Paul's commission when Paul learned of it, with the arrival of Ananias. This shift also eases the reformulation of Paul's commission in 22:14–15, allowing the introduction of new accents.

When the Lord's dialogue with Ananias disappears from the narrative, so does Ananias' role as a persecuted Christian who at first resists the Lord's command because he is afraid of Paul.[17] Instead, Ananias is presented as a devout Jew. The dominant issue has shifted. It no longer concerns Paul and persecuted Christians but Paul and the Jews.

Peter retold his story in 11:5–17 because Jewish Christians in Jerusalem objected to his behavior (11:2–3). Peter's story was his defense. It was an effective defense because it enabled Peter's critics to understand how Peter changed from a person who avoided uncleanness to one who baptized Gentiles and ate with them. Actions that appeared inappropriate out of context appeared appropriate when put back into the context of a narrative, for the narrative enabled the hearers to understand that the determinative force behind the change was God. Paul is following the same strategy in his autobiographical defense speech in 22:1–21.[18] The Jerusalem Jews can accept Paul only if they understand the change that took place in him and the force behind that change. So Paul tells his story, and he does so in a way that encourages his hearers to recognize this as the work of "the God of our fathers" (22:14).

In his speech Paul does not respond specifically to the charges in 21:28, but he is replying in a general way to the charge that he teaches "against the people." This speech is only a first step in a more extensive consideration of the charges raised against Paul by Jews. In it Paul will emphasize his Jewish roots and the Jewish roots of his mission, but his continuing loyalty to Israel will be expressed more strongly later when he emphasizes his commitment to the hope of Israel (26:6–7; 28:20). Paul speaks of the speech as his "defense ($\grave{\alpha}\pi o\lambda o\gamma \acute{\iota}\alpha$)" (22:1), and it has been compared by William Long and Jerome Neyrey to the approaches recommended for forensic defense speeches in Greco-Roman rhetoric.[19] A defense speech is designed to persuade its audience of the innocence of one who has been accused. Much of Paul's speech fits this purpose. Paul has been accused of being anti-Jewish (21:28). He begins his speech by emphasizing that he is

---

[17] See above, 115–17.

[18] See also 9:27, where Barnabas succeeds in changing the minds of the fearful apostles by telling the story of Paul's encounter with the Lord.

[19] See William Long, *Trial of Paul*, 217–29, and "The *Paulusbild*," 97–102; Jerome Neyrey, "Forensic Defense Speech," 210–24.

a zealous Jew, educated in the strict tradition of the law (22:3),[20] and continues by emphasizing the Jewish roots of his mission. However, Paul's speech ceases to be a forensic defense speech with the last verse, which is no longer designed to persuade the audience. It is followed by renewed cries for Paul's death, and this result should not be unexpected. A rhetorician might advise Paul to avoid the whole subject of vv. 17–21. In any case, the final, sharp command of the Lord need not be introduced. In the light of the actual course of the narrative as reported in Acts, Paul could honestly say that he was sent from Jerusalem to Diaspora Jews, to whom he was careful to give the first opportunity. Instead, he quotes the Lord's command to go εἰς ἔθνη μακράν ("to Gentiles [or "nations"] afar"). It may be necessary here to understand ἔθνη geographically (i.e., as the "nations," including the Jews scattered among them), as Christoph Burchard has argued,[21] but the choice of this term obscures Paul's extensive involvement in Jewish mission. At this point Paul does not choose words designed to win the hearts of his audience, as the reaction in v. 22 makes clear.

Viewed in light of its function in the narrative, Paul's speech is a review indicating how the present crisis came to pass. At the end the resulting issue is deliberately sharpened so that none will miss it. The speech says two things about Paul, which highlight a strange turn of events: (1) Paul is a zealous Jew, and his mission is deeply rooted in the world of Judaism. (2) Paul has been sent on a universal mission ("to all persons," v. 15), which, because of Jewish rejection, increasingly tends to be most fruitful in the gentile world and produce a gentile church. This tendency reinforces Jewish resistance, and Paul is now suffering the consequences. In response, Paul is able to insist that he is a true Jew, but he is not able to resolve the conflict. The mission must go forward. When it is blocked among the Jews, it must go forward among the Gentiles, as the Lord commanded.

As a defense speech, Paul's address to the crowd is a failure. The audience is not persuaded. Although this scene is not a formal trial, Paul's speech is called a "defense" (22:1), and it is made before the people, who take the role of judges. The verdict is negative. The violent reaction at the end is a dramatic indication of a persistent problem. Paul will keep trying to remove the deep suspicion against him and his mission, and the later narrative will suggest the possibility of a better result among some Jews. However, the problem will not be solved even at the end of Acts.

---

[20] According to W. Long, "The *Paulusbild*," 98–100, v. 3 is the "narrative" section of the forensic speech, which is expected to state clearly the issue of the entire case.

[21] See *Der dreizehnte Zeuge*, 165–66.

The end of the speech sharpens the problem, rather than allowing the tension to be reduced. Such a move is possible because this speech is only the beginning of Paul's defense. It begins a defense of Paul and his mission that will be cumulative, seeking to convince the suspicious by painting a portrait of Paul that will make him more understandable and acceptable to detractors sympathetic to Judaism. Points are being scored that might persuade some Jews—not an angry mob, perhaps, but those in a more reasonable frame of mind. For Christian readers of Acts these points could serve as suggestions of how Paul's essential position might be maintained without ending the possibility of conversation with Judaism.

Neyrey and Long discuss the speech's techniques of persuasion in light of the discussions of ancient rhetoricians. Neyrey discusses the need to create good will "by presenting the ethos or character of the speaker in the most favorable light," and he notes a number of features of the speech in Acts 22 that would help "secure a good hearing for Paul's testimony by presenting his ethos favorably, especially his education and piety."[22] Both Neyrey and Long comment on the references to witnesses who can corroborate particular points of Paul's account: "the high priest and the whole council of elders" (22:5) for Paul's early zeal, Paul's traveling companions for the bright light (22:9), and Ananias (an exemplary Jew) for the commission from the Lord (22:12–16).[23] Neyrey also notes that the Lord's appearance to Paul is described according to a typical form familiar from Scripture. An appearance of this type will be more "probable" to an audience accustomed to hearing of encounters with God or angels in this scriptural form.[24] These features indicate that most of the speech is carefully constructed for the purpose of persuading a Jewish audience.

To this can be added the atmosphere of Scripture and Jewish tradition that surrounds Paul's life in this speech. The indications of this include at least the following: Paul's address of the audience as "brothers" (v. 1) and use of their ethnic language (v. 2); his immediate claim to be a Jew (v. 3); his upbringing in Jerusalem and education by a respected rabbi "according to the strictness of the ancestral law" (v. 3); the claim to be a "zealot for God" (v. 3); Paul's relation to the high priest and the council of elders (v. 5); the use of ἔδαφος ("ground," only here in NT but fairly common in LXX)[25] and the LXX form of the name for Saul (vv. 7, 13); the designation of Jesus as "the Nazarene" (v. 8); the introduction of Ananias

---

[22] See "Forensic Defense Speech," 211–13.

[23] See J. Neyrey, "Forensic Defense Speech," 218–19; W. Long, "The *Paulusbild*," 101.

[24] See J. Neyrey, "Forensic Defense Speech," 219. For discussion of the typical form Neyrey refers to G. Lohfink, *Conversion of St. Paul*, 62–66; B. Hubbard, "Role of Commissioning Accounts," 187–98; idem, "Commissioning Stories in Luke-Acts," 103–26.

[25] See E. Haenchen, *Acts,* 626.

not as a Christian but as a devout Jew respected by the local Jewish community (v. 12); Ananias' address of Saul as "brother" (v. 13); the attribution in v. 14 of Paul's call to "the God of our fathers" and the reference to Jesus as "the Just One," as before Jewish audiences in 3:14, 7:52; the reference to Paul praying in the temple and receiving a vision there (vv. 17–18); the use of the verb σπεύδω ("hasten"), which is common in LXX but fairly rare in NT[26] (v. 18); the indication that Paul's activities were well known in Jerusalem (v. 19). The principal characters of Paul's narrative—himself, the Lord, Ananias—are all characterized in ways that emphasize their roots in the tradition that zealous Jews know and honor. In this way Paul attempts to speak persuasively to his Jewish audience, helping them to understand his mission as a fitting development within their own heritage. All of this is an indirect argument that Paul and his mission are not anti-Jewish. However, this careful strategy does not overcome the offense of the Lord's final command in v. 21. Paul seems to protest when first told to leave Jerusalem, an indication of his dedication to his mission in the center of Judaism (vv. 18–20). However, the Lord's requirement of a world mission cannot be ignored. So the speech ends with the tension between Jewish origins and loyalties, on the one hand, and a mission in the gentile world, on the other, at high voltage.

Reference in this speech to the Lord's command to leave Jerusalem is not an irrelevant provocation. It is a necessary warning to this audience because the people of Jerusalem are now reacting in the same way that the Lord indicated they would react when Paul first preached in Jerusalem. Jerusalem should know that it is about to lose what could have been a second opportunity to hear the good news from Paul.

Paul specifically identifies himself with his audience in v. 3: "being a zealot for God just as you all are today." This zealousness led Paul to persecute those who followed the way. Paul's audience is now doing the same thing. The old Paul and his audience are alike in their understanding of what loyalty to the God of Israel implies. Because of this common beginning point, Paul's autobiography is particularly relevant to the audience he is addressing.[27] Paul's narration of the radical change that took place in his life is an invitation to present persecutors to reevaluate Paul and Jesus and thereby be changed themselves. Furthermore, Paul is the person best qualified to testify to the power of the Lord to change persecutors. The power for change that he encountered can continue to work through retelling the story. The figure of Ananias in Paul's account is also an opportunity for his hearers. If they can understand God's

---

[26] Six occurrences, five of them in Luke-Acts. See E. Haenchen, *Acts,* 627, n. 5.
[27] See Karl Löning, *Saulustradition,* 175–76.

purpose as this devout Jew did, the present conflict will cease. Thus the
narrator presents to us a Paul who has not given up hope of appealing to
Jewish opponents.

The commission that is the foundation of Paul's whole mission is
expressed in vv. 14–15. Despite differences in wording, there are parallels
to the Lord's statement in 9:15. Paul has been especially chosen ("a vessel
of election for me," 9:15; "the God of our fathers chose you," 22:14) for a
mission of universal scope ("to bear my name before Gentiles and kings
and sons of Israel," 9:15; "a witness for him to all persons," 22:15). These
points will reappear in the third version of Paul's commission in 26:16–
17.[28] It is important to remember that Paul in Acts is not the apostle to the
Gentiles. He has been sent "to all persons," which means both Jews and
Gentiles. He is the one through whom the Lord has chosen to realize the
divine purpose of including both groups in salvation, as announced
already in Luke 2:30–32 and 3:6.

In 22:15 and 26:16 Paul is called a "witness ($\mu\acute{a}\rho\tau\nu\varsigma$)." He is qualified
to be a witness because of what he has seen and heard. Luke-Acts empha-
sizes the role of the twelve apostles as Jesus' witnesses.[29] Now we are told
that the Lord has also given this important task to Paul.[30]

Both the twelve and Paul are witnesses, but the scope of their witness
differs. The twelve are witnesses of the risen Messiah *and* of Jesus'
ministry (1:21–22; 10:39, 41). Paul shares their witness to the risen
Messiah but not their witness to Jesus' ministry. He, in turn, has a special
role that goes beyond the witness of the twelve. On the one hand, he has
seen the risen Lord just as the apostles have. Acts 22:15 and 26:16 make
clear that his witness is based on what he has seen. This was more than a
blinding light, for according to 22:14 Paul was chosen "to see the Just
One," and later the Lord says, "I appeared to you ($\mathring{\omega}\phi\theta\eta\nu\ \sigma o\iota$)" (26:16).
Paul saw not only a light but a person and therefore can bear witness to
him.[31] On the other hand, the scope of Paul's witness is special. It is a

---

[28] See below, 322–24, and see the chart, 119–20. Acts 22:15 refers to "all persons" rather than
listing Jews and Gentiles because reference to the gentile nations is being reserved for the
end of the speech, where it will provoke a violent reaction from the crowd.

[29] Cf. Luke 24:48; Acts 1:8, 22; 2:32; 3:15; 5:32; 10:39, 41; 13:31. In Luke 24:48 Jesus is
actually speaking to "the eleven and those with them" (Luke 24:33), opening the possibility
of others than the apostles acting as Jesus' witnesses. A larger group of witnesses could also
be implied in Acts 13:31. Nevertheless, the narrator is chiefly interested in the witness of
Peter and the other apostles.

[30] C. Burchard emphasizes that Paul as witness shares a role that is central to the function of
the apostles. According to Burchard, this implies Paul's fundamental equality with the
twelve. See *Der dreizehnte Zeuge,* 130–36.

[31] The parallel in 26:16 indicates that 22:14 refers primarily to the appearance on the
Damascus road, not to the following temple vision. Paul's ability to bear witness to the risen
Christ should not be questioned on the basis of 13:31. There Paul cites the apostles as
witnesses but immediately adds his own witness to the resurrection in 13:32–33. Note the
emphatic $\kappa\alpha\grave{\iota}\ \mathring{\eta}\mu\epsilon\hat{\iota}\varsigma$ ("And *we*") at the beginning of v. 32.

witness "to all persons" (22:15), that is, to both Jews and Gentiles. In 1:8
Jesus told the apostles that they would be his witnesses "to the end of the
earth." The narrative has shown that they do not fulfill this command by
themselves. After Cornelius' conversion demonstrates to the Jewish
Christians that God has cleansed the Gentiles, the apostles do not directly
participate in the gentile mission, although they have a role in verifying
the theological appropriateness of Gentiles' freedom from the law (15:1–
29). The limited scope of their witness is recognized in 13:31, where Paul
speaks of the apostles as Jesus' "witnesses to the people." This contrasts
with Paul's witness "to all persons." Thus the twelve apostles and Paul
share a witness to the risen Messiah, but there is also something distinctive about the witness of each: in the one case a witness to the ministry
of Jesus, which remains important; in the other a witness with a breadth
that corresponds to the breadth of God's saving purpose.[32] Thus the
twelve and Paul have complementary and interdependent roles in the
unfolding purpose of God.

Paul is a witness not only of what he saw but of what he heard (22:15),
and in his words the risen Lord presents himself as persecuted (twice, 22:7
and 8). Paul is called to be witness of the exalted but persecuted Lord.
Volker Stolle believes this to be important and draws a conclusion as to the
special character of Paul's witness in the defense scenes: before an audience that continues to reject Jesus and persecute, Paul must bear witness
that Jesus is nevertheless the Messiah enthroned by God.[33] Paul's defense
speech is not only a defense of himself but a witness to Jesus before a
hostile audience, as 23:11 indicates. By retelling his story, Paul is bearing
witness to the exalted Lord, who is still the persecuted. Through his past
experience Paul is specially prepared to recognize and reveal what others
cannot see, that the world is ruled by a heavenly Lord who is still rejected
and persecuted. Paul can testify to this by retelling his own story of
encounter with this Lord. The references to a "defense" in 22:1 and to
Paul on trial in following scenes place Paul's witness in a judicial context
and give it a judicial sense.[34] Paul is bearing witness for Jesus in an
ongoing trial that still involves Jesus as well as himself. Thus there may
be some justification for Jerome Neyrey's view that the trial of Jesus
continues through the trials of Paul.[35] The issues of this trial, then, extend
beyond political apologetic and defense of Paul as an individual to the
claims of the Messiah who, at present, is still accused and persecuted.

---

[32] See K. Löning, *Saulustradition,* 139–44.
[33] See *Zeuge als Angeklagter,* 209–10.
[34] See V. Stolle, *Zeuge als Angeklagter,* 141.
[35] See *Passion According to Luke,* 99–100.

Paul's witness to this Messiah will be most fully expressed in the climactic speech in Acts 26.

In being called as witness to this Jesus, Paul was also called to suffering (9:16), suffering that increasingly looks like Jesus' suffering (cf. 21:11–14; 22:22)[36] and includes an extensive series of trials and threats to Paul's life. The trials, even though extended over much more time and depicted in fuller scenes, resemble Jesus' trials. Both Jesus and Paul must appear before the Jewish council, the Roman governor, and a Jewish king. Both are repeatedly declared innocent yet not released.[37] With this in mind we can notice an interesting interplay between Paul's story in his speech and the narrator's story of Paul speaking to the people. In Jerusalem Paul's story is being replayed with different characters filling the roles. Paul the persecutor is now the persecuted believer, and the crowd that attacked Paul is now playing the role that Paul previously played.

What Paul previously announced twice (13:46; 18:6) and will announce again in Rome—a turning to the Gentiles in the face of Jewish rejection—is presented as a dialogue with the Lord in 22:17–21. The Lord instructs Paul to leave Jerusalem "because they will not receive your witness concerning me." Paul shows his commitment to a mission in Jerusalem, protesting that "they themselves know" of his previous role as persecutor. This knowledge should make his witness convincing, because he is a "reluctant witness" who has been forced to testify against his own inclination.[38] However, the Lord does not share Paul's optimism about Jerusalem and sends Paul out "to nations afar." Note that there is a significant difference between this scene and previous announcements of turning to the Gentiles: whereas the latter concern a turning from Jews to Gentiles in a particular location, 22:17–21 signals a turning from one location to another, from Jerusalem "to nations afar." This command indicates a significant shift in the cultural context of the mission. Nevertheless, Paul continues to speak to Jews, indeed, to Jews first. They are an important minority within the nations to whom Paul is sent.

When we compare this scene with the account of Paul in Jerusalem in 9:26–30, we discover that there are reasons for the Lord's command. The "Hellenists" with whom Paul had been disputing were attempting to do away with him (9:29). The departure attributed to the Lord's command in 22:17–21 is presented in terms of its human factors in 9:29–30. The "brothers" heard of the plot, and "they sent him out ($\dot{\epsilon}\xi\alpha\pi\dot{\epsilon}\sigma\tau\epsilon\iota\lambda\alpha\nu$

---

[36] See 264–66, 274.

[37] See W. Radl, *Paulus und Jesus*, 211–21, and J. Neyrey, *Passion According to Luke*, 104–5.

[38] See J. Neyrey, *Passion According to Luke*, 106. In n. 55 Neyrey cites Quintilian, *Institutio Oratoria* 5.7.15–21, in support of this interpretation.

αὐτόν)" to Tarsus. In 22:21 the same action is ascribed to the Lord, who says, "I will send you out (ἐξαποστελῶ σε)."

The narrator did not tell us of Paul's temple vision in Acts 9, where it chronologically belongs. This is an example of what Gérard Genette calls an "anachrony," a variation by the narrator from the presupposed order of events.[39] We should also note that Paul's preaching in Damascus, reported in 9:20–22, is omitted from Paul's speech in Acts 22. These variations show a desire to focus on Paul's relation to Jerusalem in Acts 22. The Lord's announcement in the vision that the people of Jerusalem will not receive Paul's witness is especially appropriate to this setting because Paul's present hearers are responding in the same way. I previously suggested that the story of Paul the persecutor was being replayed in Jerusalem with the roles changed. The story of Paul's first preaching in Jerusalem is also being replayed, without a change of roles. The rejection of Paul's witness in Jerusalem is being repeated through the attack on Paul and the outburst that will follow his speech. Perhaps the sending of Paul "to nations afar" will also be repeated through Paul's voyage to Rome. However, Paul is now a prisoner and will remain one, so it is not apparent how Paul will get there.

It is noteworthy that Paul in this speech attributes his call as a messenger to the nations to a vision in the temple, for on several previous occasions the temple has been the site of announcements that God's saving purpose will encompass the world. In the temple Simeon first announced that in Jesus God's salvation has been prepared for "all the peoples" (Luke 2:30–32), and in Solomon's portico Peter reminded his audience of the promise that "in your offspring all the families of the earth will be blessed" (Acts 3:25).[40] The temple setting gives geographical expression to the belief that this promise for the world does not conflict with Israel's calling but, in fact, is rooted in Israel's history and experience of God.

The outburst at the end of the speech shows that a Lord who directs Paul to turn from an unreceptive Jerusalem to foreign nations is highly offensive to Paul's audience. Paul and the narrator will not yield on the necessity of this turn when Jews are unreceptive, and this necessity will be emphasized again in 28:28. However, as Paul's defense against Jewish charges continues in later defense scenes, he develops a further line of thought. Paul insists that the real issue of the trial is the hope that Jews themselves affirm. This theme is a way of appealing to Jews in spite of the hardening lines of conflict. The narrator suggests that some Pharisees and

---

[39] See *Narrative Discourse*, 35–36.
[40] See J. B. Chance, *Jerusalem, the Temple, and the New Age*, 99–113, on "Jerusalem, the Temple, and the Salvation of the Gentiles."

some people like Agrippa, who believes in the prophets, may be open to
Paul's message, even if they are not ready to become Christians.

Faced with the crowd's violent protest, the tribune decides to examine
Paul under the torture of flogging. Paul protects himself by revealing his
Roman citizenship. The narrative of an action-packed day ends after this
indication that Paul is fully a member of the two worlds to which he has
been sent. He is both a devout Jew (22:3) and a Roman citizen. He even
precedes the tribune in Romanness, having been born a citizen (22:28).

Paul's arrest in Jerusalem is the beginning of a lengthy imprisonment
in which Paul's fate will again and again hang in the balance. Paul's
speeches are given a prominent place in this section of Acts, but they are
not the only important material. The surrounding narrative is important
because it shows Paul's endurance and his resourcefulness in using the
opportunities that may come to a relatively powerless prisoner. Marie-
Eloise Rosenblatt suggests that Paul "under interrogation" is "a model
and paradigm for the way a Christian could move in spiritual freedom"
while a prisoner or faced with prolonged legal jeopardy.[41] Her reflections
arise out of appreciation for the spiritual strength needed by modern
Christians who engage in civil disobedience.

---

[41] See *Under Interrogation*, chap. 6: "Before Governors and Kings: Luke's Spirituality of
Juridical and Political Witness." Quotation from 244.

PAUL BEFORE THE SANHEDRIN

The tribune has still not succeeded in discovering the cause of the animosity against Paul. He tries again by presenting Paul to the Sanhedrin. The resulting scene will both confirm the impression that Paul provokes fierce controversy and help the tribune to understand the real issues. The tribune's later letter, indicating that the accusations against Paul really concern "issues of their law," not matters that Romans would consider worthy of death or imprisonment, reports a conclusion based on the Sanhedrin hearing (cf. 23:28−29). Hence the Sanhedrin hearing will play a role in helping the tribune to distinguish between false accusations and the real issues.

In this and the following defense scenes, Paul will appear before the highest religious and political authorities of the region: the Jerusalem Sanhedrin, two Roman governors, and King Agrippa. The narrator is not content to present the powerful effect of the Christian mission in the private lives of individuals. Its cultural and political effect is also important. This aspect comes to the fore as Paul confronts high authorities of Judaism and Rome. Those who control religious and political institutions must listen to Paul and respond in some way to him.

Paul's defense before the Sanhedrin is confined to two basic statements: an assertion that he has conducted his life before God "in all good conscience" right up to the present (23:1) and a statement of what Paul considers to be the real issue in the controversy (23:6). The former assertion provokes an exchange with the high priest and his representatives (23:2-5).

Paul's assertion that he has lived with a good conscience before God "up to this day" should be understood in light of Paul's speech to the people in Acts 22. That speech reported Paul's heavenly calling but said little about Paul's response to his calling. When Paul later narrates his calling again to King Agrippa, he goes on to assert, "I was not disobedient to the heavenly vision" (26:19). Paul's statement to the Sanhedrin in 23:1 has a corresponding function and adds an important assertion to the interrupted speech in Acts 22. It indicates that Paul has lived in obedience to his heavenly call. After the Lord's instructions, only such obedience could result in a good conscience before God. Thus 23:1 is not just a general statement that Paul has been living an upright life. The narrator assumes that Paul's hearers were either present when he spoke to the people or have heard a report of his speech, for members of the Sanhedrin will comment on the story of Paul's call in 23:9. Thus they, too, would understand his initial statement to the Sanhedrin as a claim that Paul's life has been a faithful fulfillment of the calling reported in Paul's speech to the people. This reading of 23:1 is one of several indications that Paul's statements in the defense scenes are illuminated when understood as part of a progressive narrative development.[1]

The high priest's complete and immediate rejection of Paul's claim that his mission represents faithfulness to God is indicated by the command that Paul be struck on the mouth. Paul reacts with a sharply worded threat of divine retribution, but when told that he is speaking to the high priest he, in effect, retracts his statement because Scripture prohibits speaking evil of "a ruler of your people." It may seem strange that the narrator would wish to record an outburst by Paul for which he must excuse himself. However, this dialogue is able to make two points at the same time: (1) Paul is being unjustly treated by an official who is making no effort to follow the law. His conduct deserves Paul's protest. (2) In spite of the behavior of the current high priest, Paul, schooled by Scripture, respects the office of the high priest. Not only does Paul respect the temple, contrary to the accusation in 21:28, but also he respects the office that controls its operations. This scene is a good example of the lengths to which the narrator will go to show that Paul is not anti-Jewish.[2]

If we were to read Paul's statement in 23:6 in isolation from the larger narrative, we would have to say that it is a clever ploy to disrupt the proceedings by siding with the Pharisees in a long-standing debate with the Sadducees.[3] The immediate effect of his statement is discord in the Sanhedrin. Paul evidently anticipates this reaction, for he makes his statement "recognizing that one part [of the Sanhedrin] was composed of Sadducees and the other part of Pharisees." However, the subsequent defense scenes show that Paul's words are more than a tactical move for

---

[1] J. Jervell, in commenting on the defense scenes (including Acts 23), rightly states that "the four speeches form a unity, and only when they are understood from the perspective of this inner unity can one recognize the picture Luke wants to paint." *Luke and the People of God,* 163. I would add that they also show significant development.

[2] Richard Cassidy argues for an ironic interpretation of 23:5. Paul is not apologizing but "is actually indicating that it is hard to recognize this priest as God's chosen high priest because of his conduct." See *Society and Politics,* 65. The quotation of a Scripture passage that prohibits what Paul has just done speaks against this interpretation, for it turns Paul's outburst into a serious offense that he must correct.

[3] According to H. Conzelmann, "Paul's action is naively portrayed as an adroit chess move." See *Acts,* 192.

temporary advantage. Paul keeps coming back to the theme of hope and resurrection even when it no longer provokes disruption (cf. 24:15, 21; 28:20), and it will be a central theme in Paul's climactic defense speech before King Agrippa (26:6–8, 23). Paul is doing more than injecting a controversial subject into the Sanhedrin hearing. He is trying to change the entire issue of his trial, and he will persist in this effort in subsequent scenes. Therefore, the significance of Paul's statement that he is on trial "concerning hope and resurrection of the dead" can be understood only by considering the development of this theme in later scenes.

Paul's claim that he is on trial "concerning hope and resurrection of the dead" seems strange in context. No charge of this kind has been leveled against Paul. Furthermore, Paul's statement seems to ignore the real theological issue between Paul and his Jewish opponents, namely, Paul's claim that Jesus is the Messiah. In time we will discover that there is a christological core to this theme of hope and resurrection, but at the beginning this is suppressed. Paul speaks as if he were simply defending a Pharisaic doctrine.

If the narrator were merely interested in the outcome of Paul's trials, the narrative could have been much shorter than it actually is. The long narrative shows an interest in the strategy of Paul's defense. Paul's statement in 23:6 is a major move in his defense strategy. He is seeking to shift the main issue of his trial from the charges raised in 21:28 to a theological issue that will enable Paul to turn his defense into an appealing witness to suspicious Jews. Jerome Neyrey, in his treatment of Paul's defense speeches against the background of the forensic defense speech in ancient rhetoric, notes that definition of the "main question" is an expected part of the statement of facts or *narratio* in a defense speech. Furthermore, the main question of Paul's trial "is a point of considerable elaboration," for in the course of Paul's trials "it becomes clear that the main question is not the charges alleged against Paul" by his opponents. Indeed, Paul repeatedly insists that the main question is the resurrection.[4] Definition of the question is a persuasive move. It defines the case one wants to argue.[5] In 23:6 Paul shows that he is not content to accept his opponents' statement of the issues. Paul's restatement of the question in 23:6 is the beginning of a persistent effort to shift the focus of debate.

This shift will help Paul to reach important goals. Paul will succeed in

---

[4] See J. Neyrey, "Forensic Defense Speech," 214–15. Neyrey says that the main question, as Paul defines it, is "the resurrection of Jesus." However, Paul does not mention Jesus in 23:6, and this is an important part of his strategy.

[5] The persuasive significance of the rhetorical statement of facts is emphasized by W. Long, who points to Quintilian's remark that "a statement of facts is not made merely that the judge may comprehend the case, but rather that he may look upon it in the same light as ourselves." See W. Long, "The *Paulusbild*," 95, and Quintilian, *Institutio Oratoria* 4.2.21.

persuading Roman officials that the real issue behind the accusations of Paul is a Jewish religious dispute. The tribune reports in his letter that he drew this conclusion following Paul's hearing before the Sanhedrin (23:28–29). It is chiefly Paul's statement in 23:6, and its effect, that would lead to this conclusion. Governor Festus also concludes that the controversy really concerns issues of the Jewish religion, and he specifically includes a dispute over Jesus' resurrection (25:19). Thus Paul is largely successful in persuading Roman officials to see the controversy as he does.

However, the emphasis on hope and resurrection is not primarily political apologetic directed to Romans. It is primarily directed to Jews who share the Pharisaic expectation of resurrection and (as we will see later) the messianic hope. In 23:6 Paul is speaking to Jews, and his statement has an effect on his audience. Some scribes of the Pharisees are willing to defend Paul's innocence (23:9). When Paul returns to the same theme in his speech before Governor Felix, he explicitly connects it to the perspective of his Jewish opponents. This hope, he says, is one "which these people themselves await" (24:15). Paul ends his speech before Felix by challenging his Jewish accusers to accept his statement before the Sanhedrin that the real issue of his trial is the "resurrection of the dead" (24:20–21). Thus the Jewish audience is still in mind, even though Paul is speaking before a Roman governor. In 26:6–7 Paul emphasizes the passionate concern of Jews with the hope that he is discussing, and the concluding dialogue with King Agrippa indicates that one who shares the Jewish belief in the prophets might well be moved by Paul's message of the fulfillment of the Jewish hope (26:26–29). In Rome Paul will again tell Jews that his imprisonment is "because of the hope of Israel" (28:20), extending this theme beyond the defense scenes. This emphasis is not merely a way of telling Romans that the controversy is a Jewish religious matter. Making the obvious point that Paul and his accusers disagree on the claim that Jesus is the Messiah would be sufficient if this were the only goal. Instead, the audiences indicated and the emphasis on the Jewishness of this hope show that this theme is designed to appeal to Jews. This conclusion best explains the degree to which Paul is willing to stretch to show that he and non-Christian Pharisees stand on the same ground. Paul is seeking a shared starting point that will lead beyond controversy to effective witness. The narrator evidently believes that hope and resurrection can be such a shared starting point with some Jews. In contrast, pagans are pictured in Acts as reacting negatively to talk of resurrection (17:32; 26:23–24).

Reading the defense scenes as primarily a political apologetic ignores the issue highlighted at the beginning of these scenes, the charge of anti-Judaism brought against Paul (21:20–21, 28). Even if continuity with

Judaism were politically advantageous to Christianity in gaining tolerance in Roman society, it is doubtful that the narrative portrait of Paul in
the defense scenes could secure that advantage for the church. These
scenes begin by acknowledging that Paul is a renegade in the eyes of many
Jews, and the Jewish opposition continues.

Some will not be convinced by the view that Paul (and the narrator) is
seeking a basis for a further mission to Jews because they feel that the
whole emphasis on Paul's Jewish roots in the defense scenes is a response
to an internal Christian problem. The narrator, they believe, is seeking to
assure Christians that they are valid heirs of the scriptural promises in the
face of doubts raised by the disappearance of obvious connections with
Judaism.[6] I do not deny that this kind of assurance may be an important
effect of Acts and may have been a more or less conscious purpose of the
author. However, it is not an adequate explanation of Paul's defense
scenes.

First, it does not explain why Paul initially avoids christological controversy with his Jewish opponents. If the real audience is the church that
needs reassurance, there is no need to be reticent on this point. Jesus
Christ is central to the symbolic system that binds narrator and community, and placing Jesus Christ in a scriptural and Jewish context would
provide the roots that the community needs. Instead of making this point,
Paul in his defense scenes refers vaguely to "hope and resurrection of the
dead" (23:6), using the *plural* for "dead ($\nu\epsilon\kappa\rho\hat{\omega}\nu$)." Thus it is not first of
all Jesus' resurrection but a general resurrection that is indicated. The
expected reference to Jesus' resurrection continues to be absent from
Paul's statements until the very end of his speech before King Agrippa.
Instead, Paul continues to speak of the resurrection of a group, indicated
by words in the plural: $\dot{\alpha}\nu\dot{\alpha}\sigma\tau\alpha\sigma\iota\nu$ . . . $\delta\iota\kappa\alpha\dot{\iota}\omega\nu$ $\tau\epsilon$ $\kappa\alpha\dot{\iota}$ $\dot{\alpha}\delta\dot{\iota}\kappa\omega\nu$, "resurrection of just and unjust people" (24:15); $\pi\epsilon\rho\dot{\iota}$ $\dot{\alpha}\nu\alpha\sigma\tau\dot{\alpha}\sigma\epsilon\omega\varsigma$ $\nu\epsilon\kappa\rho\hat{\omega}\nu$,
"concerning resurrection of dead people" (24:21); $\dot{o}$ $\theta\epsilon\dot{o}\varsigma$ $\nu\epsilon\kappa\rho\upsilon\dot{\varsigma}$ $\dot{\epsilon}\gamma\epsilon\dot{\iota}\rho\epsilon\iota$,
"God raises dead people" (26:8). This reticence concerning Jesus'
resurrection (until 26:23) is strange and unnecessary if the narrator is
concerned only with the reassurance of Christians. However, it makes
sense if the narrator is presenting Paul as a model of a resourceful
missionary who takes account of the presuppositions of his audience. The
tendency for interpreters to overlook Paul's christological reticence in the
defense scenes results from a failure to study them as a narrative process
and rhetorical strategy. This strategy seeks to build a bridge to suspicious

---

[6] P. Esler develops this view in a new way by placing the need for "legitimation" in the
context of the sociology of sectarian groups. See *Community and Gospel*, 16–23, 46–70. This
is a helpful contribution but does not by itself explain the aspect of Acts that we are now
discussing.

outsiders before speaking of Jesus' resurrection. This insight is lost if we immediately interpret all Paul's references to resurrection in light of the final christological affirmation in 26:23.

Second, we should note that the kind of christological argument from Scripture found in the speeches of Acts 2 and 13 is remarkably absent from Paul's defense speeches. This absence is especially remarkable in the major speeches in Acts 22 and 26, which are addressed to Jewish audiences.[7] The speech before King Agrippa leads up to a point where argument from Scripture might be appropriate (see 26:27), but the speech itself follows a different strategy. There are general references to Scripture in 24:14 and 26:22, and Paul describes his call in scriptural language, but there is no attempt to mount a scriptural argument that Jesus is the Messiah. This fact is inexplicable if the real purpose of these scenes is to reassure Christians that they are the true heirs of the scriptural promise. The narrator has no trouble finding Jesus Christ in Scripture, and repeating the church's christological interpretation of Scripture would be effective reassurance for those who share the church's presuppositions. However, it is not effective witness for those who approach Scripture with other presuppositions. The strangely circuitous witness that Paul presents in the defense scenes shows awareness of this fact. This observation shows that the narrator once again presents Paul speaking in a way that is sensitive to his audience in the narrative. It also shows a real concern to find ways of breaking through the wall that is being built between Judaism and Christianity.

This view does not imply that the author of Acts anticipated non-Christian Jews as readers. Rather, Paul is being presented to Christians as a resourceful witness from whom other missionaries can learn. This view does imply that there is a continuing concern in Acts with a mission to Jews, even though relations have been poisoned by controversy. Paul is pictured as one who finds ways to speak even to hostile Jews, building a foundation for mutual understanding. In the case of King Agrippa, who is less hostile, Paul ends with a full missionary appeal (26:27–29). Paul's approach to Jews in the defense speeches is similar to his approach to cultured pagans in Athens. In both cases Paul avoids reference to Jesus until a foundation has been laid, in the one case through presenting a view of God that cultured pagans might accept, in the other case through emphasizing the hope that Paul and other Jews share. Such an approach is necessary because Paul is speaking to groups who are difficult to reach.

By seeking to shift the main question of the trial to the Jewish hope, Paul fulfills the words of Jesus in Luke 21:12–13. When you are led away

---

[7] King Agrippa is presented as a Jew in knowledge and belief. See below, 315–16.

"to kings and governors because of my name," Jesus said, "it will lead to testifying." In the course of his trials Paul will be brought before kings and governors. By seeking to redefine the main issue of the trial in 23:6, Paul is establishing a basis for turning a trial into testimony. This process is completed in the climactic scene before King Agrippa, where Paul's speech starts as a defense speech but ends as a missionary appeal.[8] Paul the prisoner is not a passive victim. He remains a resourceful witness for Jesus. His resourcefulness consists in his ability to find ways in which controversy and accusations might be turned into fruitful debate and then, perhaps, into witness. Paul on trial shows the mission working against strong cultural resistance, with powerful opponents seeking to crush it. The resourceful witness finds a way to have his message heard even within a hostile environment. The last two verses of Acts present the same picture of Paul.

Although Paul is seeking to shift the main issue of his trial away from the accusations that his Jewish opponents will bring, his emphasis on hope and resurrection is not a complete evasion of the accusations in 21:28. There Paul was accused of being anti-Jewish because he teaches against the people, the law, and the temple. In emphasizing that the hope of the Pharisees is also central to his message, Paul is indirectly responding to the charge of anti-Judaism. Taking his stand on hope and resurrection, Paul is a faithful Pharisee, affirming his family heritage (cf. 23:6). It may seem that Paul is turning a minor point of Pharisaic belief into a major one in order to prove his orthodoxy. In the perspective of Acts it is not a minor point. The hope in question is "the hope of Israel" (28:20). It is the hope for Israel's messianic kingdom, which is founded through resurrection.[9] Through continuing to bear witness to the fulfillment of Israel's hope, Paul is faithful to his people.

The narrative suggests that Paul's strategy has some effect even in the Sanhedrin. Some of the Pharisees to whom Paul is appealing come to Paul's defense (23:9). This does not mean that they are about to become followers of Jesus. Indeed, they speak from a non-Christian perspective, suggesting that Paul's vision on the Damascus road may be due to a spirit or angel, although Paul spoke clearly of the Lord Jesus. Nevertheless, they do not join the opposition to Paul and show a certain openness to Paul's views. Jewish opposition is not monolithic. The scene before King Agrippa will go further. Paul's bold witness in his final dialogue of that scene shows that he has not given up hope of convincing Jews on the basis of the prophets.

---

[8] See below, 316–17, 327–29.
[9] See below, 318–20.

The scene before the Sanhedrin ends in uproar and the tribune intervenes with his troops because he fears that Paul may be killed by mob
violence, as he almost was in the temple. Both of the defense scenes to this
point have ended in uproar that threatened Paul's life (22:22–23; 23:10).
A plot on Paul's life by determined men will immediately follow. In this
context the Lord's reassurance is especially needed. Paul receives this
reassurance in a night vision (23:11). When Jesus' witnesses were previously imprisoned, prison doors were wondrously opened for them (5:17–
21; 12:1–11; 16:23–26). That is no longer the case. The Lord's reassurance must take the place of miraculously opening doors. The divine
power that rescues from prison has become a powerful presence that
enables the witness to endure an imprisonment that lasts for years.

The Lord speaks of Paul's past witnessing in Jerusalem and of future
witnessing in Rome. It is clear, then, that Paul is speaking not merely in
defense of himself but as a witness for Jesus. "As" he did this in Jerusalem, "so" he must do it in Rome. This correlation may point not only to
the common activity of witnessing in both places but to the similar
conditions: as a prisoner. The Lord's words remind us of Paul's decision
in 19:21 to go to Jerusalem, after which he also "must (δεῖ) see Rome."
The picture is sharper now; the Lord does not speak vaguely of a plan to
"go" to Jerusalem and to "see" Rome but of the witness of Paul in these
key places. Paul has completed the first half of his journey, but he is no
longer a free man and his life is threatened. The Lord assures him that his
witness in Rome is still part of the divine plan. The course of the narrative
will seem to throw this goal in doubt. The next stage of Paul's journey is
not to Rome but to Caesarea, where Paul will remain a prisoner for a long
time. But the Lord's word to Paul reminds us that another force is at work
than the political powers who hold Paul.

On his sea voyage we will hear a third time that Paul "must" complete
his journey to Rome (27:24). This time the goal is even more distinct, for
Paul is informed that he must appear before Caesar. Jerusalem and Rome
are important as the seats of central authorities: the Jerusalem Sanhedrin
and high priest, on the one hand, the emperor, on the other. Caesarea, too,
is important as the seat of the Roman governor. Through Paul's journey
to Jerusalem and Rome the testimony to Jesus Messiah is carried to the
highest authorities by a prisoner. The journey to Rome will be especially
difficult. This difficulty is balanced in the narrative by a threefold indication of its necessity (using δεῖ in each case) at three crucial stages: when
the plan is conceived (19:21), as Paul's life is threatened in Jerusalem
(23:11), as Paul's life is threatened at sea (27:24).

PAUL ESCAPES AN AMBUSH
AND IS TAKEN
TO THE GOVERNOR

Paul's life was in danger during the riot in the temple and again as the Sanhedrin hearing began to dissolve into a riot. Jerusalem is a dangerous place for Paul. This fact is underscored by the next stage of the narrative, which presents the climactic threat to Paul's life during his short stay in Jerusalem. The narrator's desire to bring the story of Paul's perils in Jerusalem to a climax is apparent through the length and detail of the narrative of this death plot and through intensification of the threat. Paul's enemies form a careful plan of action and act with deceit. They have the support of high priests and elders who can make necessary arrangements. They are extremely determined, having bound themselves with a strict oath, and more than forty of them are ready to act.

The narrative is interested not only in vividly portraying the threat but also in giving a detailed account of how Paul escaped. It was not by his own heroic action. Paul himself does very little. His nephew takes the initiative, bringing word to Paul, and Paul simply asks a centurion to take his nephew to the tribune. Most of the action swirls around Paul, carrying him along, while minor characters in the overall narrative become the chief actors in this episode. Nor did Paul escape by the amazing intervention of some nonhuman force, as in previous prison rescues. The narrative concentrates on the plot of Paul's enemies and the countermoves of a youth and the Roman tribune. To be sure, the vision that precedes this episode in 23:11 may suggest that the Lord's purpose of bringing Paul to Rome is somehow being realized through these events. However, this purpose is being realized through the clash of human action and counteraction among persons who know nothing of the Lord's purpose for Paul.[1]

It may seem strange that the narrator would give such an extensive account of this kind of incident.[2] However, we should not deny to the narrator a real interest in the drama of human events nor an interest in

---

[1] See G. Krodel, *Acts*, 429: "Each of the players in this drama retains his freedom and all serve the purpose of God, ignorant though they be of it, except for Paul. Almost nothing is done or spoken by him and yet he remains the center of everyone's intense actions."

[2] E. Haenchen comments that the scene's "compass far surpasses its significance." See *Acts*, 649.

completing the characterization of the Roman tribune (to be discussed below). This episode is not unique in Acts. There is a series of interesting parallels between 23:12-35 and the even more detailed narrative of the sea voyage to Rome in Acts 27. Both episodes concern the transfer of Paul from one seat of authority to another under guard of the Roman military. In both the danger of the situation is vividly depicted, and suspense centers on finding a means of rescue. The emphasis on rescue from danger appears in the use of the verb διασῴζω ("bring safely through, save"), found only in connection with these two episodes in Acts (23:24; 27:43, 44; 28:1, 4). Both episodes are associated with visions reassuring Paul that it is the Lord's will that he bear witness in Rome (23:11; 27:23-24). Although God's work remains hidden behind natural forces and human decisions, the extraordinary way in which Paul escaped death on these two occasions is meant to make a vivid impression, serving as well as the opening of prison doors in testifying to God's surprising power.

The tribune Claudius Lysias is an important figure in 23:12-35. His decisive response to information from Paul's nephew saves Paul from the ambush. The narrator tells enough about Lysias' words and actions to provide an interesting characterization that shows both consistency and development. Lysias is a man of decisive action. This characteristic has worked to Paul's benefit three times: when Lysias intervened with his troops as Paul was attacked in the temple (21:31-36), when he again intervened as the Sanhedrin hearing broke into riotous discord (23:10), and now in response to the plot on Paul's life. Lysias is also a perceptive investigator. His changing reactions to Paul show that he is willing to learn about him and able to penetrate to the truth. On the first occasion Lysias intervened not because he was concerned about Paul, whom he did not know, but in order to quell a disturbance. He completely misunderstood Paul, confusing him with an Egyptian who led an uprising (21:38) and almost examining him under torture, contrary to the rights of a Roman citizen (22:24-29). There is repeated emphasis on his efforts to learn the facts about Paul (21:33-34; 22:24, 30). Through the hearing before the Sanhedrin, Lysias gains an understanding of the issues of the controversy, as he reports in his letter. He writes (23:28-29) that he brought Paul down to the Sanhedrin in order to learn the cause of the accusations against him and found that the accusations concerned issues of Jewish law and not matters punishable by death or imprisonment (under Roman law). Here Lysias states the conclusion that he drew on the basis of Paul's statement about hope and resurrection, together with the Sanhedrin's reaction. It is a perceptive conclusion. When Lysias sends Paul to Caesarea with an armed escort, he is no longer acting merely to quell public disturbances but is protecting a Roman citizen whom he believes to be innocent.

However, Lysias is more than a Roman advocate for Paul. The narrator's portrait is more complex. Through the inclusion of Lysias' letter in the narrative, we are allowed to observe him giving an official report of his own handling of Paul's case to his superior, the governor. Later, Festus will also report on his handling of Paul's case to an influential person, King Agrippa (25:14–21). In both instances there are interesting discrepancies between the report and the narrator's account of the same events. In both instances the discrepancies suggest that Roman officials need to present a public image that partially conceals the truth about their actions and motives.[3]

Lysias, reporting about his first encounter with Paul, states that when Paul was about to be killed, "I rescued" him, "learning[4] that he was a Roman" (23:27). This report suggests that Lysias from the beginning was acting to preserve the life and legal rights of a Roman citizen. However, the original narrative made clear that Lysias first suspected Paul of being a dangerous revolutionary and almost had him examined under torture, contrary to his rights as a Roman citizen. This incident is conveniently omitted from the report, and Lysias' knowledge of Paul's Roman citizenship is backdated to become the motive of Lysias' original intervention.[5] Lysias is a "round" character.[6] He has changing traits (he is ignorant but he learns) and traits of conflicting quality. He is decisive and perceptive (positive traits) but shares the tendency of those in political power structures to shade the truth for self-protection (a negative trait). As we move up the scale of political power to the governors Felix and Festus, the character flaws will become more apparent. As a result, Roman justice is also flawed.

Meir Sternberg presents a perceptive discussion of the subtleties introduced into narratives of the Hebrew Bible through repetition with variation. "This chain of repetition develops a multiple and shifting play of perspectives," he writes.[7] Two characters may give their accounts of the same events, revealing different perspectives, or a character may report events previously presented by the narrator, sometimes with subtle but

---

[3] On 25:14–21 see below, 309–13.

[4] Or "having learned." The aorist participle tends to refer to time prior to the main verb. See BDF, no. 339.

[5] R. Cassidy rightly emphasizes this discrepancy in his discussion of Lysias in *Society and Politics*, 96–100.

[6] Note the appropriation of this category from E. M. Forster in David Rhoads and Donald Michie, *Mark as Story*, 102–3.

[7] See *Poetics of Biblical Narrative*, 401.

significant differences. Because biblical literature operates with a reliable narrator, the narrator's version provides "an authorized reference-point to which we may safely appeal in order to sort out and motivate the versions originating in the other participants."[8] That is, the differences among versions encourage exploration of the reasons for departure from the authorized reference point. There are many possible reasons for differences, including appropriate shift in point of view and abbreviation or expansion in light of relevance, but biblical narrative provides ample illustration of the craft and deception of the human heart, as well as the need to bend others to one's will and deal with the powerful by flattery, through a slanted account of events. The biblical narrator can present all this without direct evaluative comment on the character. It is revealed simply by a significant discrepancy between the narrator's and the character's account of events. This narrative technique, highlighted in Sternberg's discussion of repetition in Hebrew narrative,[9] reappears in Acts' account of Lysias' letter.[10]

---

[8] See *Poetics of Biblical Narrative*, 413.

[9] See *Poetics of Biblical Narrative*, 390–440.

[10] In contrast to Lysias' report, Paul's nephew's report in 23:20–21 is quite accurate. Its accuracy is reinforced by reuse of key words in the conspirators' statement in 23:14–15. However, it is interesting that a few of the narrator's phrases from 23:12–13 also creep in. Cf. μήτε φαγεῖν μήτε πιεῖν "neither to eat nor drink" (23:12, 21); πλείους τεσσεράκοντα "more than forty" (23:13, 21).

THE TRIAL
BEFORE GOVERNOR FELIX

Lysias' decision to send Paul to Caesarea under armed guard rescues him from the assassination plot but not from legal jeopardy. Paul's case is now transferred to the highest Roman official of the province, Governor Felix. The high priest Ananias and some elders (not the whole Sanhedrin but a powerful group) are determined opponents who pursue Paul with their accusations. They use a skilled orator ($\acute{\rho}\acute{\eta}\tau\omega\rho$), Tertullus, as their spokesman, which adds to Paul's jeopardy. He is not only accused by powerful people but must face the dangerous persuasive skill of this orator.

The introductory flattery of Governor Felix by Tertullus, although conventional, is profuse. The spokesman for the high priest and his supporters then moves to the accusations, which are basically twofold: (1) The claim that Paul is "a pestilent fellow" who is "inciting uprisings among all the Jews throughout the world and is a ringleader of the sect of the Nazarenes" (24:5) portrays Paul as a danger to society. Like a plague he has been attacking the health of Roman society; this is the result of his position of leadership in a dangerous movement and is demonstrated in the uprisings that Paul causes among Jews throughout the Roman world. (2) To this sweeping accusation is added the specific charge that Paul tried to defile the temple (24:6).

When we compare Tertullus' accusation to the earlier accusation against Paul in 21:28, we see that there is a shift in a political direction. Paul's opponents in the temple charged him with teaching against the people, the law, and the temple. Tertullus portrays Paul as a danger to society, especially because he foments disturbances among Jews. Such disturbances should be the concern of a Roman governor. The Jerusalem Sanhedrin made a similar attempt to portray Jesus as a threat to Roman society when they made accusations against him before Pilate (Luke 23:2, 5).

Although the Jews accompanying him will support his accusations (v. 9), Tertullus does not cite any witnesses or evidence in his speech. Instead, he indicates that the governor himself can discover the truth of his accusations by examining Paul and securing Paul's confession (v. 8). This approach not only helps the narrator to keep Tertullus' speech short, allowing Paul to give the major address, but also strengthens Paul's counterclaim that his opponents are not able to prove their accusations (v. 13). In part this is based on the fact that Paul recognizes the high priest and his supporters as competent witnesses to what happened at the Sanhedrin hearing but not as competent witnesses to the preceding events in the temple (vv. 18–21).

Although Tertullus is supposed to be a skilled orator, Paul demonstrates his superior skill by making use of Tertullus' words to build his own case. Tertullus told the governor that "you yourself will be able to ascertain (δυνήσῃ αὐτὸς . . . ἐπιγνῶναι)" the truth of the accusations through examining Paul (v. 8). Paul picks up Tertullus' words to the governor in v. 11: "you being able to ascertain (δυναμένου σου ἐπιγνῶναι)." However, the expected results are different. Felix will ascertain that Paul came to Jerusalem only recently and has not been an agitator within his province. Paul begins his speech with the expected *captatio benevolentiae*, seeking the favor of the governor by complementing him, but his statement is sober compared to that of Tertullus and contributes directly to his defense. Felix's years of experience as governor of Judea will enable him to recognize quickly that Paul has not been an agitator within his province. Only the last twelve days come in question, and Paul readily speaks to them. In effect Paul is making Felix a witness in his own defense.

After a string of denials in vv. 11–13, Paul shifts his ground in v. 14. He mockingly makes the confession that Tertullus evidently expected ("But this I confess to you . . . ")[1] and then picks up Tertullus' reference to the Christian way as a "sect (αἵρεσις)" (vv. 5, 14). Paul's confession is ironic, for there should be nothing wrong, especially in the eyes of the accusers, with what Paul is confessing. He is confessing his faithfulness to the ancestral God and the hope of Judaism. The ironic tone reappears in vv. 20–21, where Paul defines his "crime" (ἀδίκημα, RSV: "wrongdoing") as his declaration before the Sanhedrin that he is on trial concerning resurrection of the dead.

Although Paul has previously spoken in his own defense (22:1–21; 23:1, 6), this is the first formal trial since his arrest in Jerusalem. Paul does address the charges, although briefly because he has a larger point to make. The accusation that Paul attempted to defile the temple is rejected by Paul's statements that he came to Jerusalem "to worship" (v. 11), to bring "alms and offerings" (v. 17), and was properly "consecrated" when in the temple (v. 18). Because Tertullus has not even mentioned the

---

[1] In a legal setting ὁμολογέω can mean "make a confession," that is, admit a charge, recognize one's own guilt. See BAGD, s.v. 3.a, and Otto Michel, *TDNT,* 5:200.

specific charge of bringing a Gentile into the temple, Paul need not refer to it. In vv. 11–13 the sweeping charge of inciting uprisings among Jews throughout the world is reduced to the case of the disturbance in Jerusalem since Paul's recent arrival. If Paul's mission in the Diaspora were examined, his accusers would have a stronger case, for his ministry was frequently accompanied by disturbances among Jews. Responsibility for these disturbances would be difficult to assess. Limiting the case in this way, Paul can deny that in the temple he was "discussing with anyone" (or "preaching to anyone," πρός τινα διαλεγόμενον), a possible way of provoking a disturbance. This discussing or preaching is exactly what he did do in synagogues of the Diaspora, and disturbances often resulted.[2] The narrative has given sufficient reason to regard Paul's work with suspicion, if civil calm is the primary value.[3] Such disturbances, however, fall outside Felix's area of jurisdiction, and so Paul can take the easier course of limiting his reply to events in Jerusalem. Paul is able to deny that he did anything there to incite a disturbance, either in the temple, the synagogues, or elsewhere in the city.

Nevertheless, Paul uses his ironic confession to give his own twist to the conflict. In v. 14 Paul reverts to themes from his previous defense speeches. These speeches were directed to a Jewish crowd and the Sanhedrin. From 24:14 on Paul is speaking as much to his Jewish accusers as to the Roman governor. He is arguing that he is a faithful Jew. Although the charges of Tertullus have a political slant, Paul's defense is still influenced by the charge in 21:28 that he denies the fundamentals of Judaism, the chosen people, the law, and the temple. This charge is rather clearly recalled when Paul refers in 24:18–19 to accusations by "some Jews from Asia" (see 21:27). The full relevance of 24:14–21 appears only in light of this charge (which Paul will still be denying as late as 28:17). Although Paul is now on trial before a qualified judge and some of what he says is relevant to the charges presented to this judge, the speech before Felix shows a greater concern to speak to the original charge in 21:28.

This charge accounts for Paul's claim that he "serves the ancestral God, believing in all that accords with the law and is written in the prophets." It also accounts for the claim that he shares the hope of his Jewish accusers, the hope for resurrection (24:15). In 24:14–15 Paul revives the emphasis on his Jewishness found in his speech to the Jewish crowd in Jerusalem and the specific emphasis on hope and resurrection in his statement to the

---

[2] Note the use of the same verb of Paul's work in synagogues in 17:2 (resulting in mob action and accusations before the magistrates); 17:17; 18:4 (resulting in withdrawal from the synagogue under pressure and later accusations before the proconsul); 18:19; 19:8 (resulting in withdrawal from the synagogue under pressure).

[3] Recall the repeated appearance of the public accusation type-scene, which highlights the disturbing effect of Paul's mission on the status quo. See above, 201–3.

Sanhedrin (23:6). The speech before Felix, even though addressed to a Roman governor, includes the main lines of thought established in the first two defense scenes. Paul speaks of a hope that "these men themselves await" in 24:15. In 23:6–8 the narrative made clear that a resurrection is expected by Pharisees but not by Sadducees. Now Paul ignores the possible presence of Sadducees among his accusers. He does not wish to debate with Sadducees but to show that his mission is motivated by an expectation that many Jews accept. The short declaration in 23:6 is expanded by bringing in the perspective of future judgment and its significance for present behavior. Paul's expectation of a resurrection of the just and unjust leads him to be "constantly in training (ἀσκῶ . . . διὰ παντός) to have a blameless conscience before God and humans" (24:16).[4]

In v. 17 Paul speaks of his alms and offerings. Ernst Haenchen comments, "It is only because we know about Paul's great collection from his letters that we recognize an allusion to it here."[5] Knowledge of Paul's letters can lead to a misreading of Acts at this point. Paul is not talking about a collection for the Jerusalem church. The alms are "for my nation," and the offerings are temple offerings.[6] Paul affirmed his respect for the law in v. 14; here he wishes to demonstrate his respect for the Jewish people and the temple. Thus he touches on all three of the main points in the accusation of 21:28.

Paul's denial that the Asian Jews found him in the temple "with a crowd" or "with uproar (μετὰ θορύβου)" contrasts with the behavior of the Asian Jews themselves, who according to the narrator were "stirring up all the crowd" (21:27), resulting in "uproar (θόρυβον)" (21:34). However, in v. 19 Paul is mainly concerned to point out that these Asian Jews are absent from the trial, and they are the ones who should bring accusations and be witnesses if the charge concerns Paul's behavior in the temple. To be sure, Paul is willing to let the high priest and the elders who support him bring charges, but they should speak of what they know personally: Paul's behavior before them in the Sanhedrin. If they wish, they can testify to Paul's "crime" of crying out in the Sanhedrin, "Concerning resurrection of the dead I am on trial today before you" (vv. 20–21). With this ironic reference to his crime, Paul skillfully and deliberately steers the debate back to the point that he introduced in 23:6, his affirmation of the resurrection.[7] The importance of this affirmation in this

---

[4] The suggestion of future judgment may prepare for v. 25.

[5] See *Acts*, 655.

[6] ἐν αἷς in v. 18 refers to προσφοράς and connects these offerings with Paul being in the temple.

[7] See G. Krodel, *Acts*, 441: "The irony of Paul's confession is apparent. Tertullus suggested to Felix that Paul's own confession would support the accusations of the plaintiff (v. 8). Paul now confesses his 'offense,' which has nothing to do with sedition against Rome nor

tense dialogue with Jews is shown by the place of prominence given it at the end of the speech and the preparation for this ending in v. 15. Paul, rather than wishing to forget the Sanhedrin hearing as an embarrassing incident, deliberately reminds his hearers of this scene. Again we see that Paul uses the defense scenes not merely to answer charges but to push his own agenda.

Instead of rendering a verdict, Felix adjourns the trial with the promise that he will decide the case when Lysias the tribune comes down to Caesarea, presumably to give his testimony. A brief postponement by a cautious judge who wants to have all relevant testimony before rendering a verdict would seem appropriate. At v. 27 we discover that this postponement actually stretches on for two years,[8] and Felix never does complete Paul's trial. There is a clear conflict between Felix's promise and his action, leaving us to wonder why. The narrator never supplies a clear explanation of Felix's inaction (a "gap" in the narrative)[9] but does help us form hypotheses. According to v. 26, Felix was hoping for a bribe. Delay could be a way of putting pressure on Paul and his friends to give this bribe. In v. 27 we are told that Felix left Paul in prison at the end of his term because he wished "to grant a favor to the Jews," that is, in order to placate a powerful pressure group. This suggests that the same motive caused the long delay. Felix did nothing because he neither wanted to condemn Paul nor take the political consequences of offending the high priest and his supporters. Felix's motives remain partially veiled, but there are hints of the personal and political interests at work.

The "relaxation (ἄνεσις)" of Paul's imprisonment indicated in v. 23 suggests that Felix was convinced by Lysias' letter, the trial, or both that Paul is not a dangerous man. This impression is reinforced by Felix's willingness to hear Paul's message and hold repeated conversations with him (vv. 24–26). The narrator now has the opportunity to present Paul as a witness for Jesus to governors and kings, fulfilling Jesus' prophecy in Luke 21:12–13. As we have seen, Paul the prisoner both defends himself against charges and seeks to change the minds of Jewish opponents. Now we can see a third reason why the narrator is interested in Paul's defense scenes. They demonstrate the possibility of carrying the Christian message to the high officials who control Roman society. To be sure, the

---

desecration of Jerusalem's temple, but which reveals the fundamental issue which unites (Pharisaic) Judaism and Christianity and divides non-Christian Judaism."

[8] It is preferable to understand v. 27 as referring to the length of Paul's imprisonment rather than the length of Felix's term as governor. For supporting arguments see Adolf Harnack, *Acts,* 7–9.

[9] On the significance of gaps in biblical narrative, see M. Sternberg, *Poetics of Biblical Narrative,* chap. 6 ("Gaps, Ambiguity, and the Reading Process") and chap. 7 ("Between the Truth and the Whole Truth").

narrative does not indicate that either Felix or King Agrippa was converted by Paul. Nevertheless, Paul's courageous example in speaking the Christian message to them can easily serve as encouragement to other witnesses to present their message even to high officials. Paul makes an evangelistic appeal both to a gentile and a Jewish ruler. In Acts 24 Paul's defense speech and his missionary endeavors are separate. In Acts 26 they will merge in one major scene.

We are given two indications of the content of Paul's discourse with Felix. It concerned "faith in Messiah Jesus" (v. 24) and "justice and self-control and the coming judgment" (v. 25). The former is a summary of Paul's christological preaching comparable to the references to faith in Jesus in Paul's speeches elsewhere (cf. 20:21; 26:18). The latter is more unusual. Both Peter and Paul speak of Jesus as the future world judge (10:42; 17:31), and this announcement is accompanied by a call to repentance (17:30). Paul's discussion of the coming judgment with Felix also implies the call to repentance that is a common part of mission preaching in Acts. "Justice" and "self-control" may be mentioned to indicate qualities particularly required of Felix and other rulers when they are measured in the judgment.[10] Felix's desire for a bribe and favoritism in judgment (24:26–27) can be understood as indications of his lack of these qualities.

Verse 25 puts the content of Paul's discourse in a subordinate clause in order to emphasize Felix's reaction. He is frightened by what Paul says, causing him to break off the discussion temporarily. Although recognizing the personal implications of Paul's message, Felix is not willing to make the necessary response, even though he continues to talk with Paul. Thus he deals with Paul's message in the same way that he dealt with Paul's trial: by postponing a decision that would have heavy consequences.

The portrait of Felix takes a sharply negative turn in vv. 25–27. In rapid sequence three verses provide three indications of his short-comings.[11] He is frightened by Paul's discourse on justice, self-control, and the coming judgment, for he recognizes that he could not survive such a judgment. Yet he avoids the opportunity of repentance (v. 25). His desire for a bribe (v. 26) confirms his lack of justice. Then he shows favoritism toward the powerful party in the case (v. 27). Furthermore, he fails to fulfill his promise of deciding Paul's case (v. 22). Thus Roman justice is undermined by an unjust administrator.

---

[10] See BAGD, s.v. δικαιοσύνη: "1. uprightness, justice as a characteristic of a judge," such as Felix is (24:10). It is possible, as some scholars suggest, that "self-control" is emphasized by Paul because of Felix's lack of this, demonstrated in his enticement of Drusilla away from her previous husband. See G. Schneider, *Apostelgeschichte* 2:351–52.

[11] Rightly emphasized by R. Cassidy, *Society and Politics,* 105–6.

Ernst Haenchen sees a contradiction between the positive and negative aspects of the portrait of Felix in Acts and feels that it is necessary to explain this by two conflicting needs of the narrative: Felix, like other officials, must be a witness for Paul's innocence, yet the narrative must explain why Paul was not released. Haenchen adds, "This contradiction also can admittedly be resolved by a reference to the unfathomable enigma of the human soul. But before we mount this heavy artillery, which puts an end to all discussion, we ought to reflect" on the points just mentioned.[12] However, the fact that the narrator has some appreciation for "the unfathomable enigma of the human soul" need not put "an end to all discussion." We can discuss both the literary means by which a narrator presents the contradictory tendencies within persons, causing them to be enigmas both to themselves and others, and the implied view of human beings. In the case of Felix, we are dealing with a brief and fairly simple presentation of contradictory tendencies, a presentation that should neither be overrated nor dismissed as artificial. It begins with indications of Felix's attraction to Paul, expressed through reducing the harshness of imprisonment and then through inviting Paul to speak his message. Another aspect of Felix appears when he faces the crucial decision of how he will respond to Paul's message. He is interested but protects himself from real change. Then the narrator indicates some patterns of behavior that Felix is not willing to renounce in response to Paul's call. Felix's fear indicates that he has been affected by Paul's message; thus some struggle is taking place. Furthermore, Felix continues his conversations with Paul according to v. 26, and this verse suggests mixed motives. The διό ("therefore") in v. 26 is ambiguous. It introduces a sentence that indicates the fulfillment of Felix's promise in v. 25, a sign, perhaps, of continuing genuine interest. It can also refer to Felix's hope for a bribe, providing a second, dishonorable motive for the meetings. In any case Felix's interest in Paul's message does not bear fruit. The governor withdraws from the decision at the crucial point, and the self-interested actions of an unjust judge are obvious in the final verses of this scene. We can view vv. 22–27 as a tragic plot in miniature, beginning with attraction to a great good, moving to a point of crisis, ending with tragic failure. Felix, even more clearly than Lysias, emerges as a "round" character capable of attracting our interest for his own sake.

I do not deny that Felix also has a plot function in explaining why Paul

---

[12] See *Acts*, 662–63. R. Pervo criticizes Acts even more harshly, convinced that we are simply dealing with shallow writing. He says, "In both 24:26–27 and 25:9 Luke shifts gears and thereby the characters of the respective governors. . . . Having persons change characters like coats as a means of cutting literary knots is a license taken by popular writers." See *Profit with Delight*, 33.

was not released, as Haenchen states. However, the second influence mentioned by Haenchen, the need to use Felix as a witness to Paul's innocence, is not so clear. Unlike Lysias, Festus, and Agrippa, Felix never declares Paul to be innocent, and his interest in Paul's message does not necessarily imply such an opinion. The narrator may well have been concerned to show that Paul used his imprisonment to bear witness to high officials, which would help to account for a scene in which Felix allows Paul to preach.

Felix left Paul in prison in order to "grant a favor to the Jews" (v. 27), and in the next scene the high priests and their allies will again emerge as vigorous opponents of Paul. Philip Esler's discussion of Luke-Acts in the light of a sociology of sectarianism can help us to understand the social forces behind these individual actions, suggesting that the narrative, whether based on particular historical facts or not, has some verisimilitude. His discussion should also serve as a warning against explaining Paul's imprisonment as the work of unusually evil people, for it invites us to consider the social forces at work in the relation of any "church" and its leadership with any "sect." He says,[13]

> It is very important to remember that the opposition which a sect encounters from the church from which it arose is not based solely upon doctrinal differences, for a sect threatens the position and status of the persons responsible for maintaining and servicing the church. Inasmuch as the sect raises the possibility of drawing further members out of the church and even, eventually, threatening its continued separate existence altogether, it poses a risk to the privileged position which the leaders of the church enjoy. This aspect of the antagonism a church will feel towards a breakaway group is far too often forgotten.

Furthermore, Esler refers to "the likely alliance between a religious establishment and the political authorities to suppress a new religious movement."[14] The leaders of both a religious establishment and of the state have an interest in the status quo. Esler's discussion suggests that the behavior of both the Jewish and Roman authorities is not just the result of personal evil but is the predictable result of social dynamics.

---

[13] See *Community and Gospel*, 21.
[14] See *Community and Gospel*, 49.

THE TRIAL
BEFORE GOVERNOR FESTUS

As soon as the new governor appears in Jerusalem, the high priests and other Jews of high rank (probably the same group that joined the plot against Paul in 23:14) bring charges against Paul and also make a specific request: that Paul be transferred to Jerusalem, presumably for trial. The swiftness of their action shows their continuing animosity against Paul and also suggests that they were frustrated by Felix's policy of inaction. Now they see a chance to get rid of Paul. Their request is described as a "favor ($\chi\acute{\alpha}\rho\iota\nu$)" from the governor. The possibility of Roman authorities granting a favor to Paul's powerful opponents plays an important role in developments after Felix established the precedent in 24:27. The request that Paul be transferred to Jerusalem is accompanied by a plot to kill him along the way. This is a revival of the assassination plot in Acts 23. The brief reference in 25:3 is sufficient to recall the previous vivid narrative of the plan for an ambush. The choice of words suggests that a familiar process is beginning again. Now as previously the high priests and their supporters "inform" a Roman official or "bring a charge" (using the verb $\dot{\epsilon}\mu\phi\alpha\nu\acute{\iota}\zeta\omega$: 23:15; 24:1; 25:2).[1] They are involved in a "plot" or "ambush" ($\dot{\epsilon}\nu\acute{\epsilon}\delta\rho\alpha$, $\dot{\epsilon}\nu\epsilon\delta\rho\epsilon\acute{\upsilon}\omega$: 23:16, 21; 25:3)[2] to "do away with" ($\dot{\alpha}\nu\alpha\iota\rho\acute{\epsilon}\omega$: 23:15, 21; 25:3) Paul and hope that the governor will grant them a "favor" ($\chi\acute{\alpha}\rho\iota\varsigma$: 24:27; 25:3). The speeches of accusation and defense in 25:7–8 can be summarized briefly because this part of the trial is basically a rerun of previous trial scenes, especially the trial before Felix. Thus the whole threatening process of death plot and trial seems to be starting again.

Festus does not agree to the request that Paul be brought to Jerusalem. Therefore, we have a second trial of Paul before a governor in Caesarea. Following this trial, Festus proposes that Paul stand trial in Jerusalem. Thus he reverses his position on the high priests' request. I will discuss this development below.

Festus responds to the high priests' pressure to the extent of acting with dispatch. He suggests that the accusers accompany him on his return trip

---

[1] This word occurs in Luke-Acts only in Acts 23—25.
[2] The only other occurrence of these words in the NT is in Luke 11:54.

to Caesarea, and on the day after his arrival there he brings Paul to trial. In the narrative of the trial, the speeches of accusation and defense are reduced to two verses. Only Paul is quoted in direct speech, and the quotation is one short sentence. Paul's accusers bring "weighty charges" against him, as Tertullus did in 24:5–6. Paul responded to Tertullus' charges by saying that his accusers could not prove their case (24:13), and the narrator says the same in 25:7. Then Paul denies that he has committed any offense against the law of the Jews, the temple, or Caesar. This denial responds both to the accusations of the Asian Jews in the temple (21:28) and the more political accusations of Tertullus, who presented Paul as a threat to the good order of the empire (24:5).

Like Felix, Festus does not give a verdict. Instead he asks Paul if he is willing to go up to Jerusalem and be tried there. The narrator indicates the governor's motive: Festus wants "to grant a favor to the Jews" (v. 9). Festus has adopted the policy of Felix, who left Paul in prison for the same reason (24:27). Roman justice is being undermined by political calculations. For its own purposes Rome needs to placate a powerful pressure group. Repeated use of "favor ($\chi\acute{\alpha}\rho\iota\varsigma$)" and "grant a favor ($\chi\alpha\rho\acute{\iota}\zeta o\mu\alpha\iota$)" in relation to the Roman governor (24:27; 25:3, 9, 11, 16) gives these words thematic status and makes such favoritism a major factor in the course of events.[3] The omniscient narrator's revelation of Festus' motive should be carefully noted. It will make a difference in the interpretation of following events. It means that we cannot take Festus' account of his own behavior at face value when he supplies a different reason in 25:20 for his proposal of a Jerusalem trial.

In vv. 3–5 Festus refused to grant a favor requested by the Jewish leaders of Jerusalem; in v. 9 he wants to grant the favor that he earlier refused. The narrative highlights the shift through repetition of the word "favor," suggesting that we should note the change and seek some meaning in it. It is not difficult to understand why a Roman governor would want to grant Paul's opponents a favor. They are powerful people with whom a governor must deal carefully; Paul does not have their kind of power. Nevertheless, the text leaves a gap, for it does not explain, as we might expect, why Festus would change his mind in a few days. I will suggest one possible way of filling the gap. Festus' desire to grant a favor to the Jewish leaders shows sensitivity to power relationships in his province. However, his first response to them in Jerusalem was the response of a political novice not yet aware of who holds power and what their interests are. Festus had just arrived in Jerusalem and was meeting the high priests and their allies for the first time. Their request had a hidden motive that

---

[3] See R. Cassidy, *Society and Politics*, 107–9.

Festus did not understand. He responded as if the main concern were simply to have Paul's trial soon. As Festus was returning to Caesarea, the fastest way to arrange the trial was for the accusers to accompany him and hold the trial there. Festus, however, proves to be a quick student of power. In the few days between the initial request and the trial, he has learned more about the high priests, their importance to Rome, and the strength of their conviction that Paul should be tried in Jerusalem. At the trial he seeks to rectify his first, stumbling political moves by belatedly granting the high priests' request. This suggestion for filling the gap in the text takes account of what we are told about Festus but must go beyond it in order to explain behavior that the text calls to our attention without explanation.

Paul forthrightly opposes Festus' proposal. He evidently suspects its political motivation. He says, "No one can grant me as a favor ($\chi\alpha\rho i$-$\sigma\alpha\sigma\theta\alpha\iota$) to them" (v. 11), echoing the narrator's statement that Festus wished to grant the Jews a favor. Thus he suspects the governor's bias. Festus will be no protection against the high priests in their base of power, Jerusalem. A trial has already been held. Through it Festus has learned all he needs to know. "You know very well," Paul tells the governor, that Paul has committed no wrong against the Jews (v. 10). Later Festus states that he found no evidence that Paul had committed a serious crime (v. 25), confirming that he did indeed recognize Paul's innocence at the trial, as Paul claimed in v. 10. Festus does not state this at the trial because then he would have to acquit Paul. Paul rightly believes that Festus recognizes his innocence. Yet Festus is not willing to act on this knowledge. This is further indication of his unreliability as a judge. Festus, like Felix, is not committed to justice but seeks to please the powerful. Therefore, Paul appeals to Caesar.

Ernst Haenchen has difficulty following the course of events. He says,

> In Luke's account it remains incomprehensible: 1. why after the close of the proceedings no verdict follows, but a transference of the trial is proposed, 2. why Paul does not simply insist on the continuation of the trial in Caesarea, but appeals to Caesar, 3. why Festus does not himself want to try a man charged with *laesa maiestas*.[4]

These problems arise from Haenchen's failure to take seriously the indications that Festus is a biased judge and recognized as such by Paul. If one believes, as Haenchen does, that Festus is basically "energetic and upright,"[5] the course of events is, indeed, incomprehensible, and Haenchen's own proposals for resolving the problems are insufficient.

---

[4] See *Acts*, 669.
[5] See *Acts*, 670.

Following Paul's final defense speech, Festus and Agrippa recognize Paul's innocence, and Agrippa states, "This man could have been released if he had not appealed to Caesar" (26:31–32). This statement is not a reliable indication of what Festus would, in fact, have done if Paul had chosen another course. Roman officials are quite willing to recognize Paul's innocence when they can do so cheaply, that is, when it has no effect on Paul's legal status and no political consequences. They speak of Paul's innocence as Paul passes out of their jurisdiction and they are rid of the political problem that Paul poses (see 23:29; 25:25; 26:31–32). Festus had a chance to acquit Paul at his trial. Instead he tried to please the powerful by proposing another trial in Jerusalem. Only when he is relieved of his problem by Paul's appeal does Festus publicly recognize Paul's innocence.

There may be another factor behind Paul's decision to appeal to Caesar. Paul was told by the Lord that he "must (δεῖ) also bear witness in Rome" (23:11). Since then he has spent two years in prison in Caesarea. Now he is about to be sent to Jerusalem—the wrong direction—into a situation from which he may never escape. However, by his own decision Paul can help to fulfill the Lord's purpose that he bear witness in the centers of power, including Rome.[6] Appealing to Caesar means going to Rome. It is doubtful, then, that Paul's appeal is merely the result of calculations on chances of acquittal before Festus, on the one hand, and Caesar, on the other. Nor does the appeal to Caesar imply a high estimation of Caesar as a dispenser of justice. Release from his arrest is not Paul's only goal. Bearing witness in Rome and to Caesar (27:24) is itself a controlling purpose. Paul acts to make this possible whether it improves his chances of acquittal or not.

The scene ends with Festus' decision, expressed with epigrammatic balance and terseness: "To Caesar you have appealed, to Caesar you shall go" (25:12). "Go" is the final and climactic word, highlighting what Paul has achieved. He is going to Caesar. Those who recall the preceding solemn statements about the importance of Paul reaching Rome (19:21; 23:11) will recognize that Paul's appeal is more than the legal maneuver of a desperate prisoner.

---

[6] Charles Cosgrove points out that in Luke-Acts "the divine δεῖ functions as an imperative, a summons to obedience. A great deal of the weight of its fulfillment is thrown to the human side. Jesus and Paul, as executors of the divine δεῖ are initiators and strategists of the divine purpose." See "The Divine Δεῖ in Luke-Acts," 183.

THE CLIMAX OF PAUL'S DEFENSE:
PAUL BEFORE FESTUS AND AGRIPPA

Paul's climactic defense speech is prepared by a narrative of the arrival of King Agrippa and his sister Bernice for a visit with Festus, followed by a request by Agrippa to hear Paul. This narrative first provides the framework for two fairly long statements by Festus, who reviews his handling of Paul's case first with Agrippa and then before Agrippa and assembled notables the next day. These statements by Festus considerably expand the account of his reaction to Paul and the preceding trial. They also allow us to observe Festus presenting a public image of himself as the judge in Paul's case. Comparison of this public image with the narrator's previous account of Festus' actions and motives enriches the characterization of Festus. Investigation of these matters will help us to see that the narrator's characterization of Festus is both subtle and impressive, because without the label "hypocrite" or other such epithets the conflict between public image and hidden motive emerges from the narrative.

Ernst Haenchen understands this section of Acts to have a different purpose. He says, "The preceding scene had made Paul appeal from the governor to Caesar. This introduced a wrong note—though toned down as far as possible—into the harmony which otherwise prevailed between Paul and the Roman officials."[1] Therefore, 25:13–22 has the following useful function: "Festus is personally rehabilitated before the reader. He is ultimately only a poor heathen who cannot be blamed for his lack of understanding and who indeed was so well-meaning. A bright light falls on the Roman state."[2] Thus Haenchen takes Festus' account of himself at face value. In contrast, Gerhard Krodel writes of "the shabbiness of Festus's twofold rehearsal of his deeds" and states that "Luke is at his most brilliant in sketching the hypocrisy of Festus without any overt polemics."[3] Richard Cassidy, too, states that "Festus is unmistakably portrayed presenting a summary that is decidedly biased in his own self-interest."[4] In the following I will try to show why an interpretation that is

---

[1] See *Acts*, 674.
[2] See *Acts*, 674–75.
[3] See *Acts*, 450–51.
[4] See *Society and Politics*, 111.

sensitive to the subtleties of narrative should follow the latter view of Festus rather than Haenchen's view.

The voice of the narrator must be carefully distinguished from the voices of characters within the narrative. Meir Sternberg recognizes that the narrator in the Hebrew Bible, unlike narrators in some modern literature, is "straightforwardly reliable."[5] The same holds true for Luke-Acts. The narrator's voice is authoritative. It tells the truth about the narrative world that is being described and establishes norms according to which the actions and statements of characters can be judged, for instance, by exercising selective omniscience in revealing the hidden motives of characters (as in 25:9). I am speaking here of a true view of the narrative world and of the norms that belong to it, not of historical reliability. The narrative world may be completely fictional. Yet the voice of the reliable narrator will have an important role in establishing the "facts" of the fictional world (What color was Goldilocks' hair?) and the norms in terms of which its events and characters are to be understood.[6] Certain characters within the story may also be reliable reflectors of the narrative's norms,[7] but their reliability must be established in the narrative and can always change before the end of the story. It cannot be assumed, especially with minor characters like Felix and Festus who have no past record of approval by the narrator. Furthermore, Sternberg has noted that in the Hebrew Bible the narrator and a character will sometimes give accounts of the same events. These accounts may differ in subtle but significant ways. Comparison of the accounts allows us to observe the character's conscious or unconscious distortion of events.[8] The narrator has no commitment to explain everything and certainly not all at once. So, according to Sternberg, "The narrator's own version maneuvers . . . between the truth and the whole truth but draws the line at untruth." In contrast, "The dramatis personae show no such scruples in reporting."[9] Because the narrator's account is reliable, the unreliability of the character's account can be displayed without the need for overt commentary (e.g., "Festus, distorting the truth, said . . ."). This technique, already noted in the discussion of Lysias' letter,[10] reappears in Festus' reports on his handling of Paul's case.

---

[5] See *Poetics of Biblical Narrative*, 51.
[6] As S. Rimmon-Kenan states, "A reliable narrator is one whose rendering of the story and commentary on it the reader is supposed to take as an authoritative account of the fictional truth." See *Narrative Fiction*, 100.
[7] On reliable characters as revealers of the author's norms, see Wayne Booth, *Rhetoric of Fiction*, 16–18.
[8] See *Poetics of Biblical Narrative*, 390–440.
[9] See *Poetics of Biblical Narrative*, 423.
[10] See above, 295–96.

Festus' account is partly a whitewash. He attempts to make his own handling of Paul's case look better than it was. Yet this does not explain all the differences between the narrator's and Festus' account of Paul's trial. Festus' speeches are also being used to fill out the narrator's account. In them we learn more about what Festus really thinks about Paul. We should be inclined to trust statements that go beyond the narrator's account in 25:6–12 if they do not conflict with anything there and show a perspective that harmonizes with the dominant perspective in Acts. When there is tension between the narrator's and Festus' accounts and Festus' interests are being served, however, we should suspect bias.

In 25:16 Festus states that he replied to the high priests' request in Jerusalem by citing Roman guarantees of a fair trial for a defendant. His statement suggests that Festus is strongly committed to Roman standards of justice. No such statement is included in the previous account of the incident in vv. 4–5. Nevertheless, Festus could have made such a statement. The narrator did not necessarily intend to report everything Festus said in vv. 4–5. However, Festus' assertion that he refused "to grant ($\chi\alpha\rho\acute{\iota}\zeta\epsilon\sigma\theta\alpha\iota$)" Paul to his accusers without a trial reminds us that after the trial Paul had to appeal to Caesar in order to escape Festus' plan "to grant ($\chi\alpha\rho\acute{\iota}\sigma\alpha\sigma\theta\alpha\iota$)" him to his enemies (v. 11; cf. v. 9). Festus cites the point in the narrative where he looked good. He guaranteed Paul a trial in Caesarea. However, his choice of words reminds us that he did not show the same commitment to justice when it came to the verdict.

Festus' statement in v. 17 that he held the trial without delay is accurate, but the inclusion of this unnecessary point is self-serving. In vv. 18–19 Festus goes further than the narrator previously did in indicating his reaction to the trial. Indeed, he is willing to state that the real points of dispute in the trial concerned the parties' own religion and specifically Paul's contention that Jesus is alive. Later Festus will indicate that Paul "had done nothing worthy of death" (v. 25). These two statements fit together (and are placed together in 23:29). If the trial really centers on disputes of the Jewish religion, there is no basis for a sentence of death under Roman law. Even though the narrator did not previously attribute these views to Festus, there is strong indication that they are meant to be a reliable account of Festus' judgment. On the one hand, they do not serve Festus' private interests. Indeed, they cause one to ask, If Festus perceived this to be the case, why did he not say so at the trial and acquit Paul? On the other hand, these views fit closely with views expressed elsewhere in Acts. Romans have previously expressed the view that accusations against Paul are really disputes over the Jewish law (18:14–15; 23:29). Moreover, Paul spoke of resurrection as the issue of his trial in both 23:6 and 24:15, 21. Indeed, we can now see why the narrator was content to present the speeches of accusation and defense in the trial before Festus in such abbreviated form. This trial is to be understood as basically a repetition of the trial before Felix, in which Paul briefly replied to the charges but also led his listeners back to his affirmation of resurrection of the dead.

Festus was convinced by Paul's defense. He agreed that no proof had been given of serious crimes[11] and that religious disputes about resurrection are really the heart of the matter. Indeed, his statement carries the preceding references to resurrection one step further, indicating that Jesus' resurrection, not just the general resurrection, is involved. In this respect his statement points forward to Paul's confession of faith in 26:23. Festus, however, speaks the nonconfessional language of an outsider, referring to a dispute "concerning a certain Jesus who was dead, whom Paul was claiming to be alive."

In v. 20 Festus introduces his proposal that Paul stand trial in Jerusalem with the indication that he felt "at a loss" how to investigate these religious issues. Presumably a trial in Jerusalem would make a more informed judgment possible. Here Festus supplies a different motive for his proposal than the narrator did in v. 9. Festus makes his proposal appear to be the reasonable action of a judge in a difficult case; the narrator told us that it was the biased act of an unjust judge. In that Festus hides the fact that he was acting "to grant a favor to the Jews," he is deceptive. He is presenting a public image that covers up his real motives. This does not necessarily mean, however, that he is lying when he says that he was "at a loss" in investigating this case. The two motives attributed to Festus in vv. 9 and 20 do not necessarily exclude one another. Those uncertain of their own knowledge tend to bend to the views of others. It is more convenient to bend to the views of the stronger party, in this case, the high priests and their supporters. Although both Felix and Agrippa are presented as experienced administrators well acquainted with Jewish affairs and the Christian "way" (24:10–11, 22; 26:3, 26), Festus is a neophyte who has just arrived on the scene. His statements and reactions suggest his ignorance. He refers to "a certain Jesus" (25:19), as if he had never heard of him before, and Paul's mission and witness are so strange to him that he attributes them to madness (26:24).

Thus it is quite possible to take Festus' statement of his motive in 25:20 as incomplete but valid as far as it goes. He really is at a loss because he is dealing with issues beyond his competence.[12] It is also possible that he is

---

[11] In v. 18 αἰτίαν may refer not to the "charge" (so RSV) or accusation but to a reason for punishment under the law (roughly equivalent to the proof of a charge), as in Acts 13:28; 28:18; John 18:38; 19:4, 6. Then Festus is not saying that the charges were limited to religious issues; rather he is commenting on the lack of proof of the kind of crimes that a Roman governor would expect to be brought before his court.

[12] H. Conzelmann comments on 25:20, "The reader is shown the incompetence of the

feigning ignorance in order to excuse his failure to acquit Paul. Note the difference between Gallio's and Festus' handling of Paul's case. As soon as Gallio decided that the case really concerned disputes of the Jewish religion, he threw the case out of court (18:14–15). Festus does not. The difference may be due less to the differing competence of the two Roman administrators than to the realities of political power. Gallio can afford to offend the Jews of Corinth, whereas there is a price to pay for offending the high priests and elders in Judea. The narrative leaves some ambiguity in reading Festus' motives. Nevertheless, whether Festus is weak or calculating, the narrator's statement in v. 9 holds: Festus wanted "to grant a favor to the Jews" who were accusing Paul. He has ceased to be a just judge.

In introducing Paul to the assembled dignitaries in v. 24, Festus exaggerates. He enhances the picture of the pressure that he is under from the Jews in order to present himself as unaffected by such pressure when he states his belief in Paul's innocence in v. 25. Here, as in v. 16, Festus wants to be seen as a protector of an innocent defendant's rights. The exaggeration appears when we compare Festus' statement with the preceding narrative. He speaks of "the whole multitude of the Jews" appealing to him, "shouting that he must not live any longer." There is a preceding scene in which a Jewish mob cries out for Paul's death (21:36; 22:22–23), but it is set in the temple prior to Festus' arrival. Festus is talking about appeals made to him "in Jerusalem and here." These were actually made by "the high priests and the leading men of the Jews" (25:2), some of whom later came down to Caesarea. There is no reference to a multitude shouting. Festus prefers to magnify the responsibility of the Jewish people while presenting himself as a judge who retains his independence in the midst of such public pressure.[13]

In v. 25 the reference to Paul's appeal is preceded by Festus' statement that he believes Paul to be innocent of any capital crime. This juxtaposition makes Paul's appeal seem to be an irrational act for which Festus is not responsible. Festus draws a strong contrast between his attitude toward Paul and Paul's appeal through emphatic use of personal pronouns (ἐγὼ ... αὐτοῦ δὲ τούτου ... : "I ... but this fellow himself ... "). It is incomprehensible why Paul should appeal from the jurisdiction of a judge so favorably inclined toward him, but it is only Festus' deception that creates this puzzle.

---

authorities to deal with questions of religion." See *Acts,* 207. This statement should be restricted to Festus, however. Felix and Agrippa are not presented as incompetent.

[13] Jack T. Sanders, however, takes Festus' statement in 25:24 at face value as evidence of Luke's anti-Jewish attitude. See *Jews in Luke-Acts,* 294. Narrative criticism should warn us against such hasty equation of the perspective of a character with that of the implied author.

Festus asks for Agrippa's help because he has nothing "certain" to write
to Caesar about the case. Hans Conzelmann believes this request is
unnecessary and artificial.[14] Festus' motives may be partially hidden. It is
possible that he would prefer to share responsibility for this case with
Agrippa rather than take full responsibility himself. Be that as it may,
Paul's appeal relieves Festus of one problem (having to deal with Paul's
case himself) but presents him with another. Festus himself has come to
doubt the grounds for a capital case against Paul, and he admits as much.
Yet the case is being taken to Caesar's court, and Festus must state the
basis on which Paul is being held for trial. He has nothing "firm" or
"certain (ἀσφαλές)" to write; the original charges do not now seem very
firm or certain. The immediate problem covers a potentially greater
problem, that Caesar might decide that a case with such insubstantial
charges has come to him only because of the mismanagement of his
Judean governor. It would be convenient if Festus could report some
charges of substance, justifying his failure to dismiss the case. Barring
that, it would be good at least to have his own opinion of Paul's innocence
confirmed, as he is dealing with a case where he is "at a loss" in
investigating the issues, contributing to his inability to write anything
"certain." So he asks Agrippa to hear Paul and give his opinion. Although
Festus might have preferred to have the hearing discover substantial
charges that would justify Paul's long imprisonment and the failure of two
Roman governors to acquit him, it instead confirms Festus' judgment that
Paul is innocent of the serious charges brought against him (26:31). Of
course, the need for one more examination of Paul before King Agrippa
also provides a splendid setting for Paul's climactic statement about his
mission.

The narrator shows unusual interest in Felix and Festus. They are
complex characters with conflicting tendencies. Felix is attracted to Paul
and his message, yet seeks a bribe and leaves Paul in prison to appease
Paul's enemies. Festus presents a favorable image of himself to the public,
but his handling of Paul's case is tainted with favoritism. Neither one is
willing to offend the high priests and elders by releasing Paul. The
narrator's characterization of the Roman governors contributes to a portrait of Paul as one caught in a web of self-interested maneuvers by people
who vie for support within the political jungle. However, Paul is not just a
helpless victim. As opportunity comes, he continues to bear witness to his
Lord. Although Paul continues to be denied justice and freedom, the

---

[14] See *Acts*, 207: "This verse provides the reason for this spectacle in an artificial manner.
What Festus says is self-contradictory. He had enough material!"

saving purpose of God still has use for this resourceful and faithful prisoner.

The narrator provides a setting of high ceremony for Paul's final speech to the authorities. The hearing before King Agrippa is not a private affair. Agrippa and his sister Bernice come "with much pageantry," and the "tribunes and outstanding men of the city" also assemble in the audience hall (25:23). Paul's audience is impressive and potentially intimidating. William Long detects a tendency to "bring embellishment" to the style of this speech, which would add to its persuasive effect. He writes, "While no one will maintain that Acts 26 is an example of 'grand' style as described by the ancient rhetoricians, it is reasonable to believe that Luke's ornamentation, including classical usages and extremely long sentences in ch. 26" serves Luke's purpose "to sway completely his hearers."[15] Such embellishment would be appropriate to the setting and audience depicted in the narrative.

King Herod Agrippa II is called "Agrippa" in the narrative, but his father Herod Agrippa I was called "Herod" (12:1–23). The different names obscure the relation between them.[16] Suggestions of continuity would run counter to the needs of the narrative, for the two kings play quite different roles. Herod is the evil persecutor. Agrippa is interested in Paul and willing to recognize his innocence. It is useful to bring Paul's case before a person of prestige, one whose judgment would count in the world, but the issues, as Paul has been insisting and as Festus recognized in 25:19, center around the Jewish hope. Thus the person of prestige needs also to have credentials in Judaism. King Agrippa fits this need. He is presented as Jewish in knowledge and belief. (Whether he was also a practicing Jew is ignored in the narrative.) His knowledge of Jewish affairs and of the development of the Christian "way" is emphasized in 26:3 and 26. Moreover, his knowledge is not that of an outsider with a merely professional interest in Judaism. He believes the prophets (26:27); therefore, the fulfillment of the prophetic hope is a matter of importance to him. Paul can use language of the insider with Agrippa. He can refer simply to "the people (ὁ λαός)" (26:17, 23), while he speaks only of "this nation" or "my nation" with Felix (24:10, 17).[17] Furthermore, he uses the

---

[15] See *Trial of Paul*, 237–39. Long includes items of content in such ornamentation, i.e., indications of the heightening of Paul's life story in comparison with the parallel accounts in Acts 9 and 22. With regard to literary expression, he cites the following: classical use of perfect ἥγημαι as a present (v. 2), the literary elegance of the exordium (vv. 2–3), classical ἴσασι (v. 4), classical ἀκριβεστάτην (v. 5), addition of the proverb in v. 14, genitive of the articular infinitive in v. 18, litotes (v. 19), Attic use of πειράσθαι (v. 21), classical οὐδὲν . . . λέγων (v. 22), classical παθητός = "must suffer" (v. 23).

[16] According to H. Conzelmann, *Acts*, 93, the first Agrippa "is called 'Herod' only by Luke."

[17] See G. Schneider, *Apostelgeschichte* 2:374, n. 59.

Jewish term "Satan" (26:18). Finally, the reference to "you" in v. 8 seems
to include Agrippa among the Jews skeptical of the resurrection in spite of
God's promise. Thus the speech before King Agrippa is the climax of
Paul's effort to defend himself before a Jewish audience, an effort that
began in Acts 22.

The general charge of being anti-Jewish in 21:28 is still in the background, although its specifics have faded, as have the charges raised by
Tertullus in 24:5-6. Paul's earlier speeches have dealt with these matters.
What is still needed is a clear statement on what Paul himself regards as
the main issue of the trial, the one that he has repeatedly put forward since
23:6 and that Festus acknowledged in 25:19—the issue of resurrection
and the Jewish hope. This concern will be combined with Paul's
autobiographical review of his life and mission, expanding what was said
in 22:3-16. The repeated emphasis on hope and resurrection, without
clear explanation of its bearing on Paul's situation, points forward to
some insight still to be given. This forward drive in the narrative makes
the speech before King Agrippa a moment of climax and revelation. The
climactic significance of this speech is also indicated by its impressive
setting, its length, and its position in the last of the defense scenes.

Paul's speech also serves as a climactic review and interpretation of his
mission.[18] The whole narrative of Paul's ministry—and even earlier parts
of Luke-Acts—is newly illuminated by this review. The speech before
King Agrippa is more than a defense speech. It begins as a defense speech
(cf. v. 1), and it develops aspects of previous defense speeches, but its
functions are broader. It combines themes from the defense speeches with
themes from the earlier narrative, reaching back to the missions of John
the Baptist, Jesus, and the apostles, and fashions these into a summary
statement of Paul's place in the unfolding purpose of God. Then Paul
continues his mission before our eyes as his review of his past message
becomes present proclamation, ending with a missionary appeal to King
Agrippa. A shift in function is indicated in the speech itself. Although
Paul speaks of making a defense in v. 2 and says in v. 6, "I stand on trial
($\ddot{\epsilon}\sigma\tau\eta\kappa\alpha\ \kappa\rho\iota\nu\acute{o}\mu\epsilon\nu o\varsigma$)," in v. 22 he says, "I stand bearing witness ($\ddot{\epsilon}\sigma\tau\eta\kappa\alpha$
$\mu\alpha\rho\tau\upsilon\rho\acute{o}\mu\epsilon\nu o\varsigma$)." These self-descriptions express a shift from defense to
missionary witness. The role of King Agrippa also shifts. He is not just
the prestigious authority who might help Paul by recognizing his innocence. He now represents all those who know and believe the prophets
and are not yet hardened against the gospel, that is, those Jews and God-

---

[18] On previews and reviews as interpretive keys in understanding the overall course of the
narrative, see *Narrative Unity* 1:21–22. Paul's speech also fits the third and fourth types of
material discussed there. It is an interpretive statement by a reliable character and contains
a commission statement.

fearers who might still be reached in spite of the bitter Jewish opposition that first caused Paul's imprisonment and then resisted his release. Paul the prisoner continues his mission. He does so by appealing to the prophets and to "the promise to our fathers," which "our twelve tribes" still cherish (vv. 6–7). The inclusive mission to both Jews and Gentiles, conferred on Paul by the risen Lord, continues into the present. Even though many Jews have closed their ears, Paul does not cease appealing to those who will listen, making his appeal on the basis of the Jewish hope.

As a climactic summary and review, the speech draws together material from previous speeches and clarifies relationships. It repeats the emphasis on Paul's Jewishness, his strict upbringing, and his zeal as a persecutor (26:4–5, 9–11), previously found in 22:3–5. It also shares the story of Paul's encounter with the Lord and commission as witness with the same earlier speech (22:6–16; 26:12–18). It adds to this speech the theme of hope and resurrection introduced in 23:6 and repeated thereafter. It interprets Paul's mission by emphasizing repentance and release of sins, light as a symbol of salvation, and the inclusion of both Jews and Gentiles in this salvation (26:16–18, 20, 23), using themes that appear early in Luke (Luke 1:16, 77–79; 2:30–32; 3:3, 6, 8) and in key commissioning scenes later (Luke 24:46–47; Acts 1:8). It includes the witness of Scripture and the recital of the Messiah's suffering and resurrection (26:22–23), characteristic of Peter's and Paul's mission speeches to Jews, and like Peter's Pentecost speech, it ends with a direct missionary appeal that is detached from the main body of the speech as a dialogue (2:37–40; 26:24–29). There should be much that is familiar in this speech. However, now we can see how the narrator wishes to bring it all together to present a total picture of Paul.

The speech is basically autobiographical. It is a narrative, the story of Paul's life in chronological order. At the point where Paul mentions his life as a Pharisee, a digression is inserted (vv. 6–8) that comments on the Jewish hope in resurrection to which the Pharisees are committed. This digression prepares for the speech's close: the proclamation of the Messiah who fulfills this hope as "first of the resurrection of the dead" (v. 23). Comparison with Acts 22 reveals that the figure of Ananias has been eliminated, Paul's commission is now given directly by the Lord, and it is expanded. Then the account of Paul's life is extended by a summary report of Paul's fulfillment of his commission (commission: vv. 16–18; fulfillment of commission: vv. 19–23). This report brings the story right up to "this day" on which "I [Paul] stand bearing witness" (v. 22) in fulfillment of the Lord's commission. At this point the report of past witness turns into present proclamation.

In both v. 2 and v. 7 Paul indicates that he is giving a defense concerning accusations brought by Jews. The conflict with Jewish opponents still shapes this speech, even though the accusers are not physically present. As in 22:3 Paul begins by emphasizing his Jewish roots and credentials (26:4–5). His phrases show his past and present identification with the Jewish people: "my nation," "our religion," "our fathers," "our twelve tribes" (vv. 4–7).[19] His commitment to Judaism is emphasized by citing his well-known participation in "the strictest sect of our religion," the Pharisees. When he mentions his life as a Pharisee, he immediately goes on to speak of the Jewish hope that Pharisees, especially, treasure, although this interrupts the chronological narrative of his life. He again insists that he is on trial for this Jewish hope (as in 23:6; 24:21). The transition "and now" in v. 6 emphasizes the continuity between his present faithfulness to this hope and his past origin and life as a Pharisee.[20] Paul is arguing that he has been consistent in his loyalty to the Jewish hope, whereas vv. 7–8 imply that his opponents are strangely inconsistent; what the people earnestly desire, the focus of their hope, is rejected when it arrives.

Paul heightens the irony of Jewish rejection by emphasizing the passionate intensity of Jewish hope. The promise is the promise given by God "to our fathers." It is a promise "to which our twelve tribes, earnestly worshiping night and day, hope to attain" (v. 7). Note that this promise is a corporate concern ("our twelve tribes"). The hope in question is, as Paul will say later, "the hope of Israel" (28:20). Indeed, the twelve tribes are passionately and intensely concerned with this promise and hope. It is the subject of ceaseless intercessory prayer by them. How ironic, then, that those with this intense hope accuse Paul of being anti-Jewish (21:28) and a pestilential influence among the Jewish people (24:5) when he brings word that this hope is being fulfilled. This irony is emphasized in v. 7; the very hope that the twelve tribes earnestly seek is cause of accusation against Paul. This is tragic irony because the deepest desire of the Jewish people, which rightly belongs to them by promise, is being rejected by many of them. This passage contributes to a presentation of the story of Israel that emphasizes the fulfillment of its great hope and then depicts a tragic turn away from this fulfillment. This story line stretches from the beginning of Luke to the end of Acts.[21]

This hope concerns resurrection, as v. 8 indicates. Paul's response to his

---

[19] See G. Krodel, *Acts,* 458.

[20] Note "from youth," "from the beginning" (v. 4), "and now" (v. 6), a sequence that emphasizes the continuity of past and present.

[21] See R. Tannehill, "Israel in Luke-Acts," 69–85. Klaus Haacker presents a detailed argument against E. Haenchen's view that emphasis on the hope of Israel is an attempt to show continuity with Judaism in order to gain tolerance from the Roman government. See "Bekenntnis des Paulus zur Hoffnung Israels," 438–43.

Jewish accusers may seem contrived and irrelevant because (1) the hope for resurrection is not nearly as important in early Judaism as Paul seems to imply and (2) this argument seems to ignore the central conflict over the Christian claim that Jesus is the Messiah. Both of these impressions result from a failure to grasp the full scope of this defense and appeal. The impression that the christological issue is being ignored disappears when Paul ends his speech by speaking of the Messiah as "first of the resurrection of the dead" (v. 23). Although Paul has repeatedly referred to hope for a general resurrection ("resurrection of dead persons [ἀνάστασις νεκρῶν]," 23:6; see the similar plurals in 24:15, 21; 26:8), the sign that this hope is being fulfilled is the resurrection of the Messiah, who is "first" of a communal resurrection.[22] The rejection of Paul, the proclaimer of resurrection hope, has much to do with rejection of the risen Messiah. The christological issue is not being ignored, but it is placed in the context of the hope that Paul and his accusers share, so that they may understand what is at stake.

Item (1) above, the impression that Acts is making much of a minor matter in early Judaism, may be the result of ignoring the full range of meaning of hope and promise in Luke-Acts, under the assumption that resurrection of the dead simply means life after death for individuals. Klaus Haacker argues that the theme of resurrection, whether understood metaphorically or realistically, is closely connected in Old Testament–Jewish tradition with the hopes of Israel as a people.[23] This communal hope is preserved in Luke-Acts, where hope and resurrection are linked with the reign of the Davidic Messiah, who brings salvation to the Jewish people. The hope and promise of which Paul speaks in this, his last major speech, should be understood in relation to the promise of which he spoke in his first major speech. In the synagogue of Pisidian Antioch, Paul proclaimed that Jesus' resurrection fulfilled the promise to Israel of a Davidic Messiah. From David's seed God brought to Israel a savior "according to promise" (13:23). God fulfilled "the promise to the fathers" through raising Jesus and proclaiming him "my Son" (13:32–33). This Messiah, having been raised from the dead, is no longer subject to corruption. Israel has been given "the holy things of David that are faithful," that is, lasting (13:34).[24] Paul is speaking of the renewed Davidic kingdom promised to Israel in its Scripture. This promise is tied to resurrection because Jesus is established as reigning Messiah through resurrection and his reign is characterized by resurrection life. As the

---

[22] The connection between Jesus' resurrection and communal resurrection was already suggested in 4:2 and perhaps 3:15 (Jesus as ἀρχηγὸς τῆς ζωῆς, "leader" or "founder of life").

[23] See "Bekenntnis des Paulus zur Hoffnung Israels," 443–48.

[24] See above, 166–67, 170–72.

angel said to Mary, Jesus "will reign over the house of Jacob forever, and of his reign there will be no end" (Luke 1:33). His eternal reign is a result of his resurrection, and others will be freed from corruption to share his eternal reign, for the Messiah is "first of the resurrection of the dead" (26:23). Thus the hope and promise of which Paul speaks in 26:6-7 is not merely a hope for individual life after death but a hope for the Jewish people, to be realized through resurrection.

The connection that I am drawing between the promise to the Jewish people in Paul's first and last major speeches is supported by a peculiarity of shared language. As the promise in 13:32 is τὴν πρὸς τοὺς πατέρας ἐπαγγελίαν γενομένην ("the promise made to the fathers"), so also 26:6 refers to hope τῆς εἰς τοὺς πατέρας ἡμῶν ἐπαγγελίας γενομένης ("of the promise made to our fathers").[25] It is the same promise, and Paul's synagogue speech makes clear that it concerns the Davidic Messiah who will bring to the Jewish people all the benefits of his reign. The birth narrative in Luke 1—2 dramatically portrays Jews who live in light of this promise and respond with joy to its fulfillment. Anna, in fact, is a specific example of a Jew who was "worshiping night and day" in expectation of the fulfillment of this hope (Luke 2:37), as the twelve tribes do according to Acts 26:7.[26] The intense hope that Paul describes in 26:7 is not confined to an individualistic hope for life after death. It is a hope for the Messiah's promised reign, which is established through resurrection and characterized by a resurrection life corporately shared. It includes all the benefits promised by Jesus and his witnesses (food for the hungry poor, release of sins, the gift of the Holy Spirit) and even the political freedom for the Jewish people proclaimed by Zechariah (Luke 1:69-75). Paul believes that all of this is at stake in his opponents' reaction to his message of the risen Messiah.

Paul continues his life story in 26:9-11 by describing the intensity of his former opposition to Jesus and his followers, and in vv. 12-18 he tells of the radical change that took place through an encounter with the heavenly Lord. The overwhelming power of this Lord in dealing with his balky subject is emphasized by the addition of the saying, "It is hard for you to kick against goads" (v. 14), not found in the previous accounts of Paul's call. Through this encounter Paul becomes a witness of what he has seen.

---

[25] The only use of ἐπαγγελία ("promise") between these two passages is a reference to the Roman tribune's promise in 23:21. Robert O'Toole, *Christological Climax,* 86, notes the similar wording in 13:32 and 26:6 and rightly concludes that the promise realized in the resurrection of Jesus in 13:32-33 is the same as the promise in 26:6-8. See also K. Haacker, "Bekenntnis des Paulus zur Hoffnung Israels," 447.

[26] According to K. Haacker, when Paul confesses the hope of Israel, he "steps to the side of Mary and Zechariah, Simeon and Anna, and associates himself with the disciples on the way to Emmaus" (Luke 24:21). See "Bekenntnis des Paulus zur Hoffnung Israels," 442.

A new vision of God's saving work in the world, uniting Jews and Gentiles in the promised reign of the Messiah, takes control of his life and sets him to work.

In previous discussions of the reports by Lysias and Festus, I argued that there were significant discrepancies between these reports and the narrator's accounts, suggesting that these reports were slanted for the speaker's benefit.[27] We must now consider the fact that Paul's account of his life in Acts 26 also departs from previous accounts in Acts 9 and 22. Does the narrative thereby, whether purposely or through simple ineptitude, undermine the authority of Paul's words in this climactic speech?

Most of the differences in the three accounts of Paul's call would probably not have this effect on the reader (so long as we are thinking of the ordinary reader and not of the modern, hypercritical reader whose chief preoccupation is the discovery of divergent sources and conflicting theological tendencies in a document). The addition or subtraction of details causes no problem so long as the accounts do not conflict. A narrator is free to decide how much to include. Even slight conflicts of detail are of little consequence so long as a central affirmation does not rest on them. It is the perceived attempt to score an important point unfairly that is likely to undermine credibility with hearers and readers. The fact that the narrator said that Paul's companions "stood speechless" in 9:7 whereas Paul says in 26:14 that everyone fell to the ground is a curiosity, but a fundamental point does not rest on it. The same is true of possible conflicts over what Paul's companions heard and saw (see 9:7; 22:9).[28]

Paul's commission from the Lord, however, is the foundation of his mission. Therefore, the discrepancies as to where Paul received this commission and through whom are potentially more serious. In the first account Paul's commission appears in words of the Lord to Ananias (9:15–16), in the second account Ananias conveys the commission to Paul (22:14–15), and in the third the Lord commissions Paul directly on the road to Damascus (26:16–18). The third version shows a shift of emphasis. It shows an interest in Paul's commission, which is expanded, and in his fulfillment of this commission, but there is no interest in Ananias, who drops entirely out of the story, simplifying the narrative. The omission helps Paul to move swiftly and effectively from the encounter with the Lord to the call as witness and the fulfillment of this call. However, a conflict results, for the first two accounts leave no room

---

[27] See above, 295–96, 309–14.

[28] There is no conflict between the statements that the companions saw no one but saw the light. There does seem to be a conflict in the statements about hearing, although some may think that the difference between the genitive (9:7) and accusative (22:9) of φωνή ("sound, voice") is significant.

for the commission statement at the point where it occurs in 26:16–18. In both 9:6 and 22:10 the Lord sends Paul on to Damascus, where he will be told what he must do. In 26:16–18 Paul receives his commission not in Damascus through Ananias but on the way to Damascus as part of his encounter with the Lord. The free way in which Paul reformulates the account of his commission carries a certain risk that some hearers or readers will doubt the accuracy of his account.

Evidently the narrator was not concerned about this risk and preferred to exercise some freedom in presenting Paul's speech. The lack of concern suggests that Paul, although probably a subject of debate in the Lukan environment, was not being attacked by questioning the story of his call. Furthermore, it would take some strong indications of unreliability to undermine Paul's authority at this point in the narrative. All of the previous indications (since his conversion) have been in his favor. Indeed, the statement of Paul's commission in vv. 16–18 is so closely connected with scriptural themes and previous statements of the Lord's purpose in Acts itself that it is not likely to be suspect. Although a few might be confused about where and when Paul received his commission, his role as stated so closely fits previously established norms for understanding God's purpose and Paul's role in it that most hearers and readers will not notice any conflict. This conclusion can be supported by closer consideration of vv. 16–18.

The role of Paul as a specially chosen "witness" for the Lord Jesus (v. 16) has already been presented as part of Ananias' statement of Paul's commission in 22:14–15 (see also 9:15). The Lord's commission of the apostles also highlighted their role as witnesses (Luke 24:48; Acts 1:8). Although Paul's witness partly overlaps with and partly differs from that of the apostles,[29] the emphasis in each case on being a chosen witness underscores a fundamental similarity between them.[30] The place of Paul's call in God's ancient purpose is suggested by the use of language from prophetic calls in Scripture. Those whose understanding of God's ways has been schooled in Scripture would find that Paul's call fits their expectations of the way that God calls prophetic messengers. Thus the phrase "stand on your feet" in v. 16 repeats God's words to Ezekiel when he was sent to Israel as a prophet (Ezek. 2:1–3). The connection between the Lord's sending and rescuing in v. 17 probably reflects Jer. 1:7–8, part of a prophetic call scene that has also influenced Acts 18:9–10.[31] Paul is sent "to open their eyes," and this is followed by a contrast between darkness and light (v. 18). In Isa. 42:6–7 God says, "I called you," and the

---

[29] See above, 280–81.
[30] See C. Burchard, *Der dreizehnte Zeuge,* 135–36.
[31] See above, 225–26.

resulting mission means being "a light of the nations, to open eyes of the blind (ἀνοῖξαι ὀφθαλμοὺς τυφλῶν)." A related passage in Isa. 49:6 refers again to the "light of the nations." This passage was applied to Paul's mission in Acts 13:47. Similarly, when Isa. 61:1 was used to interpret Jesus' mission in Luke 4:18, renewal of sight for the blind became part of that mission. The same imagery of enabling sight and bringing light is applied to Paul in Acts 26:18.[32] Gerhard Lohfink, noting that not just one but three of the great prophets are recalled in vv. 16–18 and that the texts chosen are vocation visions or references to the election of the Servant in Isaiah, concludes that these texts are being used purposefully and systematically to interpret Paul's mission.[33]

The language used in vv. 17–18 not only suggests the continuity of Paul's mission with the scriptural prophets but also with the mission of Jesus announced in the Nazareth synagogue. As the Lord "sends" Paul "to open their eyes," Jesus was "sent . . . to proclaim . . . to the blind new sight" (Luke 4:18). As the Lord sends Paul "so that they might receive release of sins (ἄφεσιν ἁμαρτιῶν)," Jesus was sent to proclaim "to captives release (ἄφεσιν)." The "captives" in Jesus' commission correspond, at least in part, to those under "the authority of Satan" in Paul's commission.[34] Because the apostles were also called as witnesses and to preach repentance and release of sins (Luke 24:47), Paul is being called to a task already performed by a distinguished company: the scriptural prophets, Jesus, and the apostles.

Paul's witness will be based on what he has seen and will see through the Lord's appearances to him (v. 16). The appearance of the Lord on the Damascus road has a fundamental significance for Paul's role as witness, but it is also the beginning of a continuing process of revelation. Verse 17 attaches the promise of rescue to the reference to future appearances. Besides stories of Paul's survival of stoning (14:19–20) and rescue from prison (16:19–40), which show the Lord fulfilling the promise of rescue, there is a series of appearances of the Lord or of an angel that serve primarily to sustain Paul in the face of threats (18:9–10; 23:11; 27:23–24). Paul can do more than bear witness to the risen Lord on the basis of his encounter with Jesus on the Damascus road; he can also witness to the Lord's power to sustain witnesses under threat.

Paul is promised rescue "from the people and from the Gentiles" (v. 17). Thus there will be serious opposition from both Jews and Gentiles. These same two groups are the objects of Paul's mission. The antecedent

---

[32] For further comment on the narrator's borrowing of blindness and light imagery from Isaiah see *Narrative Unity* 1:66–67.

[33] See *Conversion of St. Paul*, 71.

[34] See *Narrative Unity* 1:65–67.

of "to whom (εἰς οὕς)" is not "the Gentiles" but "the people and the
Gentiles."[35] The context of Lukan thought strongly favors this interpretation. A sending to both Jews and Gentiles is a constant part of the
narratives of Paul's call on the Damascus road (9:15; 22:15 ["to all
persons"]), and preaching to Jews is an important part of Paul's work in
the narratives of Acts 13—19. Furthermore, the description of Paul's
work in vv. 19–20 is clearly intended to show Paul fulfilling the commission in v. 17. It records Paul's work in Jewish as well as Gentile areas.
The speech ends by speaking of the risen Lord's mission "both to the
people and to the Gentiles" (v. 23). This corresponds to Paul's mission in
v. 17, for Paul is being called to participate in the Lord's inclusive mission.

Along with Ananias the healer, all reference to Paul's blinding by the
brilliant light has disappeared from this third account of Paul's encounter
with the Lord. The light is understood in this speech as a positive metaphor. It does not blind but enables sight and represents salvation. The
light that Paul encounters, according to v. 13, incorporates Paul into a
mission that brings light to others, according to vv. 18 and 23. The triple
reference to light, together with the references to seeing and to opening
eyes in vv. 16 and 18, turn light and sight into major unifying images in
the speech.[36] In dependence on Second Isaiah, light was used as an image
of salvation in Luke 1:77–79; 2:30–32; and Acts 13:47. The desire to
emphasize this image and make Paul's encounter with the light a symbol
of what all are offered through the mission appears in v. 18 and in the
description of the risen Messiah's mission in v. 23. The whole of the
Messiah's saving work can be represented as proclaiming light, a light
that reaches both Jews and Gentiles.

As a result of Paul's mission, people will "turn from darkness to light"
and "receive release of sins" (v. 18). Turning is closely related to repentance, as the combination "repent and turn (μετανοεῖν καὶ ἐπιστρέφειν)"
in v. 20 shows. Thus Paul's prophetic call leads to the familiar message of
repentance for release of sins. God's saving work is not real apart from the
actual change of human life through repentance, and v. 20 will indicate
that Paul was just as serious about this as John the Baptist, demanding
"deeds worthy of repentance" (cf. Luke 3:8: "Produce fruits worthy of
repentance"). The call to repentance for release of sins places Paul in a
prophetic succession that includes John the Baptist, Jesus, and the
apostles, whom Jesus commissioned as messengers of repentance and

---

[35] Against E. Haenchen, *Acts*, 686, and G. Schneider, *Apostelgeschichte* 2:374, who favor the
former view. Against Schneider, the images of turning to God and of opening eyes and
granting light to those in darkness (v. 18) are not reserved for conversion of pagans in Luke-
Acts. See Luke 1:16, 78–79; 4:18.

[36] See V. Stolle, *Zeuge als Angeklagter*, 172–74; and B. Gaventa, *From Darkness to Light*, 87.

release of sins in Luke 24:47. The call to repentance and offer of forgiveness then became an important part of the message of Peter and Paul (Acts 2:38; 3:19; 13:38–39; 17:30). The summaries of Paul's mission in 26:18 and 20 show once again the importance of these themes.

A place "among the consecrated ones (ἐν τοῖς ἡγιασμένοις)" comes "by faith in me," the Lord indicates. This may be a reminder of the important conclusion reached by Peter and ratified by the community at the Jerusalem conference. Peter first argued that the hearts of Gentiles were "cleansed by faith" (15:9) and then concluded by making grace and faith crucial for all: "Through the grace of the Lord Jesus we have faith so as to be saved, just as they do" (15:11).[37] Both cleansing and consecration signify acceptability to the holy God. According to 26:18, the creation of a people consecrated through faith in the Lord is an important goal of Paul's mission.

Paul continues by reporting in vv. 19–23 his fulfillment of the Lord's commission. This fulfillment is highlighted by the repetition of theme words that bind the Lord's commission and Paul's obedient response closely together (cf. "witness," "bearing witness," vv. 16, 22; "rescuing," "help from God," vv. 17, 22; "the people and the Gentiles," vv. 17, 23; "turn . . . to God," vv. 18, 20; "light," vv. 18, 23).

Paul's report of his obedience to the heavenly vision in vv. 19–20 highlights the geographical scope of his mission, listing Damascus, Jerusalem, "all the district of Judea," and "the nations" (or "Gentiles") in rapid order. The list is geographical, not primarily ethnic, and so does not exclude Paul's preaching to Jews among the nations, a preaching that the previous narrative of Paul's journeys richly illustrated. However, it does show Paul carrying out a mission to both Jews and Gentiles, in accordance with v. 17, through mentioning different areas where Jews and Gentiles predominate. The inclusion of "all the district of Judea" is striking because there is no previous indication of such a mission by Paul, nor does the account of Paul's departure from Jerusalem in 9:29–30 appear to leave a place for it. Verse 20 may be another place where a Lukan theme or pattern proves to be more important than the details in the previous narrative of Paul's actions.[38] In this case the pattern appears to be the Lord's commission to his first witnesses in 1:8,[39] where four areas of mission are also mentioned: "You shall be my witnesses not only in Jerusalem and in all Judea and Samaria but also to the end of the earth." The addition of "all the district of Judea (πᾶσαν . . . τὴν χώραν

---

[37] On 15:11 see above, 185–86.
[38] See the discussion above of the discrepancy between 26:16–18 and previous accounts of Paul's call. See also 28:17–18 and 345–46 below.
[39] Noted by R. O'Toole, *Christological Climax*, 82.

τῆς 'Ιουδαίας"; cf. "all Judea, πάσῃ τῇ 'Ιουδαίᾳ," in 1:8) to Paul's areas
of mission makes three of the four members correspond and emphasizes
Paul's concern with the Jewish homeland. The variant members of the
two lists are Samaria in 1:8 and Damascus, where Paul began his
preaching, in 26:20. Paul's mission after Damascus, as presented in
26:20, follows the course that Jesus prescribed for his witnesses in 1:8. It
begins in Jerusalem, spreads to the surrounding region, and then moves
out to encompass the world (a gigantic development that both statements
summarize in a brief phrase). Thus it is probable that Paul is being
presented as sharing the mission given to Jesus' first witnesses in 1:8.
Below we will also note echoes of Jesus' commission to his first witnesses
in Luke 24:44–48.

Paul understands this mission to be the direct cause of the attack upon
him by Jews in the temple (v. 21, "because of these things"). This attack,
then, represents a rejection of Paul's mission. In accordance with the
Lord's promise in v. 17, Paul has received "help from God" (v. 22). This
enables him to continue, even now as a prisoner standing before King
Agrippa, the work of witnessing to which he has been called. In v. 22 Paul
emphasizes the inclusiveness of this witness, not its ethnic or geographical
inclusiveness as in vv. 17 and 20 but its inclusion of all social ranks
("bearing witness both to small and to great"). It may be important to
make this clear before an audience composed primarily of the social elite.

Paul claims that his witness agrees with the predictions of Scripture,
both the prophets and Moses. It is a witness to the Messiah, whose
mission requires fulfillment of two conditions, namely, being subject to
suffering and beginning the resurrection of the dead.[40] On the basis of
these events he will then proclaim light to all, both Jews and Gentiles (v.
23). The conclusion of Paul's speech, as well as some earlier elements in
it, shows remarkable agreement with the risen Lord's solemn statement to
his first followers in Luke 24:44–48. There the Lord both reviewed his
own role and previewed the role of his witnesses, emphasizing that it was
necessary that Scripture be fulfilled (Luke 24:44–46; cf. Acts 26:22) and
dividing this fulfillment into three steps: the Messiah's suffering (παθεῖν,
Luke 24:46; cf. παθητός, Acts 26:23), resurrection from the dead (Luke
24:46; cf. Acts 26:23), and a proclamation to both Jews and Gentiles ("to
all the nations, beginning from Jerusalem," Luke 24:47; "to the people
and the Gentiles," Acts 26:23). In Luke the proclamation is in the
Messiah's name; in Acts it is the risen Messiah himself who proclaims. In

---

[40] I understand the repeated εἰ in v. 23 to express two conditions that the Messiah must fulfill
in order to complete his comprehensive saving work. Comparison with Luke 24:26 suggests
that the conditional constructions express a divine necessity, steps in the divine plan that the
Messiah must fulfill, like the ἔδει of Luke 24:26.

Luke Jesus' witnesses are to proclaim "repentance for release of sins"; in Acts the Messiah proclaims light, which is associated with repentance and release of sins earlier in the speech (Acts 26:18, 20). Jesus' statement in Luke that "you are witnesses of these things" (Luke 24:48) also parallels the appointment of Paul as witness in Acts 26:16. In these two passages we find a consistent view of mission that controls the understanding of Jesus, his first witnesses in Jerusalem, and Paul. This mission, like the death and resurrection of the Messiah, is grounded in Scripture, which discloses God's purpose of carrying salvation, including repentance and release of sins, to all peoples. This the Messiah will do through his chosen witnesses, who include the twelve apostles and Paul. In his speech before King Agrippa, Paul reports how the Lord made him a part of the mission given to the first witnesses. This mission is first of all the Messiah's mission. It is he who is proclaiming light, according to 26:23. The founder's mission continues through his witnesses; Paul's mission is a manifestation of this continuing mission of the Messiah.[41]

The conclusion of the speech in 26:22–23 shows that Moses and the prophets are being read christologically, with special attention to the death and resurrection of Jesus and the world mission to Jews and Gentiles. Earlier scenes, such as 2:14–36; 3:12–26; and 13:16–41, 47, demonstrate how scriptural argument could be brought to bear on these points. In the scene before King Agrippa, the reference to Scripture in 26:22 is related to v. 6 ("the promise to our fathers," recorded in Scripture) and prepares for v. 27, where Paul asks Agrippa if he believes the prophets. Furthermore, when Festus breaks in, moving the scene from speech to a concluding dialogue, he is probably reacting specifically to Paul's appeal to the Jewish Scripture. For him it has no authority, and he sees it as the source of Paul's madness. I am suggesting that Festus' reference to "the many letters" or "writings ($\tau\grave{a}$ $\pi o\lambda\lambda\grave{a}$ . . . $\gamma\rho\acute{a}\mu\mu\alpha\tau a$)" best fits the context if it is not a general reference to "great learning" (so RSV) but a specific reference to the Jewish Scriptures as the source of Paul's madness.[42]

Agrippa contrasts with Festus both in knowledge and belief (vv. 26–27). Paul turns back to him after correcting Festus. Agrippa's knowledge of the events of which Paul was speaking and his belief in the prophets provide an opportunity for Paul to speak boldly ($\pi\alpha\rho\rho\eta\sigma\iota\alpha\zeta\acute{o}\mu\epsilon\nu os$), which he proceeds to do by asking the king directly about his own belief in the prophets. Agrippa rightly understands this as an effort to convert him to the Christian way. The end of Acts will leave us with a picture of Paul,

---

[41] With the preceding paragraph see J. Dupont, *Nouvelles études*, 37–57, 446–56.

[42] On $\gamma\rho\acute{a}\mu\mu\alpha$ in the sense of "writing" or "book," see BAGD, s. v. 2.c.

still a prisoner, proclaiming and teaching "with all boldness (μετὰ πάσης παρρησίας)." The same view of Paul is presented more dramatically in the scene before King Agrippa. In both cases Paul shows boldness in his preaching in spite of his position as a prisoner. In Acts 26 he is even bold with a king.

Paul asks Agrippa whether he believes the prophets because he regards this as the key to acceptance of the Christian message as he has presented it. The question about belief in the prophets turns the previous emphasis on "the promise to our fathers" (v. 6) and the witness of the prophets and Moses (v. 22) into a personal challenge to Agrippa to become a Christian. This challenge is quite clear from Agrippa's reaction and Paul's final statement in v. 29. This observation confirms the fact that the emphasis on the Jewish hope, a repeated theme since 23:6, is not only defensive but also evangelistic in purpose. This was not at first apparent. Paul kept his hand concealed at first, speaking of resurrection in general, not of Jesus' resurrection. However, 25:19 shows that Paul had begun to speak of Jesus' resurrection at least by his trial before Festus, and Paul openly links the hope for resurrection to Jesus' resurrection in the climax of his speech before Agrippa (v. 23). In speaking to Agrippa, Paul moves from an emphasis on the hope of Israel to Jesus Messiah as the fulfillment of that hope, followed by a missionary appeal. Furthermore, Paul is not appealing to Agrippa alone. His challenge applies to "all those hearing me this day" (v. 29).

Ernst Haenchen claims that "Luke no longer hoped for the conversion of the Jews. . . . Although Paul speaks in Chapter 22 to the Jewish people, in 23 to the Sanhedrin and in 26 to King Agrippa, Luke with all this is not canvassing for a last-minute conversion."[43] I disagree. The vivid portrait of Paul seeking to convert a high-ranking Jew is more than a memorial to a lost past. Heroic figures (like Paul in Acts) inevitably become models of behavior, and Paul's farewell to the Ephesian elders (20:18–35) indicates awareness that Paul could be an effective model for the later church. Paul's exemplary behavior includes his dedicated witness to both Jews and Gentiles (cf. 20:21). The portrait of Paul before Agrippa has, in part, the same exemplary function.

The previous defense scenes lay the foundation for this portrait of Paul as model evangelist. The emphasis on resurrection and the Jewish hope carefully prepares for the proclamation of the risen Messiah in 26:23. The strategy is governed by awareness that common ground must be found before outsiders—especially the suspicious—will listen to a message about Jesus. Hope that some Jews might still accept the Christian mes-

---

[43] See *Acts,* 693.

sage is held open by the positive response of the Pharisees in 23:6–9 and the suggestion that Agrippa, who believes in the prophets, might thereby come to believe in Jesus Messiah. Paul appeals to Agrippa on the basis of the hope of Israel and the message of the prophets, that is, he appeals to him as a Jew. Paul is being presented as a dedicated and resourceful evangelist who is able to keep the mission to Jews alive in difficult times.

We must imagine the tone of Agrippa's response in v. 28. There are a number of possibilities, from simple surprise to sarcasm. In any case, Agrippa is seeking to turn aside Paul's appeal. Paul's reuse of Agrippa's phrase ἐν ὀλίγῳ ("in a little") seems to involve some witty interplay. If the expression is witty, the intent Paul expresses in v. 29 is quite serious. He wants all his hearers to find the light that found him, becoming what he is "except for these fetters." Paul's fetters are a dramatic emblem reminding us that Paul's bold appeal is being made while he remains a prisoner.

The principal figures withdraw, and there is a concluding conversation among them in which Paul's innocence is recognized. This final dialogue not only says something about Paul but also shows something about the officials. Once again, they are willing to declare Paul innocent after they have been conveniently relieved of responsibility for his case and can escape the political problems that freeing him might cause. The reference to "the king and the governor" in v. 30 might remind us of a saying of Jesus that Acts 26 fulfills remarkably well. To disciples led away "to kings and governors for my name's sake," Jesus promised, "it will lead to witnessing for you" (Luke 21:12–13). So it has for Paul.[44]

Acts 26 presents a climactic summary of Paul's mission as the narrator wants it to be remembered. Paul was called by the Lord to be his witness and thereby made a member of a chosen company stretching back to the scriptural prophets, a company through whom God's saving purpose in the world is being achieved. He was sent to both Jews and Gentiles, for the risen Messiah is charged with bringing God's salvation to both. Through Paul, eyes were opened to see the light of God's salvation, and people were freed from Satan's sovereignty to enjoy the sovereignty of God. They were called to repentance and received release of their sins. Although his mission exposed him to great danger from opponents, he received help from God to continue his work, and even as a prisoner he remained a bold witness for the risen Lord. The narrator helps us to envision this sort of mission by means of this dramatic scene and thereby provides both a defense of Paul against his detractors and a model for the later church.

---

[44] See R. O'Toole, "Luke's Notion of 'Be Imitators,'" 158–61.

THE VOYAGE TO ROME
AND GOD'S PROMISE
OF SALVATION FOR ALL

Why does the narrator tell in such vivid detail a story of storm and shipwreck? The only other voyage of Paul that is narrated in some detail is the last voyage to Jerusalem (20:6—21:16), and that account is mainly concerned with Paul's contacts with Christians at points along the way. There are, to be sure, other stories of adventure and rescue in Acts. The escape of Peter from prison, for instance, is a rescue story told with some vividness (12:1–19). However, this story of storm and shipwreck is longer and places Paul only intermittently in the spotlight. Paul intervenes at key points, but there is a great deal of attention to the actions of others. Julius the centurion has an important role, as do the sailors. Their efforts to save the ship are carefully noted, and these efforts are not simply the foil for divine rescue. They do not simply demonstrate the uselessness of human action.

The intermittent appearance of Paul in this episode has led to the supposition that the narrator has inserted Pauline scenes into a narrative that originally did not concern Paul at all, or in which Paul had the purely passive role of a prisoner.[1] Our task, however, is not to create a different narrative by removing parts of the present one but to see whether the present narrative may have a significant purpose or effect if considered as a whole. We must consider how the various parts interrelate and contribute to significant developments. Because this is a story of danger and rescue, we can begin by looking for indications of developing danger and also note factors that will bring the ship's company to safety. Furthermore, we must pay attention to the roles of the chief actors: Julius and his soldiers, the sailors, and Paul. In addition, a group of Christian companions of Paul designated as "we" (the "first person peripheral narrator"[2] of this section), some prisoners traveling with Paul, and perhaps

---

[1] H. Conzelmann, *Acts*, 216–21, and G. Schneider, *Apostelgeschichte* 2:387, follow M. Dibelius, *Studies in the Acts*, 204–5, in regarding the references to Paul in 27:9–11, 21–26, 31, 33–36, 43 as Lukan insertions into a prior source.

[2] A phrase used by Susan Praeder to indicate that the narrator, although a participant who is affected by events, is a passive observer rather than a principal actor in these events. See *Narrative Voyage*, 89.

some other passengers make up the company that survives this dangerous voyage.

The centurion Julius is introduced at the beginning of the episode, and v. 3 indicates his friendly attitude toward Paul, who is permitted to visit his friends in Sidon. The chief function of v. 3 is to establish a positive relationship between Julius and Paul. The visit in Sidon has no further function in the plot, but the relationship between Julius and Paul does. We will discover that the friendship and trust between Julius and Paul contribute to the rescue of the whole ship's company.

The voyage continues from Sidon, but there are numerous indications in vv. 4–8 that it is not going well. "The winds were contrary" (v. 4). From Myra they were "sailing slowly" and "with difficulty" came to Cnidus. Because "the wind did not permit us to go further," they sailed under the lee of Crete. Even so they sailed along it "with difficulty," arriving at a place with the ironic name "Good Harbors" (vv. 7–8), a place that was not a good harbor for spending the winter (v. 12). By that time the voyage was becoming dangerous because the season of safe sailing was coming to an end (v. 9). The significance of these indications of difficulty and danger crystallizes when Paul intervenes for the first time with his advice in v. 10. He predicts a disaster if the voyage continues, including much loss of life. We are not told the source of Paul's conviction. There is no reference here to a message from the Lord, the Spirit, or an angel. Perhaps this makes it easier for Paul to modify his prediction later, indicating that the ship will be lost but there will be no loss of life (v. 22). Even though there is no reference to a divine source for Paul's warning, we should take it seriously because Paul has repeatedly been presented as a perceptive and reliable person. Paul's warning prepares us, as hearers and readers, for what is coming. Skilled readers have learned to suspect that items are not included in a narrative unless they have some function in plot or characterization. In this case, it is likely that the warning of a disaster is included because it proved essentially true, and this is soon confirmed.[3] Paul's warning separates him from the foolish decision that is about to be made.[4] It is also a test of the relationship of Paul and Julius, a test that Julius fails. In v. 11 the narrator focuses on the centurion's decision as if it were the key decision. Julius may have treated Paul well previously, but he is not yet ready to trust Paul's judgment. So the ship sails off, to be caught at sea by

---

[3] S. Praeder, comparing other ancient stories of storm and shipwreck, says, "As a rule, forecasters of storm and shipwreck find no more favor with fellow sailors, passengers, or officers than Paul finds. . . . Another rule of forecasts of storm and shipwreck is that they are followed by storms and/or shipwrecks." See "Sea Voyages," 690.

[4] See S. Praeder, *Narrative Voyage,* 228: "Predictions prejudice implied audiences against those who decide to set sail."

the storm. Paul's first intervention is unsuccessful, which permits the crisis to develop.

The gentle south wind is seductive. The sailors falsely conclude that their goal of gaining a better harbor is now all but accomplished (v. 13). When the storm hits, the possibility of maneuvering the ship is greatly reduced. The crew must surrender to the storm and let the ship be carried along. The crew (perhaps with the help of the "we" group in v. 16) do what skilled sailors can to save the ship. When an islet provides brief shelter, the ship's boat is secured. Emergency measures are taken to strengthen the ship, and a sea anchor is put out to slow the ship lest it drift on the shoals of Syrtis (v. 17). As the storm continues, the ship is lightened in two stages, the last consisting of casting overboard the ship's spare tackle (vv. 18–19). By that time all has been done that can be done. These measures show skilled seamanship, but the storm continues unabated, and there is no way of calculating their course, as sun and stars are hidden. "Finally, all hope of our being saved was being taken away" (v. 20). Human skill has done what it can, and the ship is still a helpless victim of the storm. As the storm continues, hope gradually dissolves.

At this low point in the narrative, Paul intervenes a second time.[5] Although he reminds his audience of their failure to listen to his previous advice, his main purpose is to revive the hope and courage of a company that has lost hope.[6] He urges them "to cheer up" or "take heart" (εὐθυμεῖν, v. 22; cf. v. 25). Paul can encourage others because he himself has been encouraged by an angel, who said, "Do not fear" (v. 24) and assured him that it is still God's plan for him to reach Rome and stand before Caesar. Furthermore, the angel said, "God has granted you all those sailing with you." The whole ship's company will be rescued, a major modification of what Paul expected according to his earlier warning in v. 10. The reference to God granting something to Paul may suggest that this is a response to intercessory prayer.[7] If so, Paul, as well as the sailors, has been doing something for the safety of all. The announcement that all will

---

[5] Reinhard Kratz notes that Acts 27 shifts between scenes that heighten the danger and scenes in which Paul responds to this danger. See *Rettungswunder*, 323. My following discussion of the storm at sea is largely taken from a section of my article "Paul outside the Christian Ghetto: Stories of Intercultural Conflict and Cooperation in Acts," in *Text and Logos: The Humanistic Interpretation of the New Testament: Essays in Honor of Hendrikus Wouterus Boers*, edited by Theodore W. Jennings, Jr. (Atlanta: Scholars Press, forthcoming). Used by permission.

[6] H. Conzelmann complains that a speech delivered in the midst of a raging storm "is completely unreal." See *Acts*, 218. Nevertheless, it has an important literary function and follows a convention of storm scenes, as S. Praeder indicates. She says, "The usual place for such speeches is at a high point in the storm and a low point in the fortunes of the sea travelers." Paul's speech is unusual in conveying a message of hope. See "Sea Voyages," 696.

[7] So G. Schneider, *Apostelgeschichte* 2:393, n. 76.

survive is remarkable. If the narrator were simply interested in bringing Paul to Rome under divine protection, it would be an unnecessary complication to refer to the rescue of all, especially as this requires correction of Paul's previous warning. This announcement is a key to understanding the rest of the episode, for it determines what must happen, and the acts of sailors, soldiers, and Paul are to be judged in light of it. From this point on, no method of escape is acceptable that doesn't include all. Opportunities arise for the sailors to escape, abandoning the rest (v. 30), and for the soldiers to escape after killing their prisoners (v. 42). These plans are thwarted, in spite of the risk involved in trying to get the large ship close to shore and allowing prisoners to swim for their lives when they might escape. These plans are wrong not only because they endanger Paul but also because they offend against the divine plan of saving all.

Paul identifies the angel as "an angel of the God whose I am, whom I also serve" (or "worship," v. 23). He refers in this way to his own God because the majority of his audience has other gods. Thus the "all" who are promised rescue consist primarily of pagans who do not worship the one God. Nevertheless, God has decided to rescue them.

There is no indication that Paul's encouraging message has an immediate effect on his audience. The narrative continues with the approach of the island, which, although it fits Paul's prediction in v. 26, produces fear (v. 29), not encouragement. The sailors are afraid that the ship will run aground against sharp rocks. Paul's efforts to revive hope are successful only after a further intervention, when the ship's company finally does take heart (εὔθυμοι . . . γενόμενοι, v. 36), as Paul had earlier urged (vv. 22, 25). With the approach of land, the technical skills of the sailors, also noted previously in the narrative, come into play. They sense the approach of land. They confirm that shallows are approaching by taking soundings. Then they throw out four anchors from the stern to keep the ship from drifting onto rocks in the middle of the night. In all of this they are acting for the benefit of the whole ship's company. Then, however, they do something that both demonstrates disloyalty to the rest of the seafarers and failure to trust Paul's promise that God would provide a way for all to be saved. They try to "flee" from the ship in the small boat, on "pretext" of stretching out further anchors from the bow. Paul recognizes their plan in time, tells the centurion and soldiers, and the soldiers cut the ropes, letting the boat drift ashore. This is a drastic move because the boat might have been useful the next day. If nothing is done, however, the boat will only help the fleeing sailors, who are abandoning the others in a ship they cannot handle. The ship can carry all, and the divine plan is that all should be saved. The sailors are needed to sail the ship. Without them there is no hope of bringing it safely to shore. The boat must be sacrificed so that all will have a chance. Paul's alertness and the soldiers' swift action make it possible for all to reach safety.

Ernst Haenchen rejects the narrator's statement of the sailors' intentions in v. 30, asserting that "no seaman would think of leaving the safety of the ship in a boat to get to an unknown and rocky coast at night." Therefore, they must really have been planning to lay additional anchors, and the soldiers cut the boat's ropes because they mistook the sailors' intentions.[8] The story is not quite as unrealistic as Haenchen believes, for we need not accept his assumption that the sailors were sure that the ship was safely anchored for the night. The fact that they were "wishing" (or "praying," $ηὔχοντο$) that day would come (v. 29) suggests considerable anxiety about the anchors holding. Haenchen's interpretation is interesting as an illustration of how the assumption that the original story must have been realistic can combine with the license granted by historical criticism to chop up the text, resulting in a new story more to the reader's liking.

Already in v. 21 we were told that the ship's company was not eating. Seasickness in the storm could have been the cause, but there may also be a link between the loss of hope in v. 20 and the failure to eat in v. 21. The latter view is strengthened by the scene in vv. 33–38, for which v. 21 is preparation. Paul urges all to eat and begins to eat himself. The decision of the others to eat is accompanied by a change of mood; all were "taking heart" (v. 36). It is Paul who causes this change. So we find Paul, shortly before the final effort to reach shore safely, urging all to take nourishment and break their long fast. He supports his exhortation with a reason, which includes a renewed promise that all will be saved. They must eat, for it will contribute to their "salvation, for a hair from the head of none of you will perish" (v. 34). It is finally this promise plus Paul's own action that overcomes the hopelessness indicated in v. 20, replacing it with new hope and courage.

Paul takes the lead and begins to eat. The description of this is remarkable, for it echoes accounts of other significant meals in Luke-Acts: "Taking bread, he gave thanks ($εὐχαρίστησεν$) to God before all, and breaking it, he began to eat" (v. 35). The sequence of taking bread, giving thanks or blessing, and breaking the bread is also found in Luke 9:16 (Jesus feeding the multitude), 22:19 (the last supper), and 24:30 (the meal at Emmaus). Furthermore, the church's meal celebration in Acts is called the breaking of bread (Acts 2:42, 46; 20:7, 11). The reference to giving thanks makes Acts 27:35 particularly close to Jesus' last supper, and the reference to the number of participants and the indication that they were

---

[8] See *Acts*, 706, 710.

filled in vv. 37–38 are reminiscent of the feeding of the multitude (Luke 9:14, 17). The details of Paul's actions in Acts 27:35 are not necessary parts of the narrative. They could easily have been omitted if they did not have special significance. The narrative invites us to picture Paul doing what Jesus did and what the church does: give thanks to God by breaking bread and eating.

Paul's meal, then, is as sacramental as any other meal in Luke-Acts. However, the fact that Paul is eating with pagans has proved troublesome for this interpretation. Bo Reicke, who argued for the sacramental associations of this scene in 1948, nevertheless added that it could not be a real Lord's Supper because Paul is eating with pagans. Rather, Paul is allowing the people in the ship to participate in a prefiguration of the Christian Lord's Supper as preparation for later discipleship.[9] The absence of an indication that Paul distributed the bread over which he had given thanks is probably significant. Gerhard Schneider, who recognizes the eucharistic associations of this scene, is technically correct in saying that it does not depict a common meal, for Paul eats his food and the rest of the company other food.[10] To that extent the privacy of the church's celebration is maintained. The remarkable thing, however, is the effect that Paul's Eucharist has on his non-Christian companions. By eating before them, Paul finally achieves his goal of encouraging them. They take nourishment and strengthen themselves for the final effort to reach shore safely.

The promise of rescue for all in v. 24 is echoed by repeated references to all in vv. 33–37. Paul urges all to take nourishment (v. 33). He promises that a hair of none of them will perish (v. 34). He gives thanks before all (v. 35). Then all take heart (v. 36). Finally, v. 37 indicates, "All the lives in the ship, we were two hundred seventy-six." The "we" in the voyage to Rome generally refers to a small group of Christians. Here, however, the entire ship's company becomes a single "we" as the narrator numbers the company so that readers will know what "all" means. Even though the boundary of the church is not completely eliminated, the meal on the ship is an act that benefits all, Christian and non-Christian, and an act in which community is created across religious lines.

The meal can do this because of its association with God's promise for all. In v. 34 Paul repeats the angel's promise of v. 24 in other language. Then Paul takes bread and gives thanks to God. In the present context Paul's thanksgiving has particular significance. It is thanksgiving especially for God's promise of the rescue of all. Therefore, it is also an act of

---

[9] See "Mahlzeit mit Paulus," 408–9.
[10] See *Apostelgeschichte* 2:396.

trust in this promise in spite of the immediate danger. There may even be
a play on words to support a connection with the promise. The angel
announced that God "has graciously granted (κεχάρισται)" all to Paul. In
response Paul "gave thanks (εὐχαρίστησεν)."[11] Paul's gratitude and trust
are infectious. The others take heart and eat, showing the first signs that
they, too, believe in the promise.[12]

Even though the others do not share Paul's food, celebrating Eucharist
"before all" so that all will eat shows a remarkable concern to benefit non-
Christians through a central Christian practice. The use of the hyperbole
of the hair of the head in v. 34 is also remarkable. It parallels a promise of
Jesus in Luke 21:18, but there the promise applied to persecuted disciples.
Here the promise is stretched to include all, in accordance with the
repeated references to the salvation of all in the voyage narrative.

Paul told the centurion and soldiers, "Unless these [sailors] remain in
the ship, you cannot be saved" (v. 31). Paul also urged the others to eat
because this would contribute to their "salvation" (v. 34). He is referring,
of course, to being saved or rescued from the sea. These verses are part of
an emphasized theme, for there are seven references to being saved from
the sea in this section of Acts, using the verbs σῴζω (27:20, 31) and
διασῴζω (27:43, 44; 28:1, 4) and the noun σωτηρία (27:34). The rapid
repetition of the same word in 27:43, 44; 28:1 is a particular sign of
emphasis. These words are found in other accounts of sea voyages in
ancient literature.[13] Therefore, ancient readers would not find them to be
unnatural in their context. But Susan Praeder rightly discerns a double
sense in these words. She emphasizes that narratives are both created from
and read in light of a real world context of "experience and imagination"
that enters literary expression. Two such contexts have taken literary
shape and are particularly relevant to reading Acts 27:1—28:15: the
imaginative experience of ancient sea voyages expressed in sea voyage
literature and the imaginative experience of first-century Christianity as
expressed in Luke-Acts.[14] These two contexts suggest a double reading of
the thematic emphasis on salvation or rescue. In the former context the
hope for rescue from the sea is a natural part of the experience of a sea
voyage, when danger arises. The salvation or rescue may come from
various human and divine sources. In the latter context salvation takes on
a special significance. It is not only the hope of those in a storm at sea but
the purpose of God for all humanity, as announced at the beginning of

---

[11] See S. Praeder, "Sea Voyages," 698.

[12] Craig McMahan argues that "the meal shared between Paul and his shipmates constitutes
them as a community under God's protection" and that this meal is like the Lord's Supper
in serving "to constitute the covenant community and to anticipate the promised salvation."
See *Meals as Type-Scenes*, 258, 260.

[13] See S. Praeder, *Narrative Voyage*, 245–56.

[14] See *Narrative Voyage*, 95–99, 183–312.

Luke (2:30–32; 3:6). The emphasis on salvation in Luke-Acts gives to the emphasis on salvation in this sea voyage a second, symbolic sense.[15]

The narrative hints at a second sense by emphasis within the story of the voyage and by the theological importance of the terms "save, salvation" in Luke-Acts as a whole. However, the narrative does not determine for us how far we should take its suggestion. Even if we wish to remain close to the Lukan world of thought, there are two interesting possibilities to consider. First, not only does the emphasis on salvation in the voyage echo the emphasis on salvation in Luke-Acts as a whole but also the insistence that all the ship's company must be saved echoes the promise that "all flesh will see the salvation of God" in Luke 3:6.[16] Thus the fulfillment of God's promise to Paul that all those in the ship will survive the storm becomes a sign in miniature of God's promise of salvation for all flesh, which has not yet been fulfilled. Paul is conscious that he is speaking mainly to pagans when he shares God's promise with those on board the ship.[17] This unconverted audience is promised salvation from the sea. Paul makes no reference to faith in Jesus Christ as a precondition. God graciously grants salvation to all on the ship, not because of their works or their faith, but simply because it fits God's purpose. In fact, the whole narrative of the voyage to Rome is remarkable for the absence of any indication that Paul proclaimed Jesus either to his companions on the ship or to the people of Malta. The benefits that God brings through Paul do not depend on acceptance of this message. In Rome Paul will continue his work as a missionary. He has not changed his mind on the importance of this work, but the voyage narrative presents a more comprehensive vision of God's saving work, which is not limited to those who hear and accept the gospel. The mission continues within the context of this vision.

To be sure, there is little evidence outside Acts 27 that Luke-Acts anticipates the salvation of every individual. One could argue that in the context of Luke-Acts the promise to "all flesh" is a promise to large numbers of people of all kinds, but not necessarily to every individual. Indeed, the reference to "as many as were ordained to eternal life" in Acts 13:48 suggests that there are some who are not ordained to eternal life. However, if salvation in Paul's voyage to Rome does have a second level of

---

[15] G. Schneider, *Apostelgeschichte* 2:396, n. 107, recognizes that the use of the term elsewhere in Acts suggests that σωτηρία in v. 34 is "transparent" to a meaning larger than rescue from the sea. On the use of the word group "save, salvation" in Luke-Acts, see Augustin George, *Études sur l'oeuvre de Luc*, 307–20. George, however, regards the occurrences in the voyage to Rome as simply profane uses.

[16] On Luke 3:6 see *Narrative Unity* 1:40–42, where I argue that seeing God's salvation means recognizing it and responding to it, which shade over into personal participation in it. In the Lukan context Luke 3:6 (= Isa. 40:5) refers to participation in salvation by both Jews (including Jewish outcasts) and Gentiles.

[17] As noted above, Paul in v. 23 must distinguish the God he is talking about from other deities.

meaning, this section of Acts represents a new boldness of hope that anticipates salvation (in some sense) for every individual of a pluralistic community and views persons such as Paul as mediators of this promise. We cannot assume that the implied author reached theological clarity on this issue and held one view consistently. Furthermore, the nature of this salvation is not clarified. The larger Lukan context suggests that it has a second level of meaning that exceeds rescue from a storm, and the voyage narrative indicates that this salvation reaches even unconverted pagans. These observations still leave various options of interpretation, stretching from the view that Christianity is an occasional benefactor of society at large to a universalism that includes every creature in God's ultimate salvation.

Reflection on this story of the salvation of all may also move in a second direction. In the voyage narrative a remarkable amount of attention is given to the cooperative relationship between Paul and Julius the centurion and to the contributions that various parties—the sailors, Julius, and Paul—make to finally reaching safety. God's role in events is explicit only at one place: Paul receives a message from God through an angel (vv. 23-24). This message is important because it conveys a promise that enables humans to take heart and because it points to the goal toward which humans must work. Human decision and action are crucial in reaching this goal. As Paul said to the centurion, "Unless these [sailors] remain in the ship, you cannot be saved" (v. 31). Therefore, the soldiers must act. Human actions that work toward the rescue of all are acceptable contributions to the realization of God's purpose, but actions that seek the safety of one's own group while abandoning others will block this purpose until corrected. When the parties in the ship work together cooperatively for the good of all, dangers are avoided and the ship's company is finally saved. In the ship Paul and his Christian companions are a small minority within a largely pagan company, but survival depends on each party acting for the good of all. Paul does this when he warns Julius that the sailors are abandoning the ship and when he eats before all. Julius does this when he stops the soldiers from killing the prisoners, who might escape (vv. 42-43). The sailors do this when they stick to their tasks in the ship. Working together and for each other, they reach the safety that God had promised.

The implied author's interest in such a narrative could arise from concern about the role of a Christian minority in Roman society. The Christian movement is very important in the eyes of the implied author, but it will remain a minority for the foreseeable future. The possibility of salvation in the social and political sphere depends on Christians and non-Christians being willing to follow the lead of Paul, Julius, and the sailors, when they are acting for the good of all. Perhaps the Christian prophet, like Paul, will have a special role in conveying an understanding of what is possible and promised by God, but non-Christians also have important roles.

Following the meal the rejuvenated company moves into action. Remaining cargo is cast overboard so that the ship will have the best chance of passing over shoals. The efforts of the sailors (mentioned simply as "they" in vv. 39–41) are described in detail. In spite of their previous attempt to abandon the ship, they now do their duty for the good of all and steer the ship toward a beach. However, this is not a familiar harbor. The ship runs aground, and the stern begins to break up. Paul has helped by prophetic encouragement, enabling the company to respond to their situation in light of the divine promise. The sailors have done their part by protecting the ship in the storm and taking it as far as possible toward the beach. Still there is danger. The ship is breaking up and the soldiers decide to kill the prisoners, lest they escape. The soldiers, like the sailors, forget in the crisis that God's promise is for all, and they plan to save themselves by eliminating others. The community of all with mutual responsibilities is about to be violated a second time. At this point Julius the centurion makes an important contribution to the rescue. "Wishing to save Paul," he stops the soldiers and organizes the escape from ship to shore, making it possible for all to reach safety.[18] Julius' friendship with Paul makes a crucial difference at this point; he saves not only Paul but also the other prisoners. His friendly attitude was demonstrated at the very beginning of the voyage (v. 3), and the relationship was probably strengthened when Paul helped the soldiers and then the whole ship's company in vv. 31 and 33–36. Paul is a benefactor of the others on this voyage,[19] but he is also benefited. His benefits return to him as the centurion intervenes to save his life. Of course, this is part of God's care for Paul, who must stand before Caesar (v. 24), but the narrative gives careful attention to the ways that other persons contribute to and are benefited by this aspect of God's purpose. The storm narrative ends with a significant summary: "And thus it happened that all were saved (διασωθῆναι) upon the land" (v. 44). "Thus," that is, through these human actions, God's promise was fulfilled.

---

[18] H. Conzelmann, *Acts*, 221, asks whether ἐπί τινων in v. 44 should be understood as masculine, referring to the fact that some of the nonswimmers were brought ashore "on some," that is, on the shoulders of some taller persons. This might explain the shift to the genitive case following the second ἐπί. If we follow Conzelmann's suggestion, we would have a further indication that mutual concern led to the safety of all. However, it is uncertain whether τινων is neuter, referring to parts of the ship, or masculine, referring to persons.

[19] Emphasized by G. Krodel, *Acts*, 470.

The first report of events on the island emphasizes the φιλανθρωπία (kindness or friendliness toward fellow human beings) of the island's inhabitants (28:2). These people are βάρβαροι, "barbarians," who do not speak Greek or share the dominant culture of the Greco-Roman world. Yet they show unusual kindness to the strangers from the shipwreck. The friendly reception parallels the behavior of the centurion Julius, who at the very beginning of his association with Paul treats him in a kindly and friendly fashion (φιλανθρώπως, 27:3). The human kindness of Julius and the natives on the beach continues to be demonstrated by the inhabitants of Malta. Publius, the chief man of the island, receives the ship's company as his guests for three days "in a friendly manner (φιλοφρόνως)" (28:7). Both Publius and the natives on the beach help the shipwrecked party before Paul demonstrates any special powers in their presence. They are responding to the need of fellow human beings. The warm reception and helpfulness of the islanders continue after Paul's healings (28:10). The unusual emphasis on the friendly reception continues the emphasis on friendship and cooperation as key factors in saving the ship, but now a new group is included, the inhabitants of the island. Like the soldiers and sailors on the ship, the new group is not Christian.

Out of kindness toward fellow human beings, the islanders supply warmth, hospitality, and supplies for the later journey. Paul will reciprocate by healing the sick of the island. He does not do this as part of an evangelistic mission, for there is no reference to preaching or conversions. Paul is simply showing the same human kindness that the islanders showed him. Thus both the stormy voyage and the stay on Malta present suggestive images of cooperative relationships between Christians and non-Christians, to the benefit of all. On Malta the non-Christians are first to show their kindness. Although Paul is being unjustly held as a prisoner, the narrative undermines any tendency for Christians to regard the world in general as hostile and evil.

When Paul is putting brushwood on the fire, a viper seizes his hand (28:3). The following verses provide an interesting portrait of the natives of Malta. Their first, ignorant reactions to Paul are expressed in vv. 4 and 6. These verses deliberately present the perspective of the natives—what they saw, what they expected, what they said in response—and are not to be taken as indications of the views of the implied author.[20] The reference to Paul as a god in v. 6, which some have seen as striking evidence that the narrator views Paul as a "divine man,"[21] simply continues the portrait of

---

[20] Rightly emphasized by S. Praeder, "Sea Voyages," 702.

[21] Commenting on v. 6, H. Conzelmann says, "The incident is the most extreme example of the θεῖος ἀνήρ, 'divine man,' motif in Acts." See *Acts,* 223.

the natives as ignorant and prone to mistaken views. They leap to several hasty conclusions. First Paul is regarded as a murderer who is getting his just retribution even though he escaped from the sea. When Paul is not harmed by the viper, they reach the equally false conclusion that he is a god. Their pagan religious conceptions are reflected both in the reference to "Justice," an avenging goddess, in v. 4 and to Paul as a god in human disguise in v. 6. To be sure, when Paul and Barnabas were mistaken for gods in Lystra, they reacted strongly, correcting this false impression (14:11–18). There is no such correction following 28:6. The narrator evidently thought that the points just noted were sufficient indication that these natives were not reliable theologians. If the narrator wished to present Paul as a missionary preacher on Malta, it would be convenient to have him react to the mistaken views of the Maltese. This, in fact, is the way that false adulation of Peter and Paul functions in 3:11–16 and 14:11–18. Correction of these false views is part of missionary preaching, which points to the name of Jesus as the true source of power and the one God as the only true God.[22] We have seen, however, that the voyage to Rome is concerned not with missionary preaching but with the cooperative relationships that are possible between Christianity and pagan society. In this context pagans are allowed to be pagans.

The natives attribute Paul's expected death to "Justice," who avenges murder. They change their mind when he does not die. This reference to avenging Justice provides some support for the interpreters who understand the scenes of rescue from the sea and survival of snakebite as attestation of Paul's innocence.[23] Because a sea voyage was viewed as a prime opportunity for the gods to bring retribution upon the guilty, one could argue that a safe voyage was a sign of innocence. Survival of shipwreck, however, would be ambiguous evidence. Perhaps the storm was a sign of divine wrath. When the Maltese see the viper on Paul's hand, they are sure that he is being pursued by avenging Justice. The lack of any harmful effect, however, attests Paul's innocence.

Indeed, Paul proves to be a benefactor of the island during his three-month stay. After Paul healed the father of Publius, the rest of the sick on the island were coming to him and being healed (vv. 8–9). The account of Paul's healings on Malta is quite similar to the account of Jesus' healings at Capernaum at the beginning of his ministry (Luke 4:38–40). In both cases the healing of an individual is followed by the healing of "all" or "the rest" in a region. The individual, a relative of the healer's host, has been

---

[22] See G. Krodel, *Acts*, 480.

[23] See Gary Miles and Garry Trompf, "Luke and Antiphon," 259–67. Their argument is developed more fully by David Ladouceur, "Hellenistic Preconceptions of Shipwreck and Pollution," 435–49.

"seized ($\sigma v v \epsilon \chi o \mu \acute{\epsilon} v \eta$, $\sigma v v \epsilon \chi \acute{o} \mu \epsilon v o v$)" by fever. There is also reference to laying on of hands.[24] The similarities show that Jesus' healing ministry still continues through his witnesses, with benefit both to the host who receives the healer and to the whole community. A scene from the beginning of Jesus' ministry is echoed in the last description of healing in Acts, suggesting a chiastic relationship.

The narrative of the final stage of the trip to Rome in 28:11–16 is similar to the narrative of Paul's trip to Jerusalem in 20:1—21:17, although it is much shorter. In both cases the stages of the journey are carefully noted, and there is special attention to Paul's contacts with local believers along the way. As in Troas and Tyre, Paul stays with the believers in Puteoli seven days (20:6; 21:4; 28:14). A special point is made of the willingness of the Roman believers to meet Paul outside Rome and escort him to it. There is no attempt in Acts to portray Paul as the founder of Christianity in Rome.[25] Rather, it is important to the narrator that Paul is recognized and welcomed by Christians in the cities he visits after the conclusion of his missionary work in the east.

Acts 27—28 prepare the ending of Acts by providing final reflections on Paul's relations to both Jews and Gentiles. The problem of the Jews receives the climactic position as the final major scene. The voyage indicates that the narrator is also reflecting on Paul's relation to the large gentile world unaffected by Judaism. Both aspects of the narrative suggest the situation that Paul will leave behind. The major scene in Rome shows the persistence of rejection in the Jewish community, although individual Jews may still respond to Paul's message. The voyage to Rome includes a number of remarkably friendly receptions by Gentiles. Paul makes no attempt to gain conversions among these friendly people, but their open attitude is encouraging for a future mission. There are great opportunities among these Gentiles, whether they are people of status like Publius or the ordinary folk who lit the fire after the shipwreck. Paul will emphasize these opportunities in his last quoted words, in which he says that the salvation of God has been sent to the Gentiles and "they will hear" (28:28). Paul is not guaranteeing a gentile mission without problems. He himself remains a prisoner of the Romans, and the portrait of the natives of Malta shows that they have far to go in understanding and accepting central affirmations of Christian preaching. With Jews and God-fearers there is a foundation on which the missionary may build. That was lacking among the natives of Malta, and Paul's difficulties in Lystra (14:11–18), the scoffing of Athenian philosophers (17:18, 32), and the

---

[24] See further S. Praeder, *Narrative Voyage,* 153–54, and S. Praeder, "Sea Voyages," 702–3.

[25] Against E. Haenchen, *Acts,* 720, and H. Conzelmann, *Acts,* 224.

outburst of Festus (26:24) reflect the same problem. Nevertheless, good relations with Gentiles are possible. Indeed, there are Gentiles who are willing to listen to the church's message if they are approached by a missionary with the resourcefulness and dedication of Paul.

Luke-Acts is basically a story about a mission. Acts 28:28 comments on the mission's future. The narrative prepares for this comment by reports of the Gentiles' friendly response to Paul on the voyage and the Roman Jews' contrasting response. When we recognize the careful reflection on the possibilities of mission among both Gentiles and Jews in Acts 27—28, the impression that the ending of Acts is abrupt and unsuitable is considerably reduced.[26]

---

[26] On this question see further below, 353–57. S. Praeder makes a similar suggestion but refers to the mission's past. She says, "The purpose of Acts 27–28 seems to be to retrace the course of the Pauline mission to Gentiles and Jews in Acts and with it to review the universal course of first-century Christianity." See "Sea Voyages," 705–6.

PAUL AND
THE ROMAN JEWS

The last major scene in Acts presents neither Paul's trial before Caesar nor Paul's relationship to the Christian community of Rome. It focuses on Paul's message to the Roman Jews.[1] The final scene of a narrative is an opportunity to clarify central aspects of plot and characterization in the preceding story and to make a final, lasting impression on the readers. The fact that the narrator has chosen to end the work with a scene that focuses on Paul's encounter with Jews shows how extraordinarily important the issues of this encounter are to the narrator. We must recognize, however, that this final scene of Acts is actually a double scene (28:17–22, 23–28) in which Paul makes two important statements to the Roman Jews. When we acknowledge the importance of both of these statements and allow them to resonate against each other, we will see that Acts' portrait of Paul in relation to Israel is richer and more complex than often thought.

Paul's statement in 28:17–20 is a summary of the preceding trial narrative and imprisonment speeches in Acts 22—26. It presents what the narrator most wants readers to retain from that long narrative. Paul claims that he was recognized as innocent of any serious crime when examined by the Romans (28:18; cf. 23:28–29; 25:25; 26:31–32). Primary emphasis falls, however, on Paul's claim that he has "done nothing opposed to the people or the customs received from the fathers" (28:17). Such charges were made in 21:21, 28; 24:5–6, and Paul previously denied them in 25:8, 10 (cf. 24:14–15). He also assures the Roman Jews that in his appeal to Caesar he does not intend to bring an accusation against his own nation (28:19). Thus considerable stress is placed on Paul's loyalty to Israel and its way of life, and this shows continuing concern with the charges that Paul is anti-Jewish, charges that surfaced as soon as Paul reached Jerusalem in Acts 21. In 28:17 Paul is not merely saying that he is a loyal Jew like many others. He is asserting that his mission has not

---

[1] Portions of the following section are a revision of part of a previously published essay, R. Tannehill, "Rejection by Jews and Turning to Gentiles," in *Society of Biblical Literature 1986 Seminar Papers*, edited by Kent Harold Richards (Atlanta: Scholars Press, 1986), 135–41. Used by permission.

been an anti-Jewish movement. Furthermore, he remains loyal to his people in spite of the opposition he has experienced from many of his fellow Jews. Indeed, he says, "Because of the hope of Israel I wear this chain" (28:20). This statement shows the narrator's talent for presenting a vivid picture in words. It is meant to be a memorable picture that conveys the narrator's message: Paul's mission and imprisonment are acts of loyalty to Israel. In the first subscene Paul's statement begins with his claim that he has done nothing opposed to Israel or the law; it ends with his claim that he is a prisoner for the hope of Israel, thus emphasizing these two related claims of loyalty.

The theme of Israel's hope also helps to reveal the tragic irony of Israel's situation. In 26:7 Paul emphasized the Jews' intense hope in the promise and then said that he is now being accused by Jews concerning this same hope. The very hope so eagerly sought is rejected when it appears. This is ironic; it is also tragic, for Israel is losing what rightly belongs to it. The same tragic irony is conveyed by the image of Paul in chains for the hope of Israel in 28:20. The messenger who proclaims the fulfillment of Israel's hope should be honored by Israel. Instead, Paul wears a chain because of his faithfulness to Israel's hope. This means suffering for Paul. It is an even greater tragedy for Israel.[2] This sense of tragic irony carries over into the second subscene (28:23-28) of Paul's encounter with the Jews of Rome and is forcefully expressed through the quotation from Isaiah.

Paul briefly reviews the course of events since he became a prisoner. His summary of these events suggests a parallel between his own experience and Jesus' arrest and trial. He says, "I was delivered into the hands of the Romans." Because this took place "from Jerusalem," Paul may be referring to his transfer to Caesarea, and the "Romans" are the Roman governor and his officials. Paul does not say that the Jews delivered him up. The phrase "delivered into the hands ($\pi\alpha\rho\epsilon\delta\delta\theta\eta\nu$ $\epsilon\dot{\iota}s$ $\tau\dot{\alpha}s$ $\chi\epsilon\hat{\iota}\rho\alpha s$)" echoes Jesus' passion predictions (Luke 9:44; 18:32; cf. 24:7), which also influenced the prediction of Paul's sufferings in Acts 21:11. The parallel with Jesus is developed in 28:18-19 even though this causes Paul's statement to depart from the previous account of Paul's trials. It is true that Roman officials recognized Paul's innocence and Jewish leaders were pressing for his condemnation, according to the previous account. Thus the alignments for and against Paul were essentially as stated. However, vv. 18-19 make it appear that the Jews objected to an expressed intention by Roman officials to release Paul. This presentation fits the trial of Jesus

---

[2] On the tragic aspect of Israel's story in Luke-Acts, see R. Tannehill, "Israel in Luke-Acts," 69-85.

better than the trial of Paul, for Roman officials did not state an intention to release Paul but only recognized his innocence after they were no longer responsible for deciding Paul's case. Jewish pressure came not as objections to an announced plan of release but in accusations against Paul and in the political power that could make Roman governors want to grant the high priest and his supporters a "favor" (24:27; 25:9). However, the description fits Jesus' trial before Pilate quite well. After "examining (ἀνακρίνας)" (Luke 23:14; cf. Acts 28:18: ἀνακρίναντες), Pilate found "nothing worthy of death" (Luke 23:15; cf. Acts 28:18: "no reason for death") and announced that he would "release (ἀπολύσω)" him (Luke 23:16; cf. Luke 23:20: "wishing to release"; Acts 28:18: "they were wanting to release [ἀπολῦσαι] me"). To this the high priests, rulers, and people loudly objected (Luke 23:18; cf. Acts 28:19).[3] The echoes of Jesus' trial reinforce the portrait of Paul as a true follower of Jesus in facing the same sort of rejection and suffering, a portrait that has been clearly emerging since 21:11.

There are other suggestive reminders of the Jesus story in the last chapter of Acts. Not only does Paul's experience as a prisoner recapitulate Jesus' experience of rejection and suffering but also the mission of Jesus, his healing and his message, continue in Paul. We noted previously that the last recorded healings in Acts echo the early healing work of Jesus (see Luke 4:38-40 with Acts 28:8-9).[4] Now we should note that the content of Paul's preaching in Rome, like the content of Jesus' preaching, is "the reign of God" (Acts 28:23, 31; see the summary statements in Luke 4:43-44; 8:1). Jacques Dupont has pointed out that the "reign of God" occurs primarily in connection with the preaching of Paul in Acts.[5] The phrase "reign of God" links preaching in Acts to the preaching of Jesus, and it is primarily Paul's preaching that is so linked.[6] This link is especially clear at the end of Acts, where both summaries of Paul's preaching contain this key phrase. Jesus' mission of healing and proclaiming continues through Paul, and with it the experience of rejection and suffering.

The second subscene (28:23-28) reminds us of previous occasions when Paul responded to Jewish resistance by announcing a turn to the Gentiles (13:45-47; 18:6; see also 19:9). However, there are some differences. Paul is not preaching in a synagogue. This change, to be sure, simply reflects Paul's imprisonment. Paul cannot go to the synagogue, but he still ad-

---

[3] W. Radl, *Paulus und Jesus*, 252-65, and S. Praeder, *Narrative Voyage*, 160-61, discuss these parallels.

[4] See above, 341-42.

[5] See 14:22; 19:8; 20:25; 28:23, 31. The only other reference to Jesus' followers preaching the reign of God in Acts is in 8:12 (Philip).

[6] See J. Dupont, *Nouvelles études*, 128.

dresses a Jewish assembly. The difference in the description of the Jews'
reaction may be more significant. Instead of a report that Paul turns to the
Gentiles when there is public reviling or blaspheming, we are simply told
that the Jews disagreed among themselves, some being persuaded and
some disbelieving (28:24). Paul's reaction makes clear that his intensive
efforts ("from early morning until evening") have not been successful, so it
is unlikely that the reference to some "being persuaded ($\epsilon \pi \epsilon i \theta o \nu \tau o$)"
means that they have committed themselves to the Christian way. Prob-
ably the use of the imperfect is significant; they were in process of being
persuaded but had made no lasting decision.[7] Why would the narrator
want to say this when the scene is building up to the bitter words of
Isaiah? Use of the quotation would seem most justified if the rejection is
total. Furthermore, if the scene's purpose is to show that there is no longer
any hope of convincing Jews and the church must now concentrate exclusively on the gentile mission,[8] the point is undermined by portraying part
of the Jewish assembly on the verge of acceptance. The reference to some
being persuaded indicates that there is still hope of convincing some Jews
in spite of what Paul is about to say about the Jewish community of
Rome. Although the Jewish community, operating as a social entity controlled by its leadership, is deaf and blind, there are still those within it
who are open to the Christian message. This openness appears through
the text's description of the Jewish reaction as less completely negative
than we might expect.

The harsh words of the quotation are nevertheless appropriate. Paul's
preaching on this day was a special opportunity to speak to the Jewish
community of Rome, which is now departing without accepting Paul's
witness. The presence of disagreement among the Jews is enough to show
that Paul has not achieved what he sought. He was seeking a communal
decision, a recognition by the Jewish community as a whole that Jesus is
the fulfillment of the Jewish hope. The presence of significant opposition
shows that this is not going to happen. Previous scenes have shown that
the opposition of some can make preaching to the Jewish assembly impossible. Paul's closing statement in 28:25–28 is a response to this hard fact.

In spite of their failure to accept his witness, Paul still has a message for
the Roman Jews. He must take the role of the prophet Isaiah and repeat
his words,[9] words so bitter for both prophet and people that Isaiah cried

---

[7] This is the conclusion of Hermann Hauser, *Abschlusserzählung*, 64–66.

[8] See H. Conzelmann, *Acts*, 227: The scene is meant to show "that the situation with the
Jews was hopeless. . . . The time of the Gentile church has now broken in—this church has
taken possession of the inheritance of Israel."

[9] Paul is portrayed as a prophet on the model of the scriptural prophets through applying
Septuagintal language from prophetic calls to him. See Acts 18:6 (cf. Ezek. 33:4); 18:9–10
(cf. Jer. 1:7–8); 26:16–18 (cf. Ezek. 2:1, 3; Jer. 1:7–8; Isa. 42:6–7). In speaking the harsh

out, "How long?" (Isa. 6:11). Isaiah's words are full of ironic tension that expresses the tension in the plot of Acts at its end. Through repeated and emphatic statements, the people are told of a highly unnatural situation: ears, eyes, and heart, which are meant for hearing, seeing, and understanding, have lost their power to perceive. This unnatural state, in which the organs of perception contradict their own purpose, has blocked God's desire to "heal them," a desire that a perceptive people would gladly embrace. Yet God is not finished speaking to this people, for it is the prophet's uncomfortable task to show unbelieving Israel its self-contradiction. He is told to "go to this people and say" the bitter and anguished words that disclose Israel's failure. The command to go and speak is addressed to the prophet, not to the people, and it would not have been necessary to include this command in the quotation. However, its inclusion emphasizes the role of the prophet, who must not abandon the disobedient Jews but must speak to them about their disobedience. Both prophet and people are caught in a tragic situation, for the prophet is commanded to speak to a people that cannot understand, a seemingly hopeless task. Paul assumes this prophetic task. He again speaks to Israel, trying to make the people see their blindness and hear their deafness.

Acts ends on a tragic, not a triumphant note. This is not lessened by 28:28. The function of these concluding words about the Gentiles is not to justify the gentile mission, which has been done long ago, but to jar the Roman Jews by the contrast between their deafness and the Gentiles' readiness to hear. This verse is addressed to the Roman Jews ("Let it be known to you . . . "). It says, "They will hear," although you do not. This ironic reversal is strengthened by noting that Paul's announcement is a striking shift from his earlier announcement in the Antioch synagogue. There he proclaimed, "To us the word of this salvation has been sent out ($\dot{\epsilon}\xi\alpha\pi\epsilon\sigma\tau\dot{\alpha}\lambda\eta$)" (13:26), but to Jews who are deaf and blind he says, "To the Gentiles has been sent ($\dot{\alpha}\pi\epsilon\sigma\tau\dot{\alpha}\lambda\eta$) this salvation of God; *they* ($\alpha\dot{\upsilon}\tau o\dot{\iota}$) will hear."

That the close of Acts is not triumphant but tragic and anguished in tone becomes clear when we compare this scene with the purpose of God announced earlier in Luke-Acts.[10] This purpose of God provides continuity to the whole story, for all central figures are working to achieve

---

words in Acts 28:26–27, Paul is fulfilling a prophetic role well established in Israel's Scripture, where prophetic indictments of the people are common.

[10] David Moessner, "Ironic Fulfillment," 48–49, regards "tragedy" as a "misnomer" if we view the story of Israel from the perspective of the divine intention. He says, "It is exactly through the hostility against and suffering of a part of Israel, the servant, that Israel as a whole is and will be gathered." The implied author may hold on to such a hope, but the story must stop without reporting its fulfillment. The tragedy may not be ultimate, but it is still keenly felt because events do not seem to be leading to the expected gathering of Israel.

this purpose. It also establishes the norms that determine what is success and what is failure.[11] Paul's final words to the Roman Jews contain reminders of previous statements about God's purpose. The phrase "this salvation of God (τοῦτο τὸ σωτήριον τοῦ θεοῦ)" uses a neuter word for salvation, a word that is rare in the New Testament.[12] It is a reminder of promises of Isaiah quoted or paraphrased in the Lukan birth narrative, where the same rare neuter form is found (Luke 2:30; 3:6).[13] Both of these passages speak of *seeing* this salvation (σωτήριον) of God. Both speak of an inclusive salvation that will embrace Jews and Gentiles. "All flesh will see the salvation of God" (Luke 3:6). It is prepared for "all the peoples," both the "Gentiles" and "Israel" (Luke 2:30–32).[14]

However, Acts ends with a quotation from Isaiah that stands in strong tension with the promises of God in Isaiah that are highlighted in the Lukan birth narrative. Again there is reference to seeing, but the Jews of Rome fail to see; they have closed their eyes. They are unable to hear. It is the Gentiles who will hear the message of "this salvation of God." This result conflicts with God's purpose that "all flesh," including Israel, "see God's salvation." God's purpose has been blocked by human resistance, at least temporarily. Paul's commission indicates that he shares in the failure. He was sent to both Jews and Gentiles "to open their eyes" so that they might share in the "light" that the Messiah brings (Acts 26:17–18, 23).[15] Now he must confirm that the people have closed their eyes. To this extent his mission is a failure. There have, of course, been previous indications of success among both Jews and Gentiles, and the dark picture at the end of Acts is somewhat brightened by the reference to opportunity among the Gentiles and by the concluding picture of Paul faithfully continuing his preaching in spite of all difficulties. Nevertheless, the chief emphasis of the end of Acts is on the unsolved problem of Jewish rejection.

Early in Luke there were anticipations of Jewish rejection. It is possible that some of these anticipations are now reflected in the closing scene. Following his celebration of God's saving purpose, Simeon added a more somber prophecy: Jesus would be a "sign being spoken against (σημεῖον ἀντιλεγόμενον)" (Luke 2:34). The verb "speak against (ἀντιλέγω)" recurs in Acts in connection with Jewish resistance in 4:14 and 13:45 and

---

[11] See *Narrative Unity* 1:21–22.

[12] Apart from the three uses in Luke-Acts, it is found only in Eph. 6:17.

[13] J. Dupont noted this connection between the beginning of Luke and the end of Acts. See *Salvation of the Gentiles,* 14–16. See also V. Stolle, *Zeuge als Angeklagter,* 86–87, n. 108.

[14] On these two passages see further *Narrative Unity* 1:39–43.

[15] On these passages see above, 322–24. This interpretation of Paul's mission and the interpretation of God's purpose in Luke 1—2 make it impossible to accept the view of Jack T. Sanders, who reads the final scene of Acts as evidence that the Jews "were never the intended recipients of God's salvation." See *Jews in Luke-Acts,* 80.

then is used twice in the final scene (28:19, 22).[16] In the last case it is recognized that such resistance is appearing "everywhere." Furthermore, Jesus' inaugural sermon referred to Isaiah's prophecies of renewed sight, but the scene ended with Jesus' angry neighbors threatening his life.[17] The Jewish resistance anticipated early in Luke persists to the end of Acts, where it receives special emphasis.

Paul is speaking to the Jews of Rome, not to Jews everywhere. Yet the theme of Jewish rejection, followed by mission to the Gentiles, is highlighted in major scenes near the beginning (13:14–52) and at the end of Paul's mission and is repeated in other scenes. These connected scenes suggest a pattern or trend, even though there are exceptions. Building a pattern through individual scenes allows the narrator to avoid the implication that Jewish response was always the same, while suggesting the direction in which events are moving.

In previous scenes the announcement of turning to the Gentiles did not exclude renewed Jewish mission in other cities. Nothing prevents us from understanding the announcement in 28:28 as applying to Rome and leaving open the possibility of preaching to Jews elsewhere. Yet such an announcement at the end of a narrative carries extra weight. Just because the narrative ends, the narrator grants the final situation a certain permanence. The narrator may have been willing to do this because the possibility of Christians preaching to a Jewish assembly, such as Paul addressed in Rome, has become very remote.

Nevertheless, there are signs of the narrator's concern to keep a mission to Jews alive in spite of this situation. Even after Paul is forced to abandon his preaching in the synagogues of Corinth and Ephesus (in the former case, announcing that he is going "to the Gentiles" [18:6]), the narrator indicates that the mission reaches Jews of those cities (18:8; 19:10, 17–18).[18] In Ephesus, especially, there is indication of a preaching mission to Jews after Paul leaves the synagogue. There Paul preached for two years, with the result that "all those inhabiting Asia heard the word of the Lord, both Jews and Greeks" (19:10). This remark is placed after Paul's withdrawal from the synagogue. The Jews mentioned cannot be limited to those encountered in the synagogue of Ephesus before Paul's departure. Even if we allow for exaggeration, we must recognize that Paul's continuing preaching brought him in contact with a much wider circle of

---

[16] Beyond the passages cited, the word is found in Luke-Acts only in Luke 20:27, where the reading is uncertain, and in Luke 21:15.

[17] On Luke 4:16–30, see *Narrative Unity* 1:60–73. Donald Miesner believes that Luke 4:14–30 and Acts 28:17–31 are parallel. See "Circumferential Speeches," 234.

[18] These passages are noted by H. Hauser, *Abschlusserzählung*, 109.

Jews than those who attended the synagogue of Ephesus.[19] Paul's continuing mission to both Jews and Gentiles in Ephesus provides a precedent for his continuing mission in Rome, described in 28:30–31.

We have already noted that there are individuals within the Jewish community in Rome who show openness toward the Christian message (28:24). We have also noted that the lengthy imprisonment narrative presents Paul as a Jew who continues to witness to Jews in spite of their vigorous attempts to do away with him, and I have suggested that in this as in other respects Paul is a model for later evangelists.[20] The summary of Paul's continuing preaching in 28:30–31 provides some additional evidence. After the preceding contrast between Jews and Gentiles, the reference in v. 30 to Paul welcoming "all" those coming to him should not be dismissed as an idle remark. According to v. 24, some of the Jews Paul had addressed were being persuaded by his message. Their initial interest provides a motivation for some of them coming to talk to him later. All who came, whether Jews or Gentiles, were welcomed by Paul, v. 30 indicates. Note that Paul's preaching and teaching to them focus on "the reign of God" and "the things concerning the Lord Jesus Messiah." These are also the themes of Paul's preaching to the Roman Jews in 28:23. The narrator is aware that the mission cannot begin with pure Gentiles in the same way as Jews, as the distinctiveness of Paul's words in Lystra (14:15–17) and Athens (17:22–31) show. Yet Paul in Rome continues to preach the themes with which he had addressed the Jews, suggesting that Jews are at least included in his audience.

Paul's themes of "the reign of God" and "the Lord Jesus Messiah" reflect the original Jewish setting of the mission. "The reign of God" is a central theme of Jesus' preaching in its Jewish context, and in Acts "reign ($\beta\alpha\sigma\iota\lambda\epsilon\acute{\iota}\alpha$)" continues to occur primarily in statements addressed to Jews or to Christian communities (1:3, 6; 14:22; 19:8; 20:25; 28:23).[21] Some Jewish background is important for preaching God's reign because it is connected in Luke-Acts with Jesus' own reign as the Davidic Messiah. Lukan interest in Jesus' kingship appears in Luke 19:38; 22:29–30; 23:42 and in the passages that present Jesus as the successor to David's throne (Luke 1:32–33, 69–70; Acts 2:25–36; 13:22–23, 32–37). The centrality of Jesus' kingship in God's reign explains the repeated dual description of

---

[19] See F. Pereira, *Ephesus: Climax of Universalism*. Pereira emphasizes that Paul's lengthy mission in Ephesus is, according to Acts, a universal mission, directed at the same time to Jews and Gentiles.

[20] See above, 327–29.

[21] The Christian communities (see 14:22; 20:25) would include Gentiles, but there would also be opportunity to instruct them in such Jewish matters. The only additional reference to "reign" is in preaching to Samaritans (8:12).

the preacher's message in Acts 8:12; 28:23, 31. The message concerns both
God's reign and Jesus. The missionaries are not preaching about two
separate things; they are preaching about the realization of God's reign
through the enthronement of Jesus at God's right hand as royal Messiah.

It is sometimes noted that the reference to "the reign of God" in 28:31
forms an inclusion with the similar reference in 1:3.[22] The reference in
28:31 to the "Lord Jesus Messiah" also forms an inclusion with the
climax of the Pentecost speech in 2:36. "The Lord Jesus Messiah" briefly
summarizes Peter's proclamation of Jesus as "both Lord and Messiah,"
Messiah because he fulfills God's oath to David and Lord because he is
seated at God's right hand. Paul repeated this proclamation (with variations) in his synagogue sermon in Acts 13. At the end of Acts Paul is
presented as faithfully continuing the message that he and Peter preached
to the Jews in the major sermons near the beginning of the narratives
about their ministries.[23] The situation has changed in that Paul can no
longer speak in synagogues or to the Jews assembled as a community, but
he continues to welcome all people who are willing to hear his message,
including Jews.

The indication in 28:24 that some Jews are receptive and the description of Paul's activity in 28:30–31 both suggest that Paul's audience
continues to include Jews, and this view is supported by the precedent of
Paul's preaching in Ephesus after leaving the synagogue (19:10). Furthermore, this interpretation fits the portrait of Paul's mission as a whole.
To the very end Paul remains faithful to the Lord's calling to bear witness
to both Jews and Gentiles (9:15; 22:15; 26:16–18; cf. 26:23). Neither
Jewish rejection nor Roman imprisonment prevents him from preaching
"with all boldness" in response to this call. The final verses of Acts picture
Paul doing what he told the Ephesian elders he must do: complete his
ministry from the Lord in spite of the threat of death, a ministry of
witnessing to both Jews and Greeks (cf. 20:21, 24). This is the image of
Paul with which the narrator chooses to leave us.

Discussion of the Lukan attitude toward Israel must take account of
two fundamental points: a persistent concern with the realization of
scriptural promises that, the narrator recognizes, apply first of all to the
Jewish people, and the stinging experience of rejection of the message that
the hope of Israel is now being fulfilled. The resulting tension, especially
apparent in the tension between the promise in the Antioch sermon and
the bitter words at the end of Acts, is not resolved in the narrative. Acts

---

[22] See, e.g., H. Hauser, *Abschlusserzählung*, 118.

[23] According to J. Dupont, *Nouvelles études*, 487, Paul's sermon in the Antioch synagogue
gives an idea of the contents of Paul's preaching to the Roman Jews, briefly summarized in
28:23. I would add that Paul is still repeating the same message in 28:31.

offers no solution except the patient and persistent preaching of the gospel in hope that the situation will change.

The narrator expects the mission to move forward, especially among the Gentiles, but the ending of Acts is far from glib optimism. Paul continues his preaching but only after highlighting Jewish blindness and deafness. The circumstances of his mission must also be considered. He is still a prisoner, unable to circulate freely,[24] and his life is still in jeopardy. That Paul is able to preach and teach "unhindered" when visitors come is a great thing under the circumstances, but Paul must continue to endure Jewish rejection and Roman imprisonment. The final verse may suggest that for bold preachers like Paul there will be opportunities even in difficult circumstances, but the narrative does not ignore the difficult circumstances.[25]

My first volume concluded with a discussion of "closure and openness" at the end of Luke. Both terms also apply to the end of Acts. That Acts does not report Paul's trial before Caesar nor its result may seem to be a striking case of openness because the trial is the overt reason for Paul's trip to Rome and an appearance before Caesar was clearly predicted (27:24). Some scholars have found such openness intolerable in a conclusion and have sought to explain why Acts remained incomplete.[26] However, there are also strong indications of closure in the present ending, as we will note below. The resulting combination of closure and openness should not be regarded as surprising, even in ancient literature.[27] Nor does willingness to leave open certain elements of the plot necessarily represent a literary virtue.[28] In Acts the final fate of Paul is not recorded, but it is doubtful that the narrator intended to be mysterious. There are sufficient foreshadowings to enable the addressees of the work to complete what is missing. The narrator's art appears, rather, in fine control of the focus of the work in order to leave those final impressions that best fit its main concerns.

In discussing the relation of the ending of a narrative to its beginning

---

[24] Rightly noted by R. Cassidy, *Society and Politics*, 131 and n. 29.

[25] This point is even clearer if we accept R. Cassidy's interpretation of "unhindered (ἀκωλύτως)." He links it to the preceding phrase "with all boldness," understanding it as a further indication of Paul's attitude. He was "unhindered in spirit, undaunted" by his imprisonment. See *Society and Politics*, 134 and n. 37.

[26] H. Conzelmann, *Acts,* 228, discusses (and rejects) theories that Luke planned a third book or that Acts was written before Paul's trial ended.

[27] J. L. Magness discusses at length endings of ancient narratives, including portions of the Old and New Testament, that are to some degree open or "suspended." See *Sense and Absence,* 25–85. Note also the parallels mentioned by H. Cadbury, *Making of Luke-Acts,* 322–23.

[28] M. Torgovnick notes that the recent vogue of open endings in modern fiction has already become familiar and tired. Rather than extolling openness as a virtue, she asks whether the ending emerges "from the work as inevitable and right." See *Closure in the Novel,* 206.

and middle, Marianna Torgovnick distinguishes between circularity (the end recalls the beginning), parallelism (the end refers to a series of earlier points in the narrative, not just the beginning), and incompletion (the end omits one or more elements important for complete closure).[29] The ending of Acts illustrates all three of these approaches. I will first discuss indications of circularity and parallelism and then return to the issue of incompletion or openness.

Through circularity and parallelism, 28:17-31 serves as conclusion for these expanding stretches of narrative: (1) the arrest at Jerusalem and defense scenes, (2) the mission of Paul, (3) the whole of Acts, (4) the whole of Luke-Acts.[30] We have already noted some of the evidence. With reference to item (1): Paul's first statement to the Roman Jews serves as a summary and review of the defense scenes in Jerusalem and Caesarea (21:27—26:32). In circular fashion Paul's reference to the people and the ancestral customs in 28:17 recalls the initial accusation in 21:28. The reference to the hope of Israel in 28:20, concluding Paul's first statement, parallels the repeated references to hope and resurrection in the defense scenes (23:6; 24:15, 21; 26:6-8, 23), once again emphasizing this theme. (2) The sequence of preaching, resistance, and parting announcement in 28:23-28, especially the final verse, recalls the first major presentation of Paul's preaching and its result, the scene in Antioch of Pisidia (13:14-52). We have noted the contrast between 28:28 and 13:26 ("To us [Jews and God-fearers] the word of this salvation has been sent out") and the similarity between 28:28 and the announcement of turning to the Gentiles in 13:46. However, there are also parallels to what happened in Corinth (18:5-6) and Ephesus (19:8-9). (3) As to connections with the beginning of Acts, the emphasis on the reign of God in Paul's preaching in 28:23, 31, may be a particular reminder of the references to the reign of God in 1:3 and to the reign for Israel in 1:6. There are, to be sure, other references to the reign of God in Paul's preaching. The reference to salvation for the Gentiles in 28:28 anticipates the continued fulfillment through Paul and others of the mission given to Jesus' first followers in 1:8, the mission to be Jesus' "witnesses . . . to the end of the earth."[31] Paul's announcement in 13:47 showed that he applied this commission to himself, and at the end of Acts he is still working to do his part in fulfilling it. (4) Finally, there are connections with the narrative of Jesus in Luke's Gospel and specifically with its beginning. The summary in 28:17-19 links Paul to Jesus' arrest

---

[29] See *Closure in the Novel,* 13.

[30] J. Dupont, *Nouvelles études,* 483-509, discusses the relation of Acts 28:17-31 to these same four stretches of narrative, presenting the evidence somewhat differently and more fully.

[31] In 28:23 Paul is "witnessing (διαμαρτυρόμενος)" to Jews, but this is part of his comprehensive task of being Jesus' "witness . . . to all persons" (22:15).

and trial, the reference to Paul preaching the reign of God links Paul's message to Jesus' message, and we noted a parallel between Paul's and Jesus' miracles earlier in 28:8–9 (cf. Luke 4:38–40). Thus the end of Acts relates Paul to Jesus' message, miracles, and fate. The reference to the "salvation (σωτήριον)" of God in 28:28 takes us back to the beginning of Luke, where the same word was twice used in key announcements of God's purpose (2:30; 3:6). Jacques Dupont strengthens this connection by noting that both 2:30–34 and 3:4–9 add indications of resistance in Israel.[32] The contrast between the failure to see in Acts 28:26–27 and the reference to seeing God's salvation in Luke 2:30 and 3:6 is also important.

The multiple connections with key aspects of the earlier story bring the narrative to appropriate closure through circularity and parallelism. However, there is also significant openness at the end. The narrator allows readers and hearers to complete Paul's personal story in their own imaginations. Earlier parts of the narrative encourage this completion and also provide guidance. We have been led to believe that Paul would not only arrive in Rome (19:21) and bear witness there (23:11) but also stand before Caesar (27:24). Because the major obstacles of the threatened return to Jerusalem (25:3, 9) and the storm at sea have been overcome and no further obstacles are apparent, we assume that Paul does stand before Caesar. Furthermore, we have a good idea of Paul's conduct at this trial. He presents his case as he did in his previous trials, and he demonstrates the same courage and boldness that he demonstrated then and during his preaching as a prisoner at Rome (28:31). Paul's past conduct, revealing firm character, allows us to anticipate what is not written.

The narrative also provides a basis for anticipating the outcome of Paul's trial. We have noted the inclination of high Roman officials to follow political expediency rather than the requirements of justice.[33] Furthermore, in his farewell speech Paul told the Ephesian elders that they would see his face no more (20:25). This announcement produced demonstrative grief (20:37–38). It was accompanied by intimations of death. The journey he was undertaking involved renouncing life as something precious to himself in order to "complete my course" (20:24).[34] The further echoes of Jesus' passion on Paul's journey (see 21:11, 13–14) have greatest force if this journey did lead to Paul's death, even if not in Jerusalem. Thus Paul's death is foreshadowed in his farewell speech, and the echoes of Jesus' way to the cross also suggest that the pattern will be completed by violent death.[35]

---

[32] See *Nouvelles études*, 508–9.

[33] See above, 302–3, 306–8.

[34] Note the similar phrase applied to John the Baptist in 13:25.

[35] J. L. Magness refers to "suggestive foreshadowing" and "suggestive patterning" as two of

An additional argument from silence has some value in this case. If Paul had been released, this would provide the crowning evidence that the Romans really recognized Paul's innocence all along. If he were able to continue his work in new areas, this would add to the picture of Paul as world missionary, and a summary indication of his further work could have been easily added. Something happened after the two years mentioned in 28:30; it was probably not release and continued work.

Thus Paul's death is anticipated, but the ending of Acts leads away from contemplation of that harsh fact to focus on other things. Therefore, it does not highlight the injustice of Paul's death, making a final anti-government statement. Nor does it highlight martyrdom as a heroic act, as ending either with Paul's death or with a sentence of death in Caesar's trial could easily do.[36] Rather, the end of Acts directs attention to the missionary situation that Paul leaves behind and to Paul's courage and faithfulness as example for the church. It points to the opportunity among the Gentiles.[37] It underscores the crisis in the Jewish mission. It presents Paul continuing his mission by welcoming all, both Jews and Gentiles, and speaking to them "with all boldness" in spite of Jewish rejection and Roman imprisonment. This is the concluding picture of Paul's legacy.

Marianna Torgovnick indicates that "endings invite the retrospective analysis of a text and create the illusion of life halted and poised for analysis."[38] The ending of Acts invites retrospective consideration of the preceding narrative in light of the factors just mentioned.

The lack of a report of Paul's final trial and death is not the only indication of openness at the end of Acts. The narrative awakens other important expectations whose fulfillment cannot be reported. These include the completion of the mission "to the end of the earth,"[39] and the judgment of the world in righteousness by Jesus (17:31; cf. 10:42). We are reminded of one other unfulfilled expectation by the scene of Paul preaching to the Jews of Rome: the promise of salvation to the Jewish people. This expectation not only requires more time; its realization has become problematic because of Jewish rejection. Here lies the real openness of the

---

three ways that a narrative may help us to complete a suspended ending. See *Sense and Absence*, 80, 87, 107–8. In discussing the ending of Acts, Magness points to the release of Peter from prison in 12:1–17 as providing a structural pattern that suggests Paul's release at the end of Acts. See *Sense and Absence*, 85. However, the pattern of Jesus' passion is much more prominent, not only during the journey to Jerusalem but also at the end of Acts itself (28:17–19). This pattern includes death.

[36] The narrator is interested in Paul's bold witness before high Roman officials but is content to drop that interest at the end, allowing the appearance before Agrippa and Festus, rather than an appearance before Caesar, to be the climactic instance.

[37] There is preparation for this in the sea voyage narrative. See above, 342–43.

[38] See *Closure in the Novel*, 209.

[39] "The end of the earth" is not a reference to Rome. See above, 17–18, 108–9.

ending of Acts. The narrative provides a basis for completing Paul's personal story, but it does not provide a solution to the problem of Jewish rejection. Indeed, the highlighted Scripture quotations (important clues to the narrator's understanding of God's purpose) reinforce the unresolved tension with which the narrative ends, for the narrative began with the assurance that "all flesh will see the salvation of God" (Luke 3:6) but ends with the recognition that "they have closed their eyes, lest they see with the eyes," which would bring healing and a share in God's salvation (Acts 28:27–28). Because God is God, hope remains that God's comprehensive saving purpose will somehow be realized, but there is no indication of how that can happen. In the meantime, Acts can only suggest that the church welcome those Jews who are still willing to listen and continue its mission to the more responsive gentile world.

Bibliography

Adams, David Robert. *The Suffering of Paul and the Dynamics of Luke-Acts.* Ph.D. diss., Yale University, 1979.

Alter, Robert. *The Art of Biblical Narrative.* New York: Basic Books, 1981.

Anderson, Janice Capel. "Double and Triple Stories, the Implied Reader, and Redundancy in Matthew." *Semeia* 31 (1985): 71–89.

Aristotle. *The Nicomachean Ethics,* with an English translation by H. Rackham. Loeb Classical Library. Cambridge: Harvard University Press, 1962.

———. *The Poetics,* with an English translation by W. Hamilton Fyfe. Loeb Classical Library. Cambridge: Harvard University Press, 1960.

Auffret, Pierre. "Essai sur la structure littéraire du discours d'Athènes (Ac XVII 23–31)." *Novum Testamentum* 20 (1978): 185–202.

Aune, David E. *The New Testament in Its Literary Environment.* Library of Early Christianity 8. Philadelphia: Westminster Press, 1987.

Bachmann, Michael. *Jerusalem und der Tempel: Die geographisch-theologischen Elemente in der lukanischen Sicht des jüdischen Kultzentrums.* Beiträge zur Wissenschaft vom Alten und Neuen Testament. Stuttgart: Verlag W. Kohlhammer, 1980.

Balch, David L. "Acts as Hellenistic Historiography." Pp. 429–32 in *Society of Biblical Literature 1985 Seminar Papers,* edited by Kent Harold Richards. Atlanta: Scholars Press, 1985.

Barr, David L. *New Testament Story: An Introduction.* Belmont, Calif.: Wadsworth Publishing Co., 1987

Barr, David L., and Wentling, Judith L. "The Conventions of Classical Biography and the Genre of Luke-Acts: A Preliminary Study." Pp. 63–88 in *Luke-Acts: New Perspectives from the Society of Biblical Literature Seminar,* edited by Charles H. Talbert. New York: Crossroad, 1984.

Barrett, C. K. *Luke the Historian in Recent Study.* London: Epworth Press, 1961.

———. "Paul's Speech on the Areopagus." Pp. 69–77 in *New Testament Christianity for Africa and the World: Essays in Honour of Harry Sawyerr,* edited by Mark Glasswell and Edward Fasholé-Luke. London: SPCK, 1974.

———. "Paul's Address to the Ephesian Elders." Pp. 107–21 in *God's Christ and His People: Studies in Honour of Nils Alstrup Dahl,* edited by Jacob Jervell and Wayne A. Meeks. Oslo: Universitetsforlaget, 1977.

———. "Light on the Holy Spirit from Simon Magus (Acts 8, 4–25)." Pp. 281–95 in *Les Actes des Apôtres: Traditions, rédaction, théologie,* edited by J. Kremer. Bibliotheca Ephemeridum Theologicarum Lovaniensium 48. Gembloux: J. Duculot & Leuven: Leuven University Press, 1979.

———. "Apollos and the Twelve Disciples of Ephesus." Pp. 29–39 in *The New Testament Age: Essays in Honor of Bo Reicke,* edited by William C. Weinrich, vol. 1. Macon, Ga.: Mercer University Press, 1984.

———. "Faith and Eschatology in Acts 3." Pp. 1–17 in *Glaube und Eschatologie: Festschrift für W. G. Kümmel,* edited by Erich Grässer and Otto Merk. Tübingen: J. C. B. Mohr, 1985.

358

———. "Paul Shipwrecked." Pp. 51–64 in *Scripture: Meaning and Method. Essays Presented to Anthony Tyrrell Hanson,* edited by Barry P. Thompson. Hull: Hull University Press, 1987.

Barthes, Roland. "L'analyse structurale du récit à propos d'Actes X-XI." *Recherches de Science Religieuse* 58 (1970): 17–37.

Bassler, Jouette M. "Luke and Paul on Impartiality." *Biblica* 66 (1985): 546–52.

Bauer, Walter. *A Greek-English Lexicon of the New Testament and Other Early Christian Literature,* translated and adapted by William F. Arndt and F. Wilbur Gingrich. 2d ed. revised and augmented by F. Wilbur Gingrich and Frederick W. Danker. Chicago: University of Chicago Press, 1979.

Betz, Otto. "Die Vision des Paulus im Tempel von Jerusalem: Apg 22, 17–21 als Beitrag zur Deutung des Damaskuserlebnisses." Pp. 113–23 in *Verborum Veritas: Festschrift für Gustav Stählin,* edited by Otto Böcher and Klaus Haacker. Wuppertal: Theologischer Verlag Rolf Brockhaus, 1970.

Beydon, France. "Luc et 'ces dames de la haute société.'" *Études Théologiques et Religieuses* 61 (1986): 331–41.

Bihler, Johannes. *Die Stephanusgeschichte.* Münchener theologische Studien. Munich: Max Hueber Verlag, 1963.

Black, C. Clifton, II. "The Rhetorical Form of the Hellenistic Jewish and Early Christian Sermon: A Response to Lawrence Wills." *Harvard Theological Review* 81 (1988): 1–18.

Blass, F., and Debrunner, A. *A Greek Grammar of the New Testament and Other Early Christian Literature.* Translated and revised by Robert W. Funk. Chicago: University of Chicago Press, 1961.

Blomberg, Craig L. "The Law in Luke-Acts." *Journal for the Study of the New Testament* 22 (1984): 53–80.

Bock, Darrell L. *Proclamation from Prophecy and Pattern: Lucan Old Testament Christology.* Journal for the Study of the New Testament Supplement Series 12. Sheffield: JSOT Press, 1987.

Boismard, M.-É. "Le martyre d'Étienne Actes 6,8—8,2." *Recherches de Science Religieuse* 69 (1981): 181–94.

Boismard, M.-É., and Lamouille, A. *Le texte occidental des Actes des Apôtres: Reconstitution et réhabilitation.* 2 vols. Paris: Éditions Recherche sur les Civilisations, 1984.

Booth, Wayne C. *The Rhetoric of Fiction.* 2d ed. Chicago: University of Chicago Press, 1983.

Bornkamm, Günther. "The Missionary Stance of Paul in I Corinthians 9 and in Acts." Pp. 194–207 in *Studies in Luke-Acts: Essays Presented in Honor of Paul Schubert,* edited by Leander E. Keck and J. Louis Martyn. Nashville: Abingdon Press, 1966. (Reprint. Philadelphia: Fortress Press, 1980.)

Bovon, François. "L'importance des médiations dans le projet théologique de Luc." *New Testament Studies* 21 (1974–75): 23–39.

———. "Le Saint-Esprit, l'Église et les relations humaines selon Actes 20, 36—21, 16." Pp. 339–58 in *Les Actes des Apôtres: Traditions, rédaction, théologie,* edited by J. Kremer. Bibliotheca Ephemeridum Theologicarum Lovaniensium 48. Gembloux: J. Duculot & Leuven: Leuven University Press, 1979.

———. "Le Dieu de Luc." *Recherches de Science Religieuse* 69 (1981): 279–300.

———. "'Schön hat der heilige Geist durch den Propheten Jesaja zu euren Vätern gesprochen' (Act 28:25)." *Zeitschrift für die neutestamentliche Wissenschaft* 75 (1984): 226–32.

———. "Effet de réel et flou prophétique dans l'oeuvre de Luc." Pp. 349–59 in *À cause de l'évangile: Études sur les Synoptiques et les Actes offertes au P. Jacques Dupont.* Lectio Divina 123. Paris: Les Éditions du Cerf, 1985.

———. *Lukas in neuer Sicht: Gesammelte Aufsätze.* Translated by Elisabeth Hartmann, Albert Frey, and Peter Strauss. Biblisch-theologische Studien 8. Neukirchen-Vluyn: Neukirchener Verlag, 1985.

———. "La figure de Moïse dans l'oeuvre de Luc." Pp. 73–96 in *L'oeuvre de Luc: Études d'exégèse et de théologie.* Lectio Divina 130. Paris: Les Éditions du Cerf, 1987.

———. *Luke the Theologian: Thirty-Three Years of Research (1950–1983).* Translated by Ken McKinney. Princeton Theological Monograph Series 12. Allison Park, Penn.: Pickwick Publications, 1987.

Bowker, J. W. "Speeches in Acts: A Study in Proem and Yelammedenu Form." *New Testament Studies* 14 (1967–68): 96–111.

Braun, Herbert. "Zur Terminologie der Acta von der Auferstehung Jesu." *Theologische Literaturzeitung* 77 (1952): 533–36.

Brawley, Robert L. *The Pharisees in Luke-Acts: Luke's Address to Jews and His Irenic Purpose.* Ph.D. diss., Princeton Theological Seminary, 1978.

———. "Paul in Acts: Lucan Apology and Conciliation." Pp. 129–47 in *Luke-Acts: New Perspectives from the Society of Biblical Literature Seminar,* edited by Charles H. Talbert. New York: Crossroad, 1984.

———. *Luke-Acts and the Jews: Conflict, Apology, and Conciliation.* Society of Biblical Literature Monograph Series 33. Atlanta: Scholars Press, 1987.

———. "Paul in Acts: Aspects of Structure and Characterization." Pp. 90–105 in *Society of Biblical Literature 1988 Seminar Papers,* edited by David J. Lull. Atlanta: Scholars Press, 1988.

Brodie, Thomas Louis. "Greco-Roman Imitation of Texts as a Partial Guide to Luke's Use of Sources." Pp. 17–46 in *Luke-Acts: New Perspectives from the Society of Biblical Literature Seminar,* edited by Charles H. Talbert. New York: Crossroad, 1984.

———. "Towards Unraveling the Rhetorical Imitation of Sources in Acts: 2 Kgs 5 as One Component of Acts 8,9–40." *Biblica* 67 (1986): 41–67.

Brown, E. K. *Rhythm in the Novel.* Toronto and Buffalo: University of Toronto Press, 1950.

Brown, Raymond E., Donfried, Karl P., and Reumann, John, editors. *Peter in the New Testament.* Minneapolis: Augsburg Publishing House & New York: Paulist Press, 1973.

Brown, Schuyler. *Apostasy and Perseverance in the Theology of Luke.* Analecta Biblica 36. Rome: Pontifical Biblical Institute, 1969.

Bryan, Christopher. "A Further Look at Acts 16:1–3." *Journal of Biblical Literature* 107 (1988): 292–94.

Budesheim, Thomas L. "Paul's *Abschiedsrede* in the Acts of the Apostles." *Harvard Theological Review* 69 (1976): 9–30.

Burchard, Christoph. *Der dreizehnte Zeuge. Traditions- und kompositionsgeschichtliche Untersuchungen zu Lukas' Darstellung der Frühzeit des Paulus.* Forschungen zur Religion und Literatur des Alten und Neuen Testaments 103. Göttingen: Vandenhoeck & Ruprecht, 1970.

———. "Fussnoten zum neutestamentlichen Griechisch." *Zeitschrift für die neutestamentliche Wissenschaft* 61 (1970): 157–71.

———. "Paulus in der Apostelgeschichte." *Theologische Literaturzeitung* 100 (1975): 881–95.

———. "A Note on ʿPHMA in JosAs 17:1f.; Luke 2:15, 17; Acts 10:37." *Novum Testamentum* 27 (1985): 281–95.

Burger, Christoph. *Jesus als Davidssohn: Eine traditionsgeschichtliche Untersuchung.* Forschungen zur Religion und Literatur des Alten und Neuen Testaments 98. Göttingen: Vandenhoeck & Ruprecht, 1970.

Burnett, Fred W. "Prolegomenon to Reading Matthew's Eschatological Discourse: Redundancy and the Education of the Reader in Matthew." *Semeia* 31 (1985): 91–109.

Buss, Matthäus Franz-Josef. *Die Missionspredigt des Apostels Paulus im Pisidischen Antiochien: Analyse von Apg 13,16–41 im Hinblick auf die literarische und thematische Einheit der Paulusrede.* Forschung zur Bibel 38. Stuttgart: Verlag Katholisches Bibelwerk, 1980.

Cadbury, Henry J. *The Style and Literary Method of Luke.* 2 vols. Harvard Theological Studies 6. Cambridge: Harvard University Press, 1919–20.

_____. "The Summaries in Acts." Pp. 392–402 in *The Beginnings of Christianity*, edited by F. J. Foakes Jackson and Kirsopp Lake, vol. 5. London: Macmillan & Co., 1933.

_____. "Dust and Garments." Pp. 269–77 in *The Beginnings of Christianity*, edited by F. J. Foakes Jackson and Kirsopp Lake, vol. 5. London: Macmillan & Co., 1933.

_____. "Acts and Eschatology." Pp. 300–21 in *The Background of the New Testament and Its Eschatology*, edited by W. D. Davies and D. Daube. Cambridge: Cambridge University Press, 1956.

_____. *The Making of Luke-Acts.* 2d ed. London: SPCK, 1958.

_____. "Four Features of Lukan Style." Pp. 87–102 in *Studies in Luke-Acts: Essays Presented in Honor of Paul Schubert*, edited by Leander E. Keck and J. Louis Martyn. Nashville: Abingdon Press, 1966. (Reprint. Philadelphia: Fortress Press, 1980.)

Calloud, Jean. "Paul devant l'Aréopage d'Athènes. Actes 17, 16–34." *Recherches de Science Religieuse* 69 (1981): 209–48.

_____. "Sur le chemin de Damas. Quelques lumières sur l'organisation discursive d'un texte. Actes des Apôtres 9, 1–19." *Sémiotique et Bible* 37 (1985): 3–29; 38 (1985): 40–53; 40 (1985): 21–42.

Cambe, M. "La χάρις chez Saint Luc." *Revue Biblique* 70 (1963): 193–207.

Cambier, J. "Le voyage de S. Paul à Jérusalem en Act. ix. 26ss. et la schéma missionnaire théologique de S. Luc." *New Testament Studies* 8 (1961–62): 249–57.

Carroll, John T. "Literary and Social Dimensions of Luke's Apology for Paul." Pp. 106–18 in *Society of Biblical Literature 1988 Seminar Papers*, edited by David J. Lull. Atlanta: Scholars Press, 1988.

_____. "Luke's Portrayal of the Pharisees." *Catholic Biblical Quarterly* 50 (1988): 604–21.

_____. *Response to the End of History: Eschatology and Situation in Luke-Acts.* Society of Biblical Literature Dissertation Series 92. Atlanta: Scholars Press, 1988.

Cassidy, Richard J. *Society and Politics in the Acts of the Apostles.* Maryknoll, N.Y.: Orbis Books, 1987.

Causse, A. "Le pélerinage à Jérusalem et la première Pentecôte." *Revue d'Histoire et de Philosophie Religieuses* 20 (1940): 120–41.

Chance, J. Bradley. *Jerusalem, the Temple, and the New Age in Luke-Acts.* Macon, Ga.: Mercer University Press, 1988.

Chatman, Seymour. *Story and Discourse: Narrative Structure in Fiction and Film.* Ithaca, N.Y.: Cornell University Press, 1978.

Cicero, Marcus Tullius. *Orator*, with an English translation by H. M. Hubbell. Loeb Classical Library. Cambridge: Harvard University Press, 1952.

Clark, Donald L. *Rhetoric in Greco-Roman Education.* New York: Columbia University Press, 1957.

Cohen, Shaye J. D. "Was Timothy Jewish (Acts 16:1–3)? Patristic Exegesis, Rabbinic Law, and Matrilineal Descent." *Journal of Biblical Literature* 105 (1986): 251–68.

Conzelmann, Hans. *The Theology of St. Luke.* Translated by Geoffrey Buswell. London: Faber & Faber, 1960. (Reprint. Philadelphia: Fortress Press, 1982.)

_____. "The Address of Paul on the Areopagus." Pp. 217–30 in *Studies in Luke-Acts: Essays Presented in Honor of Paul Schubert*, edited by Leander E. Keck and J. Louis Martyn. Nashville: Abingdon Press, 1966. (Reprint. Philadelphia: Fortress Press, 1980.)

_____. "Luke's Place in the Development of Early Christianity." Pp. 298–316 in *Studies in Luke-Acts: Essays Presented in Honor of Paul Schubert*, edited by Leander E. Keck and J. Louis Martyn. Nashville: Abingdon Press, 1966. (Reprint. Philadelphia: Fortress Press, 1980.)

_____. "χάρις, κτλ." Pp. 372–402 in *Theological Dictionary of the New Testament*, edited by Gerhard Kittel and Gerhard Friedrich, vol. 9. Translated by Geoffrey W. Bromiley. Grand Rapids: Wm. B. Eerdmans, 1974.

———. *Acts of the Apostles.* Translated by James Limburg, A. Thomas Kraabel, and Donald H. Juel. Hermeneia. Philadelphia: Fortress Press, 1987.

Cook, Michael J. "The Mission to the Jews in Acts: Unraveling Luke's 'Myth of the Myriads.'" Pp. 102–23 in *Luke-Acts and the Jewish People: Eight Critical Perspectives*, edited by Joseph B. Tyson. Minneapolis: Augsburg Publishing House, 1988.

Cosgrove, Charles H. "The Divine Δεῖ in Luke-Acts." *Novum Testamentum* 26 (1984): 168–90.

Crampsey, James A. *The Conversion of Cornelius (Acts 10:1—11:18) : Societal Apologetic and Ecclesial Tension.* Ph.D. diss., Vanderbilt University, 1982.

Culpepper, R. Alan. "Paul's Mission to the Gentile World (Acts 13—19)." *Review and Expositor* 71 (1974): 487–97.

Dahl, Nils A. "'A People for His Name' (Acts XV. 14)." *New Testament Studies* 4 (1957–58): 319–27.

———. "The Story of Abraham in Luke-Acts." Pp. 139–58 in *Studies in Luke-Acts: Essays Presented in Honor of Paul Schubert*, edited by Leander E. Keck & J. Louis Martyn. Nashville: Abingdon Press, 1966. (Reprint. Philadelphia: Fortress Press, 1980.)

Danker, Frederick W. *Luke.* 2d ed. Proclamation Commentaries. Philadelphia: Fortress Press, 1987.

———. "The Endangered Benefactor in Luke-Acts." Pp. 39–48 in *Society of Biblical Literature 1981 Seminar Papers*, edited by Kent Harold Richards. Chico, Calif.: Scholars Press, 1981.

———. *Benefactor: Epigraphic Study of a Graeco-Roman and New Testament Semantic Field.* St. Louis: Clayton, 1982.

———. "Reciprocity in the Ancient World and in Acts 15:23–29." Pp. 49–58 in *Political Issues in Luke-Acts*, edited by Richard J. Cassidy and Philip J. Scharper. Maryknoll, N.Y.: Orbis Books, 1983.

Darr, John Andrew. *Glorified in the Presence of Kings: A Literary-Critical Study of Herod the Tetrarch in Luke-Acts.* Ph.D. diss., Vanderbilt University, 1987.

Davies, J. G. "The Prefigurement of the Ascension in the Third Gospel." *Journal of Theological Studies* 6 (1955): 229–33.

Davies, Philip. "The Ending of Acts." *Expository Times* 94 (1983): 334–35.

Decock, P. B. "The Understanding of Isaiah 53:7-8 in Acts 8:32-33." Pp. 111–33 in *The Relationship between the Old and New Testament*. Neotestamentica 14. Annual Publication of The New Testament Society of South Africa, 1981.

Dibelius, Martin. *Studies in the Acts of the Apostles.* Translated by Mary Ling. London: SCM Press, 1956.

Dietrich, Wolfgang. *Das Petrusbild der lukanischen Schriften.* Beiträge zur Wissenschaft vom Alten und Neuen Testament 94. Stuttgart: Verlag W. Kohlhammer, 1972.

Dillon, Richard J. "The Prophecy of Christ and His Witnesses According to the Discourses of Acts." *New Testament Studies* 32 (1986): 544–56.

Dinkler, Erich. "Philippus und der ANHP AIΘIOΨ (Apg 8,26–40)." Pp. 85–95 in *Jesus und Paulus. Festschrift für Werner Georg Kümmel*, edited by E. Earle Ellis and Erich Grässer. Göttingen: Vandenhoeck & Ruprecht, 1975.

Doble, P. "The Son of Man Saying in Stephen's Witnessing: Acts 6:8—8:2." *New Testament. Studies* 31 (1985): 68–84.

Dodd, C. H. "The Fall of Jerusalem and the 'Abomination of Desolation.'" Pp. 69–83 in *More New Testament Studies*. Grand Rapids: Wm. B. Eerdmans, 1968.

Dömer, Michael. *Das Heil Gottes: Studien zur Theologie des lukanischen Doppelwerkes.* Bonner biblische Beiträge 51. Cologne: Peter Hanstein, 1978.

Downing, F. Gerald. "Common Ground with Paganism in Luke and Josephus." *New Testament Studies* 28 (1982): 546–59.

Duling, Dennis C. "The Promises to David and Their Entrance into Christianity—Nailing Down a Likely Hypothesis." *New Testament Studies* 20 (1973–74): 55–77.

Dumais, Marcel. *Le langage de l'évangélisation: L'annonce missionnaire en milieu juif (Actes 13,16–41).* Tournai: Desclée & Montréal: Bellarmin, 1976.

Dunn, James D. G. *Baptism in the Holy Spirit: A Re-examination of the New Testament Teaching on the Gift of the Spirit in Relation to Pentecostalism Today.* Studies in Biblical Theology. Naperville, Ill.: Alec R. Allenson, 1970.

du Plooy, Gerhardus Petrus Viljoen. *The Narrative Act in Luke-Acts from the Perspective of God's Design.* Th.D. diss., University of Stellenbosch, 1986.

Dupont, Jacques. "'Filius meus es tu': L'intèrprétation de Ps. II, 7 dans le Nouveau Testament." *Recherches de Science Religieuse* 35 (1948): 522–43.

———. "ΛΑΟΣ 'ΕΞ 'ΕΘΝΩΝ (ACT. XV.14)." *New Testament Studies* 3 (1956–57): 47–50.

———. "ΤΑ 'ΟΣΙΑ ΔΑΥΙΔ ΤΑ ΠΙΣΤΑ (Ac XIII 34 = Is LV 3)." *Revue Biblique* 68 (1961): 91–114.

———. "Les discours missionnaires des Actes des Apôtres d'après un ouvrage récent." *Revue Biblique* 69 (1962): 37–60.

———. *The Sources of the Acts: The Present Position.* Translated by Kathleen Pond. New York: Herder & Herder, 1964.

———. *Paulus an die Seelsorger: Das Vermächtnis von Milet (Apg 20, 18–36).* Translated by Franz Josef Schierse. Kommentare und Beiträge zum Alten und Neuen Testament. Düsseldorf: Patmos-Verlag, 1966.

———. "La prière des apôtres persécutés (Actes 4, 23–31)." Pp. 521–22 in *Études sur les Actes des Apôtres.* Lectio Divina 45. Paris: Les Éditions du Cerf, 1967.

———. "Die individuelle Eschatologie im Lukasevangelium und in der Apostelgeschichte." Pp. 37–47 in *Orientierung an Jesus: Zur Theologie der Synoptiker. Für Josef Schmid,* edited by Paul Hoffmann. Freiburg: Herder, 1973.

———. "Les discours de Pierre dans les Actes et le chapitre XXIV de l'évangile de Luc." Pp. 329–74 in *L'Évangile de Luc: Problèmes littéraires et théologiques: Mémorial Lucien Cerfaux,* edited by F. Neirynck. Bibliotheca Ephemeridum Theologicarum Lovaniensium 32. Gembloux: J. Duculot, 1973.

———. "La question du plan des Actes des Apôtres à la lumière d'un texte de Lucien de Samosate." *Novum Testamentum* 21 (1979): 220–31.

———. *The Salvation of the Gentiles: Studies in the Acts of the Apostles.* Translated by John Keating. New York: Paulist Press, 1979.

———. *Nouvelles études sur les Actes des Apôtres.* Lectio Divina 118. Paris: Les Éditions du Cerf, 1984.

———. "Un peuple d'entre les nations (Actes 15,14)." *New Testament Studies* 31 (1985): 321–35.

———. "'Je rebâtirai la cabane de David qui est tombée' (Ac 15,16 = Am 9,11)." Pp. 19–32 in *Glaube und Eschatologie: Festschrift für Werner Georg Kümmel,* edited by Erich Grässer and Otto Merk. Tübingen: J. C. B. Mohr, 1985.

———. "La structure oratoire du discours d'Étienne (Actes 7)." *Biblica* 66 (1985): 153–67.

Easton, Burton Scott. *Early Christianity: The Purpose of Acts and Other Papers.* Greenwich, Conn.: Seabury Press, 1954.

Elliott, John H. "Patronage and Clientism in Early Christian Society: A Short Reading Guide." *Foundations & Facets Forum* 3,4 (1987): 39–48.

Ellis, E. Earle. "Midraschartige Züge in den Reden der Apostelgeschichte." *Zeitschrift für die neutestamentliche Wissenschaft* 62 (1971): 94–104.

Eltester, Walther. "Lukas und Paulus." Pp. 1–17 in *Eranion: Festschrift für H. Hommel.* Tübingen: Max Niemeyer, 1961.

Epp, Eldon Jay. "The Ascension in the Textual Tradition of Luke-Acts." Pp. 131–45 in *New Testament Textual Criticism: Its Significance for Exegesis,* edited by Eldon Jay Epp and Gordon D. Fee. New York and Oxford: Oxford University Press, 1981.

Esler, Philip Francis. *Community and Gospel in Luke-Acts: The Social and Political Motivations of Lucan Theology.* Society for New Testament Studies Monograph Series 57. Cambridge: Cambridge University Press, 1987.

Evans, Craig A. "The Prophetic Setting of the Pentecost Sermon." *Zeitschrift für die neutestamentliche Wissenschaft* 74 (1983): 148–50.

Exum, Cheryl, and Talbert, Charles. "The Structure of Paul's Speech to the Ephesian Elders (Acts 20,18–35)." *Catholic Biblical Quarterly* 29 (1967): 233–36.

Fenton, John. "The Order of the Miracles Performed by Peter and Paul in Acts." *Expository Times* 77 (1965–66): 381–83.

Filson, Floyd V. "The Journey Motif in Luke-Acts." Pp. 68–77 in *Apostolic History and the Gospel: Biblical and Historical Essays Presented to F. F. Bruce*, edited by W. Ward Gasque and Ralph P. Martin. Grand Rapids: Wm. B. Eerdmans, 1970.

Fiorenza, Elisabeth Schüssler. "Miracles, Mission, and Apologetics: An Introduction." Pp. 1–25 in *Aspects of Religious Propaganda in Judaism and Early Christianity*, edited by Elisabeth Schüssler Fiorenza. University of Notre Dame Center for the Study of Judaism and Christianity in Antiquity 2. Notre Dame, Ind.: University of Notre Dame Press, 1976.

_____. *In Memory of Her: A Feminist Theological Reconstruction of Christian Origins.* New York: Crossroad, 1985.

Fitzmyer, Joseph A. "The Ascension of Christ and Pentecost." *Theological Studies* 45 (1984): 409–40.

Flender, Helmut. *St. Luke: Theologian of Redemptive History.* Translated by Reginald and Ilse Fuller. Philadelphia: Fortress Press, 1967.

Francis, Fred O. "Eschatology and History in Luke-Acts." *Journal of the American Academy of Religion* 37 (1969): 49–63.

Franklin, Eric. *Christ the Lord: A Study in the Purpose and Theology of Luke-Acts.* Philadelphia: Westminster Press, 1975.

Funk, Robert W. *The Poetics of Biblical Narrative.* Foundations and Facets: Literary Facets. Sonoma: Polebridge Press, 1988.

Gärtner, Bertil. *The Areopagus Speech and Natural Revelation.* Acta Seminarii Neotestamentici Upsaliensis 21. Translated by Carolyn Hannay King. Lund: C. W. K. Gleerup, 1955.

Gager, John G. "Jews, Gentiles, and Synagogues in the Book of Acts." *Harvard Theological Review* 79 (1986): 91–99.

Gaston, Lloyd. "Anti-Judaism and the Passion Narrative in Luke and Acts." Pp. 127–53 in *Anti-Judaism in Early Christianity*, edited by Peter Richardson, vol. 1. Studies in Christianity and Judaism 2. Waterloo, Ontario: Wilfrid Laurier University Press, 1986.

Gaventa, Beverly Roberts. "The Overthrown Enemy: Luke's Portrait of Paul." Pp. 439–49 in *Society of Biblical Literature 1985 Seminar Papers,* edited by Kent Harold Richards. Atlanta: Scholars Press, 1985.

_____. *From Darkness to Light: Aspects of Conversion in the New Testament.* Overtures to Biblical Theology 20. Philadelphia: Fortress Press, 1986.

_____. "Toward a Theology of Acts: Reading and Rereading." *Interpretation* 42 (1988): 146–57.

Genette, Gérard. *Narrative Discourse: An Essay in Method.* Translated by Jane E. Lewin. Ithaca, N.Y.: Cornell University Press, 1980.

George, Augustin. *Études sur l'oeuvre de Luc.* Sources bibliques. Paris: J. Gabalda, 1978.

Gewalt, Dietfried. "Das 'Petrusbild' der lukanischen Schriften als Problem einer ganzheitlichen Exegese." *Linguistica Biblica* 34 (1975): 1–22.

Giblin, Charles Homer. "Complementarity of Symbolic Event and Discourse in Acts 2, 1–40." Pp. 189–96 in *Studia Evangelica*, vol. 6, edited by Elizabeth Livingstone. Texte und Untersuchungen zur Geschichte der altchristlichen Literatur 112. Berlin: Akademie-Verlag, 1973.

_____. *The Destruction of Jerusalem According to Luke's Gospel: A Historical-Typological Moral.* Analecta Biblica 107. Rome: Biblical Institute Press, 1985.

Glombitza, Otto. "Der Schritt nach Europa: Erwägungen zu Act 16: 9–15." *Zeitschrift für die neutestamentliche Wissenschaft* 53 (1962): 77–82.

Gnilka, Joachim. *Die Verstockung Israels: Isaias 6,9–10 in der Theologie der Synoptiker.* Studien zum Alten und Neuen Testament 3. Munich: Kösel-Verlag, 1961.

Goulder, M. D. *Type and History in Acts*. London: SPCK, 1964.

Gourgues, Michel. "Esprit des commencements et Esprit des prolongements dans les *Actes*. Note sur la 'Pentecôte des Samaritains' (Act. viii, 5–25)." *Revue Biblique* 93 (1986): 376–85.

Gowler, David B. "Characterization in Luke: A Socio-Narratological Approach." *Biblical Theology Bulletin* 19 (1989): 54–62.

Grässer, Erich. "Acta-Forschung seit 1960." *Theologische Rundschau* 41 (1976): 141–94, 259–90; 42 (1977): 1–68.

———. "TA PERI TĒS BASILEIAS (Apg 1,6; 19,8)." Pp. 709–25 in *À cause de l'évangile: Études sur les Synoptiques et les Actes offertes au P. Jacques Dupont*. Lectio Divina 123. Paris: Les Éditions du Cerf, 1985.

Grant, Robert M. *Gods and the One God*. Library of Early Christianity 1. Philadelphia: Westminster Press, 1986.

Grassi, Joseph A. "Emmaus Revisited (Luke 24,13–35 and Acts 8,26–40)." *Catholic Biblical Quarterly* 26 (1964): 463–67.

Haacker, Klaus. "Das Pfingstwunder als exegetisches Problem." Pp. 125–31 in *Verborum Veritas. Festschrift für Gustav Stählin*, edited by Otto Böcher and Klaus Haacker. Wuppertal: Theologischer Verlag Rolf Brockhaus, 1970.

———. "Einige Fälle von 'erlebter Rede' im Neuen Testament." *Novum Testamentum* 12 (1970): 70–77.

———. "Dibelius und Cornelius: Ein Beispiel formgeschichtlicher Überlieferungskritik." *Biblische Zeitschrift* 24 (1980): 234–51.

———. "Das Bekenntnis des Paulus zur Hoffnung Israels nach der Apostelgeschichte des Lukas." *New Testament Studies* 31 (1985): 437–51.

———. "Verwendung und Vermeidung des Apostelbegriffs im lukanischen Werk." *Novum Testamentum* 30 (1988): 9–38.

Haenchen, Ernst. "Judentum und Christentum in der Apostelgeschichte." *Zeitschrift für die neutestamentliche Wissenschaft* 54 (1963): 155–87.

———. "Acta 27." Pp. 235–54 in *Zeit und Geschichte: Dankesgabe an Rudolf Bultmann*, edited by Erich Dinkler. Tübingen: J. C. B. Mohr, 1964.

———. "The Book of Acts as Source Material for the History of Early Christianity." Pp. 258–78 in *Studies in Luke-Acts: Essays Presented in Honor of Paul Schubert*, edited by Leander E. Keck and J. Louis Martyn. Nashville: Abingdon Press, 1966. (Reprint. Philadelphia: Fortress Press, 1980.)

———. *The Acts of the Apostles: A Commentary*. Translated by Bernard Noble and Gerald Shinn. Philadelphia: Westminster Press, 1971.

Hahn, Ferdinand. "Das Problem alter christologischer Überlieferungen in der Apostelgeschichte unter besonderer Berücksichtigung von Act 3,19–21." Pp. 129–54 in *Les Actes des Apôtres: Traditions, rédaction, théologie*, edited by J. Kremer. Bibliotheca Ephemeridum Theologicarum Lovaniensium 48. Gembloux: J. Duculot & Leuven: Leuven University Press, 1979.

———. "Der gegenwärtige Stand der Erforschung der Apostelgeschichte. Kommentare und Aufsatzbände 1980–1985." *Theologische Revue* 82 (1986): 177–90.

Hamm, M. Dennis. *This Sign of Healing, Acts 3:1–10: A Study in Lucan Theology*. Ph.D. diss., Saint Louis University, 1975.

———. "You Are Precious in My Sight." *The Way* 18 (1978): 193–203.

———. "Acts 3:12–26: Peter's Speech and the Healing of the Man Born Lame." *Perspectives in Religious Studies* 11 (1984): 199–217.

———. "Acts 3,1–10: The Healing of the Temple Beggar as Lucan Theology." *Biblica* 67 (1986): 305–19.

———. "Sight to the Blind: Vision as Metaphor in Luke." *Biblica* 67 (1986): 457–77.

Hardon, John A. "The Miracle Narratives in the Acts of the Apostles." *Catholic Biblical Quarterly* 16 (1954): 303–18.

Hare, Douglas R. A. "The Rejection of the Jews in the Synoptic Gospels and Acts." Pp.

27–47 in *Anti Semitism and the Foundations of Christianity*, edited by Alan T. Davies. New York: Paulist Press, 1979.

Harlé, Paul. "Un 'Private-Joke' de Paul dans le livre des Actes (XXVI. 28–29)." *New Testament Studies* 24 (1977–78): 527–33.

Harnack, Adolf. *New Testament Studies III: The Acts of the Apostles*. Translated by J. R. Wilkinson. Crown Theological Library 27. London: Williams & Norgate, 1909.

Haulotte, Edgar. "Fondation d'une communauté de type universel: Actes 10,1—11,18. Étude critique sur la rédaction, la 'structure' et la 'tradition' du récit." *Recherches de Science Religieuse* 58 (1970): 63–100.

_____. "La vie en communion, phase ultime de la Pentecôte, Actes 2, 42–47." *Foi et Vie* 80 (1981): 69–75.

Hauser, Hermann J. *Strukturen der Abschlusserzählung der Apostelgeschichte (Apg 28,16–31)*. Analecta Biblica 86. Rome: Biblical Institute Press, 1979.

Hay, David M. *Glory at the Right Hand: Psalm 110 in Early Christianity*. Society of Biblical Literature Monograph Series 18. Nashville: Abingdon Press, 1973.

Hedrick, Charles W. "Paul's Conversion/Call: A Comparative Analysis of the Three Reports in Acts." *Journal of Biblical Literature* 100 (1981): 415–32.

Hemer, Colin J. "First Person Narrative in Acts 27–28." *Tyndale Bulletin* 36 (1985): 79–109.

Hengel, Martin. *Acts and the History of Earliest Christianity*. Translated by John Bowden. Philadelphia: Fortress Press, 1980.

Hickling, C. J. A. "The Portrait of Paul in Acts 26." Pp. 499–503 in *Les Actes des Apôtres: Traditions, rédaction, théologie*, edited by J. Kremer. Bibliotheca Ephemeridum Theologicarum Lovaniensium 48. Gembloux: J. Duculot & Leuven: Leuven University Press, 1979.

Hill, David. "The Spirit and the Church's Witness: Observations on Acts 1:6–8." *Irish Biblical Studies* 6 (1984): 16–26.

Holtz, Traugott. *Untersuchungen über die alttestamentlichen Zitate bei Lukas*. Texte und Untersuchungen 104. Berlin: Akademie-Verlag, 1968.

Horsley, G. H. R. "Speeches and Dialogue in Acts." *New Testament Studies* 32 (1986): 609–14.

Hrushovski, Benjamin. *Segmentation and Motivation in the Text Continuum of Literary Prose: The First Episode of "War and Peace."* Papers on Poetics and Semiotics 5. Tel Aviv: Tel Aviv University, 1976.

Hubbard, Benjamin J. "Commissioning Stories in Luke-Acts: A Study of Their Antecedents, Form and Content." *Semeia* 8 (1977): 103–26.

_____. "The Role of Commissioning Accounts in Acts." Pp. 187–98 in *Perspectives on Luke-Acts*, edited by Charles H. Talbert. Perspectives in Religious Studies Special Studies Series 5. Danville, Va.: Association of Baptist Professors of Religion, 1978.

Iser, Wolfgang. *The Implied Reader: Patterns of Communication in Prose Fiction from Bunyan to Beckett*. Baltimore: Johns Hopkins Press, 1974.

Jacobson, Glenn R. "Paul in Luke-Acts: The Savior Who Is Present." Pp. 131–46 in *Society of Biblical Literature 1983 Seminar Papers*, edited by Kent Harold Richards. Chico, Calif.: Scholars Press, 1983.

Jervell, Jacob. *Luke and the People of God*. Minneapolis: Augsburg Publishing House, 1972.

_____. *The Unknown Paul: Essays on Luke-Acts and Early Christian History*. Minneapolis: Augsburg Publishing House, 1984.

_____. "Paulus in der Apostelgeschichte und die Geschichte des Urchristentums." *New Testament Studies* 32 (1986): 378–92.

_____. "The Church of Jews and Godfearers." Pp. 11–20 in *Luke-Acts and the Jewish People: Eight Critical Perspectives*, edited by Joseph B. Tyson. Minneapolis: Augsburg Publishing House, 1988.

Johnson, Luke T. *The Literary Function of Possessions in Luke-Acts*. Society of Biblical Literature Dissertation Series 39. Missoula, Mont.: Scholars Press, 1977.

_____. *Decision Making in the Church: A Biblical Model.* Philadelphia: Fortress Press, 1983.

_____. *The Writings of the New Testament: An Interpretation.* Philadelphia: Fortress Press, 1986.

Johnston, George. "Christ as Archegos." *New Testament Studies* 27 (1980–81): 381–85.

Jones, Donald L. "The Title *Pais* in Luke-Acts." Pp. 217–26 in *Society of Biblical Literature 1982 Seminar Papers,* edited by Kent Harold Richards. Chico, Calif.: Scholars Press, 1982.

_____. "The Title *Huios Theou* in Acts." Pp. 451–63 in *Society of Biblical Literature 1985 Seminar Papers,* edited by Kent Harold Richards. Atlanta: Scholars Press, 1985.

Juel, Donald. "Social Dimensions of Exegesis: The Use of Psalm 16 in Acts 2." *Catholic Biblical Quarterly* 43 (1981): 543–56.

_____. *Luke-Acts: The Promise of History.* Atlanta: John Knox Press, 1983.

_____. *Messianic Exegesis: Christological Interpretation of the Old Testament in Early Christianity.* Philadelphia: Fortress Press, 1988.

Käsemann, Ernst. "The Disciples of John the Baptist in Ephesus." Pp. 136–48 in *Essays on New Testament Themes.* Translated by W. J. Montague. Studies in Biblical Theology. Naperville, Ill.: Alec R. Allenson, 1964.

_____. "Ephesians and Acts." Pp. 288–97 in *Studies in Luke-Acts: Essays Presented in Honor of Paul Schubert,* edited by Leander E. Keck and J. Louis Martyn. Nashville: Abingdon Press, 1966. (Reprint. Philadelphia: Fortress Press, 1980.)

Karris, Robert J. "Missionary Communities: A New Paradigm for the Study of Luke-Acts." *Catholic Biblical Quarterly* 41 (1979): 80–97.

_____. *What Are They Saying about Luke and Acts? A Theology of the Faithful God.* New York: Paulist Press, 1979.

Kawin, Bruce F. *Telling It Again and Again: Repetition in Literature and Film.* Ithaca, N.Y.: Cornell University Press, 1972.

Kaye, B. N. "Acts' Portrait of Silas." *Novum Testamentum* 21 (1979): 13–26.

Kennedy, George A. *New Testament Interpretation through Rhetorical Criticism.* Studies in Religion. Chapel Hill: University of North Carolina, 1984.

Kepple, Robert J. "The Hope of Israel, the Resurrection of the Dead, and Jesus: A Study of Their Relationship in Acts with Particular Regard to the Understanding of Paul's Trial Defense." *Journal of the Evangelical Theological Society* 20 (1977): 231–41.

Kilgallen, John. *The Stephen Speech: A Literary and Redactional Study of Acts 7,2–53.* Analecta Biblica 67. Rome: Biblical Institute Press, 1976.

_____. "Acts: Literary and Theological Turning Points." *Biblical Theology Bulletin* 7 (1977): 177–80.

Kirchschläger, W. "Fieberheilung in Apg 28 und Lk 4." Pp. 509–21 in *Les Actes des Apôtres: Traditions, rédaction, théologie,* edited by J. Kremer. Bibliotheca Ephemeridum Theologicarum Lovaniensium 48. Gembloux: J. Duculot & Leuven: Leuven University Press, 1979.

Klein, Günter. *Die zwölf Apostel: Ursprung und Gehalt einer Idee.* Forschungen zur Religion und Literatur des Alten und Neuen Testaments n. F. 59. Göttingen: Vandenhoeck & Ruprecht, 1961.

_____. "Der Synkretismus als theologisches Problem in der ältesten christlichen Apologetik." *Zeitschrift für Theologie und Kirche* 64 (1967): 40–82.

Kliesch, Klaus. *Das heilsgeschichtliche Credo in den Reden der Apostelgeschichte.* Bonner biblische Beiträge 44. Cologne-Bonn: Peter Hanstein, 1975.

Koch, Dietrich-Alex. "Geistbesitz, Geistverleihung und Wundermacht: Erwägungen zur Tradition und zur lukanischen Redaktion in Act 8:5–25." *Zeitschrift für die neutestamentliche Wissenschaft* 77 (1986): 64–82.

Kodell, Jerome. "'The Word of God Grew': The Ecclesial Tendency of Λόγος in Acts 1,7 [sic = 6,7]; 12,24; 19,20." *Biblica* 55 (1974): 505–19.

Koenig, John. *Jews and Christians in Dialogue: New Testament Foundations.* Philadelphia: Westminster Press, 1979.

———. *New Testament Hospitality: Partnership with Strangers as Promise and Mission.* Overtures to Biblical Theology. Philadelphia: Fortress Press, 1985.

Koester, Helmut. "τόπος." Pp. 187–208 in *Theological Dictionary of the New Testament,* edited by Gerhard Kittel and Gerhard Friedrich, vol. 8. Translated by Geoffrey W. Bromiley. Grand Rapids: Wm. B. Eerdmans, 1972.

Kraabel, A. Thomas. "The Disappearance of the 'God-fearers.'" *Numen* 28 (1981): 113–26.

———. "Greeks, Jews, and Lutherans in the Middle Half of Acts." *Harvard Theological Review* 79 (1986): 147–57.

———. "Traditional Christian Evidence for Diaspora Judaism: The Book of Acts." Pp. 644–51 in *Society of Biblical Literature 1986 Seminar Papers,* edited by Kent Harold Richards. Atlanta: Scholars Press, 1986.

Kränkl, Emmeram. *Jesus, der Knecht Gottes: Die heilsgeschichtliche Stellung Jesu in den Reden der Apostelgeschichte.* Biblische Untersuchungen 8. Regensburg: Friedrich Pustet, 1972.

Kratz, Reinhard. *Rettungswunder: Motiv-, traditions- und formkritische Aufarbeitung einer biblischen Gattung.* Europäische Hochschulschriften 123. Frankfurt a. M.: Peter Lang, 1979.

Kremer, Jacob. *Pfingstbericht und Pfingstgeschehen: Eine exegetische Untersuchung zu Apg 2,1–13.* Stuttgarter Bibelstudien 63/64. Stuttgart: Verlag Katholisches Bibelwerk, 1973.

———. "Einführung in die Problematik heutiger Acta-Forschung anhand von Apg 17, 10–13." Pp. 11–20 in *Les Actes des Apôtres: Traditions, rédaction, théologie,* edited by J. Kremer. Bibliotheca Ephemeridum Theologicarum Lovaniensium 48. Gembloux: J. Duculot & Leuven: Leuven University Press, 1979.

Krodel, Gerhard A. *Acts.* Augsburg Commentary on the New Testament. Minneapolis: Augsburg Publishing House, 1986.

Kurz, William S. "Acts 3:19–26 as a Test of the Role of Eschatology in Lukan Christology." Pp. 309–23 in *Society of Biblical Literature 1977 Seminar Papers,* edited by Paul J. Achtemeier. Missoula, Mont.: Scholars Press, 1977.

———. "Hellenistic Rhetoric in the Christological Proof of Luke-Acts." *Catholic Biblical Quarterly* 42 (1980): 171–95.

———. "Luke-Acts and Historiography in the Greek Bible." Pp. 283–300 in *Society of Biblical Literature 1980 Seminar Papers,* edited by Paul J. Achtemeier. Chico, Calif.: Scholars Press, 1980.

———. "Narrative Approaches to Luke-Acts." *Biblica* 68 (1987): 195–220.

Ladouceur, David. "Hellenistic Preconceptions of Shipwreck and Pollution as a Concept for Acts 27–28." *Harvard Theological Review* 73 (1980): 435–49.

Lake, Kirsopp, and Cadbury, Henry J. *The Beginnings of Christianity.* Part I, The Acts of the Apostles, vol. 4, English Translation and Commentary. London: Macmillan & Co., 1933.

Lambrecht, J. "Paul's Farewell-Address at Miletus (Acts 20, 17–38)." Pp. 307–37 in *Les Actes des Apôtres: Traditions, rédaction, théologie,* edited by J. Kremer. Bibliotheca Ephemeridum Theologicarum Lovaniensium 48. Gembloux: J. Duculot & Leuven: Leuven University Press, 1979.

Lampe, G. W. H. "The Holy Spirit in the Writings of St. Luke." Pp. 159–200 in *Studies in the Gospels: Essays in Memory of R. H. Lightfoot,* edited by D. E. Nineham. Oxford: Basil Blackwell, 1955.

———. "Miracles in the Acts of the Apostles." Pp. 163–78 in *Miracles,* edited by C. F. D. Moule. London: A. R. Mowbray, 1965.

Lanser, Susan Sniader. *The Narrative Act: Point of View in Prose Fiction.* Princeton: Princeton University Press, 1981.

Légasse, Simon. "L'apologétique a l'égard de Rome dans le procès de Paul. Actes 21,27—26,32." *Recherches de Science Religieuse* 69 (1981): 249–55.

Legrand, L. "The Areopagus Speech: Its Theological Kerygma and Its Missionary Significance." Pp. 337–50 in *La notion biblique de Dieu*, edited by J. Coppens. Bibliotheca Ephemeridum Theologicarum Lovaniensium 41. Gembloux: J. Duculot & Leuven: Leuven University Press, 1976.

Lerle, Ernst. "Die Predigt in Lystra (Acta XIV. 15–18)." *New Testament Studies* 7 (1960–61): 46–55.

Levinsohn, Stephen H. *Textual Connections in Acts.* Society of Biblical Literature Monograph Series 31. Atlanta: Scholars Press, 1987.

Liddell, Henry George, and Scott, Robert. *A Greek-English Lexicon.* Revised edition by Henry S. Jones. Oxford: Clarendon Press, 1940.

Lindars, Barnabas. *New Testament Apologetic: The Doctrinal Significance of the Old Testament Quotations.* Philadelphia: Westminster Press, 1961.

Lindemann, Andreas. *Paulus im ältesten Christentum.* Beiträge zur historischen Theologie 58. Tübingen: J. C. B. Mohr, 1979.

Lindijer, C. H. "Two Creative Encounters in the Work of Luke: Luke xxiv 13–35 and Acts viii 26–40." Pp. 77–85 in *Miscellanea Neotestamentica*, edited by T. Baarda, A. F. J. Klijn, and W. C. van Unnik. Supplements to Novum Testamentum 48. Leiden: E. J. Brill, 1978.

Löning, Karl. *Die Saulustradition in der Apostelgeschichte.* Neutestamentliche Abhandlungen 9. Münster: Aschendorff, 1973.

――――. "Die Korneliustradition." *Biblische Zeitschrift* 18 (1974): 1–19.

――――. "Paulinismus in der Apostelgeschichte." Pp. 202–34 in *Paulus in den neutestamentlichen Spätschriften*, edited by Karl Kertelge. Freiburg: Herder, 1981.

――――. "Das Evangelium und die Kulturen. Heilsgeschichtliche und kulturelle Aspekte kirchlicher Realität in der Apostelgeschichte." Pp. 2604–46 in *Aufstieg und Niedergang der römischen Welt*, edited by Hildegard Temporini and Wolfgang Haase, II Principat, vol. 25,3. Berlin: Walter de Gruyter, 1985.

Lövestam, Evald. *Son and Saviour: A Study of Acts 13, 32–37.* Coniectanea Neotestamentica 18. Lund: C. W. K. Gleerup, 1961.

Lohfink, Gerhard. "'Meinen Namen zu tragen . . .' (Apg 9,15)." *Biblische Zeitschrift* 10 (1966): 108–15.

――――. "Christologie und Geschichtsbild in Apg 3,19–21." *Biblische Zeitschrift* 13 (1969): 223–41.

――――. *Die Himmelfahrt Jesu. Untersuchungen zu den Himmelfahrts- und Erhöhungstexten bei Lukas.* Studien zum Alten und Neuen Testament 26. Munich: Kösel-Verlag, 1971.

――――. *Die Sammlung Israels: Eine Untersuchung zur lukanischen Ekklesiologie.* Studien zum Alten und Neuen Testament 39. Munich: Kösel-Verlag, 1975.

――――. *The Conversion of St. Paul: Narrative and History in Acts.* Translated by Bruce J. Malina. Herald Scriptural Library. Chicago: Franciscan Herald Press, 1976.

Lohse, Eduard. "Die Bedeutung des Pfingstberichtes im Rahmen des lukanischen Geschichtswerkes." *Evangelische Theologie* 13 (1953): 422–36.

Long, William R. *The Trial of Paul in the Book of Acts: Historical, Literary, and Theological Considerations.* Ph.D. diss., Brown University, 1982.

――――. "The *Paulusbild* in the Trial of Paul in Acts." Pp. 87–105 in *Society of Biblical Literature 1983 Seminar Papers*, edited by Kent Harold Richards. Chico, Calif.: Scholars Press, 1983.

Lowry, Richard. "The Rejected-Suitor Syndrome: Human Sources of New Testament 'Antisemitism.'" *Journal of Ecumenical Studies* 14 (1977): 219–32.

Lucian. "How to Write History." Pp. 1–73 in *Lucian*, with an English translation by K. Kilburn, vol. 6. Loeb Classical Library. Cambridge: Harvard University Press, 1959.

Luck, Ulrich. "Kerygma, Tradition und Geschichte Jesu bei Lukas." *Zeitschrift für Theologie und Kirche* 57 (1960): 51–66.

Lyons, John. *Semantics.* 2 vols. Cambridge: Cambridge University Press, 1978.

MacRae, George W. "'Whom Heaven Must Receive until the Time': Reflections on the Christology of Acts." *Interpretation* 27 (1973): 151–65.

Maddox, Robert L. *The Purpose of Luke-Acts.* Forschungen zur Religion und Literatur des Alten und Neuen Testaments 126. Göttingen: Vandenhoeck & Ruprecht, 1982.

März, Claus-Peter. *Das Wort Gottes bei Lukas.* Erfurter theologische Schriften 11. Leipzig: St. Benno-Verlag, 1974.

Magness, J. Lee. *Sense and Absence: Structure and Suspension in the Ending of Mark's Gospel.* Semeia Studies. Atlanta: Scholars Press, 1986.

Malherbe, Abraham J. "'Not in a Corner': Early Christian Apologetic in Acts 26:26." *The Second Century* 5 (1985–86): 193–210. (See also pp. 147–63 in *Paul and the Popular Philosophers.* Minneapolis: Fortress Press, 1989.)

Mánek, Jindřich. "Das Aposteldekret im Kontext der Lukastheologie." *Communio Viatorum* 15 (1972): 151–60.

Marin, Louis. "Essai d'analyse structurale d'Actes 10,1—11,18." *Recherches de Science Religieuse* 58 (1970): 39–61.

Marshall, I. Howard. *The Acts of the Apostles.* Tyndale New Testament Commentaries. Grand Rapids: Wm. B. Eerdmans, 1980.

Mather, P. Boyd. "Paul in Acts as 'Servant' and 'Witness.'" *Biblical Research* 30 (1985): 23–44.

Mattill, A. J., Jr. "The Jesus-Paul Parallels and the Purpose of Luke-Acts: H. H. Evans Reconsidered." *Novum Testamentum* 17 (1975): 15–46.

McMahan, Craig Thomas. *Meals as Type-Scenes in the Gospel of Luke.* Ph.D. diss., Southern Baptist Theological Seminary, 1987.

Mealand, David L. "Community of Goods and Utopian Allusions in Acts II-IV." *Journal of Theological Studies* 28 (1977): 96–99.

Menoud, Philippe-H. "La mort d'Ananias et Saphira (Actes 5.1–11)." Pp. 146–54 in *Aux sources de la tradition chrétienne. Mélanges offerts à M. Maurice Goguel.* Bibliothèque théologique. Neuchatel: Delachaux & Niestlé, 1950.

_____. *Jesus Christ and the Faith: A Collection of Studies.* Translated by Eunice M. Paul. Pittsburgh Theological Monograph Series 18. Pittsburgh: Pickwick Press, 1978.

Merk, Otto. "Das Reich Gottes in den lukanischen Schriften." Pp. 201–20 in *Jesus und Paulus: Festschrift für Werner Georg Kümmel,* edited by E. Earle Ellis and Erich Grässer. Göttingen: Vandenhoeck & Ruprecht, 1975.

Metzger, Bruce M. *A Textual Commentary on the Greek New Testament: A Companion Volume to the United Bible Societies' Greek New Testament.* London: United Bible Societies, 1971.

Michel, Hans-Joachim. *Die Abschiedsrede des Paulus an die Kirche Apg 20,17–38: Motivgeschichte und theologische Bedeutung.* Studien zum Alten und Neuen Testament 35. Munich: Kösel-Verlag, 1973.

Michel, Otto. "ὁμολογέω, κτλ." Pp. 199–220 in *Theological Dictionary of the New Testament,* edited by Gerhard Kittel and Gerhard Friedrich, vol. 5. Translated by Geoffrey W. Bromiley. Grand Rapids: Wm. B. Eerdmans, 1967.

Miesner, Donald R. "The Missionary Journeys Narrative: Patterns and Implications." Pp. 199–214 in *Perspectives on Luke-Acts,* edited by Charles H. Talbert. Perspectives in Religious Studies Special Studies Series 5. Danville, Va.: Association of Baptist Professors of Religion, 1978.

_____. "The Circumferential Speeches of Luke-Acts: Patterns and Purpose." Pp. 223–37 in *Society of Biblical Literature 1978 Seminar Papers,* edited by Paul J. Achtemeier, vol. 2. Missoula, Mont.: Scholars Press, 1978.

Miles, Gary B., and Trompf, Garry. "Luke and Antiphon: The Theology of Acts 27–28 in the Light of Pagan Beliefs about Divine Retribution, Pollution, and Shipwreck." *Harvard Theological Review* 69 (1976): 259–67.

Minear, Paul S. "Dear Theo: The Kerygmatic Intention and Claim of the Book of Acts." *Interpretation* 27 (1973): 131–50.

———. *To Heal and to Reveal: The Prophetic Vocation According to Luke.* New York: Seabury Press, 1976.

Moessner, David P. "Jesus and the 'Wilderness Generation': The Death of the Prophet like Moses According to Luke." Pp. 319–40 in *Society of Biblical Literature 1982 Seminar Papers,* edited by Kent Harold Richards. Chico, Calif.: Scholars Press, 1982.

———. "Paul and the Pattern of the Prophet like Moses in Acts." Pp. 203–12 in *Society of Biblical Literature 1983 Seminar Papers,* edited by Kent Harold Richards. Chico, Calif.: Scholars Press, 1983.

———. "'The Christ Must Suffer': New Light on the Jesus-Peter, Stephen, Paul Parallels in Luke-Acts." *Novum Testamentum* 28 (1986): 220–56.

———. "The Ironic Fulfillment of Israel's Glory." Pp. 35–50 in *Luke-Acts and the Jewish People: Eight Critical Perspectives,* edited by Joseph B. Tyson. Minneapolis: Augsburg Publishing House, 1988.

———. "Paul in Acts: Preacher of Eschatological Repentance to Israel." *New Testament Studies* 34 (1988): 96–104.

Morgenthaler, Robert. *Die lukanische Geschichtsschreibung als Zeugnis: Gestalt und Gehalt der Kunst des Lukas.* 2 vols. Abhandlungen zur Theologie des Alten und Neuen Testaments 14–15. Zürich: Zwingli-Verlag, 1949.

Moule, C. F. D. "The Christology of Acts." Pp. 159–85 in *Studies in Luke-Acts: Essays Presented in Honor of Paul Schubert,* edited by Leander E. Keck and J. Louis Martyn. Nashville: Abingdon Press, 1966. (Reprint. Philadelphia: Fortress Press, 1980.)

Muhlack, Gudrun. *Die Parallelen von Lukas-Evangelium und Apostelgeschichte.* Theologie und Wirklichkeit 8. Frankfurt: Peter Lang, 1979.

Mullins, Terence Y. "New Testament Commission Forms, Especially in Luke-Acts." *Journal of Biblical Literature* 95 (1976): 603–14.

Mussner, Franz. "Die Idee der Apokatastasis in der Apostelgeschichte." Pp. 293–306 in *Lex Tua Veritas. Festschrift für Hubert Junker,* edited by Heinrich Gross and Franz Mussner. Trier: Paulinus-Verlag, 1961.

———. "Wohnung Gottes und Menschensohn nach der Stephanusperikope (Apg 6,8— 8,2)." Pp. 283–99 in *Jesus und der Menschensohn: Für Anton Vögtle,* edited by Rudolf Pesch and Rudolf Schnackenburg. Freiburg: Herder, 1975.

Nauck, Wolfgang. "Die Tradition und Komposition der Areopagrede." *Zeitschrift für Theologie und Kirche* 53 (1956): 11–52.

Neirynck, Frans. "The Miracle Stories in the Acts of the Apostles." Pp. 169–213 in *Les Actes des Apôtres: Traditions, rédaction, théologie,* edited by J. Kremer. Bibliotheca Ephemeridum Theologicarum Lovaniensium 48. Gembloux: J. Duculot & Leuven: Leuven University Press, 1979.

———. "Le livre des Actes: 6. Ac 10, 36–43 et l'Évangile." *Ephemerides Theologicae Lovanienses* 60 (1984): 109–17.

———. "Acts 10,36a τὸν λόγον ὄν." *Ephemerides Theologicae Lovanienses* 60 (1984): 118–23.

Nellessen, Ernst. *Zeugnis für Jesus und das Wort: Exegetische Untersuchungen zum lukanischen Zeugnisbegriff.* Bonner biblische Beiträge 43. Cologne: Peter Hanstein, 1976.

Nelson, Edwin S. *Paul's First Missionary Journey as Paradigm: A Literary-Critical Assessment of Acts 13, 14.* Ph.D. diss., Boston University, 1982.

Neyrey, Jerome. "The Forensic Defense Speech and Paul's Trial Speeches in Acts 22— 26: Form and Function." Pp. 210–24 in *Luke-Acts: New Perspectives from the Society of Biblical Literature Seminar,* edited by Charles H. Talbert. New York: Crossroad, 1984.

———. *The Passion According to Luke: A Redaction Study of Luke's Soteriology.* Theological Inquiries. New York: Paulist Press, 1985.

Nida, E. A., Louw, J. P., Snyman, A. H., and Cronje, J. V. W. *Style and Discourse, with*

Special Reference to the Text of the Greek New Testament. Cape Town: Bible Society, 1983.

Nock, Arthur Darby. "Paul and the Magus." Pp. 164–88 in *The Beginnings of Christianity*, edited by F. J. Foakes Jackson and Kirsopp Lake, vol. 5. London: Macmillan & Co., 1933.

Nolland, John. "A Fresh Look at Acts 15:10." *New Testament Studies* 27 (1980–81): 105–15.

———. "Luke's Use of ΧΑΡΙΣ." *New Testament Studies* 32 (1986): 614–20.

Noorda, S. J. "Scene and Summary: A Proposal for Reading Acts 4,32—5,16." Pp. 475–83 in *Les Actes des Apôtres: Traditions, rédaction, théologie*, edited by J. Kremer. Bibliotheca Ephemeridum Theologicarum Lovaniensium 48. Gembloux: J. Duculot & Leuven: Leuven University Press, 1979.

O'Neill, J. C. *The Theology of Acts in Its Historical Setting.* London: SPCK, 1961.

O'Reilly, Leo. *Word and Sign in the Acts of the Apostles: A Study in Lucan Theology.* Analecta Gregoriana 243. Rome: Editrice Pontificia Università Gregoriana, 1987.

O'Toole, Robert F. "Luke's Notion of 'Be Imitators of Me as I Am of Christ' in Acts 25–26." *Biblical Theology Bulletin* 8 (1978): 155–61.

———. *Acts 26: The Christological Climax of Paul's Defense (Ac 22:1—26:32).* Analecta Biblica 78. Rome: Biblical Institute Press, 1978.

———. "Some Observations on Anistēmi, 'I Raise,' in Acts 3:22, 26." *Science et Esprit* 31 (1979): 85–92.

———. "Christ's Resurrection in Acts 13,13–52." *Biblica* 60 (1979): 361–72.

———. "Luke's Understanding of Jesus' Resurrection-Ascension-Exaltation." *Biblical Theology Bulletin* 9 (1979): 106–14.

———. "Paul at Athens and Luke's Notion of Worship." *Revue Biblique* 89 (1982): 185–97.

———. "Parallels between Jesus and His Disciples in Luke-Acts: A Further Study." *Biblische Zeitschrift* 27 (1983): 195–212.

———. "Acts 2:30 and the Davidic Covenant of Pentecost." *Journal of Biblical Literature* 102 (1983): 245–58.

———. "Philip and the Ethiopian Eunuch (Acts VIII 25–40)." *Journal for the Study of the New Testament* 17 (1983): 25–34.

———. *The Unity of Luke's Theology: An Analysis of Luke-Acts.* Good News Studies 9. Wilmington: Michael Glazier, 1984.

Overman, J. Andrew. "The God-Fearers: Some Neglected Features." *Journal for the Study of the New Testament* 32 (1988): 17–26.

Parsons, Mikeal C. *The Departure of Jesus in Luke-Acts: The Ascension Narratives in Context.* Journal for the Study of the New Testament Supplement Series 21. Sheffield: JSOT Press, 1987.

———. "The Text of Acts 1:2 Reconsidered." *Catholic Biblical Quarterly* 50 (1988): 58–71.

Patsch, Hermann. "Die Prophetie des Agabus." *Theologische Zeitschrift* 28 (1972): 228–32.

Pereira, Francis. *Ephesus: Climax of Universalism in Luke-Acts. A Redaction-Critical Study of Paul's Ephesian Ministry (Acts 18:23—20:1).* Jesuit Theological Forum Studies 1. Anand, India: Gujarat Sahitya Prakash, 1983.

Perelman, Chaim, and Olbrechts-Tyteca, L. *The New Rhetoric: A Treatise on Argumentation.* Translated by John Wilkinson and Purcell Weaver. Notre Dame, Ind.: University of Notre Dame Press, 1969.

Perrine, Laurence. *Story and Structure.* 3d ed. New York: Harcourt, Brace & World, 1970.

Perry, Menakhem. "Literary Dynamics: How the Order of the Text Creates Its Meanings." *Poetics Today* 1 (1979): 35–64, 311–61.

Pervo, Richard I. *Profit with Delight: The Literary Genre of the Acts of the Apostles.* Philadelphia: Fortress Press, 1987.

Pesch, Rudolf. *Die Vision des Stephanus: Apg 7,55–56 im Rahmen der Apostelgeschichte.* Stuttgarter Bibelstudien 12. Stuttgart: Verlag Katholisches Bibelwerk, 1966.

———. "Der Christ als Nachahmer Christi: Der Tod des Stefanus (Apg 7) im Vergleich mit dem Tod Christi." *Bibel und Kirche* 24 (1969): 10–11.

———. *Die Apostelgeschichte.* 2 vols. Evangelisch-Katholischer Kommentar zum Neuen Testament 5. Zürich: Benziger Verlag & Neukirchen-Vluyn: Neukirchener Verlag, 1986.

Pfitzner, Victor C. "'Pneumatic' Apostleship? Apostle and Spirit in the Acts of the Apostles." Pp. 210–35 in *Wort in der Zeit: Festgabe für Karl Heinrich Rengstorf*, edited by Wilfrid Haubeck and Michael Bachmann. Leiden: E. J. Brill, 1980.

Plümacher, Eckhard. *Lukas als hellenistischer Schriftsteller: Studien zur Apostelgeschichte.* Studien zur Umwelt des Neuen Testaments 9. Göttingen: Vandenhoeck & Ruprecht, 1972.

———. "Lukas als griechischer Historiker." Col. 235–64 in *Paulys Realencyclopädie der classischen Altertumswissenschaft*, Supplementband 14. Munich: Alfred Druckenmüller, 1974.

———. "Die Apostelgeschichte als historische Monographie." Pp. 457–66 in *Les Actes des Apôtres: Traditions, rédaction, théologie*, edited by J. Kremer. Bibliotheca Ephemeridum Theologicarum Lovaniensium 48. Gembloux: J. Duculot & Leuven: Leuven University Press, 1979.

———. "Neues Testament und hellenistische Form: Zur literarischen Gattung der lukanischen Schriften." Pp. 109–23 in *Theologia Viatorum: Jahrbuch der Kirchlichen Hochschule Berlin* 14 (1977–78), edited by Peter C. Bloth. Berlin: C. Z. V. Verlag, 1979.

———. "Acta-Forschung 1974–1982." *Theologische Rundschau* 48 (1983): 1–56; 49 (1984): 105–69.

Plunkett, Mark A. "Ethnocentricity and Salvation History in the Cornelius Episode." Pp. 465–79 in *Society of Biblical Literature 1985 Seminar Papers*, edited by Kent Harold Richards. Atlanta: Scholars Press, 1985.

Pokorný, Petr. "Die Romfahrt des Paulus und der antike Roman." *Zeitschrift für die neutestamentliche Wissenschaft* 64 (1973): 233–44.

Praeder, Susan Marie. *The Narrative Voyage: An Analysis and Interpretation of Acts 27–28.* Ph.D. diss., Graduate Theological Union, 1980.

———. "Luke-Acts and the Ancient Novel." Pp. 269–92 in *Society of Biblical Literature 1981 Seminar Papers*, edited by Kent Harold Richards. Chico, Calif.: Scholars Press, 1981.

———. "Miracle Worker and Missionary: Paul in the Acts of the Apostles." Pp. 107–29 in *Society of Biblical Literature 1983 Seminar Papers*, edited by Kent Harold Richards. Chico, Calif.: Scholars Press, 1983.

———. "Acts 27:1—28:16: Sea Voyages in Ancient Literature and the Theology of Luke-Acts." *Catholic Biblical Quarterly* 46 (1984): 683–706.

———. "Jesus-Paul, Peter-Paul, and Jesus-Peter Parallelisms in Luke-Acts: A History of Reader Response." Pp. 23–39 in *Society of Biblical Literature 1984 Seminar Papers*, edited by Kent Harold Richards. Chico, Calif.: Scholars Press, 1984.

———. "The Problem of First Person Narration in Acts." *Novum Testamentum* 29 (1987): 193–218.

Prast, Franz. *Presbyter und Evangelium in nachapostolischer Zeit: Die Abschiedsrede des Paulus in Milet (Apg 20,17–38) im Rahmen der lukanischen Konzeption der Evangeliumsverkündigung.* Forschung zur Bibel 29. Stuttgart: Verlag Katholisches Bibelwerk, 1979.

Puskas, Charles B., Jr. *The Conclusion of Luke-Acts: An Investigation of the Literary Function and Theological Significance of Acts 28:16–31.* Ph.D. diss., St. Louis University, 1980.

Quintilian. *Institutio Oratoria,* with an English translation by H. E. Butler. 4 vols. Loeb Classical Library. Cambridge: Harvard University Press, 1958–60.

Radl, Walter. *Paulus und Jesus im lukanischen Doppelwerk: Untersuchungen zu Parallelmotiven im Lukasevangelium und in der Apostelgeschichte.* Europäische Hochschulschriften. Bern: Herbert Lang & Frankfurt: Peter Lang, 1975.

———. "Das 'Apostelkonzil' und seine Nachgeschichte, dargestellt am Weg des Barnabas." *Theologische Quartalschrift* 162 (1982): 45–61.

———. "Befreiung aus dem Gefängnis: Die Darstellung eines biblischen Grundthemas in Apg 12." *Biblische Zeitschrift* 27 (1983): 81–96.

Reicke, Bo. "Die Mahlzeit mit Paulus auf den Wellen des Mittelmeers Act. 27,33–38." *Theologische Zeitschrift* 4 (1948): 401–10.

———. "The Risen Lord and His Church." *Interpretation* 13 (1959): 157–69.

Rengstorf, K. H. "The Election of Matthias: Acts 1.15 ff." Pp. 178–92 in *Current Issues in New Testament Interpretation: Essays in Honor of Otto A. Piper,* edited by William Klassen and Graydon F. Snyder. New York: Harper & Brothers, 1962.

Rese, Martin. *Alttestamentliche Motive in der Christologie des Lukas.* Studien zum Neuen Testament 1. Gütersloh: Gütersloher Verlagshaus Gerd Mohn, 1969.

———. "Die Funktion der alttestamentlichen Zitate und Anspielungen in den Reden der Apostelgeschichte." Pp. 61–79 in *Les Actes des Apôtres: Traditions, rédaction, théologie,* edited by J. Kremer. Bibliotheca Ephemeridum Theologicarum Lovaniensium 48. Gembloux: J. Duculot & Leuven: Leuven University Press, 1979.

Rhoads, David, and Michie, Donald. *Mark as Story: An Introduction to the Narrative of a Gospel.* Philadelphia: Fortress Press, 1982.

Richard, Earl. *Acts 6:1—8:4: The Author's Method of Composition.* Society of Biblical Literature Dissertation Series 41. Missoula, Mont.: Scholars Press, 1978.

———. "The Polemical Character of the Joseph Episode in Acts 7." *Journal of Biblical Literature* 98 (1979): 255–67.

———. "The Old Testament in Acts: Wilcox's Semitisms in Retrospect." *Catholic Biblical Quarterly* 42 (1980): 330–41.

———. "The Creative Use of Amos by the Author of Acts." *Novum Testamentum* 24 (1982): 37–53.

———. "The Divine Purpose: The Jews and the Gentile Mission (Acts 15)." Pp. 188–209 in *Luke-Acts: New Perspectives from the Society of Biblical Literature Seminar,* edited by Charles H. Talbert. New York: Crossroad, 1984.

Riesenfeld, Harald. "The Text of Acts X. 36." Pp. 191–94 in *Text and Interpretation: Studies . . . Presented to Matthew Black,* edited by Ernest Best and R. McL. Wilson. Cambridge: Cambridge University Press, 1979.

Rimmon-Kenan, Shlomith. *Narrative Fiction: Contemporary Poetics.* New Accents. London: Methuen & Co., 1983.

Ringgren, Helmer. "Luke's Use of the Old Testament." *Harvard Theological Review* 79 (1986): 227–35.

Robbins, Vernon K. "By Land and by Sea: The We-Passages and Ancient Sea Voyages." Pp. 215–42 in *Perspectives on Luke-Acts,* edited by Charles H. Talbert. Perspectives in Religious Studies Special Studies Series 5. Danville, Va.: Association of Baptist Professors of Religion, 1978.

Robinson, James M. "Acts." Pp. 467–78 in *The Literary Guide to the Bible,* edited by Robert Alter and Frank Kermode. Cambridge: Harvard University Press, 1987.

Roloff, Jürgen. *Die Apostelgeschichte.* Das Neue Testament Deutsch 5. Göttingen: Vandenhoeck & Ruprecht, 1981.

Rosenblatt, Marie-Eloise. *Under Interrogation: Paul as Witness in Juridical Contexts in Acts and the Implied Spirituality for Luke's Community.* Ph.D. diss., Graduate Theological Union, 1987.

Sabbe, M. "The Son of Man Saying in Acts 7, 56." Pp. 241–79 in *Les Actes des Apôtres: Traditions, rédaction, théologie,* edited by J. Kremer. Bibliotheca Ephemeridum

Theologicarum Lovaniensium 48. Gembloux: J. Duculot & Leuven: Leuven University Press, 1979.

Salmon, Marilyn. "Insider or Outsider? Luke's Relationship with Judaism." Pp. 76–82 in *Luke-Acts and the Jewish People: Eight Critical Perspectives*, edited by Joseph B. Tyson. Minneapolis: Augsburg Publishing House, 1988.

Sanders, J. N. "Peter and Paul in the Acts." *New Testament Studies* 2 (1955–56): 133–43.

Sanders, Jack T. "The Salvation of the Jews in Luke-Acts." Pp. 104–28 in *Luke-Acts: New Perspectives from the Society of Biblical Literature Seminar,* edited by Charles H. Talbert. New York: Crossroad, 1984.

———. "The Pharisees in Luke-Acts." Pp. 141–88 in *The Living Text: Essays in Honor of Ernest W. Saunders,* edited by Dennis Groh and Robert Jewett. Lanham, Md.: University Press of America, 1985.

———. *The Jews in Luke-Acts*. Philadelphia: Fortress Press, 1987.

———. "The Jewish People in Luke-Acts." Pp. 51–75 in *Luke-Acts and the Jewish People: Eight Critical Perspectives,* edited by Joseph B. Tyson. Minneapolis: Augsburg Publishing House, 1988.

Sanders, James A. "Hermeneutics." Pp. 402–7 in *The Interpreter's Dictionary of the Bible,* Supplementary Volume, edited by Keith Crim. Nashville: Abingdon Press, 1976. (See also pp. 63–73 in *From Sacred Story to Sacred Text*. Philadelphia: Fortress Press, 1987.)

Savran, George W. *Telling and Retelling: Quotation in Biblical Narrative*. Indiana Studies in Biblical Literature. Bloomington: Indiana University Press, 1988.

Schille, Gottfried. *Die Apostelgeschichte des Lukas*. Theologischer Handkommentar zum Neuen Testament 5. Berlin: Evangelische Verlagsanstalt, 1983.

Schlosser, Jacques. "Moïse, serviteur du kérygme apostolique d'après Ac 3,22–26." *Revue des Sciences Religieuses* 61 (1987): 17–31.

Schmidt, Daryl. "The Historiography of Acts: Deuteronomistic or Hellenistic?" Pp. 417–27 in *Society of Biblical Literature 1985 Seminar Papers,* edited by Kent Harold Richards. Atlanta: Scholars Press, 1985.

Schmithals, Walter. "Die Berichte der Apostelgeschichte über die Bekehrung des Paulus und die 'Tendenz' des Lukas." Pp. 145–65 in *Theologia Viatorum: Jahrbuch der Kirchlichen Hochschule Berlin* 14 (1977–78), edited by Peter C. Bloth. Berlin: C. Z. V. Verlag, 1979.

———. *Die Apostelgeschichte des Lukas*. Zürcher Bibelkommentare. Zürich: Theologischer Verlag, 1982.

Schmitt, J. "L'église de Jérusalem ou la 'restauration' d'Israel d'après les cinq premiers chapitres des Actes." *Revue des Sciences Religieuses* 27 (1953): 209–18.

Schnackenburg, Rudolf. "Lukas als Zeuge verschiedener Gemeindestrukturen." *Bibel und Leben* 12 (1971): 232–47.

Schneider, Gerhard. "Der Zweck des lukanischen Doppelwerks." *Biblische Zeitschrift* 21 (1977): 45–66.

———. *Die Apostelgeschichte*. 2 vols. Herders theologischer Kommentar zum Neuen Testament 5. Freiburg: Herder, 1980, 1982.

———. *Lukas, Theologe der Heilsgeschichte: Aufsätze zum lukanischen Doppelwerk*. Bonner biblische Beiträge 59. Bonn: Peter Hanstein Verlag, 1985.

Schneider, Johannes. "εὐνοῦχος." Pp. 765–68 in *Theological Dictionary of the New Testament,* edited by Gerhard Kittel and Gerhard Friedrich, vol. 2. Translated by Geoffrey W. Bromiley. Grand Rapids: Wm. B. Eerdmans, 1964.

Schubert, Paul. "The Place of the Areopagus Speech in the Composition of Acts." Pp. 235–61 in *Transitions in Biblical Scholarship,* edited by J. Coert Rylaarsdam. Chicago: University of Chicago Press, 1968.

———. "The Final Cycle of Speeches in the Book of Acts." *Journal of Biblical Literature* 87 (1968): 1–16.

Schürmann, Heinz. "Das Testament des Paulus für die Kirche Apg 20,18–35." Pp. 310–

40 in *Traditionsgeschichtliche Untersuchungen zu den synoptischen Evangelien*. Kommentare und Beiträge zum Alten und Neuen Testament. Düsseldorf: Patmos-Verlag, 1968.

Schütz, Frieder. *Der leidende Christus: Die angefochtene Gemeinde und das Christuskerygma der lukanischen Schriften*. Beiträge zur Wissenschaft vom Alten und Neuen Testament 89. Stuttgart: Verlag W. Kohlhammer, 1969.

Schulz, Siegfried. "Gottes Vorsehung bei Lukas." *Zeitschrift für die neutestamentliche Wissenschaft* 54 (1963): 104–16.

Schwartz, Daniel R. "The Accusation and the Accusers at Philippi (Acts 16,20–21)." *Biblica* 65 (1984): 357–63.

_____. "The End of the ΓΗ (Acts 1:8): Beginning or End of the Christian Vision?" *Journal of Biblical Literature* 105 (1986): 669–76.

_____. "The Futility of Preaching Moses (Acts 15,21)." *Biblica* 67 (1986): 276–81.

Schweizer, Eduard. "The Concept of the Davidic 'Son of God' in Acts and Its Old Testament Background." Pp. 186–93 in *Studies in Luke-Acts: Essays in Honor of Paul Schubert*, edited by Leander E. Keck and J. Louis Martyn. Nashville: Abingdon Press, 1966. (Reprint. Philadelphia: Fortress Press, 1980.)

_____. "Concerning the Speeches in Acts." Pp. 208–16 in *Studies in Luke-Acts: Essays Presented in Honor of Paul Schubert*, edited by Leander E. Keck and J. Louis Martyn. Nashville: Abingdon Press, 1966. (Reprint. Philadelphia: Fortress Press, 1980.)

Scott, J. Julius, Jr. "Stephen's Speech: A Possible Model for Luke's Historical Method?" *Journal of the Evangelical Theological Society* 17 (1974): 91–97.

Seccombe, David. "Luke and Isaiah." *New Testament Studies* 27 (1980–81): 252–59.

_____. *Possessions and the Poor in Luke-Acts*. Studien zum Neuen Testament und seiner Umwelt. Linz, 1982.

Seifrid, M. A. "Jesus and the Law in Acts." *Journal for the Study of the New Testament* 30 (1987): 39–57.

Sheeley, Steven M. "Narrative Asides and Narrative Authority in Luke-Acts." *Biblical Theology Bulletin* 18 (1988): 102–7.

Shuler, Philip L. "Questions of an Holistic Approach to Luke-Acts." *Perkins Journal* 40 (1987): 43–47.

Simon, Marcel. "Saint Stephen and the Jerusalem Temple." *Journal of Ecclesiastical History* 2 (1951): 127–42.

Slingerland, Dixon. "'The Jews' in the Pauline Portion of Acts." *Journal of the American Academy of Religion* 54 (1986): 305–21.

_____. "The Composition of Acts: Some Redaction-Critical Observations." *Journal of the American Academy of Religion* 56 (1988): 99–113.

Stählin, Gustav. "χήρα." Pp. 440–65 in *Theological Dictionary of the New Testament*, edited by Gerhard Kittel and Gerhard Friedrich, vol. 9. Translated by Geoffrey W. Bromiley. Grand Rapids: Wm. B. Eerdmans, 1974.

Stagg, Frank. "The Unhindered Gospel." *Review and Expositor* 71 (1974): 451–62.

Standaert, Benoît. "L'art de composer dans l'oeuvre de Luc." Pp. 323–47 in *À cause de l'évangile: Études sur les Synoptiques et les Actes offertes an P. Jacques Dupont*. Lectio Divina 123. Paris: Les Éditions du Cerf, 1985.

Stanley, David M. "Paul's Conversion in Acts: Why the Three Accounts?" *Catholic Biblical Quarterly* 15 (1953): 315–38.

Stanton, Graham. "Stephen in Lucan Perspective." Pp. 345–60 in *Studia Biblica 1978*, vol. 3, edited by E. A. Livingstone. Journal for the Study of the New Testament Supplement Series 3. Sheffield: JSOT Press, 1980.

Steck, Odil Hannes. *Israel und das gewaltsame Geschick der Propheten*. Wissenschaftliche Monographien zum Alten und Neuen Testament 23. Neukirchen-Vluyn: Neukirchener Verlag, 1967.

Steichele, Hanneliese. *Vergleich der Apostelgeschichte mit der antiken Geschichtsschreibung: Eine Studie zur Erzählkunst in der Apostelgeschichte*. Dissertation, Ludwig-Maximilians-Universität in München, 1971.

Sternberg, Meir. *The Poetics of Biblical Narrative: Ideological Literature and the Drama of Reading*. Indiana Literary Biblical Series. Bloomington: Indiana University Press, 1985.

Stolle, Volker. *Der Zeuge als Angeklagter. Untersuchungen zum Paulus-Bild des Lukas*. Beiträge zur Wissenschaft vom Alten und Neuen Testament 102. Stuttgart: Verlag W. Kohlhammer, 1973.

Stoops, Robert F., Jr. "Riot and Assembly: The Social Context of Acts 19:23–41." *Journal of Biblical Literature* 108 (1989): 73–91.

Strobel, August. "Passa-Symbolik und Passa-Wunder in Act. XII. 3ff." *New Testament Studies* 4 (1957–58): 210–15.

Strom, Mark R. "An Old Testament Background to Acts 12.20–23." *New Testament Studies* 32 (1986): 289–92.

Suleiman, Susan Rubin. "Redundancy and the 'Readable' Text." *Poetics Today* 1 (1980): 119–42.

Sylva, Dennis D. *The Lukan Jerusalem*. Ph.D. diss., Marquette University, n.d.

———. "The Meaning and Function of Acts 7:46–50." *Journal of Biblical Literature* 106 (1987): 261–75.

Taeger, Jens-W. *Der Mensch und sein Heil: Studien zum Bild des Menschen und zur Sicht der Bekehrung bei Lukas*. Studien zum Neuen Testament 14. Gütersloh: Gerd Mohn, 1982.

Talbert, Charles H. *Luke and the Gnostics: An Examination of the Lucan Purpose*. Nashville: Abingdon Press, 1966.

———. *Literary Patterns, Theological Themes, and the Genre of Luke-Acts*. Society of Biblical Literature Monograph Series 20. Missoula, Mont.: Scholars Press, 1974.

———. "Martyrdom in Luke-Acts and the Lukan Social Ethic." Pp. 99–110 in *Political Issues in Luke-Acts*, edited by Richard Cassidy and Philip Scharper. Maryknoll, N.Y.: Orbis Books, 1983.

———. *Acts*. Knox Preaching Guides. Atlanta: John Knox Press, 1984.

———. "Promise and Fulfillment in Lucan Theology." Pp. 91–103 in *Luke-Acts: New Perspectives from the Society of Biblical Literature Seminar*, edited by Charles H. Talbert. New York: Crossroad, 1984.

Tannehill, Robert C. *The Sword of His Mouth: Forceful and Imaginative Language in Synoptic Sayings*. Semeia Supplements 1. Philadelphia: Fortress Press & Missoula, Mont.: Scholars Press, 1975.

———. "The Composition of Acts 3–5: Narrative Development and Echo Effect." Pp. 217–40 in *Society of Biblical Literature 1984 Seminar Papers*, edited by Kent Harold Richards. Chico, Calif.: Scholars Press, 1984.

———. "Israel in Luke-Acts: A Tragic Story." *Journal of Biblical Literature* 104 (1985): 69–85.

———. "Rejection by Jews and Turning to Gentiles: The Pattern of Paul's Mission in Acts." Pp. 130–41 in *Society of Biblical Literature 1986 Seminar Papers*, edited by Kent Harold Richards. Atlanta: Scholars Press, 1986. A revised version appears as pp. 83–101 in *Luke-Acts and the Jewish People: Eight Critical Perspectives*, edited by Joseph B. Tyson. Minneapolis: Augsburg Publishing House, 1988.

———. "Paul outside the Christian Ghetto: Stories of Intercultural Conflict and Cooperation in Acts." In *Text and Logos: The Humanistic Interpretation of the New Testament: Essays in Honor of Hendrikus Wouterus Boers*, edited by Theodore W. Jennings, Jr. Atlanta: Scholars Press, forthcoming.

Thiering, Barbara. "The Acts of the Apostles as Early Christian Art." Pp. 139–89 in *Essays in Honour of G. W. Thatcher*, edited by E. C. B. MacLaurin. Sydney University Press, 1967.

Thornton, T. C. G. "Stephen's Use of Isaiah LXVI. 1." *Journal of Theological Studies* 25 (1974): 432–34.

———. "To the End of the Earth: Acts 1:8." *Expository Times* 89 (1977–78): 374–75.

Tiede, David L. *Prophecy and History in Luke-Acts*. Philadelphia: Fortress Press, 1980.

———. "Acts 1:6–8 and the Theo-Political Claims of Christian Witness." *Word and World* 1 (1981): 41–51.

———. "The Exaltation of Jesus and the Restoration of Israel in Acts 1." *Harvard Theological Review* 79 (1986): 278–86.

———. "'Glory to Thy People Israel': Luke-Acts and the Jews." Pp. 21–34 in *Luke-Acts and the Jewish People: Eight Critical Perspectives,* edited by Joseph B. Tyson. Minneapolis: Augsburg Publishing House, 1988.

Torgovnick, Marianna. *Closure in the Novel.* Princeton: Princeton University Press, 1981.

Townsend, John T. "The Speeches in Acts." *Anglican Theological Review* 42 (1960): 150–59.

Tragan, Pius-Ramon. "Les 'destinataires' du discours de Milet: Une approche du cadre communautaire d'Ac 20, 18–35." Pp. 779–98 in *À cause de l'évangile: Études sur les Synoptiques et les Actes offertes an P. Jacques Dupont.* Lectio Divina 123. Paris: Les Éditions du Cerf, 1985.

Trémel, Bernard. "À propos d'Actes 20,7–12: Puissance du thaumaturge ou du témoin?" *Revue de Théologie et de Philosophie* 112 (1980): 359–69.

Trites, Allison A. "The Importance of Legal Scenes and Language in the Book of Acts." *Novum Testamentum* 16 (1974): 278–84.

———. "The Prayer Motif in Luke-Acts." Pp. 168–86 in *Perspectives on Luke-Acts,* edited by Charles H. Talbert. Perspectives in Religious Studies Special Studies Series 5. Danville, Va.: Association of Baptist Professors of Religion, 1978.

Trocmé, Étienne. *Le "Livre des Actes" et l'histoire.* Études d'histoire et de philosophie religieuses. Paris: Presses Universitaires de France, 1957.

Trompf, G. W. *The Idea of Historical Recurrence in Western Thought: From Antiquity to the Reformation.* Berkeley and Los Angeles: University of California Press, 1979.

———. "On Why Luke Declined to Recount the Death of Paul: Acts 27–28 and Beyond." Pp. 225–39 in *Luke-Acts: New Perspectives from the Society of Biblical Literature Seminar,* edited by Charles H. Talbert. New York: Crossroad, 1984.

Turner, Nigel. "The Quality of the Greek of Luke-Acts." Pp. 387–400 in *Studies in New Testament Language and Text,* edited by J. K. Elliott. Leiden: E. J. Brill, 1976.

Tyson, Joseph B. "The Problem of Food in Acts: A Study of Literary Patterns with Particular Reference to Acts 6:1–7." Pp. 69–85 in *Society of Biblical Literature 1979 Seminar Papers,* vol. 1, edited by Paul J. Achtemeier. Missoula, Mont.: Scholars Press, 1979.

———. "The Jewish Public in Luke-Acts." *New Testament Studies* 30 (1984): 574–83.

———. *The Death of Jesus in Luke-Acts.* Columbia: University of South Carolina Press, 1986.

———. "The Gentile Mission and the Authority of Scripture in Acts." *New Testament Studies* 33 (1987): 619–31.

———. "The Emerging Church and the Problem of Authority in Acts." *Interpretation* 42 (1988): 132–45.

———. "The Problem of Jewish Rejection in Acts." Pp. 124–37 in *Luke-Acts and the Jewish People: Eight Critical Perspectives,* edited by Joseph B. Tyson. Minneapolis: Augsburg Publishing House, 1988.

Uspensky, Boris. *A Poetics of Composition: The Structure of the Artistic Text and Typology of a Compositional Form.* Translated by Valentina Zavarin and Susan Wittig. Berkeley and Los Angeles: University of California Press, 1973.

van Stempvoort, P. A. "The Interpretation of the Ascension in Luke and Acts." *New Testament Studies* 5 (1958–59): 30–42.

van Unnik, W. C. "Luke-Acts, a Storm Center in Contemporary Scholarship." Pp. 15–32 in *Studies in Luke-Acts: Essays Presented in Honor of Paul Schubert,* edited by Leander E. Keck and J. Louis Martyn. Nashville: Abingdon Press, 1966. (Reprint. Philadelphia: Fortress Press, 1980.)

———. "First Century A.D. Literary Culture and Early Christian Literature." Pp. 1–13 in *Protocol of the First Colloquy of the Center for Hermeneutical Studies in Hellenistic and Modern Culture*. Berkeley: 1970.

———. "The Background and Significance of Acts X 4 and 35." Pp. 213–58 in *Sparsa Collecta: The Collected Essays of W. C. van Unnik*, vol. 1. Supplements to Novum Testamentum 29. Leiden: E. J. Brill, 1973.

———. "The 'Book of Acts'—The Confirmation of the Gospel." Pp. 340–73 in *Sparsa Collecta: The Collected Essays of W. C. van Unnik*, vol. 1. Supplements to Novum Testamentum 29. Leiden: E. J. Brill, 1973.

———. "Die Anklage gegen die Apostel in Philippi." Pp. 374–85 in *Sparsa Collecta: The Collected Essays of W. C. van Unnik*, vol. 1. Supplements to Novum Testamentum 29. Leiden: E. J. Brill, 1973.

———. "Der Ausdruck ῾ΕΩΣ ᾿ΕΣΧΑΤΟΥ ΤΗΣ ΓΗΣ (Apostelgeschichte I 8) und sein alttestamentlicher Hintergrund." Pp. 386–401 in *Sparsa Collecta: The Collected Essays of W. C. van Unnik*, vol. 1. Supplements to Novum Testamentum 29. Leiden: E. J. Brill, 1973.

———."Éléments artistiques dans l'évangile de Luc." Pp. 129–40 in *L'Évangile de Luc: Problèmes littéraires et théologiques: Mémorial Lucien Cerfaux*, edited by F. Neirynck. Bibliotheca Ephemeridum Theologicarum Lovaniensium 32. Gembloux: J. Duculot, 1973.

———. "Luke's Second Book and the Rules of Hellenistic Historiography." Pp. 37–60 in *Les Actes des Apôtres: Traditions, rédaction, théologie*, edited by J. Kremer. Bibliotheca Ephemeridum Theologicarum Lovaniensium 48. Gembloux: J. Duculot & Leuven: Leuven University Press, 1979.

Veltman, Frederick. *The Defense Speeches of Paul in Acts: Gattungsforschung and Its Limitations*. Th.D. diss., Graduate Theological Union, 1975.

———. "The Defense Speeches of Paul in Acts." Pp. 243–56 in *Perspectives on Luke-Acts*, edited by Charles H. Talbert. Perspectives in Religious Studies Special Studies Series 5. Danville, Va.: Association of Baptist Professors of Religion, 1978.

Vielhauer, Philipp. "On the 'Paulinism' of Acts." Pp. 33–50 in *Studies in Luke-Acts: Essays Presented in Honor of Paul Schubert*, edited by Leander E. Keck and J. Louis Martyn. Nashville: Abingdon Press, 1966. (Reprint. Philadelphia: Fortress Press, 1980.)

Vögeli, Alfred. "Lukas und Euripides." *Theologische Zeitschrift* 9 (1953): 415–38.

Völkel, Martin. "Zur Deutung des 'Reiches Gottes' bei Lukas." *Zeitschrift für die neutestamentliche Wissenschaft* 65 (1974): 57–70.

Voss, Gerhard. *Die Christologie der lukanischen Schriften in Grundzügen*. Studia Neotestamentica 2. Brügge: Desclée de Brouwer, 1965.

Wainwright, Arthur W. "Luke and the Restoration of the Kingdom to Israel." *Expository Times* 89 (1977–78): 76–79.

Walaskay, Paul W. *'And so we came to Rome': The Political Perspective of St. Luke*. Society for New Testament Studies Monograph Series 49. Cambridge: Cambridge University Press, 1983.

Wall, Robert W. "Peter, 'Son' of Jonah: The Conversion of Cornelius in the Context of Canon." *Journal for the Study of the New Testament* 29 (1987): 79–90.

Walworth, Allen James. *The Narrator of Acts*. Ph.D. diss., Southern Baptist Theological Seminary, 1984.

Weiser, Alfons. "Das Gottesurteil über Hananias und Saphira Apg 5,1–11." *Theologie und Glaube* 69 (1979): 148–58.

———. *Die Apostelgeschichte*. 2 vols. Ökumenischer Taschenbuchkommentar zum Neuen Testament 5. Gütersloh: Gerd Mohn, 1981, 1985.

———. "Das 'Apostelkonzil' (Apg 15,1–35): Ereignis, Überlieferung, lukanische Deutung." *Biblische Zeitschrift* 28 (1984): 145–67.

———. "Tradition und lukanische Komposition in Apg 10,36–43." Pp. 757–67 in *À cause de l'évangile: Études sur les Synoptiques et les Actes offertes an P. Jacques Dupont.* Lectio Divina 123. Paris: Les Éditions du Cerf, 1985.

Wilckens, Ulrich. "Kerygma und Evangelium bei Lukas (Beobachtungen zu Acta 10,34– 43)." *Zeitschrift für die neutestamentliche Wissenschaft* 49 (1958): 223–37.

_____. "Interpreting Luke-Acts in a Period of Existentialist Theology." Pp. 60–83 in *Studies in Luke-Acts: Essays Presented in Honor of Paul Schubert,* edited by Leander E. Keck and J. Louis Martyn. Nashville: Abingdon Press, 1966. (Reprint. Philadelphia: Fortress Press, 1980.)

_____. *Die Missionsreden der Apostelgeschichte: Form- und traditionsgeschichtliche Untersuchungen.* 3d ed. Wissenschaftliche Monographien zum Alten und Neuen Testament 5. Neukirchen-Vluyn: Neukirchener Verlag, 1974.

Wilder, Amos N. "Variant Traditions of the Resurrection in Acts." *Journal of Biblical Literature* 62 (1943): 307–18.

Wills, Lawrence. "The Form of the Sermon in Hellenistic Judaism and Early Christianity." *Harvard Theological Review* 77 (1984): 277–99.

Wilson, Stephen G. "Lukan Eschatology." *New Testament Studies* 15 (1969–70): 330–47.

_____. *The Gentiles and the Gentile Mission in Luke-Acts.* Society for New Testament Studies Monograph Series 23. Cambridge: Cambridge University Press, 1973.

_____. "Law and Judaism in Acts." Pp. 251–65 in *Society of Biblical Literature 1980 Seminar Papers,* edited by Paul J. Achtemeier. Chico, Calif.: Scholars Press, 1980.

_____. *Luke and the Law.* Society for New Testament Studies Monograph Series 50. Cambridge: Cambridge University Press, 1983.

_____. "The Jews and the Death of Jesus in Acts." Pp. 155–64 in *Anti-Judaism in Early Christianity,* edited by Peter Richardson, vol. 1. Studies in Christianity and Judaism 2. Waterloo, Ontario: Wilfrid Laurier University Press, 1986.

Wittig, Susan. "Formulaic Style and the Problem of Redundancy." *Centrum* 1 (1973): 123–36.

Wolter, Michael. "Apollos und die ephesinischen Johannesjünger (Act 18,24—19,7)." *Zeitschrift für die neutestamentliche Wissenschaft* 78 (1987): 49–73.

Wuellner, Wilhelm. "Where Is Rhetorical Criticism Taking Us?" *Catholic Biblical Quarterly* 49 (1987): 448–63.

Zehnle, Richard. "The Salvific Character of Jesus' Death in Lukan Soteriology." *Theological Studies* 30 (1969): 420–44.

_____. *Peter's Pentecost Discourse: Tradition and Lukan Reinterpretation in Peter's Speeches in Acts 2 and 3.* Society of Biblical Literature Monograph Series 15. Nashville: Abingdon Press, 1971.

Ziesler, J. A. "Luke and the Pharisees." *New Testament Studies* 25 (1978–79): 146–57.

_____. "The Name of Jesus in the Acts of the Apostles." *Journal for the Study of the New Testament* 4 (1979): 28–41.

Zimmermann, Heinrich. "Die Sammelberichte der Apostelgeschichte." *Biblische Zeitschrift* 5 (1961): 71–82.

Zingg, Paul. *Das Wachsen der Kirche: Beiträge zur Frage der lukanischen Redaktion und Theologie.* Orbis Biblicus et Orientalis 3. Freiburg, Switzerland: Universitätsverlag, 1974.

Zumstein, Jean. "L'apôtre comme martyr dans les Actes de Luc." *Revue de Théologie et de Philosophie* 112 (1980): 371–90.

SCRIPTURE AND OTHER ANCIENT SOURCES

Index

Authors

Subjects